THE I TATTI
RENAISSANCE LIBRARY

James Hankins, General Editor

POGGIO
GUARINO
DEL MONTE

ON LEADERS AND TYRANTS

ITRL 99

POGGIO BRACCIOLINI
GUARINO OF VERONA
PIETRO DEL MONTE

♦ ♦ ♦

ON LEADERS
AND TYRANTS

EDITED AND TRANSLATED BY

HESTER SCHADEE and
KEITH SIDWELL

with David Rundle

THE I TATTI RENAISSANCE LIBRARY
HARVARD UNIVERSITY PRESS
CAMBRIDGE, MASSACHUSETTS
LONDON, ENGLAND
2024

Series design by Dean Bornstein

First printing

Library of Congress Cataloging-in-Publication Data

Names: Bracciolini, Poggio, 1380–1459, author. | Guarino, Veronese,
1374–1460, author. | Del Monte, Pietro, –1457, author. | Schadee, Hester,
1979– editor, translator. | Sidwell, Keith C., editor, translator. |
Rundle, David, editor, translator.
Title: On leaders and tyrants / Poggio Bracciolini, Guarino of Verona,
Pietro del Monte ; edited and translated by Hester Schadee and
Keith Sidwell, with David Rundle.
Other titles: I Tatti Renaissance library ; 99
Description: Cambridge, Massachusetts : Harvard University Press, 2024. |
Series: I Tatti Renaissance Library; 99 | Includes bibliographical references
and index. | Text in Latin with English translation on facing pages;
introduction and notes in English.
Identifiers: LCCN 2023048541 | ISBN 9780674297128 (cloth)
Subjects: LCSH: Bracciolini, Poggio, 1380–1459. Correspondence. |
Guarino, Veronese, 1374–1460 — Correspondence. | Del Monte, Pietro, –1457 —
Correspondence. | Scipio, Africanus, approximately 236 B.C.–183 B.C. |
Caesar, Julius. | Despotism — Early works to 1800.
Classification: LCC PA8477.B76 Z4613 2024 | DDC 937/.04 — dc23/eng/20240311
LC record available at https://lccn.loc.gov/2023048541

Contents

༠ঽৡ৳

· CONTENTS ·

Introduction

※※※

Poggio was born in 1380 as Gian Francesco di Poggio Bracciolini in Terranuova in the Upper Arno valley, in the countryside governed by Florence.[1] His identity was to be intimately connected with that city: his readers came to know him as Poggius Florentinus. At the end of the fourteenth century, Poggio's studies led him to Florence, where he attracted the attention of the chancellor, Coluccio Salutati (1331–1406), who was the foremost scholar of his day and a mentor to younger humanists such as Leonardo Bruni (1370–1444), Niccolò Niccoli (1364–1437), and Carlo Marsuppini (1399–1453). With Salutati's patronage, Poggio was appointed apostolic scribe in Rome (1403) and then apostolic secretary (ca. 1410). He was present at the Church Council of Constance (1414–18) in the entourage of Pope John XXIII, whose deposition in 1415 left him free—with the financial backing of Niccoli and Cosimo de' Medici (1389–1464)—to search for manuscripts of classical texts in the cloister libraries of France and the German-speaking lands. Afterward, Poggio entered the service of Henry Beaufort, bishop of Winchester, and spent four years in England. In 1423 Poggio returned to the curia of Martin V, and he followed the latter's successor, Eugene IV, to Florence in 1434, when political turmoil drove the curia from Rome. There, aged fifty-five, Poggio married Vaggia Buondelmonti, the eighteen-year-old daughter of a noble Florentine family, who bore him six children. Over time, and aided by the Medici bank, Poggio acquired substantial property, including a country villa near his hometown, which he furnished with ancient sculpture. In 1443 the papal curia returned to Rome, but in 1453 Poggio took up Cosimo de' Medici's invitation to become Chancellor of Florence. He retired from the office in 1458 and died the year after. Poggio was given a state funeral and

lies buried in Florence's St. Croce, alongside his friends and previous chancellors Bruni and Marsuppini.

The texts written and inspired by Poggio presented in this volume date to the Florentine periods of the papal curia, 1434 to early 1436 and 1439 to 1443 (the intervening years Poggio spent mostly in the pope's entourage in Bologna and Ferrara). The texts comprise an epistolary *Controversy* on the relative merits of two Roman leaders, Julius Caesar and Scipio Africanus, which, in 1435, pitted Poggio against the humanist educator Guarino of Verona (1374–1460), who had recently settled in Ferrara.[2] Five years later, a former pupil of Guarino's, Pietro del Monte (ca. 1400–1457), now papal collector, joined the debate, taking Poggio's side against his former master.[3] In that same year, 1440, Poggio published his dialogue *On the Unhappiness of Leaders*, dedicated to Tommaso Parentucelli, the future pope Nicholas V, which is set during the earlier Florentine period.[4] The works discuss different models for wielding power, the correct relationship between leading figures and the common good, the evils of corruption and other pitfalls of power, and the psychological toll and sacrifices that high office demands.

Dates of Composition and Dissemination of the Controversy

The first, short, letter on the lives and deeds of Scipio Africanus and Julius Caesar was addressed, on April 10, 1435, by Poggio to his curial colleague Scipione Mainenti of Ferrara.[5] Poggio's stated reason for writing this comparison *On the Excellence of Scipio and Caesar* is that Scipione Mainenti asked him for his judgment on both men (Poggio, *On the Excellence*, §1). This was probably as a written extension of an oral discussion, since, as Poggio writes a little later to a mutual friend (Francesco Marescalco of Ferrara, June 30, 1435: Harth 2:171):

With our Scipione of Ferrara, whom I do not merely like but love on account of his humanity and learning, I have

frequent and pleasant contact. We are quite often together chatting about many things, as is sometimes the case among men at leisure: and indeed, very often—because he is himself a very erudite man—our conversation turns to learned and eloquent men.[6]

Nor was this subject matter unusual in Poggio's curial environment: in another letter (May 4, 1435: Harth 2:168–70), he recalls the pleasant conversations he had with the entourage of Leonello d'Este, Marques of Ferrara, who visited the pope in Florence in the spring of 1435, about the qualities of the Romans and the Greeks.[7] Notwithstanding Plutarch's opinions in his *Parallel Lives*, the company agreed (Poggio informs the prince) on the greater excellence of the Romans. Other debates, too, demonstrate the fertile intellectual climate generated by the presence of the papal court and its visitors in the humanistic center Florence.[8] Quite possibly, therefore, Poggio intended no more than impressing upon Mainenti—the younger man, but a rising star in Eugene IV's curia—a private recollection of their erudite fellowship, bestowing victory on Scipione's namesake.

If so, events took a different turn. Two knights who accompanied Leonello to Florence (Feltrino Boiardo and, perhaps, Alberto della Sale)[9] brought a copy of Poggio's *On the Excellence* back to Ferrara, where it was read by the prince's former tutor, Guarino of Verona. Professing deep disappointment with Poggio's scathing treatment of Caesar, Guarino felt impelled to set the record straight, producing his *On the Excellence of Caesar and Scipio* (Guarino, *On the Excellence*, §§1–2). This rather lengthy epistolary treatise is addressed to Leonello and accompanied by a short note asking the prince to act as arbiter: neither is dated, but Leonello's departure from Florence on May 3, 1435, is the *terminus post quem*. In fact, however, Guarino may have had an inkling of what was coming, since another letter (Sabbadini 2:216–20, not included in

this volume), addressed by him to Leonello, praises the prince for having extolled Caesar in a disputation, presumably during his Florentine visit, while proffering a number of classical authorities with which to bolster his case. That debate may well have been provoked by Poggio's *On the Excellence* (written a mere three weeks before); in any case, Guarino's rejoinder to Poggio incorporates and expands on the sources cited in his much shorter letter. It is worth noting that Leonello's graduation from Guarino's tuition coincided with his wedding to Margarita Gonzaga in February 1435, and that the humanist was offered a chair in the Ferrarese *Studio* only in March 1436. Guarino's keen involvement in the *Controversy* may thus be viewed as a demonstration of his continuing usefulness to Leonello.[10]

Word of Leonello's involvement in this dispute soon reached his Gonzaga in-laws in Mantua, where Prince Carlo, a student of the humanist Vittorino da Feltre (1378–1446), addressed a brief letter in praise of Caesar to Leonello in June. Guarino replied, equally briefly, to Carlo on Leonello's behalf (Sabbadini 3:328–30, 2:254–57; these letters are not included here). Evidently, the princes or their tutors felt that praising Caesar in Latin was an appropriate pursuit for an educated ruler-to-be. Guarino's extensive rebuttal of Poggio's *On the Excellence* will have come into the latter's hands during the same summer. The two humanists had been friends for decades and formally resumed their friendship the next year (when Poggio responded positively to a letter of Guarino's on May 18, 1436: Harth 2:204–6) — proving that the dispute had produced a real rift. Poggio, reading in Guarino's text not so much a vindication of Caesar as an unprovoked attack on himself, claims that he was honor-bound to issue a *Defense* (Poggio, *Defense*, §§1–4). Moreover, just as Guarino had called upon Leonello, so Poggio asks the addressee of this text, the Venetian statesman and humanist Francesco Barbaro (1390–1454), to act as judge. In order that he might do so more effectively, Poggio bundled the three

epistles—his own letter to Mainenti, Guarino's response with the note to Leonello, and his *Defense*—along with a cover letter, likewise addressed to Barbaro. Leonello is, as it were, copied in by means of another short note, dated October 25. This is the *terminus ante quem* of Poggio's *Defense*, and it indicates that Leonello, too, received this complete dossier of what has become known as the *Controversy on Caesar and Scipio*.

The vast majority of the more than forty-five extant manuscripts preserve the *Controversy* in this format, albeit they place the cover letter to Barbaro, which Poggio intended to be read first, directly before his *Defense* (the intended reading order is restored in this volume).[11] The work traveled quickly: by January 1436 either the *Defense* or more likely the complete *Controversy* was read by Cyriac of Ancona during his travels along the Dalmatian coast, prompting him to send a letter *In Praise of Caesar* to the leading Florentine humanist Leonardo Bruni. Poggio, in turn, wrote to Bruni in March 1438, lampooning Cyriac's Latin and dismissing his authority.[12] Clearly, Poggio took an active role in the circulation of the *Controversy*: in addition to the copies for Barbaro and Leonello, he also sent the dossier to the papal collector in England, Pietro del Monte, in 1439, asking him to circulate it. Del Monte not only complied with Poggio's request but took the opportunity to compose his own lengthy anti-Caesarean tract. He had himself been a pupil of Guarino's and makes a point of this association in his response, claiming that he has firsthand experience of Guarino's incorrigible pro-Caesarean attitudes. Del Monte added his text to the dossier of the *Controversy* in the manuscript he offered in 1440 to Humfrey, Duke of Gloucester. In this format, it achieved a small circulation in northern Europe.

We do not know to whom Poggio entrusted the task of transcribing these copies. However, it follows from the stages of the *Controversy's* genesis that neither Poggio's letter to Mainenti nor Guarino's response as they were circulated in the dossier represent

the original versions of these epistles. This is in a sense also true for his *Defense*, since Poggio will have consigned the autograph of this final text to the same scribe to produce fair copies of the complete dossier. Indeed, Poggio's version of Guarino's letter contains some — probably inadvertent — alterations (see Note on the Texts); infelicities of expression in the other letters may be explained in the same way. This working method corresponds with Poggio's practice for the distribution of *On the Unhappiness of Leaders*, discussed below.

Historical Context of the Controversy

While the *Controversy* may thus have had an accidental origin, it undeniably arose in a highly charged political setting. Cosimo de' Medici had returned from his exile in Venice (September 1433– October 1434) six months before, ousting the Albizzi-led oligarchic regime that was responsible for his banishment, and exiling a number of his opponents in turn. This laid the foundations for Medici hegemony, a fragile arrangement in which the family controlled much of Florentine politics without holding an official position.[13] Poggio had long been friendly with Cosimo and his brother Lorenzo, who both took a strong interest in humanistic culture and bestowed patronage on its exponents.[14] The papal curia, welcomed to Florence by the Albizzi in June 1434, seamlessly changed its allegiance, aided by the Medici bank's services to Pope Eugene IV, the Venetian-born Gabriele Condulmer. Florence, Venice, and the pope shared, moreover, an enemy in the form of the Milanese duke Filippo Maria Visconti. For the city-states, the expansionist tendencies of the Duchy of Lombardy were a perennial danger: peace was concluded in 1433, but by the end of the decade Florence and Venice were again allied against Milan.[15] Eugene IV, reliant on the military power of the republics, supported their alliance. On his part, the pope had to contend

with the Church Council of Basel, in session since 1431, which challenged papal authority and compromised the pope's finances, and was supported by Visconti. At the same time, the encroachment of Ottoman forces on Byzantine lands led the emperor John VIII Palaeologus to seek help from Western Christendom, opening the path to reunification of the Greek and the Latin Churches, split since the Great Schism of 1054.

Against this background, Eugene IV sought to dissolve the Council of Basel and reconvene a Church Council in Italy, where it would be more easily controlled. His explicit purpose was to reunite the other Christian denominations (primarily Orthodox, but later also Coptic and Ethiopian) with the Catholic Church, that is to say, bring them under Roman authority. As early as 1433, Rinaldo degli Albizzi had expressed hopes for Florence becoming the Council's location; by 1436, various Italian cities were officially in the running.[16] The Florentine chancellor, Leonardo Bruni, wrote letters to the council outlining the city's suitability; Filippo Maria Visconti responded by threatening to refuse the delegates in Basel free movement through his domains.[17] Hosting the council would constitute an economic and cultural boost for Florence and serve as legitimation for the Medici as the city's dominant power. In the end, however, the choice fell on Ferrara, where the new council opened in January 1438 (it was moved to Florence twelve months later on account of the plague). Quite possibly Leonello d'Este's visit to the pope in Florence in spring 1435 was related to negotiations regarding the council.

Interpreting the Controversy

The ancient tradition of biographical writings (see "Sources of the Controversy," below) was revived by Petrarch in his *On Famous Men*. The longest of these biographies was the *Life of Scipio Africanus*, who was also the subject of Petrarch's epic *Africa*.[18] One rea-

son for Scipio's exalted position in Petrarch's oeuvre—besides the availability of the copious source materials also exploited by Poggio—is his heroization already in Antiquity. In Cicero's *Dream of Scipio*, well-known in the Middle Ages since it was transmitted along with Macrobius' Neoplatonic commentary, it is Africanus who foretells Rome's triumph over Carthage to his grandson and expounds on patriotic duty and its heavenly reward.

Caesar's fortune, however, was more checkered.[19] Dante, following Orosius, saw Rome's empire as a prerequisite for the coming of Christ, a view that granted Caesar a role in salvation. Caesar's successors, the Holy Roman Emperors, were to preside over a universal empire on earth, mirroring God's in heaven.[20] This form of Caesarism—which had little or nothing to do with the historical Julius—was widespread in the later Middle Ages. Furthermore, Caesar was claimed as ancestral relative or founding figure by countless dynasties and cities across Europe, including Florence prior to the research of Coluccio Salutati and Leonardo Bruni (on which more below).[21] By contrast, in the twelfth century the political thinker John of Salisbury recalled Cicero's assessment of Caesar's tyrannical behavior.[22] In the next century, competing opinions regarding Caesar were taken for granted by Brunetto Latini—Dante's teacher—who used him as example for rhetoric of praise as well as blame.[23] Likewise, Petrarch, influenced by Lucan's epic *Civil War*, initially saw Caesar's career as emblematic of overambition.[24] Yet later in life—his understanding of the historical forces in the Roman republic sharpened by Cicero's letters to Atticus—Petrarch wrote a biography of Caesar separate from his *On Famous Men*, surpassing Scipio's *Life* in length.[25] Of Caesar's qualities, besides military skill, clemency had especially exemplary value in an age of autocrats—in a Stoic mindset, furthermore, forgiving one's opponents evidences self-control—and so features in mirrors-for-princes by Petrarch and others. Caesar's excessive and (self-)destructive ambition may have been the inverse of Scipio's

patriotic service, but Petrarch detected a certain tragic yet necessary greatness in the man, whom G. W. F. Hegel, for much the same reasons, later proclaimed a "world-historical individual."[26]

Thus, even though Poggio's exchange with Guarino was unplanned, he did not innocently stumble upon a controversial subject. His letter to Mainenti says nothing novel about Scipio. But it strips Caesar of the politico-religious framework that had been constructed around him, of the world-changing greatness that Petrarch so keenly felt, and of his virtue, leaving a tyrant. The tension created by Caesar's qualities, which even his detractors granted, is largely gone in Poggio's text. While Poggio purposefully makes no reference to these inherited Caesar-receptions, which would magnify the man he seeks to reduce in size, the effect of those omissions on his contemporary readers, steeped in tradition, must have been startling. What, then, was the significance of Poggio's radically revised picture?

Naturally, scholars have tried to connect Poggio's *On the Excellence* to his Florentine environment. It has been argued that Scipio functions as alter ego of Cosimo de' Medici, with Caesar representing his opponent in Florentine politics, Rinaldo degli Albizzi.[27] Another interpretation agrees regarding Cosimo but sees in Caesar an image of the Milanese duke Filippo Maria Visconti.[28] Indeed, Cosimo and Scipio share one remarkable feature in the form of their exile, which Cosimo consistently strove to present as voluntary, as Scipio's had been.[29] This parallel was not lost on Poggio, who, in a letter to Cosimo commiserating with him on his exile, compared him to Scipio on this score (December 31, 1433: Harth 2:181–88). Poggio's presentation of Cosimo in this letter also shares some characteristics with his later Scipio, most notably the "integrity of his life" attributed to both men. But there are important differences. Scipio died in exile: hence, when Poggio wrote again to congratulate Cosimo on his return, he compared him to Cicero instead (October 28, 1434: Harth 2:192–97). More-

over, the earlier letter contrasts Cosimo's virtue not with vice, which characterizes Poggio's Caesar, but with fortune, and contends that Cosimo is better off now that he has been exiled, since freed from the burdens of political life he can devote himself to the study of letters. On both scores, this letter is closer in outlook to *On the Unhappiness of Leaders* (discussed below) than to the themes of the *Controversy*.[30]

In truth, Poggio's Scipio and Caesar are too stereotyped to produce a clear comparison with a contemporary character. This is because they embody, respectively, Stoic virtue and good citizenship versus vice and tyranny (see the Synopsis below). But that does not mean Poggio's letter to Mainenti bore no relation to his Florentine context. Inasmuch as the body of the text expounds Scipio's functioning within, and Caesar's career in opposition to the restraints of the Roman republic, Poggio's critique is aimed at usurpation, not at monarchy.[31] However, in the closing section of his letter, Poggio categorically states that Caesar's dictatorship, and the empire it inaugurated, spelled the end of Rome's liberty, and with it, the demise of Latin letters (Poggio, *On the Excellence*, §25). Here the text moves from an accusation against Caesar's morals to an incrimination of single rule. It was a bold, but not unprecedented statement: as is well known, Poggio's friend Leonardo Bruni had made the same claim, also in relation to Caesar, in his *Laudation on the City of Florence* (1404), his *Dialogues for Pier Paolo Vergerio* (ca. 1407), and his *History of the Florentine People* (Book 1, 1416).[32] Bruni, moreover, had used this contention to promote the republic of Florence as a natural heir to republican Rome, from which Bruni argued the city had been founded. Florence had long identified herself by her communal government and her liberty: in Bruni's hands, the humanist literature in which these hallmarks were celebrated — which, he argued, could flourish only under a republic — became another element of the city's self-definition.[33] It is surely relevant that Bruni's *Laudation* was recircu-

lated in 1434 as part of the Florentine campaign to host the Church Council (moreover, Bruni's letters to Basel echo its themes).[34] Following in the footsteps of Bruni, Poggio consciously placed his text in this Florentine tradition: a choice with political relevance.

Considering the connections of both Poggio and Scipione Mainenti, wider audiences to whom the tenets of *On the Excellence* may have been congenial readily suggest themselves. One of these was of course Florence's leading citizen and Poggio's friend Cosimo de' Medici, who may or may not have recognized himself in Scipio, but also, perhaps more importantly, will have recognized Poggio as a vocal exponent and propagator of Florentine culture. The other was Eugene IV, the employer of both Poggio and Mainenti. As papal secretary, it was Poggio's job to author letters on behalf of the pope, for instance regarding the Church Councils, and it was not unusual for him to labor the same themes in his personal writings.[35] The extent to which Florence's papal guest subscribed to the government's aims and literary propaganda is indicated by the fact that when Eugene or his scribe addressed a letter to King Charles VII of France in 1436, also with the intention of promoting Florence for the Council, he appropriated Bruni's *topoi*.[36] Thus, Poggio's assault on Caesar and promotion of republican liberty as cultural good in *On the Excellence* constitute the kind of "Florentine discourse" that could benefit Florence, its leading citizen, its foremost visitor, and, ultimately, Poggio himself.

Guarino, for his part, had good grounds to take umbrage at Poggio's invective against Caesar. Caesar was a favorite teaching tool and role model in his instruction of Leonello. Guarino, for instance, presented Leonello with an annotated copy of Caesar's *Commentaries*, and letters between the prince and his tutor show them discussing the text; he may also have had a hand in the portrait of Caesar by Pisanello that Leonello received for his wedding.[37] Before his employment in Ferrara, Guarino had translated

Plutarch's *Life of Caesar* and dedicated it to one of the Malatesta of Rimini, clearly believing it was a suitable mirror-for-princes.[38] Caesar, indeed, embodied the ideal of a merciful "man of arms and letters" that humanists ever since Petrarch had pressed upon their noble patrons. But what will have stung most of all is Poggio's denial that letters could thrive in a princely state. If allowed to stand unrefuted, that assertion made a farce of Guarino's role as humanist and educator at a court; furthermore, it would seem to disqualify Ferrara as location for the Church Council, which would unite leading scholars from the Greek and the Latin worlds. It is worth underlining, however, that Guarino does not extol monarchy per se, much less attack republican forms of government: on his part, the *Controversy* is never the clash of constitutions that many scholars have deemed it to be.[39]

Synopsis of the Controversy

Poggio's original letter to Scipione Mainenti has fewer than 3500 words. In its opening paragraphs (1–3), Poggio notes that ancient writers have sung the praises of Scipio Africanus as well as Julius Caesar, yet proposes a distinction between their claims to fame. While Caesar is rightly renowned for his actions in war, Poggio says, he was a scourge of the Roman state. Scipio, in contrast, was not only a great commander but also a loyal citizen and a virtuous man. Characteristically, Poggio associates love for Caesar with the common people, while more discerning men of letters will prefer Scipio. To prove these assessments, Poggio outlines the careers and characters of Caesar (4–12) and Scipio (13–20) in turn, followed by a comparison (21–24). Then, in the penultimate paragraph (25) of his letter, he strikes a new blow against Caesar: because he destroyed Rome's liberty, Poggio states, Caesar also wiped out Latin eloquence and the study of the liberal arts.

It is this claim that Guarino tackles first in his response, after a preamble (1–2) evoking his great expectations for, and deep disappointment with, Poggio's letter, which he presents as dishonest and immature. First of all, Caesar was himself a man of letters, second, many imperial authors prove the continuing vigor of all disciplines, and third, the institutions of the Roman state were not destroyed but rather restored by Caesar (3–14). Next, Guarino absolves Caesar of the calamities that did befall Rome, which were either rooted in earlier times or brought about by later emperors (15–18). He then offers his own account of Caesar's youth and early career, which claims to correct Poggio's misinterpretations, and supplies the positive achievements that Poggio left out (19–41). An excursus on Marcus Cato Uticensis (42–45) exposes the hypocrisy of Caesar's enemies. Next up are the Gallic and civil wars, which showcase Caesar's military skills and his clemency in victory; Guarino also pardons his affair with Cleopatra and magnifies the warlike prowess of the Gauls, which Poggio had slighted (46–57). This leads to the crux of the matter, namely Rome's liberty: here Guarino highlights the tyrannical designs of Caesar's enemies and the turmoil of the contemporary republic which required single rule as cure to justify his dictatorship, yet he abstains from a defense of monarchy (58–67). Guarino concludes with laudatory summaries of Caesar's achievements transmitted by ancient authors (68–70), urging Poggio to abandon his arrogant delusions and submit to their authority. In Guarino's epistolary treatise (ca. 10,000 words), Scipio has fallen almost entirely by the wayside.

In the opening of his rejoinder, Poggio explains to Francesco Barbaro that Guarino's patronizing tone and the aspersions cast on his integrity force him to defend the positions once taken (1–5). He does so, again, by distinguishing great deeds from glory, since the latter is founded on virtue (6). Ancient authorities then dem-

onstrate that Scipio was lauded for his virtue and good deeds, while Caesar was execrated for his vices and impious actions (7–19). That done, Poggio turns to a rebuttal of Guarino's specific contentions. He asserts that Latin letters did decline, even if they were not fully extinguished, and that none of the later authors reached the heights of those of Caesar's day (20–30). He denies that Caesar reinvigorated Rome's liberty, showing instead how he subverted the structures of the Roman state (31–40). He contests Guarino's interpretation of ancient authorities and defends his own (41–48). He disputes Guarino's amplification of Caesar's youthful exploits, and he reverses the moral value attached to later deeds (49–61). Scipio is vindicated against Guarino's criticism (62–64), Caesar's counsel regarding the Catilinarian conspirators is addressed with lexicographical arguments (65–68), and the figure of Cato is conjured up to chide Guarino for his attack (69–76). Poggio then diminishes Caesar's achievements in war, questions whether not killing fellow citizens merits the label clemency, disapproves of the affair with Cleopatra, and once more belittles Caesar's Gallic opponents, occasioning an etymological digression (77–85). Returning to the matter of Rome's liberty, Poggio equates single rule with tyranny (86–87). His conclusion reinstates Scipio as pinnacle of virtue and dismisses Guarino's witnesses to Caesar's accomplishments as irrelevant for virtue and hence for true glory (88–92). Although slightly longer than Guarino's text and likewise almost exclusively devoted to Caesar, Poggio's epistolary treatise (ca. 11,100 words) does not add significantly to the arguments of his original letter. Side by side with Guarino's letter, however, it does exemplify how state-of-the-art historical knowledge, philology, and literary criticism could be harnessed to argue a case and uphold a humanist's prestige.

When Pietro del Monte provides his contribution (ca. 7,300 words), he follows Poggio's line of argument, but he elaborates two elements in novel ways. First, Scipio again all but disappears

from his discussion and instead the role of Cato Uticensis is amplified further. Cato's virtue thus becomes the main foil to Caesar's depravity. The more significant intervention is to place the debate within the framework of expected behavior in such intellectual exchanges.[40] Del Monte puts into the mouth of the English prince Humfrey, Duke of Gloucester, a criticism of Guarino for his immoderate and rebarbative tone (about which Poggio had also complained). In his own voice, Del Monte questions whether even Guarino himself could believe the claims he makes for Caesar. This turns an accusation made by Guarino, namely that Poggio spoke as a show-off rather than as a true (i.e., truthful) orator, against him. Del Monte, furthermore, provides a classical precedent for such behavior in the form of the philosopher Carneades, who famously argued *in utramque partem* (on either side [of a question]). In this way, the issue of sincerity vis-à-vis the demands of genre and context (which Poggio had raised in relation to assessing Cicero's statements regarding Caesar) is elevated to a key theme by Del Monte.

Sources of the Controversy

In his letter to Scipione Mainenti, Poggio's foremost sources for his account of the lives of Caesar and Scipio are Suetonius and Livy, respectively. The model for a paired biography followed by a comparison is Plutarch. Yet, in his assessment, Poggio seeks to move away from the ambiguous portraits of Caesar proffered by his ancient biographers, arguing that Plutarch, in particular, was interested in glory, not virtue. Poggio neutralizes Cicero's praise for Caesar's clemency in his speeches *On Behalf of Marcellus, Ligarius*, and *King Deiotarus* by noting that Cicero said what was opportune for the moment, in contrast to his sincere assessment contained in *On Duties*, where he calls Caesar a tyrant. Regarding Scipio, besides Livy, Poggio draws on Valerius Maximus and Sen-

eca, but not obviously on Silius Italicus' epic *Punica*, which is devoted to the wars between Hannibal and Africanus and was rediscovered by Poggio himself during his manuscript hunt at St. Gall (Guarino, *Excellence*, §8, however refers to Poggio's find). Instead, somewhat incongruously, he bewails the "fact" that no ancient Latin life of Scipio is extant, perhaps suggesting that another one might still be found, or belittling the biography of Scipio composed by Petrarch three-quarters of a century before. Poggio does not, in any case, rely on Petrarch's text. The modern author who did leave a mark on the work is his friend Leonardo Bruni, Chancellor of Florence at the time of writing, who had indicted Caesar as cause of the decline of Latin letters in his *Laudation on the City of Florence* and *Dialogues for Pier Paolo Vergerio*.

Guarino, who had lived in Constantinople from 1403 to 1408 and was the most accomplished Hellenist of the Italians of his generation, added the Greek writers Plutarch (now cited rather than merely mentioned) and Dio Cassius as crucial authorities. Dio's *Roman History* had been brought to Italy from Constantinople by the Greek-speaking Sicilian humanist Giovanni Aurispa (1376–1459), who then moved to Ferrara on Guarino's recommendation; moreover, it was Guarino himself who had first translated Plutarch's paired biographies of Alexander the Great and Caesar into Latin (1408 and 1414).[41] Interestingly, he does not quote these translations in his letter to Poggio, but instead translates anew, producing somewhat more literal renderings than the studiedly literary versions he had previously published. By contrast, Guarino does paraphrase from his translation of Plutarch's *Life of Brutus* (1414). In addition to these Greeks, Guarino adduces further Latin authorities such as Sallust, Lucan, and Pliny, but no less of his argument hinges on the expansion and reinterpretation of evidence drawn by Poggio from Suetonius and Cicero. Additionally, a list of imperial authors aids Guarino's refutation of Poggio's

claim that the liberal arts withered away after the dictatorship of
Caesar. Besides the aforementioned authors these comprise, in order of appearance, the grammarians Donatus, Servius, Priscian,
Acron, and Asper; the poets Catullus (a chronological lapse),
Claudian, Ovid, Lucan, Statius, Silius Italicus, Vergil contrasted
with Ennius, and Persius; the historians Asconius, Lucceius (another chronological slip), Florus, Pompeius Trogus, Justin, Curtius, and Tacitus; and the philosophers Seneca and Boethius.

As Guarino, so Poggio in his *Defense* revisits the testimonies of
Cicero and Suetonius regarding Caesar, while Cicero's *Tusculan
Disputations, Philippics, On Behalf of Plancius,* and, above all, *On Duties* are his sources for the definition of glory as dependent on virtue. For Scipio, he adds further testimonies from Valerius Maximus, Aulus Gellius, Pliny, and Seneca. Not yet fluent in Greek at
the time of writing, Poggio takes issue with the standing of Guarino's Greek authors, ranking them less highly than the Latins and
scorning in particular Dio as a sycophantic flatterer of emperors.
Among the imperial authors supporting Guarino's argument about
the arts, Poggio lists the grammarian Caper and the historian
Cornelius Nepos, neither of whom Guarino mentioned, only to
"correct" his opponent by pointing out that Nepos wrote while the
republic still stood. Furthermore, he produces his own list of republican *literati,* such as the orators Lucius Caesar (although he
probably intends C. Julius Caesar Strabo Vopiscus), Hortensius,
Crassus, Antonius, and Brutus, the jurists Scaevola, Servius Sulpicius, and Trebatius (of whom no work is extant), and the grammarian Varro, claiming these surpassed the writers of the later age.

It is remarkable that neither Poggio nor Guarino makes any
extensive use of Caesar's own writings, except to prove (with reference to his lost *On Analogy*) that Caesar was a man of letters.
While Petrarch had ascribed Caesar's *Commentaries* on the Gallic
and civil wars to a Julius Celsus, their authorship had been cor-

rectly identified already by Poggio's mentor, Coluccio Salutati. They were widely read: humanists frequently list Caesar among the common historians, and, as we saw, Guarino presented Leonello with a manuscript.[42] Poggio perhaps had good reason to stay clear of Caesar's self-congratulatory campaign accounts, especially as he was interested in moral, not military matters, but it is difficult to explain why Guarino used Caesar's *Commentaries*, and the anonymous *Alexandrian War* (which he attributes to Oppius or Hirtius) features only for a couple of facts in his treatise. Poggio, for his part, in line with his strategy of depreciating Caesar's foreign enemies but based on no evidence, outright contradicts (*On the Excellence*, §22) the *Commentaries'* stated claim that the Britons were used to internal war.

Del Monte's discussion is primarily indebted to the Latin translations of two of Plutarch's lives. He provides an extended quotation from the *Life of Caesar* in Guarino's rendition (1414), ostentatiously to turn it against him. His later paragraphs follow closely the *Life of Cato Uticensis*, which had been put into Latin by Leonardo Bruni (1405–after 1407). More innovative about his contribution is its use of Cicero's *On the Republic*, the classic text the humanists never had (apart from the *Dream of Scipio* in its last book, which, as noted, had a medieval tradition, the text was rediscovered only in 1819, and then incompletely). Del Monte garners passages of it from the Church Fathers Augustine and Lactantius, and their Christian appropriation of Cicero suffuses his contribution.

Date of Composition and Dissemination of On the Unhappiness of Leaders

Poggio was in Florence in the early summer of 1440 when he composed *On the Unhappiness of Leaders*.[43] We know this from a letter to an English acquaintance of his, Richard Petworth, secretary to

the bishop of Winchester, Cardinal Henry Beaufort, dated May 24 of that year (Harth 2:378–79). He says:

> So as not to be utterly idle I spend my time writing and reading — well, what time is allowed me away from public and private worries — and I do something for my own and for the public benefit. I have recently published a book called *On the Unhappiness of Leaders*, in which I teach by reason and examples that Leaders both good (if there were ever any such) and bad are cut off from all happiness. None of those held to have been so was actually happy. Happiness — I am speaking about the human type — exists more among private individuals than among those who rule others. I am arguing thus to show that virtue is the origin and the foundation of happiness and that without it no one can be happy. But so rarely are leaders in company with virtue that they may be considered cut off from this happiness. I will give the book to your papal penitentiary to be transcribed, so that when you have read the book you may spurn the portals of the powerful and prepare yourself to pursue the happy life. I fear, though, that you may not have enough perseverance to read the book right through. If you believe me, you will consider your whitening hairs. These will encourage you to read and learn from the book.

Poggio's promise to make the book available for transcription was eventually fulfilled. A letter from Florence, dated July 30, 1442, preserved in three sources, shows that the papal penitentiary took some time to do the work, which eventually made its way to England:[44]

> Your papal penitentiary has produced a copy of my little book *On the Unhappiness of Leaders*, which I am now sending to you: but I didn't want it to arrive without my letter. You

will read it when you have the time and then give it to our mutual friend Toly to read. Believe me, it will be very useful in the goal of laying aside the desire to acquire more, but these things are not to the taste of those who care little or not at all for wisdom and whose lives have more intercourse with physical than with mental goods. You however, who are now growing heavy with age, ought to be directing your thoughts to the things that are going to help you in the next life and to dispose of those things which, as we depart, we must leave to others in such a way that they provide us with journey-money, not torments, in the coming age. This you will achieve most satisfactorily if you spend your time in continuous reading of the things that can make you a better person. But these are not minor disputations or controversies (useless even to those who write them), but precepts intended to promote living well, which remove desires and ambition, which prove the fragility of fortune on one side, and on the other the stability of matters that are in the purview of the mind. Upon these matters, my dear Richard, concentrate your thoughts: for they are the virtues and the discipline of living correctly. I would like you to have the book copied and pass it on to the Duke of Gloucester to read. Farewell and keep your affection for me. Florence, July 30, 1442.[45]

The letter also demonstrates Poggio's own style of promoting the dialogue, as well as some of his thoughts on its moral purpose and possible effect. He has a list of readers in mind, whom he wished to have sight of the piece (William Toly, another member of Beaufort's household, can read Petworth's copy when he has finished with it), and asks Petworth to have a further copy made specifically for Humfrey, Duke of Gloucester (previously the recipient of

the *Caesar-Scipio Controversy* via Pietro del Monte). He asserts, as in the earlier letter, that the work will help its recipient to reject the unhappy life of power and greed.

The dissemination of the work in England continued, as the Petworth copy was copied in its turn: we can identify three apographs made from the now lost Petworth text.[46] In addition, Poggio's letters to Bartolomeo Baldana (November 13, 1442: Harth 2:402–3), Gherardo Landriani (autumn 1442: Harth 2:396–97), and Francesco Lignamine da Padova (July 17, 1442: Harth 2:389–91) show that in this period other copies of the work were being produced and sent to friends in Italy and elsewhere.[47] The same sorts of remark about its content are also found in them.

These letters, along with the two addressed to Petworth, help to illustrate Poggio's dissemination method further. From them it appears that he transferred the responsibility of making the copies to others—in Petworth's case to his penitentiary, whoever that was, and such references to individual scribes who will or might be employed to copy the text are also found in the other letters (Gherardus and Franciscus, in the letter to Landriani; "our" Samuel, in the one to Lignamine; Nixolaus, in the letter to Baldana). Examination of some errors shared across the MS tradition,[48] and one of Poggio's own marginal corrections,[49] add to this picture, by revealing that Poggio probably handed over even his autograph to another scribe to produce the fair copy, which was the ultimate source of the extant copies.[50]

The diffusion of the dialogue was successful. Within a very short time indeed, it was accorded an ironic mention in Francesco Filelfo's *On Exile* (2.109), also published in 1440 or shortly after.[51] Within four years it had drawn a more positive reaction from Aeneas Silvius Piccolimini, whose letter *On the Miseries of Courtiers* (1444) borrows wholesale from the *On the Unhappiness of Leaders*.[52] The fifty-four extant MSS and six early-printed editions (one of

them fifteenth-century) of the work are ample testament to its wide diffusion and show that it reached England, Spain, France, and the German-speaking areas of northern Europe, as well as many places in Italy, within a very few years of its composition.

Historical Context of On the Unhappiness of Leaders

The spring of 1440 was a turbulent one for Florence. The Milanese under Duke Filippo Maria Visconti had invaded Florentine territory. The *condottiere* Niccolò Piccinino was virtually at the city's gates. In April Poggio had written to Scipione Mainenti (earlier the addressee of *On the Excellence of Scipio and Caesar*): "I see we have come to that position where a prudent man thinks of fear more than of hope" and "Now we are struck by such whirlwinds that it looks as if we have need more of divine than human counsel to save us" (April 8 and 26, 1440: Harth 2:370–71). He added a postscript eighteen days later: "I forgot to send you this when I'd thrown it onto a pile of documents because my native land was being harried by greater difficulties." Even in this turmoil of spirit, Poggio reflects on the place of study: "But you will say, we must call virtue to our aid and betake ourselves to these studies which can render us free from difficulties of this sort." This is a motif that finds an important place in the *On the Unhappiness of Leaders* (§45) and possibly helps us to locate the work between April 8 and May 24. What Poggio could not know as he sat engrossed in his studies, pessimistic about the final outcome, but taking his mind off the coming disaster by working on something, as he claims, for his private benefit and the public good, was that Count Francesco Sforza, at that point *condottiere* for Florence, would defeat the Visconti fleet on Lake Garda and that on June 29 the direct military threat to Florence would come to an end with the victory at Anghiari. This work, then, is at one level the product of the successful application of humanistic literary theory by a worried

man in the darkest days of his city's fortunes. But, as we shall, see, its inconsistent approach to political theory has caused scholars some puzzlement as to what might have motivated its central argument.

Synopsis of the Dialogue and Its Characters

The dialogue is Ciceronian in its conception. In Cicero, a group of identifiable individuals (e.g., Fannius, Scaevola, and Laelius in *On Friendship*) meets at a specific location (in *On Friendship* the house of Laelius) and proceeds to engage in intellectual conversation on a theme (in this case friendship) suggested by one of them (Fannius). *On the Unhappiness of Leaders* closely follows the template, the characters including Poggio himself (compare Cicero's *On Divination*, a dialogue between Cicero himself and his brother Quintus) and three of his friends. Of these, one, Niccolò Niccoli, had died in 1437, and Poggio had composed his funeral oration.[53] The other two, Carlo Marsuppini from Arezzo and Cosimo de' Medici, were still very much alive in 1440.[54] Marsuppini, professor of poetry, rhetoric, and Greek at the Florentine *Studio*, was a close friend of Niccoli and an important member of the Florentine humanist circle, devoted to his studies, who would, nevertheless (and despite Poggio's arguments in this dialogue) succeed Leonardo Bruni as Chancellor of Florence on the latter's death in 1444 (as Poggio would succeed Marsuppini himself after *his* death in 1453). Cosimo was acknowledged to be the city's leading citizen, through the power conferred by his banking concerns and owing to the organization of political affairs in favor of Medici interests, although he had, most of the time, no official political position. Naturally, the fact that Niccoli was no longer alive gave Poggio *carte blanche* to ascribe to him any (potentially controversial) thoughts he liked without compromising himself, but in truth he does not really use Niccoli's character as a distancing device.

The dialogue unfolds as follows. Poggio, once in Florence, has-tens to the house of his friend Niccolò Niccoli, where he finds him in his library with Carlo Marsuppini and Cosimo de' Medici, examining a manuscript of Ptolemy's *Geography* (1). After some opening remarks by Poggio, who complains about the itinerant life of the Roman curia, to which he has been attached for many years, Marsuppini counters by claiming that people like Poggio, who serve popes, are happy, as are their masters (2). Niccoli's response is to take Marsuppini to task by arguing that although Poggio and his ilk may be happy, these leaders are not and cannot be so (3). Cosimo now intervenes to support Marsuppini, who claims that at the very least the popes — as well as those who serve them — must be allowed their share of happiness (4). Niccoli once more tartly rebuts Marsuppini's view (5), which leads Cosimo to remark how critical Niccoli always is and to ask why that might be (6). Niccoli, using Lucian as support, says that he has never been wrong when blaming, only when praising, and returns to the main theme by once again asserting that all leaders are unhappy (7). Marsuppini now suggests that they use the rest of their free time to discuss this issue fully, with himself as the advocate for the happiness of leaders (8). After another sharp response by Niccoli (9), Marsup-pini once again gives grounds for his view and insists that at least popes must be considered happy (10). Poggio now intervenes to say that he agrees that if they claim to be happy, their word must be accepted, although Cosimo now brings up the counterexample of Pope Adrian IV, who claimed that no one could be more un-happy than the Bishop of Rome. Poggio responds by suggesting the discussion should bypass popes altogether, since it would be inappropriate of him in his position to say anything about their happiness (11). Now that the parameters of the discussion have been set, and the dynamics of the interaction between the charac-ters established, the pattern of the dialogue changes, and from here on it is Niccoli whose voice we principally hear (however,

there are brief interventions from the others, barring Poggio). Niccoli first argues that it is difficult for a leader to be good (12). To this Marsuppini objects that Niccoli's remarks apply to tyrants, and that ruling is by nature a good thing (13). Niccoli now responds by arguing that in fact the position of leader must be naturally bad (14). Cosimo intervenes by offering some examples of leaders considered by their own ages to have been both good and happy, focusing in particular on Augustus (15). Niccoli replies (16–35) in an extended attempt to prove by reason, authority, and examples that even good leaders are unhappy, since happiness must be associated with virtue, but virtue is rarely found in association with leaders, and they rarely give support to the studious men who could help them in their search to rule well. Power brings with it unending worries and hence unhappiness. Cosimo now once more intervenes (36) to say that Niccoli's arguments about the rarity of the good leader are generally applicable to the whole of humanity. In response, Niccoli claims that he is defining such goodness only in a pragmatic way, but that historical examples demonstrate the rarity of goodness among leaders, listing (37–39) a prodigious number of *exempla* to illustrate his point. Marsuppini briefly intervenes to challenge Niccoli's choice of examples as barbarian and pagan, but Niccoli retorts that the vices he has mentioned are still common even among Christians (40). Cosimo objects (41) that Niccoli has deliberately avoided choosing those known to have been good leaders, but Niccoli undercuts the instances he offers and continues to insist that happiness cannot accompany either bad or good leaders (41–43). Cosimo now asks about leaders in republics, to which Niccoli replies with a list of democratic and republican leaders who were conspicuously unhappy (44). In a last desperate attempt to find some comfort in Niccoli's position, Cosimo asks where happiness actually lies (45), in answer to which, in an extended cadenza that remains without reply, Niccoli demonstrates, first, that only the private individual

can be happy, and, second, that happiness is most likely to adhere to those private individuals who devote themselves "to virtue and the study of the best arts." In a final apostrophe to Poggio, he suggests that in consequence of this demonstration of the unhappiness of leaders, he should accept that those who follow the *princeps* must also necessarily be unhappy and retire to a private life of study. Niccoli has had the last word, and the discussion ends with the day's heat dwindling and the departure of the guests.

It is worth noting the relative length of contribution made by each character, although this will not always equate with their relative importance. Poggio gives himself least to say, at about 2.5 percent of the ca. 12,200 words of the spoken dialogue. Niccoli, unsurprisingly, since he is sustaining the main point at issue, speaks most, with approximately 83 percent. Marsuppini, who for the first part of the dialogue is the main interlocutor, is allowed some 9.5 percent, and Cosimo 4.5 percent. Narrative accounts for only about 0.5 percent. It is of some importance, however, that although Marsuppini is the one who initiates the idea of the formal discussion and offers challenges to Niccoli for the larger part of the piece, his last intervention is a very brief one at 40, and from then onward (at 41, 44, and 45) it is Cosimo who takes up the baton. As I shall argue below (under Interpreting the Dialogue), this pattern suggests that Marsuppini has conceded the victory, but now Cosimo, for some reason, is still anxious to continue the discussion.

Sources of On the Unhappiness of Leaders

The theme of the dialogue, the unhappiness of all leaders, arises from contemporary and personal concerns, in particular Poggio's complaint about the nomadic life of the curia, and neatly returns to them in Niccoli's closing apostrophe to Poggio (see above). But, as is the nature of humanist discourse, it is antiquity that provides

most of the material to support the discussion. Even Poggio's contemporary complaint is not made without a reference to the ancient and nomadic Scythians (1). The ancient material provides more such decoration (usually in the form of embedded and unattributed poetic quotations), but mostly is quarried either for philosophical fodder or for moral *exempla*. In the case of the philosophical matter, the authors are usually named, as they are the guarantors of truthfulness and as such need to be out in the open. The sources of the *exempla*, which in some sections pour forth like a torrent from Niccoli's mouth in particular, are not given (but usually easy to trace): one supposes that as data they are part of the common stock of knowledge. There are two references to the Bible, one to support a general proposition and the other as part of the discussion of examples (§§19 and 41). A few more recent references appear: the view of a medieval pope (sourced from Petrarch: §11), leaders' bad treatment of the famous predecessors of these Quattrocento humanists, the Florentine triad Dante, Petrarch, and Boccaccio (probably from Leonardo Bruni's *Life of Petrarch*, which is not cited: §32), and a couple to the state of affairs in Italy and Europe in general (§40). These latter references serve, it seems, to remind the reader that the theme is a universal one, as applicable in the world of 1440 as in any other period.

The named authorities are both Greek and Latin. The Greek authors specifically mentioned are, in order of appearance, Lucian, Hesiod, Aristotle, and Isocrates. Lucian was accessed directly by Poggio, as he had finally managed to gain some competence in Greek. Since Lucian was widely regarded in this period as a philosopher, though a very witty one, and was almost the first real author encountered by students of Greek, it is no surprise to find him being used as back-up.[55] The axiom from Hesiod, however, is more likely to derive from a reading of Cicero.[56] Poggio perhaps did translate, although not especially accurately, the passage from *Nicomachean Ethics* that he deploys.[57] But for Isocrates he was cer-

tainly using the Latin translation of Bernardo Giustiniani.[58] This is a bit surprising, given that Marsuppini had been the first person to render the *To Nicocles* into Latin (although Giustiniani's version was the more popular), but perhaps it is Poggio's subtle way of characterizing Niccoli's argumentative antagonism to his friend in this piece: those who could catch the slight might smile knowingly.

One other Greek is mentioned by name, Epicurus, knowledge of whom and his doctrines was available only through Latin sources, in particular from the poem of Lucretius rediscovered by Poggio and Bartolomeo da Montepulciano in 1417.[59] Canfora takes this as an indication that Lucretius is of some importance to the structure and meaning of the dialogue.[60] But Marsuppini is making only a passing reference, and to the commonplace view of Epicurus as a promoter of the physical pleasures at that. Besides, the language of this passage is not close to Lucretius, but appears to reflect more obviously a passage in Cicero's *On Ends* that discusses Epicurus. Since none of the other hints of Lucretian language or thought picked out by Canfora appear positively to demand that the reader recall Lucretius, it seems unlikely that this undercurrent is really there.[61]

The Latin writers named are Valerius Maximus, the *Augustan History* (Flavius Vopiscus and later Avidius Cassius, mistakenly mentioned for Aelius Spartianus), Terence, Justin (who is also the author most mined for the unattributed historical *exempla*), Cicero, Sallust, and Seneca. There is nothing especially remarkable about Poggio's use of these sources, which were all well-thumbed by humanists, though it seems he quite often paraphrases or misremembers them, suggesting (as does one conspicuous inconsistency between the end and the beginning of the dialogue) hasty composition.[62] In one case, however, where he has Marsuppini use Cicero's *On Duties* to support his view that the position of leader (*principatus*) is naturally good, that is not the meaning of the passage (Cicero is talking of intellectual independence, not power

over others).[63] One wonders, therefore, whether, as perhaps in the use by Niccoli of a rival version of Isocrates, Poggio is here deliberately setting up Marsuppini for a fall.

Three sources not named, but linked by their author/translator, are Xenophon's *Hiero* (a dialogue between the poet Simonides and the tyrant of Syracuse, in which the topic of the unhappiness of tyrants is predominant, which was translated by Leonardo Bruni in 1403 and was already widely diffused), and Bruni's *Life of Petrarch* and *Dialogues for Pier Paolo Vergerio*. It is difficult to explain quite why Poggio does not acknowledge Bruni (except by noting it was his habit: he fails to mention Bruni in the *Controversy* for clear borrowings from the *Laudation* and the *Dialogues*) and in particular why he does not mention Xenophon as a source. Perhaps Niccoli's poor relations with Bruni were too well known for it to be plausible that he would have cited him openly, or Poggio may be making the point, for those who knew Bruni's writings, that Niccoli cannot do without them, even if he fails, in his dudgeon, to say Bruni's name. However, in his funerary orations for Niccoli and Bruni (one composed before *On the Unhappiness of Leaders*, the other after), Poggio seems to redraw the picture of their merits slightly in favor of Niccoli, and he does, by contrast, once mention Niccoli as arbiter of Latinity in his *Defense* (§26).[64]

Two-Way Conversations

Canfora notes that Poggio's dialogue is in a conversation, as it were, with Lapo's *On the Advantages of the Papal Court* (composed two years before *On the Unhappiness of Leaders* was published) and Alberti's *Momus* (after *On the Unhappiness*).[65] It is useful to remember that these works, although pervaded with material from antiquity, were all designed to serve the interests and concerns of fifteenth-century society, however limited their use of Latin might have made access to their discourse, and that they circulated widely

among the groups to whom these matters were of relevance. It is worth adding another two-way conversation that may tell us something of interest about the meaning of *On the Unhappiness*. First of all, it is clear that Poggio picks up and interacts with material from Leonardo Bruni's *Dialogues to Pier Paolo Vergerio* (before *On the Unhappiness*). Just as clearly, Aeneas Sylvius Piccolomini's *On the Miseries of Courtiers*, written in 1444, both relies on material from Poggio and can stand as in some senses a reading of it.

In 1444, Aeneas Sylvius Piccolomini, still not in holy orders (though he would become pope as Pius II in 1458), wrote a long letter to Johann von Eich about the miseries of the life of the courtier.[66] He was at the time in the service of the Holy Roman Emperor Frederick III. There are several quite clear reuses of Poggio's dialogue in this text, and it is obvious that Aeneas Sylvius used its stimulus to compose a whole work on what was in effect merely the opening and the closing music in *On the Unhappiness*.[67] But it is also worth noting that the work may have had a personal meaning attached to it in respect of the writer's future path. In particular, his unacknowledged use of some passages by the medieval writer Peter of Blois has been taken to suggest not merely that Aeneas is tired of the court, but that his future will lie in an ecclesiastical direction.[68] The details are less important here than Aeneas' method and its implications for the way he had read Poggio: his writing was in the service of his own personal agenda, and, it is reasonable to argue, Aeneas will have supposed that the same was true of his contemporary, Poggio.

Interpreting the Dialogue

One question that arises in discussions of the meaning we should attach to *On the Unhappiness of Leaders* is to what extent Poggio agreed with the words he was putting into Niccoli's mouth. First of all, one should say that it is highly unlikely that in constructing

such a Ciceronian dialogue Poggio did not recall what Cicero had said in the introductory remarks to his *Laelius* (*On Friendship*), 1.4, about his experience of reading his own *Cato* (*On Old Age*): "and so when I myself read my own words, I sometimes have the feeling of thinking that it is really Cato and not myself, who is speaking." Cicero makes it quite clear that the central theme of the dialogues (both *On Old Age* and the current one, *On Friendship*) represents his own opinions couched in the voice of the main character, so Poggio will have understood that such dialogism was merely an imposture, allowing him to ascribe to Niccoli in this case what was on his own mind. This can be substantiated in two ways. First of all, he makes himself remark in the dialogue (11) that the popes should be believed when they claim to be happy, something undercut, it is true, by what Cosimo next says about Pope Adrian IV's view, but which nonetheless seems designed to carry an authorial message about writing in general. Second, however, in the prefatory letter to Tommaso Parentucelli, he claims paternity over the central idea of the dialogue: "It is to show, as far as my intellectual capacities have allowed, that the life of kings and leaders is entangled with many anxieties and is devoid of all happiness." It does not seem likely that, in a period in which literary theories such as we often give credence to today, which problematize the relationship between author and text, were unknown, Poggio had any more trouble than Cicero in putting his thoughts into the mouth of a fictional interlocutor (here Niccoli).

The basic problem of interpretation, however, has been to see why precisely Poggio chooses *this* theme and argument at this specific time, and why, only five years after his partisan political reading of Caesar and Scipio, where republicanism is good and monarchy bad (as discussed above, this is not the central, but it is one point of Poggio's comparison), he should produce a work in which those lines are completely blurred: popular and republican leaders, along with tyrants, kings, and monarchs of all sorts are

equally argued to be bereft of happiness, albeit for different reasons (individual power largely corrupts, whereas public responsibilities placed by the state upon selected individuals are burdens that render even good men unhappy).[69] Meanwhile, there are to be seen here and there even good monarchs (Giangaleazzo Visconti, Augustus, Marcus Aurelius, and so on).[70] His letter to Petworth of May 1440 (Harth 2:378–79) shows that he could *post factum* allow *On the Unhappiness* to be a personal directive to individuals to avoid wishing for what they cannot have (especially power).[71] And clearly, Aeneas Sylvius Piccolomini read *On the Unhappiness* this way, taking the message of the problems of courtiers as a specific prompt to tackle his own current situation. Thus, *On the Miseries of Courtiers* can be interpreted in general as a "declination" (*recusatio*) involving a personal choice to disengage from the regal curia and not to pursue those positions of power that can bring only unhappiness in their wake.

It seems reasonable to propose, however, that Poggio's original aim may have been more specific than what he claimed writing to Petworth, that is, that he was trying to persuade someone in particular of the truth of his contention that *all* leaders were unhappy. That, presumably, would have to be someone either already in such a position or known to be aiming at it. And, most likely, someone connected closely with the dialogue, that is, one of its characters, or its dedicatee. It does not appear that he was thinking of trying to persuade himself: he was not a leader in 1440, and when he finally left the psapal curia, fourteen years later, it was to become one, as Chancellor of Florence. Nor would the theme suit Marsuppini, also not a leader at the date of the dialogue, but destined also to become one (as Chancellor of Florence from Bruni's death in 1444 until his own in 1453). Moreover, the dedicatee of the piece, Tommaso Parentucelli, though destined for greatness as Pope Nicholas V, was not even a bishop in 1440, and church leaders are specifically ruled out of consideration in the work, so that

the theme would have had no special frisson in being directed specifically at him.

There is, it happens, one leader among the characters of the dialogue and only one: Cosimo de' Medici, who is specifically said to be "an outstanding leader" (*princeps*) right at the start of the dialogue, in the introductory matter before the conversation itself begins (§1). It is Cosimo who, in a desperate last attempt to burst Niccoli's bubble, asks (§44) whether even the leaders of republics are subject to his strictures. This provokes Niccoli's final and unanswered rant, in which he maintains that unhappiness is the lot of every leader of whatever political hue. If we look more closely at the specific political situation at the time of the dialogue's composition with special reference to the idea that it may particularly affect Florence's leader, Cosimo, it might be possible to make more sense of the choice of theme and the extreme view Poggio has chosen to espouse.

In 1440, then, Florence was in a parlous situation, and Poggio, pessimist that he was, seems from his correspondence of the time to have reckoned that the state had little chance of surviving with its current constitution intact. A Visconti victory would mean, of course, that Cosimo would instantly lose his position — as leader. He would then face the consequences. But what if those consequences were a blessing rather than a curse? Cosimo was wealthy and was a patron of scholars, interested, because of a good education in Latin, in humane studies. The removal of leadership could, for him, Poggio may be suggesting, mean retiring to a private life of study and therefore happiness. If this line of reasoning is correct, it may explain why the dialogue opens in a library, with Cosimo, along with Marsuppini, examining a codex of Ptolemy. This is the proper sphere for an individual of Cosimo's talents.

Significant support for this reading may be gleaned from Poggio's letter to Cosimo, which consoles him on his exile from Florence (December 31, 1433: Harth 2:181–88). On this earlier occa-

sion, Poggio uses two of the tropes that find a place in the later dialogue: the solace of the pursuit of letters (*studia humanitatis*) (ll.82–91; cf. *On the Unhappiness* §45), and the idea that high office brings servitude and, by contrast, that laying it aside offers freedom (ll.92–116; cf. §§42–43). A third idea, the notion that, while fortune can take away material things, it cannot remove the goods of the mind — such as the sense of a job well and justly done — which are lasting possessions that even death cannot remove (ll.56–71), is found in the prefatory letter to *On the Unhappiness* (§1) and clearly stands as an underlying positive to the overwhelming negatives of the dialogue itself. Seen this way, the dialogue is not really a "provocation" (*provocatio*) but rather an advance "consolation" (*consolatio*) — and perhaps it is not so surprising, then, that in such circumstances Poggio's mind went so often to the Senecan works of this genre: *To Polybius* and *To Marcia*.[72]

Once the political and military situation was resolved, of course, there was no need for such a personalized and pessimistic reading, and Poggio could continue to claim (as he already does in the preface to Tommaso Parentucelli, as well as in the letter to Richard Petworth) — and quite in line with humanist theory of reading — that he had all along intended it for his friends in various parts of the Church to help them desist from their ambitions to high office. Yet the treatment of Cosimo is egregious — both when the word "leader" is applied to him and when he becomes Niccoli's final interlocutor — and without some relation to the current political situation, this is hard to explain adequately.

At any event, that contemporaries did read the dialogue as being closely associated with Cosimo is clear from Filelfo's malicious take on it in his *On Exile* (2.109), where he ascribes to Poggio the following attack on his friend and patron:

And to amaze you even more as to his lack of self-awareness: I have written two pamphlets that I have not yet published,

one *On Nobility*, the other *On the Unhappiness of Leaders*, in which the fool fancies he is being praised when he is being excoriated by me, since I teach that he is both ignoble and unhappy.[73]

While *On the Unhappiness of Leaders* and the *Controversy* alike are thus firmly embedded in their contemporary milieu, the themes addressed by Poggio in both texts are universal. The psychology of power, the demands placed on public servants, and the dividing line between leadership and tyranny are as topical today as they were when Poggio wrote. His voice, now rhetorical, then scholarly, occasionally witty, is frequently incisive and worldly-wise, and will surely speak to a modern audience, much as it did to those of his near contemporaries who diligently read, copied, and disseminated his words.

This volume is a collaborative effort. The edition, commentary, and translation of the *Caesar-Scipio Controversy* have been prepared by Hester Schadee, those of *On the Unhappiness of Leaders* by Keith Sidwell, while David Rundle has contributed Del Monte's *Epistle*. This Introduction is also the work of Schadee and Sidwell. Without wishing to erase personal styles, Hester Schadee and Keith Sidwell have both read all sections of this book for consistency and improvement.

We are, furthermore, pleased to take this opportunity to thank Jeroen De Keyser for the unstinting collegiality with which he shared his expertise and advice regarding our editions of the *Controversy* and *On the Unhappiness of Leaders* (see Note on the Texts). Our editor, Andrew Dyck, deserves a special accolade for his close scrutiny of our final draft of the book, which has led to many improvements in every quarter. Finally, we are grateful to James Hankins, the staff at I Tatti Renaissance Library, and Harvard University Press for making this book see the light.

NOTES

1. Poggio's biography was written by Walser, *Poggius Florentinus*; see also Petrucci and Bigi, "Bracciolini, Poggio"; Revest, "Poggio's Beginnings"; and Martines, *Social World*, for the socio-economic position of Poggio and his circle. Poggio's birthplace has been renamed Terranuova Bracciolini in his honor.

2. Important studies of the *Controversy* are Crevatin, "Politica e la retorica"; Pade, "Guarino and Caesar at the Court of the Este"; Canfora, *Controversia di Poggio Bracciolini*; McCahill, "Civility and Secularism"; Pedullà, "Scipio vs. Caesar."

3. For Del Monte's contribution, see Rundle, "Carneades' Legacy"; Saygin, *Humphrey*, 90–97.

4. *On the Unhappiness of Leaders* is discussed in Kajanto, "Poggio Bracciolini's *De infelicitate principum*"; Canfora, "Topica del 'principe'"; Canfora, *Poggio Bracciolini. De infelicitate*; Schadee, "'I Don't Know Who You Call Tyrants.'"

5. Scipione Mainenti was a colleague of Poggio's in the curia of Eugene IV and appears to have been a favorite of the pope. He was among the youngest participants of the Church Council of Basel that commenced in 1431, being still a student at Bologna, and as such is likely to have been in his mid-twenties at the time of this letter. Nevertheless, Mainenti, presumably underage, was consecrated bishop of Modena in October 1436. Sabbadini, *Scoperte*, 114 and 118; Walser, *Poggius Florentinus*, 164; the date of the consecration is discussed by Bodnar and Mitchell, *Francesco Scalamonti. Vita viri clarissimi*, 158–59n165.

6. *Cum Scipione nostro Ferrariensi, quem non solum diligo sed etiam amo propter suam humanitatem et doctrinam, est mihi frequens et iocunda consuetudo. Sumus sepius una confabulantes variis de rebus, ut fit aliquando inter ociosos; sepissime vero cum ipse sit vir eruditissimus, incidit inter nos sermo de viris doctis et eloquentibus.*

7. Giovanni di Jacopo Morelli's *Ricordi*, 132, date Leonello's Florentine visit to April 30–May 3.

8. For example, the debate between Leonardo Bruni and Biondo Flavio on whether the ancient Romans spoke Latin, in which Poggio had a small part, discussed in Schadee, "Tale of Two Languages."

9. Sabbadini, *Epistolario*, 3:325.

10. Pedullà, "Scipio vs. Caesar," 291–2.

11. When the dossier was printed in 1512 as *Antilogion Guarini et Poggii*, the cover letter was omitted entirely, as was Poggio's note to Leonello, while Guarino's was included.

12. Published and translated in Mitchell, Bodnar, and Foss, *Cyriac of Ancona*, 196–221, with Poggio's response addressed to Bruni, 224–31; for discussions see Cortesi, "'Caesarea Laus'"; Schadee, "*Caesarea Laus*."

13. Kent, *Rise of the Medici*, 330–47; Najemy, *History of Florence*, 251–98; and see also the *Life* of Eugene IV by Vespasiano da Bisticci, who, however, absolves the pope of double dealings.

14. Kent, *Cosimo de' Medici and the Florentine Renaissance*, 21–27.

15. Cognasso, *Storia di Milano*, 291–93, 334.

16. Fubini, "Problemi di politica fiorentina all'epoca del Concilio," 50.

17. Müller, *Documenti*, letters from July 3, 1436, to July 15, 1437, 159–69.

18. Martellotti, *Petrarca. De viris illustribus*; Laurens, *Pétrarque. L'Afrique*.

19. For a brief overview of Caesar's afterlife, see Schadee, "After Caesar"; and James Hankins, *Virtue Politics* (Cambridge, MA-London, 2019), 124–41, for the topic among the early humanists.

20. A good starting point remains Davies, *Dante and the Idea of Rome*.

21. Baldassarri, "Like Fathers Like Sons"; Witt, *Hercules*, 246–48.

22. Nederman, *John of Salisbury. Policraticus*, 3.10 (p. 23).

23. Carmody, *Brunetto Latini. Li Livres dou Tresor*, 3.2.9 (p. 320).

24. For Petrarch's views on Caesar, see Martellotti, "Petrarca e Cesare"; and Fenzi, "Grandi infelici."

25. Crevatin, *Petrarca. De gestis Cesaris*.

26. Nisbet, *Georg W. F. Hegel. Lectures*, esp. 76–89.

27. Oppel, "Peace vs. Liberty," 220–26. Similarly, McCahill, "Civility and Secularism," 132, calls Poggio's text "a celebration of Cosimo" and Guarino's "a defense of the Este."

28. Finzi, "Cesare e Scipione."

29. Oppel, "Peace vs. Liberty," 241.

30. For a comparison of both texts, see Schadee, "'I Don't Know Who You Call Tyrants,'" 175–84.

31. This is overlooked by the many scholars who treat the controversy as a debate about opposing constitutions. The *locus classicus* of that approach is Baron, *Crisis*, 66–69; Pedullà, "Scipio vs. Caesar," rightly cautions against such readings.

32. Baldassari, *Leonardo Bruni. Laudatio*; id., *Leonardo Bruni. Dialogi*; Hankins, *Leonardo Bruni. History*; Crevatin, "Politica e la retorica," 285.

33. Schadee, "Tale of Two Languages."

34. Viti, "Leonardo Bruni e il Concilio," 511.

35. For example, his propaganda against the Council of Basel is reprised in his funeral oration for Giuliano Cesarini, published in De Keyser and Schadee, *Poggio Bracciolini. Eulogies*, 248–75, and see discussion at 53–66.

36. Viti, "Leonardo Bruni e il Concilio," 535.

37. Pade, "Guarino and Caesar at the Court of the Este"; Salmi, "'Divi Julii Effigies' del Pisanello."

38. Pade, "Guarino, His Princely Patron."

39. For example, Pade, "Guarino and Caesar at the Court of the Este," 80–88, influenced by Baron, *Crisis*, 66–69.

40. On this see Rundle, "Carneades' Legacy"; McCahill, "Civility and Secularism."

41. Pade, *Reception of Plutarch's Lives*, 1:172–27, 2:133–35.

42. For the attribution with bibliography, see Schadee, "First Vernacular Caesar," 287–88. E.g., Kallendorf, *Leonardo Bruni. The Study of Literature to Lady Battista Malatesta*, §18 (variously dated between 1405 and 1429), recommends of the historians "especially Julius Caesar, who described his own deeds with the greatest ease and elegance in his *Commentaries*" (*et in*

primis Caesarem ipsum res gestas suas Commentariis *summa facilitate venusta-teque explicantem*); the fact that Bruni's addressee was a woman shows just how run-of-the-mill an author Caesar was.

43. The word used by Poggio is *princeps* (pl. *principes*), a Latin term whose primary meaning was "first," but which developed into a noun signifying any leader, including the Roman emperor. In Poggio's day it was associated mainly with institutions in which a single individual was the main authority — what he calls in §41 and §43 *principatus*, or "princi-pates" — and so covers popes and princes (of which there were many on the Italian peninsula). But Poggio does not exclude the leaders of repub-lics from the title (see §1 and §44), so that the argument proposed by the main speaker, Niccoli, does not read exclusively as a condemnation of monarchy, even if Poggio's own view might have leaned in that direction (as witness the *Caesar-Scipio Controversy* included in this volume). Conse-quently, there is a case for seeing the main thrust of this dialogue as rather different from that of the *Caesar-Scipio Controversy*, less focused on general political principles and more personally directed toward Cosimo de' Medici, who was in a profoundly difficult situation in the summer of 1440 (see further below, under "Historical Context of *On the Unhappiness of Leaders*" and "Interpreting the Dialogue"). Because of the depoliticized use of *princeps*, then, and because the word and its cognates are absolutely central to the dialogue's theme, it has been consistently translated as "leader" wherever it occurs, and the cognate abstract noun *principatus* has been rendered "[the] position of leader" (except in the two cases where it definitely refers to principalities as concrete entities, §41 and §43). Occa-sionally, a further gloss has been added where it is clear that the word is being used to refer to the Roman emperor.

44. Berlin: Staatsbibliothek, Preussischer Kulturbesitz, MS Lat. qu. 558 (*olim* Barrois 433), ff. 42r–v (Walser, *Poggius Florentinus*, 454; Canfora, *Poggio Bracciolini. De infelicitate*, lxxviii with n. 7: his siglum is Hd); Ox-ford: Bodleian Library, MS Bodley 915, ff. 99 r–v (Canfora, *Poggio Brac-ciolini. De infelicitate*, lxxxiv–lxxxv: his siglum is Ob); Oxford: Bodleian Library, MS Rawlinson C. 298, f. 45r (Canfora, *Poggio Bracciolini. De infe-licitate*, lxxxvi: his siglum is Od).

45. Translated from the Latin text published in Weiss, *Humanism in England*, 42–44.

46. See n. 44 above, and Rundle, "Scribe Thomas Candour," 1–25.

47. See Canfora, *Poggio Bracciolini. De infelicitate*, cxli n. 40, for further examples.

48. At 9 (C20), 12 (C35), 33 (C66), 35 (C68) and 35 (C69). See notes on individual passages.

49. In the margin of Florence: Biblioteca Medicea Laurenziana, MS 47.19 (Canfora's L) of a reading at 42 (C87).

50. There can probably be no complete agreement on the weight of this evidence, though certainly in my view, the errors in 9, 12, 33 and the marginal correction in L are difficult to lay at Poggio's door.

51. De Keyser and Blanchard, *Francesco Filelfo. On Exile*, 258–59, quoted below, under "Interpreting the Dialogue."

52. See further below, under "Two-way Conversations."

53. See further translation n. 6.

54. See further translation nn. 7 and 8.

55. See translation nn. 17, 18, 23, 24, 82, 102, 104, 105, 106, and 152.

56. See translation n. 29.

57. See translation n. 60.

58. See translation n. 64.

59. See translation n. 20 for the rediscovery of Lucretius.

60. Canfora, "Topica del 'principe,'" 5–8, 81–83, and 85.

61. See translation nn. 27 and 153 for these arguments.

62. See translation n. 132.

63. See translation n. 43.

64. Published in De Keyser and Schadee, *Poggio Bracciolini. Eulogies*, 134–59 and 218–45, respectively.

65. Canfora, *Poggio Bracciolini. De infelicitate*, xx–xlvi.

66. Texts in Wolkan, *Briefwechsel*, 453–87, and Mustard, *Aeneas Sylvius*.

67. See translation nn. 77, 81, and 152, with Sidwell, "De infelicitate," and Canfora, "Topica del 'principe.'"

68. Sidwell, "Aeneas Silvius Piccolomini."

69. Canfora, *Poggio Bracciolini. De infelicitate*, xix–lxviii, for example, places a great deal of emphasis on the figure of Eugene IV and the political problems of his time in setting the context for *On the Unhappiness of Leaders*, not without noting that Poggio explicitly excuses the popes from the discussion (xlvii n. 65), or that his treatise like many others *De principe* (On Leadership) fails to address the issue of state political structures (l–li).

70. See translation nn. 97 for Visconti, and nn. 34 and 46 for Marcus Aurelius.

71. He was still urging Petworth to change his lifestyle in July of 1445 (Harth 3:3–6).

72. See Canfora, "Topica del 'principe,'" 92, for a conspectus of references.

73. *Et quo magis mireris quam est nescius sui, libellos duos scripsi, quos nondum aedidi: alterum* De nobilitate, *alterum* De infelicitate principum, *quibus homo ineptus se laudari putat cum vituperetur ab me maxime, quippe quem et ignobilem esse doceo et infelicem:* De Keyser and Blanchard, *Francesco Filelfo. On Exile,* 258–59.

ON LEADERS AND TYRANTS

Poggii Florentini
De praestantia Caesaris et Scipionis
ad Franciscum Barbarum virum clarissimum
Proemium[1]

1 Poggius plurimam salutem[2] dicit Francisco Barbaro, viro clarissimo.

Licet sciam permultas esse occupationes tuas, cum[3] publicas, tum privatas, quibus te plurimum temporis impertiri[4] convenit, audebo tamen pro nostra amicitia te interpellare paululum atque avocare a rebus seriis ad ineptias quasdam ridiculas, nescio Guarinine, viri doctissimi, an mea culpa contractas. Si tamen hac in re solitam tuam mihi prudentiam praestabis, intelliges potius culpandum esse Guarinum, qui ultro munus desumpsit neque sibi necessarium, neque congruens amicitiae nostrae.

2 Ego dudum, exercitio quodam scribendi[5] ductus, edidi epistulam quandam de Scipionis Caesarisque praestantia, in qua neque Guarini, neque cuiusquam alterius e nostris mentionem feci: usus scribendi libertate — de mortuis praesertim, qui neque rescribere possint, neque proscribere — tuli sententiam, quae opinioni meae verisimillima videbatur, linquens ceteris liberum iudicium, prout cuique libitum esset, sentiendi. At vero Guarinus, tamquam coheres Octaviani, ad quem necessario defensio Caesaris spectaret, tamquam in ea re sua existimatio versaretur, indignum id facinus[6] exclamans, insurgit adversum me, scribens superbe nimium et adroganter magis quam vires suae eloquentiae patiantur, aut

2

PROEM TO FRANCESCO BARBARO

Poggio of Florence
Proem
to the illustrious Francesco Barbaro
On the Excellence of Caesar and Scipio

Poggio warmly greets the illustrious Francesco Barbaro.[1]   1

Although I know that you have many obligations, public as well as private, to which it befits you to devote most of your time, still I will have the temerity in view of our friendship to interrupt you for a little while and call you away from serious business to some laughable trifles — occasioned either by the fault of Guarino, a very learned man, or perhaps my own. Yet if you lend me your usual insight in this matter, you will see that Guarino is more to blame, who, uninvited, took an endeavor upon himself which was neither necessary for him nor in line with the friendship between us.

A while ago, as a sort of exercise in writing, I issued a letter   2 about the excellence of Scipio and Caesar, in which I made no mention of Guarino nor of any other of our people: I used the freedom of writing (particularly about the dead, since they can neither write back nor proscribe), and I pronounced a judgment which seemed most plausible to my own belief, leaving others free judgment to think just as they pleased.[2] But Guarino — as though a fellow heir to Octavian, to whom the defense of Caesar would necessarily pertain; as though in this matter his own reputation were at stake — cried that this was a shameful deed and rose up against me, writing with excessive arrogance and more overbearingly than the strength of his eloquence permits, or his former kindness calls

pristina sua humanitas requirat. Itaque suscepit sibi laborem inanem mecum decertandi pro Caesaris causa, parum consulens iuri[7]
antiquae nostrae benevolentiae. Nulla enim in re, nullo in loco,
nullo verbo vel pauxillum a me offensus, prosiluit ad primum (ut
aiunt) tubae sonitum ad me oppugnandum veluti militem partium
Pompeianarum!

3   Quid enim urgebat Guarinum in Poggium insultare, si praetulit
Caesari Scipionem? Quid ad eum pertinuit? Quae suae partes
fuerunt mihi detrahere, mecum litigare, totiens veluti ignavum
quendam increpare, si (quod nobis ad eloquentiae studium atque
exercitationem concessum est) vel laudando, vel vituperando aliquem, remotum ab aetate nostra, non sui generis, non nominis,
non nationis ingeniolum meum volui exercere? Si Caesarem colit,
si memoriam illius caram habet, si nomen diligit, si gesta extollit,
debuit remota personarum contumelia eius suscipere defensionem
me etiam laudante, ibique quantum dicendo vel scribendo posset,
ostendere! Nam quod mihi sumpsi ad scribendi exercitium, id aliis
quoque aequo iure concessum cognosco. Sed posteaquam eo modo
mecum agere libuit,[8] ego quoque, ne desim mihi, sumpsi onus—
licet satis molestum, necessarium tamen—tum mei defendendi,
tum Guarini fortitudinem (ne dicam, ut de me scribit, audaciam)
paulum comprimendi. Etenim, cum me *audacem accusatorem magis
quam fortem* dicat, experiendum fuit an[9] hic provocator armis Vul-
caniis ab Ioveque[10] (ut ferunt) demissis in aciem descenderit.

4   Lege igitur, cum otium suppetit, primo epistulam a me con-
scriptam, quam Guarinus ridendam sibi ac[11] lacerandam putavit,
tum Guarini reprehensionem, deinde[12] defensiunculam meam.
Hoc maxime pacto vel me vel Guarinum vel utrumque aut temeritatis aut ignorantiae accusabis. Vale, et mei, ut soles, memor. Florentiae.[13]

for.[3] And so he took upon himself the vain task of fighting with me on Caesar's side, taking scant account of the law of our long-standing goodwill. For although he was not attacked by me in any matter, in any passage, or by any word, even in the slightest, he still leaped forth at the first sound of the trumpet, as they say, to do battle with me as if I were a soldier of the Pompeian faction![4]

What, indeed, drove Guarino to insult Poggio, if he ranked   3
Scipio over Caesar? What did it matter to him? Why was it his role to disparage me, to argue with me, to rebuke me time and again as some ignoble fellow, if I wanted—as we are allowed for the study and practice of eloquence—to exercise my small talents by either praising or finding fault with someone far from our time, who does not belong to his family, does not bear his name, and does not come from his nation? If he worships Caesar, if the memory of that man is dear to him, if he cherishes his name, if he extols his deeds, then he should have undertaken his defense without personal insults with me even cheering him on, and in that matter showed his mettle in speaking or writing! For what I undertook as exercise in writing, I recognize is with equal right also permitted to others. But now that it has pleased him to deal with me in this way, I have also, so as not to fail myself, taken up this burden (admittedly rather tedious, yet necessary), both to defend myself and to curb a little the courage—not to say, as he does about me, the boldness—of Guarino. And indeed, since he calls me *a bold rather than a brave accuser,* I had to test whether or not this challenger stepped down onto the battlefield with armor at hand made by Vulcan and, as the saying goes, "descended from Jove."[5]

So, when time permits, first read the letter I wrote, which Gua-   4
rino felt he had to ridicule and tear apart, then Guarino's reprimand, and finally this little defense of mine. By following this particular procedure, you will charge either me or Guarino or both with rashness or ignorance. Farewell, and remember me, as always. From Florence.

Poggii Florentini
De praestantia Scipionis et Caesaris libellus
incipit.[1]

1   Poggius plurimam salutem dicit Scipioni Ferrariensi, viro clarissimo. Rem sane arduam et imparem meis viribus postulas tibi a
me scribi, suavissime Scipio, uter scilicet vir praestantior aut excellentior fuerit et pluris extimandus,[2] Superiorne Africanus an C.
Iulius Caesar. Multa enim a veteribus rerum scriptoribus de utroque tradita sunt summa gloria et laude digna, ut difficillimum sit
inter tales principes ac tantos sententiam ferre, quamvis de altero
factum iam praeiudicium esse per Plutarchum videatur, qui Caesarem Graecorum omnium excellentissimo, Magno Alexandro,
comparavit.[3] Sed credo illum res militiae gestas et belli gloriam
secutum esse, non virtutes; nam vitia in Alexandro permulta fuisse
cognovimus.[4] Livius autem noster quid de Caesare sentiat, minime
compertum est nobis, cum ignorantia hominum aboleverit suos
illorum temporum libros; Scipionem vero 'longe clarissimum ducem et non solum suae aetatis, sed cuilibet, qui umquam fuerunt,
regum atque imperatorum parem fuisse' affirmat; qua sententia
nec Magnum Alexandrum, nec Caesarem[5] iudicare videtur Scipioni esse praeferendum. Lucianus, Graecus auctor, Hannibalem,
Scipionem ac Caesarem[6] apud inferos in certamen gloriae rerum

POGGIO BRACCIOLINI

ON THE EXCELLENCE OF
SCIPIO AND CAESAR

Poggio of Florence's Book
On the Excellence of Scipio and Caesar
begins.

Poggio warmly greets the illustrious Scipione of Ferrara.[1] It is a   1
truly challenging matter, and one beyond my powers, that you ask
me to address for you, my dearest Scipione, namely which man
was more outstanding or excellent, and to be more highly es-
teemed: the elder Africanus or C. Julius Caesar.[2] For much has
been reported by ancient writers about both men that is worthy of
the highest glory and praise, so that it is extremely difficult to pass
judgment between leaders of such quality and standing — even if it
would seem that about the latter a precedent was set already by
Plutarch, who compared Caesar to the most outstanding of all
Greeks, Alexander the Great.[3] But I believe that he was interested
in military achievements and the glory won in war, not virtues, for
we know that Alexander had many vices. What our Livy thought
about Caesar we cannot discover in any way, since mankind's ignorance has destroyed his books about those times; Scipio, however,
he asserts "to have been by far the most distinguished commander
not only of his own time, but equal to any king or general who
ever lived," from which judgment it appears that he deemed neither Alexander the Great nor Caesar to be preferred to Scipio.[4]
The Greek author Lucian playfully brought Hannibal, Scipio, and
Caesar into a debating contest in Hades over the glory of their

7

gestarum[7] disputantes ludens introduxit, ut videatur pares quodammodo eos fuisse velle sentire.

2   Caesarem, rebus bello gestis magnam gloriam adeptum, constat
fuisse civem perniciosissimum patriae, quam ceteris gentibus imperantem in servitutem redegit; et quoniam ab ea vires traditas ad
ipsius perniciem convertit, non solum non laudandum, sed tamquam patriae proditorem detestandum virum plures arbitrantur.
Scipio quoniam belli laudem cum vitae integritate coniunxit atque
omnia sua[8] consilia ad rei publicae salutem contulit eique tempore
difficillimo atque extremo paene occasu subvenit, collaudandum
eum et extollendum prae ceteris esse iudicent.[9] Ita, quamquam
multitudine ac varietate bellorum apud populum excedere videatur
gloria Caesar, tamen, si virtute et recte factis laudem et gloriam
hominum metiamur, necesse est praestare Caesari Scipionem. Illum enim ceteris praestare sapientes volunt non qui vitiis et sceleribus, sed qui virtute et honestate alios antecesserit;[10] nam vitia
aut[11] flagitia non possunt reddere hominem praeclarum, praesertim cum nulla his sit laus aut[12] gloria coniuncta,[13] quae est honeste
factorum existimatio.

3   Verum, ut quod a me petis, facilius possit perspici,[14] vita
utriusque, mores, res domi et foris gestae paucis recensendae sunt
atque invicem comparandae: tum facillimum erit discernere legen-
tibus uter alteri sit praeferendus. Hoc ut rectius explicetur, ab
utriusque adolescentia ordiamur.

4   Caesaris prior aetas, cum primum in castris versatus est, non
caruit infamia, cum 'sponda lecti Nicomedis, Bithyniae regis' et
'regina' quandoque appellaretur; quod adeo pro vero habitum est,
ut etiam sui milites post civilem victoriam ante triumphantis currum canerent: 'Gallias Caesar subegit, Nicomedes Caesarem.'

achievements, so that it seems that he was minded to view them to an extent as equals.[5]

It is evident that Caesar, despite gaining great glory from his 2 actions in war, was a thoroughly destructive citizen to his fatherland, which, while it ruled over other peoples, he reduced to slavery. Since he turned the powers it granted him to its destruction, many men reckon that he is not only not to be praised, but rather to be detested as a traitor to the fatherland. Since Scipio combined glory in war with an unblemished life, and applied all his intellectual energies to the well-being of the state, and came to its rescue during a most difficult time when it suffered an almost utter ruin: let them judge that he should be eulogized and extolled above all others. Thus, although Caesar seems to rank first in glory among the common people on account of the number and variety of his wars, still — if we measure the praise and glory of men by virtue and upright actions — Scipio necessarily surpasses Caesar. For wise men believe him to be superior who outstrips the others not in vices and crimes, but in virtue and integrity: for vices or outrages cannot make a man renowned, especially when there is no praise or glory attached to them, which is the opinion formed about deeds nobly done.

But so that what you ask of me can be ascertained more easily, 3 the life of each man and his character and achievements at home and abroad must briefly be reviewed, and these things must be compared in turn: then it will be very easy for the readers to discern which of the two is to be preferred over the other. In order to explain this properly, let us begin from the boyhood of each man.

Caesar's early years, when he first joined the barracks, were not 4 short of disrepute, for he was sometimes called "the bedstead of Nicomedes, King of Bithynia" and "queen," and this was so widely held to be true that even his own soldiers, in front of his triumphal chariot after his victory in the civil war, sang "Caesar subdued the Gallic lands, but Nicomedes Caesar."[6] In his entire youth,

· POGGIO BRACCIOLINI ·

Adolescentia omnis nihil habuit insigne, quod magnopere sit aut referendum[15] aut laudandum, praeter naturam inquietam et animum deditum factionibus et bellis intestinis; quae[16] adeo ab ipsis primoribus annis prae se tulit, ut Sullam dixisse ferant[17] 'cavendum esse puerum male praecinctum.'

5 Post annum vero trigesimum, cum ex Hispania, quo quaestor accesserat, ante tempus decessisset, Latinas colonias agitantes de civitate petenda concitavit ad novas res in Urbe moliendas. Aedilis deinde factus, cum paci atque otio infensus esset sibique etiam malis artibus potentiam quaereret, conspirasse traditur cum M. Crasso et nonnullis aliis de trucidando senatu et re publica subvertenda; cum Pisone item adolescente fertur contra rem publicam coniurasse. Ad conciliandum vero sibi plebis favorem restituit trophaea C. Marii a Sulla disiecta. C. Rabirio, quo adiutore[18] Saturninus res novas moliens oppressus fuerat, qui diem diceret, subornavit. Largitionibus profusis ac supervacuis impensis[19] ad benivolentiam infimorum et populi captandam adeo aere alieno fuit oppressus, ut pontificatum petiturus, antequam in campum ad comitia descenderet, dixisse feratur matri osculanti se domum nisi pontificem non reversurum.

6 Praeturam assecutus inter Catilinae coniurationis conscios fuisse traditur: solus certe omnium in coniuratione deprehensos conservandos censuit in senatu; quo tempore quidam ei e senatu egredienti milites exsertis gladiis mortem minitati sunt. Consul postea aetate legitima (quae erat annorum trium[20] et quadraginta) factus, pro libidine animi proque solius nutu in morem tyranni gessit consulatum. M. Bibulum collegam suis iniquitatibus adversantem domi se inclusum tenere compulit; M. Catonem,

10

there was nothing distinguished that particularly deserves to be reported or praised, except a restless nature and a mind given to faction and internal strife, which he displayed from his earliest years, so much so that Sulla is reported to have said "beware the badly belted boy!"[7]

But after his thirtieth year, having left Spain, whither he had 5 gone as quaestor, before his term was over, he incited the Latin colonies, which were engaged in seeking citizenship, to plot revolution in the City.[8] Then, having been elected aedile — since he was opposed to peace and leisure and was seeking power for himself even by wicked means — he reportedly conspired with M. Crassus and sundry others to slaughter the senate and overthrow the state; it is likewise said that he conspired against the republic with the young Piso.[9] In order to curry favor with the plebs he restored the trophies of C. Marius which Sulla had torn down.[10] He instigated someone to indict C. Rabirius, with whose help Saturninus had been crushed when he was plotting revolution.[11] Through his extravagant bribery and the excessive expenses incurred to procure the goodwill of the lowest men and of the people, he was so weighed down by debts that, when he was running for the Pontificate, before going down to the election assembly in the *campus*, he reportedly told his mother as she kissed him goodbye that he would not come home except as pontifex.[12]

When he had attained the praetorship, he was rumored to be 6 among the accomplices of Catiline's conspiracy: certainly he was the only one of all in the senate who counseled that those discovered plotting the conspiracy should be saved — at which point some soldiers with drawn swords threatened to kill him as he left the senate.[13] Afterward, elected consul at the legal age (which was · forty-three), he conducted his consulship in the manner of a tyrant, following the desires of his mind and his own whim alone. He forced his fellow-consul M. Bibulus, who opposed his iniquities, to keep himself locked in at home, and he ordered M. Cato, a

sanctissimum virum, in carcerem duci iussit actis suis et sceleribus repugnantem; quo nullum maius pessimi civis testimonium potuit afferre. Quod vero hominis rapacissimi ac furacissimi indicium fuit: tria milia pondo auri, quae erant in Capitolio, surripiens, tantundem reposuit aeris deaurati.[21]

7   Sortitus est provincias Gallias in quinquennium; quod et in aliud quinquennium prorogatum fuit: utrumque praeter leges, praeter consuetudinem, praeter maiorum instituta. Octo legiones decretae, duae ab Gn. Pompeio concessae: igitur decem legionum exercitu, magnis praeterea auxiliis, Ulteriorem Galliam ingressus primo fudit Ariovistum, Germanorum ducem, novas sibi quaerentem sedes; deinde cum Gallia omni varie[22] conflixit, tum privatis consiliis, tum communi consensu bellum renovante.[23] Saepius acie decertavit, plurima confecit bella, innumerabiles hostium copias[24] fudit, plures urbes, multa oppida vi cepit. Gallos prostravit saepius desciscentes,[25] universam Galliam (quae clauditur montibus Pyrenaeis et Alpibus, Oceano Rhenoque flumine[26]), in potestatem ditionemque Romani populi[27] victor redegit. Germanos lacessivit[28] ponte supra Rhenum constructo; Britannos aggressus pugna superans populo Romano subdidit. Quas ob res magna gloria et honore dignus videtur.

8   Sequuntur bella civilia, Pharsalicum, Africanum, Hispaniense, non digna laude, sed summa omnium hominum ac gentium exsecratione. His enim patriam suam, communem omnium parentem, oppugnavit, oppressit, perdidit; tamquam nefarius parricida. Quamquam Hispaniensis non sua virtus,[29] sed fortuna victoriam largita est: cum enim ferme[30] profligatus et victus Caesar de

most saintly man, to be cast into prison because he resisted his deeds and crimes.[14] He could not have delivered a stronger testimony of his being a thoroughly bad citizen than this. But this was evidence for him being an extremely rapacious and thieving man: secretly taking three thousand pounds of gold, which were in the Capitol, Caesar replaced them with the same amount of gilded bronze.

He obtained the Gallic provinces by lot for five years, which 7 was then renewed for another five: both against the laws, against custom, and against the traditions of the forefathers.[15] Eight legions were voted, and two handed over to him by Pompey: thus, having entered Further Gaul with an army of ten legions and great auxiliary forces besides, Caesar first routed Ariovistus, leader of the Germani, who was seeking new lands to settle.[16] Subsequently he battled the whole of Gaul in various ways, extending the war now by private counsel, now by general consent. He frequently engaged in pitched battles, completed a great number of wars, routed countless enemy forces, and took many cities and many towns by force. He frequently reduced those Gauls who were defecting, and, victorious, he brought the whole of Gaul (which is enclosed by mountains of the Pyrenees and Alps, the Ocean and the river Rhine) under the power and jurisdiction of the Roman people. After constructing a bridge over the Rhine, he harassed the Germani; he attacked the Britons and, overcoming them in battle, made them subject to the Roman people. For these things he seems worthy of great glory and honor.

Then followed the civil wars—the Pharsalian, African, and 8 Spanish wars—which were not worthy of praise, but of the utmost execration by all men and nations.[17] For in these it was his fatherland, the common parent of all, that he attacked, overwhelmed and destroyed like a heinous father-killer. Nevertheless, in the Spanish war it was not his prowess but fortune that furnished the victory: for when Caesar, all but routed and defeated,

inferenda sibi morte cogitaret, subito victores in fugam conversi sunt beneficio et ope fortunae. Pharsalicum vero bellum quam leve fuerit Cicero ipse testatur, qui plurimis in epistulis Pompeium veluti ignavum imperatorem atque imparatum[31] ducem increpans illum cum tironibus et milite collecticio adversus veteranos et robustissimum exercitum signa contulisse reprehendit. Nam Alexandrini non honorem, sed dedecus promeruit, dum Cleopatrae amore ardens incautus ferme in hostium pervenit manus; quod periculum nando effugiens evasit. Victor postmodum 'cum Cleopatra per Nilum Aethiopiam usque insanus amore penetrasset, ni[32] milites sequi se recusassent.' Pharnacis vero in Asia[33] bellum nullo labore, sola opinione confecit, una acie et[34] levi proelio hostibus superatis; quod et ipse in titulo triumphi significavit dicens 'veni, vidi, vici,' ut quodammodo citius faciliusque id bellum confecerit quam scripserit se vicisse.

9   Post civilem victoriam suscepit perpetuam dictaturam, ut solutus[35] legibus pro arbitrio suo rem publicam administraret. Atque adeo constans in retinenda fuit, ut Sullam diceret nescisse litteras, qui dictaturam deposuerit re publica constituta. Ipse litteratior[36] fuit, qui et rem publicam sustulit et populum Romanum redegit in servitutem! Omitto hastam illam et cruentam bonorum[37] venditionem civiumque[38] proscriptiones etiam ipsis victoribus deflendas; in quibus si versari velim, summa Caesaris iniquitas ostendetur.

10   Mores eius multi varie interpretantur: quidam enim commendant, alii secus tradunt. Nam prona ad principatum natura vitam multis flagitiis inquinavit; ambitio et dominandi cupido nihil ex

was considering killing himself, the victorious army suddenly took flight, owing to the kindness and help of fortune. Regarding the Pharsalian war, Cicero himself testifies to its ease, for rebuking Pompey in many letters as a cowardly general and ill-prepared commander, he reproaches him for having joined battle with recruits and hastily levied troops against veterans and a very strong army.[18] For the Alexandrian war, Caesar earned not honor but shame when, burning with love for Cleopatra, he incautiously almost fell into the hands of the enemy, a danger he escaped by swimming to safety.[19] Soon afterward the conqueror "would have sailed up the Nile with Cleopatra as far as Ethiopia, crazy with love, had not his soldiers refused to follow him."[20] Lastly, the war against Pharnaces in Asia he finished without effort through reputation alone, since the enemy were overcome in a single battle and an easy fight. This Caesar himself indicated on his triumphal placard, saying "I came, I saw, I conquered," so that he somehow finished off that war more rapidly and easily than he wrote down that he had won.[21]

After his victory in the civil wars, Caesar assumed a perpetual 9 dictatorship, so that, freed from the laws, he might govern the state according to his own will. And he was so determined to retain these powers that he said that since he laid down the dictatorship once the state had been restored, Sulla "did not know his A, B, C."[22] He was more lettered himself, he who destroyed the republic and reduced the Roman people to slavery! I pass over that auction and the bloodstained selling off of goods and the proscriptions of citizens that should be mourned even by those who were victorious—in which, if I wanted to dwell on them, Caesar's full iniquity would show itself.

Many men assess his character in various ways: some indeed 10 commend it, others report the opposite. For a nature inclined toward supreme power stained his life with many vices; ambition and the desire to rule did not permit him to act in any respect in

legibus, nihil ex utilitate publica agere permisit.[39] Facinorosos, audaces, raptores, egestate perditos, turpi iudicio damnatos in suam familiaritatem recipiens sublevabat alebatque veluti suarum cupiditatum[40] ministros. Libidine fuisse immoderata Suetonius tradit, stupra eius et adulteria referens permulta. Rapacem etiam constat fuisse et alieni appetentem, cum nonnullas civitates et oppida diripienda tradiderit militibus magis ob praedam quam ob culpam. Liberalitatem eius quidam laudando efferunt. Sed quae est liberalitas alteri per vim eripere, extorquere, furari, ut aliis largiaris? Rapina haec, non liberalitas est appellanda![41]

II   Id vero est, in quo multi Caesarem extollunt, asserentes extitisse illum[42] clementiae singularis. Verum videntur perverse nimium hoc nomine abuti. Nulla est enim clementia non trucidare eos qui, patriae libertatem tuentes, tyrannidem recusabant! Laudat noster Cicero Caesarem restituto M. Marcello multisque verbis commendat suam clementiam in civibus conservandis. Laudat item cum Q. Ligarium regemque Deiotarum defendit. At vero eas laudes non protulit veritas, sed temporum necessitas extorsit. Non enim vir excellens et amator patriae quid Caesar audire mereretur perspexit, sed quid salus civium postularet. Quamvis quae laus[43] est non iugulasse cives, cum patriae sanguinem exsorbuerit? Neque tamen ipsi sicarii et latrones hoc faciunt, ut cuius[44] spolia abstulerint,[45] vitam ac sanguinem concupiscant! At ipse Cicero, cum dicendi quae vellet ex animo libertas data est, quid de eo[46] senserit, saepius expressit: et[47] cum 'tyrannum' eum appellaverit[48] et (crudelitatis illum in quadam ad Cornelium Nepotem epistula

accordance with the laws, nor for the common good. He received into his circle men who were criminals, rash and thieving, ruined by destitution and doomed by base judgment, and raised and nourished them as agents of his own desires. That Caesar was a man of immoderate lust is reported by Suetonius, who makes reference to his very many acts of fornication and adultery. That he was rapacious and covetous of other people's property is generally agreed, since he gave a number of cities and towns to his soldiers to plunder, more for the sake of loot than because of their guilt. Some people extol his liberality with praise. But what sort of liberality is it to take by force, extort, and steal from one in order to give lavishly to others?[23] That should be called robbery, not liberality!

But there is one thing for which many extol Caesar, claiming 11 that he was a man of singular clemency. Yet they seem to misuse that title all too erroneously. For it is in no way clemency not to slaughter those who, while protecting the liberty of the fatherland, were resisting the imposition of a tyranny! Our Cicero praises Caesar for restoring M. Marcellus, and commends with many words his clemency in sparing citizens. He praises him in like manner when he defends Q. Ligarius and King Deiotarus.[24] But really, it was not the truth that called forth those words of praise, but the necessity of the times which extorted them. For that excellent man and patriot did not consider what Caesar deserved to have said of him, but what the safety of the citizens demanded. But what is the merit in not having strangled citizens once he had bled the fatherland dry? Indeed, not even cutthroats and thieves act in this way, that, once they have made off with someone's spoils, they then desire his lifeblood![25] But Cicero himself, when the liberty to say what he pleased had been granted, frequently expressed what he thought of Caesar, both when he called him a "tyrant" and, as he denounces his savagery in a letter to Cornelius

increpans) 'perditis profligatisque consiliis Caesarem usum fuisse'
adfirmet.

12   Nihil ergo reperimus in Caesaris vita, quod digne laudari me-
reatur, praeter res bello gestas; quas non possumus negare fuisse[49]
magnificas, licet patriae et civibus perniciosas. Sed obscurentur
paulo necesse est ea ipsa, qua usus est in rem publicam perfidia et
crudelitate.[50] Sed de Caesare hactenus.

13   Scipionis vitam, quod Latine nunc extet, nulli veterum scripsere: eo viri ad omnia excellentissimi gesta singula ignorantur.
Maiora quaedam sparsa reperiuntur apud varios auctores; quae,
prout facultas tulit, in hanc epistulam conieci.

14   Adolescentia eius non ignobilis fuit aut obscura, sed illustris
ac[51] praeclara, quae edidit[52] egregia facinora omnium sermone cele-
branda. Morum quidem gravitatem ab ineunte aetate, continentiam, integritatem[53] vitae, divinam quandam indolem et quasi
praematuram senectutem in eo fuisse, omnes tradunt.[54] T. quidem
Livius, qui usque ad devictam Carthaginem (quo ad bellum secundum Punicum attinet), Scipionis gesta complectitur, ait 'non tantum veris virtutibus admirabilem, sed arte quoque quadam ab
iuventa in ostentationem[55] earum compositum, pleraque[56] apud
multitudinem aut per nocturnas visa species, aut veluti divinitus
mente monita agentem; qui mos, per omnem vitam servatus, vul-
gatae opinioni fidem fecit stirpis eum divinae virum esse.'

15   Prima laus adolescentiae traditur quod, 'vixdum[57] pubertatem[58]
ingressus, patrem P. Cornelium Scipionem consulem adversus
Hannibalem apud Ticinum pugnantem[59] ac saucium interventu
suo servavit, in quo singularis pietatis officium et patriae praestitit
et patri.' Id vero adolescentis excellens[60] facinus et supra illius

Nepos, when he asserts that "Caesar had availed himself of desperate and vile counsels."[26]

Thus we find nothing in Caesar's life that deserves worthily to   12
be praised, except for his deeds done in war, which we cannot
deny were great — if we allow that they were deadly for the fatherland and the citizens. However, even these are inevitably somewhat overshadowed by the perfidy and cruelty with which he
treated the state. But enough about Caesar.

The life of Scipio — as to what is now extant in Latin — was not   13
written down by any of the ancients: hence almost every single
deed of this outstanding man is unknown.[27] Some of the greater
ones are found scattered among several authors, and these I have
brought together in this letter as far as my capacities allow.

His youth was not ignoble or unknown, but illustrious and re-   14
nowned, and gave rise to outstanding deeds that should be celebrated in the words of all. Indeed, all report that from an early age
he had a gravity of manners, a self-restraint, an unblemished way
of living, a certain innate godlike quality, and, as it were, a premature old age. Titus Livy, indeed, who covers the deeds of Scipio —
in as far as pertains to the second Punic War — up to the fall of
Carthage, says "that he was not only admirable for his true virtues,
but also, with a certain skill cultivated from boyhood, apt at their
display, performing in front of the masses many things he had seen
in nocturnal visions or been forewarned of as if by divine inspiration. This habit, which he maintained all his life, lent credit to the
common opinion that he was a man of divine stock."[28]

As the first merit of his youth it is reported that "barely into   15
puberty, he saved his father, consul P. Cornelius Scipio, when he
was fighting and wounded against Hannibal at the Ticinus by his
intervention, and in doing so rendered a singular duty of love to
both his fatherland and his father."[29] And this was truly an outstanding achievement for an adolescent, and beyond the prudence

aetatis prudentiam et robur: cum post acceptam Cannensem cladem reliquiae militum ad eum et Appium Claudium, tribunos militum, summam imperii detulissent nuntiareturque iuvenes quosdam auctore L. Caecilio Metello[61] de relinquenda Italia agitare,[62] Metelli domum petens, cum in consilium[63] iuvenum, quod erat allatum, venisset, stricto gladio mortem minitans iurare omnes coegit numquam se patriam deserturos. His duabus tantum rebus, etiam si reliqua[64] aetatis acta deessent, multorum senum, qui viri clarissimi habiti sunt, adolescentulus gloriam aequavit, primum parentem, tum patriam ab interitu[65] liberans.

16   Attamen haec leviora videntur reddere quae sequuntur. Nam cum P. et Cn. Scipionibus in Hispania interfectis, deleto[66] exercitu, adeo res perditae et desperatae essent, re publica multis cladibus afflicta, ut nemo illuc cum imperio proficisci auderet, reliquis maioribus natu cunctantibus et recusantibus, solus quartum et vigesimum annum aetatis agens, eo se iturum populo Romano ultro spopondit magna animi fiducia, maiore futurae virtutis indole, maxima patriae caritate. Non illum patris patruique interitus, non exercitus concisi, non hostium vires, non Hispaniae rebus Romanis adversae, non belli terror adolescentem deterruerunt, quominus ingenti animo, aetate etiam repugnante, eam provinciam deposceret, in qua plus timoris quam spei propositum esse videbatur. Itaque magno populi consensu, tamquam fatis ipsum ad Carthaginensium bellum deposcentibus, Hispaniae sibi decretae fuerunt, decem milia peditum, mille equites, praeter reliquias veteris exercitus concessa.[67]

17   Hac tam parva manu Hispanias aggressus Carthaginem Novam una die pugnando vi cepit; qua in re, inter cetera virtutis suae

and strength of that age: when, after the defeat suffered at Cannae, the remnants of the soldiers gave him and Appius Claudius, the military tribunes, the highest command, and it was reported that certain youngsters on the instigation of L. Caecilius Metellus were contemplating abandoning Italy, Scipio, heading for the house of Metellus, and finding the council of the young men as had been reported, forced everyone, threatening death with drawn sword, to take an oath that they would never abandon the fatherland.[30] By these two deeds alone, even if the rest of his life's actions were unknown, he equaled, as a mere youth, the glory of many old men who have been deemed renowned: freeing first his father, and then his fatherland, from ruin.

Still, the sequel seems to make these deeds slight. After P. and   16 Cn. Scipio had been killed in Spain and the army wiped out, things were so ruined and desperate, and the republic afflicted by so many disasters, that no one dared to go to Spain holding the command.[31] Then Scipio alone, being in his twenty-fourth year, while other, older men were delaying and refusing, pledged to the Roman people of his own accord that he would go to Spain, spurred by great confidence of mind, a yet greater natural bent for future prowess, and the greatest love for his fatherland.[32] Neither the deaths of his father and uncle, nor the slaughter of the armies, nor the forces of the enemy, nor the two Spains set against the interests of Rome, nor the terror of war deterred him — an adolescent — possessed as he was of a mighty spirit that did not, indeed, befit his age, from demanding that province which seemed to promise more fear than hope.[33] And so, by great popular consent, as if the fates were calling him out for the war against Carthage, Scipio was voted the two Spains and granted 10,000 soldiers and 1000 horsemen, in addition to the remnants of the old army.

After attacking the Spains with this small band, he seized New   17 Carthage by force in one day of fighting; and in this matter — besides other deeds of his virtue — he took the utmost care that the

opera, ut mulieres tutae essent ab iniuria militari, summopere curavit. Virginem eximiae formae captivam, principi Celtiberorum desponsatam, coram se adduci—licet et victor et adolescens—prohibuit eamque viro cum donis restituit intactam; qua continentia et benignitate sibi[68] Celtiberorum omnium benivolentiam devinxit. Hispanias omnes, quas Carthaginienses post patris mortem occupaverant, gentem barbaram ac feram, caesis quattuor Poenorum exercitibus, quattuor summis ducibus fusis ac fugatis, ipsis Hispanis qui desciverant subactis, in populi Romani potestatem redegit. Ad Syphacem regem potentissimum profectus ad amicitiam Romanorum traduxit; cuius violatae Syphax postea poenas dedit.

18   Devictis Hispanis, Romam rediens, consul factus est ante tempus, cum nondum trigesimum excessisset[69] aetatis annum. Consul in Siciliam primo, inde[70] in Africam transiit cum exercitu, quem nonnulli decem milia peditum, duo milia et ducentos equites, alii peditum sedecim milia, equites mille et sescentos, quidam[71] vero magis quinque et triginta milia peditum equitumque fuisse tradunt. Ubi profligatis duobus Poenorum validis exercitibus, capto rege Syphace, pluribus urbibus vi expugnatis, demum ipsum Hannibalem, excellentissimum imperatorum omnium,[72] ipsius Romani populi quindecim annis victorem, acie superavit. Quod ne levi certamine aut Marte incruento factum videatur: duodecim milia ex Romanis in ea pugna cecidisse atque Hannibalem dixisse post amissam victoriam 'se numquam struxisse aciem melius' Livius scribit. Hoc magno est argumento non cum exercitu invalido, non cum tironibus, non cum barbaris, non cum ignavo duce Scipioni certamen fuisse, sed cum robusto milite, cum veteranis, cum adsuetis Romanae militiae,[73] cum sagacissimo imperatore.

women might be safe from harm at the hands of the soldiers.[34] He forbade the bringing into his presence of a captured maiden of great beauty, betrothed to the leader of the Celtiberians, although he was both victorious and a young man, and restored her to her fiancé untouched and accompanied by gifts, and through this self-restraint and courtesy he earned himself the goodwill of all Celt-iberians.[35] All parts of the Spains—a barbarous and savage na-tion—which the Carthaginians had held after the death of his father, Scipio returned to the power of the Roman people, having vanquished four Punic armies, routed and driven to flight four supreme commanders, and reduced those Spaniards who had de-fected. After journeying to meet Syphax, a very powerful king, he brought him over into the friendship of the Romans—for the be-trayal of which Syphax later paid the price.[36]

Returning to Rome once the Spains had been conquered, 18 Scipio was made consul before the legal age, as he was not yet thirty years old.[37] As consul, he first crossed to Sicily, and then to Africa with an army which some report to have consisted of 10,000 foot soldiers and 2200 horsemen, while others say it was 16,000 foot soldiers and 1600 horse, and yet others claim it had more than 35,000 infantry and cavalry combined.[38] There, having routed two strong armies of the Carthaginians and captured King Syphax, and having taken many cities by force, he finally faced Hannibal himself—the most outstanding commander of all and triumphant over the Romans themselves for fifteen years—and overcame him in battle.[39] Lest this may seem to have been achieved in an easy contest or through a bloodless war: Livy writes that 12,000 Roman soldiers perished in that battle, and that Hannibal said, when victory was lost, that "he had never drawn up a battle line better."[40] This is strong proof that Scipio's struggle was not with a weak army, nor with recruits, nor with barbarians, nor with a cowardly commander, but with a hardy body of soldiers, with veterans, with men used to Roman warfare, and with a most

Carthaginienses pacem ab Romanis[74] petere etiam iniquis condi-
cionibus coegit. Ad triumphum inde rediit. Legatum postea fratri
in Asiam contra Antiochum regem se iturum pollicitus est, ne
fratri ad res bellicas infirmo provincia eriperetur, belloque Antiochum superavit. Haec ab eo gesta bello accepimus,[75] adeo praeclara ut nulli imperatorum secundus esse videatur.

19   Sed non minor[76] virtus eius[77] domi conspicua fuit. Summam in
eo comitatem fuisse ferunt, ad omnia ingenium docile ac promptum, mores probatissimos, auctoritatem vero permaximam. Cuius
rei illud habemus testimonium certissimum, quod, cum duo Petilii
tribuni plebis ei ad populum diem[78] dixissent, qua die iudicium
futurum erat conscendens rostra Scipio corona triumphali: 'hac die
(inquit) Quirites, Carthaginem a vobis leges pacis petere coegi:
proinde aequum est nos ire in Capitolium atque Iovi Optimo
Maximo gratias agere'; tum ex rostris adsurgentem populus uni-
versus, equester ordo et senatus in Capitolium prosecutus est, Pe-
tiliis solis in foro cum ignominia relictis. Magnitudo animi, aequi-
tas, temperantia, moderatio multis in rebus celebratur, sed tum
maxime, cum ea, quae ultro meritis eius a senatu et populo offerebantur, recusavit. Nam cum ob eius in patriam atque in singulos
cives merita singularia ad eum ornandum exquisiti honores quae-
rerentur cumque patres conscripti statuam sibi in Capitolio, in
comitio, in rostris, in curia, in ipsa cella Iovis Optimi Maximi decernere, imaginem triumphali habitu in Capitolinis pulvinaribus
collocare vellent, cum continuum consulatum, perpetuam dictaturam offerrent, nihil horum neque senatus consulto, neque plebis-
cito fieri passus est, maiori animo honores recusans quam[79]

astute general. He forced the Carthaginians to seek peace with the
Romans even under unfavorable terms; he returned thence to a
triumph. Later he promised to go to Asia as legate to his brother
against King Antiochus (lest the province be taken from his
brother, who was weak in military matters), and overcame Antiochus in war.[41] These are the things we have learned he did in war,
so illustrious that he seems to be second to none of the generals.

But his virtue at home was no less conspicuous. He was ex-   19
tremely affable, it is said, and had a keen mind responsive to all
matters, most agreeable manners, and truly a very great presence.
For this we have the following most reliable testimony: when the
two Petilii, tribunes of the plebs, had summoned him to trial before the people, Scipio, on what was to be the day of judgment,
climbed the rostra wearing his triumphal crown and said: "On this
day, citizens, I forced the Carthaginians to seek the terms of peace
from you: hence it is meet that we go to the Capitol and give
thanks to Jupiter Optimus Maximus."[42] Then the whole people,
the equestrian order, and the senate followed him as he rose from
the rostra, leaving the Petilii alone in the forum with their shame.
His greatness of spirit, his fairness, his self-restraint and sense of
measure are celebrated in many instances, but most of all at that
moment, when he refused what was being freely offered on account of his merits by the senate and the people. For when special
honors were sought with which to adorn him, because of his remarkable services to the fatherland and to individual citizens, and
the conscript fathers intended to decree him a statue on the Capitol, in the assembly place, on the rostra, in the curia, and in the
very *cella* of the temple of Jupiter Optimus Maximus, and to place
his effigy dressed in triumphal garb on the couches of the Capito-
line gods, and when they offered him a continuous consulship or a
dictatorship in perpetuity: Scipio allowed none of these things to
come to pass — neither by senate decree nor by popular vote — and
instead refused those honors with yet more greatness of mind than

effecerat, ut illis dignus haberetur. Magna viri sapientia, qui in virtute ipsa et parta laude satis praemii, satis honoris esse existimavit; maior vero prudentia, qui cavit exemplo suo, ne similium rerum cupiditas et licentia ad deteriores postmodum cives perveniret!

20   Hae virtutes tantam maiestatem Scipioni, tantam venerationem apud omnes comparaverant, ut apud Linternum[80] exsulantem[81] praedones accesserint venerabundi tamquam aliquod numen divinum; qui postem domus veluti templi alicuius venerantes, positis ante vestibulum tamquam loci sacri donis, exosculata Scipionis manu abierunt. Magna profecto vis est virtutis, ut etiam ab eis,[82] qui illam oderunt, colatur! Ego quidem hunc solum diem, hoc praedonum testimonium omnibus triumphis Caesaris antepono, siquidem unicum diem cum virtute actum ceteris gestis, a quibus abest virtus, sapientes iudicant praeferendum. Quid loquar de caritate eius in patriam,[83] quam cum[84] per omnem vitam repraesentavit, tum etiam in morte, cum eius iniurias non nisi parvo titulo ultus fuerit, quo ingratam appellavit? Illud maximi animi et amoris erga patriam insigne indicium, quod, cum sua magnitudo libertatem obumbrare videretur eoque illius opes crevissent (ut refert Seneca), ut 'aut Scipionem libertati, aut libertatem Scipioni iniuriam facere oporteret,' satius existimans patriae iniurias tolerare quam inferre, secessit Linternum[85] in exilium voluntarium, ne libertatem publicam sua praesentia violaret, ibique obiit diem suum, vir adnumerandus inter priscos heroas, quos[86] gentilis stultitia inter deos ascripsit.

21   Quoniam utriusque vitam carptim retulimus, eos nunc—ut eluceat, quod quaeritur—invicem[87] comparemus. Scipionis adolescentiam tum probatissimi mores, tum facta honorifica

that which had made him deemed worthy of them.[43] Great is the wisdom of a man who believed that there is enough reward, enough honor in virtue itself and in praises properly earned; greater still the prudence of one who took care that his example did not afterward inspire lust and license for similar things in inferior citizens!

These virtues had earned Scipio so much standing, so much veneration among all that, when he was in exile near Liternum, pirates came to him, revering him as though some divine power: they gave worship at the doorstep of his house as if it were a temple, and once they had placed gifts before the entrance as before some sacred place, they kissed Scipio's hand and left.[44] Great indeed is the power of virtue, that she is worshipped even by those who spurn her! I certainly rank this one day, this testimony of the pirates, above all the triumphs of Caesar, since indeed wise men deem one day spent in virtuous conduct preferable over all other deeds from which virtue is lacking.[45] What shall I say about his love for the fatherland, which he showed not only in his whole life but even in death, when he did not avenge his injuries except with a small inscription, in which he called it ungrateful?[46] This is a remarkable sign of a lofty spirit and love toward the fatherland: that, when his greatness seemed to overshadow liberty, and his power had grown to the extent that, as Seneca reports, "it would become unavoidable that either Scipio must injure liberty, or liberty Scipio," deeming it better to suffer injury from the fatherland than to inflict it, he left for voluntary exile in Liternum, lest by his presence he violate the liberty of the community, and there he died: a man to be numbered among the heroes of old, whom the folly of their people assigned a place among the gods.[47]

Since we have reported the lives of both men separately, let us now compare them in turn, so that the answer we seek may shine forth. Scipio's youth is marked both by the most excellent conduct

20

21

commendant, continentia, pudore, modestia plenam; Caesaris vero reprobant omnes flagitio et dedecore inquinatam. Scipioni fatali paene rei publicae tempore et eo bello, quo vires eius ferme[88] conciderant, ultro et ante tempus populus Romanus non privata ambitione, sed utilitate communi coactus detulit consulatum; in quo Urbem atque Italiam, variis cladibus attritam, ex faucibus Hannibalis liberavit. Caesar, sua aetate florente re publica nihilque adversi formidante, largitionibus, ambitu, seditiosorum[89] suffragio,[90] factione principum adsecutus est consulatum; in quo iecit fundamenta rei publicae evertendae. Scipio legibus obtemperans atque ea appetens, quae ad salutem publicam pertinerent, imperium cum suo socio partitus est, Siciliam provinciam sortitus; Caesar, conculcatis legibus, solus consulatum gessit (altero consule domi recluso), ut rem publicam propria libidine conquassaret. Scipionem illustrant virtutes permultae: iustitia, continentia, gravitas, modestia, temperantia, integritas vitae, sanctitas morum, caritas erga patriam singularis. Caesaris nomen flagitia plurima dehonestant: rapinae, furta, intestinae dissensiones, civilis sanguis, libido immoderata dominandi, stupra, adulteria, studium lacerandae patriae atque animus ad omne facinus promptus. Quo fit ut ad hanc diem nihil extet, in quo Caesar vestigium ullum virtutis suae possit imprimere, nisi forsan seditiosum esse civem, sui profusum, alieni appetentem, furem, rapacem, adulterum, factionibus et perturbandae[91] rei publicae intentum laudi dandum putamus.

22   Sequuntur deinceps res amborum bello et foris gestae. Caesar post tertium et quadragesimum aetatis annum missus est, et quidem cum decem legionibus, ad Gallos, gentem barbaram ac feram, sed bello insuetam. At is fuit exercitus, ea auxilia, is dux belli, qui

and by honorable deeds, and full of self-restraint, chastity, and modesty; but that of Caesar is reproached by all, and stained by outrages and infamy. To Scipio, during an almost fatal time for the republic in a war in which her forces had all but collapsed, the Roman people granted the consulship, freely and before his time, driven not by private ambition but by the common good: the consulship during which he freed the City and Italy, worn down by various disasters, from the clutches of Hannibal. Caesar, while the republic was flourishing in his day and fearing no misfortune, attained the consulship through lavish spending, bribery, the votes of rebels, and faction between leaders: holding that office, he laid the foundations for overthrowing the state. Scipio, complying with the laws and pursuing that which contributed to the well-being of all, shared his command with his colleague and obtained by lot as his province Sicily. Caesar, having trampled the laws under foot, conducted his consulship alone, while the other consul remained locked in at home, so that he shook the republic by his personal desire. Scipio shines with many virtues: justice, self-restraint, dignity, modesty, evenhandedness, an unblemished life, purity of conduct, and a singular love for the fatherland. Caesar's name is defiled by numerous outrages: plunder, theft, civil discord, citizens' blood, an unchecked desire for rule, fornication, adultery, a readiness to harm the fatherland, and a spirit prone to every crime. From this it stems that to this day there is nothing on record on which Caesar could leave any trace of his virtue—unless perhaps we reckon that it is laudable to be a seditious citizen, profligate with his own property and greedy for that of others, a thief, a plunderer, and an adulterer, intent on faction and throwing the republic into confusion.

Then follow the deeds done by both in war and abroad. Caesar 22 was sent when he was forty-three years old, and with ten legions at that, to the Gauls, a barbarous and wild people, but unused to war. Yet such was the army, such the auxiliaries, such the

facile possent[92] victoria potiri: Romanus contra barbarum, armatus contra inermem, veteranus contra tirones, doctus rei militaris adversus bellicae[93] artis ignaros, dux excellens adversus populos sine ducibus, sine imperatoribus bellantes, qui nihil praeter impetum animi et vires corporis ad proelia adferebant; quod et prima contra Ariovistum pugna clarissime[94] ostenditur, et multis praeterea in locis. Adiecit Romano imperio Britanniam, in qua populus vagus et sine certo duce vivebat, neque domesticis neque externis bellis adsuetus. Scipioni adolescenti provincia Hispania decreta est, cum duabus legionibus tantum ac reliquiis paterni exercitus in Hispania concisi; imperium in annum datum, sed contra Hispanos, homines feroces, exercitatos in armis, numero ac viribus fidentes, contra Carthaginiensium quattuor exercitus,[95] uni duci adversus quattuor Poenorum imperatores; quod nequaquam parvi faciendum videtur. Ducum enim in bello prudentiam, consilium, virtutem plus valere compertum est quam militum audaciam aut fortitudinem, quippe quae sine disciplina, sine duce se ipsas conficiunt. His superatis, caesis, expulsis, Hispaniam populi Romani ditioni restituit.

23   Caesari data provincia primum est in quinquennium; Scipioni in annum, et cum in Hispaniam profectus est et cum consul in Siciliam, deinde in Africam transiit — licet in alium annum imperium illi fuerit prorogatum. Sed tamen quinque annorum fiducia et animum et facultatem maiorem attulit res maximas adgrediendi quam unius anni imperium; quod an prorogari deberet erat incertum. Non enim magna facinora parvo tempore effici possunt, praesertim cum timetur successor, qui iam gloriam adeptam possit praeripere; quod et Lucculo accidit Mithridate et Tigrane regibus

commander in war, that they could easily gain victory: a Roman against a barbarian, armed against unarmed, a veteran against recruits, a man schooled in military science against men ignorant of the arts of war, an outstanding commander against people waging war without commanders, without generals, who brought nothing to the battles except the drive of their spirit and the force of their body—as was shown brilliantly both in the first battle against Ariovistus and on many other occasions. Caesar added Britain to the Roman Empire, in which lived a wandering people without a certain leader, and accustomed neither to internal nor external wars.[48] To Scipio, the province of Spain was assigned when he was a youth, with only two legions and the remnants of his father's army, which had been slaughtered in Spain; the command was given for a year, but against Spaniards, fierce men, trained in warfare, relying on their number and strength, and against four armies of the Carthaginians; it was given to one commander against four generals of the Carthaginians, which should by no means be held a small thing.[49] For in war, the prudence, counsel, and virtue of commanders is found to count for more than the boldness or bravery of the troops, which in fact without discipline and without a leader destroy themselves. Having overcome these, wiped them out, and driven them off, Scipio restored Spain to the jurisdiction of the Roman people.

Caesar was first given the province for five years; Scipio for a 23 year, when he went to Spain as well as when he went as consul to Sicily, and subsequently crossed to Africa—granted that his command was extended for another year. But still, the confidence of five years brought greater spirit and capacity for undertaking the greatest things than a one-year command, the prolongation of which was uncertain. For great deeds cannot be done in a short time, especially when one is concerned about one's successor, who can steal glory already acquired—which happened to Lucullus after he defeated the kings Mithridates and Tigranes, and Scipio

devictis, et ipsum Scipionem ferunt dubitasse, cum diceret, nisi successorem partae iam per eum gloriae timuisset, non ad peten- dam pacem, sed ad dedendam[96] civitatem compulsurum fuisse Carthaginienses. Caesar Pompeium superavit, egregium ducem; Scipio Hannibalem, praestantissimum omnium, qui umquam fuerunt, imperatorem. Caesar Iubam, regem Numidiae, devicit; Scipio Syphacem, potentissimum regem, acie superatum captum- que Romam misit. Caesar Pharnacem, regem Asiae, parva manu, levi praelio, nullo labore (ut ipsemet testatus est) profligavit; Sci- pio Antiochum, regem Asiae, insultantem belloque Romanum po- pulum lacessentem, magna cura et[97] virtute compressit.

24   Quam ob rem, quoniam virtus sola est, quae viros claros, prae- stantes, dignos gloria et laude solet efficere, vitia vero detestan- dos,[98] ne[99] utique obscurum aut dubium esse debet recte iudi- canti[100] utriusque facta atque ea aequa[101] mente expendenti virtute et recte factis Scipionem multo superiorem Caesare extitisse, glo- ria vero militari et rebus gestis nulla ex parte inferiorem. Nam al- terius vitam multis officiis et in rem publicam meritis[102] praecla- ram constat fuisse; alterius pluribus flagitiis obductam. Scipionis liberalitas, beneficentia, pudicitia, castitas; Caesaris furta, rapinae, stupra et lasciviae ostenduntur. Alter adolescentulam et ipse ado- lescens viro tradidit intactam; alter iam senex Cleopatram, alterius coniugem, abduxit. Alteri otium, pax, salus patriae, alteri discor- diae, bella et patriae pernicies cordi erant. Scipioni honores et dig- nitates ultro offerebantur; Caesar per vim et ambitum auferebat. Scipio oblatam dictaturam repulit; Caesar extorsit. Alter liberta- tem sui populi conservavit; alter redegit in miserrimam servitutem. Scipio, ne libertati patriae officeret, sponte in exilium secessit;

himself is reported to have been in doubt about this, since he said that if he had not been worried about a successor to the glory he had already accumulated, he would have compelled the Carthaginians not to seek peace, but to hand over their city.[50] Caesar overcame Pompey, a distinguished commander; Scipio vanquished Hannibal, the most outstanding of all generals who ever lived. Caesar defeated Juba, king of Numidia; Scipio overcame Syphax, an extremely powerful king, in battle, and sent him captive to Rome.[51] Caesar routed Pharnaces, king of Asia, with a small host, in a light battle, and without effort, as he himself testified; Scipio suppressed with great effort and prowess Antiochus, king of Asia, who insulted and vexed the Roman people in war.[52]

For this reason — since virtue alone is wont to make men distinguished, outstanding, and worthy of glory and praise, while vice renders them detestable — it ought to be clear and beyond doubt to anyone who correctly appraises the deeds of both men, and weighs them with a fair mind, that in terms of virtue and just deeds, Scipio was far superior to Caesar, while he was in no way inferior in terms of military glory and achievements. For it is a fact that the life of the one shone with many duties and services rendered to the state, while that of the other was obscured by many outrages. Scipio's liberality, generosity, modesty, and chastity are evident, as are Caesar's thefts, his acts of plunder, fornication, and lasciviousness. One, when he was himself a youth, restored a young girl to her fiancé untouched; the other, already an old man, carried off Cleopatra, who was someone else's wife. The former cared for peace and quiet and the security of the fatherland; the latter for discord, war, and the ruin of the fatherland. To Scipio honors and rank were freely offered; Caesar stole them by force and bribery. Scipio spurned the dictatorship he was offered, Caesar extorted it. One preserved the freedom of his people, the other reduced them to the most pitiful slavery. Scipio, lest he hinder the liberty of the fatherland, withdrew into exile of his own accord;

24

Caesar, ut libertatem eriperet, praestantissimos cives exsulare coegit. Alter ad conservandam patriam sua consilia direxit; alter ad delendam ac prosternendam.

25   Adde quod nomen Caesaris docti omnes viri exsecrari et odio habere deberent. Non enim magis patriae quam Latinae linguae et bonarum artium extitit parricida. Una enim cum libertate corruit Latina eloquentia et studia litterarum, quae in ipso flore, prius fere quam inciperent, exstincta sunt. Erat in culmine eloquentia, erant ceterarum bonarum artium[103] incrementa; quae statim prostrata re publica defecerunt. Erant complures viri doctissimi atque eloquentissimi, quos civilis clades absumpsit.[104] Vigebant studia philosophiae et ceterarum liberalium artium tempore libertatis; quam nisi delevisset Caesar, crevissent Latina ingenia neque Graecis ullo doctrinarum genere cessissent. At vero, libertate exstincta, subsecuta sunt imperatorum portenta nefaria, qui[105] et[106] doctos semper ac[107] virtutem oderunt, et adversati sunt litterarum studiis et[108] doctrinae.

26   Habes a me, iocundissime Scipio, quod postulasti. Nunc et tuum et aliorum iudicium liberum sit, ut quisque sentiat, quod[109] velit. Vale, iiii Idus Apriles, Florentiae.[110]

Caesar, in order to steal this liberty, forced the most outstanding citizens into exile. One applied his thoughts to the preservation of his fatherland, the other to its destruction and utter ruin.

Add to this that all learned men should curse the name of Cae- 25
sar and consider it loathsome. For he was no less the father-killer of the fatherland than of the Latin language and the liberal arts. Indeed, hand in hand with liberty, Latin eloquence collapsed, and the cultivation of letters — in its very blossom, almost before it began — was destroyed. Eloquence was at its peak, and there were gains in the other liberal arts, which withered away as soon as the state fell. There were many extremely learned and eloquent men, whom the civil wars destroyed. The study of philosophy and other liberal arts thrived during the era of liberty, and if Caesar had not wiped this out, the Latin genius would have grown and not have yielded to the Greeks in any discipline. But in truth, once liberty was dead, there followed the abominable monstrosities of the emperors, who always hate learned men and virtue, and are opposed to the study of letters and learning.

My dear Scipione, you have what you asked of me. Let now 26
your judgment and that of others be free, so that each may believe as he will. Be well. On the 10th of April, in Florence.

35

EPISTOLA AD
LEONELLUM ESTENSEM[1]

1 Guarinus[2] illustri[3] domino[4] Leonello Estensi salutem.[5]

Nuntius ecce novus affertur. 'Novitate movebere facti.'[6] Exortus est Caesaromastix unus, qui Caesari calumnias intendat et ei tenebras conetur offundere,[7] quem omnium gentium litterae decantant et obstupescunt, qui splendore nominis totum vel mortuus illustrat orbem. Quidni? 'Imperium Oceano, famam qui terminat[8] astris!' Id cum videatur indignum facinus, ad te provoco, princeps illustris, cum regum salus maxime regi[9] tuenda sit. Accusat ille audax potius quam fortis accusator; causam dicunt[10] scriptores nobilissimi; testes accedunt et quidem locupletes. Tu, partem cum audieris utramque, pro tua severitate sententiam[11] proferes.

LETTER TO
LEONELLO D'ESTE

Guarino greets the illustrious lord Leonello d'Este.[1]   1

Look, a new tiding is brought. "You will be moved by the novelty of the fact."[2] A single scourge of Caesar has arisen, to direct slanders at Caesar and attempt to cast shadows over him whom the writings of all peoples continually rehearse and wonder at, and who even in death brightens the whole globe with the splendor of his name.[3] Of course! "He limits his Empire by the Ocean, his fame by the stars!"[4] Since this appears a shameful deed I refer the case to you, illustrious prince, as the well-being of kings is above all to be safeguarded by a king. The accuser accuses rashly rather than bravely; the noblest authors plead the case; witnesses come forward, and substantial ones at that. You, once you have heard both sides, shall pronounce judgment in accordance with your stern character.

Guarini Veronensis
De praestantia Caesaris et Scipionis
ad Leonellum Estensem[1]

1   Guarinus Veronensis clarissimo viro Poggio, apostolico secretario, salutem plurimam dicit.[2]

Remeante proximis diebus[3] illustri principe nostro, qui visendi et salutandi pontificis maximi causa Florentiam se contulerat, egregia mihi voluptas allata est, cum—pro sua in me caritate et mea in eius maiestatem observantia—eum salvum ad nos revertisse perspexerim.[4] Accessit ad gratiam[5] laetus de te nuntius, quo et recte valere te, et res tibi secundas[6] aspirare factus[7] sum certior; quibus gratulari et perinde ac meis gaudere obvenit, pro verissima et veterrima nostra benivolentia. Adiunctus est, quasi cumulus dulcissimus, quidam[8] scriptorum tuorum fructus, qui (mihi mirificis pollicitationibus oblatus impatienti[9]) me quadam exspectatione refersit atque demulsit. Referentibus enim, seu potius buccinantibus, duobus equestris[10] ordinis viris sane splendidis et sapientissimis, didici Scipionis ac Caesaris praestantiam et differentiam ex rebus eorum gestis abs te collectam esse, et sub unum aspectum adductam. Ingenti enim spe deductus sum rem certe praeclaram contemplaturum esse me,[11] ut longa deinceps inquisitione opus non foret ad cognoscendam utriusque vitam, pro tua eximia

38

ON THE EXCELLENCE OF CAESAR AND SCIPIO

Guarino of Verona
On the Excellence of Caesar and Scipio
to Leonello d'Este

Guarino of Verona warmly greets the renowned apostolic secretary   1
Poggio.

When our illustrious prince returned a few days ago from Florence, where he had gone to meet and greet the pope, I was delighted, on account of his affection toward me and my observance toward his majesty, to see him come back to us safely.[1] Added to my pleasure were happy tidings about you, from which I learned that you are well and your affairs prosper: for this it is fitting to congratulate you and rejoice as if they were my own, given our most sincere and long-standing friendship. On top of that came, as it were as the pinnacle of my delight, some fruit of your writings, brought to me with amazing promises and, in my impatience, filling and entrancing me with some sort of expectation. For from the two truly illustrious and very wise men of the equestrian order who brought it back — or rather blew its trumpet — I learned that you had gathered from the deeds of Scipio and Caesar their excellence and the difference between them, and brought these under a single heading.[2] I was led on by a great hope that I would surely behold a noble thing, since from now on no cumbersome research would be required to learn about the lives of each man, thanks to your extraordinary learning and reading of innu-

doctrina et innumerabilium rerum lectione, in qua per aetatem atque otium versaris impensius.

2   Sic enim arbitrabar: perlato[12] autem libello et diligenter perlecto, me longe mea de te fefellit opinio. Hui quanta de spe decidi! 'Parturiunt[13] montes[14] et nascitur ridiculus mus.' Nam vel rei amplioris cura[15] perceptarum olim a te rerum memoriam obliteravit, aut in tanta iudicii tui exspectatione praevaricatus es et (ut Caesar diceret) 'non tam mendacia dicere[16] quam mentiri de me voluisti,' aut fortasse quantum tua in dicendo in re etiam ficta valeat oratio, significare delegisti. Quod si ita est, uti mox cernes, non tam oratoris, qui vir bonus et veritatis amator diffinitur a veteribus, quam in arte ostentatoris munus absolvisti. Recenseamus, si placet, quod inter nos hic dicendum sit: non dictum omne (fastidiosum namque volumen excresceret[17]), sed pauca quaedam, quibus intelligas — cum sis inter nostrates humanitatis studiis et eloquentiae deditos non postremus — eo pacto scribendum et mature disserendum, ut in ista aetate, canoque iam capite, minimum sit quod vel praesentes increpent, vel posteri.

3   Ab eo autem, quod abs te nuperrime dictum est, inchoemus; quem morem vobis hominibus dicendi vi ac ratione pollentibus inesse animadverti. Subdis enim in calce: *Adde quod nomen Caesaris docti omnes viri exsecrari et odio habere deberent. Non enim magis patriae quam Latinae linguae et bonarum artium exstitit parricida; una enim cum libertate corruit Latina eloquentia et studia litterarum.* Indignum sane[18] facinus, exstinctum doctrinae splendorem et orbatum divino lumine genus humanum; cuius profecto iactura satis deplorari et

merable matters, in which, enabled by your age and leisure, you are unstintingly engaged.

Or so I thought: but once the pamphlet was brought to me and I had carefully read it, my estimation of you turned out to have deceived me greatly. Good grief, from what high hopes I came down! "The mountains are in labor, and a laughable mouse is born!"[3] For either concern for a greater matter obliterated the memory of things you once learned, or you colluded under such great expectations of your judgment and, as Caesar would say, "you wanted not so much to tell lies, as to lie about me," or perhaps you chose to demonstrate how powerful your rhetoric is, even when speaking for a made-up cause.[4] If the latter is the case, you have, as you will soon see, acquitted yourself of the task not so much with the art of an orator, whom the ancients defined as a good man and a lover of truth, as in the manner of a show-off. Let us, if you agree, review what needs to be said between us here: not every word, for the book would grow wearisome, but just a select few, from which, since you are not the last among our compatriots devoted to humane studies and eloquence, you may grasp that one should write and debate in a mature manner, in such a way that at this stage of your life and with your head already gray there may be very little with which present or future generations can find fault.

But let us start from what you said most recently—a habit I have noticed among you people who are masters in the force and organization of your oratory. For at the very end you add: *Add to this that all learned men should curse the name of Caesar and consider it loathsome. For he was no less the father-killer of the fatherland than of the Latin language and the liberal arts. Indeed, hand in hand with liberty, Latin eloquence collapsed.*[5] Truly a shameful crime: the splendor of learning extinguished, and the race of men bereft of divine light, the loss of which cannot be sufficiently deplored, nor the outrage

indignitas accusari[19] non potest, quando nihil maius, excellentius, admirabilius vel humano excogitatum sit ingenio, vel homini divinitus attributum, seu voluptatem, seu animorum pabulum, seu fructus amplissimos, seu immortale gloriae viaticum ante oculos proponere contemplarique velimus. Ceterum quid haec ad Caesarem? Quibus id argumentis culpae Caesaris inurere posse speras? Quodnam[20] scelus 'excidit ore'? Ubinam Poggi, vir doctissime, loqui te putas? Num in convenarum barbarorum corona contionem habere te censes, qui butyrum magis et mephitim[21] quam ullum Musarum nectar redolent, et ad omne Latini sermonis vocabulum per novitatem inhiant, et prae stupore 'ab narrantis ore pendeant'?

4   Sed, ut ad te redeam: doctissimi viri, quorum iudicium pro tua moderatione tuo anteponis, Caesarem non linguae Latinae parricidam, ut tu vocas, sed (ut Tullius testatur) 'illum omnium fere oratorum Latine loqui elegantissime' praedicant. Illis testibus Caesar ad Ciceronem 'de ratione Latine loquendi accuratissime scripsit'; et alio loco[22] ita scriptum legisti: 'Caesar autem, rationem adhibens, consuetudinem vitiosam et corruptam pura et incorrupta consuetudine[23] emendat.' Sic est in *Bruto*. 'Itaque, cum ad hanc elegantiam verborum Latinorum adiungit illa oratoria ornamenta dicendi, tum videtur tamquam tabulas bene pictas collocare in bono lumine.' Complura tibi producam testimonia necesse video; qui, cum lecta meminisse nolis,[24] alios quoque rerum imperitos in fraudem ac errorem illicis, et tui nominis auctoritate circumvenis.

5   Quantus is apud Fabium Quintilianum praedicetur, scis: 'C. vero Caesar, si tantum foro vacasset, non alius[25] ⟨ex nostris⟩ contra Ciceronem nominaretur. Tanta in eo vis est, id acumen, ea

sufficiently indicted, since nothing greater, more excellent or more admirable has either been devised by the human mind or given to man by divine will — whether it is pleasure, or food for thought, or the most abundant profit, or glory's immortal journey money that we wish to consider and put before our eyes. Yet how does Caesar come into this? With what arguments do you hope to be able brand this on to Caesar's guilt? What "outrage escapes your mouth?"[6] Where on earth, Poggio, most learned man, do you think that you are speaking? Surely you do not believe that you are delivering your speech among a crowd of barbarian tramps, who smell more of butter and mephitic fumes than of any nectar of the Muses, and who gape at the novelty of every Latin word, and in stupefaction "hang on the lips of the speaker"?[7]

But to return to you: the very learned men whose judgment   4
you, in your modesty, rate higher than your own, proclaim not that Caesar was a father-killer of the Latin language, as you call him, but, as Cicero testifies, "that he spoke the most elegant Latin of almost all orators." According to these witnesses, Caesar "wrote most meticulously about the rules for speaking Latin" to Cicero; and in another passage you have read it written thus: "Caesar, by applying reason, improved vile and corrupt usage with pure and uncorrupt usage." So it says in the *Brutus*.[8] "And so when he adds to this elegance of Latin words the aforementioned rhetorical ornaments of speech, then he seems to display in a good light what one might call well-painted pictures."[9] I deem it necessary to produce a good number of testimonies for you who, since you refuse to remember what you have read, tempt others, uninformed in these matters, to delusions and error and deceive them with the authority of your name.

You know how great he is proclaimed to be by Fabius Quintil-   5
ian: "But if Caesar had been occupied only with the forum, none other ⟨of our men⟩ would be named as a rival to Cicero.[10] He has such force, such shrewdness, such animation that he appears to

concitatio, ut illum eo[26] animo dixisse, quo bellavit appareat. Exornat tamen haec omnia mira sermonis, cuius proprie studiosus fuit, elegantia'; non, ut Poggius fingit, destruit. Nonne et apud Tranquillum legis eloquentia tanta fuisse, ut aequarit praestantissimorum gloriam, aut antecesserit. 'Quid? Oratorum quem huic antepones eorum qui nihil[27] aliud egerunt? Quis sententiis aut acutior aut crebrior?[28] Quis verbis aut ornatior aut elegantior?' Plutarchus ⟨eruditissimus⟩ philosophus secundas Caesari[29] partes in dicendi potestate tribuit; qui et primas assecutus esset, si tantum eloquentiae, ad quam natura erat aptissimus, quantum armis indulsisset. Nonne et duo eius *De analogia* libri Latinorum studia iuverunt? Eos docti homines praecipua mentione minime commendassent, nisi ad testificandam Caesaris doctrinam, et in studiosos viros industriam[30] et opem pertinere cognovissent.

6   Vides, Poggi, quod et ante noveras: quanta Caesar adiumenta Latinae linguae attulerit et ornamenta; quibus factum est (nisi aut ingratus aut pervicax esse malis), ut litterarum expolitorem et munditiarum parentem verius quam parricidam appellare debeas, bene de nomine ac dignitate populi Romani meritum. Eius culpa eloquentiam Latinam et studia litterarum corruisse fingis aut iactas; contra adfirmant alii, in quibus et Cicero ad M. Marcellum: 'Sed mihi[31] crede, etiam is, qui omnia tenet, favet ingeniis,[32] nobilitatem vero et dignitates hominum, quantum et res et ipsius causa concedit, amplectitur.' Nonne et (Suetonio teste) in reformanda re publica omnium bonarum artium praeceptores honore affecit, civitate donavit et undique accivit?[33] Scire velim abs te, cum per ignorantiam[34] meam non intelligam, in quonam artium genere[35] tantus

have spoken with the same spirit as that with which he waged war. And yet he adorns all these things with a wonderful elegance of language, on which he was particularly keen."[11] He did not, as Poggio pretends, destroy Latin. Surely you also read in Suetonius that his eloquence was such that he equaled or surpassed the fame of the most outstanding men.[12] "Tell me: which of these orators who did nothing else will you prefer to him? Who was more acute or fuller in his turns of phrase, who more embellished or more elegant in his words?"[13] Plutarch, the ⟨extremely erudite⟩ philosopher, awards Caesar the second place for his mastery of speech, noting that he would have achieved even the first if he had devoted as much time to eloquence, to which he was most suited by nature, as to arms.[14] Did not also his two books *On Analogy* enhance the studies of the Latins? Learned men would certainly not have recommended these with special praise if they had not understood their relevance in showing Caesar's learning and his hard work and aid for scholars.

You see, Poggio, what you already knew before: how much sup-   6
port and embellishment Caesar supplied to the Latin language. Hence, unless you prefer to be ungrateful or obstinate, you ought more truly to call him the polisher of letters and the father of their elegance than their father-killer; a man who did a great service to the name and dignity of the Roman people. You pretend or throw out words that it was his fault that Latin eloquence and the study of letters collapsed. Others affirm the contrary, among whom is also Cicero writing to M. Marcellus: "But believe me, even he who controls all things favors talents and embraces nobility and men's honors, in as much as both the matter and his cause allows it."[15] Did he not, on the testimony of Suetonius, when reforming the state grant honors to teachers of all the liberal arts, offer them citizenship, and invite them from everywhere? I would like to hear from you, since in my ignorance I do not understand it, in which discipline of the arts such destruction took place, so that I myself

factus sit interitus, ut et tecum ipse deplorem, et atratam[36] orationem induam. Quod, si dicere nequieris, multi contra—et paene
infiniti—commemorari tibi poterunt, quibusvis in artibus excellentes, qui primum quidem circiter bella civilia, dein[37] paulo post,
tum posterioribus longe temporibus floruerunt. Quin ausim affirmare multas et quidem praeclaras artes[38] subtilius et ornatius
viguisse.

7   Vis de tenuioribus primum artificiis recognoscere? Praestantissimos fuisse non negabis virosque doctos[39] in grammaticis plurimos; qui, quanti, qualesve[40] exstiterint (etsi fato nescio quo perierint), documento sunt Donatus, Servius, Priscianus, Acron,
Asper reliquique permulti.

8   Quid de poetis? Dicerem de Catullo, Claudiano, Ovidio, Lu-
cano,[41] Statio, Silio Italico (cuius in lucem revocandi auctor exsti-
tisti), nisi omnes eos suo splendore, dignitate, admiratione unus
Vergilius obumbrasset; de quo etiam tum adolescente ab Cicerone
praeclare[42] dictum est: 'magnae spes altera Romae'; et ab alio: 'laus
quidem Maronis est, ut nullius laude crescat, nullius vituperatione
minuatur'; et 'cedite Romani scriptores, cedite Graii.' ⟨Nec imme-
rito⟩, nam 'omnia divino cantavit carmine vates,' et quem iure optimo praeponas Ennio illi, qui, antiquitatis gratia observatus, non
iniuria dictus est[43] 'vir haud magna cum re, sed plenus fidei'; 'En-
nium namque sicut sacros vetustate lucos adoramus, in quibus
grandia et antiqua robora iam non tantam habent speciem, quan-
tam religionem.' De satyris non dubitandum[44] est (Quintiliani
sententia), quin priscis illis 'tersior sit[45] ac purus[46] magis Horatius.'
'Multum et verae gloriae, quamvis uno libro, Persius meruit.' Iuvenalis non in extremis ab eruditis numeratur. Volumus et pictores

may deplore it with you and dress in mournful speech. But if you cannot say this, then against it many — in fact, almost countless — men can be cited to you outstanding in every type of art, who flourished in the first place at the time of the civil wars, next a little after, then at much later epochs. In fact, I might dare to say that many arts, and noble ones at that, thrived with more refinement and distinction!

Do you want to make a review of the lesser arts first? You will 7 not deny that there were numerous outstanding and learned men among the grammarians. Who, how many, and of what quality they were, even though their works have perished by some fate or other, is documented by Donatus, Servius, Priscian, Acron, Asper, and many others.[16]

What about the poets? I would have spoken of Catullus, Clau-8 dian, Ovid, Lucan, Statius, Silius Italicus (whom you were responsible for bringing back to light),[17] if Vergil had not single-handedly overshadowed them all with his grandeur, dignity and wonder; he who when still an adolescent was famously hailed by Cicero as "the other hope of great Rome"; and of whom someone else said: "indeed this is the glory of Maro, that he does not increase on account of anybody's praise nor diminish through anyone's invective"; and: "make way Roman writers, make way Greeks."[18] ⟨And not undeservedly⟩, since "the bard sang of everything in his divine poem,"[19] and you would prefer him with good reason to that Ennius, who, while he is honored for the sake of his antiquity, is without injustice called "not a wealthy man, but fully reliable."[20] "For we pay homage to Ennius as we do to groves sacred because of their age in which the lofty and ancient oak trees no longer possess so much beauty as venerability."[21] About the satires it cannot be doubted, in the judgment of Quintilian, that "Horace is purer and neater" than those ancients.[22] "Persius earned much true glory also, even if only with a single book."[23] Juvenal is not numbered among the least by those who are learned.[24] Nor do

non involvere silentio, quando cognata ferme sunt[47] ingenia et
'pictoribus atque poetis quidlibet audendi semper fuit aequa potestas.' Ingens nimirum et horum numerus et elegantia antiquis
non dissimilis.

9   Historicine[48] pauci ac parum incliti fuere et qui priscos sine
dubitatione post se reliquere? Nam Cicerone teste constat quantum eius aetate ab summo abesset historia, quamque genus hoc
scriptionis nondum[49] satis[50] esset Latinis litteris illustratum. Exorti
sunt Asconius, Lucceius, Sallustius,[51] L. Florus,[52] Trogus, Iustinus, Curtius, Cornelius Tacitus et (ut in uno cunctorum laudes
amplectar) T.[53] Livius ille gravis et lacteus. Philosophos taceo, cum
innumerabiles fuerint. Tamen quanti Senecam,[54] quanti Plinium,
quanti Boetium faciemus? Nonne priscis illis si non antepones,[55]
saltem aequabis?[56] Idem vere[57] de disertis et eloquentibus dicere
licet, quos defecisse tantopere deploras, ut amisso phoenice semen
et origo sit omnino sublata. Nihil[58] de Graecis commemoro, innumerabilibus[59] fere, nam si explicare superiorum saeculorum disertos homines curaveris (post civilia bella dico), 'ante diem clauso
componet Vesper Olympo'!

10   Tullius 'plura eversa quam stante re publica eloquentiae[60] volu-
mina conscripsit' et[61] ipse affirmat. Pulcherrimas et disertissimas
cum aliorum, tum Ciceronis orationes post civilia bella videmus
actas vel in senatu, vel in iudiciis. Quis recensere possit iurisconsultos, admirandos doctrina et orationis suavitate homines, qui
post illa tempora supra modum eluxere? Quot in condendis, dige-
rendis, interpretandis legibus divino quodam ingenio et ornatis-
simo scribendi genere floruerunt! Medicinam, humanae saluti
divinitus commonstratam, antiquis licet temporibus ortam, post
bella civilia et ornatam et eruditam et perfectius elimatam, ipsius

we want to envelop the painters in silence, since their talents are almost of the same kind, and "painters and poets have always had the same power to dare anything."[25] Without doubt their number was great and their elegance not dissimilar to that of the ancients.

Were the historians few in number, or of little renown, who 9 also without a doubt left the older ones behind? For on Cicero's evidence it is clear how far from its peak history was in his day, and how this genre of literature had not yet been given sufficient luster in Latin letters.[26] Then Asconius stepped forth and Lucceius, Sallust, L. Florus, Trogus, Justinus, Curtius, Cornelius Tacitus, and, to embrace the praises of all in one, the famous Titus Livy, serious and "milky."[27] I will not speak of the philosophers, since they were innumerable. Yet how greatly will we value Seneca, how greatly Pliny, how greatly Boethius?[28] If you will not prefer them to those older ones, surely you will at least put them on a par? The same may truly be said about the well-spoken and eloquent orators, whose disappearance you deplore so greatly, as though, when the phoenix has died, his seed and species have also been obliterated.[29] I make no reference to the Greeks, who are all but countless, for if you cared to list the eloquent men of ages past — after the civil wars, I mean — "the Evening Star will sooner end the day, once the heavens have closed their doors."[30]

Cicero "wrote more volumes of eloquence when the republic 10 had fallen than when she stood," even he affirms.[31] After the civil wars we see that extremely beautiful and very eloquent speeches were held both in the senate and in the courts, by Cicero as well as others. Who could take a census of the jurists, men of admirable learning and delightful speech, who after those times shone beyond measure? How many flourished in the making, ordering, and interpreting of laws, with an all but divine talent and a highly polished style of writing! The art of medicine, revealed by divine influence for the well-being of man, though it arose in ancient times, outstanding professors of the art do no deny became distin-

artis professores egregii non negant. Unum exortum est scientiae lumen, quo vel solo posteriora sic illustrata sunt saecula et mortalium mentes, ut caelitus infusa videatur. Nam sacrarum litterarum interpretes et divinarum institutionum auctores in lucem editi sunt, quorum ubertate quid copiosius, suavitate quid iocundius, dictione quid ornatius, intelligentia quid acutius, multitudine quid numerosius?[62]

11   Quae cum ita sint et ita esse inficiari nequeas, quid studiorum, bonarum artium, eloquentiae ruinam falso luges et interitum? Qua in re cave, ne te Caesaris parricidam vocare nonnulli valeant, sicut illum tu[63] litterarum insimulabas: et eo magis, quod non hac ipsa corporis vita, 'quae vere mors est,' sed gloria et nominis immortalitate eum privare[64] vis. Esto autem: *plures viri*[65] *doctissimi et eloquentissimi fuerint, quos* (ut dicis) *clades civilis absumpsit.*[66] Num idcirco litterarum et liberalium[67] praeceptores artium bello civile[68] periere? Num se e Musarum suarum[69] antris eduxerunt et togas succincti, codicibus ad telorum[70] ictus obiectis, se intra concursantes acies immiscuerunt? Tot urbes Italiae, tot peregrinae studiosis adolescentibus refertae vigebant, quae tonante civilis belli procella ne minimum[71] quidem sensere strepitum, nec ulla ex parte disciplinarum lucubrationes intermiserunt. Quot Bruti, Lentuli, Marcelli, Curiones, Sulpicii, Galbae, Polliones, Pauli peritissimi superfuere?[72] Fac Caesaris opera deletam[73] fuisse Romanorum[74] libertatem (quod tamen adhuc non concedo): numquid[75] a[76] Caesare senatus consultum factum est, quo philosophiae et ceterarum liberalium artium studiosi capite poenas luerent aut de Italicis urbibus philosophos[77] exterminavit? Quod Catonem illum

guished and learned and more perfectly polished after the civil wars. And one light of learning has arisen by which alone later ages and the minds of mortals have been so illuminated that it seems to have been poured forth from heaven. For the exegetes of sacred literature and writers of divine precepts were brought into the light, and what is richer than their abundance, what more pleasant than their smoothness, what more embellished than their diction, what more insightful than their intelligence, what more numerous than their multitude?

Since these things are so and you cannot deny that they are so, 11 why do you speciously mourn the collapse and demise of studies, the liberal arts, and eloquence? In this matter beware lest some people be able to call you the murderer of Caesar, just as you pretended he was the father-killer of letters, and the more so, in as much as you want to strip him not of this actual life of the body, "which truly is death," but of glory, and of the immortality of his name.[32] Granted, however, *there were many extremely learned and eloquent men*, as you say, *whom the civil wars destroyed*.[33] Surely therefore the teachers of literature and the liberal arts did not perish through civil war? Surely they did not emerge from the caves of the muses with their togas belted up, warding off the blows of spears with their books, and throw themselves into the clashing battle lines? So many cities, Italian and foreign, packed with studious young men continued to thrive and heard not the slightest noise while the storm of the civil war thundered, and did not interrupt their nocturnal studies in any respect. How many most expert Bruti, Lentuli, Marcelli, Curiones, Sulpicii, Galbae, Polliones, and Pauli survived?[34] Suppose that Caesar's hand destroyed the liberty of the Romans (which, however, I still do not concede): surely no senatorial decree was passed by Caesar by which students of philosophy and the other liberal arts might suffer capital punishment, nor did he banish philosophers from the cities of Italy? This we know that Cato the Censor did continually.[35] You

Censorium[78] factitasse constat. Hunc ipsum detestari et exsecrari
debueras, si tanta te studiorum tenet misericordia, quam verbis
prae te fers et quasi filiolam luges amissam. Quis variarum doctores scientiarum[79] undique allexit? Caesar. Quis praemiis orna-
vit? Caesar. Quis honore ac dignitate aluit? Caesar. Vide igitur
quam conveniat eum[80] litterarum parricidam abs te vocari!

12   'At enim sublata sunt studiorum praemia,' dices: magistratus
intercepti;[81] sententiae in senatu dicendae[82] amissa est omnis occasio, dum ad unius voluntatem cuncta reguntur; non accusandi,
non defendendi tempus locusque de more praestabatur, qui
eloquentiae campus et quasi stadium fuerat; et (ut a Cicerone dictum est) 'honos alit artes[83] omnesque incenduntur ad studia gloria.'[84] Si ita sentis aut dicis, Poggi carissime, vehementer aut fallis,
aut falleris. Finito namque civili bello[85] (Caesaris dico et Pompeii)
Romana res in pristinum adeo gradum ordinemque redacta est, ut
nulla fere iudiciis, legibus, cogendo senatui[86] videretur allata mutatio. Lege Plutarchum, diligentissimum rerum gestarum indaga-
torem, cui mira est antiquitatis notitia. Is in Dionis ac Bruti vita
comparanda haec ad verbum exposuit: 'Caesaris potentia, dum
constituebatur quidem, non parvam adversariis infestationem exhibuit, suscipientibus autem et superatis nomen dumtaxat apparuit et existimatio; ab ea nullum opus crudelitatis[87] exstitit nul-
lumque tyrannicum.' Et profecto rem ita esse comperies.

13   Vigebat senatus auctoritas; praetorum, quaestorum, censorum,
imperatorum, consulum ordinaria servabatur creatio. Quibus in
rebus, cum tu[88] diminutam seu mortuam Romanam libertatem
dicas, ego auctam et vivacem ⟨factam[89]⟩ esse contendo; longius latiusque Romani fines imperii propagatos[90] affirmo, non coniectura,

should have hated and cursed this very man, if so great a pity for studies grips you as you parade in words, mourning as if she were a deceased daughter. Who attracted instructors in the various sciences from all over? Caesar. Who decked them out with rewards? Caesar. Who nourished them with honor and dignity? Caesar. See, then, how appropriate it is for you to call him the murderer of letters!

But the rewards for studies were taken away, you will say, the magistracies were interrupted, all opportunity for delivering an opinion in the senate was lost while everything was ruled by the will of one man. No time or place was provided for prosecuting or conducting a defense in the old manner, which had been the training ground of eloquence and as it were its arena. And as Cicero said "honor nourishes the arts, and all are incited to their pursuit by glory."[36] If you think or speak like this, my dearest Poggio, you either deceive greatly or are greatly deceived.[37] For when the civil war was over — I mean the one between Caesar and Pompey — the Roman state was restored to its pristine condition and order, so that hardly any change seemed to have been introduced to the courts, the laws, or the convening of the senate. Read Plutarch, a most careful investigator of historical events, who has a marvelous knowledge of the past. In his comparison of the *Lives* of Dion and Brutus he put it literally like this: "Caesar's power, while being established, was not a little vexing to his enemies; yet to those who accepted it and were defeated, it seemed no more than a name and reputation, from which came nothing cruel and nothing tyrannical."[38]

And indeed you will find that it is so. The authority of the senate thrived, the regular election of praetors, quaestors, censors, generals, and consuls was preserved. Although you say that in these respects Roman liberty was diminished or dead, I contend that it was increased and ⟨made⟩ alive; I assert that the boundaries of the Roman Empire were extended further and wider, not from

12

13

sed scientia et eorum testimonio, qui populi Romani gesta scriptis et memoriae commendarunt: Dacas[91] subiugatos, Germanias, Pannonias, Illyricum, Dalmatiam, Africam, Aegyptum in provinciam redactam. Post Caesaris tempora his in partibus Romanum ampliatum est imperium. Num[92] Indi,[93] Scythae, Parthi, Augusto imperante in amicitiam populi Romani venere[94] obsidesque obtulere?[95] Ex quibus Parthi vindicati signa militaria, quae[96] olim magna cum nostrorum clade Crasso et Antonio ademerant, reddiderunt; quod et timoris indicium, et oboedientiae confessio est, cum vel sic victos sese faterentur et (ut dicitur) 'herbam darent.'

14   Quas ob res, cum servatum Romanum sit imperium lateque propagatum, cum magistratus et potestates consueta dignitate retentae, ut planius inferiore[97] in loco patefaciam, bonis artibus et liberalibus studiis materia[98] honos et praemia non defuerint,[99] et ea maximum susceperint[100] incrementum—tum Caesare ipso, tum Caesaris opera—non modo linguae Latinae et bonarum artium parricida C. Caesar appellari abs te non debuit—quibus ille favit et gravium historicorum testimonio famam ornamentumque contulit—sed contra linguae Latinae et bonarum artium parentem celebrare atque illustrare debent nostrorum scripta ⟨sermonesque disertorum⟩. Ad quas[101] si ingenioli mei tenuitas aspirare potuisset, litteratorum[102] nomine—pro mea virili—studiosorum[103] gratitudinem[104] testatus essem;[105] non desinam tamen, ut (quantum Poggios[106] dicendi magnitudine ac stili tuba vituperare immeritum videro) ego velut 'anser inter olores' obstrepere et commendare pergam.

conjecture but from knowledge and the testimonies of those who committed the deeds of the Roman people to their writings and to posterity. The Dacians were subjugated; and the Germaniae, the Pannoniae, Illyricum, Dalmatia, Africa, and Egypt reduced to provinces. It was after the times of Caesar that the Roman Empire was extended to include these areas. Did not the Indians, Scythians, and Parthians join the friendship of the Romans and give hostages while Augustus ruled? Of these, the Parthians, once punished, returned the military standards which they had previously, in a great defeat for our men, seized from Crassus and Antonius; which is both a sign of fear and an admission of obedience, since in this way they actually admitted themselves defeated and, as the saying goes, "offered the olive branch."[39]

Because of this, since the Roman Empire was preserved and   14 widely extended, since the magistracies and powers were retained with their customary dignity (as I will explain more clearly below), since the materials, honor and rewards for the liberal arts and the study of letters were not lacking, and since these received a very great spur both from Caesar himself and from his efforts, you should therefore not only not call Caesar the murderer of the Latin language and the liberal arts, which he favored and to which he contributed fame and honor, according to the testimony of the most trusted historians, but, quite on the contrary, it is as the father of the Latin language and the liberal arts that the writings ⟨and conversations⟩ of our ⟨eloquent⟩ men should celebrate and glorify him. And if the slightness of my small intellect could have aspired to these arts, I would have testified to the gratitude of scholars as best I could, in the name of the men of letters. Still, as it is, I will not back off, no matter how much I will see Poggios lay into him undeservedly with grandiose speech and the trumpet of their pen, from proceeding, like "a goose among swans," to shout in opposition and utter praise.[40]

15   Nunc ad institutum revocetur oratio. Litterariam ego tecum
orbitatem, et posterorum saeculorum calamitatem, lugendam esse
sentio; in qua[107] sicuti[108] Caesar omni[109] culpa vacat, ita in vitio
sunt hominum flagitia et superioris aetatis error, maxime cum[110]
invalescere coepit avaritia, quae[111] omnium malorum mater est[112]
atque materies. 'Namque avaritia (ut inquit Crispus) fidem probitatem ceterasque bonas artes subvertit.' 'At haec animos[113] aerugo
et cura peculi cum semel imbuerit,[114] speramus carmina fingi posse
linenda[115] cedro et levi servanda cupresso?' Iuventus potius et[116]
natu grandiores insuerint[117] privatim et publice rapere,[118] delubra
spoliare, sacra profanaque omnia polluere, quam ullam virtuti ac
disciplinae operam impendere; transmarinas citius quaestus gratia
peregrinationes terraeque marisque pericula subire, quam propin-
qua adire loca nullo cum discrimine, ut meliorem animum orna-
tioremque reddant. Non minimum quoque detrimentorum studiis
importavit comes ad perniciem adiuncta, luxuria, qua[119] acuta
etiam torpent[120] iuventutis ingenia; ciborumque[121] varietati pretio-
sisque[122] saporibus,[123] non artibus bonis invigilare coepit industria;
saltare, canere, alienis insidiari lectis calamistrati didicerunt ado-
lescentuli, quorum palatum prius quam linguam domesticae in-
struxerunt disciplinae. Has ipsas bonorum omnium pestes, quibus
virtus atteritur, verissime accusare, detestari[124] ac studiorum et[125]
bonarum artium parricidas exsecrari debueras, ne calumniatoris
nomen indueres.

16   *At enim libertate extincta subsecuta sunt imperatorum portenta nefaria.*
Indignum et lacrimabile facinus, cum imperio praestantissimo
atque pulcherrimo sordidos atque[126] portentuosos gubernatores
praesidere contigit! Quid, quod[127] et excellentissimi successere
principes[128] quam plurimi, seu virtutem, seu doctrinam, seu

Now let my speech be called back to its purpose. I agree with   15
you that the bereavement of letters and the catastrophe of later
ages is to be mourned, but just as Caesar is free from all guilt in
this, so the misdeeds of men and the error of an earlier age are at
fault, especially from the moment when greed, which is the mother
and the matter of all evil, began to gain strength.[41] "For avarice," as
Sallust said, "overturns faith and decency and all other good de-
meanors."[42] "But once this cancer and concern for property has
touched the mind, do we then hope that poems can be composed
to be anointed with cedar oil and preserved with light cypress?"[43]
More likely youngsters and older men would grow used to stealing
privately and publicly, to despoiling shrines, to desecrating all
things sacred and profane, rather than expending any effort on
virtue and discipline; to put up with overseas wanderings for the
sake of profit, and with the dangers of land and water, rather than
go to nearby places without any danger so that they might render
their minds better and better equipped. Not the least of obstacles
to studies, moreover, was introduced by lechery, the companion of
ruin, which slackens even the sharp minds of youth; and diligence
began to keep vigil for variety of foodstuffs and precious flavors
instead of the liberal arts; coiffed youngsters learned to dance,
sing, and ambush the beds of strangers, and it was their palates
rather than their tongues that their domestic education trained.
These plagues of all good things, by whom virtue is worn down,
you should truly have accused and decried and execrated as murderers of the liberal arts, so as not to assume the reputation of a
slanderer.

But in truth, once liberty was dead, there followed the abominable mon-   16
strosities of the emperors.[44] An outrageous and lamentable crime,
when it came to pass that base and monstrous rulers governed an
outstanding and most illustrious empire! What of the fact that
there also followed a very large number of truly excellent leaders —
whether you consider their virtue, their learning, their wisdom or

sapientiam, seu rei militaris scientiam[129] et rerum gestarum gloriam contemplere, a quibus late propagatum et saepissime ab hostili vastitate conservatum est imperium? Quos et probe nosti. Tacebo itaque Octavianum, T. Flavium, Traianum, Antoninum Pium, Hadrianum, Constantinum, Theodosium reliquosque permultos. Fac vero omnes ad unum flagitiosos post primum ac perditos evasisse Caesares: quaenam incusandi Caesaris ratio est? Erat in eius manu successoribus vitae normam praescribere et posteris quam[130] sequerentur; necessaria vivendi instituta, vel invitis, edicere? Si quis diligentissimus pater familias quaesitum industria, magnis laboribus, periculis patrimonium liberis suis legasset, ii[131] vero per socordiam illud perire sinerent, aut luxu et illecebris dilapidassent, patrem idcirco familias iustis conviciis insectarere?[132] Quod si feceris, num iusta in te odia concitaris et maledicta?

17   Ne longe abieris, primus Christi vicarius et nostrae religionis antistes constitutus est in terris Petrus, super quo Dominus noster Jesus Christus suam fundavit ecclesiam, eique pastori suas pascendas commisit oves. De cuius sanctitate reliquisque virtutibus nil[133] attinet dicere, tum quia laude non egent humana, tum quia in re tam manifesta testes sunt superflui. Petri successores non omnes Petri similes esse dices aut credis. Num igitur illum exsecraberis, quia superiori tempore nonnullos improbos vel avaritia, vel nequitia insignes exstitisse non ignoras? Eadem ratione et regium statum, et consularem, et decemviralem, et tribuniciam consulari potestate creationem atrociter increpabis, quoniam sceleratos in illis emersisse comperies? Non idcirco illorum creandorum auctores aut reprehendes, aut contumeliabere, sed eos, qui—

their knowledge of the military arts and the glory of their accomplishments—by whom the empire was widely extended and very frequently saved from devastation by the enemy? Who they were, you know perfectly well. I will therefore pass in silence over Octavian, Titus, Trajan, Antoninus Pius, Hadrian, Constantine, Theodosius and very many others.[45] Suppose all Caesars after the first one, to a man, were criminals and scoundrels: what, then, is the reason for accusing Caesar? Was it in his power to prescribe to his successors, and to later generations, the standard of life that they were to follow; to decree for them even against their will the required principles of living? If some most careful head of the family had left the patrimony he obtained with application, great labor, and dangers to his children, but these allowed it to slip away through sluggishness or had squandered it in lechery and enticements, would you therefore inveigh against that head of the household with just reproaches? And if you did so, would you then not stir fair antipathies and insults against yourself?

Lest you stray too far, Peter was appointed as the first vicar of 17 Christ and prelate of our religion on earth. Upon him our Lord Jesus Christ founded his Church and to him, as shepherd, he committed his sheep for feeding. About his holiness and the rest of his virtues there is no point in speaking, both because they need no human praise and because in a matter so evident there is an abundance of witnesses. That Peter's successors were all similar to Peter you will not say and do not believe.[46] You will surely not, then, execrate him because you are aware that, at an earlier time, there were some who were wicked or marked by avarice and indolence? Will you for the same reason also fulminate violently against the position of king, and against the election of consuls, *decemvirs*, and tribunes with consular power, because you will find that some of them turned out to be miscreants?[47] On this score you will neither reproach nor slander those responsible for appointing them, but rather those who, coming upon the opportunity and

magnarum rerum occasionem et adiumenta nacti—ad malas se
artes converterunt.

18   Videre nunc videor, amantissime Poggi, tuorum te scriptorum
iam poenitentia duci et, qui aliis placere voluisti, tibi ipsi etiam
atque etiam[134] displicere. Quod ita fit, ubi rectum consilium
mentemque calamus praecurrit.[135] Loquor tecum ingenue, quia lex
amicitiae iubet ea 'capienda esse[136] amice[137] cum benivole[138] fuerint.'[139] Et audes, catus homo, id tuum edere iudicium, ubi vagus,
non ad historiarum dictata, non ad doctorum et quidem[140] priscorum hominum sententiam, sed ad nescio[141] quem sensum volunta-
temque profers! In quo scitum[142] illud sequendum[143] abs te fuerat:
ut castum iudicis absolveres officium, persona deponenda erat
amici et iudicis induenda. Id vero quam factum a te sit, quibusdam
tecum in capitibus discutere non indignaberis. Non enim id mihi
robur easque vires inesse confido, ut solus fortissimi bellatoris incursionem uno sufferre queam impetu: reliquis etiam cohortibus
vicem relinquo, quas in subsidiis esse tibi denuntio. Quae, ubi
collata signa viderint, sublato clamore ductu Caesaris et auspicio
te[144] mox irruent. Interim, dum acies struimus, de Luciano, auctore Graeco, diligentius et apertioribus oculis animadverte,[145] apud
quem nullam de Caesare mentionem factam esse cernes.

19   Caesaris ac Scipionis praestantiam ⟨expositurus[146]⟩, hoc est uter
utri excelluerit, utriusque bona contraque turpia velut in trutina
debueras expendere: sic enim nec te iudicem, nec lectorem fefel-
lisses. Longe aliter facis, qui in altero quidem bona (quae eximia
esse non inficior) dinumeras et tollis ad sidera, in Caesare vero

means for great deeds, instead gave themselves over to evil pursuits.

Now I seem to notice, my beloved Poggio, that you already 18 regret your writings and that, having wanted to please others, you more and more displease yourself. This is what happens when the pen outpaces sound counsel and judgment. I speak frankly with you, because the law of friendship demands that things "are taken in a friendly spirit when they are done with good intentions."[48] And you dare, crafty fellow that you are, to issue this judgment of yours, even when you offer it adrift, not supported by the lessons of history or the opinion of the learned men and indeed the ancients, but according to some sort of feeling and whim! In this you should have adhered to the following neat maxim: that in order to fulfill the impartial office of judge, one must lay aside the character of the friend and put on the persona of the judge.[49] But how you have done this, you will not begrudge that I examine with you on a couple of key points. Indeed I do not trust myself to have such strength and force as to be able to withstand the assault of a very strong fighter by myself and with a single charge: I leave their turn to other cohorts which, I forewarn you, stand ready as backup. These will soon rush at you when they see the battle is joined, raising a battle cry under the command and leadership of Caesar! In the meantime, while we are drawing up our battle lines, look more carefully and with your eyes open wide at the Greek author Lucian, in whose work you will discover not a single mention of Caesar.[50]

⟨When planning to speak⟩ of the excellence of Caesar and 19 Scipio, that is to say which of the two surpassed the other, you should have weighed the good and shameful aspects of both men, as if in a balance: for in this way you would not have deceived yourself as judge, nor your reader. But you act far differently, you who for the one enumerate the good things — which indeed I do not deny were outstanding — and praise them to the skies, yet in

vitia — si qua fuerint — ita rimaris et amplificas, admirandas autem divinasque virtutes aut subtices, aut calumniaris, ut ex orationis[147] acumine potius admirationem quam veritatis pronuntiatione[148] laudem vendicare volueris; eos, qui scabie laborant imitatus, qui sinceram omittentes carnem, si quid sanie gliscat, indagant[149] et unguibus exprimunt.

20   Ecce, in comparandis Caesare et Alexandro, quia consilio[150] Plutarchi — eruditi imprimis viri auctorisque gravissimi — praeiudicium ad Caesaris commendationem pertinere cernis, cur id malignaris et quod ab homine philosopho et veritatis historiographo relatum est, id non fideliter exponis, sed in deteriorem trahis partem? Tu rem ipsam verius[151] explica, et liberum auditori relinque iudicium! *Credo*, inquis: estne in re tanta coniecturis agendum, in qua de vita certatur? Vitam enim esse non hanc, qua morimur in dies, sed gloriam, qua immortalitas[152] propagatur, sapientissimi diffiniunt; quam qui auferre conantur, longe magis furti tenentur, quam qui pistillum aut sarculum interceperit. Utque[153] comparationem minuas, Alexandrum non tam excellentissimum, quam *Graecorum excellentissimum* iactasti, ut nationi, quam 'inanissimam' ingrati quidam[154] appellare solent, comparatus[155] Caesar inferiorem[156] ab hominibus opinionem consequatur; quasi Graeci non omnium magnarum artium et insignium disciplinarum inventores exstiterint. Nec animo advertis, prae[157] cupiditate carpendi, Alexandrum Macedonem fuisse, non Graecum.

21   Et *de rebus militiae gestis, non de virtutibus* comparationem confectam[158] esse credere te dicis. Ut autem non recte credere, sed potius[159] te falsum[160] opinari videas, inspice quid in prooemio ab Plutarcho scriptum de illis est: '*Vitas*, non *Historias* conscribimus,

Caesar dig for and amplify his vices—if any there were—while passing over in silence, or slandering, his admirable and godlike virtues, in such a manner that you wanted to win admiration for the sting of your exposition, rather than praise for speaking the truth. You have imitated those who suffer skin sores, who pass over the healthy flesh, search for whatever is swollen with pus, and squeeze that out with their nails.

Look, since in the comparison of Caesar and Alexander, ac- 20 cording to the opinion of Plutarch, a man learned beyond all others and a very weighty authority, you perceive a previous judgment relevant to a commendation of Caesar, why do you malign this, and instead of honestly reporting what is recounted by this philosopher and historian of the truth, twist it into a pejorative meaning? Really, relate the matter itself truthfully and leave it to your audience to judge freely! *I believe*, you say, but should so great a matter be dealt with through conjecture, when it is a contest about life?[51] For the wisest men define life not as that in which we are dying every day, but as the glory from which immortality stems, and those who try to wrest that away are guilty of theft far more than a man who steals a pestle or a hoe. And in order to diminish the comparison, you bandied it about that Alexander was not so much the most excellent man as *the most outstanding of the Greeks*, so that Caesar, compared to that people whom certain thankless creatures like to call "wholly insubstantial," attains lower esteem from men—as if the Greeks are not on record as the inventors of all the great arts and illustrious disciplines.[52] Nor do you, in your desire to criticize him, pay attention to the fact that Alexander was a Macedonian, not a Greek.

You also claim to believe that the comparison was based on 21 *military achievements, not virtues*.[53] However, so that you may realize that you do not rightly believe but rather falsely opine, look at what Plutarch wrote about these matters in his proem: "We are writing *Lives*, not *Histories*, and there is not the slightest proof of

nec omnino[161] rebus clarissime gestis virtutis aut vitiorum inest demonstratio. Ceterum breve[162] persaepe negotium, oratio iocusve mores magis aperit, quam infinitis editis stragibus pugnae, acies maximae et urbium obsidiones.' Nec longe post addit: 'Nobis concedendum est, ut animorum[163] adeamus indicia,[164] quo per haec utriusque *Vitam* effingamus, amplissima reliquis certamina relinquentes.' Praeterea, si *Vitas* amborum percurrere[165] dedignatus[166] non esses, virtutes aut vitia magis ab eo quam res militiae gestas describi non crederes (ut ais) sed tute cerneres, et Alexandri quoque calumniam forsan[167] exorsus esses, ne socio Caesar invideret! De reliquis aut refellendis, aut purgandis, aut etiam concedendis (nec enim ipsum omnino vitio caruisse[168] ne[169] negaverim) id abs te velim impetratum, ne aut tibi tantum tribuas, ut per te de rebus tam antiquis et ab tua memoria remotis iudicium facias, aut probatis rerum scriptoribus anteponas.

22   De eo, quod *civem patriae perniciosissimum*[170] *fuisse et in servitutem patriam redegisse* dicis post videbimus, cum et posterius factum sit; verum priorem aetatem, quam adeo insectaris, examinemus. Qui mores, quae animi magnitudo, quam praeclara in Caesare eluxerit et praeluxerit[171] effigies, priores testantur anni, de quibus pauca[172] quaedam libasse sat erit. Cinnam, civem amplissimum, quater consulem dictatoremque, filiam Corneliam Caesari, vixdum annum sextum decimum[173] egresso, in matrimonium collocasse, magnae cuiusdam existimationis et praecipuae dignitatis argumentum est; non autem eius aetatis, cui nihil insigne fuisse fingis. Cui et Sulla ipse testis accedit; nam in eum, ut iam tum maximi ponderis hominem, adeo capitales exercuit inimicitias, ut perdendi

virtue or vices in exploits that were performed with the greatest renown. Rather very frequently a small matter, a speech or a joke shows up character more than massacres in which countless perish in battle, the greatest battle lines, or the sieges of cities." And not much later he adds: "Let us be given license to address the signs of people's mentalities, and so from them fashion the *Lives* of both men, leaving those very great contests to others."[54] Besides, if you had not disdained to go through the *Lives* of these two, you would not have *believed*, as you put it, that Plutarch described virtue and vices rather than military achievements, but you would have seen it for sure, and perhaps you would also have undertaken the slander of Alexander, so that Caesar might not envy his companion! Regarding the other things that are to be refuted or excused or even conceded—for I would not assert that he was entirely free of vice—I want to beg of you that you do not give yourself such license as to pass judgment, single-handedly, on matters this old and distant from your memory, or elevate yourself above sound writers of history.

About the fact that you say that *he was a thoroughly destructive* 22 *citizen to his fatherland, and reduced the fatherland to slavery* we will see later, since it also happened later; instead let us first examine his earlier life, which you attack so much.[55] What character, what greatness of spirit, and how splendid an image shone in Caesar and radiated from him is attested by his earliest years, from which it will suffice to take a few small samples. That Cinna—a citizen of the highest stature, consul four times and also dictator—gave his daughter Cornelia in marriage to Caesar when he had scarcely passed his sixteenth birthday is evidence of his high esteem and special standing, not of a period in his life in which you falsely claim that *there was nothing distinguished*.[56] And to this Sulla himself also stands witness; for he exercised such mortal animosity against him, as already then a man of very great weight, that wishing to rid himself of the boy, he sent out a great number of bounty

pueri cupidus inquisitores plurimos dimitteret, qui ad necem eum
e latebris extraherent. Nec enim minus quam Marium Sullae terrori Caesarem fuisse, ipsius Sullae testatur oratio, quem praedicare
solitum dicis 'ut male cinctum puerum praecaverent.' Quam ob
rem? 'Nam Caesari multos Marios inesse.' O ingens de Caesare
iam inde a puero praeconium, si sagacissimi ad odorandum[174] Sullae testimonio tot Marios aequabat unus! De Mario philosophus
magnus ita sentit et loquitur, ut 'in secundis rebus fortunatissi-
mum hominem, in adversis summum virum' appellet. 'Hic est qui
Cimbros et summa pericula rerum excipit et solus trepidantem
protegit Urbem.'

23   Dehinc nonne laudi maximae et adolescentis[175] ornamento
paene singulari[176] fuit, quod incliti homines, ornatissimi viri et civitatis Romanae principes pro pueri salute[177] apud Sullam inter-
cesserunt, apud eundem et virgines Vestales pro illo summis precibus contenderunt?[178] Quarum castitas et observantia maiestatis
locum in civitate Romana semper obtinuit. Quam ob causam, nisi
quod splendida in adolescentis aetate indoles generosaque pullu-
lantis virtutis nobilitas bonorum civium animos contra crudelissi-
mum tyrannum impiumque[179] commovebant? Sulla[180] namque—
cuius[181] acutissimum erat ingenium perspicaxque ac praesaga
magnifici viri coniectura—futurum Caesarem praevidebat, ab quo
sibi partibusque suis venturum exitium metuebat. Eapropter tanti
momenti iuvenem primum quidem pollicitationibus ac blandi-
mentis, deinde[182] comminationibus atque terrore ad se[183] conatus
allicere (teste Plutarcho) spretus est ab eoque contemptus: ideo
(quod reliquum erat homini carnifici) eius vitae struxit[184] insidias,
quas egregia iuvenis prudentia adhibitis remediis evitavit.

hunters to draw him out of hiding and execute him.[57] And that Sulla feared Caesar no less than Marius is proven by Sulla's very own words, since as you say he frequently declared "*that they should beware of the badly-belted boy.*"[58] Why? "Because there were many Marii in Caesar."[59] What an enormous tribute to Caesar already in his boyhood if according to Sulla, so skilled in tracing a scent, he alone equaled so many Marii! As to Marius, the great philosopher thought and spoke in such a way as to call him "in prosperous times the most fortunate man, in adversity the greatest."[60] "He is the one who bore the brunt of the Cimbri and the most dangerous turn in events, and alone protected the trembling City."[61]

Moving on, surely it was the greatest praise and an exceptional 23 badge of honor for a youngster that illustrious figures and extremely distinguished men and leaders of the Roman state interceded with Sulla for the preservation of a boy, and that even the Vestal virgins competed before the same man for his sake, deploying their most urgent prayers? The Vestal virgins, whose chastity and reverence always held a position of the highest honor in the Roman state![62] What was the reason for all this, if not that his innate brilliance at a youthful age, and the aristocratic nobility of his sprouting virtue, moved the minds of the good citizens against a thoroughly hardhearted and wicked tyrant? For Sulla, whose intellect was very sharp and perceptive, and whose conjectures warned of a formidable man, foresaw the future Caesar, by whose hand he feared that destruction would come for himself and for his faction. Because of this he strove to attract a youth of such influence to himself, first with promises and flattery, later with threats and terror; but, as Plutarch testifies, he was spurned by him and despised. Hence, since this was the only option left to this butcher, he made plots against his life, which the youth avoided with exceptional prudence by using counterstrategies.

24   Eodem tempore Sulla dictatore vehementius urgente Caesar ut Cinnae filiam Corneliam[185] repudiaret, nulla conditione compelli[186] potuit: non dotis amplissimae confiscatione, non gentiliciarum hereditatum[187] multatione, non sacerdotii[188] praestantis[189] interceptione. Quaero igitur abs te, Poggi, si adolescens virum adeo terribilem, Romani gubernatorem[190] imperii, in civium milia strages edentem,[191] contempsit et prae honestatis et officii ratione parvi fecit, num illum fortissimi viri et magnifici animi laude dignabere? Si eundem ab Cinna ex omni Romana iuventute et nobilitatis flore generum delectum, si praeterea Sullae iudicio atque verbis tanti factum aspicis,[192] audebis pervicaciter dicere quod *Caesaris adolescentia omnis nihil habuit quod magnopere sit aut laudandum aut referendum?* Melius dixisses: quod Poggio, Caesarianarum laudum detrectatori aut occultatori, placens acceptumque sit!

25   Id, ut planius[193] recognoscas, accipe. Cum aliquot Romana religio[194] flamines haberet, imprimis eximiae dignitatis et honoris flamen dialis erat, id est Iovis, παρὰ τοῦ Διός.[195] Et recte sane. Nam sicut Iovem 'hominum patrem atque deorum, rerum cui summa potestas' (ut poeta diceret) coluit antiquitas, sic et illius flaminem praestare voluerunt. Hoc itaque sacerdotium, cum plures praecipuae nobilitatis homines peterent, Caesar omnium consensu ceteris[196] praelatus est. Tanta hominum studia, pronos animos propensumque favorem meruisse, pro nihilo pones, aut insigne potius *quod magnopere sit laudandum et referendum?* Nonne ex media virtutis laude dicetur et officio?

68

At the same time, despite the enormous pressure exerted by   24
Sulla as dictator, Caesar could not be compelled on any terms to
repudiate Cinna's daughter Cornelia, either through confiscation
of the very generous dowry, or through the imposition of a fine on
his family inheritance, nor through the intervention of a high-
ranking priest. So I ask of you, Poggio, if a youngster spurned so
fearsome a man and the ruler of the Roman empire, who ordered
the slaughter of thousands of citizens, and slighted him for the
sake of honor and on the ground of duty, will you not then deem
him worthy of praise as a most brave man and an eminent spirit?
If the same youngster was chosen by Cinna from the whole Roman youth and the flower of the nobility as his son-in-law, if
moreover you see that he was deemed so important by the opinion
and words of Sulla, will you then dare obstinately to maintain that
*there was nothing distinguished in his entire youth that particularly deserves
to be reported or praised?*[63] You would have better said, "nothing that
is pleasing to and acknowledged by Poggio, detractor and con-
cealer of the glories of Caesar"!

To see the truth of this more clearly, listen to this. While the   25
Roman religion had a certain number of *flamines*, the one who was
foremost in dignity and honor was the *flamen dialis*, that is to say
the priest of Jove, *para tou Dios*. And rightly so. For just as the
ancient world worshipped Jupiter as "father of men and of the
gods, who holds the supreme power over things," as the poet
might have said, so they wanted his *flamen* to rank first.[64] And so,
even though many men of great nobility pursued this priesthood,
Caesar with the consent of all was preferred over the others.[65] Will
you deem it of no account that he earned such great favor from
men, minds so well-disposed and keen support — or rather as a
badge of honor *that particularly deserves to be reported and praised?*[66]
This will surely be said to be on account of common praise of
virtue and out of obligation, will it not?

26   Accipe et hoc, quod tute fateberis insigne. Quid frontem
contraxisti? Ne discedas, oro; abibis deinde non indoctior. Cum
Thermi, fortissimi[197] et eximii imperatoris, ductu et auspicio populus Romanus bellum in Asia gereret, in expugnatione Mytilenarum complurium strenuorum militum usus opera, enitentem
Caesaris — qui sub eo merebat[198] — virtutem habuit; in cuius rei
testimonium adolescentem corona civica donavit, 'quam (ut scis)
civis civi, a quo servatus est in praelio, testem vitae salutisque per-
ceptae dare consuevit.' Ne autem vel ignavis id praemium contigisse calumnieris, illud ipsum tradi solitum est his,[199] 'qui cum civem servaverant, eodem tempore hostem occiderant.' Sic duplicis
virtutis — et servati civis[200] et caesi hostis — insigne consecutus est
Caesar, et quidem adolescens. Vides, vir eruditissime, quot in eo
laudanda[201] sunt, cuius adolescentiam *nihil habuisse insigne* commemoras, *quod magnopere laudandum fuisse* dicis. Hoc ipsum vere insigne, et celebrandum vel in maioribus natu, facinus, si de Scipione
legisses, quanto verborum ambitu, quanta et quam luculenta oratione ⟨qua plurimum polles⟩ decorasses! Virtus ubique praedi-
canda est, seu in[202] hoste sit, seu in alterius factionis homine.[203]
Huius tam praeclari facinoris gloria tota Caesari sine ulla dubitatione tributa est, non sicut Scipionis factum de patris apud Ticinum liberatione, cum 'servati[204] consulis decus ad servum natione
Ligurem[205] ab quibusdam auctoribus delegeretur.'

27   Alterius facti venit in mentem, quod, etsi forsan alius gravate
laturus sit, insigne tamen[206] et patriae splendori et imperii stabili-
mento fuisse, negaturus non es. Regiones Asiae Romano proximas
imperio incursationibus spoliante et vastante Mithridate, rege profecto potentissimo et multos iam annos Romanis cognito ducibus,

Listen to this too, that even you will admit is distinguished.   26
Why do you frown? Do not leave, please; you will go away later
not less learned. When the Roman people fought a war in Asia
under the command and leadership of the very brave and excellent
general Thermus, who used the services of numerous vigorous
soldiers during the storming of Mytilene, he deemed the courage
of Caesar, who served under him, conspicuous, and as proof of
this he gave the youngster a civic crown, "which as you know a
citizen traditionally has given to another by whom he has been
saved in battle, as testimony that he had received from him his life
and safety."[67] But to stop you from slanderously claiming that this
prize also fell to the faint of heart, the very same one was custom-
arily given to them "who in saving a citizen had also killed an enemy."[68] And so Caesar achieved this badge of honor for the double
virtue of having both saved a citizen and slain an enemy, and this
indeed while still a young man. You see, you most erudite fellow,
how many things worthy of praise there were in the man of whose
youth you record that *it had nothing distinguished that particularly deserves to be praised.*[69] If you had read of this same achievement, truly
remarkable and praiseworthy even in those older than Caesar was,
as referring to Scipio, with how much verbal pomp, with what
long and brilliant oratory ⟨in which you excel⟩ you would have
embellished it! But virtue should be praised wherever it is met,
whether in an enemy or in a man of the other camp. And without
any doubt the full glory of so remarkable a deed was attributed to
Caesar, unlike Scipio's role in the liberation of his father at the
Ticinus, "when the distinction of saving the consul was attributed
by some authorities to a slave who was Ligurian by race."[70]

A second achievement comes to mind, which, even if perhaps   27
someone else would report it grudgingly, you nevertheless will not
deny was outstanding, both for the splendor of the fatherland and
for the steadying of the empire. Mithridates, a most powerful
king, who had been known to Roman commanders for many

Caesar, accitus ad opem ferendam, ab Rhodo profectus—quo
studiorum gratia navigarat—in Asiam traiecit, acerrimus adolescens. Ubi contractis[207] in unum adversus regios exercitus auxiliis,
Mithridatis praefectum fusis eius copiis fugavit, provinciam Romanam servavit, sociorum discrimen depulit, dubias civitates stabilivit,[208] constantes in fide tenuit. Didicerat namque —magni
cordis et optimis imbutus disciplinis adolescens—quod liberalium
artium studio ab rebus gerendis abduci, contra officium est. Prae-
termittendae etiam defensionis eas causas, ut turpes et ab[209] philosophia reprehendendas esse, cognoverat:[210] cum quis laborem re-
formidaret, aut pigritia inertiave tardaretur,[211] aut suis ipse studiis
impediretur, ut eos, quos tutari deberet, desertos esse pateretur.
Cedis[212] adhuc, an vero perstas, et *nihil insigne* in Caesaris adolescentia fuisse contendis,[213] *quod magnopere laudandum proferendumque
sit?* Hoc Caesaris factum insigne adeo populus Romanus amplexus
est, et tantopere tulit in caelum laudibus, ut—gratae mentis testimonium honore fortibus viris digno declarans—tribunatum illi
militum cunctis suffragiis tribuerit.

28   Non invitus abs te, humanissime Poggi, quaesierim, num[214] inter[215] insignia[216] colloces[217] quod a teneris[218] annis sic magnarum
rerum[219] et optimarum artium studiis invigilaverit et accuratissi-
mam operam impenderit, ut inter doctissimos Latini et Graeci
nominis homines non postremus adnumeretur; cui sane rei testis—licet inimicus—Cicero accedit: 'Omnes (inquit) superiores,
quibus honore par esset, scientia facile vicisset.' Estne insigne,
vel admirandum potius, quod 'scribere simul et legere, dictare et
audire solitum' certi auctores tradunt?[220] Quid, quod 'epistolas
tantarum rerum quaternis pariter[221] librariis dictare[222] aut, si nihil

years, was plundering and laying waste to the regions of Asia near-
est to the Roman Empire by raids.[71] Caesar had been summoned
to bring help, and setting out from Rhodes, to which he had traveled for the sake of his studies, he crossed into Asia, a very keen
young man. There, after bringing together auxiliary forces against
the armies of the king, he put Mithridates' commander to flight,
having routed his troops, saved the Roman province, removed the
allies from danger, confirmed wavering cities, and held onto those
which were steady in their loyalty. For he had learned, a young
man great of heart and already versed in the best studies, that it
goes against duty to be distracted from performing exploits by zeal
for the liberal arts.[72] He knew how shameful these grounds were
for shirking the defense, and how much to be rejected by philosophy: to wit when someone fears labor or is held back by laziness
or inertia or impeded by his own interests, and so allows those
whom he should defend to be abandoned. Do you yield yet, or do
you persist and continue to maintain that there was *nothing distinguished* in Caesar's youth *that particularly deserves to be reported or
praised?*[73] The Roman people took this outstanding achievement of
Caesar's so much to heart and so greatly extolled it to the skies
that, giving evidence of their gratitude by an honor fit for brave
men, they unanimously assigned him the military tribunate.

I would like to ask you, Poggio, cultivated as you are, if you do   28
not count it among his distinctions that from a tender age he so
held vigil and invested his efforts in the pursuit of great things as
well as the liberal arts, that he was numbered not least among the
learned men of the Romans as well as the Greeks. Cicero, even
though an enemy, testifies to this fact: "All his predecessors" — he
said — "whom he equaled in honor, he easily surpassed in learning."[74] Is it not *distinguished or rather to be admired*, that certain authors report that "he was wont simultaneously to read and write,
dictate and listen"? What about the fact that he was accustomed
"to dictating letters about such great matters to four scribes at

aliud ageret, septenis' consuetus fuerit?[223] Num *insigne aut laudandum?* Si universa Caesaris adolescentis[224] insignia complecti voluero, grande certe volumen hoc a me tempore minime destinatum confecero. Unum itaque dumtaxat praeclarum et[225] arduum facinus adiungens, reliqua valere sinam.

29   Caesar, cum Sullae furorem et acerbas in se fugiens inimicitias excedere Italia statuisset, Rhodum—praestantissimarum artium domicilium Musarumque et[226] eloquentiae nutricem imprimis—tamquam 'ad sapientiae mercaturam' enavigabat. Inter navigandum circa Pharmacusam insulam a maritimis praedonibus excipitur; ii[227] namque per id tempus, insulas oramque[228] maritimam infestantes, mare navibus innumeris et classibus ingentibus tenebant. Ab eis cum[229] dein[230] talentis quinquaginta sese redemisset, in Asiam se recepit et mox—adunatis in Milesiorum portu navibus et militibus[231] impositis, qui frequentes pro sua[232] in Caesarem pietate convenerant—in latrones fecit impetum, navalique proelio commisso fundit[233] fugatque et redactis denique in potestatem piratis cruci suffixit; quod illis ioco saepe[234] minatus fuerat, dum apud eos captivus teneretur. Hoc insigne facinus, apud non malignum virtutis aestimatorem[235] praecipuis celebrandum praeconiis, dubitari non potest, quin fortitudinis et iustae vindicationis titulis adornetur.

30   Subinde non ridere et amice interdum subirasci tibi non possum tuam perlegens epistolam, in qua, omnia in Caesarem maledicta colligens ea sic adfirmas, quasi nulla subsit dubitatio, et, cum eius magistratus percurris, si quid est cum laude gestum, tacitus omittis, sordes autem exprimis—ut, si quis eximium et celerem cursu equum adduxerit, tu 'caput argutum,' cervicem formosam,

once, or if he was doing nothing else even to seven?" Is that not *distinguished and worthy of praise?*[75] If I wanted to include all the remarkable things of Caesar's youth, I would certainly have produced a large volume, which is not at all what I intended at this time. Hence I add only one great and difficult achievement, and I shall let the others go.

When Caesar, in order to escape Sulla's rage and bitter hostilities against him, had decided to leave Italy, he sailed to Rhodes, home to the most excellent arts and of the Muses more than any other place the nurse of eloquence, as it were "for the purchase of wisdom."[76] While sailing around the isle of Pharmacusa he was captured by pirates, who at that time were infesting the islands and coasts and controlling the sea with countless ships and huge fleets. Next, when he had ransomed himself from them for the sum of fifty talents, he withdrew to Asia and when he had soon amassed ships in the harbor of Miletus and manned them with soldiers, who had gathered in great number owing to their loyalty to Caesar, he made an attack against the pirates and, after joining in a naval battle, routed them and put them to flight. Finally, having reduced the pirates to his power, he crucified them — something he had frequently threatened them with in jest when he had been held captive among them.[77] It cannot be doubted that this distinguished achievement, fit to be celebrated with high praises by an unbiased judge of virtue, should be adorned with the titles of bravery and just retribution.

I cannot help but laugh frequently and, now and then, be amicably annoyed with you while reading through your letter. For in it, as you amass every slander against Caesar, you assert these as if there were not a sliver of doubt. Likewise, running through his magistracies, you pass in silence over anything he did creditably, yet give vent to the scandals. It is as if someone brought in a splendid and speedy horse, and then you were to neglect its "short

29

30

pectus animosum, solidos pedes omittens,[236] caudae saetas te-
nuesque comas carpas. Caesarem igitur aliquotiens in coniurationis suspicionem perductum, quod Plutarchus incertum obscurum-
que fuisse dicit, quis ignorat? Scimus enim quanta inimici
eius—cives invidi et adversae factionis homines—tum malignitate,
tum metu, tum indignatione in eum machinati sunt, ut eum odio
plebis et populi, cui carissimum esse intelligebant,[237] vehementius
obicerent. Quocirca qui vitam eius scriptis et Graece et Latine
commendarunt, cum ad eum locum pervenirent, non 'conspiravit'
inquiunt, sicut 'haec gessit in Gallia' et 'in provinciae formam redegit' et 'stipendium imposuit' et 'piratas vicit,'[238] sed 'in suspicionem
venit.' Quid enim aliud est suspicio, quam incerta turpitudinis
opinio[239] et rumor inconstans? Qui eius generis est, ut nulla tam
sancta integraque persona sit, quam non suspicionibus quivis possit criminari indignumque apud iudices graves (tuique similes)
facinus habeatur, suspiciones firmamenti satis[240] habere, quas
homines aut factionibus acerbi, aut natura malivoli,[241] persaepe
confingant.

31   Cuius rei gravissimus testis est Sallustius, praestans historicus
et auctor valde bonus, qui in *Coniuratione Catilinae* suspicioni fuisse
Crassum et Caesarem scribit, cum per clarissimorum civium insidias, et calumniam variis rationibus et causis, in ea—et quidem
falso—nominati fuissent; quod a Cicerone praestantissimo cive et
amantissimo patriae consule, pro Caesaris integritate atque laudibus testimonio declaratum est.

32   Ceterum de aedilitate, praetura reliquisque magistratibus, si
quid magnifice, iuste ac forti animo gestum est, abs te mentio
nulla. Si eius praestantiam dicere velle praefatus es—cum non
mediocre vel moribus vel arti sit vitium aliud proponere, aliud

head," handsome neck, strong chest and firm feet, but carp at the
coarse hair of its tail and its thin mane.[78] Who is unaware that
Caesar was brought under suspicion of conspiracy a number of
times, though Plutarch cautions that it was uncertain and un-
clear?[79] For we know with how much malice, fear and anger his
enemies — jealous citizens and men of the other faction — plotted
against him so as to expose him the more harshly to the ill will of
the plebs and the people to whom they knew him to be very dear.
It is for this reason that those who committed his life to writing,
both in Greek and in Latin, when they reach this point, write not
"he conspired," in the same way that they write "he did these
things in Gaul" and "he reduced it to a province" and "he imposed
a levy" and "he vanquished the pirates," but instead "he came under
suspicion." For what else is suspicion but uncertain opinion of infamy and wavering rumor? And rumor is of such a kind that there
is no person so saintly and blameless that he cannot be incrimi-
nated with suspicions by anyone at all, and that among serious
judges such as yourself it is deemed an unworthy deed to take
suspicions as sufficient proof, since people often invent them when
they are either embittered by faction or malevolent by nature.

The weightiest witness in this matter is Sallust, an excellent   31
historian and a very sound authority, who writes in his *Conspiracy
of Catiline* that Crassus and Caesar came under suspicion because
they had been implicated in it through the plots and slander of
high-ranking citizens, for various reasons and motives, and indeed
falsely so.[80] This was then demonstrated, with a testimony to Caesar's integrity and merits, by Cicero, a thoroughly excellent citizen
and patriotic consul.

However, regarding his tenure as aedile, praetor, and the rest of   32
his magistracies, if anything was done with magnificence, fairness
and a strong spirit, you do not mention it. If you said at the start
that you wanted to discuss his excellence — seeing that it is no
small failing in manners or in art to propose one thing but do

commemorare — cur ornatum a Caesare comitium, forum, basilicas, porticus, cur editos magnificis apparatibus ludos, venationes,
epulas[242] reliquasque munificentias[243] nec exponis, nec significas,[244]
quae ad illius aetatis gloriam pertinebant? Ea vero vel ad peritorum iudicium, vel ad imperitorum notitiam fuerant explicanda.

33   C. quoque Caesari videris obicere, quod *ad conciliandum plebis
favorem restituit trophaea C. Marii, prius a Sulla disiecta.* Qua in re,
cum non modo vituperium nullum, sed summa pietatis laus Caesari sit,[245] quoniam quaedam illius probro suffuraris, supplendum
est, quod intercepisti. Amita[246] Caesaris Iulia, senioris uxor Marii,[247] diem suum obierat; quam nepos ipse efferre[248] honorifice
cupiens funebrem orationem (et quidem luculentam, omnium admiratione) cum[249] habuisset, ornamenta mariti ad Iuliae laudes
non parum attinere cognoscens simul et Marii statuas et trophaea
praetulit; ea posteriori tempore publice in Capitolio reposuit, quae
dudum ab inimico Sulla, et homine immanissimo,[250] disiecta la-
tuerant. Scire abs te velim, quidnam in hoc facto, quod tantum
improbas, peccatum est. Quae ab inimico per odium fuerant
abiecta, per pietatem ab amico restituta sunt; hic amitam benignus
ornabat, ille suum imperatorem ingratus dehonestabat. Qui minus
Sullae per factionem alterius honori detrahere iniuste licuit, quam
Caesari virtutis praemia iustissime[251] conservare?

34   Esto, plebis favorem Caesar adeptus est; et Sulla nobilitatis
studia extorquebat. Quod si acta Sullae rescindere flagitium est,
impie tribunicia restituta a Caesare potestas erit, 'cuius vim ac ius

another—why is there no exposition or indication of Caesar's embellishment of the *comitium*, the forum, the basilicas, and the porticos, why none at all of his production of games with magnificent splendor and of hunts and feasts and the rest of his munificent acts which contributed to the glory of that age?[81] These things should have been set forth either for the judgment of those in the know, or for the information of those who do not know.

You also seem to hold it against C. Caesar that *in order to curry* 33 *favor with the plebs he restored the trophies of C. Marius which Sulla had torn down.*[82] Since in this matter there is not only no censure against Caesar but instead the highest praise for his sense of duty, and you have secretly made away with certain details in order to abuse him, it is necessary to supply what you took. When Caesar's paternal aunt Julia, the wife of the elder Marius, had died, her nephew, wanting to give her an honorable burial himself and aware that, even when he had delivered a funeral oration (and indeed a brilliant one, to everyone's astonishment) still the honors of her husband contributed not a little to Julia's acclaim, he had carried in procession both the statues of Marius and his trophies. These he later put on public display on the Capitol: the same ones which had long lain hidden, torn down by his personal enemy, the monstrous Sulla. I should like to know from you what was wrong with this deed, of which you disapprove so much. What an enemy had torn down out of hatred a friend restored out of a sense of duty. One kindly paid tribute to his aunt, the other ungratefully dishonored his commander. How was it permitted to Sulla less unjustly to diminish the honor of another man on account of faction, than to Caesar to preserve, most justly, the rewards for his courage?

Granted, Caesar *won* the goodwill of the people; but Sulla *ex-* 34 *torted* the support of the nobility. If it is a crime to undo the deeds of Sulla, then it will be wicked for Caesar to have restored the power of the tribunes, "whose force and jurisdiction Sulla had

Sulla diminuerat,' quae una contra potentes arx[252] erat atque refugium. Res ipsa fuit argumento (de restitutis dico trophaeis) siquidem primariis et magnae auctoritatis hominibus[253] in frequenti
senatu Caesaris audaciam acerbissime incusantibus— in quibus
Lutatius Catulus—Caesar, senatu iudice, ita se purgavit adversariis confutatis, ut cunctorum laude[254] et admiratione[255] verae
magnanimitatis titulum reportarit.

35   Magnum subinde crimen intendis in Caesarem, quod *effusis* (ut
ais) *largitionibus ac supervacuis impensis populi benivolentiam captarit*,
praesertim *cum pontificatum peteret*. Huic addere[256] fidelis expositor
debuisti: cuius 'duos nactus competitores potentissimos multumque et dignitate et aetate antecedentes,' Isauricum[257] et Catulum;
et (quod ad singularem[258] Caesaris gratiam et populi in eum caritatem pertinet) 'plura Caesar in eorum tribubus suffragia solus
quam uterque in omnibus tulerit.' Ignorare videris, vel non meminisse saltem, quot liberalitatis et munificentiae modis mirabilem
populi favorem emeruit, cum id non mediocre adiumentum iis,
qui in re publica versantur, necessario comparandum esse intelligeret. Ad eum cum ludi, spectacula, convivia, tum praestita innumerabilibus patrocinia,[259] commendationes candidatorum huic vel illi
tribui, iudicibus, magistratibus, dexteritas, morum dulcedo, affabi-
litas in prensandis[260] supra aetatem dextris, ratio et omnifariam
cultus in populum valuit; quibus effectum est, ut populus invicem
novos[261] excogitaret honores ac[262] magistratus, quibus tanta in se
merita compensaret.

36   Fac autem ea largitionibus empta suffragia. Abs te quaero, Ro-
maene id peccatum sit aut deforme? Quam quidem ad inter-
rogationem antequam respondeas, et tecum diutius cogitato, et

diminished," which was the only fortress and refuge against the powerful.[83] This very matter, I mean the restoration of the trophies, furnishes another argument, inasmuch as when leading men of the highest authority, among them Lutatius Catulus, were bitterly accusing the audacity of Caesar in a packed senate, Caesar with the senate as judge so absolved himself by refuting his opponents that he won a reputation for true magnanimity, with the praise and admiration of all.

Thereafter you pin a great crime on Caesar: namely that, as you say, *through exuberant bribery and excessive expenditures he courted the goodwill of the people*, especially *when he was running for the Pontificate*.[84] To which as a truthful narrator you should have added: "facing two very powerful competitors who much surpassed him in standing and age," namely Isauricus and Catulus, and, pertinent to the unique popularity of Caesar and the people's love for him, the following citation: "Caesar carried more votes in their tribes alone than each of them in all."[85] You seem either not to know or at least not to remember with how many types of liberality and munificence he earned the marvelous support of the people, since he understood that this was a not negligible asset to those who engage in public life, and as such must of necessity be procured. This end was served by the games, the spectacles and feasts, as well as the patronage he offered numerous people and the recommendations of candidates to this or that tribe or for judicial positions or magistracies, and likewise his readiness to oblige, pleasant demeanor, and affability in shaking the hands of his elders, and his regard for and cultivation of the people in every way. It was on account of these things that the people, in turn, thought up new honors and magistracies for him, by which to repay such great services to them.

But suppose that he bought those votes with bribery. I ask you whether this was a crime in Rome, or unseemly? Before, indeed, you answer this question, you must think long and hard and con-

quosdam adsumito[263] consiliarios. Praeterea quis partiendae[264] per tribus[265] atque centurias[266] pecuniae morem introduxit? Num Caesar? Minime. Nam quid sibi[267] volunt leges antea[268] de ambitu?[269] Quid tot ambitus[270] rei superiori tempore in[271] iudicium vocati? Is vero in[272] consuetudinem inveteratus ita fuit aditus, ut optimates, ne Caesar consul designaretur, suffragatoribus[273] pecuniam spoponderint[274] atque contulerint, 'ne Catone quidem (tuo illo[275] sancto) abnuente eius generis largitionem, quam[276] e re publica fieri' profiteretur, tanto in odium Caesaris[277] deflagrabat; de quo non longe post quaedam reseranda erunt, quae ad rem pertinent.

37   Quod si quis vel sui, vel utilitatis publicae gratia sacerdotium[278] episcopatumve cuperet, nec id nisi collatis ante pecuniis atque[279] primitiis a pontifice maximo posset impetrare (quod quidem inveterato iam more omnium ferme consensu invaluit), cuinam[280] culpam obiectares? Impetrantine, an ei qui initium introduxit? Cum igitur adolescentulus Caesar competitoribus suis aetate, potentia, dignitate, opibus antecedentibus praelatus fuerit, et plura non modo in suis, sed etiam[281] in eorum tribubus suffragia consecutus sit, non largitioni, non pecuniae — qua illi superiores erant — sed gratiae, caritati, benivolentiae — quibus Caesar superabat[282] — tribuendum est. Quid tam insigne Scipioni contigisse dices? Qui[283] non principibus, ut Caesar, praepositus est petentibus, sed *desperatis ac perditis rebus,* cum nemo in Hispaniam imperium accipere *auderet.* Scipio, petere professus, temeritatis damnatus est et populum facti paenitere coepit, cum 'favor plus quam aetatis ratio valuisset' (Livio teste).

38   Caesar autem quantum caritate valuerit et benivolentia, non solum penes populum, sed etiam[284] penes senatorium ordinem, factum illud testimonio est: cum olim multitudinem, ad se sponte

sult some advisors. Furthermore, who introduced the custom of distributing money by tribes and voting units? It wasn't Caesar, was it? Not at all. For what was the purpose of the earlier laws about electoral bribery? Why were so many men accused of bribery summoned to court in earlier times? Indeed this approach was so ingrained in habit that the Optimates promised money and handed it to the voters to avoid Caesar's being elected consul, and "not even Cato," your *saintly man*, "refused this kind of bribery," which he said "was for the good of the republic," so much did he burn in his hatred of Caesar—a man about whom certain points relevant to this case will have to be disclosed a little later.[86]

If anyone were desiring a priesthood or a bishopric, be it for his   37 own sake or the common good, and he could not obtain this from the pope without gathering beforehand money or first fruits (which has indeed prevailed by longstanding custom with the consent of almost all), to whom would you apportion the blame? To the one who seeks the office, or to the person who instituted the practice? Hence when the young Caesar was preferred over competitors who outstripped him in age, power, standing, and resources, and achieved more votes not just in his own but even in their tribes, this should not be attributed to bribery or money, in which the others surpassed him, but to the popularity, esteem and goodwill, in which Caesar outstripped them. What equally outstanding thing will you claim befell Scipio? He was not, like Caesar, selected in preference over leading citizens seeking office, *but when things were hopeless and desperate* since no one *dared* to take up the command over Spain.[87] And when he had declared his candidacy Scipio was accused of recklessness, and the people began to rue what they had done since "affection had trumped the consideration of age," as Livy tells us.[88]

Yet as for Caesar, how much he was bolstered by love and good-   38 will, not just with the people but also among the senatorial order, is proven by the following deed: once, after he had restrained a

confluentem operamque sibi in adserenda[285] dignitate tumultuo-
sius pollicentem, compescuisset, 'senatus Caesari gratias per primores viros egit et accitum in curiam amplissimis verbis collauda-
vit.' Adeo utrique ordini gratiosus habebatur. Desine igitur virtutis
et laudis opera largitioni et turpitudini adsignare. Ceterum si tantum largitione ac[286] pecunia Caesarem valuisse putas, ut magistratus, imperia, dignitates usurparit aut mercatus sit: dic, oro, cur
non eadem et aliis, et Crasso ⟨quidem⟩ vel adolescenti, vel aetate
provecto contigerunt, qui re pecuniaria longe praecellebat?[287] Igitur
tam petulantissimis maledictis Romani nominis[288] splendorem insectari non debueras, sed, cum hominum comparationem[289] facere
profitearis, amborum bona malaque proferre, nec simul advocati et
iudicis officium intercipere, ne, cum utrumque reddere te incipias,
uterque esse desinas.

39   Magnam mihi desumptam video provinciam, si universis, quae
abs te depravata referuntur[290] historia vel respondere, vel detracta
supplere decrevero; verum, ut et[291] aliis vicem suam remittam, ne
'tamquam meam in possessionem venerim,' reliquos excludam,[292]
pauca quaedam deligam capita, alia nugatoria prorsus omittens.
Quod subdis, quam subdole, quam corrupte, quam venenose pro-
nuntias: *solus certe omnium in coniuratione deprehensos conservandos
censuit in senatu!* Quo me vertam? Ad Poggium? Minime. Nam
corruptus testis corruptas habet et aures. Leonellum itaque, principem gravissimum, appello, cuius integerrimo iudicio plus tribuo.
Cur Caesaris sententiam Poggius malam in partem ac sinistram
excipit,[293] cum alii de fine poenae (id est[294] morte) in coniuratos
sumendae, Caesar de poena diuturniori[295] in parricidas statuenda

multitude thronging around him of their own free will, and in disorderly fashion promising their support in asserting his honor, "the senate offered him thanks through its leading men and, after summoning him to the curia, praised him in the highest terms."[89] Such was the favor he enjoyed with both orders. So stop attributing works of virtue and merit to bribery and baseness. Besides, if you think that Caesar had such powers with regard to bribery and money that he stole, or indeed bought, magistracies, commands and honors, then please tell me why these same things did not befall others and ⟨particularly⟩ Crassus, either as a young man or at an advanced age, who far outstripped him financially?[90] Hence you should not have attacked the splendor of the Roman nation with such petulant slanders, but rather, since you profess to be making a comparison of men, you should set forth the good and the bad qualities of both and not simultaneously assume the duties of advocate and judge, lest when you start acting as both of them you cease being either.

I am aware that I will have claimed a large task for myself if I 39 decide either to respond to everything that is distorted by your account or add whatever you removed; instead, to give others a chance, too, so as not to exclude them "as though I have entered my own property," I will choose a few key issues and leave out the other trifles completely.[91] As to what you add, how cunningly and falsely and venomously do you proclaim it: *certainly he was the only one in the senate who counseled that those discovered plotting the conspiracy should be saved!*[92] Where shall I turn? To Poggio? By no means: for a corrupt witness also has corrupted ears. I therefore call upon Leonello, an extremely weighty prince, whose impartial judgment I value more. Why does Poggio interpret Caesar's opinion as bad and improper, when others counseled that the ultimate punishment, that is, death, should be inflicted on the conspirators, while Caesar thought that the longer punishment should be enacted

sentiret? Ea quo longior,[296] eo in male meritos supplicium dignius.[297]

40 *Solus*, inquit. Immo et Decimus Silanus, consul designatus,[298] idem sentiebat, idem et Tiberius Nero, idem et proconsularis homo Q. Cicero, consulis Ciceronis frater, idem et reliqui, 'nisi labantem ordinem confirmasset M. Catonis oratio,' id est[299] in Caesaris opinionem consentientem. Ergo non *solus*! 'Postquam Cato adsedit (ut ait Crispus) consulares omnes itemque magna pars senatus sententiam eius laudant.' Magna pars, inquit: non cuncti. Ergo et reliqui Caesaris sententiam probant. Non igitur *solus*, uti[300] solus Poggius affirmat; qui utinam[301] Horatianum[302] illud tenuisset: 'scribamne licenter, an omnes visuros peccata putem mea?'

41 Et, quod inconsideratius dictum ab eo est,[303] *conservandos*[304] *censuit* inquit. Conservandosne? An qui coniuratos publicatis eorum pecuniis in vinculis habendos censuit, per[305] dedecus et infamiam notatos, conservare voluit, id est salvos esse contendit? Et, ut[306] quo modo eos salvos esse voluit, constet, Caesar haec adiecit in sententia (Dione teste): 'ne quis de illorum liberatione verba in senatu facere auderet in posterum,' addita poena; 'eaque oppida unde quempiam fugisse contigisset in hostium numero haberi' censuit. Siccine liberari solent? Quis ita Latine loquitur, ut, qui intra carcerem in asperitatem vitae, in duros corporis cruciatus,[307] in salutis desperationem quempiam intruserit, saluti et conservationi consuluisse dicatur? Quod si ita est, quid ⟨Poggius⟩ Caesarem accusat, qui M. *Catonem in carcerem duci iussit*, si eo pacto Catonem conservaret? O Ciceronem, ignarum Latinae linguae[308] hominem, qui 'siccarios, veneficos, fures, peculatores non disputa-

against the father-killers? Inasmuch as it is longer, that punishment is more fitting for the miscreants.

He was the only one, he says.[93] On the contrary, the consul designate Decimus Silanus thought the same, and Tiberius Nero also, and Q. Cicero, a man of proconsular rank[94] and the brother of the consul Cicero, and the rest, "had not the speech of Cato steadied the wavering order," that is to say, agreeing with Caesar's opinion.[95] So he was not *the only one!* "After Cato sat down," as Sallust states, "all men of consular rank and in addition a majority of the senate praised his opinion."[96] A majority, he said: not all. Hence others too approved of Caesar's opinion. Not, therefore, *only* Caesar, as only Poggio asserts. If only he had stuck to this phrase of Horace: "Should I write freely, or should I consider that all will see my sins?"[97]

And, as he said more carelessly still, *he counseled that they should be saved.* Were they really to be saved? Did someone who counseled that the conspirators, their money confiscated, be held in chains, marked by shame and infamy, want to save them, that is, advocate that they be unharmed? And, so that we may be clear about the way in which he wanted them to be saved, Caesar attached the following clause to his opinion, as Dio attests. "So that no one in the future would dare to bandy words in the senate about their release" a penalty was added, and he counseled that "any town from which it chanced that anyone had fled would be classed in the category of enemies."[98] Is that the way people are wont to be freed? Who speaks such Latin that he who has cast another man into a dungeon, into a harsh life and rigorous bodily torments with no hope of salvation—that he is said to have taken counsel for his well-being and preservation? If it is so, why does ⟨Poggio⟩ accuse Caesar, who *ordered Cato to be led to prison,* if in this way he were saving Cato?[99] Oh Cicero, you ignoramus in Latin, who said that "assassins and poisoners and thieves and embezzlers are not to be worn down with philosophers' arguments but with

40

41

tione philosophorum, sed vinculis et carcere fatigandos' esse dixit, quando hac loquendi ratione conservatos significabat, quos exterminandos et poenis torquendos affirmabat. Sin diutius in vivendi acerbitate retinendos, et longiori miseria adfligendos intelligebat, quid Caesaris sententiam aut improbat, aut depravat? At eos salvos Caesar fieri curabat. Non est ita. Nam eorum, qui sententias dicebant, officium erat facienda praescribere; senatus vero decernere et rata[309] statuere. Alioquin inanis erat[310] omnis oratio![311] Nihil igitur dicit, qui coniuratos conservari ab Caesare voluisse dicit.

42   Et quoniam de Catone[312] dicturum me[313] pollicitus sum, in quo non parvam in Caesarem[314] ordiris accusationem, de homine summatim evolvam: non tibi, qui haec probe calles, sed imperitis, qui facile pelliciuntur in errorem. Complura in Catone laudibus digna viguisse contenderim, quibus ad posteritatem usque celebratus est; sed eundem tam importunum, pervicacem morosumque fuisse, ut intra Cynicorum aut Stoicorum potius angulos et altercationes quam in Romana re publica qui obversaretur[315] dignus exstiterit; qui ingenita quadam peculiari sibi duritia—fero vel ferreo potius ingenio—ardentissimi[316] spiritus virum, fax ardentissima, semper incenderit; et quem mitigare potuerat, pertinax et inexorabilis adversator irritarit.[317] Nec mirum, cum 'in ea fuerit haeresi,' quae, quam[318] semel apprehendisset,[319] 'mutare sententiam'[320] nefas esse iudicarit; non 'gratia moveri,' nemini ignoscere, misericordiam denegare constantis et vere sapientis putaret[321] officium. Quo factum est, ut quod ab ineunte aetate ab doctoribus hauserat, et acuendi ingenii ac disputationis gratia didicerat, ad immitem et scaevam[322]

chains and prison," when with this turn of phrase he indicated that those whom he asserted should be banished and tortured with punishments were saved.[100] But if Poggio understood that they were to be kept in this harsh style of living for longer and to be afflicted with a more protracted misery, why then does he disapprove of Caesar's judgment or distort it? But Caesar took care that they be saved. It is not so: for it was the duty of those who gave their opinions to suggest what should be done, but of the senate to decide and ratify it. Otherwise the whole speech was pointless! So he who says that the conspirators were intended to be saved by Caesar is talking nonsense.

And since I promised that I would speak about Cato, on whom   42
you base no small accusation against Caesar, I will set out a few things about the man, not for your sake, since you know them well, but for those who are unaware and therefore easily led into error.[101] I would argue that Cato had many qualities worthy of praise, for which he is celebrated up to the present, but that the same man was so harsh, obstinate, and cheerless, that he was worthy of going about within the corners and heated disputes of the Cynics and Stoics rather than in the Roman republic. With a sort of inborn hardness which was peculiar to him, a fierce or rather iron nature, a blazing torch always inflamed the man of blazing spirit, and him whom he might have been able to pacify, he provoked as an obstinate and relentless adversary. No wonder, seeing he was "of this school of thought" that judged it a sin to "change a position" once taken, and deemed it the duty of a consistent and truly wise man not to "be moved by favor," to forgive no one, and to deny pity.[102] And from this it came about that the lessons that he had imbibed from his teachers beginning at an early age, and had learned for the sake of sharpening his mind and for argumentation, pointed him toward a pitiless and perverse, rather than

magis quam severam vivendi normam et immobile[323] consilium
direxerit.[324] Qui sibi non pepercit, quonammodo aliis veniam
daret?

43   Tanta vero fuit eius discrepantia, infirmitas et inconstantia, ut
filium ad vivendum hortatus de Caesaris benignitate omnia spe-
rare praeceperit, cum sibi tamen prae Caesaris odio et invidia
mortem consciverit, ne de ipsius salute et conservatione Caesar
gloriaretur: quasi turpe sibi foret, quod in amantissimo et bellicoso
filio censuisset honestum. Et bonus ille vir, si diis placet,[325] prius
quam sibi manus inferret, Platonis librum *De animi immortalitate*[326]
perlegerat, quasi non Platonis instituto gravia intententur iis supplicia,

> qui sibi letum
insontes peperere manu lucemque perosi
proiecere animas. Quam vellent aethere in alto
nunc et pauperiem et duros perferre labores!

Ei tamen Pythagoricum illud instillatum esse debebat 'iniussu imperatoris, id est dei, de praesidio et statione vitae nefas esse dece-
dere.'

44   Huic sancto viro mores et instituta civitatis conformanda praebeas, qui modestissimam et probam imprimis uxorem reluctantem
ut iumentum alieno concessit viro et sanctum coniugium, pro quo
etiam bruta propugnant, profanavit? Quidnam hoc esse dices, si
lenonium[327] nequaquam appelles officium? Veluti Roma non virgines, non viduas haberet, quae Hortensio spem procreandae so-
bolis adferrent! De huius hominis moribus quid sentit Plutarchus,
subtilis earum rerum examinator, non ab re fuerit explicare. 'Cato
(inquit) non persuasu faciles, non multitudini amabiles mores
habuit, nec ad gratiam floruit in re publica.' Ceterum (ut inquit

merely a strict code of living, and to fixed policy. How can he who has not spared himself bestow pardon upon others?

Yet such was his incongruity, weakness, and changeability that, 43 though he urged his son to live and instructed him to place all his hopes on the generosity of Caesar, he committed suicide on account of his hatred and jealousy of Caesar, so that Caesar would not boast of saving and preserving him alive, as if he thought that what was honorable for his beloved and war-like son would have been shameful for himself.[103] And this good man — if it pleases the Gods! — before he laid hands on himself had read through Plato's book *On the Immortality of the Soul*, as though according to Plato's teaching grave punishments did not await those

who,
  though innocent, compassed death by their own hand and
    hating the light
  cast out their souls. How they now would wish under the high
    heaven
  to endure both poverty and harsh labors![104]

But he should have been inspired by this Pythagorean teaching: "without the order of the commander, namely God, it is sinful to depart from the garrison and guard station of life."[105]

Would you hand over the customs and principles of the state 44 for reformation to this saintly man, who gave his very modest and noble wife to another man against her will, like a draft animal, and desecrated holy matrimony for which even brute beasts fight? What will you say this is, if you will by no means call it the business of a pimp? As if Rome had no virgins and no widows who could have given Hortensius hope of begetting offspring![106] It would not be beside the point to set forth what Plutarch, a precise investigator of these matters, thought of the manners of this man: "Cato," he said, "had manners not easy to promote nor pleasing to the masses, and he did not thrive in popularity in the republic."[107]

Cicero) 'dum in Platonis magis quam Romuli re publica versa-tur'[328] ad rubricam e consulatu lapsus est. Ei obvenisse censeo, quod intempestive nascentibus accidere fructibus solet; nam ut il-los et libenter aspiciunt et mirantes, nequaquam utuntur, sic et prisci in Catone mores post multas tempestates in vitas corruptas et improbos mores incidentes, cum existimationem et gloriam ingentem vendicarint, necessariis rerum usibus minime congrue-bant; tanta erat in eo gravitas et virtutis magnitudo, nullum exsis-tentibus iam temporibus modum habens aut[329] aptitudinem.

45   Haec hominis pertinacia, quae pro tempore uti velificatione[330] noluit, dum immota tenere vela perstat nec vento cedit (quod sem-per sapientis est habitum), rectam potius mergere quam paululum obsequentem servare navem constituit. Nam Gallicas Caesaris vic-torias et propagatum imperium vel invide vel indignanter ferens, cum cetera civitas et gauderet et gratularetur, idque publicis sup-plicationibus testaretur, Cato iure iurando denuntiavit se Caesaris nomen delaturum[331] et in iudicium vocaturum; cum interim Cato non minus astutum libertatis insidiatorem et monarchiae sub dic-taturae[332] specie studentem—Pompeium—et suspicans, et dicti-tans, cum eo contra Caesarem conspiraret, et ei violatis legibus favorem omnem studiaque dicaret. Haec est illa Catonis integritas, qua *sanctissimus vir* appellari meruit, belli civilis, quantum in eo fuit, instigator et altor[333] et simultatis ultor.

46   Expediamus et paucis de Galliarum sortitione et proroga-tione,[334] cum utramque *praeter leges, consuetudinem*[335] *et instituta maiorum* factam esse contendas. Negabisne lege Vatinia et senatus auctoritate eas illi attributas? Dices id generi sui studio confectum

Moreover, as Cicero says, "living in Plato's republic rather than that of Romulus" he fell from the consulship to the cold ground.[108] In my view what happened to him was the same thing that happens to fruits growing out of season: for in the same way that people look at those with pleasure and admiringly, yet make no use of them whatsoever, so too the ancient manners of Cato, after many storms had passed, met with impure lives and improper manners, and while they won respect and enormous praise, they could not at all be squared with the necessary practical experience of the world: such was his dignity and the greatness of his virtue, but he had no measure or aptitude for the times as they now were.

And this obstinacy of the man, which prevented him from sail-   45
ing according to the season, while persevering in holding the sails unmoved instead of (as is always considered wise) giving in to the wind, caused the ship to sink on its direct course, rather than saving it by allowing it to yield a little. For Cato, responding to Caesar's Gallic victories and his extension of the empire with jealousy or indignation, while the rest of the City rejoiced as well as thanked him and attested that with public thanksgivings, announced on oath that he would prosecute Caesar and summon him to court. Meanwhile Cato, both suspecting Pompey and repeatedly calling him a no less cunning plotter against liberty and seeker after monarchy under the guise of dictatorship, nonetheless conspired with him against Caesar, and devoted to him all favor and partisanship when he violated the law. This is that integrity of Cato, for which he deserved to be called a *most saintly man*, to the best of his ability an instigator and fosterer of the civil war and avenger of rivalry.[109]

Let us also briefly deal with the allotment and extension of his   46
command over the Gauls, since you argue that both happened *against the laws, against custom, and against ancestral precedent.*[110] Will you deny that they were granted to Caesar by the *Lex Vatinia* and the authority of the senate?[111] You will say that this was achieved

fuisse; adde etiam propensis in Caesarem populi suffragiis et ardentibus in illius honores animis. Nam et tribuni[336] et consulis[337] et imperatoris[338] et alios magistratus superiori tempore precibus et commendationibus impetrari solitos, quis est qui nesciat?

47   Unum omittere non possum: te[339] ita tuo fidere iudicio, ut contra priscarum rerum[340] scriptores certam ac diffinitam pronunties sententiam. Ecce, cum aliis de bellis sapienter et fortiter administratis vulgata depraves, tum de Alexandrino *non honorem* (inquis) *sed dedecus promeruit.* Sta, oro te, gradum ne retorseris. Estne imperatoris decus primum, cum fortissimis ducibus, robustissimis militibus, ingentibus copiis terra marique pedestres[341] navalesque pugnas summo cum periculo non semel, sed pluries administrasse et inde victoriae compotem revertisse? Huius generis ab Caesare bellum illud gestum esse constat.[342] Audi, vel recordare potius, quid de illo veteres[343] sentiant, quorum supra ceteros pollet auctoritas: 'Bellum sane difficillimum gessit, neque loco, neque tempore aequo, sed hieme anni et intra moenia copiosissimi ⟨ac sollertissimi⟩ hostis, inops ipse omnium rerum atque imparatus.' Omitto intercisos aquaeductus, aquas eius[344] ingenio atque scientia restitutas; quibus, ne siti suus periret exercitus, discrimen[345] et pavor ingruerat.[346] Taceo[347] de proelio adversus Pharitas et periculo; quod cum singulari providentia[348] (non *incautus*, ut iactas, sed praesagus)[349] nando effugisset, animi magnitudine victor exstitit.

48   An parum laudis et admirationis consecutus est Caesar humanitatis, clementiae, mansuetudinis multarumque virtutum quas[350] ex eo bello reportavit? Et (ut testatur Hirtius aut Oppius)[351]

through the partisanship of his son-in-law; you should add, yet
again, by the people's votes which favored Caesar, and by their
minds burning to appoint him to office.[112] For who does not know
that at an earlier time the tribunate, consulship, generalship, and
other magistracies besides, were generally procured by requests
and recommendations?

One thing I cannot omit, namely that you so trust your own   47
judgment that you pronounce your certain and definitive opinion
in the face of the writers of ancient history. Look, you not only
pervert the common opinion about other wisely and bravely conducted wars, but about the Alexandrian war you say that it *earned
Caesar not honor but shame*. Stand your ground, I beg you, and do
not turn aside. Is it not the main glory of a general to conduct,
with very strong commanders, most vigorous soldiers, and great
armies, on land and on sea, infantry and naval battles, and to conduct them amid the gravest danger, not once but several times,
and thence to return after seizing victory? That the war fought by
Caesar was of this type is generally agreed. Listen to, or rather
recall, what the ancients, whose authority outranks that of others,
think about him: "He waged an extremely difficult war on hostile
terrain and at an unfavorable time, since it was winter and he was
within the walls of a numerous ⟨and very crafty⟩ enemy, yet himself without resources of any kind and ill-prepared."[113] I leave out
the aqueducts that were severed and the water which was restored
by his ingenuity and technical knowledge, on account of which
panic and fear arose that his army might perish of thirst. I am silent about the battle against the inhabitants of Pharos and its
danger, since when he had escaped with exceptional prudence (not
incautiously, as you claim, but with forethought) by swimming, he
emerged triumphant on account of his greatness of spirit.[114]

Or did Caesar gain too little glory and admiration for his kind-   48
ness, clemency, restraint and the many virtues that he brought
back from that war? And, as Hirtius or Oppius testifies, "he

'dignum adveniens fructum virtutis et animi magnitudinis tulit,' cum Caesar Alexandrinos hostes, sese dedentes, in fidem[352] receptos orationis suavitate consolatus est. Praeterea socios et familiares Pompeii, quoscumque[353] per Aegyptios agros errantes[354] in potestatem redegit quique, ab rege capti, coniecti in vincula fuerant, Caesar liberavit omnique beneficentiae genere prosecutus sibi conciliavit. Romam dein[355] ad familiares scribens 'maximum se ac iocundissimum victoriae fructum colligere dicit, quod ei datum est nonnullos semper ex iis[356] cives conservare, qui adversum se belligeraverint.' Hine laudi[357] an dedecori tribuendi sunt laborum et victoriarum fructus? Quos qui non laudant et admirantur invidos aut malignos appellarim, aut utrumque.

49   Quaero enim abs te: quid si cives adversariosque trucidasset? Num crudelem vocares? Utique. Cur qui eos contra salvos et incolumes reddidit et dignitate ac magistratibus insuper honestavit, non humanum, liberalem clementemque praedicas? Quia sic in suos facere Caesar debuit,[358] dices. Qua lege? Quo instituto? Benignitatis, pietatis atque[359] clementiae! Ergo quisquis earum praecepta servarit institutisque paruerit benignus, pius clemensque confitente[360] Poggio vocabitur et erit. 'Qui honeste[361] vixerit,[362] alterum non laeserit,[363] suum cuique tribuerit,'[364] iustus est, quoniam iustitiae iussa tenet. Alienos lectos invadere qui non vult, quia continentiae legibus libenter audit, num[365] continens et est, et videtur? Quid singula percurro? Quicumque virtutis sectatur officium, virtute praeditus appellatur a doctis, quia quod debebat effecit.

50   Contra te stant priscorum[366] testimonia graviora; ex quibus Cicero imprimis occurrit, quamquam — ne quid iniuriae relinquas[367] intactum — non modo Caesaris laudibus obtrectator accedis, sed

arrived reaping the worthy fruit of his virtue and magnanimity" when after receiving into his protection the Alexandrian enemies who were surrendering, Caesar consoled them with the sweetness of his speech.[115] Moreover, Caesar reduced to his power the allies and friends of Pompey, who were roaming the Egyptian country-side, and set free those who had been captured by the king and cast into chains, and he won them over to himself by bestowing all kinds of benefits on them. When he later wrote to friends in Rome "he said that he reaped the greatest and most pleasurable reward of victory, namely that he always had the opportunity to save some of the citizens who had fought against him."[116] Should these fruits of his struggles and victories be classed as merit or as disgrace? I would call anyone who does not praise and admire them envious or malevolent or both.

For I ask you: what if he had killed these citizens and enemies? 49 Would you not have called him cruel? You certainly would. So why do you not call him who, instead, returned them safe and sound and in addition decked them out with honor and magistra-cies, kind, generous, and merciful? Because Caesar had to do this toward his own men, you will say. By what law, by which custom? Those of kindness, duty and clemency! Hence whoever observes their teachings and obeys their rules will both be called, and be — if Poggio consents — kind, dutiful, and clement. "He who has lived honestly, has not harmed another, and has given each his own" is just, since he observes the commands of justice.[117] He who has no desire to get into the beds of others, because he gladly hearkens to the laws of chastity, is he not, and does he not appear to be, chaste? Why do I go through these things piecemeal? Whoever follows the requirements of virtue is said by learned men to be endowed with virtue, because he has done as he should.

Against you stand the weightier testimonies of the ancients, 50 among whom first of all Cicero comes to mind — although, so as not to leave any insult untouched, you not only approach Caesar's

et[368] Ciceronem non[369] admodum probas, qui eius virtutis testis apparet, et *eas laudes* (ais) *non protulit* veritas. Immo vero veritas Ciceronem magnas ad laudes explicandas[370] impulit; et quarum testimonium in iis,[371] quos defendebat, habebat,[372] eas etiam honorificis verbis ornabat: 'Animum vincere, iracundiam cohibere, victoriam temperare, adversarium nobilitate, ingenio, virtute praestantem non modo extollere iacentem, sed etiam amplificare eius pristinam dignitatem: haec qui facit, non ego cum summis viris comparo, sed simillimum deo iudico.'[373] Non haec idcirco vera sunt, quia a Cicerone dicta sunt,[374] sed quia vera prius — etiam Cicerone tacente[375] — fuerant, prolata fuere. Nam qui hostibus et inimicis eius, et quidem acerbissimis persecutoribus (non autem patriae libertatis defensoribus, sed potius Pompeii satellitibus, ut ostendam) vitam dederit, veniam impertierit, ad dignitates erexerit,[376] eum non magnanimum, liberalem, benignum, clementem praedicare debuit orator magnus?

51   Sed responde, quaeso. Concedamus non veritate ductum, sed temporis necessitate coactum sic[377] mentitum Ciceronem fuisse, ut suorum civium saluti consuleret et ita vivas coram voces[378] exprimendas. Acta oratione, postquam suos e periculo salvos eduxerat, quid mendacia illa scriptis edenda fuerant?[379] Ut[380] enim probe scis, post[381] causarum defensiones orationes a patronis[382] confici mos fuit. Quid tanta in mentiendo probra, quid assentationes illae parasiticae posteritati ad Ciceronis ignominiam et immortale dedecus prodendae fuere,[383] nisi veritas universorum consensu probaretur? Id ita fuisse non modo Caesaris aetate manifestum fuit, ut admirationi vox illa fuerit 'parcite civibus' medias effusa per

merits as a detractor, but you do not even fully approve of Cicero, who appears as witness to his virtue, and you say that *it was not the truth that called forth those words of praise.*[118] On the contrary, in fact the truth impelled Cicero to set forth great praises, and he even adorned those merits which he attested in his defendants with honorific words: "To triumph over one's spirit, to restrain one's anger, to temper victory, not only to lift up a fallen opponent of outstanding nobility, talent and virtue, but even to enhance his previous standing: I compare him who does this not to the greatest men, but I judge him godlike."[119] These things are not true just because they were spoken by Cicero, but rather they were mentioned because they had been true before, even when Cicero was silent. For as to a man who gave life, granted forgiveness, and exalted to offices his enemies and adversaries and indeed his fiercest persecutors (who were not, as I shall show, defenders of the liberty of the fatherland but rather the acolytes of Pompey), should the great orator not have called him magnanimous, generous, kindly, and clement?

But answer, please. Let us grant that Cicero was not led by the truth, but lied in this manner, forced by the necessity of the time, so that he might take thought for the salvation of his fellow citizens, and that therefore these words had to be spoken in Caesar's presence. When the speech was done, and he had delivered his men from danger, why then did these lies have to be published in writing? As you very well know, it was customary after the defense for advocates to write up their speeches. Why did such great outrages of dishonesty, why did these expressions of sycophantic toadyism have to be bequeathed to posterity, to the ignominy and undying shame of Cicero, unless their truth had been accepted by universal consent? That it was so was evident not only in Caesar's time, so that the famous command "spare the citizens" was spread over the midst of the battle line to general admiration, but in later

51

acies, sed et sequentibus[384] saeculis, cum odio aut invidia et amore
liberum exstitit iudicium, benignitatis et clementiae praeconia ce-
lebrata.

52   Plinius namque, locupletissimus auctor et omnium doctrinarum copia excellens, hunc in modum de[385] Caesaris clementia testatur: 'Caesari proprium et peculiare sit clementiae insigne.' Num
et hoc ad Caesaris adsentationem prolatum[386] a Plinio testimonium refelles? Accipe et illud: 'Idem[387] magnanimitatis praebuit
exemplum, cui comparari non possit aliud; illa fuit[388] vera et in-
comparabilis invicti[389] animi sublimitas: captis apud Pharsalum
Pompeii Magni scrineis epistolarum, iterumque apud Thapsum
Scipionis, ea optima concremasse fide atque non legisse.' Quid et
Tranquillus? 'Simultates contra nullos tam graves exercuit umquam, ut non occasione oblata libens[390] deponeret,'[391] cum esset in
ulciscendo[392] natura lenissimus.[393] Moderationem clementiamque
tum in administratione, tum in victoria belli civilis admirabilem[394]
exhibuit. Quotiens in Gallos, quotiens in Aegyptios, quotiens in
omnes divinam exhibuit humanitatem! Illud de ipso constat: eximium, praeter paucos admodum, nullum 'nisi praelio periisse';
omnibus suis, quem partis adversae vellent servare, concessit.
Praesto erant[395] cum aliorum, tum Plutarchi Dionisque, hominum
praestantissimorum, testimonia, nisi satis haec esse confiderem ad
detegendas[396] tuorum scriptorum praestigias, quae profecto lectorem incautum quemque deciperent.

53   Ecce enim de Alexandrino bello calumnians[397] adiungis: *non
honorem, sed dedecus promeruit, dum Cleopatrae amore ardens incautus
ferme in hostium pervenit manus.* Quasi credi velis eodem tempore in
Cleopatrae gremio apricantem Caesarem in hostilem[398] ferme potestatem pervenisse,[399] quam acuto certe ingenio et subtili coniec-

ages, too, when judgment was free from hate or envy or love, his proclamations of kindness and clemency were celebrated.[120]

For Pliny, an extremely reliable author outstandingly knowl- 52
edgeable in all domains of learning, testifies to Caesar's clemency in this way: "Let clemency be the mark that was Caesar's own and unique to him."[121] Surely you will not also reject this testimony as pronounced by Pliny to flatter Caesar, will you? Listen also to this: "The same man provided an example of magnanimity to which no other could be compared, such was the true and incomparable loftiness of his unconquered spirit, that having got hold of the letter cases of Pompey the Great at Pharsalus, and again of those of Scipio at Thapsus, he burned them in good faith and did not read them."[122] And what about Suetonius? "He never entertained hatred so serious against anybody that he did not gladly put it down when the occasion arose," since by nature he was very mild when it came to revenge.[123] He showed admirable moderation and clemency both in his conduct of the civil war and in his victory. How often did he show an almost divine humanity toward the Gauls, toward the Egyptians, toward all! This thing is agreed about him, that no outstanding man, except a very few, "died except in battle"; and that he permitted all his men to save whomever they wished from the opposing side.[124] There were testimonies at hand of others, and especially of Plutarch and Dio, those most outstanding men, if I did not trust the present number to be sufficient to reveal the trickery of your writings, which might indeed deceive any incautious reader.

And see what slanders you add about the Alexandrian war: *it* 53
earned Caesar not honor but shame when, burning with love for Cleopatra,
he almost fell incautiously into the hands of the enemy.[125] Almost as if you want us to believe that at the same time that Caesar was sunning himself in the lap of Cleopatra he almost fell into enemy hands, which surely with his sharp mind and keen powers of deduction he avoided. And he, having encouraged his men in the

tura evitavit. Qui, quoad potuit suos in pugna cohortatus, inde fugit ad navigium adnatans; quod periturum, adfluente multitudine suorum, vaticinatus, sic[400] in aliud denuo se fortiter[401] et animose nando recepit, 'elevata laeva ne libelli quos tenebat madefierent, paludamentum mordicus trahens, ne spolio potiretur hostis.'[402] Sic ergo bellavit, ut ab[403] rebus gerendis nullus eum amor aut voluptas retardarit.

54   De Cleopatra non sum, qui probare cupiam, nec tu improbare soleas, qui cantare solebas amatorium illud:[404] 'militat[405] omnis amans, et habet sua castra Cupido.'[406] Sed idem[407] contendo id eius generis esse delictum,[408] quod 'humana parum natura caveat' quodque[409] facilius sit[410] accusare quam vitare. Eo namque praeclaros et generosos viros circumventos fuisse, quis ignorat? Ut de reliquis taceam: nesciusne es virum admirandum, illustrem imperatorem et populi Romani principem, Scipionem Africanum, ancillae domesticae quondam amoribus[411] irretitum et illum, qui Hannibale superato Carthaginem colla submittere coegerat, manus amori dedisse? Quod si humanum de utroque ferendum est iudicium, uter excusatione dignior est,[412] qui reginam amavit[413] an qui ancillam? Qui formosam, qua nullam tulit aetas illa venustiorem; an qui deforme mancipium? Qui disertam, eruditam et sescentis odoribus ac lenociniis inescantem; an qui rusticam, sordidatam et popinas farinasque redolentem? Cui uxor adesset? An Caesar, cui procul erat? Multos praestantis ingenii reperies, qui neutrum incusandum, sed potius excusandum esse contendant. Nec sunt, qui audeant Cupidinis imperium increpare, 'qui iubeat caelo superos relicto vultibus falsis habitare terras' et qui de capto Iove

battle as much as he could, escaped from the scene by swimming to a ship; and having a premonition that it was about to sink as a number of his men floated to it, once more with courage and spirit betook himself to the next one, by swimming, in this way: "his left hand raised so the books that he held would not get wet, and pulling his mantle between his teeth so that the enemy might not acquire it as spoil."[126] Thus he fought in such a manner that no love or pleasure detained him from discharging his mission.

As to Cleopatra, I am not the sort of man who would want to approve, nor are you by habit the sort of man to disapprove, since you used to recite this amatory verse: "every lover is a soldier, and Cupid also has his own camp."[127] But I likewise argue that this sin is of the type that "human nature insufficiently guards against" and that is more easily berated than avoided.[128] For who does not know that renowned and noble men were beset by it? To say nothing of the others, are you unaware that the admirable and illustrious general and leader of the Roman people, Scipio Africanus, was once ensnared by love for a domestic slave and that he who, after defeating Hannibal, had forced Carthage under the yoke, surrendered to love? But if human judgment must be passed regarding both men, which of the two is more deserving of excuse? The man who loved a queen, or the one who loved a servant girl? The man who loved such a beauty that her age produced no finer, or the one who loved an ugly slave? The man who loved a well-spoken and learned woman who seduced him with a thousand perfumes and allurements, or the man who loved a countrywoman in dirty clothes who smelled of cooking shops and flour? The man whose wife was near, or Caesar whose wife was far away? You will find many men of outstanding intellect who maintain that neither should be accused but rather excused. And there is not anyone who dares assail the power of Cupid, "the sort who may order the gods to leave heaven and inhabit the earth with false faces" and may triumph over the capture of Jove.[129] Nor did the poets

triumphet. Non ab re fictum est a poetis Omphalae[414] et Iolae servisse Herculem, et Martem, intra Vulcani[415] retia deprehensum, cum Venus et ille iacuere ligati. 'Post multa virtus opera[416] lassari solet' et remissione labores instaurantur.

55   Tibi profecto condoleo, Poggi carissime. Cum tua ista tumultuaria inter doctos homines lectitatur epistola, tibi non parum auctoritatis et opinionis adimit; quem pro amore in te meo, meritisque tuis, eruditissimum praedicare soleo. Ea enim persequendi Caesareas laudes cupiditate flagras,[417] ut maturius, quae dicis, potueris advertere; quod et nonnullis olim obvenit, qui dum vitia Vergiliani carminis intentius carpunt virtutibus omissis, 'Vergiliomastiges' appellati sunt. Cum enim alia[418] permulta eius generis sint, tum vero (quod ais) *Gallos gentem barbaram et*[419] *feram, sed bello insuetam*, ab Caesare domitam. Contra exstant plurima illorum bello facinora, quibus liquet nullo eos tempore[420] a belligerando cessasse.[421] Haud immemor esse debes, ut assuetam semper armis gentem dicas, fusos fugatosque saepenumero Tuscos, florentem ea aetate gentem: 'tanta enim opibus Etruria erat, ut non[422] terras solum,[423] sed mare etiam per totam Italiae longitudinem ab Alpibus ad fretum Siculum fama sui nominis[424] implesset.' Eius fines usque ad primam Tiberis ripam tendebantur,[425] unde et dictam esse peritus nemo dubitat quasi *heteros horos*[426] (id est finis alter).' Hanc gentem ab Gallis fusam, tam late imperantem, non insuetae armis nationis argumenta dixeris.

56   Dices: 'Prisca haec.' Noviora percurre. Quotiens Romani exercitus Gallorum ductu et auspiciis magnis[427] involuti periculis! Non comparo virtutem armorum: vetustatem et adsuetam semper in

without reason invent Hercules' servitude to Omphale and Iole, and Mars' ensnarement in the net of Vulcan when he and Venus lay coupled together.[130] "After many efforts, virtue is wont to be worn out," and forces are replenished through relaxation.[131]

I do feel for you, my dearest Poggio. When your hastily-written 55 letter is read in the company of learned men it strips you of no small part of your standing and reputation, you whom on account of my love for you and your own merits I am accustomed to call most learned. For you burn with such desire to attack the merits of Caesar that you could have considered more ripely what you say. The same thing once also befell some people who rather avidly carp at the flaws in Vergil's poem while leaving out its good qualities and were then called "scourges of Vergil."[132] There are many other instances of this type, and especially where you say that Caesar subdued *the Gauls, a barbarous and wild people, but unused to war.*[133] Many of their deeds in war are on record against that claim, which make it crystal clear that at no time did they cease waging war. So that you may speak of them as a people used constantly to being under arms, you ought not to be unmindful of the fact that they frequently routed and put to flight the Etruscans, a nation flourishing at that time: "For such was the might of Etruria that the fame of its name had filled not only the lands but even the sea throughout the length of Italy from the Alps to the Sicilian strait."[134] "Their territory stretched to the first bank of the Tiber, whence no expert doubts that they were named from *heteros horos* (that is, second border)."[135] That this nation, ruling so widely, was routed by the Gauls, you might cite as proof of their being a people not unused to arms.

But you will say: "these are ancient history. Run through the 56 more recent ones!" How often did the Roman armies find themselves involved in grave danger faced with the command and leadership of the Gauls! I do not compare their virtue under arms: I show them to be an ancient people always accustomed to being

armis gentem ostendo. Peregrinemur ex Italia. Num Thracia tota, num Propontis, num Asiae pars maxima Gallicis armis domita adeo, ut per illud tempus nulla in armis natio celebratior fuerit? Plutarchus in M. *Marcelli vita* nomen antiquitus Gallicum magno Romanis terrori fuisse testatur, 'adeo, ut cum sacerdotes bellorum immunes esse decernerent, bella dumtaxat Gallorum exciperent.' Quid, posterioribus annis num[428] virtute bellica cunctis praeferebantur gentibus? Sallustius suam usque ad aetatem de militari Gallorum scientia quid sentiat, non obscurum reliquit: 'facundia Graecos (inquit) gloria belli Gallos ante Romanos fuisse'; et alio in loco: 'per idem tempus adversum Gallos ab ducibus nostris Q. Scipione et M. Manilio male pugnatum est, quo metu Italia omnis contremuerat; illique et[429] usque ad nostram memoriam Romani[430] sic habuere: alia omnia suae virtuti prona esse, cum Gallis pro salute, non pro gloria certare.'

57 His[431] atque aliis satis constare arbitror Gallorum gentem nullo tempore bellis[432] insuetam fuisse (uti[433] commemoras), sed, cum terribilis in armis fuerit—quod multorum locorum ruina, regionum vastitate, hominum strage, nationum[434] subiugatione apud rerum scriptores testatum est—concedas oportet Caesari, gentis illius domitori, immensam accessisse gloriam. Quo fit ut tua scripta diligentius perpendenda sint et, qui in proferenda sententia de Caesaris et Scipionis[435] praestantia profitebaris, sententiam de te ab lectore decepto proferri audias, ut tibi videlicet de utriusque praestantia adimi debeat auctoritas. Nam qui tam apertis in rebus

under arms. Let us move away from Italy. Was not the whole of Thrace, the Propontis, and a great part of Asia subdued by Gallic forces, so much so that throughout that time no other nation was more celebrated in arms? Plutarch testifies in his *Life of Marcellus* that in the old days the name "Gaul" had held great fear for the Romans, "so much so that when they decreed that priests were exempt from wars, they made an exception only for wars against the Gauls."[136] What about the later period, were they not then preferred over all other peoples for their martial prowess? Sallust made it quite clear what he thought of the military expertise of the Gauls even down to his own day: he said that "the Greeks ranked before the Romans in eloquence and the Gauls in the glory of war." And in another passage: "at the same time our commanders Q. Scipio and M. Manilius fought badly against the Gauls, and the whole of Italy had trembled from the fear this caused, and they and the Romans down to our own lifetime regarded the matter thus: that everything else submitted to their prowess, but that with the Gauls they fought not for their honor, but for their existence."[137]

It is sufficiently clear, I think, from these and other things, that the Gallic people were at no time unused to war (as you record), but rather, since they were terrifying in arms, as is attested by historians who document the ruin of many places, the devastation of lands, the slaughter of men, and the subjugation of peoples, you must concede that immense glory redounded on Caesar as conqueror of this people. And from this it follows that your writings should be carefully weighed and that you, who proposed to pass judgment on the excellence of Caesar and Scipio, should now hear a judgment pronounced on yourself by a reader you deceived, namely that you be stripped of your authority regarding the excellence of both men. For what will the man who understands himself to have been taken in by his faith in you in such obvious

57

tua fide sese captum intelliget, quid in obscuris et quae ignota sunt, faciet?

58 Omissis reliquis, quae muliebris cuiusdam altercationis instar habent, unum instare perspicio, quod reliqua praegravare videtur, id est libertatis amissio; qua quid dulcius, quid praestabilius, quid viro dignius mortale genus habeat, nullus dixerit. Pro ea conservanda tot arces,[436] tot moenia, tot arma, tot susceptae 'vitae dimicationes,' ut 'mori potius quam servire' optandum sit. Hoc igitur tam summum, tam caeleste bonum, quisquis interceperit, omni odiorum acerbitate persequendus est. Ceterum animum adverte et intelligentiam tuam explica, prudentissime vir Poggi, ne huius rei culpa Caesarem involvas immerito, cum diutius antea fuisset libertas exstincta, quam potentia Caesaris invalesceret, quando non illius umbra, non imago[437] vivebat ulla. Ne longius repetam: dominante Mario, quae leges, quae iudicia, quae cuiusque ordinis servata dignitas? Parva loquor: cui, vel in dominum servo, vel in principes ignobili, rapinae, incendia, caedes non licuere, in omnem sexum et aetatem stupra? 'Nobilitas cum plebe[438] perit lateque vagatur ensis et a nullo revocatum est pectore ferrum.' Haeccine[439] libertas?

59 Ubi Caesar successit amissae libertatis reparator, Sulla, 'ille quod[440] exiguum restabat sanguinis[441] Urbi hausit.' 'Tunc data libertas odiis resolutaque legum frenis ira ruit.' 'Tunc flos Hesperiae, Latii iam sola iuventus concidit, et miserae maculavit ovilia Romae.' Huius non dicam servitutis aut libertatis amissae, sed summae calamitatis iam tunc vetus origo fuerat. Compositis pace Sullana rebus (id est postquam saevire armis Sulla desiit), quot modis urbanam lacerare libertatem coepit, ut facile declararet non

matters do in the case of things that are more obscure or unknown?

Leaving the other matters aside, which amount to some quar-   58
rels among women, I see one matter looming that seems to outweigh everything else, namely the loss of liberty. No one can name
anything mankind possesses that is sweeter, more outstanding, or
more worthy of man than this: to preserve it, there have been so
many citadels, so many walls, so many arms, so many "contests for
life undertaken," that it is preferable "to die than to be a slave."[138]
Whoever, therefore, has stolen so great, so heavenly a good should
be hunted down with all the harshness of hatred. However, pay
attention and exercise your intelligence, most prudent Poggio, so
you do not blame Caesar for this matter undeservedly; since liberty had been extinguished long before the power of Caesar began
to wax, when no shadow, no semblance of it was alive.[139] To go
back no further: what laws, what courts, what dignity of each order was preserved when Marius was dominating?[140] I speak of
trifles: what slave did not have the license against his master, or
what lowly man against leading figures, for plunder, arson, slaughter, and rape against every sex and age? "The nobility perishes
with the plebs, the sword roams far and wide and the iron was not
called back from any breast."[141] Was that, then, liberty?

Where Caesar succeeded as restorer of lost liberty, Sulla   59
"drained whatever little blood was left from the city."[142] "Then free
rein was given to hatred, and freed from the restraints of the laws
anger rushed forth."[143] "Then the flower of Italy, the only remaining youth of Latium fell to the ground and stained the sheepfolds
of miserable Rome."[144] Even then the origin of this, I will not call
it slavery or lost liberty, but the supreme catastrophe had existed.
When matters were stabilized by the peace of Sulla (that is, after
Sulla ceased raging with armed force), in how many ways did he
begin to tear apart the liberty of the City, so that he easily showed

aliud quam miserabilem sub tyranno servitutem eam libertatem
esse? Sublatae leges, perempta iudicia, tribunicia potestas inter-
cepta; et, ut testimonia libertatis agnoscas, quanta (ut alia taceam
flagitia) in adolescentulum innocentemque Caesarem exercitata
persecutio, quot mortis insidiae bonorumque confiscationes!
Quaenam est servitus, si hanc appellas libertatem?

60 Clodianam subinde recense tempestatem et violentum in civitatem[442] dominatum.[443] An ulla tum lex, ullum ius, ulli possessio-
num termini fuerunt,[444] quos non contempserit, effregerit, invaserit? Tolerabilia haec. Amantissimum patriae civem, virum[445] vere
magnum, Ciceronem, ex Urbe suorum armis satellitum exterminavit, ne muttire quidem audente senatu. Audi bonae libertatis indicia: expulso Cicerone, familia eius disiecta, 'parietes perturbati,
tectis sceleratae faces illatae.' Ubi tunc libertas sopita vel sepulta
iacebat? Immo ne civitas quidem erat, sed latrocinium verius,[446]
cum leges[447] in ea nihil valebant, cum iudicia iacebant, cum mos
patrius occiderat, cum ferro pulsis magistratibus senatus nomen in
re publica non erat. Sescenta sunt extinctae iamdudum libertatis
documenta, licet in eius umbris viveretur.

61 Quid de tyrannica Pompeii vi referam? Cui cum provincia ob-
venisset Hispania, extorqueri numquam potuit, ut suam in provinciam — quam per legatos Petreium, Afranium et Varronem ad-
ministrabat — ex Urbe secederet, Catone (illo tuo sanctissimo)
reliquisque stipatoribus una conspirantibus, ne[448] per eius absen-
tiam de Romani populi cervice iugum tolleretur. Et, ut in Caesarem perniciosa tenderet retia sub belli Parthici specie duas surripiens legiones (Caesari superiori tempore ad Gallicum bellum
concessas), ut vel sic socerum exarmaret gliscentibus initio rebus,

that liberty under a tyrant was nothing but miserable slavery? The repeal of laws, the purchasing of courts, the interruption of the tribunes' power; and, so that you may recognize the proofs of liberty, to say nothing of other outrages, what great persecution was practiced against the young and guiltless Caesar, how many deadly ambushes and confiscations of goods! What indeed is slavery, if you call that liberty?

Recall the storms caused by Clodius immediately afterward, 60 and his violent control over the City. Were there any laws, any rights, any boundaries of property that he did not disdain, break and assail?[145] But those things can be tolerated. The citizen who most loved the fatherland, a truly great man, to wit Cicero, him he drove out of the city by the arms of his followers, while the senate dared not even mutter. Listen to these signs of fine liberty: when Cicero had been banished and his household dispersed, "the walls of his house were torn down and criminal torches applied to the roof."[146] Where was liberty then lying asleep or buried? In reality, that was not a state but rather a den of thieves, wherein the laws counted for nothing, the courts were defeated, ancestral custom had perished, when, with the magistrates driven out by the sword, the name of the senate was not heard in the republic.[147] There are innumerable examples to show that liberty had long since been destroyed, though people still lived in her shadow.

What shall I say about the tyrannical power of Pompey? When 61 Spain had fallen to him as a province, he could never be forced to leave the City and go to his province, which he administered through his legates Petreius, Afranius, and Varro, while that saintly Cato of yours and the rest of his acolytes conspired with him lest through his absence the yoke be lifted off the neck of the Roman people.[148] And, in order to set a dangerous trap for Caesar, stealing two legions (previously granted to Caesar for the war in Gaul) under the pretext of the Parthian war, so that he thus assuredly disarmed his son-in-law when matters first began to grow

cum Caesar de conciliandis animis litteras ex Gallia dedisset ad
consules, numquam nisi ab invitis[449] impetratum[450] est, resistente
Pompeio, 'ut in senatu recitarentur'; ubi quisquis lenius[451] aut aequius ad res tumultusque sedandos locutus fuerat, aut conviciis a
Pompeio perterritus, aut minis[452] castigatus destitisse coactus sit;
in senatum veteres Caesaris inimici vocati. Quorsum haec? Ut in-
telligamus priscam illam populi Romani disciplinam oblitteratam,[453] integritatem corruptam, ardentissimam patriae caritatem
iam pridem exstinctam.

62   Quae quidem in tempora tum Caesaris aetas incidisset, ea
vero qualia essent (auctore Plutarcho) contemplari ne pigeat, ut, si
fieri possit, hoc pacto meliorem de Caesare opinionem induas:
'Corrupta civitatis disciplina, qui magistratus petebant positis in
propatulo mensis impudentissima largitione mercantes plebem al-
liciebant. Inde conductus mercede, populus[454] pro largitore de-
scendebat, non suffragiis, sed arcubus, gladiis, fundisque certa-
turus; cruore atque cadaveribus saepenumero tribunali foedato,
nullis obsequentes, dirimebantur, civitatem veluti gubernatore
destitutam omittentes. Itaque qui mentis erant compotes, satis
habere, si tanta ex tempestate res in deteriora non exciderent, sed
ad monarchiam prolaberentur;[455] permulti etiam erant, qui in medio iam dictitare[456] auderent eo res urbanas pervenisse, ut, nisi
monarchia adhiberetur, immedicabiles essent.' Eapropter, cum status tanta perturbatione fluctuaret, ut rebus unius dumtaxat gubernationem exposceret, bene actum a fortuna secum erat, quae be-
nignissimum perinde ac medicum praestiterat. Quocirca Caesare
interfecto populus continuo Romanus, Caesaris desiderio adfec-
tus, infestum sese interfectoribus eius inexorabilemque praebuit.

fraught, even though Caesar had sent letters from Gaul to the consuls about effecting a reconciliation, permission was never granted, except unwillingly, "that they be read in the senate," since Pompey opposed it; and when anyone spoke somewhat mildly or fairly to quiet the trouble and commotion, he was forced to back down, either intimidated by Pompey's insults or chastened by threats.[149] Old enemies of Caesar were called into the senate. To what end do I say all this? So that we may understand that that ancient discipline of the Roman people had been obliterated, integrity had been compromised, and that blazing love for the fatherland had long since been extinguished.

And let us not be put off from considering what these times in 62 which Caesar's life fell were like according to Plutarch, so that in this way, if possible, you may assume a better view of Caesar: "With the community's discipline compromised, those who were canvassing for magistracies set up tables in public and enticed the plebs, buying them with unashamed bribery, and the people, hired by payments, went off on behalf of the briber, to contend not with votes but with bows, swords and slings; when the tribunal had often been befouled with blood and corpses, the recalcitrant participants were parted, abandoning a city, as it were, bereft of a helmsman.[150] Hence those of sound mind thought it sufficient if, from so great a tempest, matters did turn worse, but instead slipped toward monarchy. Indeed there were many who now dared to say in public more than once that the affairs of the city had come to such a pass that they could not be cured without monarchy being applied as medicine."[151] Therefore, since the state was tossed by such turbulence that it demanded for its affairs the rule of only a single person, it was well-served by fortune, which provided a person who was at once kindly and a physician. It is for this reason that upon Caesar's murder the Roman people, possessed by a longing for Caesar, immediately showed themselves relentlessly hostile to his killers.

63   Non adducam hunc in locum monarchiae commendationem, clarissimorum virorum et doctissimorum philosophorum disputationibus et auctoritate[457] ceteris administrandae civitatis rationibus antelatam.[458] Quid et de Caesaris facto ad Romanum imperium sentiat auctor excellens et rerum Romanarum scriptor diligentissimus, Dion, accipe; quod quam minus inepte potero, Latinis verbis conabor exponere. Is enim in initio libri XLIIII ita[459] scriptum reliquit: 'Caesar expeditionem in Parthos suscepturus hunc in modum agebat. Ceterum impius nonnullis incidens stimulus ex meritorum invidia nec non ipsius[460] odio, quem sibi honoribus praelatum esse cernebant,[461] et illum per iniquitatem interfecit, novum quoddam sceleratae gloriae nomen adsumens, et decreta populi suffragiis dissipavit rursusque[462] ex conspiratione seditiones et intestina Romanis bella paravit. Nam Caesaris interfectores et populi Romani liberatores esse prae se ferebant, re autem vera impias illi struxerunt insidias, et civitatem recte administratam[463] seditionibus involverunt. Quod si meliora longeque maiora et plura, privatimque[464] ac publice, semper ex regibus, quam ex populis obvenisse M. Brutus et[465] C. Cassius versare animo voluissent — quemadmodum[466] et barbarorum et Graecorum et ipsorum Romanorum gesta testantur — numquam civitatis praesidem curatoremque neci tradidissent, nec infinitorum sibi ipsis reliquisque mortalibus malorum causa exstitissent.

64   'Eius vero caedes huiusmodi causam habuit, nec senatus insons fuit, qui cum honorum[467] novitate et incredibili magnitudine Caesarem extolleret ac inflaret, dein[468] querelis hominem et criminationibus agitabat, quod eos Caesar libens adsumeret et ab eis intumesceret. Peccavit quidem Caesar, qui decretos sibi quosdam[469] honores desumpsit et illis vere sese[470] dignum existimavit; longe vero plurimum senatus, qui cum illi ut digno tam immensos

I will not in this place include a commendation of monarchy,   63
which is preferred above other systems for governing a state by the
arguments and authority of the most renowned and learned men.
Instead listen to what Dio, an outstanding author and a most accurate historian of Rome, thought of what Caesar did for the Roman empire, which I will attempt to set forth in Latin as aptly as
I can. For at the beginning of book 44, he left the following written account: "Caesar, about to take up the expedition against the
Parthians, was engaged in these actions. Meanwhile, a wicked urge
came over some men, due to envy of his achievements and also to
hatred of the man himself, whom they saw had surpassed them in
standing, and this urge, assuming some new name for its criminal
glory, killed him unjustly and nullified the decrees voted by the
people, and once more prepared seditious conspiracies and civil
wars for the Romans. For Caesar's murderers boasted that they
were the liberators of the Roman people, but in truth they had
laid a wicked ambush for him and involved a properly governed
state in civil war. But if M. Brutus and C. Cassius[152] had been
willing to give thought to the fact that better and by far greater
and more things both in private and in public life have always
come from kings than from the people, as the histories of the barbarians and the Greeks and the Romans themselves testify, they
would never have consigned the head and caretaker of the state to
death, nor would they have presented themselves as the cause of
countless evils to themselves and other mortals.

"His killing, in truth, had a cause of this type, nor was the sen-   64
ate without guilt, as it had first exalted and inflated Caesar with
new honors of unthinkable greatness, and then harassed the man
with grievances and accusations on the ground that Caesar will-
ingly accepted them and because of them was beginning to be
puffed up. Caesar did indeed err in accepting certain honors bestowed upon him and judging himself truly worthy of them; but
the senate erred much more since once it had begun to grant him

honores tribuere[471] coepisset, huius generis decreta ad incusationem et maledicta perduxit. Nec enim universa repudiare Caesar
audebat, ne tam ardenti studio senatus exquisitos et sibi delatos
honores aspernatus ad indignationem atque odium patres ac populum instigaret.'

65   Ex superioribus manifestum vel caeco[472] fieri puto a[473] Caesare
libertatem occupatam non esse, suamque dignitatem et caput
contra non patriam, sed factiosos patriae libertatis occupatores
defendisse, et rerum conditionem Caesaris principatum postulasse,
praeclaro testante poeta: 'victrix causa deis placuit.' Quid si
non imminutam, sed restitutam et in melius redactam libertatem
Caesaris cura, consilio et administratione comperiemus? An obscurum est Caesarem 'senatum supplevisse, praetorum, aedilium,
quaestorum, minorum etiam[474] magistratuum numerum ampliasse'?[475] Utque populariorem magisque communem statum faceret 'proscriptorum olim liberos ad honores admisit'; '⟨ob⟩ octoginta civium milia in transmarinas colonias distributa ⟨quot⟩ in
Urbem, civilibus bellis exhaustam,[476] revocavit ⟨alios non abesse
coegit?⟩; senatorum filios, ut amplior esset et in Urbe frequentia et
magistratuum communicatio, peregre proficisci vetuit'; 'omnes medicinam Romae professos et liberalium artium doctores, quo libentius et ipsi Urbem incolerent et ceteri appeterent, civitate[477]
donavit'; 'ius laboriosissime ac[478] severissime dixit, repetundarum
convictos[479] ordine senatorio movit,' poenas facinorum auxit, parricidas bonis omnibus multavit.

66   Ipsius est lex Iulia maiestatis, peculatus, ambitus, de adulteriis
aliaeque[480] quam plures. Nam cum sapientissimus rei publicae

such enormous honors as if he were worthy of them, it then turned decrees of this sort into causes for accusation and slander. For Caesar did not dare refuse them all, lest by spurning the senate's honors chosen and proffered to him with such intense enthusiasm, he might spur the fathers and the people to indignation and anger."[153]

From the above I think it becomes clear even to a blind man 65 that liberty was not seized by Caesar, and that he guarded his standing and his life not against the fatherland but against a faction intent on seizing the liberty of the fatherland, and that the state of affairs demanded the single rule of Caesar, as the renowned poet testifies: "the victorious cause pleased the gods."[154] What if we find that liberty was not diminished but restored and returned to a better condition by the care, counsel, and government of Caesar? Or is it a secret that Caesar "replenished the senate, and increased the number of praetors, aediles, quaestors, and even the lower magistrates?"[155] And in order to make the state more progressive and widely shared, "he gave the children of those who were once proscribed access to office"; "⟨because of⟩ 80,000 citizens based in overseas colonies ⟨how many⟩ did he recall to the City, which was drained owing to the civil wars, ⟨and how many others did he force to be present?⟩ He forbade the sons of senators to go abroad, so that there might be a greater abundance of them and enhanced sharing of magistracies in the City"; "he gave citizenship to all practitioners of medicine in Rome and to teachers of the liberal arts, so that they might live in the City more readily and others might move there";[156] "he applied the law in the most precise and strict manner, and removed those convicted of extortion from the senatorial order";[157] he increased the punishments for crimes, and confiscated all goods of father-killers.

From his hand is the Lex Iulia on lèse majesté, embezzlement, 66 electoral bribery, adultery and many other things.[158] For since as a very wise reformer of the commonwealth he understood that there

formator intelligeret duo[481] imprimis conservandae civitatis fundamenta esse, e medio iustitiae sinu deprompta, bonis praemia, pra-
vis supplicia, universos pro dignitate prosecutus est, hos quidem a
turpitudine deterrens, illos autem ad bonas artes animans et in-
cendens. Et ut studiosum non modo Romanae,[482] sed etiam exter-
nae pacis ac libertatis principem fateamur et praedicemus: e[483]
bellis variis non ante Romam se[484] retulit,[485] quam Syriam, Cili-
ciam, Assyriam, Bithyniam, Pontum aliasque multas domesticis
dissensionibus liberasset, iura[486] legesque acciperent, et externo-
rum hostium metum deponerent. Quotiens vivente Pompeio Caesar[487] litteris, nuntiis et legatis ab eo contendit, ut Romanae paci et
saluti publicae consulens ab armis discederet, et animum tranquillum indueret! Eius incepta secutus Octavianus Augustus, 'ad quem
rerum summa rediit, sapientia sua atque solertia, patris imitatione,
percussum undique atque perturbatum ordinavit[488] imperii corpus,
quod,' ut auctor est Florus, 'haud dubie numquam coire et consentire potuisset, nisi unius praesidis nutu quasi anima et mente
regeretur.'

67   Haec atque alia innumerabilia optime[489] formatae civitatis instituta, ademptaene seu imminutae, an restitutae et amplificatae libertatis signa sunt? Quae cum magni atque adeo admirandi viri
officia sint, quid tale de Scipione dixeris? Sane non habes. De quo,
si res bellicas tollis, nulla[490] profecto aut parva mentio fuerit; quas
etsi[491] claras et ingentes fateor, Caesaris tamen gestis et varietate[492]
et magnitudine et numero et[493] temporis longinquitate cedentes
non negabis. De Scipione me in praesentia continebo, ne tanti
hominis opinioni tuo exemplo detraham, neu una congressione
tam ingens bellum confecisse ⟨velle⟩ videar. Verum ut amborum
iudicium unam in summam paucis redigam: Scipio quidem vir

are two foremost foundations for preserving the state taken from the breast of justice, namely rewards for the good and punishments for the wicked, he dealt with each according to his merits, deterring the latter from shameful deeds, but stimulating and stirring the former to good actions. And so that we may acknowledge and proclaim him a leader keen not only on the peace and liberty of Rome but also of that of foreign nations: he did not return to Rome from his various wars until he had freed Syria, Cilicia, Assyria, Bithynia, Pontus, and many others from internal quarrels, and until they received justice and laws and laid aside their fear of external enemies. How many times, when Pompey was alive, did Caesar through letters, messengers, and legates beseech him to take thought for the peace of Rome and well-being of the state, and distance himself from arms and assume a calm demeanor? Following what he began, Octavian Augustus "to whom supreme power devolved, ordered, with wisdom and resourcefulness, in imitation of his father, organized the shattered and turbulent body of the empire," which, as Florus testifies, "without doubt never could have come together in agreement if it were not governed by the will of a single leader, as though by a soul and mind."[159]

Are these and countless other arrangements of a very well- 67 ordered state, signs of liberty abolished and diminished, or of one restored and enhanced? And since they are the services of a great and so admirable man, what of this sort could you say about Scipio? You have nothing at all. About him, if you leave out his military achievements, there would have been little or nothing to report; and while I admit that those military exploits are renowned and great, still you will not deny that they lag behind the deeds of Caesar in variety, greatness, number, and the time they took to achieve. I will restrain myself at present regarding Scipio, so as not to detract, like you, from the reputation of such a great man, and so as not to seem ⟨to want⟩ to conclude so great a war with one assault. But, to reduce the judgment on both to one brief

bonus, civis pusillanimis, imperator excellens; quod (Livii auctoritate) et adsero ipse, et tu non inficias ibis:[494] 'vir (inquit) memorabilis, bellicis tamen quam pacis artibus memorabilior.' Caesar vero civis magnanimus, princeps prudentissimus, imperator excellentissimus.

68   Quae ut maioris iudicis auctoritate quasi secundis confirmentur auspiciis, accipe, quae de Caesare eruditissimus homo Plutarchus — et Poggio Guarinoque locupletior testis — adserit et unum collegit in cumulum:[495] 'Tempus deinde[496] belligerandi ac rei militaris, qua pacatam reddidit Galliam — perinde[497] ac ipse alia capesseret initia, et alteram quandam vitae rerumque novarum viam[498] insisteret — huius[499] generis est, ut eum et bellatorem et ducem nullo ex his[500] inferiorem ostendat, quorum in ductandis[501] exercitibus singularis[502] admiratio vel praecipua exstitit amplitudo. Quod si quis Fabios, Scipiones, Metellos, et aetatis suae vel paulo superioris[503] Sullam, Marium et utrumque Lucullum Pompeiumque, cuius gloria per varias rerum bellicarum virtutes usque in caelum effloruit, comparare voluerit, rerum ab Caesare gestarum magnitudo superat. Hunc quidem locorum difficultate, in quibus ab illo[504] bella[505] peracta sunt; illum agri magnitudine, quem[506] Romano adeptus est imperio; alium multitudine hostium et viribus, de quibus victoriam reportavit; quendam immanibus[507] absurdisque gentium moribus, quas plane ad leniores[508] vivendi ritus redegit; alterum comitate[509] ac mansuetudine,[510] quibus erga victos usus est; nonnullum gratificandi ratione atque munificentia, quas in commilitones exercuit; universos denique vel hoc uno excelluit, quod plurimas commisit pugnas et plurimos adversa[511] instructos acie occidioni dedit. Annos enim minus decem intra Galliam

conclusion, Scipio was indeed a good man, a weak citizen, but an outstanding commander, as I myself assert on the authority of Livy, and as you are not going to deny: "a memorable man" — he said — "but still more memorable in the art of war than of peace."[160] Caesar, however, was a great-spirited citizen, a very wise leader, and an outstanding commander.

And so that these things may be confirmed as if under favorable   68 auspices by the authority of a greater judge, hear what the most learned Plutarch, a more trustworthy witness than Poggio and Guarino, asserts about Caesar, and has gathered together into a single conclusion: "Then the time of warfare and military involvement by which he pacified Gaul, as though he himself also was seizing upon new beginnings and pushing forward on a second path of life and of new achievements, is of such a kind that it shows him to be both a warrior and a leader second to none of these whose remarkable reputation and exceptional greatness in leading armies is on record.[161] But if anybody would want to compare the Fabii, Scipiones, Metelli, and, in his own day or a little before, Sulla, Marius, and both Lucullus and Pompey, whose glory on account of manifold virtues in matters of warfare flowered to the skies, the greatness of the exploits performed by Caesar surpasses them. One, because of the difficulty of the terrain in which he carried out his wars, the other due to the size of the area he added to the Roman empire, yet another on account of the number and strength of the enemy over which he brought back victory, another for the sake of the barbarous and incredible customs of the tribes whom he completely reduced to a more civilized way of life, and another for the affability and mildness which he practiced toward the defeated, not a few for his ways of humoring his troops and his generosity toward them, and everyone combined he surpassed in this one thing, that he undertook most battles and sent most men lined up against him to their death. For in fewer than ten years waging war within Gaul he gained control of more than

belligerans urbibus supra octingentis potitus est, gentes quadrin-
gentas subiugavit, adversus trecentas myriadas separatim iusta[512]
depugnavit acie; e quibus[513] cum centum in stragem dederit, reliquas[514] vitae reservavit.'[515]

69   Singulare[516] et conterranei mei, Plinii, magni certe viri, testimonium est de Caesare; de quo cum alia permulta, tum id profert:
'idem collatis signis quinquagies[517] dimicavit, solus M. Marcellum
transgressus, qui undequadragies dimicavit.'[518]

70   Habes, vir doctissime et amantissime Poggi, maiorum de Caesare ac Scipione iudicium; quorum auctoritate, nisi nosmet nimis[519]
amaverimus, quae sit utriusque[520] praestantia et differentia, facile
dignoscemus. Quas quidem ad res, cum tuum istud subtile excita-
veris et in se ipsum revocaveris ingenium, non dubito quin mox
palinodiam ordiaris. Sic quantum superiore[521] illa epistola, et
quidem (ut auguror) tumultuaria, facundiae laudem vendicasti,
instaurata diligentius iudicatione et docti et diserti et veri[522] scrip-
toris nomen et praeconium consequaris.[523] Vale.

800 towns, subjugated 400 peoples, fought in a pitched battle at different times against 300,000 men, of whom he put 100,000 to the sword, but left the rest their lives."[162]

My compatriot Pliny, certainly a great man, gives a remarkable 69 testimony regarding Caesar, about whom besides many other things he reports this: "he gave battle fifty times, and he alone surpassed Marcellus who gave battle thirty-nine times."[163]

There you have, my very dear and learned Poggio, the judgment 70 of the ancestors on Caesar and Scipio, by whose authority we will easily discern—unless we are too enamored of our own opinions—what the excellence of each is and what the difference between them. And indeed, once you have roused that subtle mind of yours to address these matters and restored it to itself, I do not doubt that you will soon begin a palinode. In this way, inasmuch as you have won praise for your skill in speaking with your earlier and (as I divine) hastily improvised letter, may you, once your judgment has been more carefully revised, obtain the name and reputation of a learned and eloquent and truthful writer. Farewell.

EPISTOLA AD
LEONELLUM ESTENSEM[1]

1   Poggius plurimam salutem dicit equiti insigni Leonello Estensi.

Existimo magnum pondus habere apud te, quemadmodum aequum est, Guarini benivolentiam atque auctoritatem. Nam et vir
est excellens in omni genere doctrinae, et te instituit (ut sentio)
studiis humanitatis. Sed tamen, pro tua prudentia proque[2] animi
aequitate, confido acceptius tibi esse futurum rectum iudicium
rectamque sententiam, quam ullius coniunctionis aut necessitudi-
nis affectionem.[3] Sumpsit ille onus sibi[4] superfluum redarguendi
eam epistulam, quam scripsi ad Scipionem[5] Ferrariensem; qua in
re non tantum Caesarem defendit, quantum Poggium ultro offendit, minime a me provocatus. Et quidem satius (certe prudentius)
fuerat Caesaris causam[6] tueri, me intactum relinquere, quam mecum congredi velle, qui nullo in loco, nulla in parte Guarini existimationem aut opinionem offendi. Sed posteaquam ita rigide, ita
contumeliose, ac si cum uno ex suis discipulis ageret, me reprehendit, ridet, obiurgat, dicta refellit, non tulit honor[7] meus, ut ad
hanc suam reprehensionem ipse obmutescerem.

2   Itaque rescripsi, non quidem ad eum, sed ad virum doctissimum Franciscum Barbarum, ne cum eo cogerer vel invitus decer-
tare, vel conviciis suis respondere. Ut autem ipse suae obiurgatio-
nis te[8] iudicem constituit, ita ego Franciscum defensionis meae.
Verum, quoniam nemo rectam potest[9] sententiam ferre audita
tantum accusatoris parte, mitto ad te meam defensionem:[10] tunc

LETTER TO
LEONELLO D'ESTE

Poggio warmly greets the distinguished knight Leonello d'Este.[1]   1

I appreciate that the goodwill and authority of Guarino hold great weight with you, as is fair. For he is both an outstanding man in every sort of learning and, as I understand, he has instructed you in humane studies. Nonetheless, on account of your wisdom and the fairness of your mind I trust that a correct judgment and correct opinion will be more pleasing to you than the feeling of any familiarity or obligation. He has taken upon himself the unnecessary burden of refuting the letter that I addressed to Scipione of Ferrara, in which he not so much defends Caesar as offends against Poggio, of his own accord and without any provocation on my part.[2] And indeed it would have been better (certainly more prudent) for him to defend Caesar's cause and leave me uninjured, rather than seek to clash with me, who in no passage and no section dented the reputation or prestige of Guarino. But once he started reproaching, ridiculing, and chiding me, and refuting my words so harshly, so insultingly, as though he were dealing with one of his students, my honor would not allow me to remain silent in the face of this reprimand.

As such, I have written again, not indeed to him but to the very   2
learned man Francesco Barbaro, so that I may not be compelled to fight with him against my wishes or to respond to his abuses.[3] Just as he made you the judge of his rebuke, so I have appointed Francesco as the arbiter of my defense. However, since no one can pronounce the right judgment having heard only the accuser's side, I am sending my defense to you: for you will make your judgment

enim iustissime iudicabis, cum quid a quoque dictum fuerit cognosces. Itidem ego ad Franciscum mitto priorem epistulam, Guarini oppugnationem et defensionem meam, ut, quae ab utroque adferuntur, intelligat et discutiat. Leges igitur, cum otium erit, meam hanc defensionem et, quid de hac disceptatione iudices, perscribe. Id enim, quod tu senseris, et ego sentire volo ac[11] tuo iudicio adsentiri. Vale, et mei memor. Florentiae, VIII Kalendas Novembris.[12] ·

most justly precisely when you know what was said by each of us. In the same manner, I am sending my earlier letter to Francesco, along with Guarino's assault and my defense, so that he may understand and parse the things adduced by each of us. So please read this defense of mine, when you have leisure, and write out in full your judgment about this debate. For I also want to think what you think, and to agree with your judgment. Farewell, and remember me. Florence, 25th of October.

Poggii Florentini
De praestantia Caesaris et Scipionis
ad Franciscum Barbarum defensio[1]

1   Nuper, cum exercendi ingenii causa, mi Francisce, epistulam
quandam ad Scipionem Ferrariensem scripsissem, in qua Scipionem Superiorem et C. Caesarem invicem comparans priores partes
tribueram Scipioni, Guarinus noster Veronensis,[2] vir doctissimus
et meus (ut ait) amicus, cum epistula in eius manus devenisset,
sumens causam Caesaris scripsit ad me libellum quempiam
pergrandem, in quo non tantum Caesarem tueri, quantum me
obiurgare, in me invehi velle videtur. Nam et in quodam quasi
opusculi sui prooemio, quod ei tamquam appendiculum ascribit,[3]
me *Caesaromastigen* et *magis audacem quam fortem* scribit,[4] et pluribus in locis—contra ac ius amicitiae nostrae[5] requirit—in me
acriter incursat, saepius me compellat verbis mordacibus, multa
dicens, quae sapientius atque honestius tacuisset. Equidem, nisi
Guarini nomen esset ascriptum, suum opus minime putassem: ita
enim inepte multa probare nititur, ita levibus quandoque utitur
argumentis, ita in Catonem maledictis insultat (oblitus facultatis
et ingenii sui) ut, qui scripta nesciat a Guarino,[6] a rabula quodam
foraneo[7] atque inani litigatore[8] censeat esse conficta.

DEFENSE OF
ON THE EXCELLENCE OF
SCIPIO AND CAESAR

Poggio of Florence's Defense of
On the Excellence of Scipio and Caesar
to Francesco Barbaro

Recently, my Francesco, I wrote a letter to Scipione of Ferrara, for 1
the sake of exercising the mind, in which I compared the elder
Scipio and C. Caesar to each other and awarded the first place to
Scipio.[1] When my letter had come into the hands of Guarino of
Verona, a very learned man and, as he claims, my friend, he took
up the cause of Caesar and wrote me an enormously long treatise
in which he seemed not so much to want to defend Caesar as to
reproach and assail me. For even in a sort of proem to his little
work, which he attaches to it as an appendix, he calls me *a scourge
of Caesar* and *rash rather than brave*, and in many passages he attacks
me fiercely—against what the law of our friendship demands—
and frequently addresses me with biting words, saying many things
about which he would more wisely and honorably have remained
quiet.[2] I, for one, would not have believed this to be his work had
it not been signed "Guarino." Indeed, so clumsily does he try to
prove many of his points, so slight are the arguments he uses at
times, so does he trample Cato with abuses, forgetful of his own
skills and talent, that anyone who did not know that it was written
by Guarino would reckon it had been cobbled together by some
ranter in the market place and worthless litigator.

2   Nam, cum Guarinus vir doctus atque eloquens extimetur,[9] haec
eius oratio nullam neque doctrinam, neque eloquentiam redolet.
At vero ipse, tamquam nobis phoenicem ex Arabia attulerit,[10] iac-
tat se,[11] prosilit, iurgat, sibi blanditur tamquam in choro discipulo-
rum suorum constitutus, qui, si illi adsentiuntur, si laudant doctrinam, si ingenium admirantur, si contradicere non audent,
nequaquam iudicet idem[12] alios esse facturos. Video tamen, quid
vir eruditissimus sit secutus:[13] praestantissimus atque omni laude
vir dignus Leonellus Estensis Caesaris partium est fautor; vult
ergo Guarinus, cui se totum dedit, etiam hoc novo opusculo dedi-
care, ei maxime placere studens, quem novit actorum Caesaris defensorem.

3   Sed debuit, si Caesaris patronus esse voluit et eius acta tueri,
illum laudare, extollere, magnificare atque ampliare res gestas,
postremo (si libebat) gentilium more ut deum colere, hoc facere vel
eloquenter, vel quantumvis impudenter potuit me etiam non
contradicente. Quid enim mea refert quibus laudibus Caesarem
Guarinus efferat aut ornet? Sed dum mea dicta reprehendit, dum
arguit, dum insectatur, dum in me impetum facit, non tantum
Scipionis aut Caesaris, quantum mea causa mihi ad ea necessario
respondendum putavi. Verum cum ego existimem non certamen[14]
partium, sed communium studiorum inter nos debere esse concer-
tationem ac satis esse ea adferre, quae nostram causam probabilem
reddere videantur, decrevi (licet paulum commotus animo), quam
potero, tamen modestius, defendere causam semel susceptam;
quam non solum ut deseram, rationes me Guarini non induxerunt,
sed ad tuendam sententiam ardentius ac constantius impulerunt.
Talis enim est Guarini defensio, talis argumentatio, ea testium
productio, ut qui velit Caesarem in hac causa succumbere, hunc
solum gaudeat sibi oblatum esse patronum.

For although Guarino is deemed a learned and eloquent man, 2
this oration of his gives off no scent of learning or eloquence. But
he, still, as though he has brought us the phoenix from Arabia,
boasts, leaps forth, scolds, and flatters himself as though he were
surrounded by a chorus of his students, and he does not at all
consider that, if they agree with him and praise his learning and
admire his mind and do not dare contradict him, others might do
just that.[3] I see, however, what this very learned man was aiming
at: the most excellent Leonello d'Este, a man worthy of all praise,
is a supporter of Caesar's side; hence Guarino also with this new
pamphlet wants to commit to the man to whom he has given his
whole self, keen to please above all him whom he knows to be a
defender of Caesar's deeds.

But if he wanted to be Caesar's advocate and defend his actions, 3
praise him, exalt, magnify him and enhance his exploits and finally, if he so wished, worship him as a god in the manner of the
gentiles, he should do this eloquently or as impudently as you like,
with no contradiction from me. For what is it to me, with what
sort of praises Guarino exalts or honors Caesar? But when he
criticizes my words, accuses me, harasses and attacks me, I have
reckoned I must respond to these things not so much for the sake
of Scipio or Caesar as my own. But since I believe that there
should be no partisan conflict between us, but rather a contest of
shared studies, and that it is enough to present those points that
appear to render our cause probable, I have decided, albeit somewhat shaken, to defend as best I can, yet with restraint, the cause
once taken up. Guarino's arguments have not only not induced me
to abandon it, but rather they have driven me to defend my opinion the more eagerly and steadfastly. For such is Guarino's defense,
such his reasoning and his calling forth of witnesses, that anyone
who wants Caesar to come off worse in this case would be pleased
that he was offered only this defender.

4   Si qua vero in re Guarinus violatam putabit[15] existimationem suam, in hanc[16] se culpam conferat, qui non necessario me lacessivit. Ego[17] enim satius duxi satisfacere honori meo quam illius opinioni; ad te autem, mi Francisce, institui scribere hanc meam defensionem, ne illi respondens cogerer provocatus—aliquando ut fit—par pari referre. Simul illud occurrit: cum Guarinus elegerit certum iudicem suae factionis, qui inter nos discernat, aequum[18] esse me quoque mihi comparare, qui mihi in hac causa tamquam arbiter adsistat ac rectam sententiam ferat. Scio aequitatem tuam, novi animi moderationem, perspexi rectum iudicium et, cum in praeclarissima omnium re publica sis natus atque educatus inque ea administranda plurimum versatus, confido te rectissime de hac nostra controversia—in qua de oppressa Romani populi libertate agitur, in qua pro virtute, pro honestate, pro vera gloria, quae a me defenduntur, certatur—sententiam esse laturum. Oro te autem[19] per nostram amicitiam, quo rectius tibi rationes utriusque innotescant, epistolam meam primum legas, tum Guarini libellum, deinde hanc meam defensionem: hoc maxime modo quid a me dicatur, quid ab eo obiciatur, quid a me defendatur, intelliges.

5   Sed ut iam ad nostram causam veniamus: constituendum nobis est,[20] quae Guarino mecum sit controversia, nempe de Scipionis et Caesaris praestantia. Ego Superiorem Africanum laude, virtute, gloria praestantiorem fuisse Caesare[21] contendo, Guarinus contra sentit. Hoc ut possit facilius cognosci, primum omnium[22] est nobis quid sit gloria diffiniendum; qua, si[23] et argumentis et testibus docuero excellere Scipionem, superior sim in causa necesse est. De gloria igitur et eorum[24] virtute primum erit dicendum, tum accedam ad confutandas Guarini rationes.

And if Guarino is going to feel that his reputation has been   4
tarnished in any respect, let him assign this blame to himself, who
has provoked me unnecessarily. For I have deemed it better to
satisfy my own honor than his prestige; but I have decided to address this defense of mine to you, my Francesco, so that in responding to him I may not be impelled, as sometimes happens
under provocation, to answer like with like. The following consideration also suggests itself: since Guarino has chosen a secure
judge from his side to arbitrate between us, it is fair that I also
provide myself with someone to stand with me as an arbiter in this
case and to render a sound verdict. I know your fairness, I know
the even temper of your mind, I have observed your sound judgment and, since you were born and bred in the most illustrious
republic of all and have been much involved in its administration,
I trust that you will judge most correctly regarding this controversy of ours, in which the suppression of the Roman people's
freedom is at stake, and in which battle is being joined for the sake
of virtue, honor, and true glory, which are being defended by me.
But by our friendship I beg you, in order that you may become
better acquainted with the arguments of each of us, first to read
my letter, then Guarino's treatise, and finally this defense of mine,
as in this way you will best understand what I argue, what he
counters, and what I defend.

But to come now to our case, we should set out what the dis-   5
agreement is that Guarino has with me, to wit, about the excellence of Scipio and Caesar. I contend that the Elder Africanus was
superior to Caesar in praise, virtue, and glory, while Guarino believes the opposite. So that this case can be judged with greater
ease, we must first of all define what glory is, and if I manage to
show with arguments and evidence that Scipio was superior in
this, I must necessarily win my case. So we must first discuss glory
and the virtue of these men, and then I will proceed to refute
Guarino's arguments.

6   'Gloria est' (inquit Cicero in tertio *Tusculanarum quaestionum* libro) 'consentiens laus bonorum, incorrupta vox bene iudicantium de excellenti[25] virtute.' Idem in prima *Philippicarum:* 'gloria est (ait) laus recte factorum magnorumque in rem publicam meritorum.' Igitur, cum Caesaris nullam bonorum laudem, nullam vocem incorruptam bene iudicantium de aliqua sua excellenti virtute scriptam invenerimus, recte vero facta illius admodum pauca exstiterint,[26] de re publica pessime meritus fuerit, Scipionis vero una omnium bonorum fuerit consentiens laus, unus sermo mirabilium virtutum rectequo factorum suorum inque rem publicam meritorum excellentium (ut auctores verissimi et probatissimi monumentis suis tradiderunt), necesse quidem est ut, cum virtute exstiterit longe clarior, et gloria quoque superior videatur. Ut enim idem inquit Cicero, 'multis est in virtute ascensus,[27] ut is gloria maxime[28] excellat, qui virtute plurimum praestat.'[29]

7   Si quis autem, similis Guarino,[30] dubitet de virtute Scipionis, aut quanta in eo[31] virtutum praestantia fuerit, ignoret, audiat Valerium Maximum in sexto *Memorabilium* libro: 'Scipio autem Africanus Superior (inquit) quem dii immortales nasci voluerunt, ut esset in quo se virtus per omnes numeros hominibus efficaciter[32] ostenderet'[33] et reliqua. A. Gellius[34] quoque *Noctium Atticarum* libro septimo, cum de ingenti angue, qui in cubiculo ac lecto iuxta matrem Scipionis cubare visus est absente marito, scriberet, 'Scipionem (inquit) impendio magis et rebus gestis, quam illo ostento virum esse virtutis divinae creditum est.' Alio item in loco: 'Scipio[35] Africanus antiquior, quanta virtutum gloria praestiterit et quam fuerit altus animo atque magnificus et quam sui conscientia subnixus, pluribus in rebus, quae dixit quaeque fecit, declaratum est.'

"Glory," says Cicero in the third book of the *Tusculan Disputa-* 6
tions, "is the unanimous praise of good men, the unbiased verdict
of those of good judgment with regard to outstanding virtue."[4]
The same author says in the first *Philippic:* "glory is the praise for
just deeds and great services to the republic."[5] In Caesar's case, we
have found no praise of good men, no unbiased verdict of those of
good judgment put down in writing about any outstanding virtue
of his, while his just deeds were quite scarce, and he paid dismal
service to the republic. For Scipio, however, there was unanimous
praise of all good men, a unified report of his marvelous virtues,
just deeds, and outstanding services to the republic, as the most
truthful and sound authors have recorded in their works. Since,
then, Scipio was so much more renowned for virtue, he must necessarily also appear superior in glory. Indeed, as the same Cicero
says: "for many men there is a degree in virtue, so that he excels
most in glory, who stands out most in virtue."[6]

But if anyone, like Guarino, should entertain doubts about 7
Scipio's virtue, or is unaware of the extent of the preeminence of
his virtues, let him listen to Valerius Maximus in the sixth book of
the *Memorable Deeds:* "yet the Elder Scipio Africanus," he says,
"whom the immortal gods wished to be born so that there might
be one man in whom virtue would show itself in full and to good
effect to humankind," and so on.[7] A. Gellius, too, describing in
the seventh book of the *Attic Nights* the giant snake that was
seen to sleep in the bedroom and bed next to Scipio's mother
when her husband was away, wrote that "Scipio was deemed a
man of divine virtue on account of his exertions and exploits
rather than because of that portent."[8] Likewise in another passage:
"the elder Scipio Africanus demonstrated in many matters in word
and deed how much he excelled in the glory of virtues, how high
and lofty he was in spirit, and how much bound by his con-
science."[9]

8   Haec[36] de Caesare numquam scripta legit[37] Guarinus, neque eius virtutes ab ullo auctore descriptas. Affert Plutarchum, qui Caesarem ceteris praefert ducibus Romanis magnitudine rerum gestarum; de virtutibus[38] vero magnum silentium. Neque iniuria: magnitudo enim rerum scelera et mala facinora quandoque admittit.[39] Ita non datur, ut, qui magnas res gessit, intelligatur et cum virtute gessisse. Constat igitur Scipionem, cum virtute Caesarem superarit et gloria quoque fuisse superiorem. Hoc ut fiat manifestius, alia quaedam Ciceronis de gloria[40] sententia proferenda est.

9   In oratione *Pro M. Marcello*, ex qua Guarinus multas laudes in Caesarem colligit, 'gloria est (inquit) illustris et pervagata[41] magnorum vel in suos, vel in patriam, vel in omne genus fama meritorum.' Haec diffinitio si vera sit,[42] gloria longe Scipio Caesarem antecellit. Primum[43] quae merita Caesaris in suos fuerint, referat Guarinus, qui Graecis suis delectatur; ego apud Latinos nulla fuisse[44] cognovi, nisi quod Octavianum adoptavit in filium eumque ex dodrante reliquit heredem; quod et quidam turpi amore factum tradidere.

10   De genere hominum pessime meritus est, clades perniciesque gentium ac populorum, si quidem plurimas urbes inique rapuit,[45] vastavit, diruit, diripuit ob praedam, non ob delictum. Exceptis autem civibus Romanis, quos propter[46] dedecus in rationes referri vetuit, undecies centena milia hominum sua opera interierunt; quod deplorandum videretur etiam totidem milibus ovium[47] interfectis.

11   At illud restat, ut eius[48] in patriam sint merita singularia; quam prodidit, prostravit, evertit, afflixit ac, peremptis tot triumphalibus, senatoriis, praetoriis viris, tot civium milibus trucidatis,

Guarino has never read such things written about Caesar, nor   8
his virtues described by any author. He brings in Plutarch, who
prefers Caesar to the other Roman commanders on account of the
greatness of his deeds; but about his virtues there is a deep silence.
And rightly so: for the greatness of things sometimes allows for
crimes and evil actions. Hence it is not a given that he who has
done great deeds is also understood to have done them with virtue. As such, it is generally accepted that Scipio, since he surpassed Caesar in virtue, was also superior in glory. So that this
may become more evident, another of Cicero's opinions about
glory should be cited.

In his speech *On behalf of M. Marcellus*, from which Guarino   9
draws many praises for Caesar, he says "glory is a brilliant and
widespread reputation for great services to one's family or fatherland or to the whole human race."[10] If that definition is true,
Scipio far surpasses Caesar in glory. First, let Guarino, who takes
pleasure in his Greeks, report what Caesar's services to his family
were; I have learned from the Latin writers that there were none,
except that he adopted Octavian as his son and left him three
quarters of his inheritance, which some people in fact report was
done on account of a sordid love.[11]

He did dismal service to the human race: he was a disaster and   10
ruin for nations and peoples, seeing that he looted, laid waste,
destroyed, and plundered many cities for the sake of booty, not
because of any crime on their part. Leaving aside the Roman people, whom, because of the disgrace it would have brought, he did
not allow to be included in the tallies: one million one hundred
thousand men died through his efforts, something that would
seem lamentable even if he had killed so many thousands of sheep.

But this point remains, that his services to the fatherland are   11
unparalleled — the fatherland that he betrayed, overturned, and
ruined. After completing so many triumphs, with so many men of
senatorial and praetorian rank and so many thousand citizens

populum Romanum, quadringentos amplius annos ceteris gentibus imperantem, sibi servire coegit; quamquam Guarinus ab eo
libertatem conservatam (quod suo loco refellemus) impudentis-
sime contendit, contra omnium priscorum excellentium virorum
sententiam atque auctoritatem.

12   Age, nunc Scipionis merita referantur, quamvis premar[49] inopia
scriptorum, apud quos non reperitur descripta Scipionis vita sicut
et Caesaris, cuius gesta et ipsemet et Suetonius ac Plutarchus litteris tradiderunt. Sed tamen adferentur nonnulla, quae a variis
auctoribus scripta reperiuntur. Et primum in suos merita egregia
exstiterunt. Nam et decem et octo annos natus patrem apud Ticinum (ut Livius, Valerius ac Plinius, verissimi auctores, adserunt)
singulari (ut ait Plinius in libro *Virorum illustrium*, qui ei ascribitur)
virtute servavit; et legatus fratri, ne sibi honor provinciae eriperetur, Antiochum bello superavit.

13   Quae vero in patriam fuerint Scipionis merita, tum testes sunt
permulti, tum vero Seneca gravissimus auctor, qui scribit 'Romam
soli Scipioni debere, quod[50] semel tantum fuerit ab hostibus capta';
beatus Augustinus Romanae urbis atque 'Italiae liberatorem' appellat. Silius quoque Italicus, cum[51] Caesarem multa gessisse cognos-
ceret, ex quibus suum poema ordiri potuisset, tamen, quia sciebat
virtutibus fere[52] vacua et in perniciem[53] patriae redacta, Scipionem
delegit. In quem, cum propter eius praeclara in patriam merita
multas laudes congessisset, tandem in fine sui operis eum meritis
et laudibus aequat Romulo atque Camillo, alteri conditori Urbis,
alteri restitutori.

slaughtered, he forced the Roman people, which for more than four hundred years had ruled over other nations, to be his slave; although Guarino, impudently and against the opinion and authority of all outstanding ancients, maintains that he actually preserved liberty, a contention which we will refute in its proper place.[12]

Come, let us now report the services of Scipio, even if I am restricted by a shortage of writers, among whom we find no *Life* of Scipio written out such as that of Caesar, whose deeds were committed to writing by himself as well as Suetonius and Plutarch. Nonetheless, I will adduce some things found described by various authors. First came outstanding services to his family. For, even at eighteen years of age, Scipio saved his father at the Ticinus, as Livy, Valerius Maximus, and Pliny, most truthful authors, assert; and with unique courage, as Pliny says in the book on *Illustrious Men* attributed to him.[13] Furthermore, he defeated Antiochus in war, as legate to his brother, so that the honor of his command might not be wrested from him.[14]

For his services to the fatherland there are indeed many witnesses, in particular Seneca, a most weighty author, who wrote "that Rome owes it to Scipio alone that she was only once captured by enemies."[15] Saint Augustine called him the "liberator of Italy" and of the City of Rome.[16] Silius Italicus, too, although he understood that Caesar had accomplished many things from which he could have begun his poem, still, since he knew these to be almost devoid of virtue and directed to the ruin of the fatherland, chose Scipio as his subject. And since he had heaped together much praise for him for his services to the fatherland, finally, at the end of his work, he put Scipio on a par, in terms of these services and praises, with Romulus and Camillus: one man the founder, the other the restorer of the City.[17]

14   In omne autem hominum[54] genus Scipionem meritis claruisse
constat, quae, quoniam sunt permulta — prout capta Nova Cartha-
gine custodia mulierum, restitutio nuptae adolescentulae, et alia
plurima per omnem vitam[55] — brevitatis causa omitto. Hoc Senecae dictum in quadam epistola non postponam: 'Scipionis animum
in caelum redisse (ait) ob egregiam moderationem ac pietatem,'
quam magis admiratur[56] 'cum patriam reliquit quam cum defendit.'
Transeo plura Titi Livii testimonia de virtutibus Scipionis, quoniam in priori, quam Guarinus carpit, epistola relata sunt. Hoc
solum recitabo, quod est in octavo belli Punici libro: 'cum ceteri
(inquit) laetitia gloriaque ingenti eam rem vulgo ferrent, unus, qui
gesserat inexplebilis virtutis veraeque laudis,' et reliqua.

15   Haec sunt testimonia virtutum P. Scipionis satis certa (ut
opinor); quibus cogatur adsentiri noster Guarinus laude et gloria
longe antecellere Scipionem. Adferat nunc ipse, si potest, Caesaris
virtutes: sed nullae ferme sunt, non potest. Nulli enim exstiterunt,
aut admodum pauci et ii adulandi gratia, si qui reperiuntur, qui
excepta victoria civili, qua clementer est usus, virtute Caesarem
laudarint. Guarinus solus exoritur post multa saecula, qui se ei
nimium dicarit; sed cum illum multis virtutibus claruisse dicat,
nullam profert penitus, non continentiam, non integritatem, non
iustitiam, non fortitudinem, non alterius virtutis vestigium ullum.
Sed ad ridicula quaedam descendit (quae suo loco confutabuntur)
ut, cum nando periculum evasit vestem mordicus trahens, ducit
pro fortitudine. At id non fortis viri, sed temerarii potius indicium[57] fuit, cum se in eum locum coniecisset, unde nisi nando

But it is generally agreed that Scipio was famous for his services   14
to the whole of mankind. Since they are numerous, including his
protection of the women after the capture of New Carthage, the
return of a young bride, and many other deeds throughout his life,
I omit them for the sake of brevity. But I will not disregard this
remark of Seneca's in one of his letters: "The soul of Scipio," he
says, "returned to heaven because of his outstanding temperance
and sense of duty," which he admires more "when he left the fatherland than when he defended it."[18] I leave on one side the many
testimonies about Scipio's virtues in Titus Livy, since they were
reported in my first letter, which Guarino criticizes. I will only
recall this, which is in the eighth book of the *Punic War*, where he
remarks: "while others made this matter public with delight and
enormous celebration, only the man who had achieved it was insa-
tiable for virtue and true praise," and so on.[19]

These testimonies to the virtues of P. Scipio are, to my mind,   15
sufficiently reliable to compel our Guarino to agree that Scipio was
by far superior in merit and glory. Let him now, if he can, adduce
Caesar's virtues: but there are scarcely any, so he cannot. For there
have been none or, if any are to be found, exceedingly few, who
have praised Caesar for his virtue, with the exception of the victory in the civil war, which he managed with clemency. Guarino
alone comes forward after many centuries as the one to have dedicated himself overly much to Caesar. Yet, though he says that the
man was renowned for many virtues, he actually proffers none at
all: not restraint, not incorruptibility, not justice, not courage, and
not a trace of any other virtue. Instead he stoops to trifles, which
will be refuted in their proper place; for instance, when Caesar
escaped danger by swimming, dragging his garment along with his
teeth, he takes that for courage. That, though, is not the sign of a
courageous man but rather of a rash one, since he had thrown
himself into a place from which he could not escape except by

non[58] posset evadere — siquidem fortitudo[59] est cum pericula certa
et deliberata ratione suscipimus.

16   Complectitur tamen laudes Caesaris, quae continentur in oratione habita *Pro M. Marcello,* non ab oratore (ut alias[60] scripsi), sed
a[61] tempore et causa prolatas. Nam quid Cicero de eo vere et ex
animo senserit, non videtur legisse, cui evenit, quod neglegentibus
aut captiosis solet mercatoribus, qui, cum unam paginam in libris
rationum suarum, in qua debitores conscripti sunt, legerint, reliquam, quae continet creditores, occultant; ex quo proverbium est
exortum: 'aliam paginam evolve.' Legit Guarinus Ciceronem ubi
Caesarem necessario laudavit. Audiat nunc quid scripserit vivo
Caesare, cum libere loqui potuit, et postmodum Caesare interfecto.

17   In epistola quadam ad Atticum: 'O hominem amentem et miserum (ait) qui ne umbram quidem umquam honesti viderit!' Hac
sola sententia, non ex necessitate causae, sed ex veritate etiam vivo
Caesare prolata, omnes superiores laudes obliteravit. Considera
haec diligenter, mi Francisce: nedum honestum, id est virtutem,
non fuisse in Caesare umquam, sed ne umbram quidem illum
conspexisse virtutis! Quid[62] idem post Caesaris interitum? Quid
scribit? Existimo, si haec Guarinus memoriae mandasset, paulum
fuisse de scribendi licentia remissurum. Sed Tullium audiamus
Guarini insolentiam reprimentem.

18   In *Officiorum* libro primo: 'Declaravit id modo (inquit) temeritas[63] C. Caesaris, qui omnia divina et humana iura pervertit[64]
propter eum, quem sibi ipse opinionis errore finxerat, principatum.' O magna laus, omnia divina humanaque iura temeritate
Caesaris et errore[65] eversa! In secundo autem libro: 'At vero hic
victor[66] noster, tum quidem victus cum, quae cogitarat, ea perfecit,

swimming—for courage means facing dangers with sure and deliberate counsel.

Nonetheless, he embraces the praises for Caesar contained in 16
the speech delivered on behalf of M. Marcellus, which were (as I
have written elsewhere) brought forth not by the orator, but by
the time and the case at hand. For what Cicero thought about
Caesar truly and from the heart Guarino appears not to have read,
so that what happens to him is the same as what commonly happens to careless or deceitful merchants, who, when they have read
the one page in their account books in which the debtors' names
are entered, hide the other, which contains those of the creditors
(from which practice the proverb "turn the page" arose).[20] Guarino
has read Cicero where he praised Caesar of necessity. Let him now
hear what he wrote, during Caesar's lifetime, when he could speak
freely, and a little later, after Caesar had been killed.

In a letter to Atticus he says: "oh insane and wretched man, 17
who has never seen even the shadow of moral goodness!"[21] That
single sentence, brought forth not by the necessity of the case but
by truth, even when Caesar was still alive, obliterated all the earlier
praises. Consider this carefully, my Francesco: not only was there
never anything morally good, in other words no virtue, in Caesar,
but he had not even caught sight of the shadow of virtue! What
does this same man say after Caesar's death? What does he write?
I reckon that if Guarino had committed this to memory, he would
have curbed somewhat the brashness of his writing. But let us
hear Cicero rebuking Guarino's insolence.

In the first book *On Duties*, he said: "this has of late been dem- 18
onstrated by the temerity of C. Caesar, who perverted all divine
and human laws for that position of supremacy which, by an error
of judgment, he had invented for himself."[22] Oh what great praise,
to say that all divine and human laws were overturned by the rashness temerity and error of Caesar! However, in the second book,
he adds this: "but he, our victor, was then vanquished when he

cum eius iam nihil interesset, tanta in eo peccandi libido fuit, ut hoc eum delectaret, peccare, etiam si causa non esset.' Et deinde, cum de Sulla quaedam dixisset: 'Secutus est (inquit) qui in causa impia, victoria etiam foediori,[67] non solum singulorum civium bona publicaret, sed universas provincias regionesque uno calamitatis iure[68] comprehenderet.' Hae[69] sunt verae Ciceronis voces, tunc expressae cum libere posset palam facere, quid sentiret.

19   Vides, Francisce, quantum a Tullio laudetur Caesar, si hoc laudi tribuit Guarinus, hominem amentem, miserum, nullam curam virtutis habentem, temerarium, perversorem divini humanique iuris, incensum libidine peccandi, bona civium et provincias impie publicantem describere.[70] Sed et Lucanus furentem, sanguinolentum, adulterum describit Caesarem, rara in eum virtute collata. Credo hoc in loco Guarinum tot ac talibus testibus convictum — nisi velit esse nimium impudens — procul dubio concessurum Scipionem nostrum suo Caesari gloria anteire, cum alterius virtutes[71] ante oculos conspiciat,[72] alterius scelera et delicta — nisi forsan si qua pestis ac pernicies orbis umquam fuit laudanda;[73] si qua salus, si quod praesidium vituperandum putet.

20   Quoniam non solum gravissimorum testium auctoritate,[74] sed ipsius fere virtutis[75] testimonio excellentior Caesare Scipio comprobatur, nunc ad ipsius Guarini scripta et testimonia discutienda ac reprobanda veniamus. Equidem voluissem admonuisse Guarinum verbis potius quam litteris errorum suorum, cum sint permulti; cuius ob honorem, quem vehementer diligo, tacuissem, potius quam ad hoc scribendi officium descendissem, si honor meus pateretur. Sed totiens me arguit, totiens me tamquam

brought his plans to fulfillment; although it no longer brought him any advantage, he had such a lust for doing wrong that doing wrong pleased him, even if there was no reason for it."[23] And then, after writing something about Sulla, he said: "there followed a man who, in a wicked cause and an even more sordid victory, not only confiscated the goods of individual citizens, but has comprised whole provinces and regions in a single state of catastrophe."[24] These are Cicero's true verdicts, expressed when he could freely make his thoughts public.

You see, Francesco, how much Caesar is praised by Cicero, if Guarino classes it as praise to describe a man as insane, wretched, without care for virtue, rash, subversive of divine and human law, burning with desire to do wrong, and wickedly confiscating the citizens' goods and provinces. But Lucan, too, describes Caesar as raging, bloodthirsty, and adulterous, while rarely attributing virtue to him. I believe that on this topic, since Guarino has been defeated by so many and such sterling witnesses, he will beyond doubt concede—unless he should wish to be all too brazen—that our Scipio outstrips his Caesar in glory, since of the former he sees the virtues before his eyes, but of the latter only the crimes and misdeeds, unless perhaps he reckons that a plague and ruin of the world should ever have been praised, while on the contrary its salvation and defense should have been slandered.

Since Scipio is proved to be superior to Caesar not only by the authority of the weightiest witnesses but almost by the testimony of virtue herself, let us now come to the discussion and rebuttal of Guarino's own writings and testimonies. I, for my part, should like to have admonished Guarino for his errors in words rather than writing, since they are very numerous; I would have remained silent for the sake of the honor of a man of whom I am very fond, rather than stooped to this duty of writing, had my own honor allowed it. But he censures me so often, rebukes me so often as

censorio edicto compellat, totiens me tamquam manifesti erroris castigat etiam petulantibus verbis Caesarem insectari dicens, ut necessitatem quandam mihi imposuerit ad haec rescribendi.

21 Primam omnium argumentationem Guarinus, quam ex ultimis verbis meae epistolae[76] adsumpsit, in fronte tamquam robur fortissimum totius disputationis collocavit. Dixi Caesarem non magis patriae quam Latinae linguae et bonarum artium fuisse parricidam, propterea quod sublata re publica Latina eloquentia corruisset. Haec a me[77] scripta acriter reprehendit: nullis utitur testibus ad causam accommodatis,[78] sed recenset quasdam ratiunculas inanes ac perleves, quae minime conveniunt nostrae disputationi, ut non solum non oriantur mures ex eo, in quo vagatur campo, sed ne locusta quidem!

22 Ait, *ab eo autem, quod abs te nuperrime dictum est, inchoemus*, et ultimam partem profert epistolae. Quo in loco, si vellem, possem dicere Guarinum non satis recte locutum esse Latine: 'nuperrime' enim non locum aut ordinem, sed tempus significat, neque magis quod est a me in principio positum comprehendit quam quod in fine; id 'extremum,' 'ultimum,' 'postremum' et similia, non 'nuperrime' dici solet. Item exstinctum doctrinae splendorem indignum facinus scribit: a me autem non exstinctam eloquentiam, sed corruisse est positum. Itaque mutat[79] ac[80] permiscet verba neque quid a me dicatur, neque quomodo ab eo[81] refellatur intelligens. Haec autem leviora.

23 Sed quibus tandem argumentis castigat erratum meum? Nempe luculentis[82] et ex intima arte dicendi! Adfirmat multis rationibus ac testibus Caesarem doctissimum atque eloquentissimum[83] exstitisse, multa verba effundens minime opportuna. Nam in causa certa 're non dubia utitur, testibus non necessariis.' Ego culpa Caesaris exstincta re publica Latinam eloquentiam et litterarum studia

though by censorial proclamation, castigates me so often as if for an evident error, even claiming that I am attacking Caesar with impudent words, that he has imposed a kind of obligation upon me to respond to these things.

Guarino placed his first argument of all, which he has taken 21 from the last lines of my letter, in front, as if it were the strongest point of his whole disputation. I said that Caesar was no more the murderer of the fatherland than of the Latin language and liberal arts, because once the republic had been brought down, Latin eloquence had collapsed.[25] He bitterly censures that I wrote this: he uses no witnesses appropriate to the case, but enumerates some empty, flimsy talking points which are ill adapted to our dispute, so that the field in which he roams not only yields no mice, but not even a locust!

He says: *but let us start from what was said by you most recently*, and 22 adduces the last section of the letter.[26] On this topic I could, if I wanted, say that Guarino did not speak Latin quite correctly: for "recently" refers not to place or order, but to time, and does not pertain to what I put at the beginning any more than to what I put at the end: that is usually called "last," "ultimate," or "final" and so on, but not "most recently."[27] Likewise he writes of the extinction of the luster of learning as a shameful crime, but I had said not that eloquence was extinct, but that it had collapsed. Thus he changes and mixes up words, understanding neither what I say nor how to refute it. But these are the minor points.

But with what arguments does he finally castigate my error? 23 Truly brilliant ones drawn from the heart of eloquence! He affirms with many reasons and testimonies that Caesar was exceedingly learned and eloquent, pouring out many words that are not at all to the point: for in an open-and-shut case "he uses witnesses he does not need for a matter that is beyond doubt."[28] I say that, through the fault of Caesar, Latin eloquence and the study of letters declined when the republic had been abolished. Because

cecidisse dico. Cum enim exercitium fori Romanam eloquentiam in supremum culmen eduxisset, cum apud populum ius contionandi multos ad dicendi studium excitaret, cum honor dicendae sententiae in senatu ad artem oratoriam impelleret, postquam Romani imperii potestas ad unius arbitrium pervenit, cecidit mos patrius, ut parum in foro, nihil apud populum, minimum ageretur in senatu, quod ad[84] eloquentiam requirere videretur. Nam partes populi nullae erant; senatus quod uni placuerat, decernebat; in foro pauca antiquitatis vestigia remanserunt.[85]

24   Guarinus vero Caesarem et eloquentem et multa opera scripsisse contendit.[86] Quis hoc sibi[87] negarit? Ego quoque eloquentiorem fuisse Caesarem quam ipse credat[88] affirmo. Sed quid hoc ad rem nostram pertinet? Doctissimum fuisse Alexandrum accepimus, et tamen Callisthenem philosophum interfecit. Nero fuit doctissimus, sed et Lucanum et Senecam et multos praeterea viros doctissimos interemit. Non dico Caesarem doctos viros[89] necasse, nec odio habuisse studia litterarum. Vellem Guarinus adesset: excitarem eum paulum a somno, postquam ita negligenter tamquam stertens intelligit quae a me dicuntur. Ego iterum adfirmo ex interitu rei publicae et libertatis Romanae, cuius origo et causa Caesar fuit, splendorem linguae Latinae esse collapsum.

25   Sed quam ridicule sua argumenta connectit! Ait *Ciceronem plura eversa quam stante re publica scripsisse,* et luculentas quoque orationes post victoriam Caesaris etiam[90] in iudiciis habitas edidisse; quasi ego dixerim Ciceronem post oppressam a Caesare libertatem stupidum quendam evasisse aut mutum aut elinguem! Describit multos excellentis viros qui post Caesarem exstiterunt: Sallustium, Cornelium Nepotem, Pompeium Trogum, T. Livium, Vergilium, Senecam, Horatium multosque praeterea. Sed nimium videtur rationem temporum ignorare. Primum Sallustius,

practice in the forum had carried Roman eloquence to its peak, because the right to call meetings among the people spurred many to the pursuit of rhetoric, because the honor of pronouncing an opinion in the senate drove men toward the oratorical arts, when the power over the Roman empire had fallen to the discretion of one man, the ancestral custom declined. As a result little was done in the forum, nothing before the people, and a minimum in the senate that seemed to demand eloquence. For there were no opposing sides among the people, the senate was decreeing what a single person had decided, and in the forum few traces of the old practice remained.

Guarino, however, contends both that Caesar was eloquent and 24 that he wrote many works. Who would deny it? I even assert that Caesar was more eloquent than he believes. But what has that to do with our business at hand? We read that Alexander was very learned, and yet he killed the philosopher Callisthenes.[29] Nero was very learned, and yet he took the lives of Lucan and Seneca and many other very learned men besides.[30] I do not say that Caesar killed learned men, nor that he despised the study of letters. I should like Guarino to be here: I would rouse him from his sleep a little, since he understood what I said so carelessly, as if he were snoring. I assert again that owing to the demise of the republic and Roman liberty, of which Caesar was the source and cause, the luster of the Latin language collapsed.

But how laughably he strings his arguments together! He says 25 that Cicero *wrote more when the republic had fallen than when she stood,* and that he also published splendid speeches he had delivered in the courts even after Caesar's victory—as though I had said that Cicero somehow emerged after Caesar's suppression of liberty as senseless, mute, or speechless.[31] Guarino describes many outstanding men who lived after Caesar: Sallust, Cornelius Nepos, Pompeius Trogus, T. Livy, Vergil, Seneca, Horace and many others besides.[32] But he seems to ignore the chronology all too much.

Cornelius Nepos ac Trogus floruerunt rei publicae tempore, siquidem pater Trogi cum Caesare militavit. Vergilius, Horatius, Livius,[91] Seneca orti et eruditi sunt vigente re publica: nam Titus
Livius, cum Caesar est interemptus, agebat sextum decimum aetatis annum. Seneca (ut ipse testatur) Ciceronem audire potuit de-
clamantem. Vergilius viginti et[92] quattuor annos erat natus, cum
apud Pharsaliam pugnatum est inter Caesarem et Pompeium,
Horatius vero decem et septem. Itaque qui docti vel eloquentes
postea exstitere, aut libertatis tempore orti illam priorem eloquentiam hauserunt, aut paulo post, cum aliqua prioris eloquentiae se-
mina superessent.

26   Nimium vero longius provehitur Guarinus studio mea dicta[93]
refellendi quam veritas patiatur. Ait multas et praeclaras artes post
deletam rem publicam *subtilius et ornatius viguisse*: debebat eas referre, ut sibi fides aliqua haberetur! Nicolaus enim noster pluresque viri doctissimi omnes artes in peius decidisse adfirmant.
Deinde,[94] ut *de tenuioribus* (inquit) *artificiis* loquar, *fuisse praestantissimos grammaticos, Servium, Priscianum, Donatum,*[95] *Caprum* et reliquos
adfirmat. Ego, ut doctos viros illos fuisse concedam, unam certe
Varronis *De lingua Latina* pagellam omnibus, qui post eum fuerunt,
grammaticis antepono. Comicos nullos rettulit, qui fuerint post
amissam populi Romani[96] libertatem, ne oratores[97] quidem quos
Ciceroni, L. Caesari, Hortensio, Crasso, Antonio, Bruto, ipsi C.
Caesari etiam longo intervallo possit conferre ullos refert. Pictores
non vult silentio praeterire, sed ad eos nominandos penitus ob-
mutescit. Philosophos tacere vult, cum eos nominare nequeat; et
tamen Senecae, Plinii, Boethii meminit. Seneca ex nostris est;
Plinius quid in philosophia scripserit ignoro, ut debeat inter philosophos numerari; Boethium virum doctissimum fuisse[98] nequaquam abnuo, sed nullo modo cum M. Varrone in philosophia aut
Cicerone comparandum.

First, Sallust, Cornelius Nepos, and Trogus flourished at the time of the republic, since Trogus' father fought with Caesar.[33] Vergil, Horace, Livy, and Seneca were born and raised when the republic was thriving, for Titus Livy was in his sixteenth year when Caesar was killed. Seneca, as he himself attests, was able to hear Cicero speak.[34] Vergil was twenty-four years old when Caesar and Pompey fought each other at Pharsalus; Horace was seventeen. Hence, those who later were learned or eloquent, were either born at the time of liberty and drank in that earlier eloquence, or shortly afterward, when some seeds of the earlier eloquence survived.

But in his zeal to refute my words, Guarino gets carried away   26
rather further than the truth would allow. He says that many and distinguished arts *thrived with more refinement and distinction* after the destruction of the republic: he should have named these to inspire some faith in him. In fact, our friend Niccolò, and many very learned men, assert that all arts had fallen into decline.[35] Then, to speak — he says — *about the lesser arts,* he claims *there were outstanding grammarians: Servius, Priscian, Donatus, Caper,* and others.[36] While I grant that these were learned men, I myself unhesitatingly value one page of Varro's *On the Latin Language* above all the grammarians who came after him. Guarino mentioned no comic writers who lived after the liberty of the Roman people had been lost; nor does he even mention any orators who, even by a long stretch, could be compared to Cicero, L. Caesar, Hortensius, Crassus, Antonius, Brutus, and C. Caesar himself.[37] He does not want to leave the painters unmentioned, yet falls completely silent when it comes to naming them. He does not wish to talk about the philosophers, since he cannot name them; and yet he recalls Seneca, Pliny, and Boethius. Seneca is one of ours; I do not know what Pliny wrote on philosophy that he should be ranked among the philosophers; and that Boethius was an exceedingly learned man I do by no means deny, yet he cannot be compared in any way to M. Varro or Cicero in philosophy.

27   Deficere sibi diem dixit, si disertos aut eloquentes velit commemorare; nec tamen quempiam refert in tanta copia praeter Ciceronem, tamquam fuerit et ipse tempore imperatorum. Transit ad
iurisconsultos,[99] qui *post illa* (ut ait) *tempora supra modum eluxerunt.*
Sed pervicax erit, si eos Scaevolae, si Servio Sulpicio, qui solus
centum et octoginta libros de iure civili edidit, si C. Trebatio
multisque praeterea, qui cum re publica floruerunt, existimet
comparandos! Devenit ad scientiam medicinae, quam *eruditam or-*
natamque et perfectius elimatam adfirmat; sed qui Latini medicinae
illustratores exstiterint, non profert. Postremo ad theologos descendit, *interpretes* (ut ait) *sacrarum litterarum et divinarum institutio-*
num auctores; quasi rei publicae temporibus, cum Salvator noster
nondum esset natus, hoc genus doctrinae esse potuisset! Hoc
tamen adfirmo: si[100] cum libertate Romani populi viguissent,
multo doctiores atque eloquentiores fuisse futuros.

28   Concludit tandem aliquando atque ait me falso lugere bonarum
artium et eloquentiae ruinam atque interitum. Non patiar Guarinum diutius errare in hac sua inepta conclusiuncula et, quamvis
non meminerim eloquentiam interisse a me dictum,[101] tamen, si
dixissem, testimonio Ciceronis id licuisset facere. Ego ortos stante
re publica oratores, poetas, historicos, philosophos, iurisconsultos
longe iis[102] praestare adsero, qui postmodum fuerunt, eloquentia et
doctrina; Latinam vero eloquentiam corruisse rei publicae guber-
natione submota. Guarinus vero[103] tamquam defunctam et exstinctam dixerim, in eius funere lamentatur. Non nego eos, qui
sub imperatoribus vixerunt, fuisse doctos et eloquentes, sed longe
distare a facundia atque elegantia superiorum et neque doctrina
illis neque ingenio pares. Quod si ille contentionis cupidus negabit,

Guarino said that daylight would fail him if he wanted to recall   27
all the well-spoken and eloquent men, yet still does not mention
anyone of such a great troop except Cicero, as though he also lived
at the time of the emperors. He moves on to the jurists, *who*, he
says, *after those times shone beyond measure*.[38] Yet he will be foolhardy
if he deems them comparable to Scaevola, to Servius Sulpicius —
who alone published 180 books about civil law — or to C. Trebatius and many besides who flourished along with the republic![39]
He arrives at the discipline of medicine, which he claims was *distinguished and learned and more perfectly polished*: but who these Latin
enlighteners of medicine were he does not tell us. In the end he
makes it down to the theologians, *exegetes* — as he says — *of sacred
literature and writers of divine precepts*, as if at the time of the republic, when our Savior had not yet been born, that type of learning
could have existed! Yet this I claim: that if they had thrived during
the liberty of the Roman people, they would have been far more
learned and eloquent!

At long last he draws to a close, and says that I wrongly bewail   28
the ruin and demise of the liberal arts and eloquence. I will not
suffer Guarino to err any longer in this inept little peroration of
his and, even though I do not recall that I said that eloquence had
perished, still, if I had said it, this would have been permissible on
the testimony of Cicero. My point is that the orators, poets, historians, philosophers, and jurists born while the republic stood were
far more outstanding in terms of eloquence and learning than
those who lived later, but that Latin eloquence collapsed after republican government was removed. Guarino, though, laments at
its funeral, as if I had called it dead and extinct. I do not deny that
those who lived under the emperors were learned and eloquent,
but they were far removed from the fluency and elegance of their
elders, and their equals neither in learning nor in talent. But if
Guarino, spoiling for a fight, denies that, the case will be tried

agetur[104] causa testibus praeclarissimis,[105] quorum auctoritate paulo est inferior Guarinus!

29   Et quoniam ipse me falso[106] lugere dicit eloquentiae ruinam atque interitum, adserat etiam, si audet, falso id scripsisse Ciceronem, cuius eadem est sententia. Inquit enim in libro *Officiorum* secundo: 'Admonebat me res, ut hanc[107] intermissionem eloquentiae, ne dicam interitum, deplorarem; sed tamen videmus, quibus exstinctis oratoribus, quam in paucis spes, quam in paucioribus facultas, quam in multis sit audacia.' Accipe et alios, quorum est non mea sententia, quantum Latina eloquentia fuerit diminuta. Vir doctissimus Seneca in prooemio *Declamationum*: 'quicquid (inquit) Roma facundia habuit, quod insolenti[108] Greciae aut opponat aut praeferat, circa Ciceronem effloruit; omnia ingenia, quae lucem studiis nostris adtulerunt, tunc nata sunt; in deterius[109] deinde decrescunt, sive luxu temporum, sive cum praemium[110] pulcherrimae rei cecidisset; translatum est omne certamen ad turpia.'

30   Nescio an tibi satis probatus testis Seneca videatur contra inanem Guarini opinionem! Accipe tertium quoque[111] gravissimum historici doctissimi, Cornelii Taciti,[112] testimonium, qui vel solus Guarinum deiciet ex arce (ut putat[113]) Minervae. Hic in prooemio libri decimi et septimi ita scriptum reliquit: 'Nam post conditam urbem octingentos et viginti prioris aevi[114] annos multi auctores retulerunt, dum res populi Romani memorabatur[115] pari eloquentia et libertate; postquam vero bellatum est apud Actium atque omnem potentiam ad unum referri pacis interfuit, magna illa ingenia[116] cessere, simul veritas pluribus modis infracta, primum inscitia[117] rei publicae ut alienae, mox libidine adsentandi aut odio adversus dominantes.' Cum ergo et Senecae verbis, quibus illa

with the most renowned witnesses, for whose authority he is a little less than a match!

Therefore, as he says that I erroneously bewail the ruin and 29 demise of eloquence, let him also, if he dares, claim that Cicero, whose opinion is the same, wrote this in error. For this is what Cicero says in the second book of *On Duties:* "my subject suggests that here I bewail the pause, not to say death, of eloquence. But still we see with what orators dead, in how few there is hope, in fewer still skill, and in how many shamelessness."[40] Listen to other men as well, whose opinion it is, not mine, how much Latin eloquence was diminished. The very learned Seneca wrote in the proem to his *Declamations:* "whatever Rome possessed in eloquence with which it could match or surpass insolent Greece flourished around the time of Cicero; all the talents that brought luster to our studies were born then; afterward they took a turn for the worse, either through the luxury of the times or because the reward for the fairest endeavor had fallen away; all competition was turned to base things."[41]

I suspect that Seneca seems to you a good enough witness 30 against Guarino's empty opinion! Listen to a third, also most weighty, testimony, from the extremely learned historian Cornelius Tacitus, who surely by himself will cast Guarino from what he thinks of as "the fortress of Minerva."[42] In the proem to book 17 he wrote the following: "for many authors have reported on the first 820 years since the foundation of the City, when the matter of the Roman people was being recorded with equal eloquence and freedom; but after the battle at Actium, when it was in the interest of peace that all power be handed over to one man, these great talents ceased, and at the same time truth was impaired in several ways, first by lack of knowledge of domestic affairs, since they were now in other hands, and soon by desire to flatter or hatred against those who ruled."[43] Since, therefore, it is abundantly clear both from the words of Seneca, with which he confirms that the

praeclara ingenia Ciceronis aetate nata esse, deinde in deterius decrevisse adfirmat, et Taciti testimonio, adserentis magna illa ingenia post imperium ad unum delatum[118] defecisse, apertissime constet quanta iactura secuta sit in litteris Latinis libertate amissa, verissime scripsisse me[119] dico in priori epistola Latinam eloquentiam corruisse; C. etiam Caesarem, quoniam rei publicae delendae origo et causa fuit, cuius ruina eloquentiae quoque et studiorum secum ruinam traxit, rectissime ex eo dici potuisse linguae Latinae et bonarum artium parricidam.

31   At vero instat Guarinus satis inconcinne. Negat exstinctam aut diminutam Caesaris opera[120] libertatem Romanam, sed auctam et vivacem factam esse contendit. Idem adfirmat viguisse senatus auctoritatem, praetorum, quaestorum, censorum, imperatorum, consulum ordinariam[121] servatam[122] creationem, rem Romanam adeo in pristinum[123] gradum[124] ordinemque redactam, ut nulla iudiciis, legibus, cogendo senatui videretur allata mutatio. Horum tamquam certissimum adfert argumentum, quod Romani imperii fines fuerint longius latiusque propagati; in quo pluribus quam causae suae conferat verbis evagatur.

32   In calce autem sui libelli, *quid si non imminutam, sed restitutam et in melius redactam libertatem* (inquit) *Caesaris cura, consilio et administratione reperiemus? An obscurum est* (inquit) *Caesarem senatum supplevisse, praetorum, aedilium, quaestorum,*[125] *minorum etiam magistratuum numerum ampliasse?* Argumentum restitutae et in melius redactae libertatis iudicat supplesse senatum, in quem omnem illam barbarorum faecem coniecit, unde exortum est Gallos in curia bracas deposuisse; ampliasse numerum magistratuum, quos satellitibus suis et sicariis replevit. *Octoginta civium milia* (inquit) *in*

outstanding talents were born at the time of Cicero and subsequently took a turn for the worse, and from the testimony of Tacitus, who claims that those great talents ceased when power was handed over to one man, exactly what massive destruction followed in Latin letters after liberty was lost, I maintain that in my previous letter I wrote entirely truthfully that Latin eloquence had collapsed and also that C. Caesar, as he was the origin and cause of the destruction of the republic, whose ruin also drew in its wake the ruin of eloquence and studies, could as a result quite correctly be called the murderer of the Latin language and the liberal arts.

But in truth, Guarino presses his claims rather clumsily. He 31 denies that Roman liberty was extinguished or diminished by the hand of Caesar, but contends that it was enhanced and brought back to life. He also claims that the authority of the senate flourished, and that the ordinary election of praetors, quaestors, censors, generals, and consuls was preserved, and the Roman state was returned so effectively to its former level and order that there appeared to be no change in the courts, the laws, and in the convening of the senate. And as if it were irrefutable proof of these things, he cites the fact that the boundaries of Rome's empire were extended far and wide, a matter on which he digresses using more words than befit his case.

Yet at the end of his pamphlet he says *what if we find that liberty* 32 *was not diminished but restored and returned to a better condition by the care, counsel, and government of Caesar?*[44] *Or is it a secret*—he asks— *that Caesar replenished the senate, and increased the number of praetors, aediles, quaestors, and lower magistracies as well?*[45] Here he deems it evidence of a restored and improved liberty that Caesar replenished the senate, into which he tossed the dregs of the barbarians, whence the saying came that the Gauls took off their trousers in the curia, and likewise that he increased the number of magistracies, which he filled with his hangers-on and cutthroats. *He*

transmarinas colonias distributa in Urbem civilibus bellis exhaustam revo-
cavit. O deus immortalis, ubinam gentium se scribere putat Guarinus? Nempe si apud Italos, ubi sunt plures viri eruditissimi tum
Graecis, tum Latinis litteris instituti, se loqui putasset, nequaquam suum libellum tot ridiculis somniis refersisset! Credo eum
adeo Graecis operam dare, ut Latinos neglegat, quamquam et
Graeci Plutarchus et Dion, quos commemorat saepius, si recte
inspiciat, contra se sentire videantur.

33   Sed ut hunc[126] libertatis adsertorem diligentius scrutemur, ait
se contendere *libertatem Romanam* Caesaris opere *auctam esse et viva-*
cem effectam. O vocem viro docto[127] indignam! Quid hac impu-
dentius dici potest? Loquor apud te, Francisce, quem scio haec
Guarini causa graviter ferre. Adeone sibi blanditur, adeone sibi favet et studiis suis, ut audeat totiens repetere auctam opere Caesaris libertatem populi Romani[128] contra omnium, qui umquam
scripsere, auctoritatem?

34   Tibi notus est Cicero. Nam forsan Guarinus eum[129] contemnit,
tu[130] eum quanti facias, scio. Evolve libros suos, et eos maxime, qui
sunt *De officiis,* in quibus tamquam philosophus loquitur ex ore
ipsius veritatis. 'Cum autem dominatu unius omnia tenerentur
(inquit) neque esset usquam auctoritati locus.' Et deinde: 'cum autem res publica, in qua omnis mea cogitatio, cura, opera poni
solebat, nulla esset omnino.' Alio in loco 'exstinctum senatum, deleta iudicia' queritur, in eisdem[131] etiam[132] libris: 'nec vero huius
tyranni[133] solum, quem armis oppressa pertulit[134] civitas, interitus
declarat.' Paulo autem post: 'parietes modo urbis stant hique[135] ipsi
iam extrema scelera metuentes, rem vero publicam penitus amisi-
mus.' Ipsemet Guarinus refert verba Tullii adserentis plura se

recalled—says Guarino—*80,000 citizens based in overseas colonies to the city, which was drained due to the civil wars.*[46] Oh immortal God, where on earth does Guarino think he is writing? Surely if he thought he was speaking among the Italians, where there are many highly learned men educated both in Greek and Latin letters, he would not have crammed his little book with so many ludicrous dreams! I believe he expends so much effort on the Greeks that he ignores the Latins, even though the Greeks Plutarch and Dio, whom he often mentions, seem to hold views opposed to his, if only he looked into them properly.

But, to examine this champion of liberty more carefully, Gua- 33 rino says that he maintains *that liberty was increased and made alive by the work of Caesar.*[47] Oh words unworthy of a learned man! What claim can be uttered more shameless than that? I am speaking before you, Francesco, knowing you take this badly for Guarino's sake. Does he so flatter himself, does he look so kindly on himself and on his studies that he dares to repeat over and over again that the liberty of the Roman people was increased by the work of Caesar—against the authority of everyone who ever wrote?

You are familiar with Cicero. For if perhaps Guarino disdains 34 him, I know how much you value him. Open his books, and most of all those *On Duties*, in which he speaks as a philosopher, with the words of truth itself. "But when everything was held under the control of one man," he says, "and when there was no place at all for counsel"; and then "when the republic, in which I was wont to invest all my thought, care, and effort, ceased to exist at all."[48] In another passage he complains that "the senate is extinct and the courts destroyed,"[49] and in the same books: "this is shown not only by the death of this tyrant, whom the City suffered as it was oppressed by arms."[50] And a little later: "Only the walls of the City stand, and even these now fear the worst crimes, but our republic we have utterly lost."[51] Even Guarino himself reports Cicero's

eversa quam stante re publica scripsisse; pluribus insuper in locis queritur rei publicae calamitatem. Solus ergo Cicero testis copiosus, nisi eum Guarinus reiciat, cogit illum vel reluctantem ac tergiversantem adsentiri se falsa litteris suis mandasse, cum exstinctum senatum, deleta iudicia, rem publicam amissam, eversam civitatem tyrannide[136] Caesaris oppressam totiens describit. Seneca insuper 'neque[137] Catonem post libertatem neque libertatem vixisse (dicit) post Catonem.'[138]

35   Verum ipsum aliquando suo testimonio convincamus. Superius inquit multas post Caesaris victoriam a Cicerone etiam in iudiciis esse habitas orationes. At hae solae sunt, quae pro Q. Ligario et rege Deiotaro feruntur. Si alias novit Guarinus, ipse recenseat. Qui ergo ii[139] iudices exstiterunt? Num ex ordine senatorio? Num equestri? Num per populum dati?[140] Num ipse praetor, apud quem privatae causae agebantur? Nihil minus. Quinam igitur ii[141] iudices fuerunt? Solus Caesar. Qui causam audiverunt? Unus[142] Caesar. Qui iudices sententiam tulerunt? Nempe unicus Caesar. Qui reos absolverunt? Ipsemet Caesar. O praeclarum et a Guarino productum indicium libertatis![143] Quod maius, quod manifestius, quod evidentius testimonium adferri potest libertatis amissae quam unius solius arbitrio, non auctoritate senatus, non permissu populi fieri iudicia, causas agi, reos absolvi, fori et iudiciorum more sublato? Ergo aut doceat Guarinus (quod numquam poterit) legibus id Caesari licuisse aut, velit nolit, fateatur necesse est Caesarem fuisse tyrannum exstincta populi libertate.

words when he claims to have written more when the republic was overturned than when she stood; and he laments the republic's ruin in many places besides.[52] Hence Cicero alone, an abundant witness, forces Guarino to agree, however reluctantly and unwillingly—unless Guarino were to reject him—that he has committed falsehoods to paper, since Cicero writes time and time again that the senate was killed off, the courts destroyed, the republic lost and overturned, and the state oppressed by the tyranny of Caesar. Furthermore, Seneca says that "Cato could not live after liberty nor liberty after Cato."[53]

But let us refute him finally with his own testimony. Earlier he 35 said that Cicero delivered many speeches after Caesar's victory, even in the courts.[54] But there are only these two, which were circulated on behalf of Q. Ligarius and King Deiotarus. If Guarino knows others, let him name them. So who were then these judges? Surely not from the senatorial order? Surely not from the equestrian? Surely they were not provided by the people? Surely it was not the praetor, before whom private suits were tried? Not at all. Who, then, were those judges? Only Caesar. Who were the people that heard the case? Caesar alone. Who were the judges that pronounced the verdict? To be sure, Caesar, all by himself. Who were the men that acquitted the defendants? The very same Caesar. Oh renowned sign of liberty, produced by Guarino! What greater, clearer, more evident proof can be brought forward of the loss of liberty than that it was by the will of a single man that courts were convened, cases tried, defendants acquitted, and not by the authority of the senate or the agreement of the people, once the norms of the forum and the courts had been removed? So let Guarino either demonstrate (which he will never be able to do) that this was permitted to Caesar by the laws, or necessarily admit, whether he likes it or not, that Caesar was a tyrant, since he extinguished people's liberty.

36   At propagatum esse imperium adfirmat. Quid hoc ad libertatis causam pertinet? Quasi non potuerit etiam libertate amissa Romanum[144] imperium augeri! Illud vero admodum ruditer[145] posuit: *consulum, praetorum, censorum, quaestorum, imperatorum creationem ordinariam esse servatam.* Hunc locum ut paucis absolvam, accipe Suetonii verba (quem, si legisset Guarinus, in has ridiculas ineptias non incidisset!), cum[146] de insolentia Caesaris loqueretur: 'Praegravant (inquit) cetera facta dictaque eius, ut et[147] abusus dominatione, et iure caesus existimetur. Non enim honores modo nimios recepit, ut continuum consulatum, perpetuam dictaturam praefecturamque morum, insuper praenomen imperatoris, cognomen patris patriae, statuam inter reges, suggestum in orchestra, sed et ampliora etiam humano fastigio decerni sibi passus est. Nonnullos honores ad libidinem cepit et dedit, tertium et quartum consulatum titulo tenus gessit, contentus dictaturae potestate, atque utroque anno binos consules substituit sibi in ternos[148] novissimos menses, ita ut medio tempore comitia nulla habuerit, praeter tribunorum et aedilium plebis. Pridie autem Kalendas Ianuarias repentina consulis morte cessantem honorem in paucas horas dedit. Eadem licentia spreto patrio more magistratus in plures annos ordinavit, decem praetoriis viris consularia ornamenta tribuit, civitate donatos et quosdam semibarbaros Gallorum recepit in curiam.'

37   'Nec minoris impotentiae voces propalam edebat: nihil esse amplius rem publicam quam appellationem sine corpore et specie; Sullam nescisse litteras qui dictaturam deposuerit; debere iam secum homines[149] consideratius loqui et pro legibus habere, quae diceret; adeuntes se patres conscriptos sedens excepit.' 'Adiecit ad

But he claims that the empire was extended. What does that 36
have to do with the cause of liberty? As if the Roman empire
could not have been expanded even after liberty was lost! Yet this
he wrote rather ignorantly: *that the regular election of consuls, praetors,
censors, quaestors, and generals was preserved.*[55] To deal with this passage summarily, listen to the words of Suetonius (if he had read
him, Guarino would not have fallen into these risible absurdities!),
where he spoke of the insolence of Caesar: "this was made worse
by his other deeds and words," he said, "so that he was deemed
both to have abused his absolute power and to have been justly
slain. For not only did he accept excessive honors, such as a continuous consulship, the dictatorship for life, and the censorship of
morals, as well as the forename Imperator and the epithet Father
of the Fatherland, a statue among those of the kings, and a raised
seat in the orchestra, but he also allowed honors to be bestowed
on him which were too great for a mortal man. Some honors he
received or conferred at pleasure: he held his third and fourth consulships in name only, content with the power of the dictatorship,
and in each year substituted two consuls for himself for the last
three months, in such a way that in the meantime he held no elections, except for tribunes and plebeian aediles. When one of the
consuls suddenly died the day before the Calends of January, he
gave out the vacant office for a few hours. With the same license,
and spurning ancestral custom, he appointed magistrates for several years, bestowed the emblems of consular rank on ten ex-
praetors, and admitted to the senate men who had been given citizenship, and certain semibarbarian Gauls."[56]

"No less immoderate were his public utterances: that the state 37
was nothing more than a name without body or form; that Sulla
did not know his A, B, C when he laid down his dictatorship; that
men should now address him with more consideration and regard
his word as law";[57] "when the senators approached him, he received them without rising."[58] "To the conspicuous insult of the

tam insignem despecti senatus contumeliam multo atrocius factum. Nam cum in sacrificio Latinarum[150] — revertente eo inter
immodicas[151] ac novas populi acclamationes — quidam e turba sta-
tuae eius coronam lauream candida fascia implicatam imposuisset
ac tribuni plebis Epidius Manilius[152] Caesetiusque Flavius coronae
fasciam detrahi, hominem duci in vincula iussissent, dolens seu
propter parum[153] prospere motam regni mentionem, sive, ut ipse
ferebat, ereptam gloriam recusandi, tribunos graviter increpitos
potestate privavit.' 'Comitia quoque (ut idem refert) divisa cum
populo habuit, ut pro parte dimidia populus pronuntiaret, quos
ipse dedisset.'

38   Magna quidem indicia atque opera haec sunt *libertatis adauctae
ac restitutae* (ut Guarino videtur): non adsurrexisse[154] senatui, tribuni potestate privati,[155] dictatura perpetuo sumpta, unius arbitrio
omnia administrata. *Creationem vero magistratuum ordinariam* dixisse
servatam monstri simile[156] est! Privatus comitiis populus, comitia
cum Caesare divisa, consulatus non ad ius populi sed ad suam libidinem concessi, spreto patrio more magistratus creati non ordinariam, sed libidinariam ostentant creationem. Quis haec de Mario aut Sulla legit, qui iniuriis ulciscendis ita crudeles fuerunt, ut[157]
tamen rei publicae auctoritas, magistratuum creandorum ordo et
dignitas remanerent?

39   Illud vero maxime pudet scripsisse Guarinum, in quo vel negli-
gentiam suam, vel ignorantiam testatur: ait *octoginta milia civium
Romanorum in transmarinas colonias distributa revocasse Caesarem*[158] *in
Urbem bellis civilibus exhaustam*. Nescio an ab aliquo Graeco hoc
Guarinus exhauserit. Hoc scio: Suetonii sententiam a Guarini
opinione admodum esse remotam, in quo mirari cogor Suetonium

senate he despised he added an even more monstrous act. For at
the Latin Festival, as he was returning to the city amid extravagant
and unprecedented acclamations of the people, someone from the
crowd had placed a laurel wreath with a white ribbon tied to it
onto his statue; and when Epidius Manilius and Caesetius Flavius,
tribunes of the plebs, gave orders that the ribbon be removed from
the wreath and the man taken off to prison, Caesar sharply re-
buked and deprived them of their office, outraged either because
the hint at kingship had not gone down as hoped or, as he himself
asserted, because he had been robbed of the glory of refusing it."[59]
"He held elections divided with the people," the same man also
reports, "so that for their half share the people might appoint
those men whom he had provided."[60]

Great signs and works these certainly are of a *liberty increased*
and restored, as it seems to Guarino: not to have risen in front of
the senate, the tribunes deprived of their power, the dictatorship
taken for life, all things administered by the will of one man.[61] To
say *that the ordinary election of magistrates was preserved* is akin to a
marvel! The people deprived of their elections, the elections shared
with Caesar, the consulships allotted not according to the law of
the people but at his whim, and, with ancestral custom spurned,
the elections of magistrates show not an ordinary, but an arbitrary
process. Who has read such things about Marius or Sulla, who
were cruel in avenging wrongs only to the extent that the authority
of the republic, and the order and honor of electing magistrates,
remained intact?

But this is the most shameful thing that Guarino has written,
in which he displays either his carelessness or his ignorance. He
says that *Caesar recalled 80,000 Roman citizens based in overseas colonies*
to the city, which was drained owing to the civil wars.[62] I do not know if
Guarino drew this from some Greek author or other. But I know
this: that the judgment of Suetonius is quite far removed from
Guarino's opinion, so that I am forced to wonder whether in this

ab eo hac in parte non intellectum, qui ad verbum hoc refert: 'octoginta civium milibus in transmarinas colonias distributis, ut exhaustae Urbis frequentia suppeteret, sanxit ne quis civis maior annis viginti minorve decem,[159] qui sacramento non teneretur, plus triennio Italia abesset.' Non 'revocata' scribit Suetonius, sed 'distributa'!

40   Sed dum Guarinus Caesarem tueri et ornare nititur, neque quid dicat ipse, neque quid testes, quos refert, intelligant, animadvertit. Neque hoc in loco solum, sed in multis insuper gravissimorum auctorum sententias (quos paulo post recensebo) aut non intelligit, aut nititur pervertere. Certus sum, mi Francisce, te[160] admodum mirari Guarini doctrinam, qui, studio mecum litigandi adductus, dum vult Caesaris famam servari, prodit suam.

41   Docui hucusque satis abunde, ut opinor,[161] primum anteire gloria Caesari Scipionem, tum autem culpa Caesaris Latinam eloquentiam corruisse,[162] tertio libertatem populi Romani[163] Caesaris tyrannide oppressam atque eversam. Quae ita verissimis testibus sunt confirmata, ut nulla dubitatio mentibus legentium possit haerere.[164] Nunc cetera sua refellam argumenta; non quidem omnia (nam et indigna sunt quibus respondeatur, et longior fieret oratio), sed capitaliora quaedam, quibus palmam victoriae se adeptum putat.

42   Ait *eloquentiae ruinam prodisse ex luxuria atque avaritia;* dictum Crispi Sallustii adducit[165] scribentis 'avaritiam fidem, probitatem ceterasque bonas artes subvertisse.' Quaeso, Francisce, si haec duo vitia eloquentiam everterunt,[166] ea autem Sallustii aetate tantum incrementum suscepere, ut ad summum pervenerint, cur tunc maxime viguit eloquentia, adeo in extremum culmen perducta, ut

passage he misunderstand Suetonius, who reports verbatim as follows: "having sent 80,000 citizens to colonies across the sea, in
order that the population of the drained city might be sufficient,
he decreed that no citizen older than twenty or younger than ten
who was not bound by an oath of military service should be absent from Italy for more than a three-year period."[63] Not "recalled,"
but "sent out" is what Suetonius writes![64]

Yet Guarino, striving to protect and honor Caesar, pays atten-   40
tion neither to what he says himself nor to what the witnesses
whom he cites intend. Not only in this passage but in many others
besides does he either misunderstand, or strive to bend, the opinions of the weightiest authors, whom I will review in a little while.
I am sure, my dear Francesco, that you rather marvel at the learning of Guarino who, driven by his zeal for quarreling with me, and
wishing to save Caesar's reputation, betrays his own.

Up to this point I have shown, abundantly enough in my view,   41
first that Scipio surpasses Caesar in glory, then that Latin eloquence collapsed through Caesar's fault, and thirdly that the liberty of the Roman people was oppressed and overturned by the
tyranny of Caesar. These points have been confirmed by the truest
witnesses in such a way that there can be no doubt at all lingering
in the minds of the readers. Now I shall refute Guarino's other
contentions, not indeed all of them, both because they are unworthy of a response and because my discourse would grow too long,
but some of the more important ones, through which he reckons
to have claimed the palm of victory.

He says that *the ruin of eloquence issued from luxury and greed*; he   42
adduces the words of Sallust, when he wrote that "avarice overturned faith and decency and all other good disciplines."[65] I ask
you, Francesco, if these two vices overturned eloquence, but they
underwent such an increase in Sallust's time that they reached
the highest point, why was it that eloquence was then at its peak,

maior esse non posset? Sed alia fuit causa evidentior: amisso enim rei pulcherrimae praemio, exercitium quoque illius defecit.

43   Vult extra culpam esse Caesarem, si post eum nefarii principes sunt subsecuti. Non dico illum quales posteri futuri essent, praestare debuisse. Id adfirmo: si per eum res publica stare potuisset, si illius cupiditas imperandi non adeo vires civitatis obtrivisset, ut exstinctis praeclarissimis principibus, luminibus Romanae urbis, unus quam patria esset validior, neque bonos, neque malos principes fuisse futuros.

44   Arguit me quod audeam edere (ut ait) iudicium meum, ubi *vagus, non ad historiarum dictata, non ad doctorum et priscorum sententiam, sed ad nescio quem sensum ac voluntatem* verba *proferam*, quasi vero Guarinus scripta sua[167] doctorum illorum, non somniorum suorum auctoritate[168] confirmet ac non introducat eos testes, qui in ipsum probe reiciuntur! Ego, quos auctores adhuc[169] sim secutus, magna ex parte protuli: Ciceronem, Senecam, Titum Livium, Cornelium Tacitum, Valerium, Suetonium Tranquillum; quos si despicit Guarinus, aut si me illos non recte intelligere adfirmet, aequo animo patiar esse illum in causa superiorem.

45   Verum incutere terrorem mihi se[170] credit: non solum se adversus me bellum suscepisse dicit, sed denuntiat *reliquis etiam cohortibus*, quae in me paratae sint, *vicem relinquere*. Ego[171] quantum bello valeat Guarinus experior, quantum reliquae cohortes exspecto. Quamquam male Latine locutus est: nam, cum pro sua modestia scribat non solum se incursionem meam uno impetu posse sufferre, et reliquas cohortes, tamquam si[172] ipse una cohors sit, subsidiarias esse adfirmat; nisi forsan intelligat unius cohortis munere in hoc certamine se fungi posse! Verum ego et Guarinum, et cohortes illas aperte contemno: nam ex veteranis non constant,

carried to such heights that it could not grow greater? But there was another more obvious cause, for once the reward for the fairest endeavor was lost, it also ceased to be practiced.

He wants Caesar to be free from guilt if wicked rulers succeeded him. I do not say that he should be held accountable for what sort the later ones would be. This I do say: that if he had allowed the republic to stand, if his lust for power had not sapped the strength of the state to the point that, once the most renowned leading men and luminaries of the City of Rome had been extinguished, one man was stronger than the fatherland, then there would not have been any rulers, good or bad.

He censures me for daring to issue — says he — my own judgment, where I, *adrift, offer* words *not according to the lessons of history or the opinion of the learned of old, but according to who knows what feeling or whim,* as though Guarino grounds his writings on the authority of those learned ones rather than upon his own dreams, and does not bring forward witnesses who can properly be thrown straight back at him![66] I have for the most part indicated the authors I have followed thus far: Cicero, Seneca, Titus Livy, Cornelius Tacitus, Valerius, Suetonius Tranquillus. If Guarino looks down upon them, or if he can show that I have misunderstood them, I will calmly accept that he is superior in this case.

He, however, believes that he inspires fear in me: not only does he say that he has taken up a war against me, but he proclaims that he *leaves their turn to the remaining cohorts* which stand ready against me.[67] I have experienced how strong Guarino is in war, but I await the strength of the remaining cohorts. Yet he spoke Latin poorly, since, while for the sake of his own modesty he writes that he cannot single-handedly resist my assault with a single thrust, he also asserts that the remaining cohorts are auxiliaries, as though he were one cohort himself — unless perhaps he means that in this battle he plays the part of one cohort! In truth, I openly disdain both Guarino and his cohorts, for they do not consist of veterans,

43

44

45

quos[173] tamen novi omnes, et sentiunt mecum; tironum impetum
non pertimesco.

46   Quod autem in principio meae epistolae scripseram, credere me
Plutarchum res militiae gestas et belli gloriam, non virtutes secutum in comparandis Caesare ac Magno Alexandro, longa oratione
reprehendit et, ut falsum me opinari videam, adfert testimonium
Plutarchi. Hoc mihi admodum placuit. Contra se enim illum, ut
facit saepissime, introducit. Quid inquit Plutarchus? 'Vitas, non
historias, conscribimus.' Hoc ego neque nunc[174] inficior: nam in
vita res domi et foris gestae, laus et gloria[175] continetur. Sed doceat
Guarinus, si potest, Plutarchum Alexandri ac Caesaris virtutes
comparasse, non res gestas et belli gloriam, ut scripsi. Ipse Plutarchus post priora verba refert, ut transfert Guarinus: 'nec omnino
rebus clarissime gestis virtutis aut vitiorum inest demonstratio.'
Hoc sentit vir doctissimus, Guarini testis: in caede hominum, in
strage,[176] in maximis pugnis, in expugnationibus civitatum nullam
inesse virtutem, quae, quamvis sint permagna, tamen propter hominum perniciem stragemque gentium nihil in se continere
honesti — nisi forsan cum iusta ex causa, quod tamen neque
Alexandro, neque Caesari contigit, fiant.

47   Adserit insuper virtutes magis et vitia a Plutarcho quam res
gestas describi. Hoc neque Plutarchus adserit, neque Guarinus
potest probare. Debuit non verborum inanem sonitum effundere,
sed ostendere, quod[177] honestum referat Plutarchus a Caesare,
quibus eum virtutibus exornet, quam virtutis laudem sibi tribuat.
Sed nullam adfert corrector noster. Et cum virtutes et vitia ab suo
teste describi adfirmet, silet tamen in tanta exspectatione, et in
laudibus Caesaris delitescit. Ego Plutarchum video nullum laudandi Caesaris aut Alexandri sibi officium adsumpsisse, sed mores

as I know them all and they agree with me, and I do not fear the onslaught of raw recruits.

However, as to what I wrote in the beginning of my letter, to 46 wit, that I believe that Plutarch considered military exploits and martial glory, not virtues, when comparing Caesar and Alexander the Great, he rejects this in a long speech and, so that I may see that I am wrong in my view, adduces a quotation from Plutarch. This pleased me very much indeed. For he brings him in, as he does so very often, against himself. What does Plutarch say? *"We are writing* Lives, *not* Histories."[68] I do not now deny that, for a *Life* contains achievements at home and abroad, praise and glory. But let Guarino show, if he can, that Plutarch compared the virtues of Alexander and Caesar, rather than their exploits and glory in war, as I wrote. After his earlier words Plutarch himself notes, as Guarino translates it, that *"there is not the slightest proof of virtue or vices in deeds that were done with the greatest renown."*[69] This is what this most learned man, Guarino's witness, thought: that there is no virtue present in the slaughter of men, in massacres, in the greatest battles, nor in the storming of cities, which, however great they may be, still cannot contain any moral value within them because of the ruin of men and the massacre of peoples; unless perhaps they happen for a just cause, which, however, does not apply to either Alexander or Caesar.[70]

Moreover, he claims that Plutarch described virtues, and vice, 47 rather than exploits. Plutarch does not raise this claim, nor can Guarino prove it. He should not have poured forth the empty sound of words, but should have shown what moral action Plutarch reports performed by Caesar, with what virtues he adorns him, what praise for virtue he assigns him. But our corrector cites none. And although he claims that his witness describes virtues and vices, still he is silent in the face of this great expectation and hides himself behind praises of Caesar. I judge that Plutarch did not assume the task of praising Caesar or Alexander, but rather

et res gestas descripsisse,[178] quibus nulla aut perrara est virtus admixta. Neque etiam[179] ab aliis laudatos ob eorum virtutes scio. Qui enim laudari possunt,[180] si ad philosophiam moralem animadvertamus—vivendi ducem et magistram—duo portenta orbis, duae generis humani[181] pestes, duo gentium flagella, qui nati solum esse videntur ad effusionem sanguinis, ad eversionem provinciarum, regnorum desolationem, ad communem hominum interitum atque cladem?

48   Non pugno cum Alexandro neque Graecos, qui nosti quantum audeant in historia, refello. Senecam nostrum gravissimum philosophum video multum a Guarini sententia, quo ad Alexandri laudes, differre; qui eum vesanum hominem, infelicem, furentem libidine aliena vastandi, exitium familiarium suorum, cui pro virtute fuerit[182] felix temeritas, a pueritia latronem gentiumque[183] vastatorem, tam amicorum, quam hostium perniciem propriis verbis appellat. Credo de Caesare haud dissimilia dempta crudelitate scripturum Senecam fuisse, nisi respexisset ad Neronem, qui tum imperabat. Attamen cum Plutarchus duorum, ut vult Guarinus, vitia et virtutes comparet, Alexandri autem vitia et scelera[184] a[185] Seneca referantur permulta, necesse est Caesarem quoque Alexandro copulari[186] similitudine vitiorum.

49   Devenit tandem, tamquam superiora ex animo processerint, ad laudandam Caesaris adolescentiam; qua in re multa magis ridenda protulit quam laudanda. Illud vero in primis perabsurdum:[187] *nec enim minus* (inquit) *quam Marium Sullae terrori Caesarem fuisse ipsius Sullae testatur oratio, quem praedicare solitum dicis 'ut male cinctum puerum praecaverent.' Quam ob rem? 'Nam Caesari multos Marios inesse.' O ingens de Caesare iam inde a puero praeconium, si sagacissimi*

described their character and exploits, with which no virtue or only a very small amount was mingled. I do not even know that they have been praised by others for their virtues. Indeed, if we were to turn our minds to moral philosophy, the guide and teacher of living, how could two global monsters, two plagues of the human race, two scourges of nations be praised, who seem to have been born only to spill blood, to subjugate provinces, to devastate kingdoms, for the general destruction and calamity of the human race?

I have no quarrel with Alexander, nor am I trying to refute the 48 Greeks, whose great audacity in history you know. It is our Seneca, weightiest of philosophers, whom I see differing a great deal from Guarino's opinion, as it pertains to the praises of Alexander. With his very own words, he calls him a lunatic, unfortunate, raging with a lust to destroy others' property, and himself the destruction of his intimates, who instead of virtue possessed a lucky rashness, a thief from his boyhood and a destroyer of nations, and the ruin of his friends quite as much as of his enemies. I believe that Seneca would have written hardly differently about Caesar, minus the cruelty, if he had not had his eye on Nero, who was ruling at the time. But still, given that Plutarch, as Guarino has it, is comparing the virtues and vices of both men, yet the numerous vices and crimes of Alexander are reported by Seneca, it follows necessarily that Caesar is also conjoined with Alexander by the similarity of his vices.

Finally — as if the earlier things had slipped his mind — Gua- 49 rino arrives at the praise of Caesar's youth, regarding which he proffers many things that are laughable rather than laudable. The following is especially absurd: *that Sulla — he says — feared Caesar no less than Marius is proven by his very own words, since as you say Sulla frequently declared "that they should beware of the badly-belted boy."*[71] *Why? "Because there were many Marii in Caesar."*[72] *What an enormous tribute to Caesar already in his boyhood if according to Sulla, so skilled in*

ad odorandum Sullae testimonio tot Marios aequabat unus! Haec ad verbum Guarinus, qui maximi terroris putat esse argumentum in praestantissimo imperatore puer male praecinctus, quem unico nutu, ne dicam verbo, delere potuisset. Ad te convertor, Francisce, qui vir es doctissimus: perlege diligenter Guarini verba et vide quam discrepet a recta sententia.

50   Dicit *non minus Caesarem terrori quam Marium Sullae* exstitisse. Quid hac opinione stultius excogitari potest? Unde hoc Guarinus auguratur? Quia sciret (inquit) *multos Marios inesse Caesari, qui*[188] *tot Marios aequabat*[189] *unus.* Primum, cum tot bellorum duces adversae factionis, tot cives, tot exercitus, quos aut oderat, aut timebat, delesset victor Sulla, quid negotii fuit unum delere adolescentem inopem, imbecillum, si eum tantopere extimescebat? Cui vitam amicis deprecantibus concessit, ei mortem, credo, inferre non potuit, cum victor esset et dictator! Hoc admodum ridiculum, ne dicam ineptum, voluisse Sullam iis[190] verbis unum adolescentem Caesarem, nullis rebus gestis, non uni,[191] qui fuit excellentissimus bello imperator, sed multis Mariis aequasse. Nescio an ex arte id faciat Guarinus, ut se simulet nihil scire: equidem in puerulo esset vitiosissimum tam perperam priscorum verba ad diversum et suum[192] nescio quem sensum traducere! Non enim multorum Mariorum virtutem inesse Caesari Sulla intellexit, sed ita illi in animo Marianam factionem cernebat infixam, ut etiam multos Marios partium adfectione superaret.

51   Dicit apud Sullam pro Caesare intercessisse virgines vestales propter indolem virtutis:[193] credo aut adfinium, aut amicorum precibus magis, aut aliquo turpi commercio adductas! Ad magnam laudem scribit creatum esse flaminem dialem. At vero ii,[194] qui largitione et corruptela suffragiorum factum tradunt, secus

tracking a scent, he alone equaled so many Marii![73] Thus to the letter
Guarino, who reckons that a badly-belted boy is ground for ex-
ceeding fear in an outstanding commander: a boy whom he could
have destroyed with a single nod, not to say word. I turn to you,
Francesco, since you are a very learned man: read Guarino's words
carefully and see how much he diverges from a sound opinion.

He says that *Sulla feared Caesar no less than Marius.* What can be
thought up more stupid than this opinion? From what did Guarino divine this? Because he knew — he says — *that there were many
Marii in Caesar, who by himself equaled so many Marii.*[74] First of all,
since the victorious Sulla had destroyed so many military commanders of the opposing faction, so many citizens, so many
armies, whom he either hated or feared, what trouble would it
have been to destroy a single adolescent who was without means
and weak, if he feared him so much? When he was victorious and
dictator, I suppose Sulla could not inflict death on the man to
whom he granted life on the pleas of his friends! It is entirely ludicrous, not to say inept, to suppose that with these words Sulla
meant that the single adolescent Caesar, who had achieved nothing, was equal not to one Marius, who was an outstanding commander in war, but to many Marii. I do not know if Guarino does
this from guile, so as to feign ignorance: indeed even in a school-
boy it would be a grave fault so wrongly to twist the words of the
ancients into some kind of different and peculiar meaning! In fact,
Sulla understood not that Caesar had the virtue of many Marii,
but rather that the Marian cause was so rooted in his mind that he
surpassed many Marii in his adherence to that faction.

Guarino says that the Vestal virgins interceded for Caesar with
Sulla because of his natural virtue: I believe that, instead, they
were brought in by the pleas of family and friends, or by some
shady deal! He writes that Caesar was made *flamen dialis* to his
great honor. Yet those who report that he was appointed through
bribery and a corrupt election are of the contrary opinion. But at

opinantur. Sed aliquando tandem, quo maxime modo oratorios locos tractare nosset,[195] nobis ostentare voluit. *Accipe et hoc* (inquit) *quod tute*[196] *fatebere*[197] *insigne. Quid frontem contraxisti? Ne discedas, oro: abibis*[198] *deinde non indoctior.* Ego vero ad has nugas neque frontem contraho, neque longius abibo, sed propius pedem conferam![199]

52   Verum admodum admirari[200] cogor et etiam dolere virum eruditissimum dicendi artem, quam aliis saepe tradiderit, ipsum dedidicisse,[201] et dum[202] vult oratorum colores imitari, et sine colore est et transgreditur oratorum instituta. In orationibus enim, quae habentur aut finguntur inter praesentes, cum vox nostra dirigitur ad auditores, cum loquimur coram, poni consueverunt 'sudat,' 'pallet,' 'contremiscit,' modo ne nauseat, ut de Antonio inquit Tullius. In epistola vero (qua absentem et quidem octoginta amplius milibus passuum appellat) cum me non videt, qui scit orator noster frontemne an supercilia contraham, risune an cachinno verba sua excipiam? Credit me contraxisse frontem. At ego os et totum vultum relaxavi, in maximum risum effusus! Nam quod me iis[203] suis verbis existimat fieri posse[204] doctiorem, vehementer errat: si enim ei fidem haberem, aut sibi si[205] auscultarem, multo essem quam sim stultior atque indoctior! Itaque remitto sibi hanc suam egregiam doctrinam, qua utatur inter discipulos suos in suis scholis; me stultum esse meo more permittat.

53   Sed quid tandem adfert admirationis, ut ad eius vocem et strepitum sit frons contrahenda? *In expugnatione Mytilenarum—*inquit—*donatum esse a Thermo imperatore Caesarem corona civica.* Credideram prolaturum eum aliquem triumphum insignem aut

long last he wants to show us how excellently he can handle the commonplaces of oratory. *Listen to this too*, he says, *that even you will call distinguished. Why do you frown? Do not leave, please; you will go away later no less learned.*[75] Yet in response to these trifles I neither frown nor do I intend to go further away, but instead I will go on the attack!

Indeed I am forced rather to marvel at, and even lament, the 52 fact that a very learned man has himself unlearned the art of speaking, which he himself has often taught others, and while he wants to imitate the embellishments of the orators, is both without embellishment and transgresses against the teachings of the orators. For in speeches which are truly or supposedly held before an audience, when our words are addressed to the listeners, when we speak in their presence, orators are wont to write "he sweats," "he turns pale," "he trembles," provided it is not ad nauseam, as indeed Cicero says about Antonius.[76] But in a letter in which he addresses one who is absent, at a distance of more than eighty miles, when he does not actually see me, how does our orator know whether I am frowning or raising an eyebrow, and whether it is with a smile or with a smirk that I am receiving his words? Guarino believes I have frowned. But instead I have relaxed my mouth and my whole face, having dissolved into a loud guffaw! As to his reckoning that I could grow more learned from his words, he is absolutely wrong. Indeed if I had faith in him, or were to lend him my ear, I would be much more stupid and less learned than I am! Therefore I send back to him this exceptional learning of his, for him to use in his classes among his students. Let him permit me to be stupid in my own way.

But what, finally, is this wondrous thing that he delivers such 53 that at the sound of his voice my brow should be furrowed? *That during the storming of Mytilene*, he says, *Caesar was given a civic crown by the general Thermus.*[77] I had thought that he was about to produce some exceptional triumph or the labor of some enormous

ingentis belli molem, ad cuius rei magnitudinem stupore aliquo opus esset. Sed res levissimas adsumit et quas saepissime gregarii milites edidere! At[206] Suetonius non meruisse Caesarem civicam coronam, sed ea donatum a Thermo, tamquam non meritis, sed contubernio adtributa. Quid diceret Guarinus de L. Licinio Dentato, quem quattuordecim civicis coronis a variis imperatoribus A. Gellius[207] donatum tradit? Credo illum hanc ob rem Fabio Maximo comparandum fuisse dicturum! Profecto accidit Guarino, quod cuidam amanti e nostris, qui, cum mulierem, quam deperibat,[208] occulte post ventris egestionem conspexisset nates mundantem, testatus est nihil ab ea[209] umquam pulchrius actum aut speciosius. Quicquid Caesar egit, id facinus praeclarum putat. Existimo si crepitum aliquem ventris edidisset, pro summo tonitruo Guarinum fuisse ducturum![210]

54   Hoc autem perridiculum, *praedones, qui navibus innumeris et classibus ingentibus* (ut somniat, nihil enim de his[211] legitur) *obsessum mare tenebant,* cepisse Caesarem, cum Rhodum navigaret, atque hos *a Caesare comparatis postmodum navibus[212] in Milesiorum portu commissoque navali proelio superatos atque in potestatem redactos.* Si Guarinus legisset Valerium Maximum, qui narrat mioparone[213] piratarum Caesarem captum, non circumstreperet nobis tam inani verborum apparatu, neque tot innumeris navibus et ingentibus classibus aures legentium refricasset: mioparo siquidem navicula est (ut Nonius[214] Marcellus refert) praedatoria, quam cepisse pauculis latrunculis superatis operis fuit perexigui. At Guarinus exsultat tamquam cum Xerxis aut Carthaginensium classe Caesar pugnasset.

55   At vero *stabilimentum Romani imperii me non negaturum* scribit, quod Caesar ab Rhodo in Asiam transiit praefectumque

war, at the greatness of which one is necessarily left dumbfounded. But he adduces the most trifling deeds, which are also frequently performed by common soldiers! Moreover, Suetonius says that Caesar did not earn the civic crown but that it was given to him by Thermus, as if in recognition not of his services but of his companionship. What would Guarino say about L. Licinius Dentatus, of whom Aulus Gellius reports that he was awarded fourteen civic crowns by various commanders? I believe he would put him on a par with Fabius Maximus on that ground![78] Indeed, Guarino has had the same experience as a certain lover among us, who, when he had secretly peeked at the woman with whom he was infatuated while she was wiping her bottom after a bowel movement, declared that she had never done anything more beautiful or splendid. Whatever Caesar did he deems a shining achievement. I reckon that if he had farted Guarino would reckon it the mightiest thunder!

This, however, is laughable in the extreme: there were *pirates, who controlled the waves with countless ships and huge fleets*—how he dreams, for we read nothing about them.[79] These captured Caesar, when he was sailing to Rhodes, and *when Caesar had later procured ships in the harbor of Miletus and joined a naval battle, he overcame them and brought them into his power.*[80] If Guarino had read Valerius Maximus, who recounts that Caesar was captured by a pirates' sloop, he would not be surrounding us with such noise from his empty word instrument, nor would he have irritated the ears of his readers with so many *countless ships and huge fleets*, since a *myoparon* is a small ship built for plundering, as Nonius Marcellus reports, to have captured which by routing a handful of petty thieves involved only a small effort.[81] But Guarino exults as if Caesar had battled the fleets of Xerxes or the Carthaginians.

But truly, *his steadying of the Roman empire I will not deny*, he writes, since Caesar crossed from Rhodes to Asia and, after collecting auxiliary forces, expelled Mithridates' prefect from the

54

55

Mithridatis contractis auxiliis expulit provincia. Hoc ab eo factum non abnuo, sed nugatorem quendam dico esse Guarinum, qui praefectum Mithridatis provincia expulsum, rem admodum parvam, dicat *me*[215] *non negaturum fuisse imperii stabilimentum*. Num[216] legit adeo nutasse tunc rem Romanam, ut, nisi praefectum expulisset Caesar, de imperio actum esset? Nimirum triumphasse debuit ex hoc tanto bello, tot hostium[217] milibus per somnium captis, tot trucidatis! Verum nimium effuse ac licenter has suas historias (ne dicam ineptias) Guarinus expandit, instar cantorum qui gesta Rolandi decantant in rusticorum coetu.[218] Et his suis ampullosis dictis elatus me rogat, *cedamne an perstem* in sententia? Nihil adhuc ab eo prolatum est, quod me moveat ad cedendum! Verum, si loco cedentem[219] senserit, insequatur!

56   Tribunum militum ob hanc egregiam operam factum scribit: ut sequeretur figmentum suum, triumphum decretum debuit addidisse! Sed hunc honorem multi etiam alii consecuti sunt aetate teneriori et magis dubiis in[220] rebus. Iterum ad me recurrit Guarinus et vel *ridere*, vel *subirasci* dicit, quod in epistola mea, *omnia maledicta in Caesarem colligens, si quid cum laude gesserit tacitus omittam, sordes vero exprimam*. Ego, quicquid de Caesare scripserim, me vere profiteor sensisse, nulla in re mentitum. Guarinus, dum laudes illius colligere et in melius vertere nititur, vanum se quendam confabulatorem ostendit, et[221] sibi fidem detrahens et Caesari auctoritatem.

57   Petit a me *cur non rettulerim comitium, forum, basilicas, porticus*[222] *ornatas, ludos editos, epulas* populo datas *et reliqua* generis eiusdem, quae ipse ad liberalitatem ascribit. Quoniam, cum ea

province.[82] I do not deny that he did this, but I do say that Guarino is trifling when he says *that I cannot deny that* the expulsion of Mithridates' prefect, a pretty small matter, constituted *the steadying of the empire*.[83] He surely has not read that at that time the Roman state was so unsteady that, if Caesar had not expelled the prefect, the entire empire would have been doomed? No doubt he should have won a triumph from such a great war, since so many thousands of the enemy were captured, and so many killed—in a daydream! Truth be told, Guarino elaborates his histories, not to say his nonsense, all too gushingly and with excessive license, just like those singers who recite the deeds of Roland for a crowd of peasants.[84] And puffed up by these grandiose words of his, he asks me *whether I am going to yield or am standing* by my judgment? Up to this point he has not said a single thing that might induce me to yield! However, if he has noticed me giving ground, let him give chase!

He writes that Caesar was made military tribune on account of 56 this outstanding achievement. To complete his fiction, he should have added that a triumph was decreed! But many others obtained the same honor at a younger age and in more dubious circumstances. Again Guarino returns to me and claims that he either *laughs* or *is annoyed*, on the ground that in my letter, *while collecting all slanders against Caesar, I pass in silence over anything he did commendably, yet give vent to scandals*.[85] I for my part profess that whatever I wrote about Caesar, I truly believed, without lying about any matter.[86] Guarino, while he strives to collect his merits and change them for the better, shows himself to be an unreliable story teller, who diminishes both his own credibility and the authority of Caesar.

He asks me *why I did not report that the* comitium, *the forum,* 57 *the basilicas, the porticoes were decorated, games staged, meals* given to the people, *and other things* of the same sort, which he attributes to generosity.[87] Because, since he did these things for the sake of

propter ambitionem ex rapinis undique contractis effecerit neque
ulla in parte virtutis collocari possent, censui omittenda! Neque
enim[223] liberalitati ascribi merentur quae per furta, latrocinia et
rapinas abstulit, neque ulli virtutis vestigio. Non enim liberalitas
esse potest ob aes alienum emendicata[224] suffragia, expilatio Capi-
tolii, urbium spoliatio, direptio fanorum, provinciarum venditio,
rapinae, sacrilegia, ut vel aliis dones, vel ludos populo edas, vel
plebi epulum praebeas ad eviscerationem![225]

58   Quod si videtur Guarinus ignorare Caesaris in rapiendo studium, legat, oro, Suetonium et, cum intellexerit, quid in ea parte
testetur, remittat paulum fervoris atque impetus in Caesare laudando. 'Abstinentiam (inquit) neque in imperiis neque in magistratibus praestitit, ut enim quidam monumentis suis testati sunt.
In Hispania a[226] proconsule et a sociis pecunias accepit emendicatas in auxilium aeris alieni, et Lusitanorum quaedam oppida,
quamquam nec imperata[227] detractarent[228] et advenienti portas
patefacerent, diripuit hostiliter. In Gallia fana templaque deum
donis referta expilavit, urbes diripuit saepius ob praedam quam ob
delictum. In primo[229] consulatu tria milia pondo auri furatus in
Capitolio tantundem inaurati aeris reposuit. Societates ac regna
pretio dedit, ut qui uno[230] Ptolemaeo prope sex milium talento-
rum suo Pompeique nomine abstulerit. Postea vero evidentissimis
rapinis ac sacrilegiis onera bellorum[231] civilium et triumphorum ac
munerum sustinuit impendia.' Quid ad haec respondebit Guarinus? Non Poggius, sed Suetonius evidentissimas rapinas, sacrilegia, furta, latrocinia Caesaris ostendit!

his ambition and with plunder amassed from everywhere, and since they could not be classed in any category of virtue, I judged that they should be passed over! For things that he carried off by theft, robbery and plunder do not deserve to be ascribed to generosity or to any trace of virtue.[88] Nor indeed can this be generosity: votes obtained by begging for the sake of debt, the pillaging of the Capitol, the spoliation of cities, the plundering of shrines, the sale of provinces, acts of pillage, and sacrileges, so that you may either give gifts to others or to stage games for the people or offer a meal to the plebs in order to eviscerate them![89]

But if Guarino seems to be unaware of Caesar's zeal for plun-   58
der, I beg him to read Suetonius; and, when he has understood what he reports in that passage, let him relax somewhat his desire and drive to praise Caesar. Suetonius says: "He showed self-restraint neither when in command of armies nor as a magistrate at Rome, as indeed a number of men have reported in their works. In Spain he received money that he had begged from the proconsul and from the allies to help pay his debts, and also despoiled in the manner of an enemy some towns of the Lusitanians, although they did not refuse his terms and opened their gates to him on his arrival. In Gaul he pillaged shrines and temples filled with offerings to the gods, and more often sacked towns for the sake of plunder than on account of any misdeed on their part. In his first consulship he stole three thousand pounds of gold from the Capitol, replacing it with the same weight of gilded bronze. He gave alliances and kingdoms for a price, so that he extorted nearly 6000 talents from Ptolemy alone in his own name and that of Pompey. Later he met the burdens of the civil wars and the expenses of his triumphs and entertainments with the most blatant acts of pillage and sacrilege."[90] What reply will Guarino make to this? It is not Poggio, but Suetonius who is pointing out Caesar's most blatant acts of pillage, his sacrileges, thefts, and robberies!

59   Quae est autem Guarini contumacia, ut solus post hominum
memoriam virum furem, sacrilegum, rapacem, patriae parricidam,
humani generis hostem sibi[232] laudandum putet et viro omni virtutum genere perfecto, Scipioni Africano, censeat praeferendum?[233]
Legat quantumvis Latinos auctores (nam Graecos ignoro): nullum
reperiet, qui etiam libertate deleta, cum imperatores regnarent,
Caesaris laudes sit complexus.

60   At refert Vergilii carmen: 'Imperium Oceano, famam qui terminet astris.' Quod dictum, licet Servius de Iulio Caesare intelligere
videatur, tamen plus me movent Vergilii versus sequentes, quos
ad Octavianum est necessarium referri, quam Servii auctoritas.
Considera, quaeso, vir prudentissime[234] rerum omnium, eos versus
diligenter: 'Nascetur pulchra Troianus origine Caesar, imperium
Oceano, famam qui terminet astris, Iulius, a magno demissum
nomen Iulo.' 'A magno Iulo' de Caesare dici oportet, ante quem
nullum accepimus (quod quidem meminerim), qui posset 'magnus'
vocari, 'vocabitur hic quoque votis, Aspera tum positis mitescent
saecula bellis, Cana Fides et Vesta Remo cum fratre Quirinus Iura
dabunt, dirae[235] ferro et compagibus artis,[236] Claudentur belli portae,' et quae sequuntur. Quae si ad Caesarem quis referat, videatur
desipere,[237] cuius tempora et ea, quae aliquibus annis post eum
secuta sunt, longe remota fuerunt a pace et armorum quiete; neque clausae belli portae exstiterunt, sed reseratae[238] et Furori impio
data licentia. Itaque hi versus non ad Caesaris laudem spectant,
sed Augusti, quem sibi Vergilius sumpserat extollendum.

61   Illud vero minime[239] ferendum: commendare Guarinum empta
a Caesare suffragia, tamquam id licuerit, quia ab aliis fuerit factita-
tum. Quaerit *num Caesar primus tribus ac suffragia corruperit*,[240] quasi

What, however, is this obstinacy of Guarino's, that he alone in   59
human memory thinks that he should praise a thieving, sacrile-
gious, rapacious man, a murderer of the fatherland and enemy of
mankind, and reckons that he should be ranked above Scipio Africanus, a man perfect in every type of virtue? Let him read whatever Latin author you will (for I disregard the Greeks): he will
find none, even when liberty had been destroyed and the emperors
were in power, who embraced the praises of Caesar.

But he reports this verse of Vergil: "*To limit his Empire by the*   60
Ocean, his fame by the stars."[91] As to this line, even though Servius
seems to take it as about Julius Caesar, still the following verses of
Vergil, which must refer to Octavian, sway me more than the authority of Servius.[92] I ask you, expert in all areas, consider carefully these verses: "From this splendid source a Trojan Caesar will
be born, to limit his Empire by the Ocean, his fame by the stars,
Julius, a name descended from the great Iulus."[93] "From the great
Iulus" must be said of Caesar, before whom we have no record, at
least as far as I recall, of anyone who could be called great. "He too
will be addressed in prayers; then the harsh ages will grow mild
when wars have been put to rest; white-haired Trust, and Vesta,
and Quirinus with his brother Remus will make laws; and the
gates of war, grim with iron and tight fastenings, will be closed,"
and so on.[94] If anyone were to apply these to Caesar he would
seem to be taking leave of his senses, since Caesar's lifetime and
the years immediately after him were far removed from peace and
the quieting of arms; nor were the gates of war closed, but un-
barred, and free reign was given to unholy Fury.[95] Therefore these
verses do not pertain to Caesar's praise but to that of Augustus,
whose exaltation Vergil had taken upon himself.[96]

But this is unbearable, that Guarino commends the elections   61
bought by Caesar, as if this were permissible because the same was
often done by others. He asks *whether Caesar was the first to corrupt*
the voting tribes and elections, as if I had said that the only destructive

ego solum Caesarem dixerim fuisse civem perniciosum; qui, nisi
multos socios scelerum habuisset, numquam vires patriae superas-
set. At vero suasit *M. Cato, ut Caesar consulatu deiceretur, pecuniam
populo erogari.* Hoc iuste et sancte quaerebatur contra eum, a quo
aperte videbant conculcandam populi libertatem, qui nisi tum
consul fuisset,[241] stetisset res publica nec in tot miserias culpa
Caesaris incidisset. Itaque in Catone, libertatis propugnatore, qui
consilia Caesaris aperte ad interitum rei publicae spectare conspi-
ciebat, haec largitio laudatur; in eo autem, cuius animus ad dissensiones et ad prosternendam libertatem intentus[242] respiciebat,
vituperanda est ac detestanda. Neque vero, etiam si ceteri pecca-
bant, et in Caesare quoque peccandi libido est toleranda.

62   *Sed desperatis ac perditis*[243] *rebus* (inquit)[244] *cum nemo in Hispaniam
imperium accipere auderet, Scipio petere professus temeritatis damnatus est,
Livio teste.* Si Livius in ea parte non exstaret, forsan aliquos in errorem suum posset trahere Guarinus. Sed ipse Livius, ab eo testis
productus, ipsum[245] cogit esse mendacem! Credo videri tibi, Francisce, rem indignam, quae numquam dixit Livius pro veris in hanc
causam afferri. Verum considera Titi Livii verba, quae ex illo loco
hic descripsi, et an temeritatis vel accusatum vel damnatum Scipionem dicat, adverte.

63   Scipionem viginti et quattuor annos natum professum se petere
Hispaniam in superiore[246] loco constitisse[247] dicit, 'in quem, postquam omnium ora conversa sunt clamore ac favore, ominati[248]
extemplo sunt[249] felix faustumque imperium. Iussi deinde inire
suffragium, ad unum omnes — non centuriae modo, sed etiam
homines — P. Scipioni imperium esse in Hispania iusserunt.

citizen had been Caesar, who by himself would never have sapped the force of the fatherland if he had not had numerous accomplices in crime.[97] But in truth *Cato recommended that the people were given money to keep Caesar out of the consulship.*[98] This was justly and honorably asked against the man by whom they clearly saw that the liberty of the people would be trodden underfoot; had this man not then been consul, the republic would have stood and would not have fallen into so many miseries through the fault of Caesar. Hence in the case of Cato, the champion of liberty, who perceived that Caesar's plans blatantly spelled the end of the republic, this bribery is praiseworthy. However, in the case of the other man, whose mind was keenly turned toward dissensions and the overthrow of liberty, it deserves execration and hatred. Nor, in truth, even if others did wrong, should Caesar's lust for wrongdoing also be tolerated.

But when things were hopeless and desperate—he says—*since no one* 62 *dared to take up the command over Spain, Scipio, upon declaring his candidacy, was accused of recklessness, as Livy tells us.*[99] If Livy were not extant for this passage, perhaps Guarino might be able to lead some people into his error. But Livy himself, adduced by him as a witness, forces him to be a liar! I believe it seems a shameful business to you, Francesco, to bring into this case things which Livy never said on this matter instead of the truth. But consider Livy's words in this passage, which I have written out here, and pay attention to whether he says that Scipio was either accused or condemned for recklessness.

He says in the preceding section that it was certain that Scipio 63 declared that he was seeking the command over Spain when he was twenty-four years old, "and after all faces had been turned toward him, the people by their shouts and fervor immediately predicted a fortunate and auspicious command. Then, bidden to begin voting, not only every century but all to a man ordered that P. Scipio should hold the command in Spain. But after the matter

Ceterum post rem actam, ut iam resederat impetus animorum ardorque, silentium subito ortum et tacita[250] cogitatio, quidnam egissent novi; favorem plus valuisse quam rationem aetatis maxime paenitebat. Verum cum Scipio de sua aetate imperioque mandato magno et elato animo disseruisset, rursus[251] ardorem, qui resederat, excitavit ac renovavit implevitque homines certioris spei quam quantum fides promissi humani, aut ratio[252] et fiducia rerum subicere solet. Fuit enim Scipio non veris[253] tantum virtutibus mirabilis, sed arte quoque quadam ab iuventa in ostentationem earum compositus.'

64   Haec Livius, non Poggius narrat. Ubi ergo repperit Guarinus temeritatis nomen a Livio expressum? Nullum verbum non honorificum et cum summa Scipionis laude, quem veris virtutibus dicit esse admirabilem. Proferat, si potest, tantundem de Caesare scriptum: profitebor me e[254] causa cecidisse! Sed ubinam reperiet Caesarem in populo praemiis et muneribus non corrupto aliquod imperium adsecutum? Omnia per factiones et tumultum ac bonis repugnantibus Caesari concessa sunt,[255] quae Scipio sola virtute et boni imperatoris officio est adeptus.

65   Sed audi aliud erratum meum, ut fertur a Guarino. Scripsi in epistola de Caesare: *solus certe coniurationis* reos *conservandos censuit in senatu.* Duplici me errore arguit, quod *non solus censuit neque conservandos.* Id quemadmodum probet[256] inspiciamus, ut — si fieri potest — aliquid discamus ab hoc nostro tam aequo emendatore! *Non solus,* inquit, sed Decimus Silanus, Ti. Nero, Q. Cicero idem sentiebant. Sed contra eum est Sallustius, qui scribit 'Decimum Silanum, primum sententiam rogatum, decrevisse de iis,[257] qui in custodiis tenerentur, supplicium sumendum, eum

was complete, now that the impulse and ardor of their minds had subsided, there was a sudden silence and quiet reflection on what a revolutionary thing they had done: and they regretted most of all that partisanship had outweighed the consideration of age. But when Scipio had spoken about his age and the command entrusted to him with great and exalted spirit, he again aroused the ardor which had died down and renewed it and filled the men with a more assured hope than the amount that faith in a man's promise or reason and confidence in things are wont to inspire. For Scipio was remarkable not only for his true virtues but also, from his youth, by a certain skill adept at their display."[100]

This is what Livy reports, not Poggio. So where has Guarino 64 found the word "recklessness" used by Livy? There is no word that does not attribute honor and the greatest praise to Scipio, whom he says was admirable for his true virtues. Let him produce, if he can, so great a testimony written about Caesar: I will then declare that I have dropped out of the contest! But where on earth will he find that Caesar ever attained any command among a people uncorrupted by rewards and gifts? All things were granted to Caesar through partisanship and uproar and in defiance of the good men, which Scipio obtained by virtue alone and through his service as a good commander.

But hear another of my errors, as reported by Guarino. I wrote 65 in my letter about Caesar: *certainly he was the only one who counseled in the senate that* the defendants on the charge of *conspiracy should be saved.*[101] He accuses me of a double error, because *he was not the only one who counseled,* nor *that they should be saved.*[102] Let us examine how he proves this, so that we may, if possible, learn something from this corrector of ours, so fair-minded as he is! *Not him alone,* he says, *but Decimus Silanus, Tiberius Nero, and Q. Cicero thought the same.*[103] But against him stands Sallust, who writes: "that Decimus Silanus, first asked for his opinion, had counseled regarding those held in captivity that they should be punished, and that he later,

postea, permotum oratione C. Caesaris, in sententiam Ti. Neronis pedibus ivisse, qui praesidiis additis de ea re censuerat referendum.' Q. quoque Cicero Caesaris sententiam est secutus. Ergo solus Caesar censuit conservandos: Ti. Nero,[258] Decimus Silanus diversa decreverunt, cum alter praesidiis additis[259] referendum censuisset, alter pedibus dixisset[260] in eius sententiam se iturum. Q. vero Cicero non censuit, sed sententiam alterius secutus est. Hoc non solus Poggius, sed Sallustius mecum sentit; quem si intelligeret quid[261] dicat, cum legit Guarinus, me hoc labore supervacuo liberasset.

66   Accipe et alium maiorem Guarino et praestantiorem testem solum Caesarem censuisse servandos in coniuratione deprehensos. In epistola quadam ad Atticum[262] Cicero contra Bruti opinionem scribit: 'Catonem primum sententiam putat[263] de animadversione dixisse, quam omnes antea dixerant praeter Caesarem.' Ergo[264] primus et solus Caesar: nam, si qui sententiam mutarunt[265]— qui fuere perpauci—eius verbis adhaesere, non ipsi sententiam dixerunt. At etiam referens ceteros secuturos fuisse Caesarem, *nisi labantem senatum confirmasset M. Catonis oratio*, 'labantem' exponit: hoc est *in opinionem Caesaris consentientem*. Si ita suos discipulos instruit Guarinus, multis illos[266] implicat erroribus et linguae Latinae reddit[267] ignaros! 'Labare' enim 'titubare' et 'dubitare' est; 'consentire' vero[268] 'aliquid'[269] adprobare' et 'sentire cum altero.' Dubitabat senatus quae parricidis esset[270] poena inroganda: scelus coniuratorum ultimum supplicium requirebat, oratio Caesaris animos hominum commoverat; dubitantem[271] igitur senatum, quid potissimum ageret, M. Catonis oratio confirmavit.

swayed by Caesar's speech, said that he would vote for the opinion of Tiberius Nero, who had advised that the matter be reopened once the guards had been increased."[104] Q. Cicero also followed the opinion of Caesar. Hence only Caesar advised that they be saved: Tiberius Nero and Decimus Silanus thought otherwise, since the one had advised that the matter be reopened when the guards had been increased, and the other had said that he would vote for his opinion. Q. Cicero did not propose anything but followed the opinion of another man. This is not only Poggio's view, but Sallust agrees with me; and if Guarino had understood what he said when he read him, he would have saved me from this unnecessary effort.

Read also another greater and more outstanding witness than 66
Guarino, to the effect that only Caesar counseled that those apprehended in the conspiracy should be saved. In a certain letter to Atticus, Cicero wrote, against Brutus' view: "He thinks that Cato gave his opinion about the punishment first, before all except Caesar had given theirs."[105] Hence Caesar was the first and the only one, for, if any men changed their minds — and they were very few — they clung to his words, but did not themselves give an opinion. But even when reporting that the others would have followed Caesar, *had not the speech of Cato steadied the wavering senate,* he explains "wavering": that is, *agreeing with the opinion of Caesar.*[106] If this is how Guarino instructs his pupils, he ensnares them in many errors and makes them ignorant of the Latin language! For "wavering" means "hesitating" and "being in two minds"; "agreeing" on the other hand means "approving of something" and "having the same opinion as another." The senate hesitated as to what punishment was to be imposed upon the murderers: the crime of conspiracy demanded the ultimate punishment; Caesar's speech had moved the men's minds; so the senate, hesitating as to what to do, was steadied in its resolve by M. Cato's speech.

67   Id autem inconsideratius a me dictum disputat, quod scripserim[272] conservandos censuisse. *An qui[273] coniuratos, publicatis eorum
pecuniis* (inquit) *in vinculis habendos censuit, per dedecus et infamiam
notatos, conservare voluit, id est salvos esse contendit? Quis ita Latine loquitur, ut, qui intra carcerem in[274] asperitatem vitae,[275] in duros corporis
cruciatus, in salutis desperationem quempiam intruserit, saluti et conservationi consuluisse dicatur?* Pudet me iam tantam Guarinum[276] Latinae
linguae inscitiam prae se ferre, qui, si ita reliquos docet ut scribit,
iam per me illis pecunias restituat licebit! Tecum loquor, Francisce,
qui es in Latinis peritissimus: verborum significationem rite per-
pendens, 'servare' et 'conservare,' ut nosti, idem ferme significant,
prout 'scribere' et 'conscribere' multaque praeterea, in quibus ea
praepositio ad ornatum quandoque magis[277] additur quam ad mu-
tandam verbi significationem.

68   Civica corona mos erat donare eum, qui civem servasset:[278] non
quia bona aut fortunae servata essent, sed quia civem vendicasset a
morte. Scis quoque 'servos' esse a 'servando'[279] appellatos: qui enim
in acie ab interitu servabantur, dicebantur servi; et[280] tamen ii[281] in
carceribus, in compedibus, in ergastulis nudi, in fame et siti rerumque omnium[282] inopia vivebant, verberibus[283] quoque et loris
torquebantur saepius; et tamen servati erant et ad miserias et diros[284] cruciatus.[285] Hos[286] ergo Guarini modo nequaquam servos,
hoc est 'servatos,' dici oportet! Ego, qui hoc verbum satis nossem,
dixi recte conservandos illum censuisse—hoc est ab interitu prae-
senti eripiendos—quo Silanus dignos decreverat coniuratos. Guarinus autem, dummodo mecum litiget, dummodo eloquentiam et
dicendi artem ostentet, quid loquatur aut sentiat non advertit.[287]

But he considers that I spoke rather carelessly when I wrote   67
that Caesar counseled that they be preserved. *Did someone, says he,
who counseled that the conspirators, their money confiscated, be held in
chains, marked by shame and infamy—did he want to save them, that is
advocate that they be unharmed? Who speaks such Latin that he who has
cast another man into a dungeon, into a harsh life and rigorous bodily torments with no hope of salvation—that he is said to have taken counsel for
his well-being and preservation?*[107] I am ashamed that Guarino now
parades such ignorance of the Latin language that, if he instructs
others the same way that he writes, as far as I am concerned, he
should give them their money back! I am talking with you, Francesco, as you are most skilled in Latin: if one duly weighs the
meaning of words, "to save" and "to preserve" mean almost the
same, as you know, just like "to write" and "to write down" and
many others besides, in which the preposition is added more for
the sake of ornament than to alter the meaning of the word.[108]

It was the custom to give a civic crown to him who had saved a   68
citizen from death: not because their goods or fortune were preserved, but because he had redeemed a citizen from death. You
know, too, that "slaves" (*servi*) are so called from "to (pre)serve": for
those who were preserved from death in battle were called slaves;
and even though they lived in dungeons and shackles and work-
houses, naked and in hunger and thirst and scarcity of all things,
and were frequently tormented with whips and leather straps, still
they had been preserved both for miseries and dire tortures.[109]
Those men therefore, if we follow Guarino's mode of argumentation, cannot in any way fittingly be called slaves, that is to say,
those who are preserved! I, who know this word quite well, rightly
said that Caesar counseled that they be preserved, that is be
snatched away from an imminent death, which Silanus had judged
the conspirators to merit. Yet Guarino, provided that he can quarrel with me and vaunt his eloquence and speaking skills, pays no
attention to what he says or means.

69   At ego, si vellem meo more secum agere, si non parcerem ami-
cmeo tiae, excuterem sibi fortasse[288] hanc inanem iactantiam, qua nimium tumet; docerem me *non inconsiderate, non subdole, non petulan-
ter, non venenose* (ut calumniatur)[289] scripsisse, sed vere, graviter,
mature neque cedere Guarino in cognitione linguae Latinae. Nam
si quid[290] priores de Caesare senserint sique quid mihi de eo sen-
tiendum videretur expressi — relinquens ceteris quid vellent liberum arbitrium sentiendi — quod officium, quae partes fuerunt
Guarini maledictis suis me lacessere? Ego in epistola mea neminem laesi, nullius extimationem[291] offendi; protuli quae legeram
sine cuiusquam, qui nunc exstet, contumelia. At Guarinus, tamquam nactus amplam materiam, in qua effunderet vires suas,[292]
iniit mecum certamen minime necessarium. Nisi tamen me animus fallit, reddetur sibi beneficium pro meritis suis!

70   Verum quid ego de me[293] querar, cum tanta sit superbia, ut solus post hominum memoriam Caesare excepto scribere audeat
contra M. Catonem, quem omnes, qui umquam fuerunt, summis
laudibus prosecuti sunt et tamquam virum sanctissimum celebrarunt? Dies me deficeret si omnia, quae a variis auctoribus in eius
laudem scripta comperi, vellem stilo comprehendere! Sed quaedam
postea recensebuntur. Hic autem novus morum censor, hic M.
Catonis emendator, hic non tertius, ut Iuvenalis inquit,[294] sed
quartus Cato, quid de Catone scripserit, ausculta.[295] *Importunum*
dicit, *pervicacem, morosum et dignum, qui potius*[296] *Cynicorum aut Stoicorum angulis et altercationibus quam in Romana re publica versaretur;*
eundem *fero vel ferreo potius ingenio pertinacem, inexorabilem, belli civilis
instigatorem atque altorem* appellat; *naturam immitem ac scaevam*[297]
magna discrepantia, infirmitate, inconstantia fuisse adfirmat; vitam non
probat, mortem improbat, repudium arguit uxoris.

Truly, if I wanted to deal with him in my own way, if I were not   69
to spare our friendship, I would perhaps shake this inane boastful-
ness out of him, with which he is so inordinately puffed up; I
would teach him that I did not write *carelessly or deceitfully or inso-
lently or venomously*, as he slanderously declares, but truthfully, seriously, and maturely, and that I do not yield to Guarino in my
knowledge of the Latin language.[110] For if I have expressed what
my predecessors thought about Caesar, or what I thought I should
hold about him, leaving to others their judgment free to think as
they please, what duty, what role was there for Guarino to harass
me with his abuse? I did not hurt anyone in my letter, I did not
dent anyone's reputation, I reported what I had read without any
abuse of any living soul. But Guarino, as though he had stumbled
upon ample material for pouring out his strength, entered into a
wholly unnecessary contest with me. But unless I am mistaken, he
will have the favor returned to him according to his deserts!

But why do I complain about myself, since his arrogance is such   70
that he alone in the memory of man, barring Caesar, dares to
write against M. Cato, whom all men who have ever lived have
decorated with the highest praises and celebrated as a most saintly
man? The daylight would run out on me if I wished to encompass
with my pen everything that I have found written by various authors in his praise! A number, however, will be reviewed later. But
this new censor of morals, this corrector of M. Cato, this not
third, as Juvenal said, but fourth Cato: hear what he has written
about Cato.[111] He calls him *harsh, obstinate, cheerless, and worthy of
going about the corners and heated disputes of the Cynics and Stoics rather
than in the Roman republic*; and again *with a fierce or rather iron nature*;[112] *instigator and fosterer of the civil war*,[113] and asserts that *his
nature was pitiless and perverse through incongruity, weakness and changeability*.[114] He does not approve of his life, disapproves of his death,
and finds fault with his rejection of his wife.[115]

71   Denique eo amentiae progreditur, ut Catonem lenonibus comparet Guarinus et, ut suis maledictis aliquam adferat auctoritatem, Plutarchi testimonium introducit, qui, si recte verba sua inspiciat, summis laudibus effert Catonem. Quid enim uberius a Plutarcho dici potuit quam *Catonis mores* — ut Guarinus transfert — *qui in vitas corruptas et mores improbos incidissent, ingentem sibi extimationem*[298] *et gloriam vendicasse?* Dicit insuper *non habuisse illum mores faciles persuasu aut multitudini amabiles.* Ergo Guarinus improbat mores, quos multitudo non commendat! Non legit aut non meminit multitudinem omnem exsuperantiam virtutis odisse neque etiam quantum Cicero et Seneca pluribus in locis multitudinis iudicium probent?

72   Sed (ut redeamus ad causam Catonis) non sum ego ille, qui sentiam in me tantam dicendi esse facultatem, ut audeam Catonis patrocinium sumere. Verum, ut prior Cato se ipsum vivens defendit adversus suos[299] accusatores, sic ipse posterior, exsurgens a mortuis, se ipsum tueatur adversus hunc novum calumniatorem suum. Exsurgat igitur atque astans[300] nobis illa sua prisca et severa gravitate, qua populum Romanum in ludis commovit, cum hoc novello accusatore sic agat: 'Quid tu, Guarine, quid tu, inquam, solus omnium, Guarine Veronensis, qua scientia, quo rerum usu, qua virtute, quibus facultatibus, qua confidentia mortuum accusas atque oppugnas, quem vivum[301] populus Romanus tanta habuit in reverentia, ut eius dicta pro sententiis iudicaret? Quid tu non erubescis solus inimicum Caesarem maledicendo imitari? At ille fortassis aut odio mei, aut splendore nominis, aut laudatione[302] Ciceronis, aut dicendi facilitate permotus[303] experiri voluit, quid contra Tullium posset eloquentia. Tu nulla in re a me offensus, nullius eloquentiae praesidio fulctus,[304] dicacitate tua me lacessere[305] voluisti. Quanto melius tacuisses!

Finally Guarino goes so far in his folly that he compares Cato   71
to a pimp, and, so as to lend some authority to his slanders, brings
in the account of Plutarch, who, if one were to read his words
properly, extols Cato with the highest praises. What indeed could
be said by Plutarch more fulsomely than that *the character of Cato,*
as Guarino translates, *met with corrupt lives and impure morals, and
won enormous praise?*[116] Furthermore, he says *that he had a character
not easy to promote or pleasing to the masses.*[117] So Guarino disapproves of a character that is not recommended by the masses! Did
he not read, or has he forgotten, that the masses hate all preeminence in virtue, nor indeed how much store Cicero and Seneca
repeatedly set by the judgment of the multitude?

But to return to Cato's cause, I am not one to feel that I have in   72
me such skill in speaking that I dare take up Cato's defense.
Rather, just as in earlier times, when alive, Cato used to defend
himself against his accusers, so now, in these later times, let him
rise from the dead and defend himself against his new slanderer.
Let him rise, then, and, assisting us, deal with that ancient and
severe gravity of his, with which he moved the Roman people during the games, let him deal as follows with this new petty accuser:
"Why do you, Guarino, why do you, I say, alone of all mankind,
Guarino of Verona, with what knowledge, what experience of affairs, what virtue, what abilities, and what confidence, accuse and
attack a dead man, whom, when he was alive, the Roman people
held in such reverence, that they took his words for judgments?[118]
Why do you not blush that you alone imitate his enemy Caesar in
slandering him? But perhaps Caesar was driven by hatred of me,
or by the luster of my name, or by Cicero's eulogy, or by his skill
in speaking to want to test what he could achieve with his eloquence against Cicero. You, though offended by me in no respect,
and not supported by any protection of eloquence, wanted to vex
me with your raillery. How much better if you had been silent!

73   'Non mihi curae haec sunt, cuius gloria altius ac maiori robore
fixa est quam ut tuis vocibus conquassari queat. Tibi respicio,
quem longius efferri video studio obloquendi[306] quam tua auctoritas patiatur. Sed quid tu, Guarine, quam umquam philosophiae
portiunculam[307] degustasti, ut Stoicorum sectam non probes?
Quae tua est temeritas, te,[308] qui ne extremis quidem labiis umquam philosophorum aliquod genus degustasti, reprobare Stoicorum disciplinam? Me Cynicorum disputationibus quam Romana
re publica digniorem fuisse dicis? Vide ne Cynicorum aliquis rabi-
dus te momorderit, qui te redegerit ad insaniam! Ego honestum
rebus omnibus praetuli, ego virtutem solam colui, ego tibi et ceteris recte sentiendi recteque vivendi verum iter ostendi, ego virtutem hominum esse[309] supra fortunam meo exemplo monstravi, ego
nefariis civibus semper[310] obstiti, libertatem patriae plus posse
quam unum aliquem volui; in quo si mecum ceteri[311] sensissent,
iste tuus Caesar inter sua flagitia[312] poenas patriae dedisset. Ego
patrias leges, iura, libertatem defendi, quae, postquam unius potentia exstincta sunt, mori malui quam servire.

74   'Verum quae tibi mecum est contentio? Si iniquitatem victoris
Caesaris[313] probas, quid mihi molestus es? Si servire mavis[314]
quam liber esse, quid mecum pugnas, qui superesse Romanae nolui[315] libertati? Quid autem, Guarine, tu, qui nulla in re publica es
versatus, qui nullum umquam munus cuiusquam liberae civitatis[316]
attigisti, quid Romanae rei publicae conduceret melius quam Cato
cognosti? Tu civilis belli originem, cuius me *instigatorem atque
altorem* insimulas, melius quam Cato percepisti? Quid de rebus
tibi incognitis et a tua prudentia remotis ausus es sententiam proferre? Numquid Suetonius, numquid Plutarchus, numquid ceteri,

"To me these things are of no concern, since my glory is secured   73
at a higher level and with greater strength than for it to be able to
be shaken by your words. But I am mindful of you, since I see you
are carried further in your zeal for contradicting than your authority permits. But tell me, Guarino, what little portion of philosophy have you ever tasted so as to disapprove of the Stoic school?
What is your rashness that you, who have not even with the tip of
your tongue tasted any school of philosophers, disapprove of the
teachings of the Stoics? Do you claim that I was more suited to
the disputations of the Cynics than of the Roman state? Beware
lest some rabid Cynic has bitten you and reduced you to insanity![119] I put what was morally right above everything else, I cultivated virtue alone, I showed you and the others the true path for
living and thinking correctly, I showed by my example that men's
virtue rises above fortune, I always resisted wicked citizens, I
wished for the liberty of the fatherland to outweigh any single individual, and if others had agreed with me on this matter, that
Caesar of yours with his outrages would have paid the penalty to
the fatherland. I defended the ancestral laws, justice, and liberty,
and after they were extinguished by the power of one man, I preferred to die rather than to be a slave.

"What, in truth, is your bone of contention with me? If you   74
approve of the iniquities of Caesar in his victory, why do you
trouble me? If you would rather be a slave than be free, why do
you fight with me, who refused to outlive the liberty of Rome?
But why do you, Guarino, who were never involved in government, who have never touched any task of a free city, why do you
know better than Cato what would have been fitting for the Roman state? Did you understand the source of the Civil War, of
which you pretend that I was the *instigator and fosterer*, better than
Cato did?[120] Why did you dare to pronounce judgment on matters
unknown to you and far removed from your experience? Did Suetonius or Plutarch or the others who wrote about that war, fatal to

qui de bello isto[317] funesto patriae scripsere, numquid ipse inimicus Caesar in suis commentariis hoc scriptum reliquerunt? Unde haec tua exoritur nova calumnia? Ciceronem, credo, sequi te putasti, qui mecum iocatus est in defensione Murenae; at si quid est Ciceroni et civi et mihi amicissimo in defendendo alterius capite concessum, id sibi maledicendo adsumet homo incognitus ac peregrinus? Cum ergo causam susceperis gravem, iniquam atque imparem tuis viribus, corrige te, oro, ne ab aliis castigeris, et tibi parce, tuo quoque[318] honori consule, quem, si in sententia perseverabis, omnes stultissimum iudicabunt.' Sed iam Catonem loquentem dimittamus.

75   Nescio, mi Francisce, saepius mecum recogitans animadvertere, quod fuerit[319] Guarini propositum scribere tam turpiter contra Catonem, qui est habitus ab omnibus et vivens et mortuus vir sanctissimus, siquidem Cicero noster in oratione, quae est *Pro domo sua ad pontifices*, prudentissimum virum, sanctissimum, fortissimum, rei publicae amicissimum scribit, virtute, consilio, ratione,[320] vita mirabili ad laudem prope singulari.[321] Seneca omnibus in locis Catonem[322] laudibus effert singularibus. In libro vero *De tranquillitate animi* Catonem 'virtutum veram imaginem' appellat. Sed quid ego in singulis versor? Nullum adfirmo linguae Latinae auctorem, nullum poetam, historicum, oratorem, nullum scriptorem rerum esse dico, qui maledictis Catonem incesseret, praeter unicum Guarinum.

76   Admodum tamen admiror[323] eum non legisse Sallustium in eo loco, quo Catonis et Caesaris quaedam fit vitae et morum comparatio; qui ait Catonem magnum haberi integritate vitae, constantiam laudari, ut iam paenitere debeat Guarinum contra Sallustii verba vocasse Catonem inconstantem. Catoni praeterea (inquit) studium modestiae, decoris, sed maxime severitatis erat; cum

the fatherland, or did even hostile Caesar himself in his *Commentaries* leave this written down? Whence does this new slander of yours arise? You thought, I suppose, that you were following Cicero, who jested with me in his defense of Murena. But if something is allowed to Cicero, a fellow citizen and great friend of mine, in defending another man on a capital charge, will an unknown foreigner claim the same right for himself when engaged in slanders? Since, therefore, you have taken up a serious case, an unfair one, to which your powers are unequal, I beg you, set yourself right, so as not to be castigated by others. Spare yourself and consider your own honor as well, since, if you persist in this opinion, everyone will judge you foolish in the extreme." But let us now bid farewell to Cato as a speaker.

I fail to see, my Francesco, though I was frequently thinking the   75
matter over, what Guarino's purpose was in writing so shamefully against Cato, who has been held by all to be a most saintly man, both in life and in death, especially seeing that our Cicero, in his speech *On His House before the Pontiffs*, writes that he was an extremely wise, saintly, and gallant man and very patriotic, of remarkable virtue, counsel, reason, and way of life, uniquely praiseworthy as it was. In every passage Seneca exalts Cato with exceptional praise. Indeed in his book *On Peace of Mind* he calls Cato "the true likeness of virtue."[121] But why do I linger on instances? I declare that there is no Latin author, no poet, no historian, no orator, no reporter of events who assailed Cato with abuse, apart from Guarino alone.[122]

Still I wonder greatly that he has not read Sallust in the passage   76
in which there is a certain comparison of the life and character of Cato and Caesar. Sallust says that Cato was held to be great for his incorruptible life and praised for his constancy, so that Guarino must rue the fact that he called Cato *inconstant*, contrary to the words of Sallust.[123] Furthermore, he says that Cato had a zeal for moderation, propriety, but especially for severity: he competed

strenuo[324] virtute,[325] cum honesto pudore,[326] cum innocente abstinentia[327] certabat; esse quam videri bonus malebat. Non est hoc in
loco ampliori oratione aut pluribus testibus opus ad defensionem
Catonis. Ut enim refert beatus Hieronymus Livium scripsisse,
'tanta fuit eius virtus, ut eius gloriae neque profuerit quisquam
laudando, nec vituperando nocuerit, cum utrumque summis praediti fecerint[328] ingeniis,' M. Ciceronem et C. Caesarem signifi-
cans,[329] 'quorum alter laudes[330] scripsit, alter vituperationem.'

77   Convertit se deinceps Guarinus ad bellum Alexandrinum mag-
nificandum; qua in parte, tamquam mecum congressurus, iterum
me compellat, *stare iubet, neque gradum referre*. Me admodum timi-
dum suspicatur; stare vult, ne, si acie abiero, hanc suam dicendi
palmulam amittat! Sed tota aberrat via. Non solum non disce-
dentem videbit, sed inferentem gradum et longius[331] in aciem pro-
deuntem! Interrogat sitne imperatoris decus *primum cum fortissimis
ducibus, robustissimis militibus, ingentibus copiis terra marique pedestres
navalesque pugnas summo cum periculo administrasse*. Risi verborum
iactantiam, nulla cum re admodum resonantem! Sed cum haec
omnia, quae Guarinus complectitur, concesserim, quid ad Caesaris decus conferunt?[332] Qui enim fuerunt hi[333] fortissimi duces,
robustissimi milites, ingentes hostium copiae?[334] Silentio praeteri-
tur[335] a Guarino;[336] cui ne[337] si suos solitos testes produceret, credendum esset, nedum sua[338] somnia referenti.

78   Quid autem adeo illum resonans verborum amplitudo et magni-
ficentia delectat, ut, cum plurima ampullosa verba protulerit admiratione digna, nihil probet, nihil certi adferat praeter stupendum
quendam sonitum tympanorum? At ea probare se forsan putat,
cum refert Suetonii verba: 'bellum sane difficillimum gessit neque
loco neque tempore aequo, sed hieme anni et intra moenia

with the energetic in virtue, with the honorable in decency, with the pure in abstinence; he wanted to be rather than seem good.[124] No more copious words, nor more numerous witnesses are needed here for Cato's defense. As indeed the blessed Jerome reports that Livy wrote, "'his virtue was such, that no one advanced his glory by praising it or harmed it by detracting from it, since two men gifted with the highest genius"—by which he meant M. Cicero and C. Caesar—"had done both, the former writing his praises, the latter an invective."[125]

After that, Guarino turns to exalt the Alexandrian War, and in this section, as if he is about to clash with me, he again addresses me and orders me to *stand my ground and not step back*. He suspects that I am quite timid; he wants me to stand fast lest, if I leave the line of battle, he lose his pathetic little palm for oratory! But he totally loses his way. Not only will he not see me leave, but he will see me stepping forward and advancing further into the fray! He questions whether it is *the main glory of a general to conduct infantry and naval battles with very strong commanders, most vigorous soldiers, and great armies, on land and on sea—and to conduct them amid the gravest danger*.[126] I laughed at that empty display of words that does not resonate with any content! But if I were to grant all these things which Guarino embraces, what do they contribute to Caesar's glory? Who indeed were these bravest commanders, strongest soldiers, and great hosts of enemies? This is passed over in silence by Guarino, who should not even be believed when he calls his usual witnesses, let alone when he reports his own dreams.

Why indeed does this resounding abundance of words and grandiloquence please him so much that, while he comes up with many bombastic words worthy of wonder, he does not prove them, and offers nothing reliable except some stupefying beating of drums? But perhaps he thinks he is proving them when he reports Suetonius' words: "*He waged an extremely difficult war on hostile terrain and at an unfavorable time, since it was winter and he was within*

77

78

copiosissimi ac sollertissimi hostis, inops ipse omnium rerum atque imparatus.' Sed, o magnam laudem imperatorem quempiam (ut Caesarem omittamus) inopem omnium rerum atque[339] imparatum, bellum aliquod suscepisse, neque loco neque tempore aequo! Fuitne haec imperatoria prudentia et calliditas, an summa stultitia ac temeritas? Hac tamen re bellum fuit difficillimum: quod Alexandriam se contulit Caesar imparatus, non tamquam ad bellicosum, sed pacatum locum accessurus, nullas timens[340] insidias; quod cum secus evenisset, neque loco neque tempore bellum suscipere coactus est.

79   Verum qui fuerunt hi *duces fortissimi?* Cur non nominantur? Hannibal, credo, aut Pyrrhus! Duo vilissimi spadones, et Ptolemaeus, puer belli inscius, qui nunquam castra[341] viderat. *Robustissimos milites* novo more[342] appellat Aegyptios, gentem infidam atque imbellem; quoniam vero legit 'copiosissimi ac sollertissimi hostis' ingentes copias dictum, auguratur et *fortissimos duces.* Nandi peritiam in Caesare extollit. At ea piscatorum laus esse solet, non imperatorum!

80   Redit iterum tamquam in arcem tutissimam ad clementiam Caesaris, in qua[343] admodum vires suas extendit. Me obtrectatorem Caesaris dicit, et Ciceronem non admodum probare[344] in iis,[345] quae loquitur de Caesaris clementia. Dixi antea Caesarem clementissime usum civili victoria; Ciceronem vero[346] me non probare minus vere (ne[347] dicam leviter[348]) scribit. Verba profert ex oratione Marcellina additque non fuisse causam cur Cicero vellet mentiri, cum, posteaquam actae essent causae, scriberentur. At ego iterum confirmo verba illa temporis et causae fuisse,[349] non hominis, sicut et ipse in alia oratione scribit, 'orationes suas causarum et temporum esse, non hominum nec patronorum. Nam si causae

the walls of a numerous and very crafty enemy, and was himself without
resources of any kind and ill-prepared."[127] Oh, what great praise for
any commander, not to mention Caesar, to have undertaken a war
without any resources and ill-prepared, with neither terrain nor
season favorable! Was that a commander's foresight and skills, or
the height of folly and rashness? The war was extremely difficult
for this reason: because Caesar came to Alexandria ill-prepared, as
if he was going to a pacified place rather than one at war, and fearing no ambushes; and when it turned out differently, he was forced
to undertake a war at neither the right place nor the right season.

But who were these *very strong commanders?*[128] Why are they not   79
named? Hannibal or Pyrrhus, I suppose! Two paltry eunuchs, and
Ptolemy, a boy ignorant of war, who had never seen an army
camp.[129] He calls the Egyptians, innovatively, *most vigorous soldiers,*
although they were a treacherous and unwarlike people; but since
he reads words about vast hosts of a "numerous and very crafty
enemy," he divines *very strong commanders* too.[130] He lauds Caesar's
skill in swimming. But that is thes customary praise for fishermen,
not for generals!

He returns again, as if to the safest stronghold, to Caesar's   80
clemency, on which topic he overstretches his strength. He claims
that I am a detractor of Caesar and insufficiently endorse Cicero
when he speaks of Caesar's clemency. I have said before that Caesar employed his victory in the civil war in the most merciful manner; but that I do not approve of Cicero, Guarino writes less truly,
not to say capriciously. He cites words from the oration for Marcellus and adds that there was no reason why Cicero might have
wanted to lie, since they were written down only after the arguments were concluded.[131] But I once more assert that these words
belonged to a specific time and case, not to a man, just as Cicero
himself writes in another speech that "speeches belong to their
specific cases and times, not to the men of which they speak nor
even to their advocates. For if cases could speak for themselves, no

ipsae per se loqui possent, nemo adhiberet oratorem!' Sed, cum quid sentiret de Caesare expressit, crudelem tyrannum, temerarium hominem perditum appellavit.

81   Ego tamen Senecae adsentior, qui ait: 'dedit vitam Caesar Pompeio paene,[350] si dat qui non aufert.' Itaque clementia sola est non fuisse crudelem! Nam clementiam dicimus cum quis parcit[351] ei, a quo est 'lacessitus iniuria.' Qui vero se, qui sua, qui patriam, qui libertatem defendebant: qua iniuria afficiebant Caesarem? Qui servitutis iugum recusabant,[352] quid committebant, cur poenam mererentur? Qui me nuper ceperunt praedones clementissimi dicendi sunt, qui, cum bona[353] eripuissent, vitae et sanguini pepercerunt? Laudat insuper Caesarem quod, deprehensis Pompeii et item Scipionis scrineis epistolarum, illas non legerit. Ego quoque id factum laudi tribuo. Neque enim is sum, qui dixerim nulla in re Caesarem laudandum, sed Scipioni virtute non comparandum. Ego multarum rerum laudes in eum confero, sed multo plures[354] in Scipionem. In Caesare maxima flagitia fuisse affirmo, nulla in Scipione.

82   Amorem Cleopatrae defendit etiam me consentiente longiori quam opus est sermone. Refert amorem Herculis et deorum, quasi peccantium multitudo peccatum defendat. Me versum amatorium decantare solitum scribit, quem ego neque legi umquam neque ab aliis prolatum audivi. *Scipionem Africanum irretitum amoribus* (ait) *domesticae ancillae.* Hac in re manifestus est mendax! Non enim Vulcani retibus captum Latini tradunt, sed dissimulatum ab uxore, cum intellexisset ancillam gratam Scipioni, ut Valerius refert. Gratus est mihi Guarinus, et tamen cum eo non est mihi turpis

one would use an orator!"[132] Yet, when he said what he really thought of Caesar, he called him a cruel tyrant and a reckless, irredeemable man.[133]

But I do agree with Seneca, who says: "Caesar practically gave   81
life to Pompey, if he gives something who does not take it away."[134] So it is clemency merely not to be cruel! For we call it clemency when someone extends his mercy to a man by whom he has been "injuriously provoked."[135] But those who were defending themselves, their goods, their fatherland, and liberty, with what injury were they afflicting Caesar? Those who refused the yoke of slavery, what were they doing wrong, why were they deserving of punishment? Those pirates who recently seized me, should they be called merciful because, although they carried off my goods, they spared my life's blood?[136] Moreover, he praises Caesar because, although he captured the letter cases of Pompey and likewise of Scipio, he did not read the letters they contained. I also consider this a laudable deed. Nor indeed am I the kind of person would say that Caesar does not deserve to be praised in any respect at all, only that he is not to be compared with Scipio in virtue. I attribute praise to him for many matters, but more still to Scipio. My point is that in Caesar there were very great outrages, but none in Scipio.

Guarino defends Caesar's love for Cleopatra, even though I   82
agree, with a longer speech than is called for. He speaks of the love of Hercules and of the gods, as though the number of sinners vindicates the sin. He writes that I used to sing a line of a love poem which I have never read and never heard recited by others. He says that *Scipio Africanus was ensnared by love for a domestic slave*: on this issue he is a blatant liar![137] For the Latin authors do not report that he was caught in the net of Vulcan, but that his wife covered for him, when she understood that the slave was pleasing to Scipio, as Valerius Maximus relates.[138] Guarino is pleasing to me, and yet I do not have any filthy amorous commerce with him.

amoris commercium! Quae est haec perversitas *irretitum amore*
scribere eum, cui gratam ancillam fuisse dicunt[355] idque solum
uxori notum? Formosam vero fuisse Cleopatram, ubi legerit nescio, cum contrarium Plutarchus scribat; ancillam autem defor-
mem, oculis noster Guarinus est plus quam lynceis: illi enim ultra
montes videre existimantur, huius acutior visus,[356] qui ultra mille
et quingentos annos mulierum formas[357] conspexerit![358]

83   Quod autem mihi condolet imminutam esse meam, quae
nulla[359] est, auctoritatem, propter eam quam scripsi epistolam, et
me ait maturius quae dixerim advertere debuisse: ego sibi hanc[360]
curam remitto, cum satis sibi futurum sit suam tueri et eius matu-
ritatem, quae iam in putredinem vergit, sibi[361] concedo. Scripsi
Gallos, quos domuit Caesar, gentem feram ac barbaram, sed bello
insuetam. Is contra arguit, multisque testibus causam suam[362] firmare se credit. Refert virtutem Gallorum, Italiam ab eis saepius
bello lacessitam, Graeciam, Thraciam, Asiam suis armis perdomi-
tam. Haec cum multa verbositate recitavit, me succubuisse existimat. At doceat oportet aut Gallos, quos armis exercitos, quos
vastasse Italiam et reliquas provincias dicit, eos fuisse, quos Caesar
subegit; aut eos, quos superavit, inter se aut cum vicinis bella gessisse. Quod cum neque agat, neque, si velit, possit ostendere, non
me deceptum constat (ut ait) sed se ineptum, qui tam[363] rudibus
argumentis utitur, tam multos testes, qui nihil sibi opitulantur,
ascribit.

84   At *Etruriae fines usque ad primam Tiberis ripam protendi* scripsit.
Vellem ad medium saltem flumen dixisset,[364] ne Etruscos parte

What perversity is it to write that a man is *ensnared by love* when they say that a slave girl is pleasing to him, and that this was known only to his wife?[139] Where he read that Cleopatra was pretty I do not know, since Plutarch writes the opposite, but that the slave girl was ugly, well, with his eyesight our Guarino surpasses lynxes: for those are deemed to be able to see across mountains, but his vision is sharper still, since he has seen the beauty of women across fifteen-hundred years![140]

As to the fact that he commiserates with me that my authority, 83 which is in any case nonexistent, has diminished on account of the letter that I wrote, and tells me that I should have considered what I said with more mature reflection: I return to him that same concern, since it will be enough for him to look after his own authority, and I grant him his maturity, which is already tending toward rot. I wrote that the Gauls, whom Caesar subdued, were a fierce and savage people, but unaccustomed to war. He argues against this and believes that he is supporting his case with many witnesses: he recalls the courage of the Gauls, the fact that Italy was frequently vexed by them in war, and that Greece, Thrace, and Asia were conquered by their arms. These things he has recited with great wordiness, and reckons that I have succumbed. But it behooves him to teach us either that the Gauls, whom he says were practiced in arms and laid waste to Italy and other provinces, were the same as those whom Caesar subjected, or that those whom he overcame had fought wars among themselves or with their neighbors. Since he neither argues this nor could demonstrate it even if he wanted to, it is clear that I have not been caught out, as he puts it, but rather that he is incompetent in using such crude arguments, and in adding so many witnesses who do not help his case at all.

He wrote that *the territory of the Etruscans extended to the first bank* 84 *of the Tiber.* I wish he had said "at least to the middle of the river," so as not to have deprived the Etruscans of the share of the water

aquae eis debitae privasset! Nullum insuper peritum dubitare dicit, quin *Etruria quasi heteros horos*[365] *(id est finis alter)* dicatur. Ergo imperitus Plinius Secundus, qui in *Cosmographia* sua inquit: 'adnectitur inde septima regio, in qua Etruria est ab amne Macra, ipsa mutatis saepe nominibus. Umbros exegere inde antiquitus Pelasgi, hos Lydi, a[366] quorum rege Tyrrheni, mox a sacrifico ritu lingua Graecorum Tusci sunt cognominati.' Stultus quoque M. Varro, qui eam a Ture cognominatam putat.

85   Ego insuper, licet sim omnibus in rebus indoctior, tamen ad hanc superstitiosam Etruriae interpretationem mea sponte rudis esse nolo,[367] neque credere Etruriam ab altero fine appellatam. Cum enim alter duorum sit partitivum, cur magis ab uno quam a duobus finibus cognominatur? Cur magis[368] a ripa Tiberis quam Macrae, quamvis non duobus, sed quattuor finibus clauditur Tuscia? Deliramenta quaedam somniantium haec videntur, non interpretationes! Etruscos et Tuscos idem esse dico, duabus tantum litteris additis, eadem verbi origine. 'Fluentiam' a fluente Arno antiqui appellabant, 'Florentiam' posteriores dixere, altera immutata[369] littera, altera addita. Et tamen est eadem verbi origo. Simili modo 'Pisaurum' olim, nunc 'Pensaurum'[370] dici videmus multaque alia duplici nomine[371] prolata, quorum alterum ab altero defluxit.

86   Rursus reflectit se ad *libertatem Romanam*, quam defensam et *auctam* litigat *a Caesare.* Superioribus neque[372] Marii, neque Sullae temporibus dicit fuisse aliquam populi libertatem, quam a Pompeio exstinctam omnino, a Caesare vero restitutam atque auctam longius fabulatur. Novam ipse historiam contexit; cui quantum credendum sit, ipse viderit! *Civitatis mores corruptos, priscam* (ut ait)

due to them! Furthermore, he says that *no expert doubts that Etruria was named from the Greek words* heteros horos (*that is, second border*).[141] So Pliny was an amateur, who wrote in his *Description of the World:* "the seventh region is next, in which starting from the river Macra lies Etruria, so called after many changes of name. In ancient times the Umbrians were driven out from there by the Pelasgians, and those by the Lydians, who after their king were called Tyrrhenians, but later in the Greek language, on account of their sacrificial rites, Tuscans." Also a fool is M. Varro, who reckons the region was named after *tus* meaning "incense."[142]

Though ignorant in all matters, I nevertheless do not of my   85
own volition want to be uncultured when confronted with this superstitious interpretation of the name Etruria, nor to believe that Etruria is named after *the second border*.[143] For since "the second" is the partitive of "two," why is the region named after one rather than both boundaries?[144] Why after the bank of the Tiber rather than of the Macra, although in fact Tuscany is bounded not by two, but by four borders? These seem to be the hallucinations of dreamers, not interpretations! I say that the Etruscans and the Tuscans are the same, with only two letters added, with the same etymology. *Fluentia* was named by the ancients after the flowing Arno; the moderns say *Florentia* with one letter changed, and a second added.[145] And yet the source of the word is the same. In the same way we see that *Pisaurum* is now called *Pensaurum,* and many others have been reported that have two names, of which the second derived from the first.[146]

He turns once more to the *liberty of Rome,* which he argues was   86
defended and *increased by Caesar.*[147] He says that there was no liberty of the people in the earlier times of Marius and Sulla, and tells the further tale that it was completely destroyed by Pompey, but restored and increased by Caesar. He himself has woven a new history; let him be the judge as to how far it should be believed! He says that *the morals of the community were compromised, the ancient*

disciplinam populi oblitteratam, integritatem fractam et quicquid aliud
in eam sententiam dici potest et ipse adfirmo; ad quae non est
opus Graeco testimonio,[373] cum habeamus Ciceronem nostrum
pluribus in locis mores et vitia illorum temporum deplorantem.
Erat tamen libertas, stabant iudicia, vigebant leges, populus ius
suum[374] tenebat, comitia ordine fiebant, mos patrius in creandis[375]
magistratibus servabatur.

87   Graeculum deinde adulatorem Dionem[376] historicum producit,
imperatorum adseclam,[377] virum addictum regibus, natum in servitute. Stomachatus sum, cum legi verba illius historici in hac
parte delirantis! Ait enim (ut traducit Guarinus) *plura maiora et
meliora obvenisse ex regibus quam ex populis, ut Romanorum gesta testantur.* Hic praeponit gesta regum Romanorum[378] iis,[379] quae postmodum liberata patria a servitute regia acta sunt! Unum Sallustii
dictum, qui 'regibus bonos quam malos dixit esse suspectiores,'[380]
universum Dionem confundit. Hic etiam adsentator imperatorum
M. Brutum et Cassium damnat, quod Caesarem interfecerunt. At
Cicero — verior, gravior, sanctior testis — illud factum multis in locis pulcherrimum ducit,[381] dignum gloria et laude[382] immortali. In
fine autem *Primae Philippicae:* 'si enim,' inquit, 'C. Caesaris exitus
efficere non[383] potest, ut malis carus esse[384] quam metui, nihil
cuiusquam proficiet nec valebit[385] oratio; quem qui beatum fuisse
putant, miserrimi ipsi[386] sunt. Beatus est nemo, qui ea lege vivit, ut
non modo impune, sed etiam cum summa interfectoris gloria in-
terfici possit.' Praeponat quis, si audet, Ciceroni Dionem, qui neque suam rem publicam ullam[387] habuit, neque cognovit alienam!
Sed Graeculum dimittamus et laudandos Brutum et Cassium ob
Caesaris mortem adseramus; non (ut scribit Graecus[388]) vitupe-
randos.

discipline of the people obliterated, integrity broken, and whatever else can be said to that effect.[148] I myself also affirm that this was so, and for it we need no Greek testimony since we have our own Cicero in many passages decrying the morals and vices of those times.[149] Yet there was liberty, the courts remained in operation, the laws were strong, the people had their own justice, elections were held in regular fashion, and the ancestral customs for electing magistrates were preserved.

Then he brings out that sycophantic little Greek historian Dio, 87 a hanger-on of the emperors, a man devoted to kings, born in servitude.[150] I was roused to anger as I was reading the words of this hallucinating historian in this section! For he says, as Guarino renders him, "*that many greater and better things have come from kings than from the people, as the history of the Romans testifies.*"[151] Here he raises the deeds of the Roman kings above those which were carried out later when the country had been freed from regal servitude! One line of Sallust, who said that "to kings, the good men were more suspect than the bad," refutes Dio in his entirety.[152] This flatterer of emperors even condemns M. Brutus and Cassius, because they slew Caesar. Yet Cicero, a truer, weightier, and saintlier witness, in many passages holds this deed to be the very finest, worthy of immortal glory and praise.[153] But at the end of the first *Philippic,* he says: "if indeed the end of C. Caesar cannot induce you to prefer to be loved than feared, no one's speech will do any good at all or have any influence on you. For those who deem Caesar happy are very wretched themselves: no one is happy who lives by such a principle that he can be killed not only with impunity but to the great glory of his slayer."[154] Let anyone who dares rank Dio over Cicero—Dio who had no republic of his own and never knew another! But let us dismiss the little Greek and state that Brutus and Cassius should be praised on account of Caesar's death, not, as the Greek writes, execrated.

88   *De Scipione* (inquit) *me in praesentia continebo, ne tanti hominis opi-*
nioni tuo exemplo detraham; verum, ut amborum iudicium unam in
summam paucis redigam, Scipio quidem vir bonus, civis pusillanimis, im-
perator excellens, quod (Livii auctoritate) et adsero ipse[389] *et tu non inficias*
ibis: vir (inquit) *memorabilis, bellicis tamen quam pacis artibus memora-*
bilior. Ad hoc dictum tam inconcinnum ex indignatione quadam
(quod non advertit Guarinus!) frontem atque animum contraxi.
Detrahere non vult Scipioni homo pius, non quia desit animus,
sed facultas! Quid enim ageret si illum manifestorum criminum
reum deprehendisset, cum[390] etiam nova confingat, ut eius laudes
possit inficere? Primo *damnatum* dixit[391] *temeritatis,* quod falsum
esse ostendi; tum *amore ancillae irretitum,* quod est procul a vero;
nunc civem pusilli animi adfirmat, quod testis ab eo productus
docet esse falsissimum!

89   Sed videamus quid adserat,[392] quod me credit non esse negaturum: Titum scilicet[393] Livium dixisse Scipionem civem fuisse pusillanimem. Nescio coniectura adsequi undenam Guarinus expis-
catus sit ex Livii textu,[394] quem protulit, tam mirandum sensum.
Memorabilem enim pacis artibus interpretatur esse pusillanimem!
O calumniam non ferendam! Si[395] textum Livii intelligit,[396] quid
ad diversum contrariumque sensum contorquet? Quid verbum[397]
honorificum transfert ad contumeliosum? Si non intelligit, cur in
suum dedecus profert? Cur quae nusquam scripta sunt, somniat?
Scribit Titus Livius Scipionem[398] virum memorabilem, sed memo-
rabiliorem belli quam pacis artibus. Ergo et pacis quoque artibus
memorabilis! Numquid ulla pusillanimitatis fit mentio? Quae est
haec[399] perversitas totiens Livium, Sallustium, Suetonium, Plutarchum a[400] recto sensu ad contrariam mentem[401] traducere? Quod

I will restrain myself—he says—*at present regarding Scipio, so as not*   88
to detract, like you, from the reputation of so great a man; but, to reduce
the judgment on both to one brief conclusion, Scipio was indeed a good
man, a weak citizen, but an outstanding commander, as I myself assert on
the authority of Livy, and as you are not going to deny: "a memorable
man"—he said—*"but still more memorable in the art of war than of*
peace."[155] At this statement, so ungraceful, I did—which Guarino
did not notice!—furl my brow and my mind with indignation.
This pious fellow does not want to disparage Scipio, not because
he lacks the will but the skill! What indeed would he do if he had
caught him accused of blatant crimes, since he even invents new
ones in order to stain his merits? First he said that he was *condemned for recklessness*, which I have shown to be false; then *ensnared
by the love for a slave girl*, which is far from the truth; and now he
says that he was a *weak citizen*, which the witness he called shows
to be thoroughly wrong![156]

But let us see what he asserts, which he believes I will not deny,   89
namely that Livy claimed Scipio was a weak citizen. I cannot even
hazard a conjecture whence Guarino ferreted out such a marvelous
meaning from the text of Livy that he cited. Indeed he interprets
the phrase "to be memorable for the arts of peace" as meaning "being faint of heart"! Oh insupportable slander! If he understands
Livy's text, why does he twist it to mean something different and
entirely contradictory? Why does he change a word that conveys
honor into a reproach? If he does not understand it, why does he
cite it to his shame? Why does he dream up things that were nowhere written? Livy writes that Scipio was a memorable man, but
more memorable for the arts of war than those of peace. *Ergo* he
was also memorable for the arts of peace! Is there any mention of
faintheartedness? What is this perversity again and again to twist
Livy, Sallust, Suetonius, and Plutarch from their proper meaning
into a contrary view? If he is doing it unwittingly, we should in-

si inscius[402] facit, errori indulgendum; si sciens, non leviter vindicandum!

90   Ultimo in loco, tamquam in subsidiis, collocavit extremam aciem, quae totius victoriae robur contineret: recitat Plutarchi testimonium, ab eo in Latinum conversum, qui scripsit *rerum ab Caesare gestarum magnitudinem superare Fabios, Scipiones et reliquos Romanos imperatores.* Non dixit gloriam, non laudem, non virtutem, sed magnitudinem, cui et scelera, et vitia permulta quandoque admiscentur. Idem dixit et Cicero: res gessisse Caesarem bello praeclaras, sed rei publicae calamitosas.

91   Itaque non gentes subactae, non captae urbes, non fusi exercitus, non provinciae populatae[403] gloriam possunt adferre, nisi absint procul a scelere et libidine dominandi. Quid enim laudis potest reddere sitis humani sanguinis effundendi, libido evertendarum urbium, populandarum provinciarum et rapiendi cupido? A nullis philosophis, a nullis sapientibus, a nullis historicis ea laudantur neque vero magna facinora vel[404] habenda, vel laudanda sunt, nisi iis[405] sit virtus admixta. Alioquin et magnum et laudandum facinus admisisset, qui incendit Dianae Ephesiae templum! Rem magnam gessissent[406] et laudem etiam mererentur, qui per fraudem aut proditionem vel exercitus hostium delessent[407] vel praeclaras diruissent[408] urbes! Verum nihil magnum, nihil excelsum, nihil laudabile, nihil esse gloriosum dicimus, quod non sit idem cum decore, cum honestate, cum virtute coniunctum.

92   Ut igitur, mi Francisce, reiectis Guarini argumentis iam scribendi finem faciamus, cum ea solida et vera sit[409] gloria, quae virtute et magnis vel in rem publicam, vel in omne genus hominum meritis comparatur, gloriam vero et belli, et pacis artibus homines soleant adipisci, cumque Scipionis laus per omne virtutum genus

dulge his mistakes, but if he is doing it knowingly, he should be subjected to no slight revenge!

In final position, as if among the reserve troops, he has drawn 90
up his last battle line, intending it to comprise the pièce de resistance of his whole victory: he recites the testimony of Plutarch, rendered by him into Latin, who wrote: *"that the greatness of the exploits performed by Caesar surpassed the Fabii, Scipiones, and the rest of the Roman commanders."*[157] He did not say "glory" nor "praise" nor "virtue," but "greatness," into which a great many crimes and vices are at all times mixed. Cicero also said the same, that Caesar had done deeds of distinction in war, but disastrous things with respect to the republic.

And so it is not subjected nations nor captured cities nor 91
routed armies nor despoiled provinces that can bring glory, unless they are far removed from crime and the lust for power. Indeed, what sort of praise can be gained from a thirst for spilling human blood, a lust for overthrowing cities, a desire for despoiling and pillaging provinces? No philosophers, no wise men, no historians praise these things, nor should they be regarded as great or praiseworthy achievements unless they are mixed with virtue. If it were otherwise, the person who set fire to the temple of Diana at Ephesus would have performed a great and praiseworthy deed![158] And a great thing deserving praise would have been accomplished by those who through deceit or treason had either wiped out an enemy army or razed famous cities to the ground! But we say that nothing is great, nothing lofty, nothing laudable, nothing glorious if it is not also associated with propriety, integrity, and virtue.

So now, my Francesco, having rejected Guarino's arguments, let 92
us put an end to our writing. Since that glory which stems from virtue and great services, be they to the state or to the whole of mankind, is the firm and the true one, and men are indeed wont to gain glory from the arts of war as well as peace, and since the praise of Scipio has spread over all the categories of virtue, a fact

fuerit diffusa atque id Livii, Valerii, Senecae testimonio confirme-
tur, Caesaris autem virtutum nullum nobis testem (nisi se ipsum
perlevem auctorem adferat Guarinus), prudentiae ac doctrinae
tuae erit discernere ac decernere, uter gloria, virtute[410] et belli
laude praestantior habendus sit, Caesarne an Superior Africanus,
cum in altero nullum vitium, nullum flagitium viguerit, in altero
vitia et scelera manifesta, quae a probatissimis auctoribus referuntur. Vale, et parce longitudini meae.[411]

which the testimonies of Livy, Valerius, and Seneca confirm, whereas we have no witness to Caesar's virtue, unless Guarino proffers himself as an utterly insignificant authority, it will be up to your wisdom and learning to distinguish and decide which of the two should be deemed more outstanding in glory, virtue, and praise in war: will it be Caesar or the elder Scipio, since the latter was free from vice and sin, while in the former vices and blatant crimes thrived, which are reported by the most trustworthy authors.[159] Farewell, and forgive my lengthiness.

1   Petrus de Monte,[1] apostolicae sedis protonotarius, salutem plurimam dicit Poggio secretario, viro claro.

    Proximis diebus, cum per absentiam horum principum plusculum quietis[2] a negotiis pontificis maximi nactus essem, in manus sumpsi disputationem abs te cum Guarino Veronensi,[3] viro doctissimo, de praestantia Scipionis et Caesaris habitam,[4] quam attente admodum ac diligenter perlegi. Nam antea quidem cum libellus tuo nomine mihi oblatus esset, ductus[5] tamen[6] aviditate legendi, uno paene spiritu cuncta percurreram. Legi itaque[7] imprimis epistolam tuam,[8] ex qua orta videtur esse inter te et Guarinum contentionis materia, quoniam praefers Caesari Scipionem, virum utique praestantissimum et maximis illustratum virtutibus, ac nedum patriae, sed universae Italiae liberatorem. Dehinc Guarini ipsius impugnationem, qua contra Caesarem Scipioni praeferendum esse validissimis (ut putat) argumentis contendit. Postremo tuam defensionem, ut sic, cognito quid primum a te dicatur, quid adversum te obiciatur, demum quo pacto tuam ab oppugnationibus[9] tuearis sententiam, rectius possem in ea concertatione meum tibi iudicium scribere.[10] Et quamquam parum ingenio, minus dicendi arte et eloquentia valeam, non formidabo tamen Poggio meo, hoc est amicissimo viro, meas ineptias ostendere ac quicquid in buccam venerit meis ad te litteris commendare.[11]

LETTER TO POGGIO BRACCIOLINI

Pietro del Monte, protonotary of the apostolic see, to Poggio, sec- 1
retary, renowned man, greetings.

In recent days, since I had found myself with a little more leisure from the pope's business because of the absence of those who
are the leading people here, I took into my hands the dispute between you and that most learned man, Guarino da Verona, about
the preeminence of Scipio and Caesar, which I have now carefully
and closely read. For, indeed, earlier, when the pamphlet was presented to me on your behalf, I was driven by an eagerness to read
it and had run through the whole of it nearly in a single breath.
So, first of all I read your letter from which the matter of dispute
seems to have arisen between you and Guarino, since you give
priority over Caesar to Scipio, a man certainly most outstanding
and adorned with the greatest virtues, and who was the liberator
not just of his fatherland but of the whole of Italy. From that I
turned to Guarino's counterblast, in which he claims to the contrary—with what he considers the soundest arguments—that
Caesar should be given priority over Scipio. Finally, I read your
defense, so that, knowing what you had originally said, what objections had been made against you, and how you uphold your
opinion against assailants, I could be in a better position to write
to you my judgment on this debate.[1] And although my talent may
be small and my oratorical artistry and eloquence even less, I will
nonetheless not shrink from sharing my trifles with my Poggio
(that is, with a man who is my dearest friend), and entrusting to
my epistle to you whatever will come into my mouth.

2   Illud autem imprimis dicendum censeo, magnam profecto esse
in utroque vestrum eloquentiae vim, pergrande ingenii[12] acumen,
eximiam scribendi facilitatem copiosamque[13] (ut ita dixerim) verborum supellectilem ac praeclaram sermonis venustatem[14] adeo, ut
illis priscis oratoribus, quos universi admirantur et laudant, nulla
in re inferiores iudicari debeatis. Verum non potui satis admirari et
dolere[15] Guarinum, virum (medius fidius[16]) humanissimum, qui a
primis (ut aiunt) unguiculis[17] singulari quadam loquendi modestia
semper est usus, qui suis scriptis litteris aut sermonibus[18] neminem unquam laesit, sparso iam canis capite et arata rugis fronte ac,
instar boum,[19] pendentibus a mento pallearibus, omnem paene[20]
modestiam et scribendi honestatem a se procul abiecisse, atque
effrenata quadam licentia in te, qui nullo in loco eius dignitati de-
traxeras, tam acerbe, tam contumeliose, tam aspere irruisse.

3   Cur enim, quaeso, tibi debuit iniuriari Guarinus, si Caesari
Scipionem praetulisti? Quidnam sibi ex ea re detrimenti obvene-
rat? Quid auctoritati suae detractum putabat?[21] Formidabatne se,
velut ingratum, caesarea haereditate privandum, nisi adversus te[22]
tam acerbam tamque immitem Caesaris defensionem[23] suscepisset? Tu quidem, solita scribendi libertate usus, tuum de mortuo-
rum praestantia rogatus iudicium descripsisti,[24] de quibus fas est
unicuique, nullius laesa existimatione, quod senserit libera voce
proferre. Nam ut a Satyro dictum est:

Securus licet Aenean[25] Rutulumque ferocem
Committas, nulli gravis est percussus Achilles.

Hi enim, ut pulchre inquis, *nec rescribere possunt, nec proscribere*. At
Guarinus, novitate facti commotus tanquam si ea res plurimum
sibi mali aut incommodi afferret, ita contra te vehit, ita honori tuo

First of all, it must be said, I think, that in both of you there is   2
undoubtedly a great power of eloquence, an enormous sharpness
of intellect, an exceptional ease of composition, and (so to speak)
an abundant store of words and a splendid, attractive style. You
have these to such an extent that you both must be judged in no
respect inferior to those orators of ancient times whom everyone
admires and praises. Yet at the same time I could not wonder and
bemoan enough that Guarino, as God is my witness a most humane person, who, from his earliest years (as they say),[2] has always employed a certain singular modesty of expression and who
has never wounded anyone with his writings and speeches, now,
with his head speckled with gray hair,[3] his forehead creased with
wrinkles[4] and dewlaps sagging from his chin, casts off far from
himself nearly all modesty or respectability in writing and with a
certain unbridled license inveighs so sharply, so abusively, so bitterly against you, who had nowhere slighted his dignity.

Why, I ask, did Guarino have to do you wrong if you gave pri- 3
ority to Scipio over Caesar? What loss did he suffer from that? In
what way did he feel it lessened his authority? Did he dread that
he, like an ungrateful person, would have to be deprived of Caesar's legacy unless he launched against you such a sharp and harsh
defense of Caesar? You, for your part, used your customary freedom of writing when, upon request, you wrote out your judgment
about the preeminence of the dead men, about whom anyone is
permitted to voice freely what they think, without harming anyone's reputation. For as is said by the satirist:

> You may, without concern, cause Aeneas and the fierce
>   Rutulian to join battle;
> Achilles' death will strike no one with grief.[5]

For these men, as you elegantly say, *can neither write back nor proscribe.*[6] But Guarino, who was unsettled by the novelty of the
deed,[7] as if this matter brought the worst evil and trouble upon

detrahit, teque velut ignavum quendam scriptorem totiens compellat, ut non tam Caesarem defendere — quod sibi magnae laudi
datum fuisset — quam te ultro offendere ac tui nominis gloriam
deprimere voluisse[26] videatur.

4   Fateor me Guarino multa debere, nam ab ipso prima oratoriae[27]
artis elementa suscepi.[28] Non sum adeo rerum ignarus quin in-
tellegam[29] praeceptores,[30] a quibus[31] bonis artibus[32] eruditi simus,[33] magno esse in honore habendos; quemadmodum[34] Pericles
Anaxagoram, Dion Platonem, Cicero et Caesar Apollonium, principes Italici Pythagoram, Alexander Aristotelem summo studio
coluerunt. Itaque Guarinum, qui ad haec humanitatis studia primus mihi aditum dedit, et amo et diligo.[35] Sed multo magis[36]
honestati, veritati ac iustitiae me[37] debere profiteor, a qua nullius
odium, nullius favor, gratia aut benivolentia flectere animum debet,[38] si modo viri boni[39] (ut nos decet) et esse cupimus et haberi.[40] "Nulla" enim, inquit[41] Cicero, "est excusatio peccati, si amici
causa peccaveris."

5   Et quanquam neque vos,[42] neque alius quisquam huius tam
grandis inter vos controversiae iudicem me constituerit, quia
tamen meum postulasti audire iudicium, debeo ego ex sententia
animi mei tibi rescribere.[43] Itaque (aequo animo ferat Guarinus)
necesse est, si in hac suae impugnationis acerbitate, in hoc verborum impetu, quo non lacessitus, non provocatus, te invadit[44] atque
aggreditur et contumeliis multis de honestate nititur,[45] eum nequaquam probo aut laudo, sed libera potius loquendi audacia[46]
pronuntio eum iniuriarum tibi teneri: quod primus veteris inter
vos amicitiae[47] iura violavit, quod te irridet, reprehendit, accusat,
reprobat,[48] quod denique in te ipse — tanquam caesarianarum legionum ductor[49] — quanto potest impetu ac totis viribus atrocis-
sime irruit. Potuit ille quidem — si se caesarianum esse adeo

him, so inveighs against you, so besmirches your honor and so
often upbraids you as if you were some dimwitted writer, that he
seems to have wanted not so much to defend Caesar (which would
have brought to him great praise)[8] as to find fault with you without provocation and to sully the glory of your good name.

I must admit that I owe Guarino much, for I learned from him   4
the first principles of the art of rhetoric.[9] I am not so ignorant of
the world as not to realize that we should hold in great honor
those teachers who trained us in the good arts — just as Pericles
took great care to esteem Anaxagoras, Dion Plato, Cicero and
Caesar Apollonius, the leading men of Italy Pythagoras, and Alexander Aristotle.[10] And so I love and cherish Guarino, who gave me
my first introduction to humane studies.[11] But I acknowledge I
owe much more to integrity, truth, and justice, from which hatred
or partisanship for no one, nor favor nor kindness should shake
us, if only we want (as is right for us) to be and be considered
good men. For, as Cicero says, "it is no excuse for sin that you have
sinned on behalf of a friend."[12]

Although neither you nor anyone else has made me judge of   5
this great quarrel between you, yet, because you have asked to hear
my judgment, I must write back to you with my heartfelt opinion.
Thus (may Guarino take it calmly), it is necessary to say: if in this
sharpness of his attack, in this verbal onslaught, to which he was
not incited and not provoked, he assails and attacks you, and relies
upon many slanders concerning your integrity, then I can in no
way approve of him or praise him, but rather, with a free voice I
boldly declare that he is liable for the harm done to you.[13] That is
because he was the first to break the rules of long-standing friendship that there had been between you, because he mocks, censures, accuses, and condemns you, and finally because, as if he
were a leader of the Caesarean legions, he launches a most brutal
assault on you with all his might and with as much force as he can
muster. Indeed, if he revels so much in being a Caesarean and is so

gloriatur, si tanta laudandi[50] Caesaris detinetur cupiditate — eius partes sua oratione defendere, illaesa tui nominis dignitate, idque tuo facere exemplo. Tu enim[51] in illa prima epistula tua, quam Guarinus lapidare nititur, cum luculenter et graviter (ut soles) de Scipionis et Caesaris virtutibus disserueris, neque ipsius, neque alterius viventis[52] existimationem honorem aut gloriam, ne minima quidem in re laesisti, violasti,[53] maculasti. In quo, cum maxima prudentia[54] usus sis, magna profecto laus tuo nomini accessit.

6   Neque hanc mei solius sententiam esse putes velim:[55] iudicant id uno ore omnes, qui hos libellos legunt, et cum Guarini eloquentiam, qua sane plurimum potest, magnopere extollant, illatas tamen tibi ab eo iniurias[56] damnant ac reprehendunt. Tradidi[57] ego hanc disputationem vestram[58] illustrissimo principi Humfredo, duci Gloucestriae, qui cum sit virtutis hospes, litterarum splendor et nobilitatis ornamentum, inter priscos[59] illos heroas (quos velut deos venerabatur antiquitas), si hoc nostra religionis veritas[60] pateretur, esset non immerito collocandus. Legit is eam[61] magna quadam aviditate, nam a praeclaris scriptoribus nil, nisi elegans, artificiosum atque elaboratum scribi[62] potuisse facile sibi persuadebat.

7   Paucis autem post diebus, rogatus[63] a me quale ipsius esset de ea disputatione iudicium, responsum paucis ita reddidit heros:

Ego (inquit) Poggii et Guarini eloquentiam admiror et laudo, dignosque ob eam immortali honore et gloria censeo.[64] Nam haec suavissima humanitatis studia, quae paene extincta erant,[65] eorum ingenio, labore et industria veterem splendorem decoremque recuperarunt, nostraeque aetatis hominibus magna horum exemplo spes data[66] est ad priscam

held in thrall by a craving to praise Caesar, he could have defended his position in his oration and left the honor of your name intact and so acted on your example. For you, in that first letter of yours, which Guarino strives to lambaste, while you elegantly and with dignity (as is your wont) discoursed on the virtues of Scipio and of Caesar, you did not harm, dishonor, or besmirch even in the tiniest manner the esteem, the dignity or the glory of him or any other living person.[14] In doing so, since you employed the utmost circumspection, certainly great praise has accrued to your name.

Nor would I want you to think that this is my opinion alone: 6 all who read these pamphlets judge it so unanimously, and, though they heap great praise on Guarino's eloquence, in which, to be sure, he has great power, they nonetheless condemn and censure the harm done to you by him. I gave this dispute of yours to the most illustrious prince, Humfrey, Duke of Gloucester,[15] who, since he is the patron of virtue, the splendor of letters, and the ornament of nobility, should not undeservedly be placed among those heroes of old, whom ancient times revered as if they were gods, if it were allowed by our religion. He read the debate with a certain deep enthusiasm, for he readily formed the conviction that nothing could be expressed by the most excellent of authors but that which is elegant, skillful, and well-wrought.

After a few days, when I asked him what his own judgment of 7 the dispute was, this hero gave his response briefly and in this way:

I (he said) admire and praise the eloquence of Poggio and Guarino and consider them worthy of eternal honor and glory because of that. For these most pleasant humane studies,[16] which were nearly extinct, have regained their former splendor and grace through their genius, their energy, and their hard work. By their example, great hope has been given to people of our time of coming closer to the original ele-

illam latinae linguae elegantiam propius[67] accedendi. Ceterum mordacem illum ac nimis contumeliosum scribendi modum, quem in nulla suae impugnationis parte Guarinus praetermisit, magna reprehensione dignum iudico.[68] Opinabar enim antea[69] hisce humanitatis studiis, quae (ut inquit vester[70] Cicero) adulescentiam agunt,[71] senectutem oblectant, quibus Guarinus apprime est eruditus,[72] eum gravitatem quandam morum et in omni sermone honestatem atque modestiam sibi ipsi vendicasse;[73] quod secus accidisse admiror permaxime. Licebat enim ei Caesaris causam suscipere, illam defendere, illius praestantiam ostendere, at Poggio detrahere ac maledicere nullo modo, qui pro animi sui sententia Caesari praeferre visus est Scipionem.[74]

8   Eo principis responso dolui plurimum Guarini mei causa, cuius auctoritatem apud hunc in omni genere doctrinae excellentissimum principem atque clarissimum[75] non parum diminutam esse cognovi. Quocirca quid sibi voluerit Guarinus in te tam acriter[76] invehendo? Quo magis cogito, eo minus intellego. Dum enim te laedere voluit, se ipsum proprio mucrone percussit, more sagittantis in lapidem, nam sagitta in lapidem non figitur, sed plerumque[77] resiliens percutit dirigentem.

9   Nunc, quoniam satis de hoc diximus, ad rem ipsam, cuius gratia omnis inter te et Guarinum habita disputatio est—de praestantia videlicet Scipionis et Caesaris—veniamus. Ego, mi Poggi amantissime, ex hac vestra contentione ac dimicatione litteraria maximam quandam iucunditatem laetitiamque recipio[78] ac mihi ipsi plurimum gratulor, quod te talem, tantumque ac tam[79] disertum veteris sententiae et opinionis[80] meae patronum ac defensorem (nescio qua deorum[81] providentia) nactus sum. Nunquam enim mihi persuadere potui Caesarem nedum Scipioni aut alteri

gance of the Latin language. But I judge that bitter and
overly slanderous style of writing, which Guarino has omitted from no part of his attack, deserves a severe reprimand.
Beforehand, I was of the opinion that through these humane
studies — which, as your Cicero says, occupy youth and delight old age,[17] and in which Guarino is supremely learned —
he had procured for himself a certain seriousness of character and, in all speech, probity and modesty. That this has
turned out otherwise surprises me greatly. For it was open to
Guarino to take up the cause of Caesar, defend that and
demonstrate his preeminence, but not in any way to besmirch and to slander Poggio, who, because of his own
heartfelt opinion, was seen to prefer Scipio over Caesar.

When the prince had given this reply, I was greatly saddened   8
on behalf of my Guarino, for I realized that his standing had been
not a little reduced in the eyes of this prince, who is most outstanding and famous in all forms of learning. Therefore, I ask
what Guarino might have wanted for himself in railing against you
so bitterly? The more I think about it, the less I understand it.[18]
For, in wanting to wound you, he has cut himself with the point
of his own blade, just like an archer shooting at a stone: the arrow
does not lodge in the stone but very often rebounds and hits the
shooter.[19]

Now, because we have said quite enough about this, let us come   9
to the matter itself, which is at the core of the debate between you
and Guarino, that is to say, concerning the preeminence of Scipio
and Caesar. Poggio, my very dear friend, I have gained very great
pleasure and delight from your battle and literary struggle and I
congratulate myself greatly that I have obtained — by what foresight of the gods I do not know — such a person, so great and so
well-spoken, as you as a promoter and defender of my long-
standing opinion. For I could never persuade myself that Caesar

claro viro praeferendum, sed neque ulla in re vera laude et gloria dignum, quin immo tanquam seditiosum ac turbulentum civem et pacis quietisque Romanae impatientem, deinde patriae hostem eversoremque libertatis — rei sane dulcissimae et qua nihil homini a diis immortalibus[82] utilius dari potest — summo studio vituperandum. Neque me aliquando movere potuerunt deleti ab eo quam[83] plurimi hostiles exercitus, profligatae acies, subacti reges, devictae civitates[84], reliquaque eius militaria opera et quidem praeclara atque egregia. Haec enim plurima secum vitia patiuntur neque propterea bonum, iustum, constantem, fortem ac virtuosum hominem arguunt,[85] sed tam bonis, quam malis possunt esse communia.

10   Memini cum adhuc adulescens essem (immo paene puer) et discendi cupiditate ductus[86] Guarini, doctissimi sane[87] et eruditissimi hominis, scholam frequentarem audiremque persaepe ab eo Caesareum nomen magnis laudibus extolli, praedicari atque amplificari, tacitum me ei subiratum fuisse,[88] necnon in magnam quandam deductum esse[89] admirationem, quod tam nefarium[90] hominem — cuius nullae prorsus virtutes fuere, vitia vero in omni aetate, omni vita paene innumerabilia — vir omnium historiarum et totius antiquitatis peritissimus tantopere laudaret.[91] Neque ex eo tempore in hanc usque diem aliter potui existimare[92] et cum[93] multa ipse legerim, plura quoque[94] a doctissimis viris (qui nulla in re Guarino cedunt), audiverim, nihil unquam in Caesare comperi,[95] quod quavis[96] laude et gloria dignum esset, nec nunc quidem, cum Guarinus[97] omnia eius gesta, velut in tabella quadam descripta,[98] omni studio totisque viribus[99] extollere[100] conatus est. Quin[101] ea, quae[102] libello suo complectitur, tam[103] prudenter

was — not to mention preferable over either Scipio or another famous man — but that he was worthy of true praise and glory in any respect. On the contrary, he should be censured with the utmost zeal as a factious and troublesome citizen, uneasy with Rome's peace and calm, and then the country's enemy, the overthrower of its freedom — truly the sweetest thing, than which nothing more useful can be given to man by the immortal gods.[20] Nor could I at any point be moved by his destruction of so many enemy armies, by the rout of battle lines, the overthrow of kings, the defeat of cities, and all his other military deeds which were, indeed, famous and outstanding. For these tolerate a great number of vices with them, and therefore are no proof of a good, just, constant, brave, and virtuous man, but can be common to the good and the bad alike.

I remember when I was still a youth — no, rather, not much 10
more than a boy — and, drawn by a thirst for learning I was attending the school of that truly most learned and erudite man, Guarino.[21] I would hear him so often extol with great praises, proclaim, and magnify the name of Caesar that I would quietly seethe at him. Moreover, I recall that I was induced to a great amazement that a man very well acquainted with all histories and the entirety of the ancient world could so greatly praise such an evil man, who had no virtues at all but instead throughout every stage of his life had a nearly countless number of vices. Nor have I been able from that time right up to this day to judge otherwise, and, although I myself have read many things and heard more from the most learned men (who are in no respect inferior to Guarino), I never learned of anything in Caesar which was worthy of any sort of praise and glory. Nor can I now, indeed, although Guarino has attempted with every effort and with his whole strength to extol all his deeds, as if they were depicted in a painting. Indeed, you have refuted so intelligently, so seriously and ele-

tamque graviter atque[104] ornate refellis, ut inanem quendam laborem a Guarino susceptum esse possit unusquisque facile iudicare.

II   Novi quosdam non contemnendos viros miris efferre laudibus M. Attilium Regulum eumque ceteris omnibus[105] anteferre Romanis, inter quos doctissimus et eloquentissimus nostrae religionis antistes, Augustinus, existit,[106] qui in primo *De civitate Dei* libro ita ad verbum inquit:

> Inter omnes suos laudabiles et virtutibus insignibus illustres viros, non proferunt Romani meliorem M. Regulo, quem neque felicitas corruperit, nam in tanta victoria permansit pauperrimus, nec infelicitas fregerit, nam ad tanta exitia revertitur intrepidus.

Alii sunt, qui Brutum illum, qui superbo Caesaris dominatu patriam liberare conatus est,[107] ceteris praeferunt; plerique Furium Camillum inter omnes dignitate et honore excellere contendunt, quibus ego[108] consentire soleo ob res ab eo magnifice bello gestas, quibus urbs liberata est, vitam quoque in pace integre ac laudabiliter ductam. Ad id me inducunt[109] quam plurima, tum[110] T. Livii verba huiusmodi:[111]

> Fuit Camillus vere vir unicus in omni fortuna, princeps pace belloque priusquam exulatum iret, clarior in exilio vel desiderio civitatis, quae absentis imploravit opem, vel felicitate, qua restitutus in patriam secum ipsam patriam restituit. Par deinde per quinque et viginti annos (tot enim postea vixit) titulo tantae gloriae fuit dignusque habitus, quem secundum a Romulo conditorem urbis Romanae ferrent.

gantly those things which he includes in his pamphlet that anyone can easily judge what a pointless task Guarino undertook.

I know some men, who are not to be despised, who have ex- 11 alted with amazing praises Marcus Atilius Regulus and placed him before all other Romans.[22] Among them appears the most learned and eloquent high priest of our religion, Augustine, who, in the first book of his *City of God*, speaks verbatim as follows:

> Among all their men who were praiseworthy and famous for their remarkable virtues, the Romans have no better man to offer than Marcus Regulus, who was neither corrupted by prosperity (for he remained a man of most meager means after winning so great a victory) nor broken by adversity, for he returned fearless to such an awful end.[23]

There are some who place before all others that Brutus who attempted to free the fatherland from Caesar's haughty tyranny, and a good many who argue that Furius Camillus stands out among all in worthiness and honor.[24] I am accustomed to agree with the last group on account of the great deeds he did in battle, by which the City was freed, and also the blameless and commendable life he led in peacetime. So many things lead me to that conclusion, including these words of Livy:

> Camillus was truly a singular man, whatever the circumstance; foremost in peace and war before he went into exile, more famous in exile, either by the desire of the state, which beseeched his aid in his absence, or by the good fortune with which, when he was restored to the fatherland, he restored both the fatherland itself and himself. Over the course of twenty-five years (for he lived for that many afterward), he was held to be entitled to such great glory and worthy to be known as the second founder of the city of Rome, after Romulus.[25]

12   Extollunt nonnulli Scipionem hunc nostrum Africanum, virum siquidem clarissimum et multis virtutibus exornatum,[112] alii item alios.[113] Sed qui Caesarem, perditum ac flagitiosum civem, invasorem rei publicae libertatisque subversorem, magnis efferre praeconiis ausus fuerit, in hanc usque diem praeter Guarinum cognovi neminem, nisi forte quod de ipso a Cicerone scriptum est laudi tribuendum esse Guarinus existimet. Inquit enim in libro primo *De officiis,* tanquam philosophus ex animi sententia scribens:[114]

> Nulla sancta societas nec fides regni est; nam quicquid eiusmodi est, in quo non possunt plures excellere, in eo fit plerumque tanta contentio, ut difficillimum sit servare sanctam societatem. Declaravit id modo temeritas C. Caesaris, qui omnia iura divina et humana pervertit propter eum, quem sibi ipsi opinionis errore finxit principatum.

Et audebit Guarinus tantum sibi auctoritatis vendicare, ut, quem Cicero — Latinae linguae parens ac philosophus eximius — temerarium hominem[115] ac omnium iurium divinorum humanorumque perversorem appellat, is laudet, praedicet et extollat, et (quod gravius est) Scipioni, optimo ac praestantissimo civi deque sua re publica bene merito, praeferat ac praeponat? Quae insania est? Quae feritas? Quae rabies[116] aequissimum virum, summa iustitia singularique constantia[117] et continentia praeditum, ei postponere, cuius iniquitas, iniustitia, ambitio et principatus furiosa cupido, stupra quoque et adulteria omnes replent historicorum libros, qui cum a te accurate ac diligenter enumerentur, non sunt hoc loco a me repetendi?

13   Verum unum solum[118] auctorem adducam, cui contradicere summum crimen iudicandum est,[119] qui paucis verbis omnia Guarini scripta confundit.[120] Is est divus Augustinus, in cuius libris

Not a few praise this Scipio Africanus of ours, a man certainly 12
of the utmost fame and endowed with many virtues. Others do
likewise for others. But as to who would have dared to shower
with great plaudits Caesar, a reckless and scandalous citizen, the
invader of the republic and the man who undermined its liberty:
up to this day, Guarino aside, I have known of no one—unless
perhaps Guarino thinks something written by Cicero about that
man should be considered praise.[26] For in the first book of *On
Duties*, writing from the heart as a philosopher, he says:

> There is no holy fellowship nor trust in ruling as a king. For
> in whatsoever situation it be where it is not possible for sev-
> eral people to excel, there such contention arises that it is
> very difficult to preserve holy fellowship. This was recently
> manifest in the rashness of Gaius Caesar who subverted all
> laws, divine and human, in the cause of that primacy which,
> by a mistaken opinion, he conjured for himself.[27]

But will Guarino dare to claim for himself such authority that he
will praise, proclaim, and laud the person whom Cicero—the father of the Latin language[28] and an exceptional philosopher—calls
a rash man and the subverter of all divine and human laws? Will
he dare—and this is worse—to put him before and promote him
above Scipio, the best and most outstanding citizen, who gave
good service to his republic? What madness is this? What beastli-
ness? What raging insanity that places the most righteous man,
endowed with the greatest justice, singular constancy, and self-
control below the person whose unrighteousness, injustice, ambition, and frenzied desire for primacy, as well as his fornications
and adulteries, fill all the historians' books (since you listed them
accurately and carefully, I need not repeat them here)?

But let me cite a single author, whom it must be deemed the 13
utmost crime to contradict, and who, in a few words, undermines
all of Guarino's arguments. That writer is St. Augustine, in whose

(velut in amoenissimo quodam diversorio), interdum[121] obversari soleo. Enumeratis siquidem in tertio[122] *De civitate Dei* libro paene innumerabilibus[123] populi Romani calamitatibus, bellis ac seditionibus, quibus ante Redemptoris nostri adventum conquassatum fuit illud imperium, tandem ad secundi belli Punici tempora veniens, de Scipione nostro ita[124] inquit:

> Eodem ipso ergo[125] tempore, morum optimorum maximaeque concordiae Scipio ille, Romae Italiaeque liberator eiusdemque belli Punici secundi tam horrendi, tam exitiosi, tam periculosi praeclarus mirabilisque[126] confector, victor Hannibalis domitorque Carthaginis, cuius ab adulescentia vita describitur diis dedita templisque nutrita, inimicorum accusationibus cessit carensque patria, quam sua virtute salvam et liberam reddidit, in oppido Linternensi egit reliquam complevitque vitam, post insignem suum triumphum nullo illius urbis captus desiderio, ita ut iussisse perhibeatur, ne saltem mortuo in ingrata patria sibi funus fieret.

14   Quid ad haec[127] respondebit Guarinus?[128] Quid simile de Caesare suo adducet? Nihil profecto. Nam in Caesare his tantis Scipionis virtutibus modo enumeratis contraria vitia fuere, quae illum omnibus recte sapientibus[129] abominabilem reddunt. Vis ut utriusque mutua comparatione sub quodam quasi aspectu rem[130] clariorem efficiamus? Scipionis, auctore Augustino, mores optimi; Caesaris pessimi. Scipio maxima concordia claruit; Caesar multarum discordiarum bellorum et seditionum fons fuit et origo.[131] Scipio Romae Italiaeque liberator; Caesar Romanae et Italicae libertatis saevus[132] oppressor. Scipio tam periculosi belli[133] Punici confector; Caesar civilis belli auctor. A Scipione Hannibal,

books I am wont to linger now and then, as if they were some most delightful lodging. For, indeed, in the third book of his *City of God*, after listing the Roman people's nearly countless disasters, wars, and discords, by which that empire was shaken before the coming of Our Savior, he finally comes to the time of the second Punic War, and about our Scipio has this to say:

> In that time, therefore, Scipio, a man of the best character and supreme concord, the liberator of Rome and of Italy, the famous and remarkable man who ended the Second Punic War, which had been so frightening, so destructive, and so dangerous, Hannibal's vanquisher, the tamer of Carthage, who is said from his youth to have followed a life dedicated to the gods and been nourished in their temples, yielded to the accusations of his enemies. Deprived of his fatherland, which, through his virtue, he had made safe and free again, he eked out the rest of his life in the town of Liternum and died there. After his glorious triumph, he was in thrall to no desire for his former city, so much so that he is said to have ordered that not even when he was dead should there be a funeral for him in his ungrateful fatherland.[29]

What will Guarino say in response to these words? What of 14 like kind will he cite for his Caesar? Nothing, of course. For, in Caesar, to these great virtues of Scipio that I have just listed, there were the opposing vices, which make him detestable to all who judge rightly. Do you want us to make this matter clearer by a comparison between them, as if at a glance? Scipio, on the authority of Augustine, had "the best character"; Caesar the worst. Scipio shone with "supreme concord"; Caesar was the fount and origin of many discords, wars, and insurrections. Scipio was "the liberator of Rome and of Italy," Caesar was the cruel oppressor of Roman and Italian liberty. Scipio "ended the Second Punic war, which had been so dangerous"; Caesar was the author of civil war. By Scipio,

fortissimus et prudentissimus imperator,[134] victus; a Caesare Pompeius, optimus civis,[135] profligatus omnisque senatus extinctus.[136] Scipioni subiecta Carthago fuit; Caesari Romana libertas tantique splendor ac lumen imperii. Scipionis vita fertur ab adulescentia diis dedita templisque nutrita; Caesaris vero adulescentia cum seditiosis turbulentis[137] et facinorosis hominibus ducta.[138] Scipio tanto patriae amore flagravit, ut, quorundam in se[139] civium odium cernens, voluntarium sibi exilium apud Linternum delegerit.[140] ne quam rei publicae calamitatem eius potentia afferret; at Caesar, effrenata quadam dominandi rabie detentus,[141] nedum pro patriae incolumitate[142] aemulis non cessit, sed potius furore quodam arma contra patriam, contra senatum, contra bonos omnes assumpsit, civilem sanguinem fudit et Romanam nobilitatem extinxit.

15   Vides iam, ni fallor — videre potest et Guarinus, si hanc nostram epistulam non dedignatur legere — quanta inter Scipionem et Caesarem differentia sit, quantumque alter altero sit praestantior. Quibus vero rationibus, quibus fundamentis[143] negare ausus sit Guarinus Caesarem Romanae libertatis subversorem fuisse, necdum satis intellego. Quibus auctoribus[144] probare possit, non video, neque memini apud quenquam Romanae historiae scriptorem, qui Latine scripserit, id unquam in dubitationem revocatum fuisse. Desiperet enim, qui[145] sic saperet, nisi fortasse[146] Guarinus novos quosdam codices domi habeat, quos alii penitus ignorant, quibus in hanc suam sententiam adductus est.[147] Negabitne[148] Guarinus Caesarem suum adversus senatum ac optimates rei publicae arma[149] cepisse, Romano sanguine Thessaliae[150] campos implesse atque exinde singulare sibi usurpasse urbis imperium, unde et posteri omnes imperatores[151] Caesares sunt appellati? Inficiabiturne ipsum disposuisse cuncta pro suae libito voluntatis,[152]

Hannibal, that bravest and shrewdest of generals, was vanquished, by Caesar, Pompey, the leading citizen, was overthrown, and the whole senate wiped out. It was Carthage that Scipio subdued, Caesar did the same to Roman liberty and to the splendor and light of so great an empire. Scipio's life, it is said, "from his youth was dedicated to the gods and nourished in their temples," while Caesar's youth, indeed, was spent among insurrectionary, troublesome, and villainous men. Scipio burned with such a love for his fatherland that, when he saw that the hatred of certain citizens was turned on him, he chose of his own accord to make himself an exile in Liternum, lest by his power he might cause some disaster for the republic. But Caesar, in thrall to some unbridled rage for ruling, did not even for the safety of the fatherland yield to his rivals, but, rather, in a type of frenzy, took up arms against his fatherland, against the senate, against all good people, shed citizens' blood and destroyed the nobility of Rome.

You see already, if I am not mistaken — and Guarino can see, if 15 he does not disdain to read this letter of ours — how great a difference there is between Scipio and Caesar, and how much the one is more outstanding than the other. By what reasoning and on what basis Guarino dared to deny that Caesar was the subverter of Roman liberty, I still do not sufficiently understand. I do not see by what writers he could prove it, and I do not recall any author of a Roman history in Latin by whom that was ever brought into question. Whoever had this in mind would indeed be mindless, unless perhaps Guarino has at home some new manuscripts of which everyone else is completely ignorant, and which have led him to this opinion. Will Guarino deny that his Caesar took up arms against the senate and the leading men of the republic? That he filled the fields of Thessaly with Roman blood?[30] And that subsequently he usurped for himself sole rule of the city? And that because of this all subsequent emperors have been called Caesar? Will he contest that Caesar ordered everything according to his

distribuisse magistratus spretis senatus plebisque suffragiis, spo-
liasse aerarium indeque maximum[153] auri pondus abstulisse?[154]
Haec enim[155] omnes historici concorditer scribunt. At ex his
nonne illud clarissime sequitur Caesarem libertatis Romanae op-
pressorem fuisse?

16   Cuius quidem adversus Pompeium bellum nefarium patriae
fuisse, inquit Cicero,[156] quoniam constat eo bello consules Italia
pulsos, cum hisque Cnaeum Pompeium, qui (ut idem ait) imperii
populique Romani decus ac lumen fuit; omnes dehinc consulares,
praetores, tribunos plebis, magnam partem senatus, omnem sobo-
lem iuventutis, unoque verbo rem publicam expulsam atque exter-
minatam suis sedibus. Et idem quoque alibi contra[157] Antonium
invehens, de eodem bello haec ad verbum scripta reliquit:[158]

> Tu, Antoni, C. Caesari, perturbare omnia cupienti, causam
> belli contra patriam inferendi dedisti. Quid enim aliud ille
> dicebat, quam causam dementissimi consilii sui et facti af-
> ferebat, nisi quod intercessio neglecta, ius tribunicium sub-
> latum, circumscriptus esset Antonius? Omitto quam haec
> falsa, quam levia, praesertim cum omnino nulla causa iusta
> cuiquam esse possit contra patriam arma capiendi subver-
> tendique pulcherrimam rerum omnium libertatem.[159]

Miror itaque non parum Guarinum dicere ausum fuisse libertatem
Romanam armis Caesaris non fuisse deletam, cum[160] ea, quae a
Cicerone scripta[161] sunt (teste[162] gravissimo et tantae auctoritatis,
quantae neminem Guarinus adducere poterit), contrarium manifeste demonstrent.[163] Audeo profecto dicere fuisse Romanorum

own whim, that he doled out offices, scorning the votes of the senate and the plebs, that he despoiled the treasury and took away from there a massive weight of gold? For on these things all historians write in unison. But does it not most obviously follow from these things that Caesar was the oppressor of Roman liberty?

Indeed, his war against Pompey was a crime against the fatherland, according to Cicero, since it is well known that because of that war, "consuls were forced out of Italy and with them Gnaeus Pompey" (who, as the same author says, was "the glory and light of the Roman people and their empire"), and "all men of consular rank, praetors, tribunes of the plebs, a large part of the senate, all the flower of the youth, and, in a single word, the republic was expelled and uprooted from its home."[31] And Cicero also, elsewhere inveighing against Mark Antony, wrote this verbatim about the same war:

16

> You, Antony, gave to Gaius Caesar, who desired to subvert everything, the pretext for undertaking war against the fatherland. For what else did that man say? What pretext did he provide for this most senseless policy and deed, if not that the power of interposition by the veto had been disregarded, the right of the tribunes taken away, and Antony had been restricted? I say nothing of how false, how flimsy these pretexts were, especially since there could not possibly be any just cause whatever for anyone to take up arms against the fatherland and undermining that most beautiful thing of all, liberty.[32]

I wonder not a little, then, that Guarino has dared to say that Roman liberty was not destroyed by Caesar's weapons when those statements written by Cicero (who is a most weighty witness and of such authority that Guarino will not be able to provide anyone of similar stature) obviously prove the opposite. Indeed, I dare to assert that the republic of the Romans would have lasted forever,

rem publicam aeternam futuram,[164] nisi Caesaris ambitio et principatus furiosa cupiditas[165] Romani nominis gloriam et splendorem extinxissent. Quod ut clarius doceamus, non ab re erit,
quid sit res publica describere, si forte aliquando fieri possit, ut
Guarinus desinat hunc parricidam, hunc saevissimum Italiae hostem tanto studio laudare.[166]

17   Cicero tertio *De re publica* libro Scipionem Africanum introducit
de re publica disserentem[167] dicentemque rem publicam brevi definitione esse 'rem populi, populum autem non omnem esse coetum
multitudinis sed coetum iuris consensu et utilitatis communione
sociatum.' Ex his autem definitionibus colligit tunc esse rem publicam, id est rem populi, cum bene ac iuste regitur sive ab uno rege,
sive a paucis optimatibus, sive ab universo populo. Cum vero
iniustus est rex, quem 'tyrannum' more graeco appellat, aut iniusti
optimates, quorum consensum dixit esse 'factionem,' aut iniustus
ipse populus, cui nomen usitatum non reperit nisi uti etiam 'tyrannum' vocaret, omnino nullam esse rem publicam quoniam non esset res populi, cum tyrannus eam factione capesseret.

18   Nunc Guarinum interrogo, utrum Caesarem suum regem dicat,
an tyrannum. Certe non possum mihi persuadere doctissimum
virum, qui probe discernat inter regiam potestatem et tyrannidem,
Caesarem quovis pacto regem fuisse affirmaturum.[168] Quis nescit
regem volentibus et consentientibus praeesse, tyrannum coactis et
reclamantibus; reges non nisi ex causa et necessitate[169] saevire, tyrannos ex sola voluntate?[170] Reges bonis praemia, malis supplicia
tribuunt, circa quae duo omnis, teste Aristotele,[171] legalis iustitia
vertitur; tyranni, omnia perturbantes, malis honores deferunt, bonis tormenta et cruciatus.[172] Reges omnes eorum actus ad legum

if Caesar's ambition and frenzied desire to rule had not eliminated the glory and splendor of the Roman nation. In order to spell this out more clearly, it will not be beside the point to explain what a republic is, if it could perhaps one day happen that Guarino will desist from praising with such zeal this father-killer, this cruelest enemy of Italy.

Cicero, in the third book of his *On the Republic*, introduces 17 Scipio Africanus discoursing on the republic and stating in a brief definition that the public property[33] is "the property of the people, but a people is not every assembly of the masses, but an assembly joined together by agreed laws and shared interest."[34] From these definitions, he concludes that there is a republic, that is a "property of the people," at the moment when it is well and justly ruled, whether that is by a single king, by a few of the leading men or by the whole people. When the king is unjust (whom he calls after the Greek fashion "a tyrant") or the leading men are unjust (whose unity he said is "a faction") or the people themselves are unjust (for which he does not find a name in use, unless he would style that too a tyrant), then there is no republic at all since it would not be the "people's property" because the tyrant would have snatched hold of it by means of faction.[35]

Now I ask Guarino whether he calls his Caesar a king or a ty- 18 rant. I for one cannot convince myself that a most learned man, who rightly appreciates the difference between royal rule and tyranny, would assert in any way that Caesar was a king. Who does not know that a king presides over the willing and the consenting, while a tyrant does so over the coerced and protesting? That kings do not act severely unless with good cause and out of necessity, while tyrants do it on the basis of their will alone? Kings give rewards to the good and punishment to the bad, on which two points, as Aristotle attests, legal justice turns.[36] Tyrants, confounding everything, hand honors to the bad, and tortures and torments to the good. Kings direct every act by observance of the laws,

observantiam dirigunt, quae[173] muri sunt civitatum; tyranni nihil secundum leges decernunt. Quo certe[174] tyrannum fuisse Caesarem dicendum est.[175] Ex hoc illud sequitur nullam fuisse sub eo Romanorum rem publicam, quoniam eius tyrannide ac iniusto dominatu funditus eversa desinit[176] omnino esse res populi.

19   Utinam coram cum Guarino congrederer, ut quemadmodum ab hac argumentatione Caesarem defensurus esset, ex ipsius ore audirem! Abirem enim ex eo certamine fortasse[177] non indoctior. Neque vero ab hoc tanto in patriam[178] facinore Caesarem excusat (quod prae se ferre videtur Guarinus), quod sub spe[179] Parthici belli Pompeius duas sibi surripuerit legiones, antea ad Gallicum bellum concessas, aut quod litteras Caesaris ex Gallia ad consules missas conciliandorum animorum causa Pompeius ne in senatu recitarentur, effecerit, atque saepenumero litteris et nuntiis et legatis[180] ab eo contenderit ut, Romanae paci et saluti publice consulens, ab armis discederet et animum tranquillum[181] indueret. Quid haec, quaeso, ad excusationem Caesaris attinent? Quo pacto adversus senatum, cives ac patriam iustum bellum ab eo susceptum esse defendunt? Esto quod legiones duae Pompeii artibus et factionibus[182] ei surreptae fuerint: debuitne in Romanam libertatem tam acerbe conspirare? Confiteamur litteras suas ne in senatu recitarentur Pompeium impedivisse:[183] debuitne propterea manus suas civili sanguine maculare? Cur, quod Pompeio[184] suis litteris persuadere conabatur ut ab armis discedens Romanae paci consuleret, in se ipso[185] non observabat (quo solo se optimum civem et quietis ac tranquillitatis amatorem se facile demonstrasset,[186] atque in Pompeium omnem civilis belli calumniam culpamque coniecisset)? Demus insuper[187] Pompeium odio adversus Caesarem

which are the walls of cities; tyrants decide nothing according to the laws. From which it surely must be said that Caesar was a tyrant. It follows from this that there was under him no republic of the Romans since, overturned from the root up by his tyranny and unjust domination, it utterly stopped being a "property of the people."

Would that I could meet in person with Guarino, so that I could hear from his own lips how he would defend Caesar from this line of argument! Perhaps I would indeed leave that debate more learned.[37] Truly, it does not excuse Caesar from so great an evil deed against the fatherland that—on this Guarino seems to place much weight—Pompey, in the expectation of a Parthian war, took for himself two legions which had before been assigned to the war in Gaul. Nor does it excuse him that Pompey caused Caesar's letters sent from Gaul to the consuls with the intention of winning them over to his viewpoint not to be read out in the senate,[38] nor that he repeatedly in letters and by messengers and envoys strove to obtain from him that, giving thought for Rome's peace and public safety, he would give up arms and adopt a peaceful spirit.[39] What, I ask, do these have to do with excusing Caesar? In what way do they support the claim that he undertook a just war against the senate, the citizens, and the fatherland? Granted that two legions had been taken from him by Pompey's political machinations: did that require him to conspire so bitterly against Roman liberty? Let us accept that Pompey obstructed the reading of his letters in the senate: did that require him to stain his own hands with citizens' blood? Why, when he was trying in his letters to persuade Pompey to give up arms and take thought for Rome's peace, did he not follow his own advice? By that alone he could easily have demonstrated that he was a citizen of the best sort and a lover of peace and tranquility. And he would also have thrown onto Pompey all the blame and censure for the civil war. Let us, moreover, grant that Pompey burned with hatred against Caesar,

flagrasse, ei parasse insidias, eius potentiam ac gloriam diminuere studuisse: quomodo[188] haec ab oppugnatione patriae, a subversione rei publicae Caesarem poterunt excusare?

20   Ad quam[189] conservandam tantus nobis inesse ardor debet, tantum desiderium, quemadmodum L. Lentulus conclusis Romanis ad furcas Caudinas dixisse fertur, ut eam 'tam ignominia, quam morte nostra, si opus sit, conservemus.' Nam, ut inquit Cicero sexto[190] *De re publica* libro, 'omnibus qui patriam conservaverint, iuverint, auxerint, certus in coelo ac[191] definitus est locus, ubi beatitudine sempiterna fruantur.' Debuit siquidem hic Guarinianus Caesar gravissimas et atrocissimas[192] Pompeii iniurias, persecutiones atque calumnias[193] aequo animo perpeti,[194] priusquam contra patriam, quae eum genuerat, in lucem produxerat et magnis honoribus ac magistratibus ornaverat,[195] arma tam impia, tam crudelia sumere, quae sane[196] eum infelicissimum effecerunt.[197] Nam, ut pulchre in *Philippicis* inquit Cicero, 'si quis contra rem publicam fuerit, felix esse non potest.'

21   Multo sane praeclarius[198] Themistocles ille Atheniensis, imperator prudentissimus, qui, cum bello[199] Persico servitute Graeciam liberasset, ab ingrata tamen patria in exilium missus esset, a Xerxe contra Athenienses dux belli et princeps exercitus designatus, cum maximam cladem patriae imminere cerneret,[200] hausto tauri cruore solus mori maluit, quam cum hostibus in perniciem patriae vincere. Sic Q. Sertorius, maximi vir animi et altissimi consilii, qui, oblatis sibi Mithridatis opibus et regnis, nunquam adduci potuit ut cum servitute populi Romani regnaret.[201] Cuius etiam exulantis vox illa refertur, laude[202] dignissima, malle se Romae ignobilissimum civem esse, quam exulem omnium aliarum civitatum imperatorem nuncupari. Sic profecto noster hic Scipio, qui, cum eo[203] potentiae crevisset, ut (quemadmodum scribit Seneca et a te

that he prepared traps for him, that he was keen to diminish his power and glory: how will these facts be able to excuse Caesar from his attack on the fatherland and overthrow of the republic?

There should be in us so great an ardor to preserve this, such a 20 thirst, as when the Romans were enclosed in the Caudine Forks and L. Lentulus (it is reported) said, "we should preserve the republic as much by our disgrace as by our death, if it is required."[40] Indeed, as Cicero says in the sixth book of *On the Republic*, "for all who have preserved, aided and increased the fatherland, there is a place fixed and marked out in heaven, where they may enjoy eternal bliss."[41] It certainly behooved this Caesar of Guarino's to suffer with equanimity the most serious and severe injuries, persecutions and slanders wrought by Pompey before he took up such impious and cruel arms against his fatherland, which had given birth to him, brought him into the light and adorned him with great honors and offices. His deeds definitely made him a most unhappy man. For, as Cicero elegantly puts it in his *Philippics*, "whoever has been against the republic cannot be happy."[42]

Much more excellent was the deed of that Athenian Themis- 21 tocles, a very shrewd general. Although he had liberated Greece from slavery in the Persian War, he had been sent into exile by an ungrateful fatherland. When appointed by Xerxes to be the leader in war and head of the army against the Athenians, since he realized that a very great disaster threatened his fatherland, he preferred to die alone by drinking the gore of a bull, than win with its enemies to the ruin of his fatherland.[43] Likewise Q. Sertorius, a man of great spirit and the wisest counsel, who, when offered the kingdoms and riches of Mithridates, could never be brought to rule with the Roman people as slaves. This most praiseworthy saying of his is reported during his exile: that he would rather be the meanest of citizens in Rome than be called the ruler of all other cities as an exile.[44] Thus, indeed, this Scipio of ours, when his power had increased to such an extent that—as Seneca writes and

commemoratum est) 'aut Scipionem libertati, aut libertatem Scipioni iniuriam facere oporteret,' ne quid incommodi sua praesentia res publica pateretur, secessit Linternum in exilium voluntarium.

22   Hos patriae conservatores, hos defensores, hos, inquam, libertatis auctores[204] iure ac merito dicere possumus, qui spreta propria et singulari commoditate,[205] contemptis iniuriis, quas ab ingrata patria receperunt,[206] dignitatem, gloriam ac libertatem eius[207] semper ante oculos habuerunt, nullisque honoribus, nullis praemiis, nullis iniuriis,[208] nulla denique vindictae cupiditate aut dominandi ambitione induci[209] potuerunt, ut nedum libertatem[210] opprimerent, sed ne minimum quidem mali adversus eam cogitarent. Quod cum Caesar non fecerit, sed levibus quibusdam iniuriis Pompeii pulsatus patriam hostiliter invaserit, recte eum parricidam nominasti, atque propterea non laudandum, sed quam maxime vituperandum iudicasti.

23   Quod vero Guarinus scribere non erubuit, libertatem Romanam Caesaris cura, consilio et administratione in melius restitutam ac reformatam fuisse, maximos mihi excussit cachinnos, cum quod per se ipsum id falsum est omniumque scriptorum libris ac litteris reprobatum,[211] tum quod levi quadam ratiuncula confirmatur. Putat enim Guarinus idcirco Romanam libertatem a Caesare reparatam, quia senatorum, praetorum, quaestorum aliorumque magistratuum numerum ampliaverit. Sed qualis haec ampliatio fuerit quantumque Romanam rem publicam auxerit, Cicero, optimus civis, eximius philosophus ac orator clarissimus, rogatus dicat:

Caesar (inquit) cum post civilem victoriam ignobiles quosdam in senatu delegisset, non illos honestavit, sed illa honestis ornamenta turpavit.

as you have noted—"it had become unavoidable that either Scipio would harm liberty, or liberty Scipio," withdrew into voluntary exile at Liternum so that his own presence might not cause misfortune to the republic.[45]

These men we can truly and rightly call preservers of the fatherland, its defenders and (I say) the authors of its liberty—those who, scorning their own personal and individual advantage, and disdaining the injuries which they received from an ungrateful fatherland, always had before their eyes its dignity, glory, and liberty. They could not be brought by any honors, any rewards, any insults, or, indeed, any desire for revenge or thirst for absolute rule to suppress the fatherland's liberty, nor even to think a scintilla of evil against it. Since Caesar did not act in this way but, spurred by some trivial injuries of Pompey's making, like an enemy invaded the fatherland, you rightly termed him a father-killer and because of that judged that he should not be praised but reproached in the strongest terms.

As to what Guarino did not blush to write—that Roman liberty was by Caesar's care, counsel, and administration, restored and reformed for the better[46]—that made me howl with laughter, both because this is in itself false and refuted by the books and letters of all writers, and because it is supported by some flimsy reasoning. For Guarino thinks that Roman liberty was repaired by Caesar on the grounds that he increased the number of senators, praetors, quaestors, and other offices. But what sort of increase was this, and how did it strengthen the Roman republic? Cicero, the best citizen, outstanding philosopher, and most famous orator, if asked, would say:

> Caesar (he says), when, after his victory in the civil war, he had placed some ignoble men in the senate, did not honor them, but instead soiled those marks of status for the honorable.[47]

O praeclarum Romanae rei publicae restitutorem! O magnum[212] Romanorum magistratuum ampliatorem, Ciceronis nostri testimonio! Pudet me profecto Guarini causa, cum haec verba[213] saepius lego, quae doleo ab eo unquam scripta fuisse,[214] quoniam magnum auctoritati suae plurimum detrahunt pondus.[215]

24 Sed et ante usurpatum singulare urbis imperium, quam perniciosus civis patriae Caesar[216] fuerit, quotque seditiones ac discordias concitaverit,[217] vel strictim ac breviter[218] auctore Plutarcho referendum putavi, ut evidentius ostendatur hunc semper maxima suae reipublicae incommoda importasse.[219] Caesar, inquit Plutarchus, quando absens ad petendum consulatum contra leges renitente Catone admitti non potuit:

> urbem ingressus, astutum adoritur consilium, quod praeter Catonem universos fefellit homines. Id autem extitit: Pompeii Crassique, duorum potentissimorum hominum, ex simultate in gratiam reductio; qua quidem ex ambobus non parvam in se potentiam transferens, magna permutatione rem publicam labefactavit. Inde factum est ut cum Calpurnio Bibulo consul crearetur. Is, ut magistratum iniit, leges non consuli, sed audacissimo cuipiam tribuno pertinentes ad plebis gratiam ac voluptatem tulit, nunc agri viritim dividendi, nunc largitiones impertiundae, honestissimis ac praestantissimis in senatu viris obnixe refragantibus. Itaque sublatis clamoribus obtestatus est sese ad plebem confugere, et assistentibus hinc Crasso, inde Pompeio, utrumque leges ne approbarent, interrogavit. Quibus approbare se affirmantibus oravit, ut auxilio adessent et quos adversantes cernerent, minis et gladiis absterrerent; quod hi se facturos polliciti

O, glorious restorer of the Roman republic! O, great increaser of the Roman offices, as witnessed by our Cicero! Truly, I am ashamed on Guarino's behalf when I keep reading over these words, which I regret that he ever wrote, for they very much detract from the weight of his own authority.

But even before he usurped sole rule of the City, how destruc- 24 tive a citizen to his fatherland Caesar had been, and how many plots and how much discord he had fomented I have thought to report summarily and briefly on the authority of Plutarch, so that it is shown quite clearly that this man had always caused the greatest troubles for his own republic. Plutarch says that Caesar, when in his absence he could not be allowed to canvass for the consulship against the laws, with Cato in opposition,[48]

entered the City and adopted a cunning approach which fooled all the people, apart from Cato. His plan was to turn the rivalry between Pompey and Crassus, the two most powerful men, into friendship, by which, indeed, he transferred not a little power from both of them to himself . . . and, through this great change, he overthrew the republic. Hence it came about that he was made consul with Calpurnius Bibulus. When he entered upon his office, he introduced laws fitting not for a consul but for some very daring tribune, which were to gratify and please the people: now to distribute fields man by man, now to dole out largesse, with the most honorable and outstanding members of the senate strenuously opposed. So, under loud protestations, he swore to take himself to the plebs and, with the assistance of Crassus on one side and Pompey on the other, asked them whether or not they approved of the laws. When they declared that they did approve, he begged them to provide help by identifying those who opposed and frightening them with threats and weapons — something which they promised they

sunt. Caesar quoque, ut maiorem in modum ex Pompeii potentia fructum quaereret, filiam suam Iuliam (Scipioni Servilio antea desponsatam) eidem matrimonio collocavit. Ipse paulo post Calpurniam Pisonis filiam uxorem duxit, quem successurum sibi consulem ipse crearat, obtestante multumque vociferante Catone rem haud sane tolerandam esse praeturas ac imperia per nuptiarum lenocinia vendicari. Itaque Caesaris collega Bibulus, cum frustra contra legum promulgationem intercederet et persaepe una cum Catone in foro vitae discrimen adiisset, sese domi concludens totum magistratus tempus exegit.

25   Peractis nuptiis statim Pompeius referto militibus foro ad promulgandas populo leges socium se auctoremque praestitit. Omnem subinde Caesari Transalpinam Galliam adiecto Illirico cum legionibus quatuor in quinquennium administrandam adiudicavit. Quibus rebus[220] contradicentem Catonem Caesar in carcerem adduci iussit, eum ad tribunos provocaturum existimans. Ast ubi Caesar illum ne voce quidem emissa vadentem cerneret, nec solum primores gravi et iniquo animo ferentes, sed et plebeios ob Catonis reverentiam tacitos maestosque consequentes, unum ex tribunis plebis clam obsecravit, ut Catonem e manibus lictorum auferret. Dehinc ex senatoriis viris paucissimi ad eum in curiam[221] conveniebant; reliqui, moleste tolerantes, quam procul abibant. Quod autem in Caesaris consulatu turpissime factum iudicatur:[222] creatus est tribunus plebis Clodius, ille inquietissimus vir, idque ad Ciceronis, quem primum parentem patriae Romani appellaverunt, necem atque

would do. In order to gain greater advantage from Pompey's power, Caesar also gave him in marriage his daughter Julia, who had previously been betrothed to Scipio Servilius.[49] He himself a little later took as his wife Calpurnia, the daughter of Piso, whom he had made consul in succession to himself, with Cato solemnly declaring and loudly crying that it is intolerable that praetorships and power are bartered through the pandering of marriages. And so Caesar's colleague Bibulus, since his attempts to intervene against the promulgation of laws were in vain and since he had often run the risk of being murdered in the forum together with Cato, spent his whole time in office locked up at home.

After his marriage had taken place, when the forum was filled with soldiers, Pompey immediately offered himself to the people as an ally and sponsor for promulgating laws. He then awarded to Caesar all of Transalpine Gaul as his consular province for a five-year term, adding to it Illyricum and four legions. When Cato raised objections to these arrangements, Caesar ordered that he be taken to prison, assuming that he would appeal to the tribunes. But when Caesar realized that Cato was going without even a word and that not only were the leading men taking this with heavy and unhappy hearts but also that the plebs, out of reverence for Cato, were following him silently and sorrowfully, he secretly asked one of the tribunes of the plebs to release Cato from the hands of the lictors. From this time onward, very few of the senatorial order would approach him in the senate house, while the rest, being annoyed, stayed as far away as possible. But what is judged the most sordid deed of Caesar's consulship was the election of Clodius, that most restless man, as tribune of the plebs. This was done to achieve the death and destruction of Cicero, who was the first person that the Romans called father of the fatherland. It is also said that

25

interitum; nec prius Caesar in expeditionem profectus esse
dicitur, quam Ciceronem et Clodium turbulentibus inter se
altercationibus irritasset eumque eiecisset Italia.

26   Haec ex Plutarcho (quem nobis Latinum Guarinus fecit), quibusdam praetermissis, aliis paulisper commutatis delegi, ut, si
forte ea oblivioni dederit Guarinus, haec legens reminiscatur in-
tellegatque quam laudandus fuerit hic sui Caesaris consulatus,
quantumque Scipionis consulatui comparandus. Quis non videt
Caesarem consulatum malis artibus factioneque et potentia Pompeii et Crassi assecutum fuisse? Cui non liquet, teste Plutarcho, ea
duorum amicitia fretum magna permutatione rem publicam labe-
factasse?

27   Hiccine est ille Romanae libertatis reformator, quem Guarinus
tantis efferre conatur[223] laudibus, qui ex consule plebeius factus
spreto suffragiorum ordine terroribus, minis et armorum fragore
legem tulit rei publicae quam maxime damnosam,[224] qui collegam
metu perculsum domi se continere compulit, ut licentiori furore
debaccharetur? Ille, inquam, qui Catonem, virum iustissimum ac
sanctissimum semperque commodum publicum prae se feren-
tem,[225] in carcerem duci iussit, quo in loco licet animadvertere
quanta fuerit apud Romanos Catonis auctoritas, quem tamen
Guarinus redarguere[226] non veretur (de quo posterius aliquid ex-
plicabimus). Hiccine est ille Caesar extollendus, praedicandus ac
laudandus,[227] qui simultatum ac discordiarum causam inter Ciceronem et Clodium (turbulentissimum virum!) seminavit, eumque
tribunum plebis creari[228] procuravit ad Ciceronis interitum? Quo
solo maximis conviciis insequendus[229] est, cum optimum civem
ac praestantissimum[230] consulemque vigilantissimum, qui suo

Caesar did not go on campaign until he had incited violent
disagreements between Cicero and Clodius, and had pushed
the former out of Italy.[50]

I have chosen these points from Plutarch, whom Guarino   26
translated into Latin for us, omitting some things and changing
others a little, so that, if by chance Guarino has forgotten them,
he may by reading them remember, and appreciate how much
praise should have been given to this consulship of his Caesar, and
how it ought to have been compared to that of Scipio. Who does
not see that Caesar had gained his consulship through evil meth-
ods and factiousness and by the power of Pompey and Crassus?
To whom is it not evident, on Plutarch's authority, that, supported
by the friendship of those two, he shook the republic with great
upheaval?

Is this the renowned reformer of Roman liberty, whom Gua-   27
rino attempts to exalt with so many words of praise? The man
who, transformed from a consul to a plebeian, scorned the rules
for the elections, and, through alarms, threats and the din of
weapons, carried a law which was most deleterious to the republic;
the man who forced his colleague, fear stricken, to lock himself up
in his own home so that he could run wild with more uncurbed
frenzy? The man, I say, who ordered the sending to prison of
Cato, the most just and saintly of men, who always affirmed the
public good? At this point we may note how much authority Cato
had among the Romans (although Guarino does not hesitate to
contradict him, about which we will say something later). Is it
here the famous Caesar is to be lauded, proclaimed, and praised,
who sowed the seeds of the rivalry and conflict between Cicero
and Clodius (that most disruptive of men), and who managed to
have Clodius made tribune of the people to the ruin of Cicero?
For this alone Caesar should be attacked with the greatest abuse,
since he attempted, by means of Clodius' plots, to destroy the best

consulatu[231] a perniciosa illa Catilinae coniuratione rem publicam liberavit, unicum denique lumen Latinae facundiae, Clodianis insidiis extinguere conatus est. O perfidissimum hominem! O monstrum taeterrimum! O nequissimum bonorum civium persecutorem! Hiccine Scipioni Africano anteponendus, qui multis cladibus afflicta re publica quartum et vigesimum annum agens, nullius fretus potentia, nullius auxilio, neque armatus, neque stipatus satellitibus, sed libero[232] populi consensu, magno omnium applausu consul[233] designatus est?

28   De cuius consulatu[234] cum amplissime scripseris, neque mihi, neque aliis ulteriora scribendi[235] locum ullum reliquisti. Neque vero illud praetereundum censeo, quod aerarium populi Romani a Scipione auctum atque amplificatum est,[236] adeo ut, cum per senatus consultum pecuniam ex aerario capere deberet et quaestores id ea die aperire nollent, indignatum dixisse ferant: 'Capiam vi pecuniam, quia aerarium istud a me impletum[237] est.' A Caesare vero spoliatum aerarium, quis ignorat? Cui cum se obiecisset Metellus, tribunus populi, legesque afferret, 'non idem armorum ac legum tempus est,' inquit, 'quod si has ipse res ferre non potes, hic procul abscede.'[238] Tum ad aerarii portas se contulit;[239] apparentibus nusquam clavibus fabros accersivit, quibus, portas effringere iussis, Metellus iterum obstare coepit, at in eum Caesar 'nescis,' inquit, 'adulescentule, difficilius mihi esse dicere quam facere?'; quo dicto perterritus Metellus abiit.[240] Quae[241] est in hoc Caesaris facto Guarini sententia? Laudaturusne est effractorem ac expilatorem aerarii publicumque praedonem? Quod si eum vituperabit, ut facturum[242] spero (nisi me virtutis ac prudentiae eius fallat opinio), patiatur[243] in hoc, quemadmodum et in aliis multis, Scipionem

and most outstanding citizen, the most vigilant of consuls — who in his consulship freed the republic from that destructive conspiracy of Catiline — and finally the singular light of Latin eloquence.[51] O most faithless man! O foulest monster! O vilest persecutor of good citizens! And this man should be placed before Scipio Africanus, who, when the republic had suffered many disasters, in his twenty-fourth year was made consul, not relying on anyone's power, with the help of no one, neither armed nor backed up with henchmen, but with the free agreement of the people, and everyone's great applause?

Since you have discussed his consulship most fully, you have 28 left no space for myself or others for writing anything more.[52] I do not, however, think it should pass without notice that the treasury of the Roman people was expanded and increased by Scipio, to such an extent that when it was considered necessary by the senate's decree to withdraw money from the treasury and the quaestors refused that day to open it, they say he said angrily: "I will take the money by force, because that treasury was filled by me." But who does not know that the treasury was plundered by Caesar? When Metellus, the tribune of the people, stood in his path and adduced the laws, Caesar said "arms and the law do not share the same timing," and "if you cannot bear these things, then get yourself far from here." Then he took himself to the doors of the treasury and when the keys could be found nowhere, he sent for workmen who were ordered to break down the doors. Metellus again began to stand in their way but Caesar said to him, "do you not know, young man, that it is more difficult for me to say something than do it," at which comment Metellus was terrified and fled.[53] What is Guarino's judgment of this deed of Caesar's? Will he praise the safe-breaking pillager of the treasury, its public plunderer? But if he condemns Caesar, as I hope he will (unless my opinion of his virtue and good sense is faulty), let him allow that in this as in so many other respects Scipio should be placed before his Caesar. For

suo Caesari anteferri. Nam alter omnes conatus, cogitationes ac
studia ad augendam rei publicae gloriam conservandamque libertatem, alter ad extinguendam aut suae cupiditati subiciendam
convertit.

29   Et quamquam Romanum imperium Gallia Britanniaque multis
quoque subactis[244] urbibus longe lateque ampliasse Caesar videatur, in quo sane eius res gestae admirationis et claritatis in se plurimum continent, hoc tamen solo facinore conspirationis et coniurationis in patriam, veluti caligine quadam ac nube densissima,
rerum bellicarum magnitudinem[245] splendoremque obfuscavit.
Hoc impiissimum scelus, hoc immanissimum flagitium, mi Poggi
carissime, meum semper impulit animum, ut omnibus nervis industriae meae[246] Caesarem damnarem, exsecrarem ac tanquam[247]
pestem quandam et perniciem Romani imperii[248] perhorrescerem.
Quem profecto qui extollit,[249] neque quid patriae salus, neque
quid rei publicae commodum, neque quanta libertatis dulcedo sit
meo iudicio satis animadvertit.

30   Ad id autem mihi summopere confirmandum accedit, quod[250]
ex ea civitate[251] originem duxi,[252] quae cum virtute, fortuna, potentia terras moderetur et maria sitque, quasi mundus alter,[253] commune generis humani refugium ac lucidissimum sidus Italiae — illa
tantum[254] singulari laude et gloria[255] omnes alias supersat, quod
nullius est dictioni, nullius servituti[256] atque imperio subiecta, sed
verum est et inviolatum libertatis templum. Pro qua tutanda atque
amplianda, quot terrestres navalesque paraverit exercitus, quantis
viribus quantoque conatu contenderit, ipsius servatae ac stabilitae
libertatis facile demonstrat[257] eventus. Cumque huius, de qua loquor, libertatis extinguendae[258] cupiditate saepe a summis imperatoribus ac maximis ducibus bello lacessita sit, non solum non
devicta est, sed validissimorum exercituum extitit triumphatrix.
Id enim apud nos firmissime constitutum est, ut qui libertati
finis fuerit, idem sit et vitae. Eapropter adversus tyrannorum

the former turned all his efforts, his thoughts and his energy toward increasing the glory of the republic and preserving its liberty, while the other turned them to destroying it or subjecting it to his own greed.

And although it might seem that Caesar extended the Roman 29 empire far and wide by subjugating Gaul and Britain and many cities as well, in which his deeds certainly include much deserving of admiration and fame, nevertheless by this one crime of plotting and conspiring against the fatherland—like a fog or a very dense cloud—he has obscured the greatness and splendor of his feats in war. It is this most impious evil act, this most monstrous wrong, my dearest Poggio, that always drives my mind so that with every ounce of my diligence I condemn and curse Caesar and have great horror of him as a plague and bane upon the Roman empire. Indeed, anyone who praises him in my judgment does not fully consider what the well-being of the fatherland is or the interest of the republic, or how great the sweetness of liberty actually is.

What confirms this most of all for me is that I have my roots in 30 that city which, because it rules land and sea with virtue, good fortune and power, and is (like another world) a common refuge for humankind and the brightest star of Italy, surpasses all others so much in its unparalleled praise and glory. This is because it is not subject to the rule of anyone, nor to slavery or empire imposed by anyone but is the true and pure temple of liberty. For preserving and augmenting it, how many armies on land and sea it has raised, and with what great forces and effort it has fought, the outcome—consisting of its own preserved and stable liberty—easily demonstrates. And although through a desire to destroy this liberty of which I speak the city has been challenged in war by the highest commanders and greatest leaders, it has emerged not only undefeated but the victor over extremely strong armies. For this belief is most firmly established among us: that the end of liberty would be the end to life. For this reason so many armies have been

saevissimam rabiem, tot collecti exercitus, tot instructae acies, totiens debellatum est,[259] ut (si fieri posset) nedum Venetiarum civitas, sed[260] universa Italia—quae tantis cladibus tyrannorum oppressa est[261]—aliquando pace, tranquillitate, quiete, otio, rerum
omnium mortalium dulcissima et optatissima libertate potiretur?
Quid igitur cuiquam mirum[262] videri debet, si in libertatis arce
munitissima natus, nutritus, educatus, gravissimumque ac durissi-
mum tyrannidis iugum nunquam expertus (quam ob rem diis immortalibus omnia debeo!)[263] Caesarem scelestissimum parricidam,
eversorem Romanae libertatis, hostem patriae acerbissimum[264]
pleno ore ac libera voce detestor? Ad id enim (ut dixi), etiam si
cetera deessent, me cogit compellitque natura, rerum omnium parens, quam in omni vita ducem[265] sequi a doctissimis viris admo-
nemur.

31   Sed iam reliqua prosequamur.[266] Libet nunc Guarinum paulisper interrogare, cur L. Iunium Brutum omnes[267] Romanorum de-
cantent[268] historiae summisque in coelum efferant laudibus. Credo
virum doctissimum illico responsurum[269] L. Brutum idcirco tantam sibi apud Romanos gloriam vendicasse, quod regio dominatu
et Tarquini Superbi tyrannide patriam liberavit. Id enim cum alia
permulta, tum elegantes Vergilii versus, quos mirum in modum
extollere Guarinus consuevit, pulchre declarant. Eos referre non
alienum esse a re nostra existimavi:[270]

> Vis et Tarquinios reges animamque superbam
> Ultoris Bruti fascesque videre receptos?
> Consulis imperium hic primus saevasque secures
> Accipiet, natosque pater nova bella moventes

gathered, so many battle lines arrayed and so many wars fought
and won against the most savage frenzy of tyrants in order that, if
this were possible, not just the city of Venice but the whole of Italy
(which has been subjected to such great calamities at the hands of
tyrants) might at some point obtain peace, rest, tranquility, quiet,
and calm and—the sweetest and most desired of all mortal
things—liberty. Why, then, should it seem remarkable to anyone
if I, who was born, suckled and educated in the securest stronghold of liberty and who have never experienced the most heavy
and harsh yoke of tyranny (for which reason I owe everything to
the immortal gods!), with a loud and free voice execrate Caesar,
that most wicked father-killer, destroyer of Roman liberty, and bitterest enemy of his fatherland? For, as I have said, even if the
other reasons were absent, nature, the parent of all things[54] (which
we are advised by the most learned men to follow as our leader
throughout our lives[55]), forces and compels me to this stance.

But let us now proceed with the rest. I should like now to ques- 31
tion Guarino a little about why all the histories of the Romans
laud L. Junius Brutus and praise him to the heavens. I believe that
most learned man would readily reply to this that L. Brutus
gained for himself such glory among the Romans because he freed
the fatherland from royal domination and the tyranny of Tarquin
the Proud. This indeed is beautifully expressed both in many
other places and in elegant verses of Vergil which Guarino was accustomed to extol in a remarkable way. I have considered it not
irrelevant to our matter to cite them:

> Dost wish the Kings Tarquinian to see,
> And the proud soul of vengeful Brutus, and
> Recovery of the rods and of the ax?
> He first shall take the consul's power up,
> Its savage ax blades too, and he shall call,
> A father his own sons, who stir new wars,

Ad poenam pulchra pro libertate vocabit
Infelix, utcumque ferent ea facta minores:
Vincit amor patriae laudumque immensa cupido.

Is namque[271] cernens quot mala, quot scelera, quot flagitia, stupra quoque et adulteria, furta, homicidia, spolia, rapinae ceteraque vitiorum agmina[272] in dies oriebantur, quod unius libidini et immoderatae cupiditati cuncta obtemperabant, ductus ardentissimo quodam[273] spiritu et magno libertatis amore tyrannos illos impiissimos[274] urbe fugavit;[275] simulque praecavens, ne in futurum eadem tyrannica peste affligeretur res publica, primus post exactos reges consul factus, iure iurando populum adegit neminem se unquam Romae passuros regnare. His tot tantisque in patriam beneficiis[276] dignus habitus est, cui viventi magni honores decernerentur, eius vero mortem decoram fecit publica maestitia, quae eo magis insignis fuit, quia[277] eum matronae per annum deplorarunt, quod tam acerbus ultor violatae pudicitiae fuisset.

32   Haec cum ita sint, dicat mihi Guarinus (a quo vehementer opto[278] doctior fieri), quamobrem[279] non multis quoque laudibus efferendi sint Brutus et Cassius, qui vehementi liberandae patriae a miserabili Caesaris servitute[280] amore succensi memoresque fortasse prioris illius Bruti, qui exemplum insigne recuperandae libertatis posteris reliquerat, eum[281] neci tradiderunt. Quid enim intererat[282] Tarquinius Superbus an C. Caesar singulare sibi urbis imperium vendicaret[283] omniaque suae dicioni,[284] libidini ac voluntati subiceret, cunctaque unius arbitrio interverterentur?[285] Quod si recte singula pensare ac perspicere[286] voluerimus, non formidabo illud etiam constanter asserere: longe iustiorem probabilioremque

To punishment for beauteous freedom's sake.
Unhappy man! Howe'er posterity
Report these deeds, the victory shall stand
To love of land and huge desire for praise.[56]

For when he saw how many evils, how many crimes, how many outrages, violations as well as adulteries, thefts, killings, despoliations, plunderings, and a procession of other vices arose daily because everything was submitted to the lust and uncontrolled desire of a single person, Brutus, driven by a brightly burning spirit and a great love of freedom, chased those most impious tyrants from the city. At the same time, taking precautions to avoid the republic suffering the same menace of tyranny in future, after being elected as the first consul after the ejection of the kings, he forced the people to promise that they would not allow anyone ever to be king in Rome. On account of these many and great benefits to his fatherland, he was considered worthy of being given great honors in his lifetime; but his death was made honorable by a public mourning, which was all the more notable because the matrons bewailed his passing for a whole year, as he had been such a fierce avenger of violated virtue.[57]

As these things are so, let Guarino—by whom I strongly desire 32 to be made more learned—tell me why Brutus and Cassius should not also be exalted with much praise. They burned with a strong passion to free their fatherland from the miserable servitude of Caesar, and perhaps mindful of that earlier Brutus, who had left to posterity a shining example of the recovery of freedom, they consigned Caesar to death. For what difference did it make whether it was Tarquin the Proud or Julius Caesar who claimed for himself sole rule of the city, and subjected everything to his own power, caprice and will, and turned everything upside down at the discretion of a single person? If we want to consider and perceive the particulars correctly, I will not shrink from resolutely

fuisse causam Caesaris occidendi, quam Tarquinii repellendi.[287] Tarquinius enim neque novum regnandi modum, neque prius inauditam imperii[288] potestatem sibi usurpavit. Nam ab urbe condita ad eius usque tempora regio dominatu urbs Romana semper subiecta fuit.[289] At Caesar contra leges maiorumque instituta multorumque annorum rem publicam, quae aut consulum, aut aliorum magistratuum imperio gubernata fuerat, suae tyrannidi subicere non expavit.[290] Tarquinius voluntariis civibus; Caesar coactis ac contradicentibus imperavit. Tarquinius nulla contra patriam arma, ut regno potiretur, sumpsisse fertur;[291] Caesar vi et armis ac civili cruore libertatem oppressit. Tarquinius Romanum imperium auxit, Caesar post civilem victoriam dominandi cupiditate extinxit.[292] Itaque si superior ille Brutus, quem pulchrae libertatis desiderium ad pellendam ex urbe regum tyrannidem[293] impulit, iure ac merito laudatur, ut ex superioribus facile apparere potest,[294] cur non multo ampliori[295] laude et gloria Brutus posterior et Cassius laudandi[296] sunt, quod patriae servitutem, magistratuum contemptum, legum omnium comitiorumque perturbationem ferre diutius non valentes, cum in dies magis ac magis Caesaris insolentiam, fastum ac libidinem augeri cernerent, eius morte rem publicam eo[297] horrendo monstro liberare non formidarunt? Quod quidem optimorum civium[298] factum nunquam satis digne extollere[299] possem, etiam si mihi linguae centum essent oraque centum.[300]

33   Et ne forte me proprio sensu haec scribere Guarinus existimet,[301] Ciceronis verba, pluribus in locis sparsa, in unum[302] collegi, ut ipsius de morte Caesaris iudicium[303] memoria repetens desinat aliquando eum tantis laudibus[304] extollere. Inquit enim imprimis mortem Caesaris factum fuisse gloriosissimum; item omnes boni

asserting even this: the case for killing Caesar was far more just and persuasive than that for expelling Tarquin. For Tarquin did not usurp for himself a new mode of ruling or a previously unheard of power of rule. Indeed, since the foundation of the City right up until his own time the City of Rome had always been subjected to royal lordship. But Caesar, contrary to the laws and practices of the forefathers which had existed for many years, did not scruple to subject to his own tyranny a republic, which had been governed by the power of consuls or other magistrates. Tarquin ruled willing citizens, Caesar ones who were forced and objecting. Tarquin is not said to have taken up arms against the fatherland in order to gain the kingship; Caesar by force of arms and the shedding of citizens' blood crushed freedom. Tarquin expanded Roman rule, Caesar after the civil victory destroyed it through his desire to wield control. Thus, if the earlier Brutus, whom the yearning for beautiful freedom drove to expel the tyranny of kings from the City, is rightly and deservedly praised (as can easily be seen from the facts mentioned above), why should the later Brutus and Cassius not be showered with much greater praise and glory? For they could no longer bear the enslavement of the fatherland, the spurning of the magistracies, the overthrowing of all the laws and elections, and since they realized that day by day Caesar's insolence, haughtiness, and caprice were growing more and more, they did not shrink from freeing the republic from that dreadful monster by his death. In fact, I could never praise worthily enough that deed of the best citizens, even "if I had a hundred tongues and a hundred mouths."[58]

In case Guarino by chance imagines that I write these things 33 solely as my own opinion, I have gathered together the words of Cicero which are scattered in various places, so that he may recall Cicero's judgment on the death of Caesar and finally cease to laud him with such great praise. In the first place, Cicero says that the death of Caesar was the most glorious deed; also (he says) all good

(ait), quantum in ipsis fuit, Caesarem occiderunt: aliis consilium, aliis animus, aliis occasio defuit, voluntas nemini. Alibi factum Bruti et Cassii laudans, inquit:

Quae res unquam (pro sancte Iuppiter) non modo in hac urbe, sed in omnibus ceteris est gesta maior? Quae gloriosior? Quae commendatior erit hominum memoriae sempiternae?

Et iterum:

Quodsi[305] se ipsos illi nostri liberatores e conspectu nostro abstulerunt, at exemplum facti reliquerunt. Tarquinium Brutus bello est persecutus, qui tum rex fuit, cum esse Romae regem liceret. Sed Sp. Cassius, Sp. Mellius, M. Manlius[306] propter suspicionem regni sunt necati. Hi autem primum cum gladiis non in regnum appetentem, sed in regnantem[307] impetum fecerunt; quod ipsum factum, cum per se praeclarum atque divinum est, tum expositum ad imitandum, praesertim cum illi eam gloriam consecuti sunt, quae vix coelo capi posse videatur.

Haec Cicero in *Philippicis* graviter et luculenter, ut solet, quae si Guarinus animadvertisset, nequaquam (ut arbitror) tam vehemens fuisset in eo laudando, cuius mortem Cicero[308] factum quoddam gloriosissimum, praeclarum atque divinum appellat.

34   Illud autem omnem admirationis modum excedit, quod Guarinus, studio laudandi Caesaris aut tibi contradicendi adductus, grande quoddam scelus committere non exhorruit.[309] Nam Catonem Uticensem, divinum quendam sanctum[310] atque integerrimum virum, cuius nomen in hanc usque diem[311] apud omnes—

men killed Caesar, as far as they were able: some lacked the resolution, some the spirit, some the opportunity, but nobody the will.[59] Elsewhere, praising the deed of Brutus and Cassius, he says:

> What greater thing has ever been done, oh sacred Jove, not only in this city but in all others? What more glorious? What worthier to be assigned to the perpetual memory of humankind?[60]

And again:

> But if those our liberators have taken themselves out of our sight, still they have left the example of their deed behind them. Brutus harried Tarquin in war, who was then king when it was permissible to be king of Rome. But Spurius Cassius, Spurius Mellius and Marcus Manlius were killed on the suspicion of wanting to be king. These men [Brutus and Cassius], on the other hand, were the first to take up swords and make an attack, not upon a person seeking kingship but on one who was reigning. This deed is not only splendid and superlative in itself but also exhibited for imitation, especially since they have gained such glory that it seems heaven can hardly contain it.[61]

Cicero said these words in the *Philippics* authoritatively and brilliantly, as is his wont. If Guarino had taken them into account, he would (I think) have been by no means so strident in praising the man whose death Cicero called a "most glorious," "splendid," and "superlative" deed.

What, however, goes beyond any measure of astonishment is 34 that Guarino, led by his eagerness either to praise Caesar or to contradict you, did not shrink from perpetrating a certain huge and heinous act. For he accuses, rebukes and snipes at Cato Uticensis, a godlike, saintly, and most upright man, whose name to this very day is celebrated by everybody — Caesar excepted — with

Caesare excepto—magna veneratione[312] celebratum est, accusat, reprehendit, mordet atque importunum dicit, rigidum, pervicacem, morosum, pertinacem, inexorabilem ceterisque multisque vitiis refertum, quae mediusfidius hic repetere non potui,[313] quoniam eorum recordatione abhorret animus ac incredibili quadam molestia premitur, cum animadverto Guarinum niti lumen unicum Romanae gravitatis, modestiae, iustitiae et continentiae[314] et integritatis suis verbis extinguere.[315] Idque non aliam ob rem facere eum arbitror,[316] nisi quia Cato, tanquam verus libertatis patriae defensor caesarianarumque factionum et coniurationum[317] propugnator acerrimus (quoniam ex ipsis evertendam rem publicam[318] prudentissimus vir longe ante praevidebat), a Caesare maximo semper odio habitus est. Qua ex re facile assequor coniectura Guarinum tam immoderata laudandi Caesaris cupiditate detineri, ut nedum Catonem ipsum, quem omnium scriptorum annales praedicant ac venerantur, verum omnes Romanae urbis optimates, universum paene senatum, quam plurimos praestantissimos cives et de re publica optime meritos—quibus in multis rebus Caesar inferior extitit[319]—quoniam ad reprimendam Caesaris furiosam dominandi[320] ambitionem Pompeii castra secuti sunt, damnaturus sit eosque ignavos et improbos homines appellaturus.

35   O indignum facinus! O novum calumniae genus! O magnam ingenii caecitatem![321] Quorsum ruit Guarini oratio?[322] Quorsum praecipitat, ut[323] virum sanctum,[324] iustum, severum, constantem,[325] nullis minis, nullis[326] terroribus, nullis precibus, nullius odio aut gratia a recto atque honesto declinantem, tam turpiter tamque ignominiose nominare ausus sit?[327] An ignorat Guarinus, quod Cato hic noster in sermone semper fuit verax, in iudicio iustus, in consilio providus, in commisso fidelis, in proposito constans, in bonitate conspicuus, in universa morum honestate praeclarus?[328] An nescit, quod Catonis bona mens, purum pectus, innocens vita omnium consensu laudatur? Ferunt a pueritia eius constantiam et severitatem conspicuam fuisse vimque habuisse

great veneration.[62] Guarino calls him troublesome, rigid, willful, peevish, stubborn, relentless, and stuffed full with all and every vice,[63] which (by my faith), I could not repeat here, since my soul shudders at the memory of them and it is overcome with an unbelievable vexation when I consider that Guarino with his words strives to snuff out the unique shining light of Roman dignity, modesty, justice, temperance, and integrity. I think he did so for no other reason than that Cato—as a true defender of the freedom of the fatherland and the bitterest battler against Caesar's factions and conspiracies (because he, a very shrewd man, had long before foreseen that these very things must undermine the republic)—had always been most deeply hated by Caesar. From this I easily infer that Guarino is so held in thrall by his immoderate desire to praise Caesar that he was bound to damn and call cowardly and wicked not just Cato, whom all writers' histories proclaim and honor, but all the leading men of the city of Rome, nearly the whole senate and as many as possible of the most outstanding citizens and benefactors of the republic (to whom Caesar was in many respects inferior) since, in order to curb Caesar's frenzied ambition for absolute rule, they joined Pompey's camp.

Oh outrageous crime! Oh new type of slander! Oh great mental blindness! To what end does Guarino's speech rush? To what end does it plunge that it has dared so foully and so shamefully to arraign a man who was saintly, just, austere, constant, who did not diverge from what is right and honorable because of any threats, any fear, any prayers, or the hatred and favor of anyone? Or is Guarino not aware that this man, our Cato, was always truthful in speech, just in judgment, farsighted in advice, trustworthy in an undertaking, constant in a plan, distinguished in goodness, splendid in the complete respectability of his character? Or does he not know that Cato's good mind, pure heart and guiltless life are praised by the agreement of everyone? They say that from early childhood he was notable for his constancy and gravity, and had a

35

ultra aetatem eius incepta:[329] adulantibus siquidem asper fuit; tardus ad risum, ut usque ad significationem dumtaxat os eius rideret idque perraro;[330] ad iram non facile labens sed, cum in eam devenerat, implacabilis.[331] Erat praeterea gravis atque terribilis iustitiae custos; in ceteris vero moribus mitissimus atque humanissimus. Auctor horum omnium nobis est Plutarchus, quem si Guarini iudicio praeferendum censeo, nihil est, quod mihi subirascatur. Is etiam refert eum tantae integritatis tantaeque iustitiae apud Romanos habitum fuisse, ut multi hoc ipso condemnati fuerint, quod Catonis iudicium recusando non satis sua innocentia confidere visi sunt. Multis quoque in magni opprobrii partem obiectum ait, quod Catonem, iudicem oblatum, recipere noluissent. Quod, quaeso, praeclarius, quod laudabilius testimonium de cuiusquam viri virtute dici aut referri posset? Ego hoc populi Romani iudicium, hanc de Catone existimationem cunctis Caesaris victoriis censeo esse praeferendam. Eam enim non armorum terror, non instructae acies, non militum robur, non locorum opportunitas,[332] non ipsa fortuna — quae magnam in rebus bellicis sibi partem vendicat[333] — sed virtus, integritas, bonitas et innocentissime acta vita Catoni comparavit.

36   Maiestas vero eius et auctoritas tanta apud Romanos fuit, ut P. Clodio, turbulentissimo cive, virgines vestales apud populum accusante, Cato earum suscepta defensione tantam sua gravitate et auctoritate accusatori verecundiam iniecerit, ut urbem relinquere cogeretur. Qua de re cum ei Cicero gratias ageret, non sibi inquit Cato, sed rei publicae gratias agendas, cuius causa illa fecisset. O divinum hominem, qui omnia eius consilia, actiones omnes in rem publicam conferebat![334] Amor vero eius in patriam, quibus verbis potest explicari? Omnium siquidem bonorum, omnium oppressorum defensor fuit, gratuitam unicuique operam suam

determination beyond his years.[64] He was indeed harsh toward flatterers, so slow to laugh that his mouth would only form a token smile, and that only on rare occasions; he did not easily slip into anger but when he had, he was implacable. He was, moreover, a serious and fearsome guardian of justice; for the rest of his character, he was truly the mildest and most humane of men. The author of all these points is Plutarch, and if I consider his judgment preferable to that of Guarino, there is no reason he should grow angry with me. Plutarch also tells us that Cato was held among the Romans to have so much integrity and justice that many were condemned by this very fact, that, by objecting to Cato's judgment, they seemed to lack sufficient confidence in their own innocence. He also says that it was cast for many as a great reproach that they had refused to accept Cato when he was offered as the judge for their case.[65] What, I ask, could be said or cited as a more splendid or more praiseworthy testimony to any man's virtue? I think this judgment of the Roman people, this opinion of Cato should be placed before all Caesar's victories. For it was not the fear of arms, not the forces arrayed, nor the soldiers' might, nor the advantage of location, nor fortune itself—which plays a large part in matters of war—but virtue, integrity, goodness, and a life led blamelessly that won it for Cato.

His greatness and authority with the Romans were, indeed, so 36 great that when Publius Clodius, that most disruptive citizen, was accusing the Vestal virgins before the people and Cato took up their defense, he put the accuser to such great shame by his gravity and authority that Clodius was forced to leave the city.[66] When Cicero gave him thanks for that act, Cato responded that thanks should go not to himself but to the republic for the sake of which he had done those things. O divine man who devoted all his counsels and actions to the republic! Can any words express his love for the fatherland? For he acted as the defender of all who were good, of all who were oppressed, expending his effort, free of charge, for

impendens;[335] neminem sibi blandiciis conciliavit; in senatu libere
dixit; utilitatem publicam cunctis rebus semper anteposuit; nullis
muneribus coinquinatus est;[336] omnes factiones colligationesque,[337]
velut paci et tranquillitati rei publicae adversas, detestatus est.[338] In
senatum primus veniebat, postremus abibat.[339] Quod autem maximum amoris eius in patriam indicium est: Caesaris audaciae et
furori se totis viribus obicem posuit, idque persaepe cum magno
vitae suae discrimine. Praevidebat enim vir prudentissimus eum
ignem, nisi in initio[340] extingueretur, ingens incendium suscitatu-
rum; cuius consilio ac voluntati si paritum fuisset, nunquam profecto res publica in eas calamitates incidisset. Quo in loco facile
discerni potest, quanto maior Romae[341] fuerit eius quam Caesaris
auctoritas, cum adversus eum, quem sibi infestissimum experieba-
tur suisque cupiditatibus tantopere[342] resistentem, nihil unquam
asperioris mali exercere ausus fuerit, quoniam eum ab omni senatu
et universo populo, velut intrepidum libertatis publicae defensorem, maxima veneratione coli atque honorari[343] cernebat.

37   Pompeii vexilla secutus est, quoniam ea bonos omnes sequi in-
tuebatur ipsumque adversus Caesarem pro libertate Romana dimi-
caturum existimabat. Is sane non adeo Caesarem odio persequeba-
tur, quam civium, qui cum eo erant, salutem et incolumitatem
optaret. Pompeianis namque ob Caesarem aliquando in fugam
versum, laetitia exultantibus, solus ipse plorabat calamitosam patriae fortunam, ambitionem detestatus, cuius causa multi ac boni
cives in acie cecidissent. Ferunt eum, a qua die Pompeii castra ingressus est, neque capillos neque barbam deposuisse, luctum vero
pro tantis rei publicae cladibus semper observasse.[344] Sed[345] quid
in singulis tam clarissimi viri virtutibus immoror, quas si omnes[346]

anyone; he did not ingratiate himself with anyone through flattery; he spoke his mind in the senate; he always put the public welfare before all other things; he was not corrupted by any bribes; he abhorred all factions and leagues as being against the peace and tranquility of the republic. He was the first to arrive at the senate and the last to leave. Yet, the greatest sign of his love for the fatherland is that he placed himself with all his might as an obstacle against Caesar's audacity and frenzy, and by so doing often put his own life in great danger. For that most wise man foresaw that that fire, if it was not extinguished at the start, would raise a huge conflagration. If his counsel and will had been obeyed, then the republic would never indeed have fallen into such disasters. At this point it is easy to recognize how much greater his authority was at Rome than Caesar's, since Caesar dared not ever orchestrate anything truly hurtful against Cato, whom he had found by experience to be most hostile to himself and so firmly resistant to his desires, because he realized that he was honored and held in the highest respect by all the senate and the entire people as the fearless defender of public liberty.

Cato followed Pompey's standards because he observed that all 37 good men were following them and reckoned that he himself would battle against Caesar for the sake of Roman freedom. Truly, he did not so much harry Caesar out of hatred but rather wished for the safety and well-being of the citizens who were with him. Thus, on one occasion when Pompey's supporters were celebrating with delight because Caesar had finally been put to flight, he alone deplored the disastrous fortune of the fatherland, abhorring the ambition for the sake of which many good citizens had died in battle. They say that from the day he entered Pompey's camp, he trimmed neither his hair nor his beard and always observed mourning because the calamities befalling the republic were so great.[67] But why do I linger on the individual virtues of such a famous man, when if I wanted to delineate them all, time and words

explicare vellem, tempus et sermo mihi deficeret, siccareturque
fons ille mellifluus Ciceronianae eloquentiae? Si cuncta, quae in eo
laudabilia fuere sua vellet oratione complecti,[347] unum solum Lucani, non ignobilis poetae, testimonium adducam—praeter ea,
quae a te et verissime et eleganter in defensionem sanctissimi hominis scribuntur—quod Guarinum, in hac parte graviter errantem
(ut cum eius bona venia loquar), vincit, superat et confundit.[348]
Inquit enim poeta ille de Catone loquens:

> Iustitiae cultor, rigidi servator honesti
> In commune bonus nullosque Catonis in actus
> Irrepsit partemque tulit sibi nata voluptas.

Quantas, quaeso, quamque admirabiles laudes Catonis his tribus
versibus[349] conclusit poeta doctissimus? Plurimas profecto, quae
unumquemque optimum ac praestantissimum[350] decorum redde-
rent ac gloriosum.

38   Proferat nunc Guarinus tale de suo Caesare testimonium, et
ego illico me errasse fatebor eiusque sententiae acquiescam. Id autem cum non possit, quemadmodum ex ipsius libello evidenter
apparet,[351] cedat aliorum auctoritati—praesertimque veterum, qui
omnes adversus eius opinionem sentiunt[352]—desinatque aliquando
invasorem patriae, hostem Romanae libertatis ac civilis sanguinis
effusorem extollere, qui, ut ab eodem poeta scriptum est:[353]

> Caesar in[354] arma furens nullas nisi sanguine fuso
> Gaudet habere vias.

Desinat, inquam, hunc Scipioni, integerrimo viro, praeponere. Desinat postremo eius causa Catonem, hominem divinum, iustum,
immaculatum[355] et publicae utilitatis defensorem,[356] suis calumniis

would fail me, and the famous honeyed fountain of Ciceronian eloquence would dry up?[68] If one wished to embrace in one speech all the other things which were praiseworthy about him, I would cite (apart from those things which you write so very truly and elegantly in defense of this most holy man) one testimony alone, that of Lucan, a not undistinguished poet. And this defeats, overcomes, and routs Guarino, who gravely errs in this matter (to speak with his good leave). For speaking of Cato, that poet says:

> He cultivated justice and preserved
> Uncompromising honor. He was good
> For the common weal, and into Cato's deeds
> There never once crept in and stole a share
> That creature, pleasure, born to suit itself.[69]

I ask: how many praises of Cato did the most learned poet encompass in these three verses and how remarkable are they? So very many, indeed, and such as would ennoble and glorify any excellent and outstanding man.

Now let Guarino offer a similar piece of evidence for his Caesar, and I will immediately admit I have erred and accept his opinion. But since he cannot do that (as it obviously appears from his own pamphlet), let him yield to the authority of others, and particularly of the ancients, who all hold an opinion against his view. And let him finally cease praising that invader of the fatherland, that enemy of Roman freedom, the spiller of citizen blood, who, as the same poet wrote:

> Caesar, raging for arms, rejoices that he has
> No other path than that by shedding blood prepared.[70]

Let him cease, I say, from placing this person before Scipio, that most blameless man. Let him cease at last to trouble, for Caesar's sake, Cato with his slanders — that divine, just, and spotless man, that defender of the public benefit — turning the virtues of such a

38

275

confundere virtutesque tanti viri in vitiorum nomina permutare.[357] Nam constantem in proposito (quod philosophi maximae laudi tribuunt, dicentes nihil tam congruere viri sapientis gravitati, quam nullis terroribus de sententiae proposito posse depelli[358]) Guarinus pertinacem; gravem vero, tardum ac morosum; nullum ab honesto flexibilem precibus, durum et inexorabilem mira quadam tam clarissimarum virtutum in vitiorum vocabula transformatione (quam Ovidius ignoravit), persaepe in suis scriptis[359] appellat.

39   Itaque, ut aliquando scribendi finem faciam (modum enim grandioris epistolae[360] iam videor excessisse), sentiat[361] Guarinus, praeceptor meus, vir sane eruditissimus et eloquentissimus,[362] quod sibi libet,[363] nunquam profecto me in suam sententiam trahere poterit, quae ab omnibus, qui ante nos de hisce rebus scripserunt quam maxime deviat;[364] praesertim cum nullo pacto[365] mihi persuadere possum ipsum ex animi sententia ea omnia scripsisse, sed magis fortasse ad eloquentiae suae vim[366] ac potentiam ostendendam, ea in re Carneadem, Academicae sectae philosophum, imitatus, qui, cum legatus ab Atheniensibus Romam missus esset, disputavit de iustitia copiose audiente Galba et Catone Censorino maximis tunc oratoribus. Idemque disputationem suam postridie contraria disputatione subvertit et iustitiam, quam pridie laudaverat, sustulit,[367] non quidem philosophi gravitate (ut ait Lactantius[368]), cuius firma et stabilis[369] debet esse sententia, sed quasi oratorio exercitii genere in utramque partem probabiliter disserendo.[370] Non enim magnum negotium esse videtur[371] virum omni genere laudis et gloriae praestantem sua oratione extollere, neque in hoc ars plurimum pollet.[372] At nefandissimum ac scelestissimum hominem praedicare eiusque vitia miro dicendi artificio

great hero into charges of vices. For a man who was constant in
his purpose—a virtue to which philosophers accord the greatest
praise, saying that nothing so becomes the seriousness of a wise
man as not to be deflected from his stated purpose by any
threats[71]—Guarino in his writings very often calls "obstinate" and
a serious man "slow and cheerless" and one who is unwilling to be
swayed from what is honorable by entreaties, "harsh and relentless."[72] What an amazing metamorphosis—one which Ovid did
not know—of such most splendid virtues into the terminology of
vices.

And so, to put an end, at last, to my writing (for I seem already   39
to have gone beyond the measure of even a longish letter): let
Guarino, my teacher, a man truly very learned and eloquent, think
what he pleases, but he will never be able to draw me to that opinion of his, which diverges as much as is possible from that of all
who have written before us about these things. In particular, I can
in no way convince myself that he has written all those things with
heartfelt conviction, but maybe more in order to make a display of
the skill and power of his own eloquence, imitating in that regard
Carneades, a philosopher of the Academy, who, when he was sent
to Rome by the Athenians as their ambassador, discoursed fulsomely about justice in the hearing of Galba and Cato the Censor,
who were then the leading orators. The next day, the same man
undermined his own position with the contrary one, and destroyed that justice which he had praised the day before. As Lactantius says, he did that not with the seriousness of a philosopher,
who should be firm and constant in his opinion, but as in a kind
of oratorical exercise framing a probable argument on either side.[73]
For it would not seem a significant undertaking to praise in his
speech a man who was outstanding in every type of praise and
glory, nor is this where the art of rhetoric has its greatest power.
But to laud the most heinous and wickedest man and by a certain
remarkable skill in speaking to hide his vices as if in a cloud of

quodam[373] — quasi virtutum nube — obfuscare idque quam pluribus ita fuisse posse[374] persuadere, excellentis sane ingenii et eximii artificis indicium est.[375]

40   Tuum vero, mi Poggi dulcissime, in tanta concertatione rectissimum[376] (per immortalem Deum!) iudicium probo, confirmo ac laudo omninoque sequendum censeo, neque ullius persuasione ab ea unquam discedam sententia, dum spiritus hos reget artus, quoniam verissime te scripsisse existimo, quin potius certo scio et ita scio, ut ceteros desipere putem, qui tecum in ea controversia non sapiunt.[377] Tu enim iure ac merito Scipionem Africanum, virum utique iustitia, modestia, gravitate, continentia, temperantia, integritate et (quod maximi facio) caritate in patriam singulari, quam difficillimo tempore exhaustis paene rei publicae viribus totque deletis exercitibus ab hostili Hannibalis oppugnatione liberavit, Caesari praefers,[378] quem rapinae, furta, homicidia, adulteria, stupra, seditiones, civilis sanguis et — quod omnium scelerum immanitatem excedit — extincta patriae libertas, aliaque innumerabilia flagitia cunctis abominabilem reddunt.[379]

41   Magnas tamen Guarino gratias ago, quoniam suis minis, iniuriis magnoque illo verborum impetu, quo adversus te usus est, quodam quasi stimulo ac flagello ita te ad scribendum concitavit, ut veritatem (quam antea nullis urgentibus stimulis[380] paucis argumentis confirmaveras), ea Guarini acerba impugnatione postea provocatus admirabili quadam sermonis elegantia et sententiarum gravitate[381] clariorem lucidioremque effeceris; adeoque scribens gladiolos tuos (ut vulgo fertur) acuisti, ut nihil dubitationis in ea re, de qua inter vos disceptatum est,[382] oriri possit, quod illa tua disertissima et luculentissima defensione non enodaveris. Cuius

virtues and to be able to convince as many as possible that this was so — that is a sign of a truly excellent talent and of an outstanding artist.

Your judgment however, my most charming Poggio, in this 40 great controversy I approve of as wholly right (by the immortal God!); I support and praise it and reckon it should be followed entirely. Nor will anyone's persuading ever make me stray from this opinion for as long as there is life in these limbs, because I judge that you have written must truly; indeed, I know this for certain and I know it so firmly that I think that others are fools who do not share your wisdom in this debate. For you justly and with good reason prefer Scipio Africanus to Caesar: Scipio, a man of such justice, modesty, seriousness, moderation, temperance, blamelessness and (what I regard as most important) singular love of the fatherland, which, in very trying times — when the forces of the republic were nearly exhausted and so many armies annihilated — he freed from Hannibal's hostile attack, versus Caesar, whose robberies, thefts, murders, adulteries, defilements, seditions, the shedding of citizen blood, and (what surpasses all other crimes in its monstrousness) the destruction of the freedom of the fatherland, and countless other outrages, make him despicable to all.

To Guarino, however, I give many thanks because by the 41 threats, insults, and the great onslaught of words that he has used against you he has stirred you to writing as if by some sort of goad and whip. Hence, provoked later by that bitter attack of Guarino's you made the truth clearer and more lucid, with a remarkable elegance of speech and seriousness of expression, whereas before, when there was no insistent prompting, you had confirmed it with a few arguments. In writing, you sharpened your daggers (as the saying goes) to such an extent that no point of doubt can arise about that matter that was debated between you, which your very fluent and brilliant defense has not resolved. Indeed, all good and

quidem laboris tui causa boni omnes ac docti viri plurimum
tibi debent. Publicam enim causam agendam ac defendendam
suscipiens, quamquam fortissimum adversarium habueris, cuius
peritiam et eloquentiam multi formidassent, nunquam tamen
deseruisti, sed constanter ac viriliter resistens gloriosam ex ea dimicatione[383] meo iudicio victoriam reportasti.

42   Ex te vero scire cupio vehementer, quid in ea re vir clarissimus
et Graecae ac Latinae linguae peritissimus, Franciscus Barbarus,
quem tu iudicem tibi[384] constituisti, iudicaverit, senserit quidve
rescripserit. Maximum enim pondus apud me habet eius viri sententia.[385] Itaque si me amas, da operam, ut eius ad te epistolam
videam.[386] Novi enim ipsius humanitatem[387] prope singularem, qui
etsi multis magnisque rei[388] publicae negotiis, curis et occupationibus[389] in praefectura Brixiensi per id tempus detentus fuerit,[390] ad
te tamen responsum aliquod dare non praetermisit.[391] Vir enim
est, qui in negotio quocumque otium sibi sciat vendicare. Illud
postremo scias velim, me hunc libellum, quem misisti, pluribus[392]
legendum exemplandumque tradidisse, ut etiam apud hos homines,[393] quorum quidam (licet perpauci) non abhorrent ab hisce
artibus atque humanitatis studiis, tuae virtutis gloria innotesce-
ret[394] laudereturque praestantia tua in extremis terrae. Quam—
mihi crede, qui tibi nec adulari volo, nec scio—neque Guarinus
obfuscare potuit, neque ulla unquam delebit vetustas aut oblivio,
quin potius semper honos nomenque tuum laudesque manebunt.
Vale et parce ruditati atque ineptiae meae.[395]

Ex Londoniis pridie Kalendas Februarias.

learned men are much indebted to you for your effort. In taking up a public cause that had to be pleaded and defended, although you had the strongest adversary, whose knowledge and eloquence would have intimidated many, still you never gave up but constantly and manfully stood your ground and from that conflict you brought back, in my judgment, a glorious victory.

I would dearly like to know from you what judgment was 42 passed by that most famous man and most learned in both Greek and Latin, Francesco Barbaro, whom you appointed as your judge, what he thought or wrote back, for that man's opinion carries very great weight with me. And so, if you love me, put in the effort to let me see his letter to you. For I know the nearly unique kindness of the man who, even though he was preoccupied at that time in many and great affairs of state, cares, and business in the governance of Brescia, nonetheless did not neglect to give you some response.[74] For he is a man who knows how to find for himself some leisure, whatever business occupies him. Finally, I would like you to know that I have given this pamphlet, which you sent, to many people to read and copy, so that among these men—some of whom (though they are very few) do not shun these arts and humane studies—the glory of your virtue may shine and your excellence may be praised at the ends of the earth. This excellence— believe me, who do not want and would not know how to flatter you—Guarino could not obscure, nor will age or forgetfulness ever destroy it; rather, your honor, name, and praises will endure. Farewell, and forgive my rusticity and gaucheness.

From London, January 31 [1440].

Ad doctissimum et clarissimum virum
Thomam de Serezano
Poggii Florentini
De infelicitate principum liber
incipit feliciter.[1]

C1   1. Rem minime probatam vulgo et quae haud persuaderi nisi admodum paucis queat, hoc libello aggressus sum, vir clarissime Thoma, ut ostendam quantum facultas ingenii tulit regum ac principum vitam multis confectam angoribus omni felicitate carere. Difficile id quidem et prorsus a communi existimatione alienum. Nam pervetus est et[2] ea communis omnium gentium mentibus infixa opinio, illos solos beatos ac felices esse, quos fortunae munus in sublimi rerum statu prae ceteris collocavit; quae res a teneris usque annis adeo nobis est insita, ut votis singuli omnibus opes, honores, magistratus, dignitates, imperia expetant, tanquam in his beatae sit finis vitae constitutus. Eo autem hanc tam late patentem insaniam pervulgatam videmus, ut, qui virtutum et bonarum artium studiis procul ab externarum rerum cupiditate dediti haec adumbrata fortunae beneficia contemnant, aut vecordes

C2   aut imbecilli animi aut stulti esse dicantur. Etenim omnes ferme mortales veluti ex loco inferiori suspicientes hos ex altissima, ut

POGGIO BRACCIOLINI

ON THE UNHAPPINESS
OF LEADERS

Here with good fortune begins
Poggio of Florence's book
On the Unhappiness of Leaders[1]
dedicated to Tommaso of Sarzana,[2]
a most learned and illustrious man.

1. In this book, most illustrious Tommaso, I have tackled a position C1
not at all generally approved of and of which only a very few can
be persuaded. It is to show, as far as my intellectual capacities have
allowed, that the life of kings and leaders is entangled with many
anxieties and is devoid of all happiness. Of course, this is difficult
and completely foreign to the general view. In fact it is an age-old
and common opinion that is firmly imprinted upon the minds of
all nations that the only people who are blessed with happiness are
those whom fortune's gift has placed before others at the pinnacle
of affairs. This opinion is so implanted in us right from our earliest years that in all their prayers individuals beg for riches, honors,
magistracies, positions of influence, and commands, as though the
goal of the happy life were founded upon these elements. Indeed,
so broadly disseminated do we see this widespread insanity to be
that those who are far from desire for the external goods and despise these shadowy benefits of fortune, because they are given
over to the pursuit of the virtues and the liberal arts, are said to be
either crazy or weak in the head or stupid. For the fact is that C2
almost all mortals, looking up as if from a lower place at these

videntur, basi suspensos rerum dominos admirantur atque obstupescunt inhiantesque ad exteriorem principum pompam atque ornatum quales oculis cernuntur, tales interius esse putant. Virtutem vero et bene vivendi disciplinam pauci appetunt, pauciores quaerunt, satis superque satis sibi sapientiae et prudentiae inesse vel potius superesse ducentes, dummodo ea assequantur, quae praeclara ac speciosa vulgo publica insania fecit. Sed pars maxima nostrae infelicitatis stultitia est, qua in tantum mentes hominum a vero procul abducuntur atque opinionibus fallacibus excaecantur, ut nil[3] sincerum, nil rectum possint discernere, id tantummodo expetendum esse ducentes, ad quod vulgaris appetitus communi errore labatur. Nos vero (quos doctrinam sapientum virorum sequi atque eorum praeceptis obtemperare decet) longe aliter a communi stultitia sentire vitamque felicem non in fortunae arbitrio, sed in virtutis praesidio constituere debemus. Non enim rebus externis et fortuitis, sed animi bonis felicitas tribuenda est. Cui quidem sententiae multi excellentes ingenio viri inhaerentes abiectis propriis fortunis philosophiae studio vacarunt, ut veram felicitatem assequerentur. Et certe sicubi ea est, in virorum doctrina et sapientia praestantium domicilio reperitur, qui procul a cupiditatibus nihil alieni appetentes, aetatem suam in virtutis contentione posuerunt. Sed caeca mens hominum, quibus nihil est pensi virtutis iter,[4] quibus nihil cum animo est commune, ad illecebras corporis deflexa, in iis solum quae fortunae temeritati parent[5] felicitatem sitam esse arbitratur.[6] Horum ergo fallacem opinionem tum pro communi utilitate, tum pro veritate tuenda paulum mihi reprimendam existimavi docendumque id quod luce clarius est: nihil verae solidaeque felicitatis eiusmodi bonis inesse, sed illam quaeri a bonis animi oportere, quae sola nostra sunt et

masters of the universe who seem to be supported on an elevated pedestal wonder at them and are dumbstruck and, gaping at the external pomp and show of leaders, think that inside they are as they appear to the eyes.[3] But few strive for virtue and the knowledge of how to live well, and fewer actually seek it, thinking that they have enough and more than enough wisdom and prudence in them (or rather considering it to be superfluous), so long as they get hold of the things which public insanity generally has made splendid and attractive. But the greatest part of our unhappiness is the folly by which the minds of men are led so far from the truth and blinded by false opinions that they can see nothing which is genuine and honest, considering that the only thing worth seeking is that toward which, by a common error, the taste of the mob sinks. We, however, whom it befits to follow the teaching of wise men and to obey their precepts, ought to take a very different view from the general idiocy and to reckon the happy life not to be in fortune's remit, but under the protection of virtue. It is not to external and fortuitous things but to the goods of the mind that happiness is to be attributed. And many intellectually gifted men, sticking fast to this view, throwing away their own fortunes have made time for the study of philosophy in order to gain true happiness. And to be sure, wherever this happiness exists, it is found in the dwellings of men outstanding for their learning and wisdom, who far from desires and grasping after nothing belonging to others have invested their lives in the battle for virtue. But the blind minds of men[4] who do not value the path of virtue at all, and who have no common bond with mental pursuits, turn aside toward the snares of the body and think that happiness is located only in those things which obey rash fortune. Their false opinion, both for the common good and to preserve the truth, I have considered I should try to repress a little and to teach what is clearer than daylight: that there is no true and solid happiness present in goods of this sort, but that it needs to be sought by the goods of the

C3

nec auferri possunt dum vitam agimus, et mortuos non derelinquunt.

C4   2. Ad te autem, mi Thoma, quem scio pro tua sapientia mecum adversus vulgarem temeritatem pro virtutis causa sentire, hoc opusculum inscripsi, ut habeat te suum apud eos qui contra sentiunt defensorem. Nam cum ad philosophiam atque optimarum artium studia, quibus ab adolescentia imbutus fuisti, addideris theologiae scientiam ita, ut illis priscis doctissimis viris sis procul dubio omni doctrinarum genere comparandus, nequaquam est consentaneum ut pluris fortunae dona facias quam virtutem aut ullam[7] statuas felicitatem quae sit ab honesti ratione seiuncta. Id autem me maxime movit ut tibi hoc opusculum dicarem, quod, sicut ex vita et verbis tuis saepius cognovi, videris cupiditatibus modum statuisse ac recte iudicare in philosophiae praeceptis ac multarum rerum cognitione et doctrina, quibus alitur animus noster, plus adiumenti ad bene vivendum quam in ullis his quae tantopere expetuntur dignitatibus contineri. Siquidem hae nihil secum praesidii ad virtutem ferunt potiusque cupiditatum et voluptatum irritatrices quam ministrae continentiae et honestatis esse consueverunt. Philosophiae vero (hoc est sapientiae) studia[8] fortunam contemnere, rectam rationem ducem vivendi sequi, rebus modum imponere, animi dotes omnibus imperiis anteferre docent et ad veram perducunt felicitatem.

C5   Hanc autem disputationem olim inter doctissimos viros habitam nunc paulum otiosus litteris tradidi, ut, si qui de his uberiora vellent scribere, latior eis facultas hac nostra veluti provocatione tribueretur.[9]

ON THE UNHAPPINESS OF LEADERS ·

mind, which alone are ours and cannot be taken away while we live and do not leave us when we are dead.

2. I have dedicated this little work to you, my dear Tommaso, C4 whom I know because of your wisdom to hold the same view as I do against vulgar chance and in favor of the cause of virtue, so that it might have you as its defender among those who think otherwise. For since to philosophy and the pursuit of the liberal arts in which you were imbued as a boy you have added such a knowledge of theology that in every type of learning you are undoubtedly to be compared with those famous most scholarly men of the past, it is in no way reasonable for you to consider the gifts of fortune of higher worth than virtue or think anything to be happiness which is separated from a policy of uprightness. However, the thing that most induced me to dedicate this work to you was the fact that, as I know from many examples in your life and words, you seem to have placed a limit on your desires, and rightly to consider that there is more help toward living well in the precepts of philosophy and the knowledge of many things and learning, by which our minds are nourished, than is to be found in any of these positions of importance which are so often sought. In fact, these do not bring with them any predisposition toward virtue and are usually rather stimulants to the desires and pleasures than ministers of continence and uprightness. On the contrary, the study of philosophy, that is, of wisdom, teaches us to despise fortune, follow right reasoning as our guide to living, to impose a limit upon possessions, to prefer the gifts of the mind to any position of command, and leads us toward true happiness.

This disputation was held among very learned men some time C5 ago. Now that I have a little leisure, I have committed it to paper so that if anyone wants to write more fully on the subject, they may be given a greater opportunity to do so because of this — what shall I call it? — "challenge" of mine.

287

C6   1. Cum ex mea consuetudine, qua primum aestate pontifex Euge-
nius ex Urbe Florentiam concessit, meridie ad clarissimum virum
Nicolaum Nicolum,[10] cuius domus commune doctissimorum hominum diversorium erat, me contulissem, doctissimum ibi Latinis
Graecisque litteris virum[11] offendi, Carolum Aretinum, et item
Cosmum de Medicis, cum in hac nostra re publica egregium principem, tum optimum ac praestantissimum civem. Hos ego Ptolo-
maei *Geographiam* inspicientes cum in primis, ut mos est, consalu-
tassem, una in Nicolai bibliotheca consedi et simul cum illi quo in
statu nostrae cum publicae, tum privatae res essent percontarentur,
coepi paululum[12] de temporum conditione communique calami-
tate, tum etiam mea, qui paulo[13] antea e[14] praedonum manibus
evasissem, queri, ceterorum vitam nostrae praeferens, qui Scytha-
C7   rum more semper instabiles vagaremur. 'Infelices enim quodam
modo sumus,' inquam, 'quibus non datur uno in loco residere
diutius, sed mutare regiones cogimur et varias in diem sedes tanquam novi coloni quaerere.[15] Nam cum annos iam amplius quattuor et triginta fuerim Romanae curiae incola, nunquam integrum
triennium una in urbe egimus, vagi semper ac loca varia pera-
grantes.'

C8   2. Hic subridens paulum Carolus: 'Tu,' inquit, 'eam damnas vitam, Poggi, quam multos summo studio appetere, in qua maxima
laboris[16] et industriae proposita esse praemia videmus, quae felix
prae ceteris esse videtur, tum[17] multis voluptatibus et commodis
referta, tum iis molestiis curisque vacua, quibus ceteri affliguntur.
Ego enim et te et reliquos qui pontificibus obsequuntur (quantum

On the Unhappiness of Leaders

1. In the summer when Pope Eugene[5] first left Rome for Florence,   C6
as usual I took myself off at midday to see the most famous Niccolò Niccoli,[6] whose house was a general place of resort for scholars. There I came across Carlo Marsuppini of Arezzo,[7] a man
deeply learned in both Latin and Greek, and also Cosimo de'
Medici,[8] at one and the same time an outstanding leader in our
republic and an excellent and most distinguished citizen. They
were examining a copy of Ptolemy's *Geography*.[9] When I had
greeted them in the customary manner, I sat down with them in
Niccoli's library.[10] As soon as they started inquiring about the position of both my public and private affairs, I began to complain a
very little about the state of the times and our shared misfortune
and also about my own (I had very recently escaped from the
hands of bandits).[11] I said I preferred the life others led above that
of people like myself, who are always wandering about, with no
fixed abode, like the Scythians.[12] "We are rather unfortunate," I   C7
said, "since we are not allowed to stay in one place very long, but
are forced to change our locations and like new colonists to search
for different bases every day. I have been in the Roman curia for
more than thirty-four years, but we have never spent a whole
three-year stretch together in Rome.[13] We are always wandering
and crisscrossing different regions."[14]

2. Here Carlo Marsuppini smiled a little and said: "The life you   C8
are condemning, Poggio, is one we see many people seeking with
great zeal and in which we see very great rewards for hard and
diligent work laid out. It appears to be happier than the other
available lives, both because it is filled with many pleasures and
advantages and because it is free from those difficulties and worries with which the others are rife. I consider both you and the
rest of those who serve popes, as far as I can tell by conjecture, to

assequor coniectura) beatos iudico, procul ab his nostris census et
tributi continua vexatione constitutos.[18] Etenim et felices videntur
esse pontifices tali honore ac dignitate, quos omnes colunt et[19] pro
diis adorant, et qui[20] eos sequuntur, quos illi consueverunt, cum
volunt, duobus tantum verbis felices reddere ac fortunatos. Nam
tum[21] omnes principes magna existimo felicitate frui, tum vero
maxime pontifices, cum nulla cura, nullo labore, nulla opera, nullo
periculo eum statum adipiscuntur, qui habetur maximus inter
mortales, absque ullo paratur negotio, nullo sudore retinetur,
quandoquidem pro armis auctoritate Christi et signo crucis utuntur, quod est tutissimum, si eo uterentur, propugnaculum. Verbis
enim quam ferro tutiores esse consueverunt. Itaque felices procul
dubio censendi sunt ii, quibus datur parva industria tantum adipisci imperium, minore partum retinere.'

C9   3. 'Vide,' inquit Nicolaus, 'ne longe te fallat opinio, quanquam
existimo haec a te colloquendi inter nos gratia dici. Tu felices appellas et pontifices et eos qui degunt in principatu. Ego, secus
sentiens, eiusmodi homines miseros duco neque ullius verae compotes felicitatis. Illos qui adstant principibus, qui latus circumdant,
qui aures occupant, qui vendunt, ex aliqua parte dixerim forsan
felices, cum ii soli laborum principum fructus percipiant. Ad hos
enim sollicitudo, curae, timores, anxietas, pericula descendunt; illi
quaestui vacant et voluptatibus, ad contrahendas opes ac divitias
intenti, et tanquam muscae ad mel advolant, ita isti ad explendas
varias cupiditates ad aulas[22] regum ac principum concurrunt. Rari
hominem, plurimi fortunam sequuntur. Felices itaque videtur ac
beatos alios reddere qui ipse prae ceteris est infelix! Nam si qua

be blessed, situated far away as you are from our men with their unending struggles over incomes and taxes. And indeed, popes appear happy because of such honor and position, since everyone worships them and adores them like gods, and so do those who follow them, whom popes have usually been able to make happy and fortunate at a whim, with just two words. For I reckon that, first, all leaders enjoy great happiness, and second, popes in particular do so, since they obtain the condition which is regarded among mortals as the greatest, with no worry, no hard work, no effort, and no danger. Moreover, this position is gained with no strain, and is retained with no sweat, since instead of arms they use the authority of Christ and the sign of the cross, which is the safest bulwark, if they were using it.[15] For they have usually been safer with words than with weapons. So without doubt we ought to consider people happy who are allowed to obtain such great power with little effort and to keep what they have gained with less."[16]

3. "Beware," said Niccolò, "not to be badly deceived by your C9 opinion (though I think you have said these things so as to generate a discussion among us). You call 'happy' both popes and those who spend their lives in the position of a leader. I have a different view. I hold men of this sort to be miserable and incapable of any true happiness. Those who assist leaders, stand by their sides, hold their attention and sell it, I would perhaps call happy in some respects, since they alone reap the harvest of the leaders' labors. For the latter have to deal with worry, responsibilities, fears, anxiety and dangers, while their followers are free to enjoy their income and pleasures, focusing their attention on getting together wealth and riches. As bluebottles fly toward honey, so these people flock to the courts of kings and leaders to fulfill their various desires. Few are those who follow the man, but very many who follow his fortune. Thus the person who is himself unhappy before all others appears to make others happy and blessed! Any joviality,

iocunditas, si qua oblectatio, si qua quies, si qua voluptas, si qua remissio inest principatui, eam illi decerpunt maxime, qui sunt principibus grati. Quicquid vero laborum, molestiarum, dolorum, angoris principatus affert, id solum principibus haeret, voluptates rarae et quae etiam ab animis curarum mole oppressis minime degustentur.'

C10   4. 'Formicis,' inquit Cosmus, 'Indicis (ut aiunt[23]) similes esse principes dicis, quae suo labore aurum ex harena effodientes aliis percipiendum atque utendum tradunt, ipsae omni usu fructuque auri destitutae. Ridiculum quippe videtur eos qui imperent infelices, qui vero serviunt felices putare. Equidem, si mihi detur optio, mallem illo pacto infelix quam hoc, ut putas, felix esse. Nam si qua est in nobis felicitas, ea magis principum quam reliquorum

C11 videtur familiaris.' Hic Carolus, 'Ut omittantur,' inquit, 'ii de quibus aliquid addubitari potest, de pontificibus saltem concedas, Nicolae, oportet, ut vere dici possint felices. Cum enim sanctissimi et beatissimi appellentur, nemo autem non solum beatissimus, sed ne beatus quidem possit esse non felix, consentaneum videtur pontifices omnis, quoniam beati felix est vita, recte felices appellari posse. Illud quoque mihi concedes, opinor: illos qui domestici eorum vocantur, esse huiusmodi felicitatis participes. Fieri enim nequit ut qui cum felice ac beato familiarius vivant, sint expertes eius quocum degant felicitatis.'[24]

C12   5. 'Longe aliter se res habet atque existimas,' Nicolaus inquit, 'quamvis te mecum iocari arbitrer et Socratica ironia uti. Nam haec quae modo sanctitatis ac beatitudinis nomina rettulisti et pleraque alia quae adulantium turba in pontifices et reliquos excelsos viros congessit ad aucupandam principum benivolentiam, ab his[25] conficta atque adinventa sunt, quibus ea ars[26] quaestui est,

any amusement, any rest, any pleasure, any relaxation involved in the position of a leader is enjoyed most of all by those who are pleasing to leaders. Any labors, troubles, and pains that being in the position of a leader brings, attach only to leaders. Their pleasures are rare and such as cannot be truly tasted by minds oppressed by a mass of worries."

4. "Like Indian ants, as the saying goes," Cosimo de' Medici interjected, "that's what you are claiming leaders are, the ones who dig gold from the sand by their own efforts and hand it to others to take and use, deprived themselves of any use and enjoyment of the gold.[17] It seems ridiculous to consider those who rule as unhappy and those who serve as happy. At any rate, if I were given the option, I would prefer to be unhappy in that way than happy the way you think. If there is any happiness to be had among us, it seems more at home with leaders than with the rest." At this point Carlo said, "Let's leave aside those in respect of whom there can be some doubt. You must at least concede, Niccolò, that popes can be said truly to be happy. For since they are called most holy and most blessed, yet no one even called blessed, let alone 'most blessed,' can fail to be happy, it seems reasonable to say that all popes can rightly be called happy, since the life of the blessed man is happy. You will allow me this point also, I think, that those who are called their servants are sharers in this happiness. For it cannot be that people who live in close contact with a happy and blessed man do not experience the happiness of the person with whom they live."

5. "Things are very different from what you suppose," Niccolò replied, "although I think you are joking with me and employing Socratic irony.[18] These names of 'holiness' and 'blessedness' which you reported just now as well as lots of others heaped up by the crowd of flatterers upon popes and other lofty men have been engineered and invented to ensnare the goodwill of leaders by people to whom this skill is profitable, seeking as they do to applaud and

qui per adulationem (optimam regum conciliatricem) applaudere illis et gratificari quaerunt. Adeoque haec inolevit abusio, ut non C13 his verborum praestigiis uti turpe ac nefas putetur. Sed ego hos nostros[27] pontifices sive quosvis alios dominos eorumque fucata nomina contemno, a quibus ad ostentationem omnia, paucissima ad veram laudem et gloriam fiunt. Nulla enim (vel parva admodum) his bonarum artium cura est, nulla doctrinae, nulla sapientum ac doctorum virorum, nulla virtutis. Simulata in quibusdam C14 quaedam signa virtutis apparent, nulla impressa vestigia. Suscepit hic'—me intuens—'olim diligentiam et laborem peragrandae Alamaniae librorum perquirendorum gratia, qui in ergastulis[28] apud illos reclusi detinentur, in tenebris et carcere caeco; qua in re multum profuit Latinis Musis eius industria. Nam octo Ciceronis orationes, integrum Quintilianum, Columellam, qui antea detruncati ac deformes apud nos erant, et item Lucretii partem pluresque alios Latinae linguae auctores praeclaros restituit nobis. Plures quoque[29] ex diris carceribus, quibus inviti obsoletique opprimuntur, eruisset—sunt enim multi vinculis et foedo carcere abstrusi—nisi fortunae defuissent. Haec cum ab eo fuissent in lucem edita cumque uberior et quasi certa spes proponeretur ampliora inveniendi, num quis postea aut princeps aut pontifex vel minimum operae aut auxilii adhibuit ad liberandos praeclarissimos illos[30] vi-C15 ros ex ergastulis barbarorum? In voluptatibus, in rebus nulla laude dignis, in bellis (re pestifera et perniciosa hominibus) aetatem et pecunias consumunt. In pervestigandis vero excellentium virorum monumentis, quorum sapientia et doctrina ad vitam beatam et veram felicitatem perducimur, obtorpescunt atque obdormiunt, vitam plerique more pecorum agentes. Insanis cupiditatibus et variis ambitionibus acti, mirum de virtutibus aut sapientia aut aliqua

gratify them by means of the very best conciliator of kings, adula-
tion. This abuse is so inveterate that it is considered base and
wrong not to use these delusory forms of words. I, however, con-   C13
demn these popes or other masters of any kind of ours and their
counterfeit names. They arrange everything for show, but hardly
anything to aim at true praise and glory. They have no care, or a
very slight one, for the liberal arts, none at all for learning, none
for wise and learned men, and none for virtue. In some of them
some counterfeit signs of virtue appear, but no properly stamped
impressions. Poggio here," he said, looking at me, "long ago under-   C14
took the diligent task of traversing Germany to look for books
which were being kept locked inside dungeons there 'in shades and
prison dark.'[19] In this matter his industriousness was of great benefit to the Latin Muses. For he restored to us eight speeches of
Cicero, the complete Quintilian and Columella, which before that
had been with us only in truncated and deformed versions, and
likewise also a part of Lucretius and many other famous writers of
the Latin language.[20] And many more he would have brought into
the light from the harsh prisons in which, unwilling and decayed,
they are being held prisoner (for there are many that have been
thrust away in chains and foul incarceration) had his financial resources not failed him. When these had been brought into the
light by him and there was greater, indeed an almost certain, hope
of finding more, did any leader or pope give even the most paltry
effort or aid to free these outstandingly famous men from the
dungeons of the barbarians? No. They keep on spending their   C15
lives and their resources on pleasures, on things worthy of no
praise, on wars, a pestilent thing and harmful to mankind. But in
exploring the written legacy of the great men, by whose wisdom
and learning we are led to the blessed life and true happiness, they
languish and fall asleep, most of them living their lives like cattle.[21]
Driven by insane lusts and diverse ambitions, about the virtues or
wisdom or any of the arts of living well they preserve a miraculous

bene vivendi arte silentium agunt, ut non principum aut felicium, sed portentorum sint nomine appellandi. Neque de nostris[31] tantum saeculis queror, quae nostra religio reddidit mitiora: semper etiam priscis temporibus eiusmodi mores cogitationesque dominantium extiterunt, ut non videatur mirum esse nullum fuisse iis commercium cum felicitate commune.'

C16   6. Tum Cosmus, graviter ut assolet: 'Facillime,'[32] inquit, 'Nicolae, qui mos tuus est, laberis ad detrahendum. Equidem minime miror si quando es in privatos dicacior, cum in ipsos principes tam facile inveharis. Et tamen nullius iniuria aut in te contumelia facit, ut tam sis promptus aut copiosus in eorum obiurgationem. Ego nonnullos novi qui abs te excipi deberent ab reliquorum caterva, viri docti, egregii omnique laude et commendatione dignissimi. Verumtamen mecum saepius ipse cogitans addubitare cogor quaenam sit potissimum causa, cur in vituperando sis quam in laudando proclivior.'

C17   7. 'Hoc facile est ad explicandum,' Nicolaus inquit, 'quod longa aetas et ante acta vita me docuit. Nam in laudandis hominibus saepius deceptus sum, cum ii deteriores essent quam existimaram;[33] in vituperandis vero nunquam me fefellit opinio. Tanta enim inter homines versatur[34] improborum copia, ita sceleribus omnia inficiuntur, ita hypocritae superabundant, qui videri quam esse boni malunt, ita quilibet sua vitia aliquo honesti[35] velamento tegit, ut periculosum sit et mendacio proximum quempiam laudare. Plures ad me adeunt importune, qui suam stultitiam a me commendari volunt: afferunt nescio quid ab eis editum, insulsum penitus, inconditum, inconcinnum, certe dignum quod ad latrinas deferatur; quaerunt aestimationem[36] meam. Ego liberior in loquendo — nam poetam, si malus, nequeo laudare — verum effero, moneo ne efferant, interdico, vitia ostendo; non eloquentiam, non gravitatem, non ornatum, non prudentiam, non Latinae linguae

silence, to such an extent that rather than leaders or happy men they ought to be called monsters. And I am not just complaining about our own times, which our religion has made milder. It was always the case in olden days too that the character and thought of leaders were of such a kind that it does not seem a wonder that they had no common commerce with happiness."

6. Then Cosimo said, in his usual serious manner, "Niccolò,   C16 you very easily slip into criticism. It's your usual way. I for one do not wonder if you are sometimes rather satirical toward private individuals, seeing that you so easily inveigh even against leaders. Yet no one has harmed you or criticized you to such an extent that you should be so ready and eloquent in their dispraise. I know some men who ought to be excepted by you from the mob of others. They are learned individuals, outstanding and most worthy of every praise and commendation. Howbeit, I have quite often thought to myself and am constrained to question what the real reason is that you are more prone to blame than to praise."

7. "That is easy to explain" said Niccolò. "I have been taught to   C17 do so by my long years and the life I have already lived. For I have quite often been deceived in praising men, when they were worse than I had reckoned, but my opinion has never let me down when I have criticized people. There is dwelling among men such a host of wicked people, everything is so infused with criminality, there are so very many hypocrites, who wish to seem rather than to be good,[22] people so cover their vices with some veil of goodness, that it is dangerous and the next thing to a lie to praise anyone. Lots of people come to me begging to have me praise their stupidity. They bring something they have written, completely inane, confused, inelegant and certainly only worth taking to the latrines. They ask for my assessment. I speak quite freely (for if a poet is bad, I can't praise him), I tell the truth, I advise them not to publish it, I forbid its dissemination, I point out the faults. I assert that there is in it no eloquence, no gravity, no ornament, no wisdom, no propriety

proprietatem, non integritatem in suis scriptis esse affirmo. At quidam, proterva elatione temerariaque inflati, abeunt irati, sub-murmurantes me invidia commoveri. Quid loquar de moribus nostris ac vita, cum multi recessus sint animorum adeoque in oc-culto[37] siti, ut potius divinare quam affirmare de laudibus homi-num possis? Hanc ob causam, cum pauci vix ferendi, stultorum vero plena sint omnia, satius esse duco in eam partem declinare,[38] in qua verior sim futurus. Accusatae apud Lucianum divitiae quod nunquam se ad honestos viros conferant, non sua id culpa fieri, sed bonorum raritate respondent. Nam, cum caecae vagentur ne-que selectione aliqua uti possint, usu venit ut saepius in malos, qui undique circumfluunt, incidant quam in bonos, quorum paucitas raro obvios elidit. Alio item in loco, cum laudandi vituperandique artem aeque callere se dicat, alterius iam desuetudine oblitum, in altera se admodum exercitatum vitio hominum describit. Nihil igitur vanitati stultitiaeque propius esse videtur quam laudare quempiam, de cuius probitate ac virtute non tibi exactissime constet. Qua in opinione multorum nequitia in diem me reddidit[39] firmiorem. Quod si privatorum, quibus parvula licent, qui legibus coercentur, maxima pars vitiorum mole urgetur,[40] quid in tanta dominorum licentia, quibus pro lege est appetitus, putas contin-gere? Itaque — ut eodem redeat unde nostra defluxit oratio — mea quidem sententia est, hos vestros[41] principes (hoc enim nomine imperatores, reges, duces ceterosque qui aliis dominantur, compre-hendi volo) etiam si boni sint, et esse et censeri recte posse infe-lices ac miseros, quantumvis fortunae obtegantur bonis. Nam mali nullo modo felices erunt, a bonis vero, propter rerum quas

C18 *(marginal note)*

in their use of the Latin language, and no integrity to their works. But still some of them, inflated with an obstinate and thoughtless pride, go away angry, and muttering that I am motivated by jealousy. What am I to say about our characters and our lives, since we have many mental recesses, and so well hidden away, that it would be easier to guess than to assert firmly in the case of praising men. It is for this reason, when there are so few who are barely bearable, and everything is filled with stupid people, that I think it is better to veer toward the side where I am likely to be more truthful. In Lucian, Wealth is accused of never going to honorable C18 men.[23] He says that this is not his fault, but is due to the rarity of good men. For since he walks round blind and cannot use any principle of selectivity, it happens that he more often stumbles upon bad men, who are floating about everywhere, than good, whose scarcity rarely drives them into his path. Likewise Lucian in another place, although he says that he is equally proficient in the arts of praise and blame, represents himself as having forgotten the former through lack of use, but as pretty adept at the latter because of the viciousness of men.[24] So nothing seems closer to vanity and idiocy than to praise someone about whose honesty and virtue there is not the most precise agreement. In this opinion the wickedness of the majority has made me firmer by the day. But if the majority of private individuals are beset by a mass of vices, even though they have few opportunities to indulge them and are held in check by the laws, what do you think happens in the situation of unbridled opportunity enjoyed by lords, for whom the law is their desire? And so to bring my speech back to its source,[25] my view is that these leaders of yours, and under this heading I want to include emperors, kings, dukes and the rest who hold sway over others, even if they are good men, can rightly be considered and actually are unhappy and miserable, however much they are covered by fortune's favors. For there is no way bad men will be happy. But even the good lack all happiness because of the weight

sustinent pondus (maius enim Atlante onus ferunt), propter infinitas curas, molestias, anxietates, labores quibus cruciantur, omnis felicitas abest. At multi felices existimantur: obumbrat enim ampla fortuna multorum vulnera et cicatrices. Nos autem non aestimationem[42] vulgi, sed veritatem quaerimus, quae plane dictitat nullam felicitati cum principibus esse societatem.'

C19   8. 'Nimis quidem in arto, Nicolae,' Carolus inquit, 'hos circumscribis (vel potius proscribis) ita, ut neminem tibi assensurum putem. Quis enim tibi concesserit multos ex priscis illis, qui a suis dicti sunt, non fuisse felices? Enumerari enim plures[43] possunt, quos sua aetas felicissimos iudicavit. Verum, quandoquidem et aestus diei est et otium superest, discutiamus paulum, Nicolae,[44] si libet, et id colloquendi causa, utra sit verior ac probabilior sententia. Tu principes infelices et eorum vitam miseram putas; ego contra felices iudico ac beatos.'

C20   9. Hic arridens Nicolaus: 'Hic noster Carolus,' inquit, 'aperte somniat et secus ac sentit loquitur. Quomodo enim viro doctissimo licet dicere eos esse felices,[45] quos ne homines quidem quandoque audeat appellare: ignavos, imperitos, indoctos, impotentes, avaros, superbos, iracundos, crudeles, libidinosos, adulatorum et stultitiae servos, qui ambitione nescio qua effrenata, tanquam ad pestem mortalium nati, bellis semper indulgent, pacis atque otii hostes? Non licuit Italiae nostris temporibus ab armis quiescere propter nonnullorum principum aliena rapiendi cupiditatem. Mitto alia vitia, in quibus quantumlibet per me versentur, dummodo[46] infra eorum domos contineantur; quos tu qua ratione felices nuncup⟨av⟩eris,[47] ignoro.'

of the affairs that they carry (for in fact they bear a burden greater than Atlas')[26] on account of the infinite worries, troubles, anxieties and labors which torment them. Of course, many are reputed to be happy, because their wounds and scars are hidden in shadows by their great wealth. However, we are not looking for the popular judgment, but the truth, which plainly tells us over and over that there is no bond between leaders and happiness."

8. "You are circumscribing them too narrowly, Niccolò," said   C19
Carlo, "or rather proscribing them, in such a way that I don't think anyone will agree with you. Who is going to concede, for instance, that many of those ancients claimed by their peers to be happy were not? For quite a few people can be listed whom their own epoch judged extremely happy. Now, since it is the hottest time of the day and we still have some free time left, why don't we have a short discussion, if you like, Niccolò, just for the sake of conversation, about which opinion is truer and more probable. You think that leaders are unhappy and that their lives are miserable. I on the contrary judge them happy and blessed."

9. At this Niccolò smiled and said, "Our Carlo here is obviously   C20
dreaming and voicing the opposite of his true opinion. For how can any man of true learning say those are happy whom he would not dare even to call *men*, cowardly beings, unskilled, uneducated, violent, greedy, haughty, prone to anger, cruel, lustful, slaves to flatterers and folly, who through some unbridled ambition, as though they were born to afflict mankind, continually indulge in wars and are the enemies of peace and tranquility. In our lifetimes Italy has not been allowed to have a respite from arms because of the desire of some leaders to seize other people's property. I will say nothing of the other vices, in which they may indulge as much as they please as far as I am concerned, provided that they are kept within the confines of their homes. These you have called happy, though I do not know on what argument."

C21   10. 'Parcas oro maledictis,' Carolus inquit. 'Non enim iurgio
haec, sed ratione disserenda sunt. Istis quippe vitiis nullam felicitatis partem ascribi posse concedo, sed non ea in omnibus esse
videntur. Male enim nobiscum ageretur, si tam dura conditio omnium principum esset. Rari sunt in quibus non aliqua virtus eluceat. Quare mihi recte consideranti felices principes esse videntur,
quibus adsunt omnia quae sunt hominibus maxime exoptanda
quaeque solent efficere beatam vitam. Nam possident opes, divitias, dignitates, imperia; est summa in eis rerum licentia,[48] summa
beneficiorum facultas, summa liberalitatis occasio. Adsunt—si
quid ad rem pertinet, sed approbat Epicurus—diversae corporis
atque animi voluptates, aurea atque argentea mensa, varii magnifi-
cique apparatus, ludorum et cantus plura genera ad aurium ani-
C22   mique iocunditatem exquisita. Coluntur atque adorantur ab reliquis; quae maxima habetur voluptas. Iusti praeterea, sapientes,
temperati, boni esse possunt, sicuti multi quoque[49] habiti sunt, et
virtute praediti; quibus ex rebus patefit ampla ad felicitatem via.
At tu principes omnis, bonos malosque, in una eademque infelicitatis damnatione constituis. Saltem huius'—me intuens—'gratia
summos pontifices excepisses, quos iniquum est aestimare[50] felicitate privatos. Cum enim se honesti et optimarum rerum cura oc-
cupatos, cum salutis communis, cum pacis populorum, cum omnium gentium quieti se consulere in suarum litterarum prohemiis
quotidie profiteantur, cum salvatoris vice fungantur in terris rebus-
que caelestibus mentem applicent, qui possunt, tam sanctis dediti
cogitationibus, non esse felices? Sunt praeterea[51] divinarum rerum
antistites, quarum cultu nemini dubium est felicitatem hominibus

10. "Please spare us your curses," said Carlo. "These things have   C21
to be discussed rationally, not by brawling. I admit that those vices
cannot be ascribed even the tiniest portion of happiness. But they
do not appear to exist in everyone. We would all be doing pretty
badly if the condition of all leaders were so hard. The sort in
whom some virtue does not shine forth are few and far between.
So I am thinking rightly when I say that leaders seem happy to
me, since they have everything men most desire and which usually
makes life happy. For they possess resources, wealth, positions of
influence and power, and they have the greatest freedom of action,
the greatest opportunity to do good to others, and the greatest opportunity for generosity. In addition, if it is at all to the point
(though Epicurus at any rate approves), they have in their presence the various pleasures of body and of mind, a gold and silver
table, diverse and magnificent trappings, and many types of games
and song, specifically designed to please the ears and the intellect.[27] They are worshipped and adored by the rest, and this is re-   C22
garded as the greatest pleasure. Besides, they can be just, wise,
temperate and good, just as many of them also have been considered to be, and endowed with virtue, through which qualities a
wide road to happiness opens up. But you condemn all leaders,
good and bad, to the same lack of happiness. At least for his sake,"
here he looked at me, "you might have granted an exception to the
popes, whom it is unjust to reckon bereft of felicity. For since every day in the prefaces of their letters they declare themselves involved with the care for decency and the best matters, combined
with our common deliverance, with peace between the peoples,
and the tranquility of all nations, because they are operating as the
Savior's regents on earth and applying their minds to the affairs of
heaven, how can men dedicated to such holy thoughts *not* be
happy? Besides, they are the exponents of religious rites, through
the observance of which no one doubts that happiness is given to

elargiri. Idem et nostro huic pontificis secretario videri convenit,
cuius plurimae pontificiae epistolae sunt in eorum commendationem.'

C23   11. Tum ego, 'In litteris,' inquam, 'meis id primum adverto, quod
pontificis esse oporteat[52] officium aut munus, eas laudes eis tribuens, quibus vacare non debent. De felicitate vero ipsismet existimo esse credendum.[53] Si enim has suas cogitationes esse af-
firmant, litteris autem eorum fidem praestandam esse ipsi suis
legibus sanxerunt, non sum ego adeo arrogans, ut eorum decretis
existimem esse ullo modo fidem abrogandam. Itaque per me feli-
cissimi appellentur licebit, cum ego illos beatos credam, qui se esse
C24   beatos putant.' Tum Cosmus, 'Atqui,' inquit, 'nuper[54] legi longe secus iudicasse pontificem Hadrianum, virum prudentem et vitae
sanctitate praestantem. Solitum enim dicere frequenter accepimus
neminem videri sibi Romano pontifice miserabiliorem nulliusque
deteriorem conditionem esse. Asserebat cathedram illam, in qua
residerent pontifices, spinis refertam, pallium, quo amiciretur,
consertum aculeis acutissimis tantaeque molis, ut etiam robustissimos premeret, mitram vero igneam, quae caput gestantium ureret.
Hic aperte professus est qualem felicitatem pontifices assequantur
C25   (eos dico, qui munus pontificium amplecti volunt).' Tum ego, 'Missos,' inquam, 'pontifices faciamus, in quibus[55] plures quam in reliquis imperiis et felices et Deo accepti reperti sunt, sermonemque
nostrum convertamus ad reliquos, de quibus honestius liberiusque
inquiri potest. Verum me, qui in maximi omnium principis obse-
quio versor, aequius est hac de re silere quam loqui. Hic noster
Nicolaus, in libera civitate liberior ceteris, nullius obnoxius cupiditati, qui unus semper prae se tulit summam dicendi licentiam neque veretur quo animo sua dicta accipiantur, dummodo quod
sentit proferat, audacius uberiusque suum iudicium explicabit.'

men. And it is fitting that our papal secretary here holds the same view, who has written many papal letters in their praise."

11. Then I replied, "In my letters I focus primarily upon what the job or duty of a pope should be, and I only bestow on them praises which they ought not to be without. Concerning their happiness, however, I think we ought to believe the men themselves. For if they assert that these are their thoughts, and they have sanctioned by their laws the notion that their written words should be trusted, I am not so arrogant as to think that belief in their declarations should in any way be denied. So as far as I am concerned, it will be allowable to call them extremely happy, since I believe blessed those who think themselves blessed." Then Cosimo said, "But I recently read that Pope Adrian, a wise man and outstanding for the holiness of his life, had a far different opinion. The tradition is that he frequently said that no one seemed more unhappy to him than the Bishop of Rome, and no one's situation worse. He used to claim that the throne upon which the popes sit was filled with thorns, the robe which they wore full of the sharpest needles and so heavy that even the strongest were weighed down by it, and that the miter was made of fire and burned the heads of those who wore it.[28] He openly admitted the sort of happiness popes achieve, those I mean who wish to embrace the duty of the papacy." Then I said, "Let us leave aside the popes, among whom are found more happy men and men acceptable to God than in the other positions of power, and let us turn our conversation to the rest, about whom we can inquire more honorably and freely. As for me, since I am in the service of the greatest leader of all, it is more reasonable for me to stay silent on this matter than to speak. Our Niccolò here, a man more at liberty than the rest in a free city, who depends on no one's desires, who alone has always exhibited the highest degree of freedom of speech, and is not afraid of the way his words may be taken, so long as he says what he thinks, will reveal his judgment more boldly and fully."

C23

C24

C25

C26   12.1 'Mihi quidem,' Nicolaus inquit, 'cum his vestris rerum dominis nulla unquam privata consuetudo fuit, neque enim magna ex parte ii sunt, de quibus aequa mente possim audire. Quamvis enim raro hanc urbem exierim, tamen et omnium qui ubique sunt principum mores et vita mihi innotescunt, et eorum qui hactenus fuerunt gesta perlegi. Itaque tum vita eorum,[56] tum ratio et veritas mihi persuadent ut credam nihil dici posse miserius principantium vita; quam recte ac penitus intuenti licet inspicere ambitiosam, anxiam, turbulentam, maximis cruciatibus calamitatibusque ac malis facinoribus plenam. Carolus bonos posse esse principes et nonnullos habitos[57] dicit, ego non qui esse possunt, sed qui fuerint perquiro, quos nondum ulla aetas sortita est.

C27   12.2 'Nam si veteri[58] Hesiodi sententia difficile est bonum esse, id multo in regibus et imperio difficilius fiet, quos plura vitiorum irritamenta ab exercitio virtutum subducunt. Eluxit aliquando, sed tamen perraro, in aliquibus quidam virtutum splendor. Sed scriptorum nonnullorum assentatio, qui adulationis praemia a principibus expectabant, ex parvula scintilla virtutis maximum incendium excitarunt, ampliantes ea verbis, quae tenuia rebus erant. Valerius Maximus, adulatorum scriptorumque omnium adulantissimus, de Iulio Caesare in gratiam Tiberii saepius aperte mentitur, in laudibus suis tanquam de deo loquens, non de eo cuius acta in omni vita, armorum gloria excepta, a bonis reprobata extitere. Sed licet pauci paulum emerserint a consuetudine aliorum, tamen, si qua in eis virtus enituit, ea multorum flagitiorum caligine obumbrata est. Invenies quosdam humanos sed luxuriosos, alios prudentes sed

12.1 "I have never," said Niccolò, "had any private intercourse   C26
with these masters of affairs of yours, and for the most part they
are not the sort of men I can listen to people talking about with
equanimity. For even though I have rarely left this city, nonetheless
the life and character of all leaders everywhere have become known
to me. And I have read about the doings of those in the past. So
it is both their lives and reason and truth which persuade me to
believe that nothing can be called more miserable than the life of
those who act as leaders, which the right-minded enquirer who
looks deeply into the matter may see as ambitious, anxious, turbulent and filled with the greatest trials and calamities and with evil
deeds. Carlo says that leaders can be good and that some have
been regarded as such, but I am not inquiring about who can be
thought good, but who actually have been. No age has ever yet
been allotted such people.

12.2 "For if, according to the old saw of the poet Hesiod, it is   C27
difficult to be good,[29] this will become much more difficult among
kings and in a position of command, because more incentives to
vice draw them away from the practice of virtue. Occasionally, but
very rarely indeed, there has dawned in some men a sort of bright-
ness of virtues. But through their obsequiousness some writers,
who were looking for the rewards of flattery from leaders, have
made a huge conflagration out of a small spark of virtue, amplify-
ing by their words what was tenuous in actuality.[30] Valerius Maximus, the most adulatory of the all the adulatory writers quite often
openly lies about Julius Caesar to please Tiberius, speaking in his
praise as though he were God, not about the man whose deeds
during his whole life (the glory of his military achievements excepted) have been criticized by good men.[31] But even if a few men
have managed to rise up a little away from the ways of the rest,
nevertheless, any virtue which shone out in them was overshadowed by the darkness of their many crimes. You will find that
some were humane, but dissolute, others prudent, but cruel, these

crudeles, hos iustos sed deditos avaritiae, nonnullos magnificos sed raptores, quosdam liberales sed ira fervidos et impotentes. Ita quoquo verteris, nihil purum, nihil sincerum in eis reperies, nihil castum, nihil absolutum, sed ita infecta omnia, ut longo intervallo virtutes a vitiis superentur.

C28   12.3 'Neque hoc tantum natura[59] hominum, quantum ipsius evenit vitio principatus. Nam tum natura fragiles sumus atque imbecilles, qui facillime[60] ad lasciviam et vitia labamur, tum principatus re ipsa et licentia malus est malorumque opifex ac minister. Sed in hac omni nostra disputatione praedictum velim me nihil adversus personas, sed de re ipsa sentire quod loquor; quae, cum plurima vitia secum trahat, necesse est etiam bonos viros aut corrumpat aut defatiget adeo, ut nullam felicitatem degustare queant. Sunt enim in regno quaedam tanquam in aetate adolescentum ac senum natura insita vitia; quae qui tollit aut mitigat, divino potius fungitur munere quam suo. Sicut enim ignis, quicquid illi haeret, aut calefacit aut urit, ita et imperium quos apprehendit, aut malos reddit aut certe deteriores. Deliniuntur enim homines illius consuetudine et contagione inquinantur. Quo fit ut, etiam si probi, casti, pii, humani ad illud evehantur,[61] inficiantur eius moribus et malignitate evadantque impii, scelesti, inhumani, periuri, crudeles.

C29   12.4 'Neque solius Nicolai est haec, sed Flavii quoque Vopisci sententia, qui ad Diocletianum imperatorem in *Aureliani Vita*[62] scribens: "Vide, quaeso," inquit, "quam pauci fuerint principes boni, ut bene dictum sit a scurra quodam Claudii mimico unico[63] anulo omnis bonos principes describi ac depingi posse. Quaeritur quae res malos principes[64] faciat? Iam primum licentia, deinde rerum copia, amici improbi, satellites detestandi, eunuchi

here just, but given to avarice, some magnificent, but robbers, some liberal, but burning with anger and violent. Hence, whichever way you turn, you will find nothing pure and nothing sincere in them, nothing chaste, nothing perfect, but everything so infected that their virtues are by a long way overborne by their vices.

12.3 "And this does not come about so much through the nature   C28
of man, as through the fault of the position of leader itself. For we are by nature fragile and weak, so as easily to slip into lasciviousness and vice, and at the same time the position of leader by its very nature and its license is bad, and an incitement to and servant of evil. However, in the whole of our discussion I would like it to be understood at the start that what I am saying does not reflect my feelings against individuals, but about the thing itself, which, since it brings in its train very large numbers of vices, is bound either to corrupt even the good or to wear them out so thoroughly that they can have no taste of happiness. For there are in kingship as in adolescence and old age some naturally inherent faults, and anyone who removes or mitigates these is enjoying a gift which comes from God rather than from himself. For just as fire heats or burns whatever is in contact with it, so power too makes bad or certainly worse those whom it takes hold of. Men are bewitched by its company and polluted by its contagion. Hence it happens that even if honest, chaste, pious, and humane individuals were to come to power, they would be infected by its malign character, and turn out impious, criminal, inhumane, perjurers and cruel.

12.4 "Nor is this just the opinion of Niccolò, but also of Flavius   C29
Vopiscus, who said, writing to the emperor Diocletian in his *Life of Aurelian*: 'Consider, I ask you, just how few the good leaders [emperors] have been, so few that a jester of Claudius' court produced the *bon mot* that all good emperors [leaders] could be described and depicted on a single ring. You ask what it is that makes leaders bad. First of all, their complete freedom of action, next the abundance of their possessions, their dishonest friends,

avarissimi, aulici vel stulti vel detestabiles." Ex quo Diocletianum dixisse commemorat nihil esse quam bene imperare difficilius. "Colligunt se," inquit, "quatuor aut quinque atque in unum ad imperatorem capiendum consilium coeunt, dicunt quid probandum aut improbandum sit. Imperator, qui domi clausus est, vera non novit, facit iudices quos fieri non oportet, amovet a re publica quos debet[65] retinere. Ita bonus, cautus, optimus venditur imperator." Quas ob res nil rarius bono principe esse testatur.

C30   12.5 'Idem Saturninum, quem Aegyptii ad imperium assumendum cogebant, locutum memorat: "Nescitis, amici, quid mali sit imperare? Gladii pendentes cervicibus imminent, hastae undique, undique spicula; ipsi custodes timentur, ipsi comites formidantur. Adde quod omnis aetas[66] in imperio reprehenditur." M. Aurelius Antoninus Pius, quem per omnem vitam philosophantem inter omnes qui unquam imperarunt palmam tulisse virtutis historiae ferunt, sanctimonia certe vitae excelluit omnes. Ab Hadriano adoptatus in imperium, magis doluisse quam laetatus esse traditur; iussus autem ex privatis hortis in domum principis migrare, invitus accessit. Et cum ab eo domestici quaererent, cur tam maestus in tantam adoptionem transiret, multis verbis disputavit quae

C31   in se mala imperium contineret. Diocletianus vero, cum post depositum imperium in privata villa agro colendo intentus degeret, rogatus a Licinio ut ad imperium rediret, id recusavit, disserens, ostenso horto quem planarat, quam dulcis et iocunda ea vita esset, quam vero misera et anxia in imperio constituta. Videtis quam naturam principatus esse affirmaverint et sapientes viri et ii qui et

their detestable henchmen, their avaricious eunuchs, and courtiers who are either stupid or abominable.' As a result of this, Vopiscus recalls that Diocletian said that nothing was more difficult than ruling well. 'Four or five people gather together,' he said, 'and go in together to advise the emperor, and they say what is to be approved and what not. The emperor, who is shut inside his home, does not know the truth, makes people he ought not into judges, and removes from the state those whom he ought to keep. Thus a good, careful and outstanding emperor is bought and sold, and it is for these reasons he says that nothing is rarer than a good leader [emperor].'[32]

12.5 "The same writer mentions that Saturninus, whom the C30 Egyptians forced to take power, said: 'Do you not know, my friends, what a bad thing it is to rule? Hanging swords threaten your neck, everywhere there are spears and everywhere arrows, your very guards are feared and your very comrades terrify you. What is more, every age is criticized when it comes to empire.'[33] Marcus Aurelius Antoninus Pius, who, as he practiced philosophy all his life, the histories agree took the palm for virtue among all those who have ever ruled, certainly surpassed all others in the sanctity of his life. When he was adopted as the emperor's successor by Hadrian, he is said to have lamented rather than rejoiced, and when ordered to leave his private gardens and go to the emperor's [leader's] palace, he agreed unwillingly. And when his servants asked him why he was making the transition to such a great adoption so sadly, he argued in a long speech the evils that ruling contained within itself.[34] Indeed, when, after abdicating the impe- C31 rial power, Diocletian was living in his private villa, concentrating on farming his land, upon being asked by Licinius to return to rule, he refused, setting out, as he pointed to the garden which he had leveled out, how sweet and pleasant was that life, and indeed how unhappy and anxious was the one spent ruling.[35] You see what the nature of the position of leader has been said to be both

ipsi summi et boni principes extiterunt. Etenim, veluti fuligo com-
maculat tangentes, sic regnum possidentes corrumpit multitudine
morborum animi; quos si quis sanae mentis penitus prospexerit,
haud sane multum illius cupiditate flagrabit. Non enim solum
quae Terentianus ille adolescens querebatur in amore vitia, iras,
suspiciones, inimicitias, bellum, pacem rursum, sed multo in eo
acerbiora atque asperiora perspicax animus intuebitur: impotentiam, fastum, superbiam, libidines, odia, crudelitatem, ambitionem dominandi, cupiditates, veneficia et quicquid aliud ad perniciem mortalium nequitia hominum excogitavit.

C32   12.6 'Quod si quis eo robore, ea firmitate animi, divino quodam
munere fretus, ad principatum adeat, ut omnis eius illecebras virtute superaturus esse videatur, tamen, ut sessor bonus in equo re-
trogrado ac calcitroso excutietur dilabeturque aliquando, ita qui ad
imperium ascendet,[67] diffluet vel invitus rerum licentia ac luxu et,
tot insidiis tum hominum, tum vitiorum circumventus, declinabit
a gubernaculo et, tanquam vehementi actus tempestate, vi fluc-
tuum iactabitur ad scopulos, in quibus allidetur periclitabiturque
omnis bene vivendi ratio et disciplina. Nam quod Carolus ad
comparandam felicitatem contulit divitias, opes, rerum licentiam,
beneficiorum facultatem, imperia, dignitates voluptatesque et alia
plura quae retulit, ista quidem potius infelicitatis quam felicitatis
irritamenta instrumentaque esse videntur. Verum opibus ac divitiis
non magis utuntur principes quam privati, neque magis quam
quantum homini fiat satis.[68] Victum habent pretiosiorem et
cultiores vestes, sed venena in his formidantur et amicorum insidiae. Suspiciosae sunt epulae atque potus raroque sapiunt, tum

by wise men and those who themselves also have been supreme and good leaders. For just as soot marks those who touch it, so ruling corrupts its possessors with a multitude of mental diseases, so that if any sensible person examines these properly, he will surely not burn greatly with desire for it. For it is not just the vices of which the young man in Terence complains in respect of love, the fits of anger, suspicions, enmities, war, the peace that follows,[36] but the perceptive mind will see in it much bitterer and harsher things, impotence, contempt, arrogance, lusts, hatred, cruelty, the ambition to lord it over others, desires, acts of poisoning, and whatever else human wickedness has devised for the destruction of mortals.

12.6 "But even if someone comes to the position of leader with C32 such strength, and such firmness of mind, relying on them as a divine gift, that he appears to be bound to overcome all its snares by his virtue, nonetheless, as a good rider on a backing and recalcitrant horse will sometimes be thrown or fall off, so the man who climbs to power will even unwillingly succumb to license and lust, and, surrounded by so many snares both of men and of vices, he will leave the helm, and as though driven by a violent storm he will be thrown by the force of the waves against the rocks, on which he will be crushed, and all his theory and practice of good living will be in danger.[37] For the things which Carlo cited as conducive to gaining happiness, namely riches, resources, the ability to do things, the opportunity to do good turns, positions of power, offices, pleasures and all the other things he set out, these seem rather to be incitements to and instruments of unhappiness than of happiness. Indeed, leaders do not use wealth and resources more than private individuals, and no more of them than as much as would be enough for a human being. Leaders have more costly food and better-cut clothes, but in the midst of all this they fear poison and ambushes set by their friends. Feasts and drinking sessions engender suspicion and they rarely taste good, since they are

mixtae curis, tum continuo usu neglectae. Nam voluptates, quo magis affluunt, eo ex copia ac satietate fiunt[69] insuaviores; praeterea[70] non idem qui reliquis gustus neque appetitus. Quod si quando esuriens cibum capit, non sinunt variae cogitationes percipere ciborum suavitatem. Venerea multis suspicionibus implicantur; multi enim, hoc veluti laqueo capti,[71] perierunt. Licentia nihil felicitatis importat; nam scitis, veteri proverbio, ea fieri solere homines deteriores.

C33   12.7 'Beneficiorum facultas est nobis optanda, sed plurima pars hominum eam ad maleficia convertunt. Non est dignum beneficii nomine quicquid principes donant.[72] Effusio aliquando et inconsulta largitio beneficium appellatur. At in dando beneficio ratio personarum et temporis constet oportet. Illi autem ut plurimum tribuunt non egenis, sed turpibus et indignis. Dant tamen quod tenere non possunt: dignitates, praeturas, magistratus; in pecuniis vero, quae servari possunt, sunt multo remissiores. Mensa aurea argenteaque et ceteri apparatus nihil afferunt subsidii quo simus felices. Non enim aegritudines animi levant, sed praestant curiosiorem: plus ea aspicientes delectant quam possidentes. Hoc verissime ausim dicere, in quo et multi sapientes conveniunt:[73] nullum esse ex corporis sensibus, in quo non a privatis principes voluptate exsuperentur. Quare longinqua erit ab his vitae felicitas, quos et nulla vera ac solida sequitur voluptas et multi circumstant mentis cruciatus.'

C34   13. Tum Carolus, 'Tyrannorum,' inquit, 'non regum aut imperatorum vita iis cruciabitur quae dixisti malis, quoniam et Iustinus affirmat tyrannos semper vitiis abundare; ideoque et esse infelices necesse est. At vero ceterorum, qui recto iustoque iudicio pro

either mingled with worries or despised because of daily use. For the more pleasures abound, the less sweet they taste because of their abundance and satiety. Furthermore, they do not share the same taste and appetite as others have.[38] But if ever they actually do take food because they are hungry, their diverse concerns do not allow them to sense the pleasure of their food. Love affairs are filled with many suspicions, and many have died as a result of them, caught there as though in a net. License contributes nothing to happiness, for you know the old proverb: it usually makes men more wicked.[39]

12.7 "We ought to wish for the power to do good, but most men turn it to wicked ends. What leaders give is not worth the name of beneficence. An occasional gift or a spontaneous act of generosity is called 'beneficence.' But in giving gifts, one must take account of persons and occasions. For the most part, however, they give not to the needy, but to the base and unworthy, and even so they only give what they cannot keep, namely honors, praetorships and magistracies. They are much more remiss in relation to money, which they can keep. A golden and silver table and the rest of such pomp bring us no help in gaining happiness, for they do not lighten the sicknesses of the mind, but make it more careworn: they delight those who look at them more than those who possess them.[40] This I would dare to say most truly, and many wise men would also agree, that there is none of the bodily senses in which leaders do not receive less pleasure than private individuals.[41] And so happiness in life will be far away from these, who have no true and stable pleasure and who are surrounded by many mental tortures." C33

13. Then Carlo said, "It is the life of tyrants and not of kings or emperors that will be tormented with the ills you speak of, since Justin, too, affirms that tyrants always abound in vices,[42] and so it follows that they must also be unhappy. But the state of the rest, who with right and just judgment rule for the common good, C34

communi utilitate regnant, longe alia videtur esse conditio; qui, cum sint legum ac iustitiae ministri, nec privato sed publico commodo dent operam, cum pacem colant, cupiditatibus statuant modum, viros doctos ament, cum quasi parentes eorum quibus praesunt appellari mereantur, quid his abest quin et dici et esse felices queant? Nam quod arbitraris natura malum esse principatum, vide ne longius quam ratio suadeat a vero seducaris. Natura insitum nobis principandi appetitum Cicero noster tradit, ut animus bene a natura institutus et subesse nolit et cupiat praeesse. Indidit enim nobis sive deus sive parens natura desiderium laudis et gloriae, quam maximam consequimur praestantia et imperiis, quibus eminentia quaedam animique excellentia iudicantur. Cernis natura ipsa duce gestire animum nostrum ac laetari cum reliquos etiam bonarum artium certamine antecellit; etenim extollimur gloria quadam, si prudentia, consilio, doctrina vel arte egregia ceteris praestamus. Cum enim id scire videmur, quod alios fugiat, tum maxime erigimur ad laudis cupiditatem. Itaque singulis in rebus insitus nobis est praeeminentiae appetitus[74] et cupiditas imperandi. Quae autem natura nobis insunt, omni culpa et reprehensione vacant neque etiam mala appellari[75] decet. Cibi enim ac potus venereorumque[76] appetitus, cum e natura prodeat, nullo modo est vitiosus. Sed quemadmodum horum usus non necessarius, si ad voluptatem referatur, non caret crimine, ita, si quis principatu abutatur, quando labitur ab ordine rationis, datur vitio. Nullum igitur crimen, nullum delictum ascribendum est principatui, cum sit eius appetitio a natura, neque etiam ulla infelicitas tribuenda, sed iis potius,[77] qui per abusum rem optimam ad vitia detorquent et iniuriam ceterorum. Nam quid utilius, quid optabilius tribuit

C35

C36

seems very different, since these men are servants of the laws and justice, and pay heed not to the private, but to the public interest, and, since they cultivate peace, place a limit upon their desires and cherish learned men, since they deserve to be called almost the parents of those whom they lead, what is to stop them from being able to be called, and actually being, happy? As to the fact that C35 you think that the position of leader is by nature a bad thing, take care that you are not straying further from the truth than reason dictates. Our Cicero tells us that the desire to act as leader is ingrained in us by nature, so that a mind well trained by nature both refuses to be subordinate and desires to lead.[43] Either God or Mother Nature has instilled in us the desire for praise and glory, which we obtain at its greatest by excellence and from the positions of power through which our eminence and excellence of mind are judged. You can see that, with nature herself as our guide, our spirit exults and rejoices when it outruns others in the contest of the liberal arts, for we are raised up by a sort of glory if we excel others in wisdom, counsel, learning or in an important skill. For when we appear to know something that escapes others, then we are most of all aroused to desire praise. And so in each individual domain the appetite for preeminence is born in us and so is the desire to rule. But those things which are within us naturally are free from all blame and fault and it is inappropriate to call them bad. The desire for food, drink and sexual intercourse is in C36 no way vicious, seeing that it comes from nature. But just as the unnecessary use of these things is not free from blame, if it is purely for pleasure, so if anyone abuses the position of leader, when he slips from the path of reason, it is put down to vice. To rule itself, therefore, we should attach no accusation and no crime, since the appetite for it is natural, nor even is any unhappiness to be attributed to it, but rather to the people who through abuse turn a very good thing toward vices and the injury of others. What more useful gift has God given us, or more desirable and more

nobis deus, quid ad virtutum exercitia propensius,[78] quam eam
facultatem potestatemque, qua liberales esse, benefici, magnifici,
qua multorum commoda procurare et tum in homines, tum in
ipsos deos pietatem exercere valeamus? Hac datur protegere op-
pressos, afflictos erigere, subministrare egenis, opem ferre amicis,
praemia tribuere virtuti, prodesse quam plurimis. Quare nequaquam amplius dixeris aut malum natura esse principatum, cum
tanta assit bene agendi[79] facultas, aut infelicitatis causam nisi malis
praebere.'

C37   14. Tum Nicolaus: 'Quos tu quidem tyrannos appelles, nescio.
Hoc certe scimus: nonnullos eorum fuisse regibus meliores ius-
tiusque in subditos imperium exercuisse. Non enim nomine, sed
re distinguuntur. Verumtamen si recte regum, imperatorum cete-
rorumque principantium vitam ac mores perpendes, dignos reperies permultos qui tyrannorum potius quam regum nomen
mereantur. Nam boni illi, qui ad publicam utilitatem intendant
secluso privato commodo, qui bonos et doctos diligant, qui parentis animum gerant, qui fuerint, in nostris litteris non continentur,[80] et si quos ulla aetas produxit, rariores Stoicorum sapiente
extiterunt. Sed quod regnandi appetitum naturalem et ob eam
causam principatum minime malum dixisti, hoc tibi affirmo: quae
C38   bona natura sunt, mala esse non posse. Principatus vero qualis sit,
exempla principum docent, quos te non fugit ut plurimum reprehensione quam laude digniores. Neque etiam consentaneum est ut
quod natura bonum sit, malos reddat possidentes; naturalia enim,
etiam repugnantibus nobis, vim suam exercent. Enumerasti, Ca-
role, bona quae possunt prodire ex principatu, oblitus (credo) quot
calamitatibus illius cupiditas orbem terrarum afflixit, ut exsecrandi
illi esse videantur,[81] qui quod omnium erat, ad unum primi

favorable to the exercise of the virtues, than that ability and power through which we are enabled to be liberal, beneficent, and noble, and through which we can serve the advantage of the many, and practice piety toward both men and the gods themselves? Through this we are enabled to protect the oppressed, to raise up the afflicted, to give succor to the needy, to help our friends, to pay virtue its proper reward, and to aid as many as possible. For these reasons, then, please say no more either that the position of leader is by nature bad, since it has such a power for doing good, or that it provides a cause of unhappiness, except to the wicked."

14. Then Niccolò said, "I don't know whom you are actually C37 calling tyrants. But we know certainly that some of them were better than kings and exercised their power more justly over their subjects. For it is not by their *name*, but by their deeds, that they are distinguished.[44] However, if you weigh up correctly the life and character of kings, emperors, and the other people acting as leaders, you will find many who deserve the name 'tyrant' rather than 'king.' For as to those good rulers, the sort who aim at the public good, setting aside their private comfort, who cherish good and learned men, and who behave like parents, any who have existed are not contained in our literature, and if some era has produced any, they have been rarer than the Stoics' sage. But as to your argument that the desire for the position of leader is natural and for that reason rule is not a bad thing at all, this I declare to you, that things good by nature cannot be bad. However, what the position C38 of leader is like is shown by the examples of leaders, who, it does not escape you, are more often worthy of blame than praise. Nor is it reasonable to argue that what is good by nature makes its possessors bad. For natural qualities exert their own force upon us even against our will. Carlo, you have listed the good things which can come from the position of leader, forgetting, I suspect, with how many disasters the desire for power has afflicted the world, so that those men appear worthy of execration who first gave to one

detulerunt libertatemque sub qua nati erant servituti subicientes, unum aliquem plus quam omnes posse maluerunt. Quamvis regum quod primum imperii nomen in terris fuit sanctum est habitum apud priscos illos, dum sua cuique placebant, nomen quidem mite laborisque et officii plenum. Sed sicut omnia mala exempla a bonis initiis orta sunt, ut Crispus ait, sic in imperiis nomen regis tantum mansit, res funditus periit ad tyrannidemque defluxit. Itaque, cum principatus possessio, si veteribus historiis, si rationi credimus, possessores improbos efficere soleat, et principatum quoque malam rem esse putandum est.'

C39   15. 'Nonne,' Cosmus inquit, 'ab hoc tuo decreto excipis multos, quos felices ac bonos sua aetas existimavit? Ut barbaros missos faciamus: divum Augustum, Vespasianum, Titum, Antoninum Pium, M. Aurelium, Alexandrum Severum, Traianum, optimos ac iustissimos principes, quorum vita merito felix dici potest. Augusti quidem felicitatem omnes historici, omnes annales decantant, pace per universum orbem terra marique parta; quare huic saltem felicitatem tribuas necesse est, ne videaris in omnibus velle esse contentiosus.'

C40   16. 'Tu mihi,' Nicolaus inquit, 'phoenicem nescio quam affers, multis inauditam saeculis atque invisam. Antiqua monumenta paucos istiusmodi principes recensent, permultos vero illos, quorum flagitia ac scelera plures mortales et regna conquassarunt. Verum nihil affert momenti, quin dici omnes debeant infelices,[82] paucorum (si qua ea fuit) virtus. Una enim hirundo, ut dicitur, ver non designat. Sed tamen, si qui paulo tolerabiliores aut etiam, ut vultis, boni extiterint,[83] id ita perraro contingit,[84] ut portenti loco

man what belonged to everyone and who, subjugating the freedom under which they were born to slavery, preferred one person to have more power than everyone else. Nevertheless, 'king,' which was the earliest name given on earth to power, was held to be sacred by those ancients, while everyone was content with what was his, a gentle word indeed, full of hard work and duty. But just as, in the words of Sallust, all bad examples start from good beginnings, so in relation to power, only the name of king remained, while the thing itself perished utterly and was swallowed up by tyranny.[45] Therefore, since the possession of the position of leader usually makes its holders corrupt, if we believe the ancient histories and our reason, it follows that we must regard the position of leader itself as a bad thing also."

15. "On this principle," said Cosimo, "are you not leaving out   C39 many whom their own age considered happy and good? Leaving aside the barbarians, there are the divine Augustus, Vespasian, Titus, Antoninus Pius, Marcus Aurelius, Alexander Severus, Trajan, all excellent and most just emperors [leaders], whose life can justly be called happy.[46] At any rate in Augustus' case all the historians and annalists proclaim his happiness, since he obtained peace by land and sea throughout the world.[47] So you must attribute happiness at least to him, if you don't want to seem contentious on all issues."

16. "You are bringing me some phoenix or other," said Niccolò   C40 "which has not been heard of or seen for many centuries. The ancient records report very few such leaders, but numerous whose crimes and sins have shaken many mortal men and kingdoms. However, it produces no important evidence to counter the claim that all leaders are unhappy that a few have possessed such virtue, if indeed any at all has really existed. As they say, one swallow does not signify the spring.[48] However, even if there have been some slightly more tolerable leaders or even, as you claim, good ones, this happens so rarely that it can be looked upon as a

haberi possit. Nam saepius monstra hominum terra quam bonos principes produxit. Natus est nuper infans bovis capite, alter vero cati; hic mancus manu oritur, alter digitis multiplicatis. Quae omnia longe a natura hominum distant. Eodem pacto, cum principatus natura sit malus, inventi tamen longo intervallo sunt[85] aliqui qui paulum[86] descisceret[87] ab illius naturae institutis, sed monstris ac portentis rariores. Neque vero[88] hos ipsos felices fuisse iudico, sed vacuos felicitate. Non enim extrinsecus aut a fortunae indulgentia venit felicitas, neque ut alii, sed ipsimet de sua felicitate existiment oportet.

C41

17.1 'Expendamus illum ipsum Augustum, quem, ut ais,[89] felicissimum omnia saecula celebrarunt, et qua vixerit felicitate consideremus. Prima illius aetas, in civili bello diutius versata, nulli pepercit crudelitati. Certe triumvirum ultimus[90] proscribendis civibus modum statui passus est. Nonnullos etiam proscribendos nominatim curavit ad eorum expilandas domos, donec, sublatis iis qui rem publicam[91] salvam vellent quique suis cupiditatibus obstabant, cum Antonio et Lepido libertatem eripuit civitati. Non refero patriae proditionem, a qua armatus imperioque praeter aetatem Ciceronis opera potitus, et arma et imperium in patriae perniciem ac viscera convertit. Tum sociorum altero senatus auctoritate ab insignibus imperii deiecto, interfectoque[92] altero per civilem sanguinem oppresso, solus rerum potitus est. At is saepe[93] insidiis etiam suorum appetitus, saepius diversorum in se coniurationes expertus est; quo tempore vitam diutius sollicitam duxit et inquietam, mortis et insidiarum metu, donec, Liviae uxoris consilio usus, cum Pisoni pepercisset, hac clementia

C42

miracle. For the earth has more often produced human monsters than good leaders. Lately a child was born with a bull's head, another with a cat's. One was born with one hand, another with extra fingers. These are all a far cry from man's nature. In the same way, although the position of leader is by nature a bad thing, nonetheless once in a long while some men have been found who have deviated a little from the basis of its nature, but they have been rarer than monsters and miracles. Nor do I consider that C41 even these men have been happy, but rather devoid of happiness. For it is not from outside or by the indulgence of fortune that happiness comes, nor must we judge what others think, but what the people themselves feel about their own happiness.

17.1 "Let us ponder the famous Augustus, whom, as you say, all ages have called most happy, and consider in what happiness he lived. His early years, passed for rather a long time in civil wars, spared no cruelty. Certainly he was the last of the triumvirs to allow a limit to be placed on their proscriptions of citizens. He even made sure that some were proscribed by name so as to plunder their houses, until, having removed those who wanted to save the republic, and who stood in the way of his desires, along with Antony and Lepidus he snatched away the freedom of the state.[49] I will not mention his betrayal of the fatherland, from which he acquired an army and gained *imperium*, with Cicero's help, below the minimum age, only to turn his arms and power to the destruction of his fatherland and into its very vitals. Then, having used the senate's authority to cast one ally down from the insignia of power and the other having been killed, defeated in civil conflict, he took charge of affairs on his own. But still, he was often at- C42 tacked by traps set by his supporters, and more often experienced the conspiracies of various individuals against him, during which period he lived for rather a long time an anxious and worried life, fearful of death and plots, until, when on the advice of his wife Livia he had pardoned Piso, by this act of clemency he made the

reliquam sibi vitam securam praebuit. Hucusque nulli datus est inter tot timores felicitati locus. Age, postquam timere desiit, quae felicitas subsecuta est? Primum (quae magna ducitur felicitatis portio) caruit filiis qui imperio succederent. Tum multiplici dolore per omnem vitam affectus fuit: sororem Octaviam amisit, Marcellum ac Drusum nepotes, quos imperio destinaverat, magnae virtutis atque indolis adolescentes, immatura mors eripuit. M. Agrippae generi ac Maecenatis, quos carissimos ac fidissimos expertus erat, funera prosecutus est. Filias ambas, ab se domi optime educatas, ob meretriciam frequentibusque adulteriis infamem vitam, edicto palam proposito, ad insulas relegavit; quo facto, cum se, cum domum, cum familiam dehonestasset, propria detegens[94] dedecora, tantum postea doluit, ut saepissime[95] Maecenatis Agrippaeque, qui sibi verum dicere soliti erant, interitum defleverit, questus multotiens sibi deesse qui vera ex animo loquerentur.

C43 Subsecuta est Germanici exercitus, Quintilio Varo duce, clades, magnum rei publicae vulnus. Quis cum his aerumnis felicitatem coniunget?[96]

17.2 'Adice his, quibus per omnem vitam torquebatur, plurimas atque ingentes tum publicas, tum privatas curas, adeo omni quiete otioque et animi et corporis sublato, ut saepius ad deponendas undique urgentes[97] molestias de restituenda re publica cogitarit; quod et fecisset requietem appetens, nisi vitae insidias timuisset. Haec quippe maxima dicenda[98] principum infelicitas, ut e rerum statu descendere absque capitis periculo nequeant, quod et Diocletianus et Maximianus pluresque alii vitae discrimine sunt ex-

C44 perti. Sed ut Augusti felicitatem discutiamus, accipite quid vir

rest of his life free from care.[50] Up to this point, there was no room provided for happiness among so many fears. Well then, after he stopped being afraid, what happiness followed? First of all he had no sons to succeed to his power, a thing reckoned to constitute a large part of happiness. Then he was afflicted throughout his life by a multitude of griefs: he lost his sister Octavia;[51] his nephews Marcellus and Drusus, whom he had groomed for power, youths of great virtue and talent, were snatched away by an untimely death.[52] He followed the funeral processions of his son-in-law Marcus Agrippa and of Maecenas, whom he had found to be very dear and most loyal to him.[53] Both his daughters, whom he had brought up excellently in his home, he banished to islands by a public decree, for leading a life redolent of prostitution and infamous for many acts of adultery.[54] And when by this action he had dishonored himself, his house and his family by uncovering personal disgraces, he afterward grieved so much that he very often bewailed the deaths of Agrippa and Maecenas (who used to tell him the truth), complaining over and over again that he had no one to tell him the truth from his heart. There followed the disaster of the army in Germany under the command of Quintilius Varus, a great blow to the state.[55] Who will be prepared to conjoin happiness with these sufferings? C43

17.2 "Add to these the enormous public and private worries with which he was tormented throughout his life, which took away all the peace and leisure of his mind and body to such an extent that quite often he thought of restoring the republic in order to lay down the great problems which pressed upon him from all sides. And he would have done this, in his search for peace, had he not feared plots against his life.[56] I suppose that this should be said to be the greatest unhappiness of leaders, that they cannot relinquish power without personal danger,[57] something which Diocletian, Maximian and many more learned at risk to their lives.[58] But to C44 dispel the idea of the happiness of Augustus, listen to what the

sapientissimus Seneca de eius felicitate senserit in eo libro, quem scripsit *De brevitate vitae*:

> Potentissimis, inquit, et in altum sublatis hominibus exci-
> dere voces videbis, quibus otium optent, omnibus suis bonis
> praeferant, cupiant interim ex illo suo fastigio, si tuto liceat,
> descendere. Nam, ut nihil extra lacessat aut quatiat, magna
> in se ipsa fortuna ruit. Divus Augustus, cui dii plura quam
> ulli praestiterunt, non desiit quietem sibi precari et vacatio-
> nem a re publica petere. Omnis eius sermo ad hoc semper
> revolutus est, ut speraret otium. Hoc labores suos etiam si
> falso, dulci tamen oblectabatur solatio, aliquando se victu-
> rum sibi. In quadam ad senatum epistola, cum sibi otium
> polliceretur, etiam ex verborum dulcedine se voluptatem per-
> cipere affirmabat. Tanta otii cupido incesserat ut illud, quia
> usu non poterat, cogitatione praesumeret, et qui omnia vide-
> bat ex se pendentia, qui gentibus fortunam dabat, illum diem
> laetum demum cogitabat quo magnitudinem suam exueret.
> Expertus erat quantum illa bona, per omnes terras fulgentia,
> sudoris exprimerent, quantum occultarum sollicitudinum te-
> gerent.

C45 Haec Seneca, qui deinde labores anxietatesque, quibus etiam senex agitabatur, describit, ut omnino infelicem vitam per omnem
aetatem egisse videatur.

18. 'Haec tam multa de Augusto rettuli, ut ex beatissimo principum sumatur omnium coniectura. Nam si quem consensus hominum pro felicissimo atque optimo duxit adeo agendorum mole
premebatur, ut nihil sibi magis quam ea vita displicere videretur,
quid de aliis censendum est, qui ad Augusti virtutem et laudes

wise Seneca thought about his happiness, in the book he wrote *On the brevity of life*:

> 'From the most powerful men, he says, and those elevated to high position, you will see words slipping out by which they pray for leisure, putting it before all their goods, desirous for a while of climbing down again from their high pinnacle, if they could do so safely. For great fortune collapses upon itself to ensure that nothing outside harms or shakes it. The divine Augustus, to whom the gods gave more than to any other person, never stopped praying for peace for himself and seeking free time from affairs of state. Every word of his always returned to this, his wish for leisure. With this solace, however false, yet sweet, he continually lightened his labors, that one day he would live for himself. In a letter to the senate promising himself some free time, he affirmed that he took pleasure from the mere sweetness of the words. So far had his desire for leisure gone that he enjoyed it in thought since he could not do so in practice, and the man who saw everything hanging on him and who gave their fortune to the peoples, considered that day would finally be happy when he could lay aside his greatness. For he had experienced how much sweat those goods, which shine throughout the world, required, and how many hidden cares they concealed.

Thus Seneca, who goes on to describe the labors and anxieties with which Augustus was burdened even as an old man, so that he appears at every age to have lived an altogether unhappy life.[59]   C45

18. "I have said so much about Augustus to allow us to conjecture about everyone else on the basis of the most happy of all leaders. For if the one whom the general consensus among men has considered as the happiest and the best was so oppressed by a heap of duties that nothing seems to have displeased him more than that life, what must one think of the rest, who have been a

longa intercapedine accesserunt? Nempe infelices fuisse dicemus nulloque in loco minus reperiri vitam felicem quam ubi maxime esse putatur. Nam si inter bonos non versatur, nec in malis quidem reperietur. Refugit enim omnem improborum societatem.

C46   19. 'Verum, quoniam felixne sit vita principum quaeritur, primum quid sit felicitas, deinde an domicilia principum sequatur discutiendum. Felicitatem esse vitam seu operationem secundum virtutem, scribit vir sapientissimus Aristoteles, et exercitio virtutum felicitatem comparari. Cicero noster vult eam esse honestarum rerum prosperitatem vel fortunam, adiutricem bonorum consiliorum; quibus qui non utatur, nullo pacto felix esse queat. Ubi ergo virtutes aut bona consilia desunt, ubi adsunt vitia, ibi nequit esse ulla felicitas. Non enim tam diversa interque se repugnantia coniunguntur. Sed virtutis raram[99] coisse cum principibus familiaritatem, praeteritorum exempla docuerunt; ut vero improbi malique sint, ratio, qua constat vitiis facilem aditum ad

C47   principes patere, nobis persuadet. Igitur et infelices erunt. Vellem doctorum ac bonorum virorum gratia ut sapientiae darent operam principes illiusque praeceptis obtemperarent. Sed cum his nulla sapientiae cura sit, nec virtutes quidem cognoscere aut earum usu ad vitae subsidium uti possunt. Fugit ignorantiam virtus et rationi sapientiaeque inhaeret. Ea cum sit principum contubernalis, careant virtutibus oportet. Hoc sentiens divina veritas, quae mentiri nequit, per os prophetae iterum repetens hanc sententiam: "Homo," inquit, "cum in honore esset non intellexit, comparatus est iumentis insipientibus et similis factus est illis." Quid aliis testibus, alia ratione, alia auctoritate opus est ad demonstrandum virtutem seorsum habitare a principibus et ob eam rem esse

long way from approaching Augustus' virtue and praises? Of course, we will conclude that they were unhappy, and that the happy life is found nowhere less than where it is most reckoned to be. For if it does not dwell with the good, then it will not be found among the bad ones either. Indeed, it avoids all association with the wicked.

19. "However, since we are inquiring whether or not the life of   C46
leaders is happy, we should first discuss what happiness is, and then whether it is to be found in the houses of leaders. That happiness is life or activity in accordance with virtue is what the very wise man Aristotle tells us, and that happiness is obtained through the exercise of the virtues.[60] Our own Cicero wishes it to be prosperity in honorable matters or a fortune which aids good counsels, and the person who does not experience these cannot by any means be happy.[61] Hence where virtues or good counsels are lacking, where vices are present, in that place there cannot exist any happiness. For such different things, so diametrically opposed to each other, cannot be joined together. But examples from the past have shown that familiarity with virtue rarely coexists with leaders. Indeed, that they are dishonest and evil, reason, which shows that leaders have easy access to vices, persuades us. Therefore, they will also be unhappy. For the sake of learned and good men I   C47
would wish that leaders paid attention to wisdom, and obeyed its precepts. But since they do not care at all about wisdom, they can neither recognize virtues nor use them to help their lives. Virtue flees from ignorance and sticks fast to reason and wisdom. Since ignorance dwells with leaders, they needs must lack virtues. Divine Truth, which cannot lie, holds this view, repeating this opinion again through the mouth of the prophet. 'A man,' he says, 'has no understanding when he is in a position of honor. He can be compared to stupid beasts and becomes like them.'[62] What need is there of other witnesses, other reasoning, or another authority to show that virtue dwells apart from leaders, and that it is for this

infelices? Stultitia enim summa infelicitas est, cum a divino dei oraculo iumentis insipientibus similes esse dicantur. Non intellegere eos dixit, qui in honore consistunt; excaecatur enim mens eorum splendore dignitatis et imperii, ut et[100] stultitiae ac insipientiae pateat et rara sit virtus in illis.

C48   20. 'Nam si dixeris fortitudinem in illis esse, id prorsus negabo. Cum enim fortitudinis opus sit adire pericula pro communi salute ad iniurias propulsandas armisque decernere pro salute patriae, principum autem cura sit pro privato commodo et augendis imperii finibus arma capere, quantumvis ardua pericula subeant, fortitudinis laude atque opere[101] carebunt. Si temperatos dixeris, multi ridebunt, cum illorum voluptates, luxuriam, libidines legerint atque audierint. Iusti vero nequaquam sunt; nam cum ea virtus versetur circa poenam ac praemia tribuenda, poenam quidem inferunt cum eorum statui conducit. Non enim sontes puniunt, sed persaepe extollunt propter admissum scelus. Praemio vero nequaquam afficiunt bene meritos, sed quos libido persuadet, qui ut

C49   plurimum sunt reprobi ac nefarii viri. Prudentia plures videntur excellere, quoniam quae adversus inferiores machinantur, possunt perficere. Versutos ego, callidos, astutos multos audivi, prudentes vero nullos, siquidem prudentia est reliquarum virtutum moderatrix et veluti quidam auriga. Sed cum[102] reliquae virtutes procul absint ab eorum vita, et prudentia quoque deerit. Sapientia vero quae potest regibus ac principibus inesse, qui neque litteris neque doctrina illam percipiunt,[103] neque sapientum[104] praeceptis neque doctorum hominum vocibus neque bonorum consuetudine neque integritate vitae? Satis illi ex magnitudine imperii se sapere arbitrantur, partim temerarii atque insulsi, partim feminis molliores.

reason they are unhappy? For folly is the greatest unhappiness, since by the divine oracle of God they are compared to stupid beasts. Those who are in positions of honor do not understand, he said: for their mind is blinded by the splendor of their dignity and power, so that it lies open to stupidity and foolishness, and virtue rarely appears in them.

20. "For if you claim that bravery exists among them, with that C48 I will disagree profoundly. For since it is the task of bravery to approach dangers for the common good in order to drive away acts of aggression and to fight with arms for the safety of the fatherland, but the care of leaders is for their private convenience and to take up arms to increase the territory under their control, whatever arduous dangers they undergo, they will lack praise for bravery as well as its work. If you say they are temperate, many will laugh, since they have read and heard of their pleasures, lechery and lusts. They are indeed by no means just: for while that virtue turns on punishment and the giving of rewards, they inflict punishments when it enhances their position. For they do not punish the guilty, but often exalt them because of a crime they have admitted to. They by no means bestow a reward on those who deserve it, but upon those their whims persuade them to honor, who for the most part are vile and wicked men. Quite a few leaders C49 appear to excel in prudence, since they can bring to fruition their plots against inferiors. I have heard of many clever, cunning and astute leaders, but no prudent ones, since prudence is the moderator of the other virtues and acts like a charioteer.[63] But since the other virtues are far distant from their lives, prudence will also be absent. But what wisdom can there be in kings and leaders, when they do not receive it through literature or education, nor through the teachings of the wise, nor through the words of learned men, nor through the company of good men, nor through integrity of life? They think they know enough just from the size of their empire, although some are rash and foolish, and others weaker than

Multos liberales vulgus existimavit, quoniam multis condonarunt. At ii stultitiae potius quam liberalitatis laudem meruerunt. Inconsulta enim elargitio et pecuniarum temeraria effusio vituperanda est. In liberalitate quidem loci, temporis, personae ratio habetur. Adeat regem vir doctus et sapiens, munus petens: contemnetur; adeat fatuus, ridiculus aut histrio: vestibus donabitur atque auro. Non honestis viris aut egenis tribuunt, sed procacibus, improbis, importunis. Itaque dum liberalitatis nomen assequi volunt, in temerariae effusionis culpam prolabuntur. Virtutes igitur ferme omnes, tanquam proscriptae, regum ac dominantium animos reliquerunt seseque ad humiliores homines contulerunt.

21. 'Rationibus ista hucusque a nobis[105] acta sunt. Adiciamus si C50 placet et auctoritatem. Isocrates, gravissimus auctor testisque religiosus, in eo libro quem de regno *Ad Nicoclem* scripsit:

Permulta sunt, inquit, quae privatos homines inducant[106] ad bene honesteque vivendum. In primis quidem illorum vita non otio, non luxu, non divitiis frangitur, sed pro quotidiano victu comparando laboribus ac vigiliis insudant. Legibus etiam, quibus immoderatae cupiditates hominum frenantur, parere[107] coguntur. Adde quod inter aequales liberiore quadam licentia loquendi utuntur, qua et amicorum errata reprehendere et in inimicos invehere queunt. Accedunt ad haec institutiones quas veteres illi clarissimique poetae de vita et moribus tradiderunt. Haec omnia privatorum mentes ad meliorem vitam inducunt, quibus adiumentis destituti reges esse videntur. Neque enim in tanto fastu tantaque rerum licentia moneri se aut emendari patiuntur.

women. The common view has judged many generous, because they have given to a great many. But these deserve praise for folly rather than for generosity. Ill-advised largesse and rash prodigality with money is reprehensible. Where generosity is concerned, account must be taken of place, time, and individual. If a learned and wise man approaches a king asking for a gift, he will be despised. If a fool, a jester, or an actor does the same, he will be rewarded with clothing and gold. They do not give to honorable or poor men, but to the forward, dishonest and importunate. So when they want to gain a name for generosity, they fall into the vice of rash prodigality. Hence, almost all the virtues, as though proscribed, have left the minds of kings and rulers and betaken themselves to humbler men.

21. "So far we have dealt with the matter by arguments. If you agree, let us also add authority. Isocrates, a most serious author and a scrupulous witness, wrote in the work on kingship *To Nicocles*: C50

'There are very many things,' he says, 'to induce private individuals to live well and honorably. First of all, their lives are not broken by leisure, lechery or riches, but they sweat for their daily bread, laboring and staying up at night. They are obliged also to obey the laws which rein in the immoderate desires of men. Add to this the fact that they can employ a more unrestrained liberty in speaking among their peers, by means of which they can both criticize their friends' mistakes and attack their enemies. Added to this are also the instruction on life and morality which those ancient and famous poets have handed down. All these things lead the minds of private individuals toward a better life, but of these aids kings appear to be deprived. Nor amid such great contempt and free access to resources do they allow themselves to be advised or corrected.'[64]

C51 Haec ille. Perversum igitur nimis hominum genus est et humanitati adversum eorum qui sanas respuunt monitiones. Viri non omni honesto vacui admoneri se arguique gaudent, ut exinde meliores fiant. Cum enim in multis offendant omnes — homines enim sumus — grata ac iocunda est iis, qui se[108] emendari, qui se ad honestatem comparare volunt, reprehensio erratorum suorum, quo[109] meliorem vitam sequantur; ob eamque rem gratias solemus agere monitoribus nostris, magni loco beneficii habentes ea vitia in nobis ostendi, a quibus ipsi minime abstinemus, morbo animi impediti.

22. 'At vero regibus imperatoribusque quam grata sit vitiorum suorum admonitio, plures miserabili exemplo docuerunt. Hostes enim sunt veritatis, adulatoribus atque assentatoribus se penitus tradentes; quae maxima est infelicitas. Magnum sane consummatae nequitiae signum est suos monitores et recta consilia odisse.

C52 Quo in vitio[110] plures insanierunt. Rex Persarum Cyrus (ut recentiores praetermittam), Harpalo[111] familiari ob reprehensum in se vitium filios epulandos in convivio dedit et, ne parentis mors filiis adiceretur, epulas illas laudare ut suavis coactus est. Cambyses cuiusdam ex carissimis filium ob admonitam in eo ebrietatem sagitta transfixit. Alexander Magnus, vesanum animal, Callisthenem philosophum, condiscipulum suum, Persarum in eo mores culpantem, omnibus detruncatum membris in cavea more inclusum beluae discruciavit. Refertae sunt historiae casibus illorum qui, suorum principum vitia emendare cupientes, mortis supplicio affecti sunt. Non enim patiuntur monitiones qui spernunt virtutem, sed sana consilia aut acerbo odio aut tormentis prosequuntur.

23. 'Constare arbitror tum ratione, tum auctoritate, tum exemplis

C53 quam raram cum principibus virtutes ineant societatem. Quid?[112]

This is what Isocrates said. It is a most perverse breed of men and   C51
contrary to the nature of humanity which rejects sane advice. Men
who are not altogether devoid of honor rejoice in being challenged
and admonished, so that they may become better because of it.
For since all of us offend in many areas (for we are human), criticism of their faults is pleasing and delightful to those who wish to
improve and prepare themselves for probity, so that they may follow a better life. For this reason, we usually thank our advisors,
considering as a great gift the revelation of those faults from which
we ourselves least refrain, hindered by a mental sickness.

22. "However, how pleasing to kings and emperors is the criticism of their vices, not a few have demonstrated through their
pitiable example. For they are enemies of the truth and hand
themselves over completely to sycophants and flatterers, which is
the greatest unhappiness. Indeed, it is a great sign of their con-
summate wickedness that they hate their advisors and proper advice. And embroiled in this failing, many have been driven completely mad. Cyrus, King of the Persians (to pass over more recent   C52
examples) gave his friend Harpalus his own children to eat at a
feast because he had criticized a fault in him, and, so that the
death of their father might not be added to that of the sons, he
was forced to praise the food as delightful.[65] Cambyses transfixed
with an arrow the son of one of those closest to him because he
had raised the issue of his drunkenness.[66] That mad animal Alexander the Great, when his fellow-pupil Callisthenes the philosopher accused him of living like a Persian, cut all his limbs off, shut
him into a cage like a wild beast, and tortured him to death.[67] The
histories are packed with the misfortunes of men who have been
punished by death for desiring to correct their leaders' faults. For
those who spurn virtue do not put up with advice, but punish
sound counsel either by bitter hatred or by torture.

23. "I think it is agreed by reason, authority and examples how
rarely the virtues enter into association with leaders. What am I   C53

Vitia quam familiaria illis esse videntur! Cogita primum quantum
ira sit malum, quam atrox facinus, quam crudele, quot eius exempla a regibus in perniciem gentium edita. Non recito[113] Sullae
iussu quattuor ob iram legiones civium uno edicto ferro absump-
tas, non stragem Praenestinorum, non multa ab eo in cives impetu
irae facta. Transeo Alexandrum, qui Clitonem, senem familiarem,
in convivio lancea transfodit, qui Lysimachum amicum leoni obiecit. Non recenseo multorum rabiem qui humanum sanguinem,
quia ore non poterant, oculis exhauserunt. Hoc affirmare ausim:
nullum taetrius malum, nullum scelestius, nullum periculosius
protulisse naturam. Atqui haec pestis nefaria in regibus ac principibus praecipue domicilium collocavit. Puerulis sunt ad iracundiam faciliores. Quicquid eorum animos offendit, scelestum iudicant. Nefas ducunt[114] eorum cupiditatibus aut dictis contrairi.
Parvulo excitato vento, incenduntur ira ad hominum cruciatus;
fortunae enim beneficio tumidi, cum appetitu pro ratione utantur,
etiam in rebus parvulis profundunt iram. Nam comitem fortunae
felicis iracundiam esse, viri sapientes tradunt, et magnam fortunam maiorem iram testantur sequi. Periculosa ac turbulenta sunt
principum vitia, sed ira maiorem stragem edit facultati rerum coniuncta.

C54   24. 'Bene praestanterque scribit Seneca perire funditus omnia,
ubi quantum ira suadet, fortuna permittit. Darius, Persarum rex,
bellum adversus Scythas moturus, offensus Ortobazi nobilis senis
precibus in solacium senectutis rogantis unum e tribus liberis
sibi relinqui, plus quam peteret pollicitus se daturum, omnis tres
in eius conspectu occisos obiecit. Xerxes, cum Graecis gesturus

saying! How at home among them the vices appear to be! Consider firstly how great an evil is anger, what a dreadful crime, how cruel, and how many examples of it have been perpetrated by kings to the destruction of their subjects. I will not mention the four legions of citizens put to the sword on the orders of Sulla by one edict because of anger, nor the massacre of the people of Praeneste, nor the many things done by him against the citizens under the impulse of anger.[68] I pass over Alexander, who put a lance through his associate the aged Clitus at a feast, and threw his friend Lysimachus to a lion.[69] I will not review the madness of many who have drunk human blood with their eyes, because they could not do it with their mouths. This I would venture to say, that nature has produced no viler evil, none more criminal, and none more dangerous. And yet this nefarious plague has taken up its dwelling especially among kings and leaders. They are more easily angered than small children. Whatever offends their minds, they consider a crime, and they think it wrong for their own desires or words to be opposed. When a tiny breeze gets up, they are set on fire by anger to torture men. For, puffed up by the favor of fortune, since they follow their appetites rather than their reason, they pour out their anger even in tiny things. For wise men tell us that a propensity to anger is the companion of good fortune and they bear witness to the fact that greater anger follows great fortune. The vices of leaders are dangerous and turbulent, but anger wreaks greater havoc when it is allied to the power given by material resources.

24. "Seneca puts it outstandingly well,[70] writing that everything C54 perishes completely, when fortune permits all that anger urges. Darius, the Persian king, when he was about to make war on the Scythians, offended by the request of the old nobleman Ortobazus, that to comfort his old age one of his three sons should be left to him, promised that he would give him more than he asked and had all three killed in his sight and thrown down in front of him.[71]

bellum, parenti quinque filiorum unius vacationem petenti, ira
motus, quem vellet eligendi potestate concessa, eum quem delege-
rat in duas partes consectum[115] ab utroque viae, qua exercitus
transiturus erat, latere suspendi iussit. Transeo nostros principes,
ne quem mea notet[116] oratio; attamen requirebat multorum salus
illos fuisse paulum ab ira remissiores.

C55   25. 'Cuperem ut hoc uno tantum urgerentur malo. Sed multa
illam vitia consequuntur. Primum vesana ambitio (malus officii
magister), quae eos, semper ampliandi proferendique dominii cupiditate incensos, in aliorum perniciem stragemque irritat atque
impellit. Hinc cum vicinis bella, hinc caedes, incendia, nationum
populationes et provinciarum vastitas descendunt. Ubi enim imperandi cupiditas regnat, ibi pacis aut otii ratio esse non potest. Tum
vero luxuria et libidines variae, quae cum etiam doctissimos ac sapientis[117] viros quandoque ab officio declinare coegerint, quid in
principibus virium atque[118] auctoritatis habere putatis, in quibus
licentia cum stultitia admiscetur, qui, sensuum voluptatibus potius
quam rationi obtemperantes, non solum illas coercere, sed etiam
allicere consueverunt?[119] Blandum id quidem malum et quod
propter multi iam fuerunt e principatu pulsi. Quid autem turpius
(ne dicam infelicius) Alexandro et priscis regibus, qui cohortes
uxorum exoletorumque libidinis causa habebant?

26. 'Adde his superbiam atque impotentiam, quae raro a principibus recedunt. Adde avaritiam (dominantium sectatricem), qua
omnes ferme ducti in divitum fortunas impetum faciunt. Adician-
tur quoque multiplices cupiditates, quae mentem eorum semper
C56   affligunt. Quid de conscientia scelerum loquar, qua nullum Seneca

As Xerxes was on the point of war against the Greeks, when a father of five sons asked for one to be released from service, moved by rage he first of all allowed him to choose which one he wanted and then killed and cut in half the one he had chosen and ordered the parts to be hung up on each side of the road on which the army would pass.[72] I pass over our own leaders, so as not to impugn any of them in my speech: the safety of the majority of them, however, required them to be a little slacker in their anger.

25. "I would have wished that they were only beset by this one   C55 evil. But many faults follow in the wake of anger. First of all, crazy ambition, a bad teacher of duty, which is always provoking and driving them, inflamed by the desire continually to increase and expand their dominion, to the destruction and massacre of others. Hence come wars with one's neighbors, murder, conflagrations, and the devastation of nations, peoples and provinces. For where the desire for power holds sway, in that place no account can be taken of peace or quiet. Secondly, since lechery and the various lusts have occasionally even driven the most learned and wise men to defect from their duties, what strength and authority do you think they have with leaders, in whom license is mingled with folly, given that they, obedient to the pleasures of their senses rather than to reason, are accustomed not only not to hold them in check, but actually to invite them in? It is a pleasant set of vices and one which has caused many to be expelled from the position of leader. What is viler, not to say unhappier, than Alexander and the early kings, who kept cohorts of wives and male lovers because of lust?[73]

26. "Add to these vices arrogance and insolence, which rarely leave the side of leaders. Add avarice, the follower of rulers, led by which virtually all make attacks on the fortunes of the wealthy. There should also be added the multiplicity of desires which always afflict their minds. What shall I say about the knowledge of   C56 their crimes? Seneca writes that there is no greater punishment

gravius esse supplicium scribit? Numquid vobis parvus[120] videtur
esse in principibus cruciatus? At ii[121] qua conscientia vivant, satis
constat, nempe ea quam ipsorum facinora requirunt. Ingratitudo
quoque eorum domestica est; qua in re praestant reliquis etiam in
agenda, nedum in referenda, gratia insolentes. Quicquid eis operis,
quicquid muneris, quicquid beneficii impenditur, id debito iureque
fieri putant et, ne quid cuiquam debeant, sibi omnia deberi arbitrantur.

27. Adiciuntur his malis suspiciones, metus, timores, qui iugiter
animos principum lacerant: servi, familiares, domestici, amici, noti
atque ignoti formidantur; non uxor, non liberi, non fratres, non
cognati sunt extra suspicionem. Horum namque singulorum
conspiratione et fraudibus plures principes interierunt. Nullus his
locus tutus est, nulla regio, nulla ora;[122] ubique insidiae timentur.
Dies solliciti, insomnes noctes aguntur, tum vitae, tum imperii
amittendi metu; qua vita, tot malis implicita, nihil prorsus potest
infelicius excogitari. Audite, quaeso, quid in hanc sententiam in
eodem libello dicat Isocrates: "Si metus illorum," inquit, "sollicitu-
dinesque et pericula consideres, si nonnullos ex regibus aspicies ab
iis necatos, quos fidissimos cogitabant, si item reges ipsos in eos
animadvertisse crudelius quos singulari familiaritate caros habuissent, aliis vero contigisse ut, postquam in suos saevissent, ab suis
postea occiderentur, quamvis potius vitam quam hanc,[123] tot tantisque periculis coniunctam, censeas eligendam."

28. Illud quoque nequaquam est in minimis ipsorum malis ad-
numerandum: quod suavissimo omnium fructu amicitiae privantur. Ipsi neminem nisi inconsulto quodam impetu diligunt a nulloque diliguntur. Inter pares quidem amicitia versatur et eos in

C57

than this.[74] Does this seem to you a small torture in leaders? It is well known, however, with what consciences they live, namely, that which their crimes require. Ingratitude is also at home with them, in which they excel others, insolent as they are even in giving, not to mention returning thanks. Whatever effort, gifts, or favors are bestowed on them, they think are theirs of right and are owed them, and to avoid owing anything to anyone, they consider that everything is owed to them.

27. "There are added to these evils the suspicions, fears and anxieties which abundantly tear at the minds of leaders. They fear their slaves, the members of their household, their servants, their friends, people known to them and unknown. No one is above suspicion, not their wives, not their children, not their brothers nor their relatives. For many leaders have perished through the conspiracy and deceit of each of these. No place, no region, no shore is safe for them; everywhere they fear plots. Their days are passed anxiously and their nights sleeplessly, either through fear of losing their lives or their empire. One cannot think of any life more unhappy than this one, wound up as it is in many troubles. Listen, I ask you, to what Isocrates says in the same book on the same subject: 'If you think of their fears, anxieties and dangers,' he says, 'if you see that some of the kings have been killed by those whom they considered most trustworthy, and that equally kings themselves have exacted crueler punishment on those whom they had considered dear to them by virtue of an unusual intimacy, but that it has happened to others that after they had raged against their family members, they were killed by them, you would consider any life whatsoever as your choice before this one so tied up with so many great dangers.'[75]   C57

28. "Nor is it by any means to be counted the least of their problems that they are deprived of the sweetest fruit of all, that of friendship.[76] Leaders never love anyone except through some spontaneous impulse and they are loved by no one. Friendship simply

quibus eadem bonarum artium vigent studia. At ii[124] non solum
non amant pares, sed cum eis regnandi gratia[125] decertant. Bonis
artibus quantum vacent, palam nobis est. Cum inferioribus nulla
esse potest amicitia; nam timeri a suis quam diligi principes malunt. Sed quem metuunt, et oderunt, veteri sententia. Itaque nullus apud ipsos amicitiae locus est. Amici quippe est ex animo et
vera loqui; at illi veritati sunt omnino infesti, cum nihil nisi quod
libeat eorum aures patiantur. "Sed videmus," inquies, "multos amicorum nonnulla praebere officia." Id quidem nullo fit principis
amore, sed ob utilitatem privatam. Sectantur enim quem saepius
oderunt, sed utilitas superat malivolentiam. Concurritur enim ad
eos tanquam ad aurifodinam, quaestus et lucri causa. Non igitur
amantur, sed venerantur ac metuuntur.

29.1 'Satis eis est laudari colique ab adulatoribus et iis quos veluti canes ad latrandum alunt. Bonos et veritatis cultores penitus
respuunt, cum aliena sit eis virtus suspecta. Triplex enim—
ut principum felicitatem cognoscatis—genus hominum est eis
maxime acceptum ac familiare. Hos inter primas partes adulatores
tenent atque assentatores, non homines sed portentuosae beluae
atque immanes veri dicendi hostes, qui mentiendo blandiendoque
adeo principum mentes infatuant, ut parum distent ab insanis.
Consilia principis commendant, quantumvis perniciosa ac turbulenta, cum sit consilii inops; prudentiam admirantur, cum sit
stultus; illum plus quam ceteros sapere profitentur, cum haud
procul absit ab amentia; eoque eum suis assentationibus abducunt,
ut, nihil verum audiens, suae sapientiae fidens, prolabatur

operates among equals and those in whom the same enthusiasms for the noble arts operate. But leaders not only do not love their equals,[77] but actually compete with them for the sake of ruling. How much time they devote to the liberal arts is obvious to us. They can have no friendship with their inferiors, for leaders prefer to be feared rather than loved by their subjects.[78] But it is an old proverb, that people also hate the man they fear.[79] So there is no place among them for friendship. For it is the job of a friend to speak from the heart and to speak the truth, yet leaders are completely opposed to truth, since their ears will only allow in what pleases them. 'But,' you will object, 'we see many of their friends doing various good turns.' However, this happens not because of love for the leader, but for private interests. For they are in the train of a man they quite often hate, but their own interests overcome their ill will. People flock to leaders as they do to gold mines, for income and profit. Hence they are not loved, but worshipped and feared.

29.1 "For leaders it is enough to be praised and worshipped by sycophants and by those whom they feed like dogs for barking. They completely reject good men who cultivate the truth, since virtue is suspect and alien to them.[80] For (so that you may recognize the happiness of leaders) there are three types of men that are most pleasing to and friendly with them. Among these, first place goes to the sycophants and flatterers, who are not human beings, but portentous monsters and immense enemies of telling the truth, who by their lies and flatteries so infatuate the minds of leaders that they are not far from insanity. However pernicious and turbulent a leader's counsels, they praise them, though he is devoid of good sense. Though he is stupid, they praise his wisdom. They say he has more wisdom than others, though he is not far from madness, and they lead him by their flatteries to the point where, because he hears nothing true, through trusting his own wisdom he slips most often into the most unfortunate disasters.

C58

C59

saepissime in miserrimos casus. Neque enim ad ullam sapientiae cognitionem pervenire possunt quibus ab assentatoribus persuasum est iam se ad sapientiam pervenisse. Obsessi ab adulatoribus, omni veritatis cognitione privantur. Nam si quem iniuria princeps affecit, id pro summa iustitia assentatores comprobant. Luxuriam dicunt oblectationem naturalem, usu et consuetudine gentium permissam. Avaritia parcitas, prodigalitas liberalitatis nomine appellatur. Crudelitatis culpam leniunt specie severitatis. Nullum est tam taetrum facinus, nullum tam nefarium in regibus vitium, quod non adulatores alicuius obtegant virtutis velamento. Quo fit, cum malus ab nequissimis laudetur, ut, cumulata stultitia multorum comprobatione, vitiis pro virtutibus abutatur. Qua in re summa est infelicitas.

C60   29.2 'Hos sequuntur voluptatum ac luxuriae ministri, quibus secretiora domus permissa sunt: cum his occulta colloquia et interiora, quae lucem fugiunt, consilia credita. Tertiam aciem perquirendae comparandaeque pecuniae architecti conficiunt, gratum regibus ministerium. Horum suasu impulsuque nova vectigalia, divitum insidiae, proscriptiones, rapinae, spolia subsequuntur. Accumuletur his quartum genus, idque pestiferum, delatorum, ingens malum et in bonorum atque innocentum virorum perniciem promptum; quibus non solum principes improbi, sed modesti quoque habiti aures praebuerunt. Apud Hadrianum certe imperatorem adeo valuere delatorum voces, ut amicos, quos ad summum provexerat, postea habuerit hostium loco.

C61   30. 'His ergo tam bonis, tam sanctis ministris, tam fidis satellitibus suffulta principum consuetudo, quam iniqua conditione agitur! Mihi credite, non ingreditur limen horum ulla felicitas, sed tormenta et variae calamitates. Ab his amicitia exclusa est, repulsa veritas, adulatio accita. Nam quod Carolus doctos ab eis viros

For people who have been persuaded by flatterers that they have already arrived at wisdom cannot arrive at any understanding of wisdom. Beset by sycophants, they are deprived of all understanding of the truth. For any injury inflicted on anyone by a leader is approved as supreme justice by the flatterers. Lechery they call a natural delight, permitted by universal custom and usage. Avarice is called thrift and extravagance generosity. They lessen the fault of cruelty by masking it as severity. There is no crime so vile, no vice so criminal among kings which the sycophants do not hide under the veil of some virtue. Hence it comes about that when an evil man is praised by evil men, once folly has been piled up by the approval of many, he makes use of vices as though they were virtues. Here is the greatest unhappiness.

29.2 "These are followed by those who pander to their pleasures C60 and lechery, to whom the more secluded parts of the palace are open, since to them are entrusted the secret conversations and more intimate plans, which flee the light of day. The third rank consists of the architects of seeking and acquiring money, a function pleasing to leaders. It is at their prompting and impulsion that new taxes, ambushes on the wealthy, proscriptions, thefts, and pillaging follow. To these let there be added a fourth type, and a destructive one too, the great evil of informers, which is ready to destroy good and innocent men, to whom not only bad leaders, but also those who have been held to be moderate have lent their ears. Certainly the words of informers had so much power with the emperor Hadrian that he later regarded as enemies friends whom he had raised to the highest positions.[81]

30. "Supported by such good and such holy servants, and such C61 faithful underlings, under what bad conditions is the social life of leaders conducted! Believe me, no happiness crosses their threshold, only torments and various calamities. By them friendship is shut out, truth driven off, and flattery invited in. For as to Carlo's recent point that the learned are loved and cultivated by them, it

diligi colique paulo ante dixit, longe tota aberrat[126] via. Nam neque litterarum studia apud reges et dominos, nisi admodum paucos, unquam viguerunt, neque ab eis doctrina ac sapientia praediti aut culti aut magni habiti. Diversa sunt principum excellentiumque virorum studia; quorum virtus semper fuit regibus formidolosa. Perstringit enim dominorum veluti lippientes oculos alienae virtutis fulgor, ut, a quo se superari sentiunt, aut odiant aut nequaquam diligant. Non autem neque apud Graecos neque apud Latinos tanta doctissimorum eloquentissimorumque virorum copia viguisset neque adeo sapientiae parens philosophia esset exculta, nisi et Athenae et urbs Roma diutina in libertate vixissent. Loquendi enim vivendique libertatem litterarum studia expetunt et sequuntur, servitutem fugiunt atque abhorrent. Plures doctrinae studiis deditos viros qui sub regibus orti erant legimus Athenas se contulisse, ubi et virtuti honor et libertati locus erat.

31. 'Quomodo enim cari esse principibus viri sapientes possunt, qui (quod maxime est dominis invisum) vitae libertatem prae se ferunt? Nam cum principes, assentatoribus stipati, veritatem horreant, viri autem studio sapientiae dediti, veri cultores, adulationem ut vitium pessimum aspernentur, necesse est ut aut reiciantur aut pereant. Iam dixi[127] Callisthenem ab Alexandri temeritate ob sanas monitiones crudelissime necatum. Plato, vir sanctissimus,[128] a Dionysio, Siciliae tyranno, per doctrinae speciem vocatus, tyranni opera venundatus est. Zenonem philosophum, senem admodum, Phalaris tyrannus omni cruciatus genere dilaceravit. Anaxagoras, nobilis philosophus, a Nicocreonte, Cypriorum rege, occisus est.[129] Socrates, tyrannorum tempore damnatus, veneno periit. Boethius, vir doctissimus atque innocentissimus, Theoderici regis

C62

strays a long way from the proper path. For study of literature has neither flourished among kings and lords (save a very few), nor have men endowed with learning and wisdom ever been cultivated or considered important by them. Leaders always have different enthusiasms from those of the best men, whose virtue has always been feared by kings. For the gleam of someone else's virtue stings the eyes of leaders as if they were inflamed, with the result that they either hate or certainly do not love those by whom they feel themselves surpassed. For neither among the Greeks nor the Romans would so great a number of very learned and eloquent men have flourished, nor would philosophy, the mother of wisdom, have been so developed, had not Athens and the city of Rome lived long in freedom. For the study of literature demands and follows upon freedom of speech and life, but flees from slavery and shrinks from its approach. We read of very many men dedicated to learned studies, who were born under kings, but betook themselves to Athens, where respect was given to virtue and a place provided for freedom.[82]

31. "For how can wise men be dear to leaders, when they parade the thing most hated by their masters, a life of freedom? For since leaders, with their serried ranks of flatterers, shudder at truth, yet men devoted to the study of wisdom as cultivators of the truth reject sycophancy as a dreadful vice, they must either be banished or killed. I have already mentioned the cruel death of Callisthenes through the rashness of Alexander because of his good advice. That most holy man Plato, after being summoned by Dionysius the tyrant of Sicily because of the glory of his learning, was sold into slavery upon the tyrant's orders.[83] When Zeno the philosopher was a pretty old man, the tyrant Phalaris tore him to pieces by means of every type of torture.[84] Anaxagoras the famous philosopher was killed by Nicocreon, King of the Cypriots.[85] Socrates[86] was condemned to death in the period of the tyrants and died from poison.[87] Boethius, a most learned and innocent man, lost

C62

iussu vitam amisit. Quam de reliquis coniecturam sumemus, cum divus Augustus, qui bonorum principum principatum tulit, tam crudelis in Ovidium, poetam egregium, fuerit? Quem cum in Pontum ob levem nescio quam offensiunculam relegasset, nun-

C63 quam ut rediret ab se impetrari passus est. Non amant principes nisi suis moribus congruentes. Quem vero legimus aut a regibus[130] aut imperatoribus aut ceteris dominantibus honore, opibus, dignitate amplificatum fuisse excellenti doctrina virum? Quid Augustus in Virgilium aut T. Livium contulit, alterum poetarum, alterum historiae Romanae patrem? Vir eloquentissimus Quintilianus Romae publicam scholam unde viveret tenuit. Lactantius Firmianus, vir praestans doctrina et arte dicendi, qui Crispum, Constantini imperatoris filium, litteris erudivit, adeo pauper vixit, ut plerumque necessariis egeret. Haec cura praestantissimorum doctrina virorum imperatoribus fuit.

C64   32.1 'Sed quid ego antiquiora recenseo? Tulit aetas superior tres viros praeclarissimos qui sapientia et doctrina magnum lumen Italiae attulerunt. Prior Dantes eluxit ingenio singulari, cuius exstat poema praeclarum neque, si litteris Latinis constaret, ulla ex parte poetis superioribus postponendum. Is patria ob civiles factiones pulsus, cum nihil secum praeter virtutem asportasset, contulit se ad Canem, veterem principem Veronensem, cuius tum liberalitas prae ceteris ferebatur. Susceptus ab eo Dantes ac victus quotidianus, ut reliquis ex familia, tributus. Vacabat vir doctissimus ingenio, scribendi curae intentus: nulla in eum dignitas, nullus honor, nullae opes collatae. At Florentinus quidam, per facetias et dicacitatem multas a domino — ut mos est fere principum,[131] quibus plus stulti quam sapientes placent — divitias consecutus,

his life on the command of King Theoderic.[88] What are we to conjecture about the rest, when the divine Augustus, who took the position of leader among the good leaders, was so cruel to the outstanding poet Ovid? When he had exiled him to Pontus for some tiny little misdeed or other, he never allowed himself to grant a petition for his return. Leaders only love those who suit C63 their ways. Indeed, which of those we read were enhanced in honor, wealth, or dignity either by kings. or emperors or other rulers was a man of outstanding learning? What did Augustus bestow on Vergil or Titus Livius, the one the father of Roman poetry, the other of Roman history? The most eloquent Quintilian ran a public school at Rome to get his living.[89] Lactantius Firmianus, a man outstanding in learning and the art of speaking (who trained Crispus the son of the emperor Constantine in literature), lived so poorly that for the most part he lacked the bare essentials of life.[90] This was how important men outstanding in learning were to the emperors.

32.1 "But why am I listing off the more ancient examples? The C64 previous century brought forth three very famous men, who brought a great light to Italy through their wisdom and knowledge. The first, Dante, shone with a singular genius, and there is a famous poem of his extant which would in no way be inferior to those of earlier poets, if it had been written in Latin.[91] Exiled from his native land because of factional strife within the city, since he had brought nothing with him except his virtue, he betook himself to Can Grande, the former leader of Verona,[92] whose generosity was famed above that of everyone else. Dante was received by him, and provided with his daily meals (like the rest of the household). This most learned man had time to indulge his genius, intent upon the task of writing: no dignity, no office and no wealth were, however, conferred upon him. Still, a Florentine who had gained great wealth from his master for his jokes and ready wit (as is the way with almost all leaders, to whom fools give more pleasure than

cum in aula Canis a Dante quaesisset cur ipse, qui nullas nosset litteras, tam dives evasisset, Dantes vero tali sapientia et doctrina pauper esset, "Quando," inquit Dantes, "ego meis studiis moribusque principem similem[132] invenero sicuti tu tuis, et ipse me praedivitem reddet."[133] Quibus verbis offensione principis contracta abiit. Ac[134] tandem vir excellentissimus omnique laude dignissimus, cum multa peragrasset loca parvique ipsius fieret virtus, Ravennae diem suum obiit. Magnum profecto Italiae dedecus, nullum ex tot principibus—permulti enim tum erant—repertum, qui talis viri pro dignitate nominis alendi ornandique curam suscepisset.

C65   32.2 'Hunc secutus est paulo inferior aetate Franciscus Petrarcha, vir priscis illis sapientia atque eloquentia comparandus, cuius ingenio haec nostra humanitatis studia, quae multis seculis sopita iacuerant,[135] adeo excitata sunt, ut priorem ferme dignitatem ac vires recuperarint.[136] Plures tum Italia principes alebat, sed praestabat unus omnibus honore, potentia, dignitate Robertus, rex Neapolitanus; ad quem cum Petrarcha accessisset, tenui honore susceptus—omnia enim regi eius viri virtute erant antiquiora—tantum viatico adiutus ad lauream in Urbe suscipiendam Romam[137] venit; acceptaque laurea in villa privata meliori vitae deditus, spretis principibus, consenuit, ubi et defunctus est.

32.3 'Eadem ferme aetate et Iohannes Bocatius, vir singularis ingenii, sed doctrina impar superioribus, floruit; cuius plurimi extant libri ad institutionem legentium editi. Contulit se is quoque Neapolim, vir tenui censu, ad quendam ex primoribus apud reginam principibus, spe, quoniam ab eo accersitus esset, maiora

wise men), when he had asked Dante at the court of Can Grande why it was that he, who was illiterate, had emerged so rich, while Dante, despite possessing such wisdom and knowledge, was poor, Dante replied: 'When I find a leader who matches my enthusiasms and ways as you have found one who matches yours, he too will make me extremely rich.'[93] Having by these words earned the disapproval of the leader, he left the court. And in the end, this outstanding man, most worthy of every praise, when he had traversed many regions, and his virtue had been valued at little, died at Ravenna. It is indeed a great disgrace to Italy that out of so many leaders (and there were a great many then) none was found to take on the care of such a man for the distinction of cultivating and enhancing his reputation.

32.2 "Dante was followed by the slightly younger Francesco   C65 Petrarca,[94] a man comparable to the ancients in wisdom and eloquence, through whose genius those humane studies of ours, which had lain dormant for so many centuries, were awoken to such an extent that they have virtually recovered their former dignity and strength. Italy at that time was the nursemaid of many leaders, but one stood out from the rest in honor, power and dignity, namely King Robert of Naples.[95] When Petrarch had come to him, he was received with small honor (for everything was more important for the king than the virtue of this man), and, helped only with his traveling expenses, he came to Rome to collect the laurel crown in the city. When he had received the laureate, he devoted himself to a better life in a private house, having rejected leaders, where he grew old and died.

32.3 "At about the same time lived Giovanni Boccaccio also, a man of unique genius, but less learned than the other two, many of whose books are available which were published for the instruction of readers.[96] He also betook himself to Naples, a man of small means, to one of the queen's leading nobles, in the hope of gaining greater rewards, since he had been summoned by him. But

quaedam consequendi. Sed haud diutius accola eius urbis fuit, tum contemptus sui impatiens, tum offensus principis illius moribus. Itaque Florentiam reversus aequo animo paupertatem tulit atque aulas deinceps principum aspernatus, mores quoque eorum suis scriptis detestatus, vixit sibi et Musis.

C66   33. 'Legite[138] quantumlibet veterum annalium monumenta: rarissime reperietis vel philosophum vel oratorem vel quempiam litteris et sapientia praeditum, aut ditatum a regibus aut opibus ac dignitate auctum, vel ad praestanda consilia vel ad praecipiendam[139] vitae disciplinam vel ad componendos mores fuisse accersitum. Quaedam ab his ad iactantiam quandam oblata vel data accepimus. Sed nullae unquam illis praefecturae a regibus demandatae, nulli honores habiti, nulli magistratus commissi, nulla graviora consilia credita. Neque id (ut opinor) iniuria. Sciunt enim ipsos nequaquam suarum cupiditatum futuros esse ministros. Taceo de nostris; a quibus quanti aut eloquentes aut docti aestimentur,[140] minime est obscurum. Unum tantum hac nostra aetate scimus in honore habuisse coluisseque egregios viros: superiorem ducem Mediolanensem, quos undique ad se praemiis pellectos[141] et dignitate et opibus affecit. Ceteri vero apparent tanquam rari nantes in gurgite vasto.

C67   34. 'Verum reliqua prosequamur quae principum vitam infelicem praestare videntur. Haud exigua felicitas ducitur[142] filios habere ac relinquere imperii successores. At malos principes exemplis constat improbitatem suam in filios infundere et efficere similes sui. Nam ut in regno, ita et in parentum vitiis filii videntur succedere. Ex malis ergo filiis nulla ad patres felicitas perveniet. Boni si quos legimus aut caruere filiis, sicut Augustus, Titus, Traianus, Antoninus Pius, aut eos genuere quibus fuisset satius defecisse.

he was not an inhabitant of that city for very long, both because
he could not bear the disrespect in which he was held and because
that leader's way of life offended him. And so, returning to Florence, he bore his poverty with equanimity, and, spurning from
then onward the courts of leaders and cursing their ways in his
writings, he lived for himself and the Muses.

33. "Read as much as you like of the records of ancient history, C66
you will very rarely find either a philosopher or an orator or anyone gifted in letters or wisdom who was either enriched by kings,
or had his wealth or dignity increased, or was summoned to give
advice, or to teach the discipline of life, or to provide moral education. We do learn that some things were offered or given by them
so that they could boast about it a little. But they were not entrusted with prefectures by kings at any time, no honors were held
by them, no magistracies given them, and no important counsels
were put into their care. Nor, I think, was this a wrong decision.
Kings know that these individuals will in no way be the servants
of their desires. I say nothing of our own leaders: what value is
given by them to eloquent or learned men is by no means obscure.
There is only one in our epoch whom we know to have held in
honor and cultivated outstanding men, the last Duke of Milan.[97]
He enticed them from everywhere with rewards and gave them
status and resources. The others 'appear like swimmers here and
there in the vast torrent.'[98]

34. "But let us move on to consider the other things that seem C67
to make the life of leaders unhappy. It is considered no small happiness to have sons and to leave successors to one's empire. Example proves, however, that bad leaders pour their own wickedness
into their sons and make them like themselves. For sons seem to
inherit their fathers' vices just as they inherit kingdoms. So from
bad sons no happiness will come to their fathers. Any good emperors [leaders] we read about have either lacked sons, like Augustus, Titus, Trajan, and Antoninus Pius, or have begotten those it

Avidius Cassius, in *Vita Severi imperatoris*: "Neminem magnorum
virorum," ait, "bonum et utilem filium reliquisse et eos aut interi-
isse sine liberis aut tales reliquisse, ut humano generi fuisset utilius
non esse natos." Magna est ergo vitae principum felicitas et admodum reliquis appetenda, quae aut deserta virtutum comitatu aut
oppressa vitiis, tum adulatoribus obsessa, tum curis anxia, quietis
inops, liberorum voluptate carens, nullius est expers calamitatis!
Sed stultum atque imperitum vulgus non haec eorum damna animadvertit nec conspicit miserias interiores: ex basi suspensos ac
sublimes prospectat. Opes, aurum, vestes, argentum, famulantium
catervas obstupescens, exteriorem ornatum intuetur, non intro novit quibus exagitentur malis.

C68 35. ʼSapientissime de his scribens Seneca: "Isti," inquit, "quos pro
felicibus aspicitis, si non qua currunt,[143] sed qua latent videritis,
miseri sunt, sordidi, turpes, ad similitudinem suorum parietum
extrinsecus culti." Lucianus autem, Graecus auctor, in *Alectrione*
suo Micillum,[144] qui et ipse aliquando rex fuisset, interrogatum a
Gallo num quidnam felix regum vita esset quemadmodum vulgo
aestimaretur,[145] habens quod bonorum maximum homines puta-
rent, ita respondentem introducit:

> Imperabam equidem pluribus provinciis tum multitudine
> hominum atque ubertate, tum vero amoenitate urbium refer-
> tis, fluminibus insuper navigio aptis et portuoso mari. Exer-
> citus habebam permultos; non pauci stipatores ac satellites
> corpus custodiebant. Abundabam auro, navibus et iis rebus
> omnibus, propter quas principes existimantur[146] esse felices.
> Quotiens prodibam[147] domo, multi me veluti deum quen-
> dam intuebantur atque adorabant. Alii praeibant cursu

would have been better to be without.[99] In his *Life of the Emperor Severus*, Avidius Cassius says: 'None of the great men left a good and useful son and they either died without children or left the sort that it would have been more useful for humanity if they had not been born.'[100] Great therefore is the happiness of the life of leaders and quite to be desired by others, when it is either deserted by the company of the virtues, or oppressed by vices, both beset by sycophants and worried by anxieties, bereft of peace and quiet, lacking the joy of children, and untouched by no calamity! Still the stupid and ignorant mob does not notice these disadvantages of theirs, nor does it see the miseries within: it only sees them supported on their pedestals and raised on high. Dumbstruck by their wealth, their gold, their clothing, silver and cohorts of servants, it looks upon the external display and does not realize with what evils they are beset within.

35. "Seneca writing very wisely about this, says: 'Those whom you see as happy, are, if you do not look where they are on show but where they lie hidden, miserable, dirty, base, and, rather like their walls, plastered on the outside.'[101] In his *Cockerel*, the Greek author Lucian introduced Micyllus, who had once been a king himself, replying as follows to the cockerel's question whether the life of kings was happy as was generally assumed, containing what men consider the greatest of good things: [102]

C68

> At all events, I used to rule a large number of provinces filled both with a multitude and proliferation of men and with lovely cities, with navigable rivers to boot, and a sea with many harbors. I had many armies, not a few bodyguards and servants protected my body, and I had enormous quantities of gold, ships and all the other things on account of which leaders are reckoned to be happy. Whenever I left the house, many looked upon me and worshipped me as though I were a god. Some ran ahead of the rest and others climbed

ceteros, alii tecta conscendebant, ut me inspicerent, magni facientes[148] videre currum quo vehebar, vestes, diadema, tum eos qui ordine praeibant ac sequebantur. Ego autem, mihi ipsi conscius quantae me res[149] torquerent, affligebar animo, illorum stultitiae ignoscens. Mei vero miserebar, qui essem similis magnis illis colossis, quos Phidias aut Myron sculpserat. Hi enim Iovem aut Neptunum ex auro vel ebore sculpunt, fulmen aut tridentem in manibus tenentes. At si quis introspexerit, videbit informe corpus, vectibus ferreis, clavis, cuneis et luto piceo compactum, in quibus mures et C69 mustelae diversorium habent. Eiusmodi profecto regnum est.[150] Quid tibi formidines enarrem, timores, suspiciones, domesticorum odia, insidias quibus abundat regia? Quid levem brevemque somnum et insomnia turbulenta? Quid varias ac multiplices cogitationes? Quid spes malas, vitam inquietam? Quid pecuniarum curam, litigia, expeditiones, mandata, leges, quae ne parvulam quidem somni quietem sinunt capere? Necesse est unum pro omnibus curam gerere ac sescentis[151] laboribus detineri. Neque enim dulcem, ut Homerus ait, somnum capiebat Menelaus, multa versans pectore, cum Graeci reliqui sterterent. Torquet Croesum filii surditas, Artaxerxem Clearchus, qui Cyro cum exercitu affuit, Dionysium Syracusium Dion tyrannide expellens, alium Parmenion, Perdiccam Ptolomaeus, Ptolomaeum Seleucus. Quod autem malorum est omnium maximum:[152] contemnant reges sibi amicissimos oportet et eos timeant, ne quid ab eis patiantur adversi. Hic enim ⟨a⟩ puer⟨o⟩ veneno periit,[153] hic ab amatore occisus est, hunc forsan mors similis occupabit.

rooftops to catch a glimpse of me, thinking it a great thing to
see the chariot in which I was riding, my clothing and my
diadem, as well as those who came ahead of me and those
who followed. However, I myself, conscious of what a lot of
problems afflicted me, was cast down in my mind, pardoning
their stupidity. It was myself, however, that I pitied, since I
was like those huge statues which Phidias or Myron had
carved.[103] They sculpt Jupiter or Neptune out of gold or
ivory, holding a thunderbolt or a trident in their hands. But
if anyone looks inside, he will see an ugly body, held together
by iron beams, nails, bars, wedges and pitchy clay, where
mice and weasels have their dwelling. This is what ruling is   C69
actually like.[104] Why should I tell you of the fears and worries, the suspicions and hatred of servants and the plots with
which the palace abounds? Why should I mention the light
and brief sleep and the turbulent dreams, why the diverse
and multifarious thoughts, why the bad prospects and the
life without peace? Why should I speak of the worry about
funds, the lawsuits, expeditions, charges, laws, which allow
us to get not even a tiny grain of peaceful sleep? One person
is obliged single-handedly to take responsibility for everyone
and to be occupied with countless labors. For, as Homer tells
us, not even Menelaus was enjoying sweet sleep, as he turned
over many things in his heart, while the rest of the Greeks
were snoring. Croesus is tormented by his son's deafness,
Artaxerxes by Clearchus, who was with Cyrus' army, Dionysius of Syracuse by Dion driving him from his tyranny,
someone else by Parmenion, Perdiccas by Ptolemy, Ptolemy
by Seleucus.[105] But the greatest ill of them all is that kings
must despise those most friendly to them and fear them in
case they suffer some wrong at their hands. One has died
from poison ⟨administered by his slave⟩, another has been
killed by his lover. Another will perhaps die a similar death.

357

In libro autem *De Calumnia* regum et principum aulas maxime abundare calamitatibus dicit, in quibus invidiae et suspiciones semper vigeant, adesse quoque adulatores gratum illis genus, ut facile detur calumniandi locus. Quamobrem tum ratione, tum auctoritate fateri cogimur miseram atque infelicem esse principum vitam.'

C70   36. Tum Cosmus: 'Cupiebam,' inquit, 'te paulum ante interpellare, qui mihi risum moveris, cum veluti rem pergrandem ac mirandam tibi visus es dicere, bonos principes instar esse portenti. Nam istud non magis in principibus quam reliquis monstri loco habendum est, bonum esse. Cicero quidem tuus in *Divinationis*[154] libris: "Si quae rarissime fiunt, monstra putanda sunt,' inquit, 'magis monstrum erit vir bonus quam partus mulae." Ita perraro evenit ut vir bonus reperiatur. Quod si virum bonum portenti simile Cicero arbitratur, quid tu in principibus putas contingere, quos plura quam privatos homines vitiorum irritamenta molliunt ac seducunt pluraque circumstant oblectamenta corporum, virtutibus inimica?[155] Rara virtus est in omni hominum conditione et statu, siquidem omnia praeclara rara. Itaque non magis in principibus quam in aliis deesse bonitatem experimur.'

C71   37. 'Non quaero,' Nicolaus inquit, 'bonum aut sapientem illum Stoicorum, qui nondum est inventus. Hos sentio bonos, quos usus et vita hominum comprobat, in quibus satis est inesse aliquam etsi non perfectam virtutem, ac saltem speciem et adumbratam effigiem earum virtutum, quas civilis vitae ratio requirit. At id ita rarum in illis reperitur, ut monstrum videatur, si quis bonus repertus sit. Difficulter enim perveniunt ad virtutis possessionem, quibus opes, divitiae, imperia, voluptatum vitiorumque illecebrae peccandi facultatem subministrant. Scitis fortunam fingi a sapientibus caecam, quae et illos quoque caecos reddit, quos amplexatur.

In his book *On Calumny*, however, Lucian says that the courts of leaders and kings are especially full of calamities, in which hatreds and suspicions are always rife and there is present that tribe pleasing to them, the sycophants, so that an occasion for slander is easily provided.[106] Hence we are forced both by reason and by authority to admit that the life of leaders is miserable and unhappy."

36. Then Cosimo said, "I wanted to interrupt you a little earlier, since you caused me to smile when you thought you were enunciating a great and admirable thing saying that good leaders were like a miracle. For being good is no more to be considered a portentous event among leaders than among the rest. At any rate your Cicero says in his books *On Divination* that if anything that appears very rarely is to be considered a portent, then a good man will be more of a portent than the offspring of a mule.[107] So very rarely does it happen that a good man is found. But if Cicero thinks a good man is like a portent, what do you think happens with leaders, who are softened and seduced by more incitements to vice than private individuals and surrounded by more bodily pleasures, which are the enemies of virtue? In every condition and state of men, virtue is a rarity, since all outstanding things are rare. So we find that goodness is no more lacking in leaders than in others." C70

37. "I am not searching," said Niccolò, "for the famous good man or sage of the Stoics, who has not yet been discovered. I regard as good those whom the experience and life of men approves of, in whom it is sufficient for there to be, if not perfect virtue, at least some semblance and sketched-out appearance of those virtues, which the way of civic life requires.[108] But in leaders this is so rarely found that it seems a portent if any of them has been found to be good. For it is with difficulty that they come to possess virtue to whom resources, wealth, power and the snares of pleasures and vices provide the opportunity for wrongdoing. You know that fortune is imagined by the wise as blind, since it renders blind also C71

Libidine enim pro ratione abutuntur, ad id prompti quod rerum licentia permittit. Quo fit ut, posthabita honesti cura, cum ad vitia deflectantur, saepissime de statu rerum cadant et a fortuna deserantur; quo nihil esse potest infelicius. Omitto antiquas tragoedias, principum infelicitatis copiosissimas testes, *Oedipodem, Troadem, Atreum, Thyestem, Medeam, Agamemnona* ceterosque permultos, quorum exemplo Graeci illi sapientissimi poetae infelicitatem quasi familiarem principibus expresserunt et, ut vulgo essent notiora, in scaenis decantari eorum exitus voluerunt ad reprimendam eorum stultitiam, qui felicitatem cum magna fortuna coniunctam putant. Non referentur a me quos varii fortunae impetus, dum felices haberentur, absumpsere. Multi bello, plures veneno, plurimi gladio, quidam in vinculis interierunt. Testes sunt Croesus, Syphax, Iugurtha, Perseus, Mithridates ceterique infelicitate insignes. Ad perniciosiora enim tendit oratio.

C72

38. 'Primum quidem ita duce natura imbuti atque instituti sumus, quod etiam in ceteris animantibus vim praecipuam obtinet, ut nihil nobis carius liberis esse possit. Carissima est coniunx, carissimi parentes, fratres, cognati et qui ex eodem sanguine manant; iocundissimam etiam aequalium consuetudinem et sanctissimum amicitiae vinculum effecit. Quae ita nascuntur nobiscum, ita usu comprobantur, ut qui ea neget, non homo, sed belua videatur. At regum et principum effera immanisque crudelitas, quae etiam ferarum asperitatem superaret, artissima iura naturae, amicitiae vincula, omnes communis societatis leges ob imperandi cupidinem abrupit. Non filiis a parentibus, non viro ab uxore nec e contrario,

C73

those whom it embraces. For they use lust instead of reason, ready
to do whatever free access to resources permits. Hence it happens
that putting aside the care of the honorable, since they turn aside
to vice, they very often fall from their positions of power and are
deserted by fortune. There can be nothing more unhappy than
this. I leave aside the ancient tragedies, which are most ample wit-   C72
nesses to the unhappiness of leaders — *Oedipus, Troas, Atreus, Thyestes, Medea, Agamemnon* and the huge number of others by whose
example those incredibly wise Greek poets represented unhappiness as almost a family member for leaders, and, to make them
more generally known, wanted their ends to be sung upon the
stage, to counter the stupidity of those who think that happiness is
conjoined with great fortune.[109] I will not report those whom various attacks of fortune snatched away while they were considered
happy. Many have died in war, more by poison, very many by the
sword, some in chains, as the examples of Croesus, Syphax,
Jugurtha, Perseus, Mithridates and others famous for their unhappiness testify.[110] For my discourse is heading toward more destructive territory.

38. "First of all, then, we are on nature's impulsion so constituted and trained (and we can see the same central force obtaining
also among other living things) that nothing can be dearer to us
than our children. Our spouse is very dear, as are our parents,
brothers, relations and those who derive from the same blood.
Nature has made intercourse with one's fellows most enjoyable
and the bond of friendship most sacred.[111] These are so born in us
and are so approved by habit that the person who denies them
seems to be not a human being, but a wild beast. But the wild and   C73
inhuman cruelty of kings and leaders, of a sort to surpass even
that of wild animals, has broken asunder the tightest laws of nature, the bonds of friendship, and all the laws of communal living
for the desire to rule. It has left nothing at all safe, not to sons
from their fathers, not to husbands from their wives, or the op-

non fratri a fratre, non sociis, non amicis, non cognatis quicquam tutum reliquit, sed abegit atque impulit in mutuas caedes.

39.1 'Ninus (ut a primis exordiar) non pepercit maternae neci. Artaxerxes, Persarum rex, cum vivens Darium filium per indulgentiam sibi in regnum, donatis imperii insigniis, substituisset, eundem, cum quinquaginta ex fratribus parricidium parantem, cum coniuratis occidi imperavit. Alexander, maior Philippi Macedonum regis frater, cum regno potiretur cum fratre Perdicca, per insidias Euridicae matris occiditur. Philippus, post multarum urbium gentiumque excidia, post defatigatum sanguine ac caedibus animum, Olympiadis uxoris opera ab adolescente Pausania interfectus est. Eodem modo et Candaules,[156] Lydorum rex, uxoris fraude periit. Xerxem, Persarum regem, bello adversus Graeciam infeliciter gesto in patriam reversum, Artabanus praefectus admodum regi fidus interemit. Dionysius Secundus, Siciliae tyrannus, qui postmodum pueros docuit Corinthi, cum maior fratribus natu a militibus ad regnum assumptus esset, primo avunculos, tum vero fratres e medio abstulit. Ptolomaeus, Aegypti rex, cognomento Philopater, patre ac matre interfectis, addita etiam fratris ac sororis caede, regno potitus est. Haud dissimile fuit scelus Nicomedis, Bithyniae regis, qui patrem regno spoliatum peremit. Eodem ductus furore alter Aegypti rex Ptolomaeus, cum propter multiplices crudelitates, quibus grassatus in multos fuerat, timeret ne populus maiorem natu filium odio sui regno praeficeret, illum vita privavit. Alterum filium iuniorem, ex Cleopatra uxore eademque sorore genitum, die natali in membra discerptum, inter epulas et convivas

C74

C75

posite, not to brother from brother, not to comrades, friends, or relatives, but it has driven and urged them toward mutual slaughter.

39.1 "To begin from the beginning, Ninus did not spare his mother from death.[112] Artaxerxes, the King of the Persians, although he had substituted his son Darius for himself as ruler while he was still alive through fondness, giving him the insignia of power, ordered the same individual, when he was organizing an act of father-killing along with fifty of his brothers,[113] to be put to death along with his co-conspirators. When Alexander, the elder brother of Philip, King of Macedon, got hold of power with his brother Perdiccas, he was killed by a plot of their mother Eurydice.[114] Philip, after the destruction of many cities and peoples, C74 after his spirit had become fatigued with blood and slaughter, was killed by the youth Pausanias at the behest of his wife Olympias.[115] In the same way Candaules too, King of the Lydians, died through his wife's deceit.[116] Xerxes, King of the Persians, having waged an unsuccessful war against Greece, when he had returned to his homeland was killed by the prefect Artabanus, who had been pretty loyal to the king.[117] Dionysius the second, tyrant of Sicily, who later taught boys in Corinth, after being chosen to rule by the army as the eldest brother, first of all did away with his uncles, then indeed with his brothers.[118] Ptolemy, King of Egypt, known as Philopater, gained power by killing his father and mother, then adding also the murder of his brother and sister.[119] No different was the crime of Nicomedes, King of Bithynia, who killed his father after robbing him of power.[120] Driven by the same madness, C75 the second King Ptolemy of Egypt, when he was afraid, because of the manifold cruel acts which he had perpetrated against many, that the people through hatred of him might appoint as ruler his elder son, deprived him of his life. His second, younger son by his wife and sister Cleopatra, he cut into pieces and served to Cleopatra on her birthday amid the feast and guests.[121] Not infe-

Cleopatrae obtulit. Non inferior impietate fuit filius Eucratidis, Bactrianorum regis, quem victorem ab Indis redeuntem particeps regni factus interfecit. Adicitur[157] his exsecrabile scelus Phraatis, regis Parthorum, qui, cum a patre Orade solus ex triginta fratribus in regnum adscitus esset, quasi nefas duceret absque nefario facinore imperare, primum patrem admodum senem, tum fratres omnes occidi imperavit. Deinde superiorum cladibus addidit filii adulti necem, veritus ne ob tantorum scelerum invidiam rex a populo constitueretur.

C76   39.2 'Quid Attalum commemorem? Qui populum Romanum reliquit heredem, qui, cum a patre Eumene regnum florentissimum accepisset regiamque cognatorum atque amicorum caede foedasset, furiis postmodum ac dementia agitatus, veste squalida, promissa barba, capillo neglecto, omissa regni administratione, primum fodiendo serendoque horto, tum aerariae artis studio se dedit, aere fodiendo intentus; qua ex re morbo contracto periit. Qua ergo tantorum scelerum conscientia, quo mentis furore, quo turbine animi eos agitari necesse fuit, qui sanctissima naturae iura tam taetris, tam atrocibus flagitiis violarunt? An tu inter tot et tam foeda atque immania facinora ullum residere felicitatis vesti-

C77   gium putas? Quam felix extitit Alexander Magnus, qui regni futuri auspicia iecit fratris Carani morte, qui amicorum pariter atque inimicorum pestis, paternis amicis crudelissime occisis, praedo gentium ac regnorum pestis,[158] non magis vino quam sanguine humano inebriari solitus fuit? Mihi quidem cum ei maxime favit fortuna, tum praecipue expers felicitatis fuisse videtur. Nam cum vitiis potentiam adderet, cum insanior in diem fieret, cum ebrius

rior in impiety was the son of Eucratides, King of the Bactrians, whom he killed on Eucratides' victorious return from India, although he had been made a partner in Eucratides' realm.[122] To these can be added the execrable crime of Phraates, King of the Parthians, who, when he alone of thirty brothers had been called to the throne by his father Oras, as though he thought it impious to rule without a nefarious deed, ordered first his father, who was quite old, and then all of his brothers, to be put to death. Then to the calamities of the above he added the death of his grown up son, fearing that the people might make him king because of their hatred of such great crimes.[123]

39.2 "Why should I mention Attalus, who left the Roman people as his heir, who, when he had received the kingdom in a flourishing state from his father Eumenes and had befouled the palace with the slaughter of relatives and friends, driven later by the furies and madness, in dirty clothing, with a long beard and his hair neglected, having lost the government of his kingdom, gave himself up first to digging and sowing his garden, then to learning the bronze smith's art, concentrating on mining bronze? From this he contracted a disease and died.[124] So by what consciousness of such great crimes, by what mental derangement, by what disturbance of mind must those have been driven who violated the most sacred laws of nature by such vile and atrocious crimes? Do you think that among so many and so foul and monstrous crimes any trace of happiness is left? How happy was Alexander the Great who laid the foundations for his future kingdom with the death of his brother Caranus, who was a plague equally to friends and enemies, having killed his father's friends most cruelly, a pirate of nations and a pestilence to kingdoms, accustomed no more to the drunkenness induced by wine than to that induced by human blood? To me at any rate it was at the moment when he was most favored by fortune that he seems to have been most untouched by happiness. For when he added power to his vices, when he became madder by

C76

C77

365

debacchabatur[159] in suos, cum se adorari ut deum mandabat, cum
se Iovis filium mentiretur, quae poterat in tanta dementia esse felicitas? Atqui hos fructus parit principatus, haec opera suadet, hos
satellites[160] tum parandi sui, tum conservandi subministrat, ut
nihil videatur exsecrabilius quam principatus nomen.'

C78   40. 'Barbarorum,' Carolus inquit, 'haec feritas atque immanitas
fuit, qui et hodie quoque in suos saeviunt imperandi gratia. Nostros humaniores ac temperatiores fides Christi reddidit longeque
C79   ab eiusmodi crudelitate removit. 'Haec vitia,' Nicolaus inquit,
'videntur esse et barbaris et Graecis et Latinis communia. Possem
multas excitare tragoedias ex quibusvis gentibus eorum qui neque
suo neque alieno sanguini pepercerunt, nisi nonnullorum pudore
impedirer. Malo quippe silere quam refricare cicatrices, iam vetustate atque oblivione obductas. Nonnullorum autem recentiora vestigia ac propinquiora sunt, ut verissime dictum sit nullam sanctam
societatem neque fidem regni esse. Etenim in Italia fraternas caedes vidimus ob dominii cupiditatem et inter propinquos saevo
Marte certatum. In Gallia, Germania, Britannia, Hispaniis saeva
arma et plus quam bella civilia exarsere, non a domestico, non a
cognatorum, non a proprio sanguine temperatum, plus quam civili
odio et cladibus propinquorum omnia foedata. Itaque et nostri
quoque principatus, vitia experti, documento esse possunt, nullam
regni neque fidem neque felicitatem esse.'

C80   41.1 Tum Cosmus, 'Hic noster Nicolaus,' inquit, 'diligenter et
malos multos principes collegit et eorum expressit vitia; de bonis
vero aut eorum virtutibus penitus verbum nullum. Nonne tu ab
eorum numero secernis et quos paulo ante rettulit Carolus, et
David regem, pluresque ex Hebraeis, et e nostris optimos quidem

the day, when he drunkenly raged against his own people, when he commanded that he be worshipped as a god, when he put out the lie that he was the son of Jupiter, what happiness could there be in such great lunacy?[125] But these are the fruits that the position of leader brings, these are the works it urges, these are the servants it provides both for its attainment and for its retention, so that nothing appears more execrable than the words 'the position of leader.'"

40. "This is the savagery and brutality of barbarians," said C78 Carlo, "who today too rage against their own people in order to rule.[126] Our rulers have been made more humane and temperate by the Christian faith and far removed from cruelty of this kind." "These vices," said Niccolò, "seem to be common to barbarians, C79 Greeks and Romans. I could cite many tragedies from any people you like of those who would have spared neither family nor outsiders' blood, if I were not held back by shame for some of them. But I really prefer to be silent than to reopen wounds already healed by time and oblivion.[127] Yet there are more recent and nearer traces from some to prove how very true is the saying that rule knows no sacred tie or trust. For in Italy we have seen brother kill brother through desire for rule and a fight involving cruel war between relatives.[128] In France, Germany, Britain, and Spain, savage wars and more than civil conflicts[129] have burst into flame, with no mercy shown to the blood of household members, relatives, or close family, and everything befouled by more than civil hatred and the deaths of one's closest.[130] Hence even our own principates when they have undertaken the path of vice can be used as proof that in ruling there is no loyalty[131] and no happiness."

41.1 Then Cosimo said, "Our Niccolò here has diligently collected many bad leaders and articulated their vices, but about the good or their virtues, there was not a single word. Surely you are leaving out of their number the ones mentioned just now by Carlo,[132] as well as King David and several more of the Hebrew

illos principes Arcadium, Honorium, Theodosium, Carolum
Magnum multosque praeterea vitae sanctimonia et omni virtutum
genere illustres? Quid oppones Roberto, regi Neapolitano, quem
nostri maiores modestum principem et felicem regem iudicarunt,
de quo Petrarcha noster multa scripsit in eius commendationem?
Cave hos infelices dixeris, ne nimis pervicax videaris.'

C81   41.2 'Non abnuo,'[161] Nicolaus inquit, 'multa extitisse in multis
principibus laudanda, sed felicitatem affirmo ab eorum vita prorsus abfuisse, eamque esse principatus conditionem, ut nulla ei cum
felicitate possit esse communio. Robertus quidem is quem modo
nominasti (ut omittam consortes regni, sollicitudines ac molestias,
animi maerores, turbulenta consilia, quibus etiam felices vestri[162]
necessario distrahuntur), qui potuit esse felix, cum fuerit avaris-
simus ac semper ad cumulandum aurum intentus? Quod adeo
appetivit,[163] ut omnia apud eum fuerint venalia. Tantum vero auri
argentique in aerario condidit, ut hodie quoque, qui ditissimum
quempiam designare velit, eo[164] locupletiorem dicat. At scitis
quantum malum, quam turpe in rege praesertim et quam foedum
sit avaritia, cuius sociam esse felicitatem, nullus sanae mentis affir-
mabit.

C82   41.3 'Nam et gentiles omnes, quos Carolus recensuit, et Chris-
tianos quoque, nisi quos Dei pietas extulit, felicitate caruisse
contendam. Sed divino quodam munere suffulti quidam, non
principatus opera aut favore, sed nutu et dono Dei praeclari ac felices evasere. Pauci tamen, "quos aequus amavit Iuppiter aut ardens
evexit ad aethera virtus." Dei enim providentia, ut fides nostra aliquando stabilita a persecutione conquiesceret, bonos quosdam esse
voluit, quorum auctoritate fides roboraretur. Nam quod David

kings, and from ours those excellent emperors [leaders] Arcadius, Honorius, Theodosius, Charlemagne and many besides who were famous for the sanctity of their lives and every kind of virtue?[133] What will you say against Robert, King of Naples, whom our ancestors judged a modest leader and a happy king, about whom our Petrarch wrote much in praise?[134] Take care not to judge these unhappy, for fear of seeming stubborn."

41.2 "I am not saying," said Niccolò, "that there have not been   C81 many praiseworthy qualities in many leaders. I am contending that happiness was completely absent from their lives and that the position of a leaders is such that it can have no communion with happiness. Take Robert, whom you have just mentioned, to say nothing of those participants in his kingdom, the worries and annoyances, sadnesses of mind, the turbulent plans by which even your happy men are necessarily pulled apart, how could he be happy when he was incredibly avaricious and always intent upon the accumulation of gold? This he desired so much that everything in his court was for sale. Indeed, he hid so much gold and silver in his treasury that even today when someone wants to call a person really rich, he says 'richer than Robert of Naples.'[135] Yet you know how great an evil and how base and foul a thing is avarice, especially in a king. No one in his right mind will claim that happiness has any truck with it.

41.3 "For I shall contend that all the pagans whom Carlo listed   C82 and the Christians too, except those whom their godly piety elevated, were lacking in happiness. However, relying on some divine gift, a number have turned out famous and happy, not with the aid of the position of leader but through the will and gift of God. They are few, however, 'those loved by a fair Jupiter or raised to the ether by a burning virtue.'[136] For divine providence has willed, so that our faith, at long last stabilized, might come to rest from persecution, that there be some good kings, by whose authority our faith might be underpinned. As to King David, whom you named,

regem nominasti et alios quibus similis vita[165] contigit, non possumus de iis, quae occulto Dei iudicio aguntur, humanam sententiam ferre. Verumtamen et ipsum David ad stuprum et homici-
dium (quae vitia a principatus natura manare videntur) labi divina
sapientia permisit. Non attingit nostra prudentia haec altissimi
C83   Dei secretiora consilia. Id tamen aperte constat: imbecillitatem
conditionis humanae fieri in principatu multis vitiorum illecebris
imbecilliorem et ad mala quam ad bona promptiorem. Quamobrem caelesti ope, non sua principes quidam vitae felicitatem sunt
assecuti. Affuit enim illis superna virtus, quae ipsos deflecti ad
turpia aut decipi regni delinimentis[166] non permisit.

41.4 'Nam in principatu tot incommoda, tot tormenta insunt,
tantum rerum pondus ei incumbit, ut omnem a se felicitatem ex-
cludant adeoque etiam illos, qui boni felicesque sunt habiti ac
beati, exagitat ac conterit, ut nulla felicitate fruantur. Id ipsum
quidem multis praeesse ac dominari et unum pro omnibus intentum esse, sollicitum, vigilantem, anxium, ad infinita quaedam
C84   negotia distractum, magnum est infelicitatis argumentum. Non
sequor Stoicorum doctrinam, qui virum bonum nimis artis
circumscribunt spatiis. Hunc assumamus, qui minimis vitiis urgetur,[167] qui bonus existimetur[168] ab reliquis. Regem istum constitue
et bono, ut aiebas, publico vacantem agentemque omnia quae boni
principis officium requirit: felix dicetur, ea scilicet felicitate, qua
secundus fortunae cursus appellatur. Verumtamen ego felicem
eum — quod non fortuna, sed animus praestet necesse est — nulla
ratione nominabo. Animum enim quietum, liberum felicitas sequitur et omni perturbatione vacuum. At vero principes tot
curis, vigiliis, molestiis, anxietatibus, sollicitudinibus, angoribus

and the others who chanced to have a similar life, we cannot cast a human vote on matters which are done through the secret judgment of God. Nonetheless, divine wisdom allowed even David himself to slip into adultery and murder, vices which appear to derive from the nature of the position of leader.[137] Our wisdom does not reach these more hidden counsels of the loftiest divinity. But we can obviously agree that the weakness of the human condition becomes weaker in the position of leader, because of its many temptations to vice, and more prone to the bad than to the good. For that reason it is through divine aid and not their own that some leaders have achieved happiness in life. For they had a virtue from above, which did not allow them to be deflected toward base deeds or to be deceived by the blandishments of power.

41.4 "For there are so many inconveniences and tortures in the position of leader and such a weight of affairs presses upon it that they exclude all happiness from themselves, and it so harries and wears down even those who have been regarded as happy and blessed that they enjoy no happiness. Indeed the very fact that they are in charge of many people, rule and have sole responsibility for everyone, are worried, awake, and anxious, as well as pulled into an infinite number of items of business, is a great proof of their unhappiness. I am not following the doctrine of the Stoics, who confine the good man within excessively narrow bounds.[138] Let us take the one who is oppressed by fewest vices, who is considered good by others. Make him king, who devotes himself to the common good, as you said, and does all the things which the duty of a good leader requires. He will be called 'happy' in the same sense in which the favorable flow of fortune is called happiness. However, I shall by no means call him happy, since it must be his mind and not fortune which provides happiness. For happiness follows a mind which is peaceful, at liberty and free of all disturbance. But leaders are torn apart by so many worries, sleepless nights, difficulties, anxieties, cares, and tribulations that their

C83

C84

distrahuntur, ut lacer animus ac fessus, nihil quietis percipiens, nullam in se admittat felicitatem.

C85   41.5 'Illa ipsa quam vulgo felicitatem opinantur, infelix est. "Nihil," inquit Seneca, "infelicius est eo, cui nihil unquam[169] evenit adversi." Et alio in loco magnae felicitatis[170] tutelam, ut nihil de futuro timeatur, esse sollicitam scribit moleque sua premi. Quid quod eiusmodi felicitas tenebris quibusdam nos obfundit caliginemque menti obicit, qua veri videndi[171] atque ex recta ratione iudicandi facultate privamur? Num ea parva infelicitas esse videatur?[172] Adice quod principes boni — etiam de his enim loquimur — maximo omnium bono et quod beluae etiam appetant, vivendi libertate, privantur. Hac quidem re sola carent, cum cetera bona circumfluere videantur. Et qui dominari se putant, sunt omnium servi; quae res parum distat ab infelicitate.

C86   42. 'In libro *De animi tranquillitate* Seneca "Magna servitus[173] est," inquit, "magna fortuna." Non somnum extendere in partem diei licet, non a rerum tumultu in otium quietum confugere, non assidua laboriosi officii statione fatigatum corpus voluptuaria peregrinatione recreare, non spectaculorum varietate animum detinere aut ex tuo arbitrio diem disponere. Multa tibi non licent, quae minimis et in angulo iacentibus licent. "Non licet tibi quicquam[174] arbitrio tuo facere. Audienda sunt tot hominum milia, tantus

C87   rerum ex toto orbe congestus." Haec erit igitur optimi quoque principis felicitas, ut omnium veluti publicum sit mancipium, ut unus pro omnibus gravibus affligatur curis. Soli enim pro singulis est vigilandum. Audiendae multorum querelae, constituenda iudicia, iustitia servanda, salus omnium procuranda, subditorum

mind, mangled and weary, gaining no peace, admits no happiness to itself.

41.5 "The actual happiness which most people think is happi- C85
ness is in fact unhappy. 'Nothing,' Seneca says, 'is unhappier than the man to whom nothing bad has ever happened.'[139] In another place he writes that protecting one's own great happiness so that there is no fear regarding the future is a worrisome thing and collapses under its own weight.[140] What of the fact that such happiness overwhelms us with shadows and brings darkness into our minds, by which we are deprived of the ability to see the truth and judge correctly. Surely this would not seem a small unhappiness? Add the fact that even good leaders (it is of these that we are still speaking) are deprived of the greatest good of all, such as even wild animals seek, namely a life of freedom. It is this thing indeed alone that they lack, when the rest of the good things appear to be in abundant supply. And those who think they are in control, are in fact the slaves of everyone, a situation that is not very far from unhappiness.

42. "In his book *On Peace of Mind*, Seneca says: 'Great fortune is C86
great slavery. You cannot extend your slumbers into a part of the daytime, or escape the tumult of business into quiet leisure, or refresh your body fatigued from the assiduous perseverance at a laborious duty with a pleasure trip, or beguile your mind with a variety of spectacles, or arrange your day using your own judgment. You cannot do many things which even the lowest and those who lie in a corner can do. You cannot do anything for yourself using your own judgment. You have so many thousands of people to listen to, and such a pile of business from all over the world.'[141]
This then will be the sort of happiness even a good leader has, to C87
be as it were the public slave of everyone so that he alone is afflicted on everyone's behalf with serious cares. For he alone has to be on the watch for everyone. He has to listen to the complaints of many, set up courts, preserve justice, take care of the safety of all,

iniuriae propulsandae, ratio belli ac pacis habenda, otio consulendum, uni omnium cura gerenda, mali terrendi poenaque afficiendi,[175] boni praemio alliciendi. Huic vitae tam sollicitae, tam occupatae, tam inquietae, tam molestae, tam variis rebus distractae, quae felicitas tribui potest? Hunc ego veluti alterum Ixiona, rotae[176] affixum, potius vertigine mentis agitatum dixerim quam ulla felicitate affectum. Haec fuit causa quamobrem Augustus otium sibi et quietem tantopere expeteret. Haec Antiochum, regem Asiae potentissimum, quem Scipio bello victum superavit, ultra Taurum montem regnare iussum, dicere coegit se magnam gratiam habere Romano populo, quod se nimis magna ac molesta procuratione Asiae liberasset. Haec eadem pluribus ex Gallia Britanniaque ac ceterarum gentium regibus occasionem praebuit, ut abiecta regni cura ad liberiorem vitam confugientes religioni Deique cultui se dedicarent.

C88

43.1 'Magno illi quidem[177] animo atque excelso divino freti munere, ea repudiarunt, quae tanto studio,[178] tanto errore, tanta insania, tanta cupiditate a ceteris appetuntur. Paucorum tamen hoc est munus hominum. Rari enim qui virtutem intuentur, rariores qui exquirant, et qui assequantur rarissimi. Sed maxime tamen principibus via virtutis ignota est, quorum cogitationes alio deflectere regna cogunt quam ad virtutis indagationem. Ita[179] tum[180] illi beati existimantur, quos nulla imperandi cupido detinet, tum illos aetas omnis beatissimos putavit, quibus Dei munificentia largita est ut, regna verae felicitati postponentes, virtutem et beatam vitam potiorem insignibus[181] imperii iudicarent. Nam ii quibus regni cupiditas carior fuit, omni felicitate exciderunt. Malos enim refugit; ad bonos, quoniam continuis occupationibus, curis, negotiis vexantur, adire non potest. Hoc modo aeque boni ac mali

C89

ward off attacks on his subjects, take thought about peace and war, look out for civic order, single-handedly take care of everyone, frighten the evil and inflict punishments upon them, entice the good with rewards. To this life, so anxious, so busy, so full of stress, so uncomfortable, so pulled apart by various things, what happiness can be attributed? Him I would rather name almost a second Ixion tied to his wheel, assailed by a spinning mind, than the recipient of any happiness.[142] This was the reason why Augus-   C88
tus so intensely sought leisure and peace for himself.[143] It was this that forced Antiochus, the most powerful King of Asia, whom Scipio overcame when he defeated him in war, when ordered to rule beyond the Taurus mountains, to say that he was very grateful to the Roman people for having freed him from the too great and difficult task of governing Asia.[144] This same motive also provided an opportunity to many Kings of Gaul, Britain, and other races, to set aside the trouble of ruling, and, fleeing to a freer life, to dedicate themselves to religion and the worship of God.[145]

43.1 "It was indeed by relying on a great spirit and a lofty gift from God that those men rejected the things which with such great enthusiasm, such great error, such great insanity, and such great cupidity are sought by others. But this is the gift of few men.   C89
Rare are those who have virtue in view, rarer those who seek it out, and rarest of all those who attain it. Nonetheless, it is most of all to leaders that the road to virtue is unknown, since their kingdoms force them to turn their thoughts elsewhere than to the search for virtue. So it is both that those are adjudged blessed whom no desire for power holds back, and that every age has considered most blessed those to whom god's munificence has allowed to put ruling second to true felicity and judge virtue and the happy life preferable to the insignia of power. For those to whom the desire for rule was dearer forfeited all happiness. For it flees from the bad, yet it cannot approach the good, because they are harried by continual tasks, cares, and business. In this way the good and

C90 erunt infelices. Neque vero arbitror efflagitare hanc meam sententiam ampliores probationes eorum quae sunt tum nota rationibus,
tum exemplis notissimis manifesta. Constat enim vitam principum[182] tragoediam quandam esse, calamitatum plenam, ex qua
multi actus confici possent ad repraesentandam tanquam in
theatro eorum infelicitatem. Nam varii casus rerum, dubia regna,
suspensa in diem atque instabilis fortuna, anceps consiliorum
eventus, adulatorum fraus, ambitio amicorum, domesticorum pro-
ditiones, insidiae filiorum, uxorum perfidia, incerta fratrum voluntas, dubia multorum fides, levitas vulgi, bellorum incertus finis,
pax suspecta, ipsa regni sollicitudo et anxii metus, quibus rebus
quassari mentes principum videmus, manifesto arguunt principes
omnis quadam infelicitatis conditione damnatos.

C91 43.2 'Nec mihi inconstans stultorum opinio aut vulgi temeritas
(in quo nullum consilium, nulla ratio viget) aliquid affert, quominus haec nostra opinio verissima videatur. Quae cum sint conspicua et veluti palam in conspectu omnium sita, quis sanae mentis
abnuerit, cum principatus, regna, imperia etiam bonis viris gravia
et turbulenta omnem adimant vitae iocunditatem ac quietem, quin
illorum tanquam rei infelicis cupiditas aspernanda nobis sit ac
penitus fugienda? Nam, cum videamus principes partim ira et
libidine fervidos, partim sanguine et suorum caede efferatos,
alios cupiditate ambitioneque flagrantes, alios afflictos timore,
hos suspicione metuque dubios, illos tormentis cruciatuque hominum saevientes, quosdam voluptatibus luxuriaque diffluere, hos
ignavia torpere, omnes fere amicis destitutos inter adulatorum
assentatorumque turbam stupere, ⟨ut⟩[183] nonnulli curis exedantur,
suos, alienos, domesticos suspectos habeant, hos belli rabies

bad will be equally unhappy. Nor do I consider that this view of   C90
mine demands further proof for things which are both known
by arguments and clear from very well-known examples. We can
agree that the life of leaders is a tragedy full of calamities, from
which many scenes could be drawn, to represent their unhappiness as though in the theater. For the diverse outcomes of events,
their shaky kingdoms, their unstable fortune, which is in suspense
every day, the uncertain outcome of their plans, the deceit of their
flatterers, the ambition of their friends, the betrayals by their servants, the plots of their sons, the treachery of their wives, the uncertain disposition of their brothers, the doubtful loyalty of many,
the fickleness of the mob, the uncertain outcome of wars, suspicions in peacetime, the troubled rule itself, and the anxious fears
by which we see the minds of leaders being shaken clearly prove
that all leaders are condemned to a condition of unhappiness.

43.2 "Nor does the wavering opinion of fools or the temerity of   C91
the mob (in which there is no force either of counsel or of reason)
give me any grounds for doubting that my view is absolutely true.
And since these things are obvious and, as it were, openly placed
in the sight of everyone, what sane person will deny, since princi-
pates, kingdoms and empires, heavy and turbulent burdens, take
away all the joy and peace of life even from good men, that we
should reject and completely avoid desire for them as though for
an unhappy thing? For since we see leaders partly burning with
anger and lust, partly made savage by the bloody slaughter of their
own people, some on fire with desire and ambition, others afflicted
with fear, these wavering through fear and suspicion, those raging
by inflicting tortures and crucifixion on men, that some are carried
away on the tide of pleasure and lechery, that others are languid
from sloth, that almost all, bereft of friends, stand stupefied in a
crowd of sycophants and flatterers, how some are eaten away by
worries and consider suspect their own people, outsiders, and the
members of their household, some have been borne off by the rage

absumpserit, alii veneno perierint,[184] multi aut filiorum aut amicorum fraudibus sint deleti, alii, variis fortunae fluctibus iactati, nulla quiete, nullo otio potiantur: profecto nihil potest dubii nostris mentibus residere, quin principes omnis, nisi quibus divina pietas affulsit, cum eorum vita nullius sit expers molestiae, infe-

C92 lices ac miseri iudicentur. Si enim etiam illi quos bonos fuisse iudicamus, multis oppressi curis, pluribus conflictati molestiis, defatigato animo, mente inquieta, non suo, sed aliorum arbitrio, non privato, sed publico otio et quieti vacare cogantur, cum non dominii, sed continuae servitutis sit bonis onus subeundum, quid aliud aestimandum[185] est, nisi naturam principatus malam ac perniciosam etiam sapientum animos defatigare, ut, cum imperio et opibus abundent, felicitatis inopia urgeantur? Facessat igitur a nobis illius appetitus et dominorum quoque consuetudo, neque nos illis committamus, qui possint obesse, si velint.'

C93   44. Tum Cosmus, 'Quid tu,' inquit, 'Nicolae, censes de illis, qui in sua re publica civitatis principes extiterunt? Num eos quoque

C94 iis quibus reliqui principes malis obrui putas?"Decernant hoc ipsimet,' inquit Nicolaus,[186] 'qui, quanta illis felicitas tribui debeat, experti sunt. Alcibiades, Themistocles, Pericles, Aristides, Hannibal, Camillus, Q. Metellus, Scipiones, Rutilius, Caesar,[187] Pompeius, M. Antonius, Lepidus multique praeterea ex priscis et e nostris nonnulli testes[188] copiosissimi, quantum felicitatis ex altiori gradu et fortunae favoribus contrahatur. Nam quamvis Sulla felicem se dici voluerit, tamen tantum a felicitate abfuit, quantum fuit crudelitati propinquus. Nihil enim sibi accidere potuit infelicius quam male faciendi facultas ac libido, quibus se felicem putavit.

of war, others have died from poison, many have been wiped out by the plots of sons or friends, and others, tossed upon the diverse waves of fortune, gain no rest and peace, there can be absolutely no doubt left in our minds as to the fact that all leaders (except any upon whom the divine piety has shone down), since their lives are free of no form of trouble, should be judged unhappy and miserable. For if even those whom we judge to have been good, oppressed by many cares, harassed by many troubles, mentally worn out and with no peace of mind, are forced to serve not their own judgment, but that of others, and not their private peace, but that of the public, since the good have rather to undertake a burden not of overlordship but of continual slavery, what other judgment must we make than that the evil and pernicious nature of the position of leader tires out even the spirits of the wise, so that, although they abound in power and wealth, they are oppressed by a paucity of happiness? Let therefore desire for it depart from us and also acquaintance with potentates, and let us not put ourselves in the hands of those who could harm us if they wished."   C92

44. Then Cosimo said, "What do you think, Niccolò, about those who have been leaders of the state in their republics? Surely you don't think that they too are overwhelmed by the same ills as the rest of the leaders?" "Let them be the judges themselves," Niccolò replied, "who have experienced how much happiness ought to be attributed to them. Alcibiades, Themistocles, Pericles, Aristides, Hannibal, Camillus, Quintus Metellus, the Scipios, Rutilius, Caesar, Pompey, Marcus Antonius, Lepidus, and many more besides of the ancients and some of our own are most eloquent witnesses as to the amount of happiness which is drawn from higher stations and the favors of fortune.[146] For although Sulla wished to be called happy, nonetheless he was as far from happiness as he was near to cruelty. For nothing unhappier could have befallen him than the capacity and lust for doing evil, the things he thought made him happy. For to proceed with the   C93   C94

Grassari enim caede ac sanguine civium, proscriptorum[189] capitibus oculos pascere, bona proscribere, irae imperio regi summa infelicitas fuit. Marius et cum pulsus est[190] miser, et infelix cum rediit, qui, civis patriae perniciosus, ea in cives effecit, quae ne hostes
quidem patriae crudeliora expetivissent. Quare et iis quoque felicitas defuit, quibus fato datum fuit ut in suis urbibus decederent et
vita insulsae plebis iudicio ac popularibus factionibus addicti; quo
nihil potest esse miserius.'

C95   45.1 'Ubinam ergo,' Cosmus inquit, 'versari illam arbitramur?
Num residet apud mortales? An quemadmodum de Astraea ferunt
fabulae, relictis hominibus ad superos migrasse dicemus?'

C96   45.2 'Nusquam,' inquit ille, 'minus quam ubi maxime esse putatur. Legistis (ut opinor) quem olim Apollinis oraculum[191] felicem
esse responderit. Nam cum Gyges, rex Lydorum, qui sibi prae ceteris fortunatissimus videbatur, Apollinem consuluisset quis eo
tempore felix esset, contempsit oraculum regias opes atque apparatus, et Aglaum[192] quendam Arcadem, parvuli ruris cultorem, qui
metas agelli sui nunquam cupiditate excesserat, felicem iudicavit.
Repressit Apollo regis superbiam, et qui se felicissimum omnium
arbitrabatur, a rustico agri cultore dei iudicio superatus est, qui
nullum regem, nullum imperatorem, nullum principem, sed priva-
C97 tum quendam agricolam felicem iudicavit. Ante Valerium Maximum reges multi, imperatores nonnulli fuerant. Nullum ex his, ne
divum quidem Augustum, posuit inter felices, sed unum tantum
privatum civem Romanum, Q. Metellum, ut nulla dubitatio residere in nobis[193] queat non in principibus, sed in privatis viris aliquando felicitatem esse repertam.

bloody slaughter of citizens, to feast one's eyes on the heads of the proscribed, to proscribe goods, to be ruled by the power of anger was the greatest unhappiness.[147] Marius was miserable both when he was exiled and unhappy when he returned, since, himself a citizen destructive of his fatherland, he inflicted upon his own citizens such things that not even his fatherland's enemies would have desired crueler. Hence those too were deprived of felicity to whom was granted by fate the gift of dying in their own cities, their lives bound over to the judgment of the foolish plebs and the popular factions. There can be nothing unhappier than this."[148]

45.1 "Where on earth, then," said Cosimo, "do we suppose happiness to be? Surely it does not dwell among mortals, does it? Or shall we say, as the story goes about Astraea, that it has left mankind and moved to the gods?"[149]   C95

45.2 "Nowhere less," Niccolò replied, "than where it is most deemed to be. You have read, I suppose, about the man whom the response of Apollo's oracle said was happy. For when Gyges, King of the Lydians, who thought he was fortunate before all others, had asked Apollo who at that time was happy, the oracle disdained kingly pomp and circumstance, and judged happy a certain Arcadian called Aglaus, who cultivated a very small country plot and had never out of greed overrun the boundaries of his little field. Apollo checked the arrogance of the king and the one who considered himself the happiest was outdone by a rustic soil tiller in the judgment of the god, who ruled no king, no emperor, and no leader happy, but a farmer, a private individual.[150] Before Valerius Maximus' time there had been many kings and several emperors, but none of these, not even the divine Augustus, did he place among the blessed, only one private Roman citizen, Quintus Metellus, so that we cannot remain in doubt that it is not among leaders, but among private individuals that happiness is sometimes found.[151]   C96   C97

45.3 'Hanc et Lucianus in suo *Menippo* sententiam probat. Menippus enim, cum adolescens[194] legisset apud Homerum Hesiodumque et alios poetas deorum bella, adulteria, furta, rapinas, stupra aliaque eiuscemodi mala facinora, credebat ea licita esse atque honesta, postquam deorum exemplo atque auctoritate corroborarentur. Deinde adolescentiam egressus, cum audisset ea a legum latoribus tanquam inhonesta et turpia suis sanctionibus prohiberi, incertus animi utri rectius sentirent, philosophos adiit, ut ab eis sciscitaretur quaenam esset vita optima. Sed cum illos quoque conspiceret admodum sibi ipsis dissentientes — nam hi voluptatem, hi vacuitatem doloris, virtutem alii, quidam animi corporisque et[195] fortunae bona vitam beatam efficere volunt — incertior multo quam antea ac diffisus vivorum sapientia mortuos consulere decrevit. Igitur ad inferos penetravit, sciscitaturus a Tiresia, qui et ipse vates ac divinator fuisset, sententiam quam quaerebat. At ille, primo cum id nefas esse scitu respondisset, tandem mollitus Menippi verbis ad aurem insusurrans[196] apud privatos viros optimam vitam (hoc est felicitatem) inveniri dixit.

C98   45.4 'Si quo igitur in loco habitat, inter privatos diversorium habet, procul a regum culmine et fastigio imperandi. Virtutes enim effectrices sunt vitae felicis, quae, a principum domiciliis exclusae, si quando casu aut errore limen ingrediuntur, e vestigio aufugere coguntur, perterritae moribus, ministris, artibus quibus apud eos vivitur. Cum privatis vero, cum in eis vigeant studia sapientiae et doctrinae, cum litterarum otio occupentur, quorum animus, remotus ab ambitione, liber a cupiditate, suis contentus est, non appetens aliena, libenter versantur et felices reddunt suos

45.3 "This view Lucian also approves of in his *Menippus*.[152] For Menippus, since as a young man he had read in Homer and Hesiod and the other poets of the wars of the gods, their adulteries, thefts, rapes, sexual misdemeanors, and other wicked deeds of this sort, believed these things were allowed and honorable, corroborated as they had been by the authority and example of the gods. Then, having left his youth behind, when he had heard that these things were prohibited by the sanctions of the lawgivers as dishonorable and disgraceful, uncertain in his mind about which of the two views was the more correct, he went to the philosophers to ask them which was the best life. But when he saw that they too differed pretty much among themselves (for some thought it was pleasure, others freedom from pain, others virtue, and yet others the benefits of mind, body, and fortune which made life happy), now much less certain than before and mistrusting the wisdom of the living, he decided to consult the dead. Therefore he went down to the underworld, to ask Teiresias, who had been himself both a seer and a prophet, for the opinion he was looking for. Though at first he had replied that this knowledge was taboo, nonetheless, eventually, softened by Menippus' words, whispering into his ear, he said that the best life, that is, happiness, is found among private individuals.

45.4 "And so, if it lives anywhere, happiness has its dwelling   C98
among private men, far from the lofty pinnacles of royal power. For the virtues are what make life happy, but these, shut out of the houses of leaders, if ever they by chance or error cross the threshold, are forced instantly to flee, terrified by the morals, servants and arts by which life is lived among them. With private individuals, indeed, since it is among them that the pursuit of wisdom and learning flourish, since they are occupied by the leisure they devote to literature, and their mind, removed from ambition, free from desire, is content with what is their own, not seeking what is someone else's, they live freely and make their adherents happy.

cultores. Hi enim soli virtutis iter cognoverunt, hi bene vivendi praecepta nobis tradiderunt, hi qui esset vitae cursus optimus tum exemplo, tum litteris demonstrarunt; ab his naturae cognitio defluxit, horum opera variae artes ad usum hominum repertae, hinc disciplinarum omnium ratio, hinc astrorum caelique motus adinventi, hinc iura, leges et rerum publicarum gubernacula emanarunt, ab his rerum omnium quae ad victum, quae ad cultum corporis, quae ad dignitatem, quae ad tutelam, quae ad mores spectant, origo ducitur. Horum consiliis secundam fortunam moderate ferre docemur, forti animo adversam. Horum studiis, cura, vigiliis, animi morborum medela, corporum aegrotantium salus inventa est. Ab his sapienter et honeste vivendi praecepta sumus assecuti. Hi, tanquam virtutum sacerdotes, pacis atque otii amici, soli felicem vitam assequuntur. Posthabitis enim atque abiectis opibus, imperiis, dignitatibus, contemptis divitiis, in excolenda matre virtutum, philosophia, in rerum occultarum pervestigatione versati, ad liberalium artium disciplinas et humanitatis studia velut in portum tranquillum confugerunt, ubi nullo impetu, nulla fortunae iactati temeritate, vitam beatam ac felicem adepti sunt. Hos, quantum possumus, imitemur operibus nostris, cum sint eorum sectatoribus uberrima praemia constituta.[197]

C99

45.5 'Principes vero, a quibus eiusmodi studia abfuerunt,[198] a quibus raro boni quippiam ad homines pervenit, quorum cupiditas, ambitio, alieni appetitus infinitis aerumnis et calamitatibus orbem afflixit, qui otium, pacem, quietem reformidant, qui hanc vitam veluti peregrinantes transeunt, contemnamus. Etenim perpetua oblivione sepulti essent, nisi eos doctorum virorum

For it is these that are the only ones who know the path to virtue, it is they who have handed down to us the instructions for living well, it is they who have shown both by example and in their writings what the best way of life is, it is from them that knowledge of nature has flowed, through their efforts that the various arts were discovered for men's use, from this source that the method of all disciplines derives, from this source that the movements of the stars and the heavens were discovered, from this source that rights, laws, and the government of republics emanated and from them that we trace the origin of all things which relate to food, which relate to the care of the body, which relate to dignity, to safety, and to morals. It is through their counsels that we learn to bear good fortune moderately, and bad fortune with a brave heart. It is through their studies, care, and vigils that care for mental ills and cures for ailing bodies have been discovered. It is from them that we have obtained the precepts for wise and honorable living.[153] They, the priests, so to speak, of the virtues, the friends of peace and calm, are the only ones who achieve the happy life. For putting behind them and rejecting resources, power, and office, and spurning wealth, spending their time in the cultivation of philosophy, mother of the virtues, and in the investigation of hidden knowledge, they have fled, as into a quiet harbor, to the disciplines of the liberal arts and humane studies, where they have achieved the blessed and happy life tossed by no random assault of fortune.[154] Let us imitate these men, as far as we can, in our works, since for their followers there are very rich rewards established.

C99

45.5 "Leaders, though, from whom these types of study have been absent, and from whom rarely does anything good come to mankind, whose cupidity, ambition, and desire for what is another's have afflicted the world with countless problems and disasters, who fear leisure, peace and quiet, and who pass through this life like travelers—let us despise them.[155] And indeed, they would have been buried in perpetual oblivion, had not the works of

C100 monumenta ab interitu vindicassent. Hi soli praestant ut magnorum virorum memoria non una cum corpore intereat. Horum
lumine verborum res gestae illustrantur, horum scriptis nomen
augetur, horum vocibus et praeconio gloria virorum excellentium
celebratur. Qua in re dominorum iniquitas culpanda est, quibus,
cum immortalitas quaedam doctorum hominum studio et vigiliis
tribuatur, tamen eos ita parvi faciunt, ita contemnunt, ut mirum
videatur in tanta ingratitudine (ne dicam stultitia) principum
quempiam scribendi et eorum res gestas litteris mandandi laborem
C101 aggredi voluisse. Sed sapientes illi, qui virtutis praemia in ea ipsa
norunt esse constituta, nihil extra se quaesiverunt, virtute et scribendi laude contenti. Hi nihil sperant a regibus, nihil appetunt,
nihil concupiscunt, virtuti et optimarum artium studiis dediti, hi
beati ac felices dici possunt, quibus solis datur ut ea contemnant,
ad quae reliqui, veluti caeci, insano impetu concurrunt. Hi tanquam ex superiori loco in quadam specula positi, tum ceteros, tum
praecipue reges veluti personatos quosdam homines ac ridiculos
spernunt ac despiciunt. Vident enim infra se positos quibus in
sordibus, quibus in flagitiis, quibus in passionibus perturbationi-
busque versentur, vident eos extrinsecus ornatos et, qua conspi-
ciuntur ab hominibus, claros ac conspicuos haberi, intus vero sordidos, miseros, incultos, afflictos et variis animi morbis laborantes,
quorum vita, nisi scriptorum splendor accederet, perpetuo situ et
squalore sordesceret.

C102 45.6 'Hunc vero' — me intuens — 'non modo non felicem, sed
miserum puto, alieni nutus (ne dicam voluntatis) servum, cui ad
praescriptum alterius est vivendum.'[199] Neque vero ipse solus est

learned men rescued them from death. These are the only ones   C100
who can guarantee that the memory of great men does not perish
together with their bodies. It is by the light of their words that
historic deeds are made to shine forth, it is by their writings that
names are made famous, and it is by their words and commendation that the glory of excellent men is celebrated. In this matter
the wickedness of rulers is to be faulted, since, although they receive a sort of immortality through the studies and vigils of learned
men, they nonetheless hold them in such low esteem, they so despise them, that it seems incredible, amid such ingratitude, not to
say stupidity, among leaders, that anyone has wanted to approach
the task of composition and of committing their deeds to writing.
But those wise men who knew that the prizes for virtue were es-   C101
tablished in virtue itself, did not seek anything outside themselves,
content with their virtue and praise for their writing. It is these
that hope for nothing from kings, ask for nothing, and desire
nothing, devoted to virtue and the study of the best arts, it is these
that can be called blessed and happy, to whom alone it is granted
to despise the things toward which the others run in a mad rush,
like blind men.[156] It is these who, as though from a higher vantage
point, placed on a watchtower, despise and spurn both the rest and
particularly kings, as though they were actors and clowns. For they
can see amid what filth, what sins, and what passions and pertur-
bations those placed below them dwell, they see them decorated
on the outside and, where they are gazed upon by people, regarded
as famous and striking, but on the inside filthy, unhappy, unre-
fined, afflicted and laboring beneath various mental diseases,
whose lives, had not the brilliance of writers been added to them,
would have become begrimed with perpetual neglect and squalor.

45.6 "Poggio here," at this point he looked at me, "I consider   C102
not merely not happy, but unhappy, the slave of someone else's approval, not to say will, who must live at the behest of another. Nor
indeed is he himself alone bereft of happiness, but so are all those

felicitatis expers, sed ii omnes, qui principibus dicati nihil sibi liberae vitae relinquunt, ut ea assequantur, quibus potiti multo sint
quam antea miseriores. Primum dignitates quas adipiscuntur, cum
hae[200] nihil virtutis secum portent, felicitatis sunt vacuae. Nihilo-
minus opes ac divitiae, quibus timores, curae, vigiliae, sollicitudines, molestiae sunt commixtae, insuper invidiae subdita haec
omnia sunt, quae multos deiecit e[201] culmine ac fastigio rerum et
reddidit contemnendos. Itaque non magis principes infelices dixerim quam eos qui, rerum externarum cupiditate, nutum principis
observant. At vero infelicem vitam nescio an infelicior obitus co-
mitetur. Quamobrem, si qui felicitatem appetunt, non in principatu, sed in virtute et beata vita collocatam intelligant. Hanc
omnes, principatum pauci adipisci possunt.

C103   45.7 'Sed iam tempus admonet ne[202] simus verbosiores. Hic
tamen noster, si—quod saepius suasi—in otium se litterarum li-
beramque vitam conferret, procul a publicis curis, quae maxime
studiis adversantur, sique parvo contentus, quod doctorum[203] hominum virtus requirit, posteritatis memoriae vacaret, tum vere felicis nomen mereretur. Non tamen vereor, si tranquillioribus rebus
uti unquam licebit, quin quod suasimus, esse nos aliquando ei
persuasuros.'[204] Quae cum essent dicta et diei aestus remissior
esset, discessimus.

who by devoting their lives to leaders leave themselves no life free to acquire the things which, when they have acquired them, will make them far unhappier than before. First of all, the positions of prestige which they seek to acquire, since they bring no virtue with them, are empty of happiness. No less are resources and wealth, with which are mixed in fears, anxieties, sleepless nights, worries and troubles, in addition all subject to envy, which has thrown many down from the topmost pinnacle of affairs and rendered them contemptible. So I would not call leaders more unhappy than those who hang on the leader's nod in their desire for external things. Indeed, I rather think that an unhappy life may be followed by an unhappier death. For this reason, if any people seek happiness, they should realize that it has its abode not in the position of leader but in virtue and the blessed life. Everyone can have this, while few can gain the position of leader.

45.7 "But now time warns us not to be too verbose. Yet if our friend Poggio here did what I have often urged and betook himself to the peace offered by literature and a free life far from the public duties which are the chief obstacles to study, and if 'contented with little,' as the virtue of learned men requires, he concentrated his attention on the things posterity will remember, then truly he would deserve the name 'happy.'[157] I have no doubt that if we ever have a chance to enjoy more peaceful circumstances, we will one day persuade him to take the advice we have offered." When these things had been said and the heat of the day had become less oppressive, we departed.

C103

Note on the Texts

❧❦❧

CONTROVERSY ON CAESAR AND SCIPIO

All texts of the *Controversy on Caesar and Scipio* between Poggio and Guarino have been edited before. Guarino's letter is included in his *Epistolario* curated by Remigio Sabbadini (1916), the text of Poggio's *On the Excellence* was established by Giuliana Crevatin (1982) based on a census of eighteen manuscripts, and the whole corpus was published by Davide Canfora (2001) (o), who reissued the two previous editions — in the case of *On the Excellence* collating Crevatin's version with Vatican City: BAV MS Urb. lat. 224 (U) — side by side with his own text of Poggio's *Defense*, based on U and fifteen other manuscripts. Consequently, the collection of the three epistles presented by Canfora reflects different textual witnesses and editorial principles (which in Sabbadini's case remain unstated) for its three constituent parts. This matters not merely for consistency, but also because both *On the Excellence* and Guarino's response have archetypes that differ from the dossier put together by Poggio when, after writing his *Defense*, he bundled the latter with the former two epistles and dispatched all three together, with cover letters, to Francesco Barbaro and Leonello d'Este. At this stage Poggio or his copyist might, either willfully or by mistake, have altered his own or Guarino's work. Furthermore, my spot-check demonstrated that, in the process of copying the texts established by Sabbadini and Crevatin, Canfora introduced new errors, not found in their editions nor in the cited manuscripts (some are significant indeed, such as the failure to print the first lines of Guarino's note to Leonello). Weeding out these errors would have required a serious effort to collate the printed texts, only to result in an edition that is still effectively a miscellany. On balance, it seemed better to invest the time in collating manuscripts and produce a new edition rigorously based on Poggio's dossier. This also allowed me further to regularize spelling, adapt punctuation, allocate paragraphs, and add subdivisions — marked with an asterisk in the translation — as I saw fit.

Naturally, the I Tatti series is not the place for a full critical edition based on all (forty-five plus) witnesses. I have therefore decided to limit my collations to a number of sound witnesses representing different families located high in the stemma, that is to say, close to Poggio. To identify these, I have relied on Crevatin's detailed discussion of the tradition of *On the Excellence*, which, on the basis of an error in §7, she groups into two primary families. From the first, I chose to collate Crevatin's "best codex," Florence: Biblioteca Marucelliana MS B.V.9 (M), and Canfora's favorite, U, which belongs to the same family. From Crevatin's second family, I selected Ferrara: Biblioteca Comunale Ariostea MS Cl.II.125 (F), which her apparatus showed to have few unique errors and which she described as in an elegant hand. Finally, I partially collated several manuscripts unseen by Crevatin that all offer a different, third reading precisely in this critical passage. This is the English branch comprising Cambridge: CUL MS Gg.i.34 (C); Cambridge: Trinity College, MS O.9.8 (T); and Oxford: Bodleian Library, MS Bodley 915 (Ob), which also contain Pietro del Monte's epistle to Poggio, on which more below. Of this branch, I chose fully to collate C, which is the dedication copy prepared by Pietro del Monte for Humfrey, Duke of Gloucester, of Poggio's dossier and his own response, rather than its misbound—though not significantly more corrupt—sibling T, which includes (mis)corrections by the scribe of the slightly inferior Ob, Thomas Candour (see also for *On the Unhappiness*).

In this way, I hoped to have identified three different families, represented, respectively, by M + U, by C, and by F. My collations later complicated this picture, but not, I think, in a disconcerting manner. First of all, I immediately noticed what appeared to be a conjunctive error between the uncorrected text of C (and of T and Ob for that matter) and F in the first line of Guarino's letter, where all leave out the required word *diebus*. However, the collation of a total of 25,000 words has not yielded any other significant conjunctive errors, so that one can only hypothesize a flaw in Poggio's archetype (e.g., *diebus* written as marginal insertion), which generated identical but independent omissions.

Second, I was alerted to the slim volume London: BL MS Harley 3340 (H), which contains nothing but Guarino's letter, albeit misbound, and might thus be supposed to represent his original text before its inclusion in Poggio's dossier. I decided also to collate this manuscript, not, obviously, in order to return to a mixed edition, but to be able to report any significant redactions made by Poggio. The results were twofold. On the one hand, H does indeed contain unique readings against M U C F that must be correct, and so almost certainly derives directly from Guarino's epistle without Poggio's intervention. Yet it does not appear that Poggio purposefully tampered with the text of his opponent, since none of these variations change the content or the force of Guarino's argument, with one single exception (in Guarino §65, cf. Poggio's *Defense* §§32, 39) which may be unintentional. On the other hand, I found that H also shares a significant number of readings with F, against M U C. All of these, in themselves, constitute equally plausible alternatives, and in the absence of H one would thus discard F against the authority of M + U and C. With H, however, accounting for half the stemma of Guarino's letter, its agreement tips the balance in F's favor, meaning M U C are wrong. This, in turn, is possible only when they derive from the same ancestor: in other words, they do belong to one family, instead of two, after all. The stemma may be visualized thus:

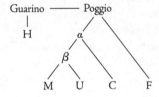

The practical consequences are that, in the case of Guarino's letter, it is in principle legitimate to follow the readings of H against M U C F. In the light of my decision to publish Poggio's dossier, however, I have, faced with equal probability, consistently favored M U C F, following H only on the handful of occasions where the text of M U C F is clearly

wrong. M U C F's omissions compared to H, meanwhile, have been included between angle brackets ⟨ ⟩.

Similarly, for *On the Excellence* and the *Defense*, where such an "external" witness is not available (for I have not found, in Crevatin's study of *On the Excellence*, evidence of an earlier redaction), it is in principle legitimate to follow the readings of F against M U C. Yet in the case of Guarino's text, comparison of F and M U C against H showed the ratio of correct (i.e., agreeing with H) readings of F and M U C to be approximately 1:3. In the other two epistles, in case of equal probability, I have therefore followed M U C.

I have reported scribal corrections (*ante* and *post correctionem*) only where the *apparatus criticus* also notes errors or omissions; otherwise they remain unreported. Also not reported are some unique errors in single witnesses and most spelling variations — particularly in proper names — and hypercorrections typical of fifteenth-century practice.

Collated MSS of the Controversy

C   Cambridge: Cambridge University Library, MS Gg.i.34
       (Photographs courtesy of Carlotta Barranu)

F   Ferrara: Biblioteca Comunale Ariostea, MS Cl.II.125

H   London: British Library, MS Harley 3340 (Photographs courtesy of Jeroen De Keyser)

M   Florence: Biblioteca Marucelliana, MS B.V.9 (Photographs courtesy of Jeroen De Keyser)

Ob   Oxford: Bodleian Library, MS Bodley 915 (Photographs courtesy of David Rundle)

T   Cambridge: Trinity College, MS 0.9.8 (Photographs courtesy of Keith Sidwell)

U   Vatican City: Biblioteca Apostolica Vaticana MS Urb. lat. 224

⟨ ⟩   text in H omitted in M U C F

H. S.

LETTER OF PIETRO DEL MONTE TO POGGIO

Pietro del Monte, then papal collector in England, wrote to Poggio on January 31, 1440, thanking him for having sent the *Controversy* and giving

his own opinion. Short extracts of the epistle were published by Haller, *Piero da Monte*, 142–43. Haller employed solely Vatican City: BAV, MS Vat. lat. 2694 (V), as did Riccardo Fubini when printing the full text in the fourth volume of Poggio's *Opera omnia*. This was an understandable choice, as it is in the author's hand, in the collection of his speeches and letters he made for himself when he had returned to Italy. However, an earlier manuscript, Cambridge: CUL, MS Gg.i.34 (C), should have priority because it is the copy that del Monte had made in England of the whole *Controversy*, including his contribution, for the English prince, Humfrey, Duke of Gloucester. It was the version of the text in C that gained a wider circulation. V is, in effect, a later light revision of C: it sometimes provides short passages omitted — presumably by scribal error — in C, but in other instances, particularly in the later pages, it is not as full as C. C is therefore taken as the base text here, collated with V and with the few minor mistakes in Fubini's transcription noted with the siglum f.

LIST OF MSS OF THIS LETTER KNOWN TO BE EXTANT

Berlin	Staatsbibliothek, MS lat. fol. 366, 62v– 69v (England, s. xv^2) (*Iter* 3:481b)
T (see above)	Cambridge: Trinity College, MS 0.9.8, 44–57v
C	Cambridge: Cambridge University Library, MS Gg.i.34, 89v–115 (England, 1440) (D. Rundle, "Two Unnoticed Manuscripts from the Collection of Humfrey, Duke of Gloucester," *Bodleian Library Record* 16 [1998]: 211–24)
Ob	Oxford: Bodleian Library, MS Bodley 915, 169–87 (D. Rundle, "The Scribe Thomas Candour and the Making of Poggio Bracciolini's English Reputation," *English Manuscript Studies 1100–1700* 12 [2005]: 1–25 as no. 6)
San Daniele del Friuli	Biblioteca Civica Guarneriana, MS 50 (s. xv^{med} [1464 × 1466]) (*Iter* 2:567a; L. Casarsa et al., *La Liberia Di Guarnerio d'Artegna* [Udine, 1991]: 254–57)
Trier	Bibliothek des Priester-Seminars, MS. 44, 162v–75 (Low Countries, s. xv$^{3/4}$) (*Iter* 3:713b)

V   Vatican City: Biblioteca Apostolica Vaticana, MS Vat.
lat. 2694, 207–18 (*recte* 157–68) (Italy, s. xv^{med} [ca. 1450
× 1457])

Wolfenbüttel   Herzog August-Bibliothek, MS. Guelf. 857 novi (s. xv)
(H. Butzmann, *Kataloge der Herzog August Bibliothek
Wölfenbuttel: Die Mittelalterlichen Handschriften der
Gruppen Extravagantes, Novi und Novissimi* [Frankfurt
am Main, 1972] 401; *Iter*, 3:736b)

A further manuscript, formerly at the Sorbonne (MS 229), is now lost.

{}   deletion

^^   interlinear or marginal additions

D. R.

ON THE UNHAPPINESS OF LEADERS

The text of *On the Unhappiness of Leaders* was originally intended to be based on that of Davide Canfora (1998). But close examination of his edition revealed a series of problems: with his assessment of the MS tradition (where he does not provide a viable stemma), with the accuracy of his reports of the MSS, and with his judgment on various cruces and other critical issues. In addition, his articulation of the text into paragraphs often obscures continuity of thought and subject matter. Thus the text presented here is the result of a new set of collations of a select group of MSS, a new — if necessarily only preliminary — assessment of the MS tradition based on those collations, and a reexamination of the various textual cruces. Its presentation involves a fresh set of divisions of the work into paragraphs (including separate numbering for dedication letter and dialogue). Where these idea-units seemed to be overlong (at 12, 17, 29, 32, 39, 41, 43, and 45), I have split them into subparagraphs. Nonetheless, for the sake of continuity and easy cross-reference, I have used Canfora's sigla for the MSS (with the exception of his C, here named Cb to distinguish it from the C MS of the *Controversy* and Del Monte's *Epistle*), and I have inserted his paragraph numbers in the form (C1–103).

There are fifty-four extant MSS of *On the Unhappiness of Leaders* plus a further six printed editions (the earliest Paris, 1474), but the autograph is

lost. Canfora reduces the tradition to two main groups of MSS, λ—represented through *eliminatio codicum* by Florence, L, with marginal insertions, it seems, by Poggio himself—and ζ, which consists of only three MSS (Paris, Za; Brussels, W; and Bern, B). The remaining forty-three MSS and four printed editions he calls a "costellazione," α, which is defined solely by the criterion of not belonging to either λ or ζ. His rationale for the identification of ζ as a separate group is that these MSS are the only ones that contain (part of) the phrase (which Canfora deems essential) *eruditi qui voluptatibus* at 14 (C37).

Canfora, however, makes a strange choice in identifying L as "in general the most correct of all the witnesses." Even with Poggio's own corrections (which can be found on ff. 45r, 45v, 48r, 50r, 50v, 56v, 60v, and 64v), it still has six omissions not apparent in the ζ group and the α constellation, as well as some other egregious errors: at 13 (C36) *venenorumque* instead of *venereorumque*, at 32.2 (C65) *Romani* for *Romam*, at 41.5 (C85) *infelicitatis* instead of *felicitatis*, and at 45.3 (C97) *insursans* instead of *insusurrans*. L and its apographs, then, are a distinct group, but cannot be regarded as especially trustworthy.

As for Canfora's treatment of the ζ group, although he is quite right to distinguish it from the rest on the grounds that it contains (part of) the phrase *eruditi qui voluptatibus* as well as the subjunctive verb *contineantur*, he nowhere examines closely the reading of the consensus, or regards it as suspicious that the phrase is found only in three relatively late MSS, all of transalpine origin. In fact, the reading of the other MSS, *continentur*, strongly suggests that we are looking at an interpolation in the ζ group. The ζ group reading is as follows (with the variants unique to ζ in italics):

Nam boni illi, qui ad publicam utilitatem intendant secluso privato commodo, qui bonos et doctos diligant, qui parentis animum gerant, qui fuerint in nostris litteris *eruditi, qui voluptatibus* non *contineantur*, et si quos ulla aetas produxit, rariores Stoicorum sapiente extiterunt.

(For those good ones, the sort who put aside their private interests and concentrate on the public good, who act like fathers, who have been educated in our literature, who are not hindered by their

lusts, even if any era has produced some, have been rarer than the Stoics' sage.)

The consensus reading is:

> Nam boni illi, qui ad publicam utilitatem intendant secluso privato commodo, qui bonos et doctos diligant, qui parentis animum gerant, qui fuerint, in nostris litteris non continentur, et si quos ulla aetas produxit, rariores Stoicorum sapiente extiterunt.

> (For as to those good ones, the sort who put aside their private interests and concentrate on the public good, who act like fathers, [sc. any] who have existed are not contained in our literature, and if some era has produced any, they have been rarer than the Stoics' sage.)

The difficulty supposedly emended by the additional phrase is the use of *qui* in *qui fuerint* to mean *si qui*; a difficulty enhanced by mistaken punctuation (*qui fuerint* [,] *in nostris literis*). This will have provoked the supposition that something was needed to complete the phrase (viz., *eruditi*), and in turn the need to invent a further generic clause to balance the earlier ones, changing the mood of *continentur* and filling it out with *voluptatibus* (thus repeating in different terms the sense of the first *qui* clause). This hypothesis finds support in the fact that of the ζ group, Za has *eruditi* only and omits *qui voluptatibus*. The resulting reading of the ζ group is difficult and not entirely suitable to the context.

The consensus, however, produces excellent sense, for Poggio's point is that good rulers *if they have existed at all* are rarer than Stoic sages. This is amplified and clarified by the second colon of the sentence (*et . . . sapiente*). Moreover, the idea is both anticipated by Niccoli's statement at paragraph 12.1, *Carolus bonos posse esse principes et nonnullos habitos dicit, ego non qui esse possunt, sed qui fuerint perquiro, quos nondum ulla aetas sortita est* ("Carlo says that leaders can be good and that some have been regarded as such, but I am not inquiring about who can be thought good, but who actually have been"), and backed up by Niccoli's later statement (37): *'Non quaero,' Nicolaus inquit, 'bonum aut sapientem illum Stoicorum, qui nondum est inventus'* ("I am not searching," said Niccolò, "for the famous good man or sage of the Stoics, who has not yet been discovered"). And the

same skeptical notion in regard to the existence of happy *principes* is also echoed in Poggio's letter to Richard Petworth, written shortly after he finished writing the dialogue (see Introduction). These ζ group ·MSS, then, follow the lead of an emended copy, unless one of them was itself the originator of the interpolation, and so will be represented in the proposed stemma as deriving from a lost ζ. They have no especially authoritative place in the textual transmission.

The two main legs of Canfora's reconstruction of the MS tradition are thus rendered null as far as their authority to provide a sound text is concerned. Since it was not possible for the present edition to reexamine all fifty-four witnesses, I have collated only six in full, choosing two exempla, L and Za, from the two distinct groups identified by Canfora (λ and ζ), and four other early witnesses that are independent of each other. These are: Oa, written in Ferrara in 1446 by Richard Bole from a copy presumably housed there; Ob, written by Thomas Candour, probably in England ca. 1450, an apograph of the copy sent by Poggio to Richard Petworth in 1440; Od, also an apograph of the copy sent by Poggio to Richard Petworth in 1440, written in London ca. 1447 by Milo de Carraria (the independence of Ob from Od is demonstrated among other things by the retention of *nuncuperis* at 9 [C20] by Od and its correction to *appelles* by Ob); and Vc, a Vatican MS written in the pontificate of Nicholas V (1447–55). In addition, I have checked some relevant passages in Cb, though this is datable only to ca. 1460–80, because it contains material not found in MSS of Canfora's main groups.

I have suggested in the Introduction, on the basis of shared errors in all branches of the MS tradition that I find hard to ascribe to Poggio himself, that he had a fair copy made from which the rest of the tradition derives. The autograph I shall call A, and this slightly faulty apograph I shall call A^2. In a significant number of places, the consensus of the selected MSS (including Za, despite the interpolation discussed above) provides readings arguably superior to those of L. Sometimes these are omissions in L (e.g., *quo vitio* at 22 [C51], where the consensus is *quo in vitio*), sometimes they are the egregious errors mentioned above (e.g., at 13 [C36] L *venenorumque*). This means that L (and its apographs) is an inferior offshoot of A^2, while ζ and the other selected MSS remained

closer to it. L's usefulness is therefore highly questionable, except at 42 (C87), where Poggio himself corrected the consensus, and at 5 (C14), where Poggio's marginal correction is shared by Od and Vc, but not by Oa, Ob, and Za. I have therefore been inclined to see the consensus of selected MSS as likelier to reproduce the reading of A² than L.

Thus we can construct a limited stemma, based on the selected witnesses as well as reasoned supposition regarding their historical genesis (with π = the lost copy sent by Poggio to Richard Petworth in 1442; ϕ = the lost or unidentified Ferrarese copy used by Richard Bole in 1446 for Oa; δ = the copy used by the scribe of Vc: possibly the lost dedication copy?), as follows:

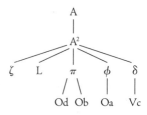

Further down the stemma we can place the apographs of L, such as Vg, and the surviving apographs of ζ, B W and Za. Though much more work would be required to establish further branches, it does on these arguments seem rather less likely that phrases in, for example, Cb, which do not occur in the selected MSS, originated from Poggio's pen, as occasionally argued by Canfora, who appears to consider any expanded text as somehow necessarily deriving from the author's hand. Indeed, interference by later scholarly conjecture on the basis of reading the Greek text of Herodotus is almost certain in the cases of the readings *Candaules* in Vc at 39.1 (C74), where other MSS read *Cadualus*, and *Arpago* for *Arpalo* in Da Db Hb at 22 (C52). One might also conjecture that the insertion of *Nero Senecam ac Lucanum mori coegit* after *occisus est* in Cb and related MSS at 31 (C62) was due to a later reader's cross-reference to Poggio's *Defense*. Less clear is how or why the phrase *armis ac ferro* in Cb and related MSS at 28 (C57) entered the text, but its presence would spoil the

neat and succinct antithesis by unnecessary padding, so perhaps it was a marginal comment to explicate *decertant*, subsequently incorporated into the text of this subbranch.

The *apparatus criticus* reports mostly significant divergences in the textual tradition based on my collation of the MSS listed below, with a few additional pieces of information taken from Canfora, in cases where I have been unable to check the MSS in question for myself.

Collated MSS of De Infelicitate Principum

L   Florence: Biblioteca Medicea Laurenziana, MS 47.19 (datable to mid-fifteenth c. Italian)

Oa   Oxford: Balliol College, MS 136 (datable to fifteenth c., *DIP* datable to January 28, 1446. Ferrara [Richard Bole]) (Photographs courtesy of David Rundle)

Ob   Oxford: Bodleian Library, MS 915 (datable to ca. 1450. England [Thomas Candor]. Copied from Richard Petworth's MS, sent to him in 1440 by Poggio) (Photographs courtesy of Jeroen De Keyser)

Od   Oxford: Bodleian Library, MS Rawlinson C. 298 (datable to ca. 1447. London [Milo de Carraria]. Copied from Richard Petworth's MS, sent to him in 1440 by Poggio) (Photographs courtesy of David Rundle)

Vc   Vatican City: Biblioteca Apostolica Vaticana, MS Vat. lat. 186 (datable to the pontificate of Nicholas V [1447–55]: see the heading of the text. Italian)

Za   Paris: Bibliothèque nationale de France, MS lat. 14845. (datable to fifteenth c. French. Owned by Abbey of Saint-Victor, Paris)

List of Other MSS of De Infelicitate Principum Mentioned, with Canfora's Sigla

B   Bern: Burgerbibliothek MS 562 (datable to 1450–70. French)

Cb   London: British Library, MS Harley 2500 (datable
[Canfora's C]   to 1460–80. Flemish)

Da	San Daniele del Friuli: Biblioteca Civica Guarneriana, MS 44 (datable to 1455–66. Italian [Guarnerio d'Artegna])
Db	San Daniele del Friuli: Biblioteca Civica Guarneriana, MS 47 (datable to 1449–56. Italian [Battista da Cingoli]. Apograph of Da)
Hb	Berlin: Staatsbibliothek, Preussischer Kulturbesitz, MS Lat. oct. 175 (*olim* Phillips 2750) (fifteenth c.)
Hd	Berlin: Staatsbibliothek, Preussischer Kulturbesitz, MS Lat. qu. 558 (*olim* Barrois 433)
Vg	Vatican City: Biblioteca Apostolica Vaticana, MS Urb. lat. 224 (datable to 1460 or 1465. Italian [Nicolaus Riccius Spinosus, with titles and marginal corrections by Jacopo Bracciolini]. Apograph of L)
W	Brussels: Bibliothèque Royale Albert Ier, MS IV, 928 (datable to 1468–69)

K. S.

NOTE ON ORTHOGRAPHY

For various reasons the editors have decided to "normalize" the Latin according to the standards common in Latin dictionaries such as *OLD* and text series such as *OCT*. For those who wish to see for themselves what normal orthography was in the fifteenth century, this can be done easily now by following some of the links to the MSS consulted for this edition given in the bibliography. As for Poggio's own practice, while we do not have Poggio's autograph MSS of these works, we have a considerable body of his own handwriting, as he was one of the most important developers of humanist script (Ullman, *The Origin and Development of Humanistic Script*). His own orthographic habits can be sampled in the photographs in Ullman (plates 13–27) and the digital versions of Vat. lat. 1843 (online at https://digi.vatlib.it/view/MSS_Vat.lat.1843) and Vat. lat. 1849 (online at https://digi.vatlib.it/view/MSS_Vat.lat.1849), Poggio's own transcriptions of Livy's first and third decade, done around 1425/6.

Notes to the Texts

❧❦❧

1. Poggio . . . proemium] *as reported in* U
2. plurimam salutem] salutem plurimam F
3. cum] tum M F
4. impertiri] impartiri U
5. quodam scribendi] scribendi quodam U *o*
6. id facinus] facinus id M
7. iuri] viri M
8. libuit] libunt M
9. an] in M
10. Ioveque] Iove M
11. sibi ac] ac sibi F
12. deinde] dein F
13. Florentiae] *om.* F

POGGIO, *ON THE EXCELLENCE OF SCIPIO AND CAESAR*

1. Poggii . . . incipit] *as reported in* U
2. extimandus] existimandus F aestimandus *o*
3. comparavit] compararit F *o*
4. fuisse cognovimus] esse cognovimus *o*
5. Caesarem] Caesarem quidem *o*
6. ac Caesarem] ac Alexandrum F
7. rerum gestarum] rerum ab se gestarum F
8. sua] *om.* F

9. iudicent] iudicant *o*

10. antecesserit] antecesserint *M*

11. aut] et *o*

12. aut] et *F*

13. gloria coniuncta] coniuncta gloria *U*

14. facilius possit perspici] possit facilius perspici *F*

15. aut referendum] anteferendum *U*

16. quae] quod *o*

17. ferant] ferunt *M C*

18. adiutore] auctore *F*

19. impensis] expensis *U*

20. trium] tria *o*

21. deaurati] inaurati *o*

22. omni varie] omni *M om. U*

23. bellum renovante] renovante bellum *F*

24. hostium copias] copias hostium *F*

25. desciscentes] desistentes *F*

26. montibus . . . flumine] Pyrenaeis montibus Oceano Rhenoque flumine et Alpibus *M U o*: montibus Pyrenaeis Oceano Rhenoque flumine et Alpibus *C*: Alpibus Pyrenaeis Oceano Rhenoque flumine et Alpibus *F*

27. Romani populi] populi Romani *F*

28. lacessivit] lacessunt *U*

29. virtus] virtutus *M*

30. ferme] fere *U o*

31. imparatum] imperatum *U*

32. ni] in *M*: nisi *o*

33. in Asia] *om. M U C o*

34. et] *om. F*

35. solutus] solutis *F*

36. litteratior] litterator *U o*

37. bonorum] bonorum bonorum *F*

38. civiumque] civium *M U*

39. permisit] promisit *M*

40. cupiditatum] cupidinum *U*

41. est appellanda] appellanda est *F*

42. illum] eum *F*

43. laus] salus *U*

44. cuius] quibus *F*

45. abstulerint] abstulerit *M*

46. eo] Caesare *U*

47. et] ut *F*

48. appellaverit] appellavit *F*

49. fuisse] non fuisse *M U o*

50. et crudelitate] *om. U*

51. ac] et *o*

52. edidit] eddidit *M*

53. ab . . . integritatem] et *M U*

54. Omnes tradunt] tradunt *U o*

55. in ostentationem] inoscentationem *M*

56. pleraque] pluraque *F*

57. vixdum] vix *F*

58. pubertatem] per ubertatem *M*: ubertatem C^{ac}

59. pugnantem] repugnantem *U*

60. excellens] *om.* C^{ac}

61. auctore L. Caecilio Metello] *om. o*

62. agitare] consilium agitare *F o*

63. consilium] concilium *o*

64. reliqua] reliquae U

65. ab interitu] *om. o*

66. deleto] delecto U*ac*

67. praeter . . . concessa] reliquiae veteris exercitus concessi F

68. sibi] *om. F*

69. trigesimum excessisset] excessessit trigesimum U

70. inde] deinde *o*

71. quidam] qui *M U C*

72. imperatorum omnium] omnium imperatorum U

73. cum . . . militiae] *om. U*

74. pacem ab Romanis] ab Romanis pacem *M U o*

75. accepimus] suscaepimus F

76. minor] minus *o*

77. virtus eius] eius virtus U

78. ei . . . diem] diem ei ad populum F

79. quam] *om. F*

80. Linternum] Liternum *M U o*

81. exsulantem] exulantes F

82. eis] illis C

83. loquar . . . patriam] de caritate eius in patriam loquar U

84. cum] tum U

85. Linternum] Liternum *M*

86. quos] quo C*ac*

87. invicem] *om. o*

88. ferme] *om. o*

89. seditiosorum] seditione U

90. suffragio] flagitio *M U C*

91. perturbandae] perturbendae *M*

406

92. possent] posset F

93. bellicae] belli U

94. clarissime] *om.* M U C o

95. quattuor exercitus] exercitus quattuor F

96. dedendam] delendam M: dedandam U^{ac}

97. cura et] cum C

98. detestandos] destestanda sunt o

99. ne] neque F

100. iudicanti] iudicandi F

101. aequa] *om.* U

102. et . . . meritis] in rem publicam et meritis F

103. artium] *om.* U

104. absumpsit] assumpsit M U^{ac}

105. qui] quae C

106. et] *om.* F

107. ac] et F

108. et] ac F

109. quod] quid F o

110. Vale . . . Florentiae] *om.* F

GUARINO, *LETTER TO LEONELLO D'ESTE*

1. Guarini . . . Estensem] *adapted from* U's Guarini Veronensis de Praestantia Caesaris et Scipionis ad Leonellum Estensem

2. Guarinus] Guarinus Veronensis o

3. illustri] illustrissimo o

4. domino] principi o

5. salutem] salutem plurimam dicit F

6. Nuntius . . . facti] *om.* o

7. offundere] effundere F

8. terminat] terminet *H o*

9. maxime regi] regibus maxime *F*

10. dicunt] dicant *M*

11. severitate sententiam] sententiam severitate *H*

GUARINO, ON THE EXCELLENCE OF
CAESAR AND SCIPIO

1. Guarini . . . Estensem] *as reported in* U

2. plurimam dicit] plurimam salutem *M U C*

3. diebus] *om.* C^{ac} *F*

4. perspexerim] prospexerim *o*

5. gratiam] gloriam *F*

6. tibi secundas] secundas tibi *F*

7. factus] *om.* U

8. quidam] quidem *U*

9. impatienti] impatientiae *F*

10. equestris] equestribus *M C*

11. me] *om. o*

12. perlato] perlecto *M U*

13. Parturiunt] Parturierunt *U C*

14. Hui . . . montes] *om. F*

15. cura] causa *o*

16. dicere] *om. o*

17. volumen excresceret] excresceret volumen *o*

18. sane] certe *C*

19. et . . . accusari] et indignitas deprorari accusari M^{ac}: *om.* C

20. Quodnam] Quidnam *M U* C^{ac}

21. mephitim] nephitim *U*

22. alio loco] alio in loco *C*

23. vitiosam . . . consuetudine] *om.* M U

24. nolis] nobis M

25. alius] aliter H

26. eo] eodem H

27. nihil] nil H

28. crebrior] acerbior F

29. Caesari] Caesaris F

30. industriam] industria F

31. mihi] mi H

32. ingeniis] ingenius H

33. accivit] acuit U^{ac}

34. ignorantiam] ignorationem H *o*

35. genere] *om.* M U C

36. atratam] attritam C: atram *add. marg.* C: attractam H

37. dein] de inde M: deinde *o*

38. artes] arte *o*

39. doctos] *om.* F

40. qualesve] quales ut M: qualesve sint *o*

41. Lucano] *om.* C

42. praeclare] *om.* U

43. est] *om.* C

44. dubitandum] dubitanda M U C

45. tersior sit] sit tersior M U C

46. purus] purius C

47. ferme sunt] sunt ferme M U C

48. Historicine] Historici nec U^{pc}

49. nondum] num dum H

50. satis] *om.* C

51. Asconius Lucceius Sallustius] Asconius Lucceius U: Lucceius Sa-
lustius Asconius H

52. L. Florus] Lucius Florus F

53. T.] om. M

54. quanti Senecam] om. M U

55. antepones] anteponis o

56. aequabis] aequalis M

57. vere] vero F

58. Nihil] Nil o

59. innumerabilibus] immemorabilus F

60. eloquentiae] om. F o

61. et] ut et C^{pc}: ut o

62. multitudine quid numerosius] om. C

63. tu] om. M U C

64. privare] privari U

65. viri] om. U

66. absumpsit] assumpsit M U^{ac}

67. litterarum et liberalium] liberalium et litterarum U

68. bello civile] om. F o

69. suarum] om. o

70. telorum] teloris M

71. minimum] nimium F o

72. superfuere] superfuerunt U

73. deletam] delatam U: delectam H

74. Romanorum] Romanam C F

75. numquid] num quod H

76. a] ab H

77. philosophos] populos U

78. Censorium] Cesarinum M: Censorinum U C F

79. scientiarum] sententiarum *U C*

80. eum] *om. M U C*

81. intercepti] intercepi *M U^{ac}*

82. dicendae] dicendo *M*

83. artes] artis *o*

84. gloria] gloriae *H*

85. civili bello] bello civili *F*

86. senatui] senatu *F*

87. opus crudelitatis] crudelitatis opus *H*

88. tu] tum *U*

89. factam] *om. M U C F*

90. propagatos] propagatio *U^{ac}*: propagato *C^{ac}*: prorogatos *M o*

91. Dacas] Dicas *F*

92. Num] Non *F*

93. Indi] Inde *M U C*

94. venere] venerunt *F*

95. obtulere] tulere *o*

96. quae] cum *C*

97. inferiore] inferiori *M C*

98. materia] materiam *U*

99. defuerint] defuerunt *H*

100. susceperint] susceperunt *U*

101. quas] quos *o*

102. litteratorum] litterarium *U*

103. studiosorum] studiorum *M U*

104. gratitudinem] magnitudine *U*

105. essem] esse *M*

106. Poggios] Poggius *M*

107. qua] quas *F*

108. sicuti] sicut *H o*

109. omni] omnium *M U F*

110. cum] tum *M U*

111. quae] *om. U*

112. mater est] mater *U*: fuit mater *F*

113. animos] *om. F*

114. imbuerit] imbuerit animos *M U C F H*

115. linenda] linienda *F*: livendra *C^{pc}*

116. potius et] et potius *F*

117. insuerint] insueverunt *F*

118. rapere] inpere *M om. U*

119. qua] quam *H*

120. etiam torpent] torpent etiam *C*

121. ciborumque] ciborum *H o*

122. pretiosisque] prociosisque *M*

123. saporibus] soporibus *M H*

124. detestari] destestarique *U*

125. et] *om. F*

126. atque] ac *U C*

127. Quid quod] Quitque *M*: Quique *U*: Qui que *C^{ac}*

128. successere principes] principes successere *U*

129. rei militaris scientiam] militaris scientiam *M U C^{ac}*: militaris rei scientiam *C^{pc}*

130. quam] qui *F*: quae *o*

131. ii] hi *H*

132. insectarere] insectare *U^{ac}*

133. nil] nihil *C*

134. atque etiam] *om. M U*

135. praecurrit] praevertit *o*

136. esse] *om.* F

137. amice] *om.* C T

138. benivole] bene vole *o*

139. fuerint] fiunt U *o*

140. quidem] quid M

141. ad nescio] nescio ad H

142. scitum] situm F

143. sequendum] sequendus U

144. te] in te U^{pc} C^{pc}

145. animadverte] animadvertere *o*

146. expositurus] *om.* M U C F

147. orationis] ornationis F

148. pronuntiatione] pronuntiationem U

149. indagant] indagat M C^{ac}: nudant F

150. consilio] in consilio F

151. verius] verum *o*

152. immortalitas] mortalitas M U C^{ac}

153. Utque] Ut U

154. quidam] quidem F

155. comparatus] comparatas M U^{ac}

156. inferiorem] inferioribus F

157. prae] pro C

158. confectam] factam U

159. potius] *om.* C

160. te falsum] falsum te M U C *o*

161. omnino] animo M U

162. breve] brevem U^{ac}

163. animorum] animarum *U*

164. indicia] indiciam *M*

165. percurrere] percurres *M U*

166. dedignatus] dignatus *F*

167. forsan] *om. M U C*

168. caruisse] carere *M U C*

169. ne] *om. M U C F H o*

170. perniciosissimum] pervitiosissimum *M*

171. praeluxerit] praeluserit *H*

172. pauca] parva *o*

173. annum sextum decimum] sextum decimum annum *M U C*

174. ad odorandum] adodorandum *M*: adorandum *F*

175. adolescentis] adolescenti *o*

176. singulari] singularis *o*

177. salute] salutem *o*

178. contenderunt] contempnerunt *M*: *om. U*

179. impiumque] imperiumque *C*

180. Sulla] Sullae *U^{pc}*

181. cuius] *om. M U*

182. deinde] de inde *M*

183. se] sese *F*

184. struxit] instruxit *F*

185. Corneliam] *om. o*

186. compelli] comdicu *H*

187. hereditatum] hereditatis *U*

188. sacerdotii] sacerdotis *F*: sacerdotu *H^{ac}*

189. praestantis] *om. H*

190. gubernatorem] gubernationem *C*

191. edentem] et dentem M

192. aspicis] aspicias H

193. planius] Plinius F

194. religio] regio F

195. παρὰ τοῦ Διός] *attempt to transliterate* M C: *left blank* U

196. ceteris] Caesaris C*ᵃᶜ*: *om.* C*ᵖᶜ*

197. Thermi fortissimi] fortissimi Thermi M

198. merebat] nitebat U: inhaerebat F

199. his] iis M U C *o*

200. servati civis] civis servati U

201. laudanda] laudabilia U

202. in] *om.* U*ᵃᶜ*

203. factionis homine] hominis factionis homine M C*ᵃᶜ* F*ᵖᶜ*: hominis factione homine F*ᵃᶜ*

204. cum servati] conservati F

205. Ligurem] Ligure *o*

206. tamen] tum M

207. contractis] contra actis U

208. civitates stabilivit] stabilivit civitates C

209. ab] *om.* U: ab eo *o*

210. cognoverat] cognoveras M U

211. tardaretur] traderetur F C*ᵃᶜ*

212. Cedis] Credis M U C: Caedis H

213. contendis] contemnis M

214. num] unum M U

215. inter] *om.* F

216. insignia] in signa M: signa U

217. colloces] colores F

218. a teneris] atteneris M

219. rerum] *om. M U C*

220. tradunt] tradant *H*

221. pariter] paternis *C*

222. dictare] dictaret *M U*

223. fuerit] fuit *F*

224. adolescentis] adolescentiae *U*

225. et] ut *o*

226. et] *om. U*

227. ii] *om. M U*: hii *C*: hi *F*

228. oramque] omniaque *F*

229. cum] cura *M*

230. dein] deinde *U*: *om. F*

231. militibus] indicibus *F*

232. sua] tua *M U^{ac}*

233. fundit] fudit *F*

234. ioco saepe] saepe ioco *M U C*

235. aestimatorem] extimatorem *M U*

236. omittens] omictes *M*: omittes *U C^{ac}*

237. intelligebant] intelligebat *M*

238. sicut . . . vicit] *om. U*

239. opinio] oratio *o*

240. firmamenti satis] firmanentum satis *C*: satis firmamenti *H^{pc}*: satis momenti *H^{ac}*

241. malivoli] malevola *H*

242. epulas] epistolas *M C F*

243. munificentias] magnificentias *M*

244. significas] magnificas *M U*

245. Caesari sit] sit Caesari *C*

246. Amita] Amica *M*

247. Marii] mariti *M C F*

248. efferre] et ferre *M U*

249. admiratione cum] cum admiratione *F*

250. immanissimo] humanissimo *M*: inhumanissimo *U*

251. iustissime] *om. F*

252. arx] ars *M U*

253. hominibus] honoribus *M U*

254. laude] *om. M U C^{ac} F*

255. admiratione] admirationem *U*

256. addere] adere *M*

257. Isauricum] Is auricum *H*

258. singularem] secularem *M*

259. patrocinia] patrociniam *M*

260. prensandis] prehensandis *F*: presandis *H*

261. novos] nous *M*

262. ac] de *C*

263. adsumito] assumpto *M*

264. partiendae] patiendae *M*

265. Per tribus] partibus *F*

266. centurias] centuriis *F*

267. sibi] *om. U*

268. antea] antea latae *o*

269. ambitu] amitu *M*

270. ambitus] amitus *M U^{ac}*

271. in] *om. M U^{ac}*

272. in] non *F*

273. suffragatoribus] suffragiatoribus *M U C*

274. spoponerit] spoponerint *M*

275. tuo illo] illo tuo *M U C*

276. quam] qua *U*

277. Caesaris] Caesaris furore *o*

278. sacerdotium] sacerdotum *M*

279. pecuniis atque] *om. F*

280. cuinam] qui nam *M*

281. etiam] et *M*

282. superabat] imperabat *C*

283. Qui] Quid *F*

284. etiam] *om. C*

285. adserenda] adsequenda *C^{pc}*

286. ac] et *F*

287. praecellebat] praecellebant *F*

288. nominis] romanis *U*

289. comparationem] comparationes *H*

290. referuntur] feruntur *F*

291. ut et] et ut *M*

292. excludam] exclaudam *M U*

293. excipit] excepit *o*: trahit excipit *F^{ac}*

294. id est] *om. M*: et *F*

295. diuturniori] diuturniore *M U*

296. quo longior] colonior *M U*

297. dignius] dignus *C^{ac}*: dignum *F*

298. designatus] *om. C^{pc} F*

299. id est] idem *M U C*

300. uti] ut *o*

301. utinam] nunc *C*

302. Horatianum] orationum *M C*: oratianum *add. marg C*

303. dictum ab eo est] dictum est ab eo *F*: ab eo dictum est *H*

304. conservandos] conservandos esse *F*

305. per] et per *o*

306. ut] *om. U*

307. cruciatus] cruciatos *o*

308. Latinae linguae] linguae latinae *F*

309. et rata] erratas *M U*

310. inanis erat] erat inanis *H*

311. oratio] ratio *M U*

312. de Catone] detone *M U a c*

313. dicturum me] dicturus *M U*

314. in Caesarem] Caesaris *F*

315. obversaretur] observaretur *M U C F*

316. ingenio ardentissimi] *om. H*

317. irritarit] tritarit *M U C^{ac}*: territarit *C^{pc}*

318. quae quam] quamquam *U*

319. apprehendisset] apprehenditione *M*: apprehendissione *U*

320. sententiam] sententiam sentiam *U^{ac}*: sentiam *U^{pc}*

321. putaret] constaret *M U C F*

322. scaevam] saevam *U o*

323. immobile] innobile *M U C F*

324. direxerit] dillexerit *U*

325. si diis placet] si displiceret *F*

326. animi immortalitate] immoralitate animi *U*

327. lenonium] lenonum *M U C F*

328. versatur] versaretur *F o*

329. aut] *om. M U*

330. velificatione] vellificatione *M C^{ac}*

331. delaturum] elaturum *M*

332. sub dictaturae] subdictore *M*: sub dictore *U*

333. altor] auctor *M U o*

334. prorogatione] propagatione *F*

335. consuetudinem] consuetudines *o*

336. tribuni] tribuno *U^{ac}*: tribunos *U^{pc} C^{pc} F*

337. consulis] consules *M U C F*

338. imperatoris] imperatores *M U C F*

339. te] et *M U F*

340. priscarum rerum] rerum priscarum *U*

341. pedestres] pedestras *M U^{ac}*

342. esse constat] constat esse *F*

343. veteres] vetere *M*

344. eius] enim *F*

345. discrimen] discrimine *M U*

346. ingruerat] ingluerat *M U*

347. Taceo] Ratio *M*

348. prudentia] providentia *C F^{pc}*

349. praesagus] praesagiis *M U*

350. quas] *om. M U C F H o*

351. Oppius] Appius *F*

352. fidem] fide *M U*

353. quoscumque] quosque *U C*

354. errantes] errantem *M*

355. dein] deinde *U F o*

356. iis] hiis *C*: his *H*

357. laudi] an laudi *F*

358. facere Caesar debuit] Caesar debuit facere *U*

359. pietatis atque] atque pietatis atque *M*: atque pietatis *U C F H*

360. confitente] confidentie *M U*

361. honeste] honestate *M*

362. vixerit] vixerint *M C^{ac} F*

363. laeserit] laeserint *F*

364. tribuerit] tribuerint *F*

365. num] non *F*

366. priscorum] *om. M U*

367. relinquas] reliquens *M U*

368. et] si *M U F*: nec *C*

369. non] *om. C^{pc}*

370. explicandas] *om. U*

371. iis] hiis *C*: his *F H*

372. habebat] *om. C*

373. iudico] iudicio *M*

374. sunt] sint *M U*

375. Cicerone tacente] tacente Cicerone *F*

376. erexerit] errexerit *H^{ac}*: evexerit *o*

377. sic] sit *M*

378. coram voces] voces coram *F*

379. fuerant] fuerunt *M U*

380. Ut] Unum *M U*

381. post] per *F*

382. a patronis] apatrocus *M*

383. fuere] fuerunt *F*

384. sequentibus] frequentibus *C*

385. de] *om. F*

386. prolatum] prolatum est *F^{ac}*

387. Idem] Universale *F*

388. fuit] fuerit *M U C*

389. invicti] in vicii *M*

390. libens] liberis *F*

391. deponeret] deponerent *F*

392. ulciscendo] vulciscendo *M*

393. lenissimus] benissimus *M*: benignissimus *U*: levissimus *C H*

394. admirabilem] admirabile *H*

395. erant] erunt *U^{pc}*

396. detegendas] tegendas *U F*

397. calumnians] calumnias *U*

398. hostilem] hostium *o*

399. pervenisse] provenisse *U*

400. sic] sit *U*

401. denuo se fortiter] se fortiter denuo *F*

402. hostis] ostis *M*

403. ab] a *M U C*

404. amatorium illud] *om. F*

405. militat] militas *M*

406. Cupido] cudo *M*

407. idem] iam *o*

408. delictum] deluctum *M*: deductum *U*

409. quodque] quidque *U*

410. sit] sic *M*

411. amoribus] *om. F*: a maioribus *H^{ac}*

412. est] sit *M U C F*

413. amavit] amarit *M*

414. Omphalae] Oniphale *F*

415. Vulcani] Vulgani *M U^{ac}*

416. opera] opem *M U*

417. flagras] flagrus *M*

418. alia] *om. H*

419. et] ac *C*

420. nullo . . . tempore] eos tempore nullo *F*

421. cessasse] cessare *U*

422. non] *om. M C^{ac}*

423. non . . . solum] non solum terras *U F*

424. nominis] nobis *U*

425. tendebantur] detinebantur *F*

426. heteros horos] hetereos horos *U*: ἕτερος ὅρος *F*

427. magnis] magis *F*

428. num] non *F*

429. et] ut *F*

430. Romani] *om. U*

431. His] Hiis *M*

432. bellis] bello *U*

433. uti] ut *o*

434. nationum] natione *M U*

435. Caesaris et Scipionis] Scipionis et Caesaris *C*

436. arces] artes *F*

437. imago] in magno *F*

438. plebe] phebe *M*

439. Haeccine] Hoccine *M U^{ac}*

440. quod] apud *M U*

441. sanguinis] sanguis *U*

442. civitatem] civitate *M*

443. dominatum] dominantum C

444. fuerunt] fuerant M U C

445. virum] *om.* U

446. verius] potius U

447. leges] *om.* M U

448. ne] nec F

449. invitis] inimicis C

450. impetratum] imperatum F

451. lenius] levius C

452. minis] nimis M

453. oblitteratam] obliceratam M

454. populus] populus romanus F

455. monarchiam prolaberentur] monarchiam auderent eo res urbanas pernevenisse prolaberentur U[ac]

456. dictitare] dictatore M U

457. auctoritate] auctoritatis U

458. antelatam] antelata M

459. ita] *om.* U

460. ipsius] impius M U

461. cernebant] cernebat o

462. rursusque] rursus M U F

463. administratam] administrandam o

464. privatimque] privatim U

465. et] *om.* U

466. quemadmodum] quamadmodum M U[ac]

467. honorum] bonorum M U C

468. dein] deinde U o

469. sibi quosdam] quosdam sibi o

470. sese] se U

471. tribuere] tribueret U

472. caeco] ecce F

473. a] ab H

474. etiam] et M U F

475. ampliasse] ampliavisse F

476. exhaustam] inexhaustam M

477. civitate] civitati M

478. ac] et M

479. convictos] coniunctos M: convinctos U^{ac}

480. aliaeque] aliae F

481. duo] divo H

482. Romanae] Romae F

483. e] et F

484. Roman se] se Roman F

485. se retulit] se re retulit M

486. iura] vita M

487. Caesar] *om.* F

488. ordinavit] ordivit M U

489. optime] optimae F

490. nulla] in illa M

491. etsi] si U^{ac}: si et U^{pc}

492. varietate] varie M U C^{ac}

493. et] *om.* U

494. inficias ibis] inficiabis M: inficias U

495. unum . . . cumulum] in unum collegit cumulum F

496. deinde] dein H

497. perinde] plode M: clade U

498. viam] tuam M: *om.* U

499. huius] cuius *U*

500. his] hiis *C*

501. in ductandis] inductantis *M*

502. singularis] singulis *M U F*

503. superioris] superiores *M U C^{ac} F H*

504. illo] ipso *U*

505. bella] *om. M U*

506. quem] quae *M U*

507. immanibus] in manibus *cH*

508. leniores] leviores *C*

509. comitate] comitare *M U*

510. ac mansuetudine] *om. U*

511. adversa] adversarios *F*

512. iusta] iuxta dixta *M U*

513. e quibus] equibus *F*

514. reliquas] reliquasque *C*

515. reservavit] servavit *M U*

516. Singulare] Simile *F*

517. quinquagies] quinquageties *F*

518. solus . . . dimicavit] *om. U*

519. nimis] nimium *U*

520. utriusque] veriusque *M*

521. superiore] superiori *o*

522. veri] viri *M U C F*

523. consequaris] consequeris *F*

POGGIO, LETTER TO LEONELLO D'ESTE

1. Poggii . . . Estensem] *as reported in U*

2. proque] pro *F*

3. ullius . . . affectionem] benivolentiam Guarini *M U o*

4. onus sibi] sibi onus *C*: onus *F*

5. Scipionem] Scipionem Mainentem *F*

6. Caesaris causam] causam Caesaris *F*

7. honor] honos *o*

8. te] *om. F*

9. rectam potest] potest rectam *U o*

10. meam defensionem] defensionem meam *F*

11. ac] a *M*

12. Florentiae . . . Novembris] *om. F*

POGGIO, DEFENSE OF ON THE EXCELLENCE
OF SCIPIO AND CAESAR

1. Poggii . . . Defensio] *instead of U's incorrect* Poggii Florentini de prae-stantia Caesaris et Scipionis ad Leonellum Estensem

2. noster Veronensis] Veronensis noster *F*

3. ascribit] ascribit et pluribus in locis, contra ac ius amicitiae nostrae requirit, in me acriter incursat, saepius me compellat U^{ac}: scribit *F*

4. me . . . scribit] *om. C*

5. amicitiae nostrae] nostrae amicitiae *M C*

6. a Guarino] agunrino *U*

7. foraneo] *om. M U C*

8. inani litigatore] litigatore inani F^{ac}

9. extimetur] existimetur *F*

10. attulerit] tulerit *F*

11. se] *om. U*

12. idem] item *M C*: ita *U o*

13. sit securus] secutus sit *F*

14. existimem non certamen] certamen existimem non *F*

15. putabit] putabat *F*

16. culpam] hanc culpam *F*

17. Ego] Egone *U^{ac}*

18. aequum] contra aequum *F*

19. te autem] autem te *F*

20. nobis est] est nobis *F*

21. fuisse Caesare] Caesare fuisse *C*

22. omnium] *om. C*

23. qua si] quasi *F*

24. et eorum] eorum et *F*

25. excellenti] excellente *F*

26. pauca exstiterint] exstiterint pauca *U M o*

27. ascensus] assensus *F*

28. gloria maxime] maxime gloria *F*

29. praestat] potest *U M· o*

30. similis Guarino] Guarino similis *F*

31. eo] eodem *F*

32. efficaciter] efficacior *F*

33. ostenderet] ostenderetur *F*

34. A. Gellius] Agellius *M U C*

35. Scipio] Scipio item *M U*

36. Haec] Hoc *o*

37. legit scriptum] *M U C o*

38. virtutibus] virtute *M*

39. admittit] admittunt *U*

40. Ciceronis de gloria] Ciceronis gloria *M*: Ciceronis *C*: de gloria Ciceronis *F*

41. pervagata] provagata *M*

42. sit] est *F*

43. Primum] primum quod *U o*

44. fuisse] esse *C*

45. rapuit] *om. F*

46. propter] per *F*

47. ovium] civium *F*

48. eius] *om. F*

49. premar] praemia *M*

50. quod] qui *M*

51. cum] cum cum *F*

52. fere] fore *F*

53. perniciem] pernitium *M*

54. hominum] *om. C*

55. vitam] vitam acta *U o*

56. admiratur] admiramur *F o*

57. indicium] iudicium *U C^{ac}*

58. non] *om. F*

59. fortitudo] fortitudine *U o*

60. alias] aliquando *F*

61. a] ad *M*

62. Quid] Quod *F*

63. temeritas] *om. F*

64. pervertit] evertit *C*

65. Caesaris et errore] et errore Caesaris *F*

66. victor] auctor *M*

67. foediori] foediore *F*

68. iure] genere iure *F*

69. Hae] Haec *U C*

70. describere] describeret *F*

71. virtutes] virtus *F*

72. conspiciat] concupiscat *F*

73. laudanda] laudandum *C*

74. auctoritate] auctore *F*

75. virtutis] veritatis *F*

76. meae epistolae] epistolae meae *M*

77. a me] autem *F*

78. ad causam accomodotis] accomodatis ad causam *F*

79. mutat] permutat *F*

80. ac] atque *F*

81. ab eo] *om. U*

82. luculentis] loculentis *M*

83. doctissimum . . . eloquentissimum] eloquentissumum atque doctissimum *F*

84. quod ad] quo *M*: quod *C*

85. remanserunt] remanserant *C*

86. contendit] contempnit *M*

87. hoc sibi] sibi hoc *F*

88. credat] credit *F*

89. doctos viros] viros doctos *F*

90. etiam] et iam *M*

91. Livius] *om. F*

92. et] *om. C*

93. mea dicta] dicta mea *M U o*

94. Deinde] Demum *F*

95. Donatum] *om. F*

96. Romani] *om. C F*

97. oratores] auctores *F*

98. fuisse] *om. U*

99. ad iurisconsultos] adiuris consultos *M*

100. si] *om. C*

101. dictum] non esse dictum *F*

102. iis] his *F*

103. vero] *om. F*

104. agetur] augetur *M*

105. testibus praeclarissimis] praeclarissimis testibus *M U o*

106. me falso] falso me *F*

107. hanc] in hoc quoque loco *F*

108. insolenti] etiam insolenti *F*

109. in deterius] ment *followed by blank space F*

110. praemium] primum U^{ac}: praemum U^{pc}

111. tertium quoque] quoque tertium *F*

112. Taciti] *om. F*

113. putat] puto *F*

114. aevi] tui *M*

115. memorabatur] memorabantur *C*

116. illa ingenia] ingenia illa *F*

117. inscitia] in Scitia *M*

118. magna . . . delatum] magna post imperium at unum delatum ingenia *M U o*

119. scripsisse me] me scripsisse *F*

120. opera] *om. F*

121. ordinariam] ordinatam *F*

122. servatam] conservatam *F*

123. pristinum] pristinitum *M*

124. gradum] statum *C*

125. aedilium quaestorum] quaestorum aedilium *F*

126. ut hunc] ut *M U C*: hunc *F*

127. viro docto] docto viro *U o*

128. populi Romano] Romani populi *C*

129. Guarinus eum] eum Guarinus *F*

130. tu] ut *F*

131. eisdem] eis *U*

132. etiam] *om. o*

133. tyranni] tyrandi *M*

134. pertulit] protulit *M U*

135. hique] atque *F*

136. tyrannide] tyrannidem *M*

137. neque] *om. F*

138. dicit post Catonem] post Catonem *M*: post Catonem refert *U o*

139. ii] *om. F*

140. Num . . . dati] *om. U*

141. ii] hi *F*

142. Unus] Solus *M U o*

143. et . . . libertatis] *om. M*: libertatis auctorem *U o*: et a Guarino indicium productum libertatis *F*

144. Romanum] etiam Romanum *F*

145. admodum ruditer] ruditer admodum *F*

146. cum] quom *F*

147. et] *om. C*

148. in ternos] internos *M C^{ac} F*

149. secum homines] homines secum *M U o*

150. Latinarum] latiorum *F*

151. imodicas] modicas *F*

152. Manilius] Marullus *o*

153. parum] patrum *F*

154. adsurrexisse] asurrexisse *M*

155. privati] perpetui *F*

156. simile] similem *M*

157. ut] *om. U o*

158. Caesarem] *om. C*

159. decem] sexaginta *o*

160. te] et *M*

161. satis . . . opinor] ut opinor satis abunde *U o*

162. tum . . . corruisse] *om. F*

163. populi Romani] Romanam *F*

164. haerere] inhaerere *U o*

165. adducit] aducit *U*: adicit *o*

166. everterunt] evertunt *M*

167. sua] sunt *M*

168. auctoritate] auctore *M*

169. auctores adhuc] adhuc auctores *F*

170. se] si *U*

171. Ego] Ego autem *C*

172. si] *om. F*

173. quos] quas *F*

174. nunc] non *F*

175. gloria] gloria in historia *o*

176. in strage] instinge *M*

177. quod] quid *o*

178. sed . . . descripsisse] *om. F*

179. etiam] et *F*

180. possunt] possint *U C o*

181. generis humani] humani generis *F*

182. fuerit] fuit *C*

183. gentiumque] gentium *U C o*

184. scelera] scelera et scelera *M*

185. a] *om. F*

186. Alexandro copulari] cupulari Alexandri *U*: copulari Alexandro *o*

187. perabsurdum] est perabsurdum *C*

188. qui] cui *M U C*

189. Marios aequabat] aequebat *F*

190. iis] his *F*

191. uni] uno *C F*

192. et suum] suum et *F*

193. indolem virtutis] virtutis indolem *F*

194. ii] hi *F*

195. nosset] noscet *F*

196. tute] tu *F*

197. fatebere] fatebre *C*

198. abibis] abilis *M*

199. conferam] paene conferam *F*

200. admodum admirari] admirari *U o*: admodum *F*

201. dedidicisse] didicisse *M*: dedicisse *U o*

202. et dum] dum enim *U o*

203. iis] his *F*

204. fieri posse] posse fieri *F*

205. si] *om. F*

206. At] Ac *M*

207. A. Gellius] Agellius *M U C*^{ac}

208. depiribat] deperiebat *U*

209. ea] eo *U*

210. ducturum] dicturum *U*

211. his] hiis C

212. navibus] in navibus F

213. mioparone] in oparone M

214. Nonius] Nunius M

215. me] non M

216. Num] Non F

217. hostium] histium M

218. in rusticorum coetu] *om.* M U *o*

219. cedentem] credentem M

220. in] *om.* C

221. et] *om.* F

222. porticus] *om.* C

223. enim] *om.* C

224. emendicata] mendicata F

225. eviscerationem] eius scelerationem M: eius orationem F

226. a] *om.* F

227. imperata] imparata F

228. detractarent] decertarent F

229. primo] ipso F

230. uno] uni *o*

231. bellorum] *om.* F

232. sibi] *om.* M U *o*

233. censeat praeferendum] conferendum C

234. prudentissime] peritissime M

235. dirae] durae C

236. artis] arctis M F

237. desipere] despicere F

238. reseratae] reserare M: reservatae U^{ac}

239. minime] minimo *M*

240. corruperit] corrupit *F*

241. fuisset] fuisse *M*

242. intentus] intentum *U*

243. perditis] proditis *U o*

244. inquit] in inquit *M*

245. ipsum] eum *M*

246. superiore] superiori *F o*

247. constitisse] se constituisse *F*

248. ominati] ominanti *C*

249. exemplo sunt] exemplo sunt *C*: sunt extemplo *F^{ac}*: ex templo sunt *o*

250. tacita] tanta *C*

251. rursus] rursum *M o*

252. ratio] *om. M*

253. non veris] *om. M*

254. e] a *F*

255. Caesari concessa sunt] concessa sunt Caesaris *C*

256. probet] praebet *M*

257. iis] his *F*

258. Ti. Nero] Ti. Neronis *U^{ac}*: enim vero *F*

259. additis] *om. M*

260. pedibus dixisset] dixisset pedibus *U o*

261. quid] quit *M*

262. ad Atticum] adacticum *M*

263. sententiam putat] putat sententiam *U M*

264. Ergo] Ego *U*

265. mutarunt] immutarunt *U o*

266. illos] *om. F*

267. reddit] redigit *F*

268. vero] *om. M U*

269. aliquid] *om. U*

270. esset] esse *M*

271. dubitantem] dubitabat *F*

272. scripserim] scripserint *M*

273. An qui] Atqui *F*

274. carcerem in] carceris *M U*

275. vitae] *om. C*

276. Guarinum] Guarini *U*

277. quandoque magis] magis quandoque *U o*

278. servasset] servasset a morte *U^{ac} o*

279. servando] servandos *o*

280. et] *om. o*

281. ii] his *F^{ac}*: hi *F^{pc}*

282. omnium] *om. U F o*

283. verberibus] xiberibus *F*

284. diros] adiros *M*: ad diros *U*: ad duros *o*

285. cruciatus] cruciatos *o*

286. Hos] Hoc *M*

287. advertit] animadvertit *F*

288. sibi fortasse] fortasse sibi *U o*: sibi forte *F^{ac}*

289. ut calumniatur] non calumnianter *F*

290. quid] ego qui *F*

291. extimationem] existimationem *F*

292. suas] *om. U*

293. ego de me] de me ego *F*

294. inquit] ait *C*

295. ausculta] abstulta *M*

296. qui potius] potius qui *F*

297. scaevam] saevam *M U C o*

298. extimationem] existimationem *F*

299. defendit adversos suos] adversus suos defendit *F*

300. astans] adstans *o*

301. vivum] unum *o*

302. laudatione] laude *F*

303. aut . . . permotus] aut dicendi facultate permotus *U*^{ac}: permotus aut dicendi facilitate *F*^{ac}

304. fulctus] flucitus *F*

305. lacessere] licessere *M*

306. obloquendi] eloquendi *F*

307. portiunculam] particulam *F*

308. te] et *M*

309. esse] ego *F*

310. civibus semper] semper civibus *F*

311. mecum ceteri] ceteri mecum *F*

312. flagitia] flagella *F*

313. victoris Caesaris] victoris *U o*: Caesaris victoris *F*

314. mavis] maius *M*

315. nolui] volui *M U*

316. liberae civitatis] civitatis liberae *F*

317. isto] illo *M*

318. tuo quoque] tuoque *C*

319. fuerit] fuerat *C*

320. consilio ratione] ratione consilio *F*

321. singulari] singularem *F*

322. omnibus in locis Catonem] Catonem omnibus in locis *M U o*

323. admiror] admodum admiror *F*

324. strenuo] strenua *M*^{pc}: strenue *M*^{ac}

325. virtute] de virtute *U o*

326. pudore] de pudore *U o*

327. abstinentia] de abstinentia *U o*

328. fecerint] fuerint *F*

329. significans] *om. F*

330. laudes] laudem *F*

331. longius] logius *C*

332. conferunt] conferuntur *M*: conferant *F*

333. Qui enim fuerunt hi] Inde *F*

334. hostium copiae] copiae hostium *C*

335. praeteritur] praeterit *F*

336. a Guarino] *om. F*

337. ne] nae *F*

338. sua] *om. F*

339. atque] *om. M U o*

340. timens] totiens *F*

341. nunquam castra] aciem armatam nunquam *U o*

342. more] amore *M*

343. qua] quo *F*

344. probare] probat *U*

345. iis] his *F*

346. vero] *om. F*

347. ne] ut *C F*

348. dicam leviter] leviter dicam *F*

349. fuisse] verba fuisse *M*

350. paene] poene *F*

351. parcit] pepercit *F*

352. recusabant] accusabant *F*

353. bona] *om. F*

354. plures] plura *C*

355. dicunt] dicant *F*

356. visus] est visus *U C o*

357. formas] formam *C*

358. conspexerit] conspexit *U C o*

359. nulla] tamen nulla *C*

360. hanc] ob hanc *F*

361. sibi] *om. M*

362. suam] *om. C*

363. tam] tot *C*

364. dixisset] duxisset *F*

365. heteros horos] eteros horos *M*: etheros horos *U*: etheros choros *U^{ac}*: ἕτερος ὅρος *F*

366. Lydi a] Lidia *U^{ac}*: Lidii *U^{pc}*

367. nolo] volo *U o*

368. ab . . . magis] *om. C*

369. immutata] mutata *F*

370. Pensaurum] Pensarum *M*

371. nomine] ratione *F*

372. neque] atque *C*

373. opus Graeco testimonio] Graeco testimonio opus *F*

374. suum] summum *o*

375. creandis] servandis *C*

376. adulatorem Dionem] Dionem adulatorem *C*

377. adseclam] assedam *M*: secula *F*

378. gesta . . . Romanorum] *om.* U: gesta testantur. Hic praeponit gesta Romanorum regum F

379. iis] his F

380. suspectiores] suspiciosiores M U o: suspiciores C

381. ducit] dicit F

382. gloria et laude] laude et gloria M U o

383. non] hoc non M

384. carus esse] esse carus F

385. nec valebit] ne valebit M: valebitve U o

386. ipsi] *om.* F

387. ullam] nullam F

388. Graecus] Guarinus U o: *om.* F

389. ipse] et ipse F

390. cum] quom F

391. dixit] dicit U o

392. adserat] afferat F

393. scilicet] *om.* o

394. textu] testu o

395. Si] Sed F

396. intelligit] non intelligit F

397. verbum] verum F

398. Scipionem] *om.* F

399. est haec] haec est M

400. a] *om.* F

401. mentem] memoriam M: sententiam U o

402. inscius] inscitia M U o

403. populatae] popularem F

404. vel] *om.* F

405. iis] his F

406. gessissent] gessisset *F*

407. delessent] delesset *M U*: dell delesset *U^{ac}*

408. diruissent] diruisset *M U*

409. solida et vera sit] sit solida et vera *F*

410. virtute] et virtute *o*

411. meae] meae. VI Kl Octobris MCCCC XLIIII Io de Sanggans scripsit etc. *M*: meae. Finis *Uh*

DEL MONTE, *LETTER TO POGGIO BRACCIOLINI*

1. de Monte] *om. V*

2. quietis] ocii *V*: officii *f*

3. Veronensi] Veronense *C*

4. habitam] habitam {quam cum superioribus mensibus ad me misisses meumque postulasses de illa iudicium, per occupationes perfecte non potueram ac propterea meam de ipsa sententiam ad te scribere distuli. Nunc autem, cum per quietem a rebus publicis liceret [*f*: fieret], attente admodum legi ac diligenter perlegi.} *V*

5. esset ductus] esset tuque meum postulasses de illo iudicium, etsi per occupationes perfecte legere ac singula, ut decebat, considerare non possem, ductus *V*

6. tamen] tamen rei novitate et *V*

7. percurream. Legi itaque] percurream Nunc vero, cum per quietem a rebus publicis mihi licere animadverti, legi *V*

8. epistulam tuam] epistulam tuam ad Scipionem Ferrariensem *V*

9. oppugnationibus] oppugnantibus *V*

10. scribere] *obliterated by damp in C*

11. ac quicquid . . . litteris commendare] *added in margin by del Monte in C*: ac quicquid . . . litteris {deferre} commendare *V*

12. ingenii] ingenium *f*

13. copiosamque] copiosamque et ornatam *V*

14. ac . . . venustatem] *om.* V

15. dolere] dolere cum vidi V

16. medius fidius] certe V

17. a primis . . . unguiculis] *om.* V

18. aut sermonibus] et orationibus V

19. instar boum] *om.* V

20. paene] porro V

21. putabat] esse sentiebat V

22. te] te pro Caesaris dignitate V

23. immitem Caesaris defensionem] contumeliosam defensionem V

24. descripsisti] scripsisti V

25. Aenean] eneam C V

26. voluisse] *om.* V

27. oratoriae] rhetoricae V

28. suscepi] suscepi, bonis me praeterea moribus instruxit V

29. intellegam] sciam V

30. praeceptores] scriptores *f*

31. a quibus] qui nos V

32. artibus] artibus et egregiis moribus V

33. eruditi simus] erudierunt V

34. quemadmodum] sic V

35. Itaque . . . diligo] *om.* C

36. multo magis] *om.* V

37. me] me multo maiora V

38. debet] debent C

39. boni] boni officium V

40. et esse . . . haberi] agere volumus et implere V

41. inquit] ut inquit V

42. vos] nos *f*

43. Et quanquam . . . rescribere] *om.* C

44. te invadit] te ultro provocat et invadit V

45. atque aggreditur . . . nititur] nihilque tale timentem aggreditur V

46. loquendi audacia] voce V

47. amicitiae] benivolentiae V

48. reprobat] improbat V

49. in te . . . ductor] velut caesarianarum legionum ductor adversum te V

50. laudandi] extollendi V

51. Tu enim] Nam V

52. viventis] inventis *f*

53. gloriam . . . violasti] gloriam laesisti aut V

54. prudentia] prudentia et modestia V

55. esse . . . velim] putes V

56. iniurias] iniurias magnopere V

57. Tradidi] Dedi V

58. vestram] nostram *f*

59. priscos] veteres V

60. religionis veritas] religio V

61. eam] libellum V

62. scribi] dictari V

63. diebus rogatus] diebus cum ad eum rediissem rogatus V

64. ob eam . . . censeo] eos [*f:* vos] censeo gloria immortali V

65. erant] videbantur V

66. nostraeque . . . data] magnaque nostrae aetatis hominibus horum exemplo [*f omits* horum exemplo] spes data V

67. propius] proprius V

68. mordacem . . . iudico] Guarinum magna reprehensione dignum iudico, quod in nulla impugnationis suae parte iniurias contumelias et
maledicta in Poggium praetermisit *V*

69. antea] *om. V*

70. vester] *om. V*

71. agunt] *sic in C V for Cicero's* alunt

72. apprime est eruditus] per omnem aetatem operam dedit *V*

73. vendicasse] usurpasse *V*

74. quod secus . . . Scipionem] *om. V*

75. atque clarissimum] *om. V*

76. tam acriter] tam acriter tam ignominiose *V*

77. plerumque] interdum *V*

78. laetitiamque recipio] laetitiamque [*f:* laetitiam] suscipio *V*

79. talem . . . tam] talem tamque *V*

80. et opinionis] *om. V*

81. deorum] divina *V*

82. a diis immortalibus] ab immortali Deo *V*

83. quam] *om. V*

84. devictae civitates] civitates devictae [*f:* devinctae] *V*

85. bonum . . . arguunt] hominem probant esse virtuosum *V*

86. ductus] *om. V*

87. sane] *om. V*

88. tacitum . . . fuisse] tacitum ei subirasci solere *V*

89. deductum esse] venisse *V*

90. tam nefarium] tam scelestum, tam nefarium *V*

91. tantopere laudaret] tanto studio extolleret ac laudaret *V*

92. existimare] iudicare *V*

93. et cum] cumque *V*

94. plura quoque] pluraque *f*

95. comperi] invenire potui *V*

96. quavis] ulla vera *V*

97. Guarinus] *om. V*

98. descripta] depicta inducere solent *V*

99. studio . . . viribus] cura et diligentia *V*

100. extollere] Guarinus describere *V*

101. quin] nam *V*

102. quae] quae ipse *V*

103. tam] adeo vere *V*

104. tamque . . . atque] et *V*

105. ceteris omnibus] multis *V*

106. existit] extitit *f*

107. liberare conatus est] liberavit *V*

108. ego] ego interdum *V*

109. inducunt] inducere solent *V*

110. tum] tum vero *V*

111. huiusmodi] istiusmodi *V*

112. multis virtutibus exornatum] virtutibus decoratum *V*

113. alii item alios] *om. f*

114. scribens] loquens *V*

115. hominem]*om.* C

116. Quae feritas? Quae rabies] Quae dementia? Quae mentis alienatio? *V*

117. constantia] modestia *V*

118. solum] praeter Ciceronem *V*

119. summum . . . iudicandum est] nefas iudicabitur *V*

120. scripta confundit] fundamenta subvertit. *V*

121. interdum] libenter *om. f*

122. tertio] quarto *V*

123. innumerabilibus] multis magnisque *V*

124. ita] ita ad verbum *V*

125. ergo] igitur *V*

126. mirabilisque] admirabilisque *V*

127. Quid ad haec] Haec ille. Ad quae quid *V*

128. Guarinus?] Guarinus? {Quid simile de Caesare suo adducet?} Quem tantae auctoritatis testem in iudicium vocabit? *V*

129. sapientibus] iudicantibus debent *V*

130. rem] rem nostram *V*

131. fons . . . origo] auctor fuit *V*

132. saevus] *om. V*

133. belli] secundi belli *V*

134. imperator] hostis *V*

135. civis] vir *f*

136. extinctus] paene extinctus *V*

137. turbulentis] *om. V*

138. ducta] ducta et multis coinquinata sceleribus. *V*

139. in se] *om. C*

140. apud . . . delegerit] elegerit *V*

141. detentus] adductus *V*

142. incolumitate] salute *V*

143. quibus fundamentis] quo fundamento *V*

144. auctoribus] auctoritatibus *V*

145. qui] quicumque *V*

146. fortasse] forsitan *V*

147. quibus . . . adductus est] qui . . . adduxerunt *V*

148. Negabitne] Negarene potest *V*

149. arma] ostilia arma *V*

150. Thessaliae] pharsalicos *V*

151. imperatores] *om. V*

152. pro suae libito voluntatis] pro libito *V*

153. maximum] magnum *V*

154. abstulisse] subtraxisse *V*

155. enim] *om. V*

156. Cuius quidem . . . Cicero] Quod Ciceronis quoque testimonio convincitur, qui Caesaris bellum adversus Pompeium nefarium dicit fuisse patriae et perniciosum libertati *V*

157. alibi contra] adversus *V*

158. haec . . . reliquit] inquit *V*

159. subvertendique . . . libertatem] *om. C*

160. cum] {Et} cum *V*

161. scripta] paulo antea dicta *V*

162. teste] teste sane *V*

163. manifeste demonstrent] evidenter ostendant *V*

164. fuisse . . . futuram] aeternam esse potuisse Romanorum rem publicam *V*

165. cupiditas] cupido *V*

166. laudare] extollere ac laudare. *V*

167. disserentem] disputantem *V*

168. Caesarem . . . affirmaturum] regem fuisse Caesarem ulla ratione dicturum *V*

169. necessitate] necessitate aut utilitate publica *V*

170. sola voluntate] libidine et praecipitatione *V*

171. omnis . . . Aristotele] ut docet Aristoteles omnis *V*

172. tormenta et cruciatus] tormenta, vincula, cruciatus et coetera eiusmodi *V*

173. quae] quae ut inquit Cicero *V*

174. certe] certa [*sic*] C

175. Quo certa . . . dicendum est] Ex his tyrannum fuisse Caesarem quis non videt? V

176. desinit] desunt V

177. fortasse] forsitan V

178. in patriam] *om.* V

179. spe] spem C

180. litteris et nuntiis et legatis] litteris et nuntiis V

181. tranquillum] tranquillorum V

182. et factionibus] *om.* V

183. Confiteamur . . . impedivisse] Confiteamur Pompeium impedivisse ne in senatu eius litterae legerentur V

184. Pompeio] Pompeius *f*

185. in se ipso] ipse primus V

186. demonstrasset] ostendisset V

187. insuper] praeterea V

188. quomodo] quonam modo V

189. Ad quam] Cum ad eam V

190. sexto] quarto *f*

191. ac] aut *f*

192. et atrocissimas] *om.* V

193. iniurias . . . calumnias] iniurias ac persecutiones V

194. perpeti] pati V

195. ornaverat] decoraverat V

196. sane] profecto V

197. effecerunt] reddiderunt V

198. Multo sane praeclarius] *om.* V

199. imperator . . . bello] cum imperator bello V

200. esset a Xerxe . . . cerneret] *om.* C

201. populi . . . regnaret] populum Romanum regeret *V*

202. laude] omni laude *V*

203. cum eo] cum virtute ac rebus pro patriae salute feliciter gestis eo *V*

204. auctores] amatores *f*

205. commoditate] voluntate *V*

206. contemptis . . . receperunt] *om. C*

207. libertatem eius] excellentiam patriae *C*

208. nullis iniuriis] nulla dominandi ambitione *V*

209. cupiditate . . . induci] cupiditate adduci *V*

210. libertatem] patriae libertatem *V*

211. omniumque . . . reprobatum] *om. f*

212. magnum] egregium *V*

213. verba] ab eo scripta *V*

214. ab eo . . . fuisse] eum scripsisse *C*

215. magnum . . . pondus] auctoritati suae plurimum detrahunt *C*

216. Caesar] *om. C*

217. concitaverit] excitaverit *V*

218. ac breviter] *om. V*

219. importasse] attulisse *V*

220. Quibus rebus] Quibus in rebus *f*

221. in curiam] *om. V*

222. factum iudicatur] factum {videtur} iudicatur *V*

223. efferre conatur] effert *V*

224. damnosam] perniciosam *V*

225. iustissimum . . . ferentem] iustissimum semper publicae utilitati inservientem *V*

226. redarguere] laudandi Caesaris immoderato studio redarguere *V*

227. extollendus . . . laudandus] extollendus *f*

228. creari] creare *f*

229. insequendus] insectandus *V*

230. ac praestantissimum] *om. V*

231. suo consulatu] *om. V*

232. libero] liberi *f*

233. consul] imperator *V*

234. consulatu] rebus gestis *V*

235. ulteriora scribendi] *om. V*

236. atque amplificatum est] ditatum ac repletum est *V*

237. impletum] repletum *V*

238. Cui cum . . . abscede] *om. V*

239. contulit] contulisset *V*

240. quibus portas . . . Metellus abiit] eisque ut portas effringerent imperavit. O bonum civem! O virum laude dignum, qui pecuniam publicam surripuit, ut adversus rem publicam ductaret exercitum! *V*

241. Quae] Quaenam *V*

242. facturum] factum *f*

243. patiatur] patiatur obsecro *V*

244. subactis] in potentiam redactis *V*

245. magnitudinem] spem *C*

246. industriae meae] ingenioli mei *V*

247. tanquam] veluti *V*

248. Romani imperii] *om. f*

249. extollit] extollit pace eius loquor *V*

250. Ad id . . . quod] Accedit ad [*f supplies:* hoc] naturalis quaedam vis et innata mihi libertatis conservandae cupiditas cum enim *V*

251. ex ea civitate] ex ea ^Venetiarum^ civitate *V*

252. duxi] ducam *V*

253. quasi mundus alter] *om. V*

254. tantum] *om. V*

255. et gloria] *om. V*

256. servituti] potestati *V*

257. facile demonstrat] declarat *V*

258. extinguendae] extinguendae aut opprimendae *V*

259. totiens debellatum est] *om. V*

260. nedum . . . sed] *om. C*

261. oppressa est] opprimitur *V*

262. cuiquam mirum] mirum Guarino aut cuipiam *V*

263. gravissimumque . . . debeo] *om. V*

264. acerbissimum] acerbissimum quietis et pacis impatientem *V*

265. ducem] *om. ƒ*

266. Sed iam . . . prosequamur] *om. C*

267. omnes] *om. V*

268. decantent] celebrent *V*

269. responsurum] res pensurum *ƒ*

270. mirum in modum . . . existimavi] apud Guarinum decantare solebam, manifeste declarant. Hi sunt eiusmodi *V*

271. namque] siquidem *V*

272. quot scelera . . . agmina] scelera flagitia stupra quoque et adulteria regio dominatu *V*

273. ductus . . . quodam] ductus generosi anima ardenti *V*

274. impiissimos] *om. V*

275. fugavit] fugavit et regium nomen una cum potestate extinxit *V*

276. His tot . . . beneficiis] Hoc tanto in patriam beneficio *V*

277. quia] quo *V*

278. opto] cupio *V*

279. quamobrem] cur *V*

280. qui vehementi . . . servitute] qui Caesaris libidinem ac tyrannidem in dies crescere intuentes vehementi liberandae patriae a tam perniciosa servitute V

281. eum] Caesarem V

282. intererat] ad opprimendam libertatem intererat V

283. vendicaret] usurparet V

284. dicioni] dictioni C V

285. interverterentur] non tam regerentur quam perverterentur V

286. perspicere] animadvertere V

287. repellendi] effugandi V

288. prius inauditam imperii] ab eo institutam regiam V

289. regio . . . subiecta fuit] reges in urbe regnaverunt. Fertur enim Romae regnatum fuisse ab urbe condita usque ad liberatam annos ducentos quadraginta quatuor V

290. tyrannidi subicere non expavit] tyrannidi ac potestati subiecit V

291. sumpsisse fertur] accepit V

292. dominandi cupiditate extinxit] extinxit vel saltem debilitavit. Tarquinius tunc regnavit cum Romae licebat regnare, Caesar cum nullo pacto liceret. V

293. regum tyrannidem] regiam potestatem V

294. ut ex superiorbus facile apparere possunt] superiora facile demonstrant V

295. ampliori] maiori V

296. laudandi] extollendi V

297. eo] tam V

298. optimorum civium] optimorum ac fortissimorum civium V

299. extollere] extollere ac laudare V

300. etiam si . . . centum] om. V

301. existimet] existimet quamvis talia sint quae probatione non egeant V

302. sparsa in unum] dispersa V

303. iudicium] iudicium Guarinus *V*

304. tantis laudibus] *om. V*

305. Quodsi] Etsi *f*

306. Manlius] Mallius *V*

307. propter . . . regnantem] *om. V*

308. Cicero] *om. C*

309. grande . . . exhorruit] in magnum quendam errorem videtur incidisse *V*

310. sanctum] *om. V*

311. in hanc . . . diem] *om. V*

312. omnes . . . veneratione] maxima *V*

313. quae mediusfidius . . . potui] quae in eius libello continentur ea hic repetere ideo nolui *V*

314. iustitiae et continentiae et integritatis] continentiae et integritatis *V*

315. extinguere] quasi quadam densissima nebula obfuscare *V*

316. facere . . . arbitror] *om. V*

317. et coniurationum] *om. V*

318. evertendam rem publicam] subversionem rei publicae secuturam *V*

319. quibus in multis . . . extitit] *om. V*

320. dominandi] *om. V*

321. O magnam . . . caecitatem] *om. V*

322. Quorsum . . . oratio?] Quorsum labitur Guarinus? *V*

323. ut] quonam modo *V*

324. sanctum] {sanctum} *V*

325. severum, constantem] severum, integrum, constantem *V*

326. nullis] *om. C*

327. tam turpiter . . . sit] turpiter ac ignominiose appellare ausus est *V*

328. Guarinus quod . . . praeclarus] Guarinus Catonem fuisse semper in sermone veracem, in iudicio iustum, in consilio providum, constantem in

proposito, conspicuum in bonitate, in universa morum gravitate praeclarum *V*

329. vimque . . . incepta] *om. V*

330. ut usque . . . perraro] *om. V*

331. sed cum . . . implacabilis] *om. V*

332. non locorum opportunitas] *om. V*

333. vendicat] solet vendicare *V*

334. Maiestas vero . . . conferebat] *om. V*

335. impendens] impedens *f*

336. nullis muneribus . . . est] *om. V*

337. colligationesque] conspirationesque *V*

338. velut paci . . . detestatus est] praesertim potentum velut rei publicae perniciosas semper damnavit *V*

339. In senatum . . . abibat] *om. V*

340. nisi in initio] nisi parvus esset *V*

341. Romae] apud Romanos *V*

342. suisque . . . tantopere] ausibus tanto studio *V*

343. honorari] observari *V*

344. Pompeii vexilla . . . observasse] *om. V*

345. Sed] *om. C*

346. omnes] *om. C*

347. siccareturque . . . complecti] *om. V*

348. vincit . . . confundit] succumbere causa facit *V*

349. his tribus versibus] virtutes in angustum quendam locum *V*

350. optimum ac praestantissimum] virum *V*

351. quemadmodum . . . apparet] *om. V*

352. qui omnes . . . sentiunt] scriptorum *V*

353. extollere . . . scriptum est] tot laudibus prosequi. De quo idem poeta sic cecinit *V*

354. Caesar in] Caesar C

355. divinum . . . immaculatum] rectum V

356. defensorem] auctorem V

357. virtutesque . . . permutare] inter quos quantum distet vel superiora de utroque Lucani carmina ostendunt evidenter. Sed neque debuit Guarinus studio laudandi Caesaris et vituperandi Catonis huius tanti viri virtutes in vitiorum nomina commutare. V

358. dicentes . . . depelli] om. V

359. mira quadam . . . scriptis] nescio qua contraria commutatione V

360. faciam . . . epistolae] om. f

361. sentiat] sentiat scribat dicat V

362. sane eruditissimus et eloquentissimus] doctissimus V

363. libet] libet sibique de Caesaris laudibus quantum vult blandiatur V

364. quae ab omnibus . . . deviat] quoniam a clarissimis auctoribus qui ante nos scripserunt plurimum adversatur V

365. praesertim . . . pacto] accedit quod nulla ratione V

366. eloquentiae . . . vim] eloquentiae aut ingenii vim V

367. ea in re Carneadem . . . sustulit] om. V

368. ut ait Lactantius] om. V

369. firma et stabilis] firma stabilis ac vera V

370. in utramque . . . disserendo] falsa pro veris et iniusta pro iustis et mala pro bonis probabiliter defendendo V

371. videtur] videtur non praecipuae cuiusdam artis, non excelsi ingenii V

372. neque . . . pollet] om. V

373. quodam] quadam [sic] C

374. quasi virtutum nube . . . posse] tegere et quod maius est quadam virtutum specie decorum ac pulchrum et formosum reddere idque multis V

375. indicium est] opus esse censendum est V

376. concertatione rectissimum] concertatione in hoc litterato certamine iudicium, et quidem rectissimum

377. neque ullius . . . sapiunt] *om.* V

378. praefers] praeferendum statuis V

379. aliaque innumerabilia . . . reddunt] aliaque pene innumera flagitia cunctis debent abhominabilem reddere. V

380. nullis . . . stimulis] nemine urgente V

381. sententiarum gravitate] rerum copia V

382. nihil dubitationis . . . disceptatum est] omnem materiam praecideris nihilque V

383. resistens . . . dimicatione] in suscepta a te semel iusta causa perstitisti, ac tandem ex ea dimicatione V

384. tibi] huius litis V

385. Maximum . . . sententia] Plurimi enim facio tanti viri sententiam V

386. eius ad te . . . videam] sciam quale fuerit ipsius iudicium V

387. humanitatem] humanitatem et sapientiam V

388. rei] nostrae rei V

389. et occupationibus] ac periculis V

390. Brixiensi . . . fuerit] Brixiensi {. . ..} tentus fuerit C

391. non praetermisit] nulla ratione debuerit praetermittere V

392. pluribus] quibusdam C

393. homines *corrected by del Monte over an erasure that probably read* barbaros C

394. tradidisse . . . innotesceret] dedisse qui inter hanc barbariem aliquid de latinae linguae lepore vel summis labiis degustarunt quosque magnum tenet desiderium has artes atque haec humanitatis studia perdiscendi ut tuae virtutis gloria etiam in hisce mundi finibus cognosceretur cognita celebraretur V

395. Vale . . . meae] *om.* f Vale . . . meae tecum enim familiarissime locutus sum. Iterum vale V

POGGIO, *ON THE UNHAPPINESS OF LEADERS*

1. AD . . . FELICITER] AD DOCTISSIMUM ET CLARISSIMUM VIRUM THOMAM DE SEREÇANO POGGII FLORENTINI DE INFELICITATE PRINCIPUM LIBER INCIPIT L. AD DOCTISSIMUM VIRUM THOMAM DE SEREÇANO POGGII FLORENTINI DE INFELICITATE PRINCIPUM LIBER INCIPIT *Oa*: Ad clarissimum virum Thomam de zeresano Poggii Florentini de infelicitate principum liber incipit. Feliciter lege *Ob*: Pogii de infelicitatibus principum ad clarissimum virum Thomam zarzanensem liber incipit qui nunc ad Nicolaum V pontificem maximum *Vc*: *No headings Od Za. For the headings in the other MSS, see further Canfora 1998, cxlvii–cxlix. According to him, of the two other* ζ *MSS, B has* Liber de principum infelicitate *and W* Ad doctissimum et clarissimum virum Thomam de Sarezano Pogii Florentini de infelicitate principum liber incipit feliciter. *The titles reported are extremely diverse, but usually distinguish—at the very least by the use of decorated capitals and the capitalization of the first line or two—between the prefatory letter to Thomas and the dialogue itself (which I have done here, numbering the dedication letter's paragraphs separately from the text of the dialogue, though Canfora does not do this in his edition). The consensus of selected MSS, where they preserve titles, seems to suggest that A probably had the heading* Ad doctissimum et clarissimum virum Thomam de Serezano Poggii Florentini de infelicitate principum liber incipit feliciter.

2. et] ut *Oa*

3. nil] nihil *L*: nichil *Vc*

4. quibus . . . iter] quibus nihil est pensi virtutis nitet *Za*: *om. L*

5. parent] patent *Oa*

6. arbitratur] arbitrantur *Vc*: arbitramur *L Vg*

7. ullam] nullam *Oa*

8. studia] studium *Od*

9. tribueretur] tribuetur *Oa*

10. Nicolaum Nicolum] Nicholaum Nicoli *Ob*: Nicolaum *Od*: Nicholaum *Za*

11. virum] *om. Ob*

12. paululum] paulum *L Oa*

13. paulo] palum *corr. in margin to* parum *Oa*

14. e] *om. Oa*

15. sedes tanquam novi coloni quaerere] tanquam novi coloni sedes quaerere *Ob*

16. laboris] et laboris *Oa*

17. tum] cum *Oa*: quum *Vc*

18. ab his nostris . . . constitutos] *Canfora:* ab his nostris . . . ⟨constrictis⟩ constitutos *Mariotti (cf. Sen. Dial. 1.4.16: ipsa enim vexatione constringitur):* ab his nostris censibus . . . constitutos *Martelli:* ab hac nostra . . . constitutos *Rizzo:* ab his nostris . . . constitutis *Tateo*

19. et] ac *Oa*

20. et qui] et item qui *Ob*

21. tum] cum *Oa Ob Od*: quum *Vc*

22. aulas] aurales *Vc*: aulares *Ob Od*

23. ut aiunt *after* Formicis, *corr. by dots beneath and* ut aiunt *written also after* Indicis *Oa*

24. felicitatis] *om. Oa*

25. his] iis *Oa Od*

26. ars] res *Oa*

27. nostros] vestros *Ob*

28. ergastulis] ergastolis *Canfora*

29. alios . . . Plures quoque] alios Latinae linguae auctores praeclaros restituit nobis. Plures quoque *L*^(corr. Poggio) *Od Vc*: alios linguae Latinae auctores praeclaros restituit nobis. Pluraque *Oa Ob Za: om. L*

30. praeclarissimos illos] illos preclarissimos *Ob*

31. nostris] ipsis *Ob*

32. Facillime] facile *Ob*

33. existimaram] existimaveram *Od Za*: existimarem *Vc*: extimaram *L*

34. inter homines versatur] versatur inter homines *Ob*

35. honesti] honesto *Oa*

36. aestimationem] extimationem (*corr. to* estimationem) *L*: estimationem *Od*: estimacionem *Oa Ob Vc*: existimationem *Za*

37. occulto] occultis *Oa*

38. in eam partem declinare] in eam declinare partem *Ob*

39. in diem me reddidit] in diem me reddit *Ob Od Vc*: me in diem reddidit *L*

40. urgetur] urgentur *L*

41. vestros] nostros *Ob*

42. aestimationem] extimationem *Oa Ob Od Vc Za*: existimationem *L*

43. plures] *om. Ob*

44. Nicolae] *om. Ob*

45. Quomodo enim viro doctissimo licet dicere eos esse felices] *om. Ob*

46. dummodo] *om. Ob*

47. nuncup⟨av⟩eris] nuncuperis *L Oa Od Za*: appelles *Ob*: nuncupes *Vc*

48. rerum licentia] licentia rerum *Ob*

49. quoque] *om. Ob*

50. aestimare] extimare *L Oa Ob Od Za*: *om. Vc*

51. praeterea] propterea *Oa Od*

52. esse oporteat] esse oporteant *Ob*: oporteat esse *Oa Vc*

53. existimo esse credendum] esse credendum existimo *Ob*

54. inquit nuper] nuper inquit *Ob*

55. in quibus] in quis *L Oa*

56. vita eorum] eorum vita *Ob*

57. habitos] habitos esse *Oa*

58. Nam si veteri] Nam si vetere *Za*: Nam veteris *L*$^{corr.}$: Nam veteri *L*^{ac} Canfora

Canfora claims the insertion of si belongs to his α group of MSS, but it is also there in Za, which is one of his ζ MS. Poggio certainly liked the formulation nam si (see paragraphs 3, 4, 18 [twice], 20, and 29). But he also uses the adjective vetus

in the ablative twice more in a similar phrase (paragraphs 12 veteri proverbio *and 28* veteri sententia), *so that it seems better to reject* veteris.

59. hoc tantum natura] hec tantum natura *Vc*: hec natura tantum *Za*: tantum hoc natura *L*

60. facillime] facile *Ob*

61. evehantur] evehuntur *Oa Vc*

62. In Aureliani vita] in Aureliam vitam *Oa Vc*: in Aureliam ita *Ob Od*

63. mimico unico *Ob*: inimico unico *Od Vc Za*: numico unico *Oa*: mimico uno *L*

Canfora cxxii prefers L's uno *here, on the grounds that it is the reading of Poggio's source (Historia Augusta) as written out by Poggio himself in Florence, Biblioteca Riccardiana MS 551. But the consensus of selected MSS suggests rather that Poggio was aiming for a smoother phrasing, with a jingle echoing* mimico, *and L has (perhaps influenced by the* HA *passage) normalized it to* uno.

64. malos principes] principes malos *Oa*

65. debet] *Hist. Aug. has* debeat *here, which we might have expected rather than* debet, *the reading of the consensus of the MSS.*

66. omnis aetas] etas omnis *Ob*

67. ascendet] ascendit *Oa*

68. satis] fas *Oa*

69. fiunt] sunt *Oa*

70. praeterea] propterea *Oa*

71. capti] *om. Oa Vc*

72. principes donant] princeps donat *Oa Od*

73. conveniunt] convenerint *Oa*

74. insitus . . . appetitus] insitus . . . appetitio *L Oa Vc Za*: insita . . . appetitio *Ob Od*

The incorrect gender of the adjective in L Oa Vc Za suggests that Poggio wrote appetitus *originally, but a scribe let his eye slip a few lines down to* eius *appetitio. Oa Ob then correct the gender of the adjective from the incorrect masculine. The widespread acceptance of* insitus . . . appetitio *suggests, since Poggio is*

highly unlikely to have written it, that this shared error derives from A², the copy Poggio commissioned from his autograph.

75. mala appellari] appellari mala *Ob*

76. venereorumque] venenorumque *L*

77. iis potius] potius hijs *Ob*

78. quid ad virtutum exercitia propensius] *om. Oa*

79. bene agendi] beneagendi *L*: beneagere *Od*

80. qui fuerint, in nostris literis non continentur] qui fuerint in nostris literis eruditi, qui voluptatibus non contineantur *BW (according to Canfora)*: eruditi non contineantur *Za (omits qui voluptatibus)*

81. esse videantur] iudicantur *Ob*

82. omnes debeant infelices] debeant omnes infelices *Oa*

83. extiterint] extiterunt *Oa Ob Od*

84. contingit] contigit *Oa Ob Od*

85. inventi tamen longo intervallo sunt] inventi sunt tamen longo intervallo *Ob*

86. paulum] paulo *Canfora*

87. desciscerent] disciscerent *L Oa Za*: discisserent *Ob*: dissererent *Od*

88. vero] non *Oa*

89. ut ais] *om. Oa Od Vc*: ut *Ob*

90. triumvirum ultimus] triumvirum ultimis *Oa*: tribuens vires ultimo *Od*

91. rem publicam] ad rem publicam *Oa*

92. altero senatus auctoritate ab insignibus imperii deiecto, interfectoque] *om. L*

93. saepe] ipse *Oa*

94. detegens] detegentes *Oa*

95 saepissime] sepe *L*

96. coniunget] coniungeret *Oa*

97. urgentes] *Cb Da*: ingentes *L Oa Ob Od Vc Za*

See Canfora 1998, cxxxii and cxlii. The repetition of ingentes is an infelicity (not the only one of this type, however: see n. 158 below, on 39.2), perhaps due to dittography, and undique appears to support urgentes; ingentes may have been an error of A² and therefore shared widely in the tradition. Canfora argues that urgentes may be a later authorial correction, though he does not explain why it should appear in only this group of MSS, which are fairly distant from Poggio himself. If it is correct, it will be a (good) guess by someone in this part of the later tradition.

98. dicenda] dicendi Oa

99. raram] raro Oa: rarum L (see 33.1 for the same phrase, where the MSS agree on raram)

100. ut et] et ut Oa: ut Za

101. quantumvis ardua pericula subeant, fortitudinis laude atque opere] om. L^{ac}

102. cum] enim Oa

103. litteris neque doctrina illam percipiunt] litteris doctrinam ullam percipiunt Ob

104. sapientum] sapientium Oa

105. a nobis] om. Ob

106. inducant] indicant Oa

107. parere] patere Oa

108. se] sic Oa

109. quo] qui Oa

110. quo in vitio] quo vitio L

111. Harpalo] Harpalo Vc: Arpalo L Oa Ob Od Za: Arpago Da Db Hb
    See Canfora lxi–lxiv and cxxxiii–cxxxiv for the hypothesis that the reading Arpago derives from a later scholarly intervention, possibly by Guarino, on the basis of Herodotus.

112. Quid?] Quidni? Ob

113. recito] recto Oa

114. ducunt] dicunt Oa

115. consectum] *Canfora*: confectum *Ob*

116. notet] vocet *Vc*: noceat *Oa*

117. sapientis] sapientissimos *Oa Za*

118. atque] & *Oa*

119. non solum . . . consueverunt] (*om.* illas) *L Oa Ob*: non solum illas coercere, sed etiam allicere consueverunt *Od B Vc*: non modo illas non coercere, sed allicere consueverunt *C W Za*

 With Canfora I retain the reading of most MSS. His justification (1998, cxxv) refers to TLL VIII 1321, 33 ff., where the example of the omission of non *rests on Varro 9.7:* non modo videatur esse reprehendenda, sed etiam . . . sequenda. *Scholars from Stephanus on, however, have doubted the validity of this construction (Stephanus inserted a second* non *in his text of Varro). The addition of* non *is probably to be placed well after the divergence of selected MSS from A², since in ζ it does not occur in B, but is there in W Za, while in the selected group it does not occur in the early Oa Ob Od (but it does appear in the later C).*

120. vobis parvus] parvus vobis *Ob*

121. ii] hi *Vc Za*

122. ora] ora *Canfora*: hora *L Oa Ob Od Vc Za* (*This spelling may well indicate* ora *in any case, since aspiration is fairly random in fifteenth-century orthography, and the focus here is upon place, not time.*)

123. quam hanc tot tantisque periculis coniunctam] quam tot tantisque periculis coniunctam *L*

 Cf. Isocrates, Ad Nicoclem, *trans. Giustiniani, London, British Library, MS Royal 10 B IX, fol. 81r:* quamvis potius vitam eligendam arbitraris quam tot tantisque in periculis universae Asiae imperatum ire. *If Poggio was staying close to Giustiniani's translation, he might well have omitted* hanc. *But this is one of a number of instances where the selected MSS seem to preserve a better reading than* L.

124. At ii] At hi *Ob Za*: Ac hi *Oa*

125. regnandi gratia] *C (and others linked to it) inserts* armis ac ferro *after* gratia (*most probably this was originally a marginal or interlinear gloss explicating* decertant *that has slipped into the text*).

126. aberrat] aberat *Oa Od Vc*

127. iam dixi] ut iam dixi *Ob*

128. sanctissimus] sapientissimus *Oa*

129. occisus est] *C* (*and others linked to it*) *have* Nero Senecam ac Lucanum mori coegit *after* occisus est. *Canfora* (1998, *cxxx–cxxxi n. 24*) *includes this sentence, arguing that it might have been a later addition by Poggio, rather than a scribal interpolation. The latter seems more likely, as it only begins to appear in this later stage of the transmission and the same* exemplum *is used by Poggio in the* Defensio (*see this volume,* §24, *p. 128*).

130. aut a regibus] a regibus *L Canfora*

131. fere principum] omnium fere principum *Ob*

132. principem similem] similem principem *Ob*

133. reddet] redderet *Od*

134. Ac] *Od Za:* At *Oa*

135. iacuerant] iacuerunt *L*

136. recuperarint] recuperarunt *Oa*

137. Romam] Romani *L*

138. Legite] musice *Za*

139. praecipiendam] percipiendam *L Oa Ob Od Za* (*this is very likely an error derived from the copying of the autograph*)

140. aestimentur] extimentur *L Oa Ob Za:* estimentur *Vc:* existimentur *Od*

141. pellectos] perlectos *Od:* pollectos *Vc:* pollicitos *Ob:* preelectos *Za*

142. ducitur] dicitur *Oa Vc*

143. currunt] *Modern texts of Seneca,* De Providentia *1.6.3 write* occurrunt, *which certainly makes better sense, though presumably Poggio and his contemporaries understood it here in the sense of* occurrunt. *See further Canfora 1998, lxiv, on the textual tradition of Seneca.*

144. Micillum] Miciclum *L Oa Ob Od Za:* Micyclum *Vc* (*others, according to Canfora, have* Micidum *and one* Mitiolum). *The consensus of selected MSS is* Miciclus, *but Poggio was working from the Greek text (see Sidwell "Sodalitas"), and is likelier to have written* Micillus, *which* A^2 *then copied as* Miciclus.

145. aestimaretur] extimaretur *L Ob Od*: extimarent *Za*: existimaretur *Oa Vc*

146. existimantur *Oa Ob Od Vc*: extimantur *L Za*

147. prodibam] prodiebam *L*

148. magni facientes] magnificantes *Oa Za*

149. quantae me res] quante res me *Ob*

150. Eiusmodi profecto regnum est] *om. Ob*

151. sescentis] sexcentis *L Oa Ob Od Za*

152. est omnium maximum] omnium est maximum *Ob*

153. Hic enim ⟨a⟩ puer⟨o⟩ veneno periit] Hic enim puer veneno periit *Oa Ob Od Vc Za*: Hic enim veneno puer periit *L*

 Poggio is still following Lucian (Gall. 25) closely here (though see n. 105 on the translation for some divergences), but the text given by MSS here makes no sense and does not represent any Greek MS reading of Gallus reported in the editions. There is, however, a major divergence in the textual tradition at this point, with modern editions (e.g., Macleod 1972–87) printing the text ἐγὼ γοῦν ὑπὸ τοῦ παιδός ἀπέθανον ὑπὸ φαρμάκων *"I (i.e., the cockerel when I was king) was poisoned by my slave" and the divergent text reading* ὁ μὲν ὑπὸ τοῦ παιδός ἀπέθανεν ὑπὸ φαρμάκων *("One died from poison at the hands of his slave"). Poggio was clearly using a MS that contained the second reading. But even with a still imperfect knowledge of Greek, he would hardly have written something so nonsensical in Latin as "This man died from poison as a boy," or "This boy died from poison," when the context is all about the way monarchs are killed in their prime. So the Latin text should read* Hic enim ⟨a⟩ puer⟨o⟩ veneno periit. *A² will have garbled Poggio's version, probably by omitting* a *and then hypercorrecting the grammar without consulting the Greek text. It is notable that here too, the independent evidence of the Greek text suggests that the selected MSS with the exception of L have preserved at least part of the correct reading (the place of* puer *in the Greek word order).*

154. divinationis] divinationibus *Oa*

155. oblectamenta corporum, virtutibus inimica] *Canfora punctuates* oblectamenta, corporum virtutibus inimica. *But this links* corporum *with* virtu-

tibus. *A more natural link is between* oblectamenta *and* corporum, *so I have relocated the comma after* corporum.

156. Candaules] Cadualus *L Oa Ob Od Za:* Candaules *Vc:* Candualus *Canfora (from Poggio's own copy of Justin). It would be interesting to know whether other copies within his reach (in Florence or the Vatican library, for example) also had this reading. Names are notoriously badly transcribed and some of the MSS have the more correct versions. But the agreement of the selected MSS suggests that this is most likely the reading of* A^2. *If this accurately represents the autograph, however, it seems to show that Poggio was not yet paying much attention even to his Lucian reading, since* Candaules *occurs at Asinus 28 (a work Poggio translated around the same time as he wrote DIP: see Sidwell "Sodalitas," 147–48), as well as not even having dipped a toe into Herodotus (the story is at 1.8). In concert with the note on the name Micillus in paragraph 35 above, I incline to the view that this is probably an error introduced by* A^2, *and that Poggio originally wrote* Candaules, *which the scribe deformed into the more familiar form* Cadualus.

157. Adicitur] Adicitus *Oa*

158. qui amicorum pariter atque inimicorum pestis, paternis amicis crudelissime occisis, praedo gentium ac regnorum pestis] *Poggio was normally more careful about repetitions without rhetorical effect (here,* pestis . . . pestis). *I wonder whether in fact this might be dittography, with the second* pestis *replacing* pernities. *If so, it is probably an error introduced by* A^2. *But cf. n. 97 above, on 17.2.*

159. debacchabatur] debacharetur *Ob*

160. satellites] satelles *Oa Od Za*

161. abnuo] ab uno *Oa Ob (Oa corr. in marg.)*

162. vestri] nostri *OaOb (Oa corr. in lin.)*

163. appetivit] appetunt *L Oa*

164. eo] eo loco *L Oa Od Vc. The addition of* loco *is presumably just an anticipation of* locu- *in* locupletiorem. *The readings in Ob Za show that the error could have been corrected at any stage by a thoughtful scribe. Given that it is shared, however, by four of the selected MSS, we might postulate that* A^2 *introduced this error.*

165. similis vita] vita similis *Ob*

166. delinimentis] *The word as written in the MSS is an alternative spelling for the CL word* delenimentis *(OLD s.v.* delenimentum *1 "blandishment," "enticement," e.g., Tac. Agr. 21.3,* paulatim . . . discessum ad delenimenta vitiorum, *"little by little they departed towards the blandishments of vice"). Consequently, it is translated here as* delenimentum. *Cf.* deliniuntur *at paragraph 12 above.*

167. minimis vitiis urgetur] minimis urgetur vitiis *Ob*

168. existimetur] existimetur *Oa Ob Od Vc Za*: extimetur *L*

169. Umquam . . . nihil] *om. Za*

170. felicitatis] infelicitatis *L*

171. videndi] vivendi *L*

172. videatur] videtur *Ob*

173. servitus] virtus *Oa*

174. tibi quicquam] sibi quicquam *Od*: quicquam tibi *L Oa. The word order in the source text is, as reported by the majority of the selected MSS, against L.*

175. terrendi poenaque afficiendi *L*[c Poggio]: terrendi poena afficiendique *L*[ac] *Oa Ob Od Vc Za*

176. rotae] recte *Oa*

177. illi quidem] quidem illi *L Od*

178. tanto studio, tanto errore] tanto studii errore *Za*

179. Ita] Itaque *Canfora*

180. tum] cum *Oa*

181. insignibus] in singulis *Oa*

182. vitam principum] principum vitam *Ob*

183. ut *Tateo*: cum *Rizzo*

The MSS have no conjunction introducing the middle part of this long period, which is constructed as follows: the opening clause cum videamus . . . stupere *has a long series of adjectives, participles, and infinitive phrases dependent on* videamus; *the second clause switches to a series of subjunctive verbs (*exedantur, habeant, absumpserit, perierint, sint, potiantur); *the main clause follows*

(nihil potest dubii) *and introduces a further series of interlocking subordinate clauses which provide the conclusion from the preceding premises ("there is no doubt princes cannot be happy"). Rizzo suggested* cum, *"since," in anaphora with the opening* cum *clause;* Tateo *ut, consecutive, representing these clauses as the results of the opening proposition.* cum *is certainly an easy supplement: one could argue that its assumption is what has led to its omission. Against it is the lack of variation it imparts, when the sentence appears to be building up steam. Against Tateo is the lack of preparation (some such word as* adeo*), though with so many different aspects, this is not really surprising — one would have wanted the preparation in everything that precedes, which would have diminished the rhetorical effect. In favor of consecutive* ut *is the variation achieved by this switch of construction and the sense of a rhetorical movement from observation through consequences to conclusion: "since we see all the following data, which result in the following types of evil consequence, ergo there is no doubt that princes are unhappy." The lack of preparation for a consecutive* ut, *however, argues strongly against this interpretation. On the other hand,* video *can be used with* ut *in indirect questions (see* OLD *s.v.* video *14c), and this interpretation of Tateo's conjecture works more easily.*

184. perierint] perierunt *Oa Vc Za*

185. aestimandum] extimandum *L Oa Ob Od Za*: estimandum *Vc*

186. inquit Nicolaus] inquit *L Oa Za*: om. *Od Vc*

187. Caesar] Iulius Cesar *Za (om. Rutilius)*

188. testes] testes sunt *L*

189. Grassari enim caede ac sanguine civium, proscriptorum *L Ob*: Grassari enim caede ac sanguine, civium proscriptorum *Canfora*

190. et cum pulsus est] et compulsus est *Vc*: etenim pulsus est *Oa*

191. oraculum Apollinis] Appolinis oraculum *Ob*

192. Aglaum *L Ob Vc*: Aglum *Za*: Agalum *Oa Od*

193. residere in nobis] in nobis residere *Ob*

194. cum adolescens] adolescens cum *Ob*

195. et] om. *Za*

196. insusurrans] susurantis *Vc*: insursans *L*

197. constituta] *om. Ob*

198. a quibus eiusmodi studia abfuerunt] *om. L*

199. vivendum] videndum *Oa*

200. hae] hic *Oa*: hee *Ob*

201. e] a *Oa Za*

202. ne] ut ne *L. Although L's reading is the* lectio difficilior, *the consensus of the other MSS against L, as in a number of other instances, suggests that the simpler* ne *may be the correct reading (though, of course,* ut *could easily have dropped out after* –et).

203. doctorum] doctissimorum *Ob*

204. Non tamen vereor . . . quin . . . esse nos ei persuasuros]. *The use of acc. + inf. after* quin *is nonclassical (see Hofmann-Szantyr, 679, and Canfora 1998, cxliv), so that the text does not require correction (which would in any case have to be quite harsh:* quin quod suasimus ⟨simus⟩ nos aliquando ei persuasur⟨i⟩ *and therefore, despite its unclassical feel, not a likely error for copyists to have made).*

Notes to the Translations

ABBREVIATIONS

BAV   Biblioteca Apostolica Vaticana
Iter   P. O. Kristeller, *Iter Italicum*, 6 vols. (London-Leiden:
          E. J. Brill, 1963–97)
OLD   P. G. W. Glare, ed. *Oxford Latin Dictionary* (Oxford:
          Oxford University Press, 1982)

POGGIO, *PROEM TO FRANCESCO BARBARO*

1. Francesco Barbaro (1390–1454) was a Venetian statesman and humanist from a patrician family. He frequently served as governor of Venice's subject cities and as the republic's ambassador. Barbaro had studied under several well-known humanist educators, including Guarino, and was himself the translator of two *Lives* of Plutarch, and the author of *On the Business of a Wife* (1415). In the manuscripts, this proem is placed directly before Poggio's *Defense*, also addressed to Barbaro, but it is clear from Poggio's words in §4 that he intended it as cover letter, to be read before his own *On the Excellence*, Guarino's response, and his *Defense*, in that order.

2. Publius Cornelius Scipio Africanus (236–183 BCE), also known as Scipio Africanus the Elder, and Gaius Julius Caesar (100–44 BCE).

3. Gaius Octavius Thurinus (63 BCE–14 CE, after 27 BCE called Augustus) was the great-nephew of Caesar. Following Roman law, after his adoption by Caesar he took Caesar's name, to which the second cognomen Octavianus was added.

4. Verg. *Aen.* 5.139–40. Gnaeus Pompeius Magnus (106–48 BCE), better known in English as Pompey the Great, was Caesar's adversary in the Civil Wars (49–45); his side, comprising much of Rome's political elite, continued the fight against Caesar after Pompey's death in 48.

5. In Guarino's *Letter to Leonello*, §1; Verg. *Aen.* 9.148.

POGGIO, *ON THE EXCELLENCE OF*
SCIPIO AND CAESAR

1. Scipione Mainenti of Ferrara, who was a colleague of Poggio's in the curia and a favorite of Pope Eugene IV (see Introduction, "Dates of Composition and Dissemination of the *Controversy*").

2. Publius Cornelius Scipio Africanus (236–183 BCE), also known as Scipio Africanus the Elder, and Gaius Julius Caesar (100–44 BCE).

3. Alexander III of Macedon (356–323 BCE), better known as Alexander the Great, figured as the Greek counterpart to Caesar in Plutarch's *Parallel Lives*.

4. Livy 30.30. This is a sleight of hand of Poggio, as Livy in fact compares both Scipio and Hannibal to the commanders who came before them.

5. Lucian's *Dialogues of the Dead* 25 (12) in fact features Alexander, Hannibal (247– 183/1 BCE), and Scipio but not Caesar, as pointed out in Guarino, *Excellence*, §18. Poggio did not begin his Greek studies in earnest until around 1438, so he probably read Lucian's dialogue in Giovanni Aurispa's loose translation of 1425, in which Scipio (rather than Alexander, as in Lucian's original) was the winner.

6. Suet. *Iul.* 49. Caesar was ambassador at the court of Nicomedes IV Philopator of Bithynia (r. ca. 94–74 BCE) in 80.

7. Suet. *Iul.* 45. Lucius Cornelius Sulla (ca. 138–78 BCE) was dictator of Rome in 81, temporarily concluding the struggle between the oligarchic Optimates and the populist Populares in favor of the former.

8. Caesar was quaestor in Spain in 69 or 68 BCE. Poggio follows Suet. *Iul.* 8.

9. Caesar was elected aedile in 66 BCE; some of his expenses in this position appear to have been covered by the famously rich Marcus Licinius Crassus (ca. 115–54 BCE), the third man in his future triumvirate with Pompey. A conspiracy, sometimes called the First Catilinarian Conspiracy, was rumored to be on hand after the invalidation of the consular

elections of 66 owing to accusations of corruption leveled at the consuls designate. Poggio follows the account of Suet. *Iul.* 9 regarding Caesar and Crassus as well as Gnaeus Calpurnius Piso.

10. Gaius Marius (157–86 BCE) staved off the incursions of the Germanic Cimbri and Teutones and held the consulship an unprecedented seven times. He belonged to the faction of the Populares and was married to Caesar's aunt Julia.

11. Caesar incited Titus Labienus to indict Gaius Rabirius in 63 BCE for the murder of Lucius Appuleius Saturninus, a tribune and ally of Marius, in 100 BCE. Rabirius was defended by Cicero in a speech that survives. Poggio follows Suet. *Iul.* 12.

12. Caesar ran for and won the office of Pontifex Maximus, chief priest of the Roman College of Pontiffs, in 63 BCE. The anecdote is from Suet. *Iul.* 13.

13. The Catilinarian Conspiracy of 63 BCE, unmasked by the then-consul Cicero. Poggio follows Suet. *Iul.* 14.

14. Caesar was consul in 59 BCE together with Marcus Calpurnius Bibulus (ca. 102–48 BCE), an Optimate who shortly after this consulship married Marcus Porcius Cato's (95–46 BCE) daughter Porcia, the future wife of Marcus Brutus.

15. Caesar was voted the provinces of Gallia Narbonensis, Gallia Cisalpina, and Illyricum in 59 BCE; the command was renewed in 56, to run until 49.

16. Caesar's then ally and eventual enemy Gnaeus Pompeius Magnus, or Pompey the Great (106–48 BCE). Suet. *Iul.* 24 does not report the number of Caesar's legions at the start of his command, but Poggio's figures feature in ibid., 29, pertaining to the negotiations before the Civil Wars.

17. The Great Roman Civil Wars (49–45 BCE), also known as Caesar's Civil Wars, comprise the Battle of Pharsalus (48), in which Caesar defeated Pompey, Caesar's African campaign against Metellus Scipio and Marcus Cato, which concluded with the Battle of Thapsus (46), and his Spanish campaign culminating in the Battle of Munda (45), in which

Caesar routed the last of the Pompeians. Poggio probably lists them in this manner—rather than adopting the sequence of the Caesarean corpus in which three books on the *Civil Wars* are followed by one each on the *Alexandrian*, *African*, and *Spanish Wars*—because they pitted Caesar against Roman commanders, unlike the operations in Alexandria and Pontus.

18. For example, Cic. *Att.* 7.3.2.

19. The Alexandrian War (48–47 BCE) was fought between Caesar, supporting the interests of Cleopatra, and her brother Ptolemy XIII. For the risky escape, see Suet. *Iul.* 64.

20. Suet. *Iul.* 52.

21. Suet. *Iul.* 37. Pharnaces II of Pontus (97–47 BCE) defected and was defeated by Caesar in 47.

22. Suet. *Iul.* 77.

23. Poggio follows Cicero's assessment of Caesar's actions in *Off.* 1.14.43.

24. In Cicero's *On Behalf of Marcellus*, *On Behalf of Ligarius*, and *On Behalf of King Deiotarus*, respectively.

25. Poggio borrows the comparison from Cic. *S. Rosc.* 50.146.

26. Ammianus Marcellinus, 21.16.13 (= Epist. fr. II.5 Mueller).

27. While there is indeed no ancient biography of Scipio, Livy's ample account of Africanus' deeds, which Poggio himself relies on in what follows, falsifies his assertion that these were barely known. Valerius Maximus' *Memorable Deeds and Words* is another key source for Poggio's account. Poggio passes in silence over the fourteenth-century *Life of Scipio* by Petrarch in his *On Famous Men*, as well as his epic *Africa* (see also Introduction, "Interpreting the *Controversy*" and "Sources of the *Controversy*").

28. Livy 26.19. The Second Punic War between Rome and Carthage (218–201 BCE), also known as the Hannibalic War, is most fully reported in Livy's *From the Foundation of the City*, Books 21–30.

29. Val. Max. 5.4.2. Scipio's father, then consul, Publius Cornelius Scipio, led the Roman troops at the Battle of Ticinus (218 BCE) in Northern Italy against Hannibal.

30. Scipio and Appius Claudius Pulcher (d. 211 BCE) took charge of the estimated ten thousand Roman survivors of the Battle of Cannae (216 BCE) against Hannibal in modern Puglia. Poggio follows Livy 22.53.

31. Both Scipio's father (Publius) and his uncle Gnaeus Cornelius Scipio Calvus were killed in the Battle of Upper Baetis (211 BCE) in Spain against Hasdrubal Barca, brother of Hannibal.

32. At this time (211 BCE) Scipio was in fact twenty-five years old.

33. The two Roman provinces Nearer and Further Spain.

34. Carthago Nova (mod. Cartagena) was founded in 227 BCE and was the center of Carthaginian power in Spain; Scipio took the town in 209.

35. This episode, recounted in Livy 26.50, had a rich afterlife in early modern literature, music, and the visual arts as *The Continence of Scipio*.

36. Scipio met Syphax in 206 BCE; the price paid by the king was his death in captivity at Tibur (mod. Tivoli) in 203/2.

37. In 205 BCE; Scipio was in fact thirty-one years old, and Livy 28.38.6, which recounts Scipio's election, makes no reference to his age. Perhaps Poggio is thinking of Scipio's election to the aedileship in 213, when he was under the legal age.

38. Poggio follows the discrepancy in numbers reported in Livy 29.25.1–2.

39. Scipio decisively defeated Hannibal at modern Zama, Tunisia (202 BCE), reducing Carthage to a Roman vassal, fifteen years after Hannibal's victory at Cannae; Poggio counts inclusively.

40. Livy 30.35.3 in fact gives a loss of 1500 men on the Roman side; the figure 12,000 is cited in Livy 30.29.7, as reported by Valerius Antias for Hannibal's losses shortly before the battle of Zama. Livy's same chapter, 30.35.5, states that it was Scipio who reckoned that Hannibal had drawn up a particularly fine battle line (*confessione etiam Scipionis omniumque peritorum militiae illam laudem adeptus [sc. Hannibal] singulari arte aciem eo die instruxisse*). Livy's epitomizer Florus I.22 reports that both generals maintained this about each other (*Constat utriusque confessione nec melius instrui aciem nec acrius potuisse pugnari*).

41. See discussion of §19 below.

42. Livy 38.51.6–12; Poggio's source is Val. Max. 3.7.1e and g. Poggio merges two incidents. In 187 BCE, Scipio's brother Lucius Cornelius Scipio Asiagenes, for whom he had been a deputy, was challenged by the two tribunes over the accounts he had kept of the tribute paid by the Seleucid king Antiochus III the Great (ca. 241–187 BCE); Africanus then tore up the account books in his brother's defense. In 185, he was himself accused of having accepted bribes from Antiochus, which accusation he answered by reminding the people of his victory at Zama. Quintus Petillius and Quintus Petillius Spurinus acted on the instigation of Scipio's opponent Marcus Porcius Cato the Elder.

43. These honors were offered to Scipio after his return from Zama.

44. Shaken by the opposition he faced in Rome, Scipio withdrew to his villa in Liternum, Campania, in 184 BCE, where he died probably the year after. Poggio paraphrases Val. Max. 2.10.2b.

45. Poggio echoes Cic. *Tusc.* 5.5.

46. Scipio declined burial in the family tomb in Rome, on the Appian Way, instead inscribing his tombstone in Liternum with the words "*Ingrata patria, ne ossa quidem habebis*," or "Ungrateful fatherland, you will not even have my bones."

47. Sen. *Ep.* 86.3.

48. Poggio contradicts *BGall.* 5.9.4, where Caesar suggests that the Britons were involved in an internal war before his arrival.

49. The four Carthaginian armies are reported in Livy 28.38.3.

50. Lucius Licinius Lucullus (118–57/6 BCE) lost his command in the Third Mithridatic War against Mithridates VI the Great of Pontus (135–63 BCE) and Tigranes II of Armenia (140–55 BCE) to Pompey; his triumph was thwarted by Pompey's ally Gaius Memmius. Scipio's comment paraphrases Livy 30.44.3.

51. Juba I of Numidia (ca. 85–46 BCE) sided with Caesar's enemies during his African campaign.

52. As noted regarding §8 above, Pharnaces was in fact king of Pontus, which had been merged with Bithynia to become the Roman province of

Bithynia and Pontus after the defeat of his father, Mithridates, by Pompey in 63 BCE.

GUARINO, *LETTER TO LEONELLO D'ESTE*

1. Leonello d'Este (1407–October 1, 1450) was an illegitimate son of Niccolò III d'Este and succeeded his father as Marquess of Ferrara in 1441, ruling until his sudden death. Leonello received an exemplary humanist education with Guarino, starting from the latter's arrival in Ferrara in 1429. In February 1435 Leonello married Margarita Gonzaga, daughter of the lord of Mantua; among his wedding gifts was a portrait of Caesar by Pisanello, Salmi, "'Divi Julii Effigies' del Pisanello," 91–95. In 1444 Leonello became the son-in-law of Alfonso of Aragon, king of Naples. His reign and patronage mark a period of cultural flourishing in Ferrara.

2. Ovid *Met.* 7.758.

3. *Caesaromastix* (scourge of Caesar) is Guarino's coinage, modeled after *Homeromastix* and *Vergiliomastix*; see Guarino, *Excellence*, §55.

4. From Verg. *Aen.* 1.287, where the mood is subjunctive, as is the case in MS H. This possibly reflects Guarino's author copy of the letter, but a well-known quotation like this is easily regularized by a scribe.

GUARINO, *ON THE EXCELLENCE OF CAESAR AND SCIPIO*

1. Giovanni di Jacopo Morelli's *Ricordi* give April 30 to May 3, 1435, as the dates of Leonello d'Este's Florentine visit (see Introduction, "Dates of Composition and Dissemination of the *Controversy*"). Pope Eugene IV and his curia, including Poggio, had resided in Florence since a rebellion in May 1434 forced them to flee Rome. Leonello's visit may have been connected to negotiations to reconvene the Church Council of Basel in Ferrara, a plan that came to fruition in 1438 (the next year it was transferred to Florence on account of the plague). The Council of Ferrara and Florence briefly succeeded in reuniting the Greek and the Latin Churches.

2. The two knights are identified as Feltrino Boiardo and, perhaps, Alberto della Sala by Sabbadini, *Epistolario*, 3:325, comm. on letter 670.

3. Hor. *Ars P.* 139.

4. Cf. Gell. *NA* 11.11. The distinction is that someone who "lies" intends to deceive, whereas someone who "tells lies" may himself be deceived and unwittingly spread falsehoods. Both Aulus Gellius and Nonius Marcellus 441 M. attribute this doctrine to P. Nigidius, not Caesar.

5. Poggio, *Excellence*, §25.

6. Verg. *Aen.* 2.658.

7. Verg. *Aen.* 4.79.

8. Cic. *Brut.* 252, 253, 261. The reference is to Caesar's treatise *On Analogy*, whose Greek title Cicero here paraphrases in Latin.

9. *Brut.* 261.

10. The forum stands as synecdoche for the practice of forensic oratory.

11. Quint. *Inst.* 10.1.114.

12. Suet. *Iul.* 55.1. Like all humanists, Guarino frequently indicates ancient authors by a different part of their Roman names from that in use today.

13. Guarino cites a letter from Cicero to Cornelius Nepos (Epist. fr. II.4 Mueller).

14. Plut. *Caes.* 3.2.

15. Cic. *Ad fam.* 4.8.2.

16. Aelius Donatus (fl. 350 CE), tutor of St. Jerome and author of the *Art of Grammar*, which was ubiquitous as a basic textbook for Latin instruction in the Middle Ages; Maurus Servius Honoratus (fl. 400 CE), best known for his commentary on Vergil; Priscianus Caesariensis (fl. 500 CE), author of the *Institutes of Grammar*, which served as standard textbook; Helenius Acron (ca. 3rd century CE), a grammarian to whom in the fifteenth-century scholia on Horace were attributed; Aemilius Asper (ca. 1st or 2nd century CE) wrote commentaries on Terence, Sallust, and Vergil.

17. Guarino is on shaky ground with Gaius Valerius Catullus (ca. 84–ca. 54 BCE), since he flourished before Caesar's dictatorship, while Marcus Annaeus Lucanus (39–65 CE) wrote the much-read anti-Caesarian epic *Pharsalia* (*Bellum civile*). Claudius Claudianus (ca. 370–ca. 404 CE)

was well known in the fifteenth century, particularly for his panegyrics; Publius Ovidius Naso (43 BCE–17/18 CE), most famous for the *Art of Love* and *Metamorphoses*, was among the most influential Latin poets during the Middle Ages; Publius Papinius Statius (ca. 45–ca. 96 CE), author of the *Thebaid* and other works was also widely known; by contrast, the *Punica* of Silius Italicus (ca. 28–ca. 103 CE), an epic devoted to the wars fought by Scipio Africanus and others against Carthage, was only discovered by Poggio in the monastery of St. Gall in 1417.

18. Publius Vergilius Maro (70–19 BCE), author of the *Eclogues, Georgics,* and the *Aeneid;* these judgments are reported in Serv. *Ecl.* 6.11; Macrob. *Sat.* 1.24.8; Prop. 2.34.65.

19. This judgment on Vergil, attributed to Ovid, appears in several late medieval Italian sources, such as the respective *Commentaries* on Dante's *Divine Commentary* of Pietro Alighieri and Benvenuto da Imola, and, with *monstravit* (showed) as verb, the *Life of Dante* of Filippo Villani and the *Life of Vergil* of Domenico Bandini (d. 1418; the life is part of his encyclopedic *Font of Memorable Things of the Universe*). The actual source for this latter version is a tetrastich summary of Vergil's *Georgics* 3, in Shackleton Bailey, *Anthologia Latina,* 1.1:12–13, no. 2.III.

20. Cic. *Sen.* 1.1 = Enn. *Ann.* v. 335 Skutsch. Only fragments of the epic *Annals* of Quintus Ennius (ca. 239–ca. 169 BCE) are extant. The quoted verse, written by Ennius, refers not to Ennius himself, but to a shepherd who guided T. Flamininus during his campaign against Philip V of Macedonia. The identification of *ille vir* (that man) with Ennius expressed by Guarino was made by the scribes A² and V²; see Powell, *Cicero. Cato Maior de Senectute,* on *Sen.* 1.1.

21. Quint. *Inst.* 10.1.88.

22. Quintus Horatius Flaccus (65–8 BCE), author of satires, epistles, and epodes, was much read throughout the Middle Ages.

23. Quint. *Inst.* 10.1.94. Aulus Persius Flaccus (34–62 CE) is the author of a book of satires that circulated widely in medieval Europe, often together with Juvenal.

24. Decimus Iunius Iuvenalis wrote satires in the late first and early second century CE; see previous note.

25. Hor. *Ars P.* 9–10.

26. Cic. *De or.* 2.13.55.

27. That is, rich: Quint. 10.1.32. Quintus Asconius Pedianus (ca. 9 BCE–ca. 76 CE) wrote historical commentaries on Cicero's orations, five of which were discovered by none other than Poggio at St. Gall in 1416; Lucius Lucceius was in vain solicited by Cicero to write a laudatory history of his consulship; Gaius Sallustius Crispus (86–ca. 35 BCE) is the author of the *Jugurthine War* and the *Conspiracy of Catiline,* much read in the later Middle Ages, as well as a mostly lost *History of Rome;* Lucius Annaeus Florus (ca. 74–130 CE) wrote a popular *Epitome of Roman History* mainly based on Livy; Gnaeus Pompeius Trogus (d. after 9 CE) composed a universal history centered around the kings of Macedon, which is lost but known through the *Epitome* produced by Marcus Junianus Justinus Frontinus (fl. 2nd century CE), which was much used in the Middle Ages; Quintus Curtius Rufus (fl. 1st century CE) wrote a *History of Alexander the Great* very popular in the Middle Ages and Renaissance; Cornelius Tacitus (56–ca. 120 CE) is the author of the *Histories* and *Annals,* which slowly came back into circulation (missing *Annals* 1–6) only after the death of Giovanni Boccaccio (1375), who owned the manuscript, as well as of three minor works, which were recovered in the 1450s; and Titus Livius Patavinus (64 or 59 BCE–12 or 17 CE), the author of the monumental *From the Foundation of the City,* whose missing parts were avidly sought but not found by Poggio and other Quattrocento humanists.

28. Lucius Annaeus Seneca (ca. 4 BCE–65 CE), known as Seneca the Younger, the Stoic philosopher and tragedian; Gaius Plinius Secundus (23–79 CE), known as Pliny the Elder, the author of the encyclopedic *Natural History;* and Anicius Manlius Severinus Boethius (ca. 477–524 CE), who was born shortly after the deposition of the last Roman emperor and served as Roman senator and consul under the Ostrogothic king Theoderic the Great until he was jailed and executed on suspicion of treason. In jail, Boethius composed the *Consolation of Philosophy,* a Platonist text with an enormous afterlife in the Middle Ages and the Renaissance.

29. In Greek mythology, the phoenix is a long-lived bird that periodically dies and is reborn — in some versions, from the ashes of his prede-

cessor after self-combustion. Since ancient authors regularly used the phoenix as metaphor for rare phenomena, in the current context Guarino may be thinking of Cicero as an exceptionally gifted orator, whose legacy, however, was kept alive in subsequent generations.

30. Verg. *Aen.* 1.374.

31. Cic. *Off.* 3.4. These were primarily philosophical works, not oratory, as the term *eloquentia* may seem to imply.

32. Cic. *Tusc.* 1.75.

33. Poggio, *Excellence*, §25.

34. Guarino lists some of the leading families of Rome who produced statesmen, orators, and writers.

35. Marcus Porcius Cato (234–249 BCE), known as Cato the Elder or Cato the Censor, guardian of ancient Roman propriety against Greek innovations; he infamously urged the expulsion of the Skeptic philosopher Carneades from Rome. He was the great-grandfather of Caesar's opponent Cato Uticensis.

36. Cic. *Somn.* 14; *Tusc.* 1.4.

37. This distinction was drawn at §2.

38. Plut. *Comp. Dion. Brut.* 2.1. Plutarch's *Life of Brutus* was the first Plutarchan biography to be translated into Latin, by Iacopo Angeli da Scarperia in 1400, but the *Life of Dion* and the *Comparison of Dion and Brutus* were first published by Guarino himself in 1414 and dedicated to Francesco Barbaro, later the addressee of Poggio's *Defense* (Pade, *Reception of Plutarch's Lives*, 1:183–91). Guarino here paraphrases this translation, which runs: *Caesaris vero potentia, dum constituebatur, quidem non modicas adversantibus turbas atque molestias praebuit. Postquam a victis suscepta est, nomen et opinio dumtaxat apparuit; nullum ex ea crudele facinus, nullum denique tyrannicum extitit* (Oxford, Bodleian Library, MS. Bywater 38, fols. 63r–v; Vatican City, BAV, MS Pal. lat. 919, fols. 104v–5r); cf. §§21, 62, 68.

39. Serv. *Aen.* 8.128; see also Otto, *Sprichwörter*, 161 s.v. herba 2. Marcus Licinius Crassus (ca. 115–54 BCE) led the Romans to a crushing defeat against the Parthians in the Battle at Carrhae in 54. Marcus Antonius (83–30 BCE), better known in English as Mark Anthony, Caesar's parti-

san and later partner of Octavian and Lepidus in the second triumvirate, was not in fact involved in this expedition, but he did campaign against the Parthians between 40 and 33 BCE.

40. Verg. *Ecl.* 9.36.

41. Guarino's choice of topic recalls Poggio's dialogue *On Avarice* from 1428.

42. Sall. *Cat.* 10.4.

43. Hor. *Ars P.* 330.

44. Poggio, *Excellence*, §25.

45. Medieval authors deemed Octavian (63 BCE–14 CE, after 27 BCE called Augustus) a good ruler for instituting peace at Rome and so preparing for the birth of Christ; and Titus (39–81 CE) for conquering Jerusalem; while Trajan (53–117 CE) was ranked among the "virtuous pagans"; Antoninus Pius (86–161 CE) acquired the epithet "dutiful" already upon ascension and continued the peace of the reigns of Trajan and Hadrian (76–138 CE); Constantine the Great (272–337 CE) converted Rome to Christianity; Theodosius the Great (347–395 CE) was the last emperor to rule both the Eastern and the Western Roman Empire.

46. Guarino's argument hinges on the Catholic notion of apostolic succession, which holds that episcopal and more particularly papal authority and grace are transmitted through a lineage going back, via St. Peter, to Christ. As long-standing member of the papal curia, Poggio was well placed to know the human foibles of the prelates he served; Guarino may implicitly refer to Pope John XXIII, Poggio's former master, who was deposed as the Council of Constance in 1415.

47. The *decemvirs*, as the name indicates, were special commissions in Roman republican government comprising ten men. The consular tribunate was an office in the fifth and fourth centuries BCE, which later Roman writers relate either to the "Conflict of the Orders" or to Rome's military expansion in Italy.

48. Cic. *Amic.* 88.

49. Cf. Cic. *Off.* 3.43.

50. See Poggio, *Excellence*, §1.

51. Poggio, *Excellence*, §1.

52. Poggio, *Excellence*, §1. Cf. *Rhet. Her.* 1.1.

53. Poggio, *Excellence*, §1.

54. Plut. *Alex.* 1.2–3. Guarino translated Plutarch's *Life of Alexander* by 1408, during his stay in Constantinople, and published *Alexander and Caesar* as a pair by 1414 (Pade, *Reception of Plutarch's Lives*, 1:172–77; 2:133–35). Remarkably, Guarino does not here quote his own translation, which runs *quippe cum non historias sed vitas perscribere in animo sit. Praeterea non usque quaque clarissima gesta virtutem flagitiaque declarant. Verum exigua persaepe res ac verbum iocusque quispiam mores magis aperit, quam hostes infiniti proelio caesi, ingentes acies et expugnata oppida"; "sic et nobis indulgendum est, ut animorum signa ineamur, per ea utriusque vitam significantes, eorum amplitudines ac res bellicas aliis reliquentes.* (Vatican City, BAV MS Vat. lat. 1879, fol. 1r; Vatican City, BAV MS Vat. lat. 1880, fol. 1r); cf. §§12, 62, 68.

55. Poggio, *Excellence*, §2.

56. Poggio, *Excellence*, §4. Lucius Cornelius Cinna (d. 84 BCE) was consul four consecutive times (87–84), but was not, in fact, dictator. He was instrumental in the return to Rome of Gaius Marius (157–86 BCE), who had been exiled by Lucius Cornelius Sulla (ca. 138–78 BCE). Marius was married to Caesar's aunt Julia, and Caesar's betrothal to Cinna's daughter Cornelia continued these political affiliations.

57. Sulla, although later leading the oligarchic Optimate cause to victory, rose to power as officer serving under Marius, who belonged to the populist faction (the Populares). After a civil war against Marius' allies, Sulla became dictator of Rome in 81 BCE.

58. Suet. *Iul.* 45.3.

59. Suet. *Iul.* 1.3.

60. Cic. *Parad.* 16.

61. Juv. 8.249–50. Marius defeated the Germanic Cimbri and Teutones in 102–101 BCE.

62. Suet. *Iul.* 1.2. A college of female priests dedicated to Vesta, goddess of the hearth, the Vestal virgins had to take a vow of chastity.

63. Poggio, *Excellence*, §4.

64. Verg. *Aen.* 1.254; 10.18; 10.100.

65. Guarino seems to confuse Caesar's nomination as *flamen dialis* by the consuls Marius and Cinna in 86 BCE with his contested election as *pontifex maximus* in 63, Suet. *Iul.* 1 and 13.

66. Poggio, *Excellence*, §4.

67. Gell. *NA* 5.6.11. Marcus Minucius Thermus served as propraetor of the province of Asia in 80 BCE; Caesar began his military career in his service, winning the civic crown for his performance during the siege of Mytilene.

68. Gell. *NA* 5.6.13.

69. Poggio, *Excellence*, §4.

70. Livy 21.46.10. This episode is recounted in Poggio, *Excellence*, §15, to demonstrate Scipio's virtue.

71. Recounted in Suet. *Iul.* 4. Mithridates VI the Great of Pontus (135–63 BCE) faced off with the Romans in the First (88–84), Second (83–81), and Third (75–63) Mithridatic Wars.

72. Cf. Cic. *Off.* 1.19.

73. Poggio, *Excellence*, §4.

74. Cic. *Off.* 2.65. This is a mistake on Guarino's part: the reference is to the unnamed Servius Sulpicius (consul in 51 BCE), not to Caesar.

75. Pliny, *HN* 7.91–92; Poggio, *Excellence*, §4.

76. Cic. *Off.* 3.6.

77. Drawn from Suet. *Iul.* 4, and Plut. *Caes.* 1.3–2.4.

78. Verg. *G.* 3.80.

79. Cf. Plut. *Caes.* 7.4.

80. Sall. *Cat.* 49.1.

81. As described in Suet. *Iul.* 10.

82. Poggio, *Excellence*, §5.

83. Suet. *Iul.* 5.

84. Poggio, *Excellence*, §5.

85. Suet. *Iul.* 13. Publius Servilius Vatia Isauricus (ca. 122–44 BCE) and Quintus Lutatius Catulus (ca. 120–61/60 BCE); the date is 63 BCE.

86. Poggio, *Excellence*, §6. Suet. *Iul.* 19.

87. Poggio, *Excellence*, §16.

88. Livy 26.18.10–11.

89. Suet. *Iul.* 16.2. Early in 62 BCE, Caesar supported a bill by the tribune of the plebs Q. Caecilius Metellus Nepos in opposition to the senate, which Suetonius reports led to the suspension of his praetorship; Caesar then de-escalated the threat of disorder posed by his supporters, after which the senate reinstated him. Morstein-Marx, *Julius Caesar and the Roman People*, 99–109, deconstructs Suetonius' account.

90. Crassus was known for his great wealth.

91. Cic. *Off.* 1.134.

92. Poggio, *Excellence*, §6.

93. Poggio, *Excellence*, §6.

94. At the time of the meeting (December 5, 63 BCE), Q. Cicero was in fact praetor designate; he would become proconsul only in 61 BCE.

95. Suet. *Iul.* 14.2. Decimus Junius Silanus was consul in 62 BCE; Quintus Tullius Cicero, brother of Marcus, was praetor in the same year; Tiberius Claudius Nero was praetor by 63, since he spoke as a man of praetorian rank in these deliberations. Guarino knew Silanus' opinion from Suet. *Iul.* 14.1, and Nero's from Sall. *Cat.* 50.4; he inferred Quintus Cicero's opinion from Cic. *Cat.* 4.3.

96. Sall. *Cat.* 53.1.

97. Hor. *Ars P.* 265–66.

98. Dio Cass. 37.36.2.

99. Poggio, *Excellence*, §6.

100. Cic. *Off.* 3.73.

101. See §36.

102. Cic. *Mur.* 61–62.

103. Cato the Younger's son, also called Marcus Porcius Cato (73–42 BCE), was pardoned by Caesar after the Battle of Thapsus, while his father killed himself.

104. Verg. *Aen.* 6.434–37. Guarino's knowledge of Cato's reading matter derives from Plutarch's *Cato minor* 68.2. This text was first translated by Leonardo Bruni, 1405–after 1407 (Pade, *Reception of Plutarch's Lives*, 1:133–41), but Guarino would have read the Greek original.

105. Cic. *Sen.* 73.

106. Plut. *Cat. Min.* 25.2–5. Quintus Hortensius Hortalus (114–50 BCE) sought the hand of Cato's daughter in 56; Cato refused but offered Hortensius his own wife, Marcia, instead. After Hortensius' death, Marcia moved back into Cato's household.

107. Plut. *Cat. Min.* 49.4.

108. Cic. *Att.* 2.1.8.

109. Poggio, *Excellence*, §6.

110. Poggio, *Excellence*, §7.

111. The *Lex Vatinia de provincia Caesaris* (Vatinian Law on Caesar's Province) was approved by the Roman people and provided Caesar with the provinces Cisalpine Gaul and Illyricum (to which Transalpine Gaul was added by the senate) for five years from March 59 BCE.

112. Caesar's son-in-law, married to his daughter Julia, was Pompey.

113. Suet. *Iul.* 35.1. In the *Defense*, §78, Poggio cites these lines in the version reported by MS H.

114. Poggio, *Excellence*, §8.

115. *BAlex.* 32.3–4.

116. Plut. *Caes.* 48.2.

117. Ulp. 1.1.10.

118. Poggio, *Excellence*, §11.

119. Cic. *Marcell.* 8. Cicero's speech *On Behalf of Marcellus* (46 BCE) celebrates Caesar's leniency; it was not part of a trial, and there was no de-

fendant. Perhaps Guarino was writing from memory — cf. Poggio's lapse regarding Lucian, *Excellence*, §1, derided by Guarino in §18 above — or he relied on a commonplace book, which would preserve the precise quotation but not its context.

120. Suet. *Iul.* 75.2; Flor. 2.13.50.

121. Pliny, *HN* 7.93.

122. Pliny, *HN* 7.94.

123. Suet. *Iul.* 73.

124. Cic. *Lig.* 19; *Deiot.* 33.

125. Poggio, *Excellence*, §8.

126. Suet. *Iul.* 64.

127. Ov. *Am.* 1.9.1. Guarino takes a jab at Poggio's love life, since he fathered fourteen children with his common-law wife, Lucia Panelli, before wedding the young Vaggia Buondelmonti in 1436.

128. Hor. *Ars P.* 353.

129. Sen. *Phaedr.* 294–95.

130. Hercules was ordered by the Delphic oracle to serve Queen Omphale of Lydia for a year, carrying out feminine tasks and wearing women's clothes; in Ovid's version, the same resulted from his erotic captivity to Iole, *Her.* 9.

131. Sen. *Her. F.* 476.

132. Serv. *Ecl.* 2.23.

133. Poggio, *Excellence*, §22.

134. Livy 1.2.5.

135. Isid. *Etym.* 14.4.22, where *primam* (first) is an interpolation. The Greek name for the territory of the Etruscans given by Isidore is *Heterouria*.

136. Plut. *Marc.* 3.4.

137. Sall. *Cat.* 53.3 (cf. Cic. *Off.* 1.38); *Iug.* 114.1–2, which, however, names the commanders as Quintus Caepio and Gnaeus Mallius, while their

defeat in 105 BCE was at the hands of the Germanic Cimbri, thought at the time to be Gauls.

138. Cic. *Planc.* 77 and *Pis.* 16.

139. Cf. Cic. *Off.* 3.81.

140. Namely, the three orders of the Roman people: the senatorial order, the equestrian order, and the commoners.

141. Luc. 2.101–2.

142. Luc. 2.140.

143. Luc. 2.145–46.

144. Luc. 2.196–97. The *ovilia* (lit. "sheepfolds") were used as voting booths in Rome.

145. The patrician Publius Clodius Pulcher (ca. December 93–52 BCE) was adopted into a plebeian family in 59, in order to allow him to stand for election as tribune of the plebs for the year 58. In this position he secured the exile of Cicero, avenging the latter's execution of the Catiline conspirators. In 62, during the Bona Dea festival—a women-only celebration hosted by the wife of the *pontifex maximus* Caesar, Pompeia—Clodius had been found in Caesar's house, having reportedly gained access by cross-dressing. He was accused of having seduced Pompeia, which caused Caesar to divorce her, yet both men remained political allies.

146. Cic. *Parad.* 28.

147. Cf. August. *De civ. D.* 4.4, where it is argued that kingship without justice is nothing but thievery.

148. Lucius Afranius, Marcus Petreius, and Marcus Terrentius Varro were Pompey's legates in Hispania, which was granted to Pompey for five years in 55 BCE; see Broughton, *Magistrates*, 2:215, 220, and 625.

149. Caes. *BCiv.* 1.1.

150. Cf. Cic. *Off.* 2.22.

151. Plut. *Caes.* 28.3–4. Again, Guarino does not quote his own published translation, which runs *tum ex saeva romanae rei publicae tempestate*

nactus. Nam qui honores principatusque petebant, omni abiecta prorsus verecun-
dia, epulum publice largitionesque distribuebant in populum. Qua propter corrup-
tum mercede populum ad comitia descendentem cerneres, non suffragiis, sed arcu,
gladio fundaque pro largitore decertantem, et tribunalia saepenumero sanguine ca-
daveribusque foedantem rem inter se petulantissime decernere, cum interim civitas,
amisso rectore sicuti navis relicto clavo fluctuans, agitaretur. Idcirco qui animo et
ratione valebant, satis fore existimabant, si ex ea hominum insania et tanta rerum
tempestate nihil truculentius quam monarchia tantisper emergeret (Vatican City,
BAV MS Vat. lat 1879, fol. 41v; Vatican City, BAV MS Vat. lat 1880, fol.
34v); cf. §§12, 21, 68.

152. Marcus Junius Brutus (85–42 BCE) and Gaius Cassius Longinus
(before 83–42 BCE), the most famous of Caesar's tyrannicides.

153. Dio Cass. 44.1–3; Guarino provides his own translation, excerpting
and rearranging the order. Dio Cassius' *Roman History* was first brought
to Italy from Constantinople by Giovanni Aurispa, who translated a
speech from it in 1425. A few years later he moved to the court of Ferrara
on the recommendation of Guarino.

154. Luc. 1.128.

155. Suet. *Iul.* 41.1.

156. Suet. *Iul.* 42.1. In his *Defense*, §39, Poggio takes Guarino to task for
presenting Suetonius as stating that Caesar recalled people, instead of
him prohibiting their prolonged absence. But as the words between angle
brackets show, MS H of Guarino's letter, in all likelihood reflecting Guarino's author copy (since it is a stretch to think that the copyist would
have emended the text through consultation of Suetonius, and see Note
on the Texts), mentions both scenarios, the former perhaps proleptically
referring to Suetonius' claim, in the next line, that Caesar sought to attract doctors and scholars to Rome. It is possible that Poggio purposefully misquotes Guarino, but I am inclined to think that there was a
scribal error in the letter received by him from Guarino (which will itself
have been a transcript of Guarino's author copy).

157. Suet. *Iul.* 43.1.

158. The Julian law on adultery was in fact enacted by Augustus, not Julius Caesar.

159. Flor. 2.14.3: "in imitation of his father" (*patris imitatione*) is Guarino's addition.

160. Livy 38.53.9.

161. "Second path of life" renders *rerumque novarum viam*: though the usual meaning of *res novae* is "revolution," this is a direct translation of Plutarch's *pragmatōn kainōn hodon*.

162. Plut. *Caes.* 15.1–3. Again, Guarino does not quote his own published translation, which runs "*Tempus autem bellorum quae deinceps gessit et expeditionum quibus pacatam reddidit Galliam aliud quoddam vitae principium ac gerendorum novam quasi viam instituit, ita ut summorum virorum et clarissimorum ducum neminem huic et bellatori, et imperatori preponendum censeas. Nam siquis Fabios, Scipiones, Metellos et, aetatis suae aut paulo post, superiores duces Sullam, Marium utrumque Lucullum et ipsum denique Pompeium, cuius omnimoda in re militari virtus et gloria ad caelum usque perfloruit, comparandos duxerit, profecto Caesaris gesta superant. Hunc quidem locorum asperitate, in quibus ab eo decertatum est, illum regionum amplitudine, quas Romano adeptus est imperio, alium a se domitorum hostium vi ac multitudine, quendam pacatarum ab eo nationum feritate atque perfidia, alium mansuetudine et clementia, quas erga victos exercuit, aliquem gratia et munificentiis, quibus suos prosecutus est commilitones, universos autem vel hoc ipso superavit, quod et longe plura commisit proelia et plures in acie obtruncavit hostes. In Gallia siquidem, nec totum belligerans decennium, octingenta viribus cepit oppida, tercentos subiugavit populos, adversum tercentas partim instructus myriades, centum quidem ferro caesis, totidem vitae reservatas captivas habuit.*" (Vatican City, BAV MS Vat. lat 1879, fol. 36v; Vatican City, BAV MS Vat. lat 1880, fol. 30v); cf. §§12, 21, 62.

163. Pliny, *HN* 7.92.

POGGIO, LETTER TO LEONELLO D'ESTE

1. On Leonello, see Guarino's *Letter to Leonello*, §1.

2. On Scipione Mainenti, see Poggio's *Excellence*, §1.

3. On Francesco Barbaro, see Poggio's *Proem*, §1.

POGGIO, *DEFENSE OF ON THE EXCELLENCE
OF SCIPIO AND CAESAR*

1. On Francesco Barbaro and Scipione Mainenti, see, respectively, Poggio's *Proem,* §1, and Poggio's *Excellence,* §1.

2. Guarino, *Letter to Leonello,* §1.

3. See Guarino, *Excellence,* §9.

4. Cic. *Tusc.* 3.3.

5. Cic. *Phil.* 1.29.

6. Cic. *Planc.* 60. Modern editions of this passage read *in virtute multi sunt adscensus, ut is maxime gloria excellat qui virtute plurimum praestet* (There are many degrees of virtue so that he excels most in glory who is most outstanding in virtue). With one exception, the manuscripts agree with Poggio's *multis,* but all have *sunt* rather than *est.*

7. Val. Max. 6.9.2.

8. Gell. *NA* 6.1.5 (not Book 7, as Poggio claims).

9. Gell. *NA* 4.18.1.

10. Cic. *Marcell.* 26. (Most manuscripts have *in suos cives,* "toward his fellow citizens," but a small group of manuscripts, evidently including Poggio's source, omits *cives.*)

11. This was reportedly alleged by Mark Antony, Suet. *Aug.* 68.

12. Poggio refers to to the quadruple triumph celebrated in September 46 BCE, followed by the triumph over Spain celebrated in 45.

13. See Poggio, *Excellence,* §15; Guarino, *Excellence,* §26. The treatise *On Illustrious Men* has been attributed to Pliny the Elder and Pliny the Younger, Cornelius Nepos, Suetonius, and Sextus Aurelius Victor; the reference here is to §49.4.

14. See Poggio, *Excellence,* §18.

15. Sen. *Ep.* 86.5. Rome was captured by the Gauls in 390 BCE.

16. August. *De civ. D.* 3.21.

17. Sil. 17.651–52.

18. Sen. *Ep.* 86.1. The allusion is to Scipio's self-imposed exile at Liternum.

19. Livy 28.17. On the occasion of the expulsion of the Carthaginians from Spain.

20. Cf. the proverb *utramque paginam facit* ("enters both columns," sc. in a ledger), discussed by Erasmus, *Adagia* 1315 = 2.4.15, based on Plin. *HN* 2.22.

21. Cic. *Att.* 7.11.1. This letter, written in 49 BCE, in fact predates Cicero's *On Behalf of Marcellus.*

22. Cic. *Off.* 1.26.

23. Cic. *Off.* 2.84.

24. Cic. *Off.* 2.27.

25. Poggio, *Excellence,* §25.

26. Guarino, *Excellence,* §3.

27. Poggio is hypercritical: Cicero himself uses *nuper* in the same sense in *Inv.* 1.25.

28. Cic. *Off.* 2.16.

29. Callisthenes of Olynthus (360–328 BCE), a great-nephew of Aristotle, was appointed by Alexander the Great as historian of his Asiatic campaign. Callisthenes' growing criticism of Alexander, and implication in a plot to kill him, led to his imprisonment and death, either from torture or natural causes.

30. The emperor Nero (37–68 CE) was tutored by the Stoic philosopher and playwright Lucius Annaeus Seneca (ca. 4 BCE–65 CE), known as Seneca the Younger, whose nephew was the poet Marcus Annaeus Lucanus (39–65 CE). With time, Seneca's influence over Nero waned, and he unsuccessfully tried to retire from court in 62 and 64. Lucan initially won Nero's patronage but later incurred his enmity, perhaps on account of critical verses. Both men were implicated, probably wrongly in Seneca's case, in the Pisonian Conspiracy against Nero of 65 and forced to commit suicide. Both opened their veins in the bath and bled to death, their death scenes described in moving detail by Tacitus.

31. Guarino, *Excellence*, §10; Cic. *Off.* 3.4.

32. For the historians Sallust, Trogus, and Livy, see Guarino, *Excellence*, §9; Cornelius Nepos (ca. 110–ca. 25 BCE) is not in fact mentioned there. For the poets Vergil and Horace, see Guarino, *Excellence*, §8; for Seneca see §24 above.

33. Justin 43.5.11–12.

34. But in fact did not do so: Sen. (the Elder) *Controv.* 11.

35. The reference is to Poggio's friend Niccolò Niccoli (1364–1437), who was a famed arbiter of ancient and contemporary authors, even though he wrote nothing himself. He was the main speaker in Leonardo Buni's *Dialogues for Pier Paolo Vergerio* (ca. 1407), as he would again be in Poggio's own *On the Unhappiness of the Leaders*, and in the former text he espouses the position Poggio attributes to him here.

36. For Servius, Priscian, and Donatus, see Guarino, *Excellence*, §7. Flavius Caper (fl. 150 CE), whose works are lost but whom Poggio would know of as highly regarded by Priscian, is not actually mentioned in that passage by Guarino, who instead refers to Acron and Asper.

37. Lucius Julius Caesar, cousin of Gaius, was consul in 64 BCE and is reported as speaking in favor of the death penalty for the Catilinarian conspirators in Cic. *Cat.* 4.13; he was not, however, known as an orator and does not appear in *Brutus*, Cicero's history of oratory in dialogue form. Poggio probably meant to refer to C. Julius Caesar Strabo Vopiscus, who was one of the speakers in Cicero's *On the Orator*. Quintus Hortensius Hortalus (114–50 BCE), consul in 69, was an Optimate and mentor of Cicero, who depicted him in his lost dialogue (and see §70 below); the intended Crassus and Antonius are probably Lucius Licinius Crassus (140–91 BCE) and Marcus Antonius (143–87 BCE), both protagonists in Cicero's dialogue *On the Orator*, rather than their namesakes in the first and second triumvirates; Marcus Junius Brutus (85–42 BCE) is Caesar's killer and the dedicatee of Cicero's *Brutus* and other works.

38. Guarino, *Excellence*, §10.

39. Probably Quintus Mucius Scaevola Pontifex (d. 82 BCE), founder of the study of Roman law and author of an eighty-volume work on civil

law, but Poggio may also be thinking of his relative Quintus Mucius Scaevola Augur (d. ca. 87 BCE), who features in several of Cicero's dialogues; Servius Sulpicius (ca. 106–43 BCE), a correspondent of Cicero's and quoted in the *Pandects*, although his own legal works are lost; and Gaius Trebatius Testa (fl. 1st century BCE), dedicatee of Cicero's *Topics* and recommended by him as legal advisor to Caesar, who is likewise cited by later lawyers while his own works are lost.

40. Cic. *Off.* 2.67.

41. Sen. (the Elder) *Controv.* 1.6–7.

42. Ov. *Met.* 8.250.

43. Tac. *Hist.* 1.1 (Poggio takes Tacitus' *Histories* to be a continuation of—or indeed the same work as—his *Annals*, since in the manuscripts both appear together under the title *From the Death of the Divine Augustus*, with *Histories* 1–5 listed as Books 17–21). In Tacitus' text, *res* is plural and means "affairs" or "acts." This passage was also quoted by Leonardo Bruni in his *Laudation on the City of Florence*, as discussed in the Introduction, "Interpreting the *Controversy*" and "Sources of the *Controversy*."

44. Guarino, *Excellence*, §65.

45. Guarino, *Excellence*, §65. Poggio prefers to leave unmentioned the source of Guarino's facts, which is Suet. *Iul.* 41.1, while the conclusion about liberty is Guarino's own.

46. Guarino, *Excellence*, §65. As above, Poggio leaves unmentioned the source of Guarino's statement, which is Suet. *Iul.* 42.1, but he makes the attribution in §39, where he accuses Guarino of misquotation; see ad loc.

47. Guarino, *Excellence*, §13.

48. Cic. *Off.* 2.2–3.

49. Cic. *Off.* 3.2.

50. "This," that is, the superiority of affection over intimidation as a means of securing one's rule, Cic. *Off.* 2.23.

51. Cic. *Off.* 2.29.

52. Guarino, *Excellence*, §10.

53. Sen. *Dial.* 2.2.2 (= *On Constancy*).

54. Guarino, *Excellence*, §10.

55. Guarino, *Excellence*, §13.

56. Suet. *Iul*. 76.

57. Suet. *Iul*. 77.

58. Suet. *Iul*. 78.

59. Suet. *Iul*. 79.1 (modern editions read Marullus and Flavus).

60. Suet. *Iul*. 41.1.

61. Guarino, *Excellence*, §§13, 65.

62. Guarino, *Excellence*, §65; Suet. *Iul*. 42.

63. Suet. *Iul*. 42.1 (*decem*, "ten," is a crux in Suetonius' text faithfully copied by Guarino and Poggio; some more recent manuscripts and the 1533 Basel edition give *quadraginta*, "forty"; Isaac Causabon's 1595 Geneva edition *lx*, "sixty").

64. As noted regarding Guarino, *Excellence*, §65, this apparent misreading of Suetonius almost certainly did not occur in Guarino's authorial letter, but probably stems from the copy of it with which Poggio worked. Poggio's accusation is thus baseless but not, I think, in bad faith.

65. "The ruin . . . greed" is from Guarino, *Excellence*, §41. Sall. *Cat*. 10.4.

66. Guarino, *Excellence*, §18.

67. Guarino, *Excellence*, §18.

68. Guarino, *Excellence*, §21; Plut. *Alex*. 1.2.

69. Guarino, *Excellence*, §21; Plut. *Alex*. 1.2.

70. Poggio selectively paraphrases Guarino's translation in *Excellence*, §21, of Plut. *Alex*. 1.2.

71. Suet. *Iul*. 45.3.

72. Suet. *Iul*. 1.3.

73. Guarino, *Excellence*, §22.

74. Guarino, *Excellence*, §22.

75. Guarino, *Excellence*, §26.

76. Cic. *Phil*. 2.84, *sudat, pallet*, but not *contremiscit*.

77. Guarino, *Excellence*, §26.

78. Lucius Sicinius Dentatus (d. ca. 450 BCE), as described by Aulus Gellius, *NA* 2.11.2; Pliny, *NH* 16.5.14, gives the family name as Siccius. Quintus Fabius Maximus (ca. 280–203 BCE), named *Cunctator* (the Delayer), was consul five times, was dictator, and famously harried Hannibal with a kind of guerilla warfare, refusing pitched battle.

79. Guarino, *Excellence*, §29.

80. Guarino, *Excellence*, §29.

81. Val. Max. 6.9.15; Non. 534.16.

82. Guarino, *Excellence*, §27.

83. Guarino, *Excellence*, §27.

84. An Italian version of the Old French *Song of Roland* existed before Matteo Maria Boiardo's *Orlando in Love* (1483–95) and Ludovico Ariosto's *The Frenzy of Orlando* (1516–22).

85. Guarino, *Excellence*, §§27 and 30.

86. Guarino, *Excellence*, §2.

87. Guarino, *Excellence*, §32. The *comitium* in the Roman forum was a meeting place for assemblies, where much judicial and electoral activity took place.

88. For this principle, see Cic. *Off.* 1.43.

89. Poggio appears to misremember Suet. *Iul.* 54.1, which speaks of *a sociis pecunias accepit emendicatas in auxilium aeris alieni*, "money he received from the allies obtained by begging to help his debt."

90. Suet. *Iul.* 54.

91. Guarino, *Letter to Leonello*, §1; Verg. *Aen.* 1.286.

92. Serv. *ad Aen.* 1.287.

93. Verg. *Aen.* 1.286–88.

94. Verg. *Aen.* 1.290–94.

95. Poggio borrows "unholy Fury" from Verg. *Aen.* 1.294.

96. Poggio reaches this conclusion by selective quotation and ignoring the structure: he does not quote *hunc tu . . . caelo . . . accipies* ("you will

receive him into heaven," Verg. *Aen.* 1.289–90), referring to Caesar, and does not note that *tum* (1.291) marks a chronological progression.

97. Guarino, *Excellence*, §36.

98. Guarino, *Excellence*, §36.

99. Guarino, *Excellence*, §37, citing Livy 26.18.

100. Livy 26.18.8–19.3.

101. Guarino, *Excellence*, §39; Poggio, *Excellence*, §6.

102. Guarino, *Excellence*, §§40, 41.

103. Guarino, *Excellence*, §40.

104. Sall. *Cat.* 50.4.

105. Cic. *Att.* 12.21.1.

106. Guarino, *Excellence*, §40.

107. Guarino, *Excellence*, §41.

108. Poggio's argument is that *servare*, "to save," means practically the same as *conservare*, "to preserve," regardless of the prefix.

109. Poggio uses the legal definition given in Just. *Inst.* 1.3.3, *servi ex eo appellati sunt, quod imperatores servos vendere, ac per hoc servare, nec occidere solent*, "slaves are named from the fact that commanders are wont to sell, and thus save, slaves, and not to kill them."

110. Guarino, *Excellence*, §39.

111. Juv. 2.40.

112. Guarino, *Excellence*, §42.

113. Guarino, *Excellence*, §45.

114. Guarino, *Excellence*, §§43, 42.

115. The reference is to Cato's divorce of his wife Marcia so that she could marry Hortensius, see Guarino, *Excellence*, §44.

116. This is not Guarino's translation of Plutarch, as Poggio claims, but Guarino's own assessment in *Excellence*, §44.

117. Guarino, *Excellence*, §44; Plut. *Cat. Min.* 49.4.

118. Modeled after Cic. *Cael.* 33–34. Cato and the games: Val. Max.

2.10.8. "They took his words for judgments" is inferred from the *Distichs of Cato*, which date to the third or fourth century.

119. Poggio puns on the name "Cynic," κυνικός in Greek, meaning "dog-like."

120. Guarino, *Excellence*, §44.

121. Sen. *Tranq.* 16.1.

122. Poggio appears to forget that Hirtius and Caesar each wrote an *Anti-Cato*.

123. Guarino, *Excellence*, §43.

124. Sall. *Cat.* 54.5–6.

125. Hieron. Migne, *PL* 25.861A (*In Hoseam*).

126. Guarino, *Excellence*, §47.

127. Guarino, *Excellence*, §47; Suet. *Iul.* 35.1.

128. Guarino, *Excellence*, §47.

129. The eunuchs Ganymede and Pothinus and the Egyptian boy-king Ptolemy XIII Theos Philopater (62–47 BCE), all involved in Caesar's Alexandrian war.

130. Guarino, *Excellence*, §47.

131. Guarino, *Excellence*, §6.

132. Cic. *Clu.* 139.

133. Cic. *Off.* 1.26, 2.23, 3.82–83.

134. Sen. *Ben.* 2.12.1. The reference is not to Julius Caesar and Pompey the Great, as Poggio implies, but to the emperor Gaius Caligula and Pompeius Pennus.

135. Cic. *Off.* 3.76.

136. See also Poggio, *Excellence*, §11.

137. Guarino, *Excellence*, §54.

138. Val. Max. 6.7.1. The wife was Tertia Aemilia.

139. Guarino, *Excellence*, §54.

140. Poggio confuses the name of the legendarily farsighted Lynceus of Messene with the word "lynxes"; see Erasmus, *Adagia* 1054 = 2.1.54.

141. Guarino, *Excellence*, §55; this assertion is not, as Poggio implies, Guarino's own, but a quotation from Isid. *Etym.* 14.4.22.

142. Pliny, *HN* 3.50. The origins of Etruria had been studied by Leonardo Bruni in the first book (1416) of his *History of the Florentine People*, where the same Plinian passage serves as the (unattributed) source (Hankins, *Leonardo Bruni. History*, 1:13). The etymology from Greek *thuein*, "to sacrifice," is also found at Serv. *ad Aen.* 2.781 and is attributed to Varro at *Grammaticae Romanae fragmenta*, p. 352 no. *405. Varro, *Rust.* 2.4.9, offers an etymological discussion of the same verb in relation to nuptial sacrifices in Etruria, but does not connect this to Etruria's name. Poggio may misremember, or infer a connection.

143. Guarino, *Excellence*, §55.

144. Poggio uses grammatical terminology: *partitivus* was used in medieval grammar to indicate part of a whole.

145. That is, Florence. The same etymology is given in Hankins, *Leonardo Bruni. History*, 1:3.

146. That is, Pesaro.

147. Guarino, *Excellence*, §§13, 58–62.

148. Guarino, *Excellence*, §§62, 61.

149. For example, Cic. *Ver.* 2.4.56; *Cat.* 1.2; *Dom.* 137; *Deiot.* 31.

150. Lucius Cassius Dio, also known as Dio Cassius (ca. 164–ca. 229 CE) wrote an eighty-volume *Roman History* in Greek. Born in Nicaea, in the province of Bithynia, he was a Roman senator, governor of Pergamum and Smyrna, and twice consul. He was politically active under the emperors Commodus to Severus Alexander.

151. Guarino, *Excellence*, §63; Dio 44.2.2.

152. Sall. *Cat.* 7.

153. For example, Cic. *Phil.* 2.25.

154. Cic. *Phil.* 1.35.

155. Guarino, *Excellence*, §67; Livy 38.53.9.

156. See §§62 and 82 above.

157. Guarino, *Excellence*, §68; Plut. *Caes.* 15.2.

158. This occurred in 356 BCE. Honoring the Ephesians' decision not to bestow fame on the arsonist, Poggio's probable source Valerius Maximus does not transmit the name (which Theopompus reports was Herostratus). Val. Max. 8.14 ext. 5.

159. For "firm and true glory," see Cic. *Ad Brut.* 9.2.

DEL MONTE, *LETTER TO POGGIO BRACCIOLINI*

1. Del Monte here shows that he read the previous contributions in the order advised by Poggio, *Proem*, §4.

2. Del Monte uses the idiomatic phrase "*a primis unguiculis*," literally meaning "from the first fingernails."

3. Presumably, an intentional echo of Guarino, *Excellence*, §2.

4. Jer. *Ep.* 10.2.

5. Juv. 1.162–63, with the Rutulian being the tribe's king and Aeneas' enemy in single combat, Turnus.

6. Poggio, *Proem*, §2.

7. Del Monte here echoes Guarino's phrasing in the covering letter to Leonello accompanying his *On the Excellence*.

8. For why it might have brought Guarino praise, see §39 below.

9. Poggio, in his *Defense*, e.g., §66, mused on what education Guarino gave his students. Del Monte, who was one of those students (see n. 21 below), takes up this prompt.

10. Del Monte here cites famous cases from antiquity of leading figures and their teachers, but he also alludes to Guarino's own injunction to his students to cultivate the reputation of their schoolmaster. On this trope, see Rundle, "Beyond the Classroom."

11. Here Del Monte provides an early instance of the phrase *humanitatis studia* being used to evoke an educational program: see Kohl, "Changing Concept."

12. Cic. *Amic.* 37.

13. Del Monte alludes to his legal training and to the "action for harms" (*actio iniuriarum*) under civil law: *Digest* 47, tit. x.

14. Del Monte here echoes Poggio, *Defense*, §69.

15. Humfrey (1390–1447) was the youngest son of Henry IV and, at this point, the protector of the realm during the minority of his nephew, Henry VI, as well as being the heir presumptive to the throne. Del Monte had already cultivated him by presenting to him his dialogue, "On the Differences among the Vices" (*De vitiorum inter se differentia*): see Rundle, "Carneades' Legacy," and Pellizzari, *Variae humanitatis silva*.

16. That praise for a devotion to *humanitatis studia* is applied equally to Poggio (never a teacher) as to Guarino shows that a looser sense of the term than the educational is employed here, in contrast to above (see n. 11).

17. Cic. *Arch.* 16.

18. Cf. Cic. *Nat. D.* 1.60.

19. Jer. *Ep.* 52.14.

20. Two Ciceronian topoi are combined here: the "sweetness" of liberty (e.g., Cic. *Cat.* 4.16) and philosophy as the best gift of the gods (e.g., Cic. *Fam.* 15.4.16, *Ac.* 1.7).

21. This was presumably during Guarino's time of teaching in Venice, between 1414 and 1419, when Del Monte was in his midteens.

22. Marcus Atilius Regulus was consul in 267 BCE and again in 256, and a general in the First Punic War. Captured by the Carthaginians in 255, he was later sent by them to Rome as an envoy to arrange an exchange of prisoners, but instead he urged the senate to reject the proposal. Augustine follows earlier writers saying that he voluntarily returned to his captivity and was tortured to death: see, e.g., Cic. *Off.* 3.99–111.

23. August. *De civ. D.* 1.24.

24. That is Marcus Brutus (?85–42 BCE), the conspirator against Julius Caesar who is discussed below, at §32. Marcus Furius Camillus, appointed by the Romans dictator during the invasion by the Gauls in 387/6 BCE; cf. Poggio, *Defense*, §13.

25. Livy 7.1.9.

26. Guarino had invoked other passages of Cicero in support of his praise of Caesar: *Excellence*, §§51–52.

27. Cic. *Off.* 1.26; cf. Poggio, *Defense*, §16.

28. An allusion to Plin. *HN* 7.117.

29. August. *De civ. D.* 3.21. As is clear from the sequel, Del Monte takes the genitives at the opening of this passage — *eodem tempore morum optimorum maximaeque concordiae* (at the same time of best manners and maximum harmony) — to refer to Scipio, when Augustine is using them, with characteristic irony, of the time in which he lived. Augustine's irony is directed at Sallust, who has just been cited for his idealized view of the earlier republic: Sall. *Cat.* 9.

30. A reference to Caesar's defeat of Pompey near Pharsalus (present-day Farsala) in Thessaly in 48 BCE.

31. Cic. *Phil.* 2.54.

32. Cic. *Phil.* 2.53, but with the last phrase about liberty being, notably, Del Monte's own addition.

33. Here *res publica* is translated literally as "public property" (as opposed to *res privata*, "private property") to clarify the logic of the quotation from Cicero.

34. The quotation is actually from Cic. *Rep.* 1.39, repeated more briefly at Cic. *Rep.* 3.43. The text of Cicero's philosophical work, except for a part of Book 6 (the "Dream of Scipio" [*Somnium Scipionis*]), was not available to the humanists, and Del Monte's source is August. *De civ. D.* 2.21.

35. Cf. Cic. *Rep.* 3.43, also known indirectly from August. *De civ. D.* 2.21.

36. Arist. *Eth. Nic.* 5.7 (1134a32).

37. Del Monte echoes here the phrasing of Guarino, *Excellence*, §26, to which Poggio responds in his *Defense*, §§51–52.

38. Guarino, *Excellence*, §61.

39. Guarino, *Excellence*, §66.

40. Livy 9.4.15.

41. Cic. *Rep.* 6.13 = 17 Powell.

42. Cic. *Phil.* 2.64.

43. Plut. *Them.* 31. There were two Latin translations of this life available at the time of this letter. The one that gained a wider circulation was by Lapo da Castiglionchio, and that was certainly available to Humfrey, Duke of Gloucester, at the time Del Monte was writing. However, an earlier version was that by Guarino of Verona, and Del Monte's phrasing of *hausto tauri cruore* quotes Guarino's version (e.g., BAV, MS. Vat. lat. 1875, fol. 18), rather than Lapo's rendition (which has *epoto taurino sanguine:* see the *editio princeps* [Rome, 1470], fol. 89v).

44. Plut. *Sert.* 22. The one translation available was that by Leonardo Bruni, which was available in England while Del Monte was there, as Bruni had sent a copy of his Plutarch translations to Humfrey, Duke of Gloucester; the manuscript is now London: British Library, MS. Harl. 3426.

45. Sen. *Ep.* 86.1–3; cf. Poggio, *On the Excellence,* §20.

46. Guarino, *On the Excellence,* §65.

47. A fragment from an unidentified work of Cicero's recorded in Jer. *Ep.* 66.7.

48. Plut. *Caes.* 13–14. As Del Monte himself says later, he is using Guarino's translation, and this long passage is a précis of Guarino's Latin.

49. This is the name given in Guarino's translation, although it was actually Quintus Servilius Caepio.

50. On Clodius, see Guarino, *Excellence,* §60.

51. The precise phrase *Romanae lumen facundiae* was used of Priscian by Eutyphus, *Ars de verbo* 1.8 (= *Grammatici latini,* 5:456), but Del Monte probably also had in mind praise of Cicero such as *facundiae Latiarumque litterarum parens* (the parent of eloquence and Latin letters), Plin. *HN* 7.117.

52. Poggio, *Excellence,* §§18, 21.

53. Plut. *Caes.* 35, closely paraphrasing Guarino's translation.

54. Plin. *HN* 37.205.

55. A Stoic doctrine often invoked by Cicero, e.g., *Off.* 1.22.

56. Verg. *Aen.* 6.817–23.

57. Livy 2.7.4.

58. Verg. *G.* 2.43.

59. Cic. *Phil.* 2.29.

60. Cic. *Phil.* 2.32.

61. Cic. *Phil.* 2.114.

62. Del Monte takes his lead from Poggio, *Defense*, §§70–76.

63. Guarino, *Excellence*, §42.

64. This and the immediately following sentences are a quotation from Plut. *Cat. Min.* 1.2, in a close paraphrase of the translation by Leonardo Bruni (which, in discussing Cato's smile, has difficulty in rendering the Greek original).

65. Plut. *Cat. Min.* 48, using Bruni's translation.

66. A reference to Clodius' prosecution of Fabia for *incestum* in 73 BCE, briefly mentioned by Plut. *Cat. Min.* 19. However, Moreau, *Clodiana religio*, 233–37 (followed by Tatum, *The Patrician Tribune*, 44), refers the key piece of evidence, Plut. *Cat. Min.* 19.5–6, to the year 61, rather than 73.

67. Plut. *Cat. Min.* 53.

68. Cf. Cic. *Brut.* 322.

69. Luc. 2.389–91.

70. Luc. 2.439–40.

71. Cf. Hor. *Carm.* 3.3.1–8.

72. Guarino, *Excellence*, §42.

73. Lactant. *Div. inst.* 5.15, a quotation repeatedly used by Del Monte: see Rundle, "Carneades' Legacy."

74. On Barbaro, see Poggio, *Proem*, §1. Del Monte's original phrasing claims as a fact that Barbaro (with whom he was acquainted) gave his judgment on the controversy, but no such response is known to survive. When Del Monte later came to transcribe and revise his letter, he

changed the phrasing to "ought not to have neglected to give you some response."

POGGIO, *ON THE UNHAPPINESS OF LEADERS*

1. The rationale for the translation of the Latin terms *princeps, principes,* and *principatus* are given in the Introduction, n. 43.

2. Tommaso Parentucelli of Sarzana (1397–1455), appointed bishop of Bologna in 1444 and cardinal in 1446, became Pope Nicholas V in 1447, in succession to Eugene IV (see n. 5). A poor boy, educated in Bologna, he was made a member of the household of Niccolò Albergati, bishop of Bologna, in 1420, where he graduated in arts (1421) and then theology (1423). He followed Albergati to Florence in 1434, after the pope's expulsion from Rome (see n. 5), where he became a close associate of the Florentine humanists, including Poggio, Leonardo Bruni, and Carlo Marsuppini (who appears as a character in the dialogue: see n. 7). A prominent supporter of humanist studies, he collected the nucleus of what would become the Vatican Library.

3. This point is elaborated at 45.5.

4. "The blind minds of men," *caeca mens hominum,* cf. Luc. 2.14–15, Stat. *Theb.* 5.718–19, *caeca futuri / mens hominum* (mind of men blind to the future). These are not mentioned by Canfora in his edition, although they are much closer to Poggio's words than Lucr. 2.14, *o miseras hominum mentes, o pectora caeca* (O wretched minds of men, O blind hearts), which Canfora cites in his apparatus of sources and makes part of his wider discussion of Lucretian influences (Canfora, "Topica del 'principe,'" 74; see also 5–8 and 67–68, 71, 73–75). For further skepticism about the role of Lucretius in *The Unhappiness of Leaders,* see nn. 27, 153, and 156, and Introduction.

5. Gabriele Condulmer (1383–1447), a Venetian, appointed bishop of Siena in 1407, then cardinal of San Clemente in 1408, succeeded Martin V in 1431 as Pope Eugene IV. His disagreements with the Council of Basel led to its appointment of the antipope Felix V in 1439. But Eugene in response had established his own council, at Ferrara in 1437, moving it later to Florence, which ignored Basel and negotiated a reunification

agreement with the Greek Church, signed in July 1439. His disagreements with the Colonnas, the family of Martin V, led to his expulsion from Rome in 1434 and his move to Florence, which ought, then, to be the date at which the dialogue is set (but see n. 13 below).

6. Niccolò Niccoli (1365–1437) was a major figure in the humanist circle of Florence. Though he wrote only one (now lost) work, *On Orthography*, he made a major contribution toward the development of the humanistic script perfected by Poggio. His circle of friends included Coluccio Salutati, Leonardo Bruni, and Poggio. But he had a reputation for outspokenness, which led to many quarrels, including with Bruni and Francesco Filelfo, who wrote a satire attacking him. He was famous for his support of Poggio's search for Latin manuscripts (mentioned by him in section 5: see n. 20) and was an avid collector — and transcriber — of them. His library of Greek and Latin manuscripts, which features in this dialogue as the setting for the conversation, was left on his death to the Convento di San Marco in Florence. Despite his own reticence in writing, Niccoli appears as an interlocutor in dialogues by Valla (*On Pleasure*) and Tortelli (*On the Excellence of Medicine and the Laws*), as well as in several by Poggio (*On Avarice, Whether One Ought to Marry, On Nobility,* and *On the Unhappiness of Leaders*).

7. Carlo Marsuppini of Arezzo (1398–1453) studied in Florence under Guarino of Verona and later taught the sons of Cosimo de' Medici (see next note). Appointed professor of poetry, rhetoric, and Greek in 1431, replacing Francesco Filelfo, he played an important role in the Florentine humanist circle as a close friend of Niccoli (see n. 6), Ambrogio Traversari, and Poggio. In 1444, he succeeded Bruni as Chancellor of Florence, a post he held until his death, being succeeded in turn by Poggio. Like Niccoli, he was a reluctant writer, though he was responsible for some translations from the Greek (the *Battle of Frogs and Mice*, the Homeric *Hymn to Mars, Iliad* 1 and 10, and Isocrates' *To Nicocles*: see n. 64), a small number of Latin poems, a prose *Consolation* on the death of the mother of Cosimo and Lorenzo de' Medici, and some letters (to Pontano, Tortelli, and Valla among others). The perception of his central role in the humanist circle, however, like that of Niccoli, can be gauged by his appearances in Latin dialogues by Giovanni Lippi (*On the Excellence of the*

Laws and Medicine) and Poggio (*Symposiastic Debate* and *On the Unhappiness of Leaders*), as well as by the false attribution to him of several works (Alberti's *Tale of Philodoxus* and the *Table-Talk* named *Virtue*, and Guarino's version of Isocrates' *Life of Evagoras*).

8. Cosimo de' Medici (1389–1464) was for many years head of the wealthy and influential Medici bank, his position at which brought him and his family great influence in Florence. But his rivals, the Albizzi, managed to have him exiled in 1433 and attempted to change the republic's government so as to reduce Medici power. Cosimo went into exile in Venice, where there was a branch of his bank, and was recalled late in 1434 (so *after* the supposed date of the conversation reported in *On the Unhappiness*: see n. 13 below), when the pope's intervention had undermined a planned coup by the Albizzi. After his return, Medici control over the reins of the state steadily increased, although Cosimo was never in any formal way a head of state. Further attempts by the now exiled Albizzi, in league with Filippo Maria Visconti, Duke of Milan, to undermine Cosimo's position came to an end after the battle of Anghiari on June 29, 1440, soon after Poggio had completed *On the Unhappiness of Leaxders*. Cosimo was an important patron of the arts and literature, who knew Latin, consorted with Florence's leading scholars—Traversari, Bruni, Niccoli, and Poggio—had Latin works dedicated to him (for example, Panormita's *Hermaphrodite* and Bruni's translation of the *Economics* attributed to Aristotle), and was the patron of Marsilio Ficino, the translator of Plato.

9. Poggio had alluded to Niccoli's competence in Greek and Latin, his love of learning, and his grasp of ancient history (all crucial for Poggio's portrayal of him here) in his 1437 funeral oration, published in De Keyser and Schadee, *Poggio Bracciolini. Eulogies*, 134–59, §18: "He worked very hard on Greek letters; Latin letters he grasped so well that no one better understood the teachings of all disciplines of the liberal arts in which men are commonly instructed. He had all the histories of old so firmly in his mind that he almost seemed to have been present at the events" (*Graecis litteris plurimum insudavit; Latinas ita tenuit, ut nemo melius omnium disciplinarum, quibus homines liberaliter institui solent, doctrinam percepit. Priscas historias ita omnes memoriae fixas habuit, ut illis ferme interfuisse vi-*

deretur). Poggio also mentioned the use of Niccoli's house as a meeting place for scholars, §26: "Learned men saw his house as their home and as it were a shared resort for letters" (*Domum suam docti viri suum domicilium existimabant et tamquam commune diversorium litterarum*). He also focused attention on Niccoli's particular enthusiasm for cosmography, §18: "He made such a study of geography that he knew the regions, cities, lands, places and areas of the whole world better than those who had long resided in them" (*Cosmographiae adeo operam dederat, ut toto orbe terrarum singulas provincias, urbes, situs, loca, tractus denique omnis melius nosset quam ii, qui in eis diutius habitassent*). Given the close ties between Niccoli and Poggio and their shared passion for books, it is likely that Poggio is thinking here of a quite specific MS. It might well be the Latin version of Ptolemy's *Geography* (Canfora, "Topica del 'principe,'" 66) translated ca. 1406–9 by Jacopo Angeli da Scarperia, another student of Salutati and Chrysoloras, since the surviving Greek MSS are mostly now in the Vatican Library. In any case, Niccoli was fascinated by geography, and presumably Cosimo and Carlo are being portrayed as eager fellow enthusiasts.

10. The setting may be modeled on that of Cic. *Fin.* 3, where Cicero encounters Cato in Lucullus' library. We owe this insight to Andrew Dyck.

11. After Eugene's retreat from Rome to Florence in May 1434, Poggio had fallen into the hands of Piccinino's soldiers near Narni, but managed to regain his freedom and reach Florence after paying a large ransom (*On the Variety of Fortune*, in Fubini, *Poggii Opera omnia*, 2:92; Walser, *Poggius Florentinus*, 157–58).

12. The Scythians were a nomadic people, located by Greeks and Romans in the lands to their north and east, from the Danube to the Don, Caucasus, and Volga. Among the passages in classical writers from which Poggio may have derived his notion of their lifestyle is Val. Max. 5.4 ext. 5.

13. Poggio entered the curia as a scribe toward the end of 1403, or in early 1404 (Walser, *Poggius Florentinus*, 20), so his calculation is a little out if he is thinking of the summer of 1434 as the fictive date for the dialogue

(as two of his time indicators suggest: see nn. 5 and 11 above). Perhaps he was thinking of the *year* in which he set the dialogue (1434)? But in any case, he had spent the years 1418 to 1423 in England in the service of Henry Beaufort, bishop of Winchester, hardly to be counted as a curial appointment. So it could be that he was thinking of the actual date of writing: 1403 to 1440 is thirty-eight years, counting inclusively, from which he has subtracted the four years of his English service, to reach the figure "more than thirty-four." Adding 1403 + 34 (inclusively), however, would give us 1436 as the fictive date, which contradicts the specific time markers mentioned in nn. 5 and 11, but may in fact be a better answer, since Cosimo could not have engaged in this debate in Florence in the summer of 1434, being still in exile (see n. 8). The self-contradictory evidence provided by Poggio for his supposed fictive date may be another indication of hasty composition (see also nn. 132 and 146).

14. The papal court was in constant motion. For example, in the early years of Poggio's service (1405–10), the curia visited Viterbo, Siena, Lucca, Rimini, Pisa, Pistoia, and Bologna (Sabbadini, *Scoperte*, 75). At the dramatic date of the dialogue, it had been ejected from Rome and settled in Florence (see nn. 5 and 11 above).

15. This sardonic reflection probably relates to the way in which popes still regularly used arms in their struggles to retain authority over the Papal States.

16. "People happy who are allowed . . . gained with less" (*ii quibus datur parva industria tantum adipisci imperium, minore partum retinere*): cf. Sall. *Cat.* 2.4: "For power is easily retained by the same arts as were employed to obtain it in the first place" (*Nam imperium facile eis artibus retinetur, quibus initio partum est*).

17. Plin. *HN* 11.36.111. These creatures were first mentioned by Herod. 3.102–5, but the fact that the wording and the concept of the Indians stealing it from them here echo Pliny's account strongly suggests that he is the source. Herodotus was in any case not available in Latin translation until Lorenzo Valla's version was produced (some time after 1455?), and while Poggio might have been able to read Herodotus in the original,

he was still in 1440 studying Lucian (and so only in the early stages of his renewed Greek studies: see nn. 23, 24, 102, 104–6, and 152), while Pliny would have been well known to him.

18. Socrates' famous irony is mentioned by Cic. *De or.* 2.270, *Brut.* 292, and *Off.* 1.108, and Quint. *Inst.* 9.2.46, but it is just possible that Poggio may be thinking of the passage in Lucian, *Dial. mort.* 20 (6).5, where Socrates himself mentions the trait to Menippus.

19. Verg. *Aen.* 6.734.

20. During his period of service at the Council of Constance (1414–17), Poggio took time out to travel four times in search of copies of lost or damaged works of Classical Latin literature. The reference here is to his discovery of Cic. *Caec.* (at Langres), *Leg. agr.* 1–3, *Rosc. Am.*, *Rab. perd.*, *Rab. Post.*, and *Pis.* (some in France, some in Germany), and to a complete Quintilian, a complete Columella, and a Lucretius (at St. Gall). However, it must not be forgotten that, although Poggio here claims all these finds for himself through Niccoli, on two of those journeys he had been accompanied by others, whose letters contain details of the discoveries — in 1416 by Cencio de' Rustici and Bartolomeo da Montepulciano, and in January 1417 by Bartolomeo da Montepulciano. Among the other major literary finds from these journeys in Germany and France were Ammianus Marcellinus, Silius Italicus, Manilius, Statius' *Silvae*, and Valerius Flaccus, but also a number of previously unknown classical grammatical works and commentaries, as well as some Christian works, e.g., Lactant. *Opif. Dei* (Walser, *Poggius Florentinus*, 48–61; Sabbadini, *Scoperte*, 75–84).

21. This image is perhaps borrowed from Sall. *Cat.* 1.1: "so that they should not pass their lives in silence like cattle" (*ne vitam silentio transeant veluti pecora*).

22. "Who wish . . . good" (*videri . . . malunt*). Cf. Sall. *Cat.* 54.6: "he preferred to be good, rather than simply seem so" (*esse quam videri bonus malebat*).

23. The reference is to Lucian of Samosata, a second-century CE Greek satirist. His works were brought to Italy in the first place by Manuel Chrysoloras, who taught Greek in the Florentine *Studio* between 1397 and

1400, and naturally transferred his teaching materials from the Byzantine tradition to the West (see further Sidwell, *Lucian of Samosata*; Mattioli, *Luciano e l'Umanesimo*; Marsh, *Lucian and the Latins*; Berti, *Luciano di Samosata*). This reference is to §25 of his dialogue *Timon*, which was one of the earliest of his works to be translated, certainly before 1403 (by one Bertholdus, probably a student in Chrysoloras' classes). The dialogue dramatizes the idea that wealth is blind and cannot discriminate in the distribution of his gifts, using the template of Aristophanes' *Wealth*, through the story of Timon the misanthrope, later used by Shakespeare in *Timon of Athens*. Poggio had studied Greek at various stages earlier in his life but had returned more seriously to these studies since the Council of Ferrara-Florence, at which in 1439 the Eastern and Western Churches had agreed a reconciliation. This dialogue shows that Poggio had been reading some Lucian texts not yet translated (such as *Pisc.*, *Gall.*, and *Men.* — see nn. 24, 102, 104–6, and 152). Indeed, his Latin version for Tommaso Parentucelli (dedicatee of this dialogue) of *Iupp. ref.* belongs to this period (as does perhaps his version of *Lucius vel Asinus*: note that Walser's attribution [*Poggius Florentinus*, 231] of a version of *Ver. hist.* to Poggio is wrong; it was repeated by Canfora, "Topica del 'principe,'" 2 and 86, but silently corrected in his edition *Poggio Bracciolini. De infelicitate principum*, lvi with n. 2). Poggio moved on to bigger things with his abbreviated version of Xen. *Cyr.*, completed in 1446. See further Sidwell, "*Sodalitas*."

24. Lucian, *Pisc.* 20. This dialogue was later translated by Jacobus Perleo of Rimini, but must have been accessed by Poggio directly from the Greek text (see n. 23).

25. "And so . . . to its source," *eodem . . . oratio*. Cf. Cic. *Tusc.* 5.28.80: "But let your speech keep within bounds and return from whence it diverted from its path" (*Sed adhibeat oratio modum et redeat illuc unde deflexit*); Hor. *Sat.* 1.108: "I am going back to where I started" (*illuc unde abii redeo*).

26. Atlas was the mountain on whose shoulder the heavens were supposed to be supported. cf. Verg. *Aen.* 8.136–37, 141.

27. Epicurus (341–270 BCE), a moral and natural philosopher, who propounded the "atomic" theory, later argued in detail by Lucretius in his *On*

the Nature of the Universe. He is remembered here for his doctrine that the greatest good was pleasure. "In addition . . . the ears and the intellect," *Adsunt . . . exquisita.* Canfora's edition suggests as a parallel Lucr. 2.20–53, but it has no linguistic and very little material relationship to what Poggio writes here. In fact, the phrase *corporis atque animi voluptates* appears rather to be modeled on Cic. *Fin.* 2.27.89: "in bodily — and if you like I shall add mental — pleasure" (*in voluptate corporis — addam si vis animi*), and this passage actually does deal with the central proposition of the philosophy of the Epicurus, that pleasure is the greatest good, so is more likely to be what Poggio had in mind. See further nn. 4 and 153 and Introduction.

28. "But I recently read . . . who wore it," *Atqui . . . ureret* (Rossi, *Petrarca. Le familiari,* 9.5.25–28). The pope in question, whose words are probably paraphrased here from Petrarch's letter (Petrarch claims he picked this up "among some philosophical trifles" [*inter philosophicas nugas*]), was Pope Adrian (or Hadrian) IV, born Nicholas Breakspear (ca. 1100–1159), the only Englishman to have held the papacy. His tenure ran from 1154 to 1159.

29. "It is difficult . . . good," *difficile . . . esse.* Cf. Hes. *Op.* 289–92. Canfora's edition suggests Lucian, *Hermot.* 25 as the source, but the quote is found more accessibly in Cic. *Fam.* 6.18.5 and was also used by other humanists (e.g., Guarino of Verona in a letter to Francesco Barbaro, Constantinople, ca. 1408, in Sabbadini, *Epistolario,* 1:7, ll. 64–69).

30. The grammatical subject here, *assentatio,* gives way to plural verbs, so that de facto *scriptores* becomes their subject.

31. "Valerius Maximus . . . god," *Valerius . . . loquens.* Cf. Val. Max. 1.6.13. See Strasburger, *Caesar,* who collects the (mostly negative) assessments of Caesar's contemporaries.

32. "Consider, I ask you . . . than a good leader," *vide . . . testatur.* Paraphrased from *Hist. Aug., Aurelian* 42.5; 43, which was ascribed at the time to Flavius Vopiscus.

33. "The same writer . . . to empire," *Idem . . . reprehenditur.* Paraphrased and slightly précised from *Hist. Aug., Four Tyrants* 10.1–3.

34. Marcus Aurelius, Roman emperor from 161 to 180. "Marcus . . . within itself," *M. Aurelius . . . contineret.* Paraphrased from *Hist. Aug., Aurelius* 1.1; 5.3–4.

35. Diocletian (C. Aurelius Valerius Diocletianus), Roman emperor (284–305 CE). Ill-health forced his abdication. "Indeed, when . . . spent ruling," *Diocletianus . . . constituta.* Slightly misremembered from Aur. Vict. *Caes.* 39.5–7, where it is Herculius and Galerius, not Licinius, who ask him to return to power. See also §17.2 with n. 58.

36. "The young man . . . follows," *ille . . . rursum.* Slightly misremembered from Ter. *Eun.* 59–61: "In love all the following vices are present, insults, suspicions, fallings out, truces, war, the peace that follows" (*in amore omnia haec insunt vitia: iniuriae, / suspiciones, inimicitiae, indutiae, / bellum, pax rursum*).

37. "So the man . . . in danger," *qui . . . disciplina.* Canfora's edition compares Cic. *Att.* 2.7.4, but the only point of contact is the idea of losing control of the helm (of state) "when I had not relinquished the helm, but had it snatched away from me" (*non abiectis sed ereptis gubernaculis*), and Cicero continues the thought by expressing a wish to watch the ensuing shipwreck safely from shore.

38. "Leaders have . . . as others have," *Victum . . . appetitus.* Canfora's edition compares Xen. *Hier.* 1.17–19 and 4.2 (translated by Leonardo Bruni in 1403 and sharing the major theme of the unhappiness of rulers with this dialogue). The theme of the differentiation of food quality and the fear of poisoning are treated in different parts of Xenophon's dialogue, however.

39. "It . . . wicked," *ea . . . deteriores.* Ter. *Haut.* 483: "for we are all of us the worse for license" (*nam deteriores omnes sumus licentia*).

40. "For they do not lighten . . . possess them," *Non enim aegritudines . . . possidentes.* Canfora's edition compares Lucretius (an author Poggio had rescued from oblivion: see above, n. 20) 2.45–46 and 2.48. But 2.37–39 are more apposite: "Therefore since neither wealth nor nobility nor the glory of power produce any benefit in our bodies, it remains to be reckoned that they do not benefit our minds either" (*Quapropter quoniam nil*

nostro in corpore gazae / proficiunt neque nobilitas nec gloria regni, / quod superest, animo quoque nil prodesse putandum), although even this is not exactly what Poggio is saying here.

41. "That there is . . . individuals," *nullum . . . exsuperentur.* Canfora's edition compares Xen. *Hier.* 1.27–28, but in that passage Hiero is specifically refuting the superiority of the tyrant to the private individual in the realm of sexual satisfaction.

42. "Tyrants . . . vices," *tyrannos . . . abundare.* Just. *Epit.* 21.5.9. The sentiment occurs in a passage devoted to the fall of Dionysius of Syracuse.

43. "Cicero tells . . . to lead," *Natura . . . praeesse.* Cf. Cic. *Off.* 1.4.13, although the concept expressed in this passage as *principatus* is intellectual independence rather than acquisition of power over others. See Introduction.

44. "For it is not . . . distinguished," *Non enim . . . distinguuntur.* Sen. *Clem.* 1.12.1: "But the tyrant is distinguished from the king by his deeds, not by his title" (*Tyrannus autem a rege factis distat, non nomine*).

45. "Nevertheless . . . by tyranny," *Quamvis . . . defluxit.* Sall. *Cat.* 2, 51.27.

46. Augustus, the first Roman emperor (d. 14 CE); Vespasian (emperor, 69–79); Titus, son of Vespasian (emperor, 79–81); Antoninus Pius (emperor, 138–161); Marcus Aurelius (emperor, 161–180); Marcus Aurelius Severus Alexander (emperor, 222–235); Trajan (Marcus Ulpius Traianus; emperor, 98–117).

47. "Since . . . the world," *pace . . . parta.* Livy 1.19.3.

48. "One swallow . . . spring," *Una . . . designat.* Arist. *Eth. Nic.* 1.6 (= Bekker 1098a, 18–19).

49. Antony: M. Antonius (83–31 BCE); he along with M. Aemilius Lepidus (d. 13 or 12 BCE) and Augustus (C. Octavius) formed the triumvirate in 43, which defeated Caesar's assassins, Brutus and Cassius, at Philippi in 42. This passage as a whole is modeled on Sen. *Clem.* 1.9–11, with the help of other bits from Seneca and Suetonius (noted at the appropriate place).

50. Poggio misremembers his source (Sen. *Clem.* 1.9), which names the conspirator pardoned at Livia's behest as Gn. Cornelius Cinna Magnus

(Cinna), and erroneously substitutes C. Calpurnius Piso, the figurehead of the conspiracy against the emperor Nero in 65 CE.

51. Octavia died in 11 BCE. Sen. *Ad Polyb.* 15.3.

52. M. Claudius Marcellus, son of C. Claudius Marcellus and Octavia, Augustus' sister, and regarded as a possible heir to his uncle, died in 23 BCE. Nero Claudius Drusus, younger brother of the future emperor Tiberius, died in 9 BCE. Sen. *Ad Polyb.* 15.3 (Marcellus); *Ad Marciam* 2.3–5 and 3.1–3 (Marcellus and Drusus).

53. M. Vipsanius Agrippa, a strong supporter of Augustus and entrusted with his signet ring during the emperor's illness in 23 BCE as his chosen successor, died after returning from campaign in Pannonia in 12. C. Maecenas, a close friend of Augustus', but perhaps most famous for his patronage of the poets Vergil and Horace, died in 8 BCE. Sen. *Ben.* 6.32.2–4; cf. Suet. *Aug.* 66.3.

54. In fact, Augustus had only one daughter, Julia, whom he banished for her infamous lifestyle. Sen. *Ben.* 6.32.1. But his granddaughter, also called Julia, was involved in the scandal too, and Poggio, in making this error, was probably thinking of Suet. *Aug.* 65.1: *Iulias filiam et neptem omnibus probris contaminatas relegavit* (He exiled the two Julias, his daughter and his granddaughter, befouled as they had been by every sort of vice).

55. P. Quinctilius Varus, legate of the Rhine army, was attacked as he marched through the Teutoburg Forest by Arminius, war chief of the Germanic Cherusci, and all three of his legions were wiped out. Varus took his own life. Poggio's sources probably include Sen. *Ep.* 47.10 and Suet. *Aug.* 23, but perhaps also Flor. 2.30.

56. On the conspiracies that plagued Augustus, cf. Sen. *Brev. vit.* 4.5–6; Suet. *Aug.* 17 and 19.

57. "That . . . danger," *ut . . . nequeant.* Cf. Xen. *Hier.* 7.12.

58. For Diocletian, see n. 35. Maximian (Marcus Aurelius Valerius Maximianus), Roman emperor alongside Diocletian from 286 to 305 CE (he abdicated at the same time as Diocletian). "Something . . . to their lives," *quod . . . experti.* Aur. Vict. *Caes.* 39.5–7.

59. "But to discuss . . . they concealed," *Sed ut Augusti . . . tegerent.* Sen. *Brev. vit.* 4.1–5. The first part (down to *victurum sibi* is quoted word

for word (more or less), but from *In quadam . . . tegerent* Poggio paraphrases.

60. *Eth. Nic.* I.7.14–15 (= Bekker 1098a, 7–18), where Aristotle actually says, "The good of man is the active exercise of his soul's faculties in conformity with excellence of virtue, or if there be several human excellences, in conformity with the best and most perfect among them."

61. Cicero's dictum, attacking Caesar's cruelty, paraphrased in this passage, is preserved in Amm. Marc. 21.16.13 (= Epist. fr. II.5 Mueller): "Nor is there any happiness at all . . . unless it is prosperity derived from honorable dealings. Or to define the matter another way: happiness is the fortune which aids good counsels, and if a person does not make use of these there is no way he can be happy" (*neque enim quidquam est felicitas . . . nisi honestarum rerum prosperitas. Vel ut alio modo definiam: felicitas est fortuna adiutrix consiliorum bonorum, quibus qui non utitur, felix esse nullo modo potest*). Ammianus was one of the authors discovered by Poggio and Bartolomeo da Montepulciano at St. Gall in 1417 (see n. 20).

62. Psalm 48:13 and 21 (Vulgate): *Et homo cum in honore esset non intellexit; comparatus est iumentis insipientibus, et similis factus est illis.*

63. "Since prudence . . . charioteer," *prudentia . . . auriga.* Cf. Jer. *Adv. Iovinian.* (CPL 0610) 2.10 col. 312, l. 34, "The corporeal senses are like horses, running along without the aid of reason, while the soul like a charioteer holds their reins as they run" (*sensus corporum quasi equi sunt, sine ratione currentes, anima vero in aurigae modum retinet frena currentium*), a motif ultimately derived from Pl. *Phaedr.* 246a–b.

64. "There are very many things . . . corrected," *permulta . . . patiuntur.* Isoc. *Ad Nicocl.* 2–4. Canfora, "Topica del 'principe,'" 20, claims the translation is literal, although it is more of a close paraphrase (for example, *reges* is used to render *tyrannois*). Carlo Marsuppini, to whom Niccoli addresses his arguments and *exempla*, was in fact the first to translate this work (1430), of which eleven MSS survive. Bernardo Giustiniani, a pupil of Guarino, wrote another version in 1431, and this is preserved in twenty-five MSS. A third version Poggio might have known was that of Lapo da Castiglionchio, made in 1436, of which thirteen MSS survive. These data are taken from Gualdo Rosa, "Traduzioni latine dell' *A Nico-*

cle," 275–303, who does not mention the use of the Isocratean work in our text. Nonetheless, because at 281–82 of this article she fortuitously gives samples from this very passage of Isocrates, of the versions of Marsuppini, Giustiniani, and Lapo, it is possible to see (1) that Poggio is using a translation already to hand, rather than giving his own version, and (2) which translation it was. It is somewhat surprising, then, that he appears to be using—and slightly adapting or misremembering—not Marsuppini's, but Giustiniani's text: *Etenim permulta sunt, o Nicocles, quae privatum quenque ad bene honesteque vivendum inducant. In primis quod illorum vita non ocio, non luxu, non delitiis frangitur, sed quotidiano pro victu comparando laboribus vigiliisque inserviunt. Legibus deinde, quibus immoderata hominum frenatur cupiditas, parere coguntur.* Marsuppini's version is quite different: *Multa etenim sunt quae privatos erudire possunt ac illud inprimis quod non in luxu atque deliciis vivunt, sed per singulos dies certare atque laborare de iis quae ad victum pertinent necessario coguntur; inde suarum civitatum leges, quibus obtemperare necesse est.* The Giustiniani passage can be found in London, British Library MS Royal 10 B IX, fol. 81r–v and also id. fol. 148v. See also n. 75 below.

65. Cyrus the Great (d. 530 BCE), the founder of the Persian Empire. "Cyrus . . . delightful," *Rex Persarum . . . coactus est.* Sen. *Ira* 3.15.1.

66. Cambyses, son of and successor to Cyrus the Great. "Cambyses . . . drunkenness," *Cambyses . . . transfixit.* Sen. *Ira* 3.14.1–2.

67. Alexander the Great, that is, Alexander III of Macedon (356–323 BCE), conqueror of huge swathes of the Near East, which became the successor kingdoms under the Seleucids, Ptolemies, and Attalids. "That mad . . . to death," *Alexander . . . discruciavit.* Just. *Epit.* 15.3.3–5.

68. "I will not . . . of anger," *non recito . . . impetu ire facta.* Val. Max. 9.2.1.

69. For Alexander see n. 67. "I pass over . . . to a lion," *Transeo . . . obiecit.* Sen. *Ira* 3.17.1–2; Val. Max. 9.3 ext. 1; Just. *Epit.* 12.6.3 (Clitus), 15.3.7 (Lysimachus).

70. Sen. *Ira* 3.16.4.

71. Darius I (d. 486 BCE), king of Persia, defeated at Marathon by the Athenians in 490. "Darius . . . of him," *Darius . . . obiecit.* Sen. *Ira* 3.16.3.

72. Xerxes (son of Darius I), king of Persia (486–465 BCE), who invaded Greece and was defeated at Salamis (480) and Plataea (479). "As Xerxes . . . would pass," *Xerxes . . . iussit.* Sen. *Ira* 3.16.4.

73. "What . . . lust?," *Quid . . . habebant?* Cf. Just. *Epit.* 12.3.10, but Poggio is thinking more broadly, since this passage alludes only to Alexander and only to his *female* lovers.

74. "What . . . than this," *Quid . . . scribit.* Cf. Sen. *Clem.* 1.13.2–3 (this is not a direct quotation).

75. "If you think . . . great dangers," *si metus . . . eligendam.* Isoc. *Ad Nicocl.* 5. Once more Poggio appears to be using Giustiniani's translation: *Cum vero contra metus illorum solicitudines periculaque considers, cumque cogitando recenseas ex regibus aliquos quidem ab iis necatos quos sibi crediderant singulari fide devinctos regesque item ipsos in eos animadvertisse crudelius quos intimissime quadam familiaritate caros habuissent, aliis vero utraque simul hoc obtigisse . . . quamvis potius vitam eligendam arbitraris quam tot tantisque in periculis universe Asie imperatum ire.* (London, British Library MS Royal 10 B IX, fol. 81r, and also id. fol. 149r: see also n. 64 above).

76. "Nor is it . . . friendship," *Illud . . . privantur.* Cf. Xen. *Hier.* 3.5–6 (see n. 64).

77. For reuse of this passage, see Aeneas Silvius Piccolomini, *On the Miseries of Courtiers* (Wolkan, *Briefwechsel,* 482). See also nn. 81 and 152, and Introduction.

78. "For leaders . . . subjects," *nam timeri . . . malunt.* Cf. Cic. *Off.* 2.7.23.

79. "But it is . . . they fear," *Sed . . . oderunt.* Cf. Sen. *Clem.* 1.12.4.; also Cic. *Off.* 1.28.97.

80. "For leaders . . . alien to them," *Satis est . . . suspecta.* Cf. Xen. *Hier.* 5.1–2. See also §31, "Leaders . . . learning," *Non amant . . . virum,* and §33, "Read . . . education," *Legite quantum . . . accersitum.*

81. Hadrian (Publius Aelius Hadrianus), Roman emperor (117–138 CE). *Hist. Aug., Hadrian* 15.1–2, thought in Poggio's time to have been written by Aelius Spartianus. Poggio still had a copy of this work at his death (Walser, *Poggius Florentinus,* 420n30). This passage is also used by Aeneas Silvius Piccolomini in his *On the Miseries of Courtiers* (Wolkan, *Briefwech-*

sel, 460), almost certainly directly from Poggio's dialogue (see further nn. 77 and 152, and Introduction).

82. As possible sources here for "We read . . . freedom," *Plures . . . locus erat*, Canfora's edition suggests Thuc. 2.37 and 39, from Pericles' funeral speech, and Pl. *Menex*. 240d and 244e. Neither of these texts was yet available in Latin translation (Valla's Thucydides was begun only in 1448), so that Poggio's access to them would probably have had to be directly from the Greek. Although it is doubtful he had got much beyond Lucian at this stage of his studies (see nn. 23, 24, 102, 104–6, and 152, and Sidwell, "*Sodalitas*"), he moved among people who might have been able to pass on such information.

83. Plato (ca. 429–327 BCE), Athenian philosopher, whose works were now beginning to circulate more widely once again. Canfora's edition suggests Plato's *Seventh Letter* as the source for this anecdote: Bruni had translated Plato's *Letters* for Cosimo de' Medici between 1423 and 1427. But Poggio might also have got this story from Diog. Laert. 3.19, the Latin translation of which which had been completed by Ambrogio Traversari in 1433 and also dedicated to Cosimo.

84. Zeno of Elea, a fifth-century BCE philosopher, who lived long after the tyrant Phalaris. The source for the anecdote must be Val. Max. 3.3 ext. 2, the only place that mentions Phalaris' torture of Zeno. But Poggio has recalled—or read—too hastily, as Zeno appears from Valerius to have survived his ordeal (Valerius apppears to have drawn this inference from Cic. *Tusc*. 2.52, where the tyrant is not named).

85. Anaxagoras of Clazomenae (500–428 BCE), a philosopher who settled in Athens. Poggio is clearly recalling, inaccurately, the very next section of Valerius Maximus (3.3 ext. 4), where, however, the name of the executed philosopher is Anaxarchus. Nicocreon was king of Salamis in Cyprus at the time of Alexander the Great's conquests (336–323 BCE).

86. In some late MSS, the sentence "Nero forced Seneca and Lucan to their deaths," *Nero Senecam ac Lucanum mori coegit*, is inserted before *Socrates*. Lucius Annaeus Seneca (ca. 4 BCE–65 CE), tutor of the emperor Nero and then his political advisor, was forced to commit suicide for his alleged part in the conspiracy of Piso. His moralistic writings are often

cited by Poggio. Marcus Annaeus Lucanus (39–65 CE), author of the epic poem *On the Civil War*, was also forced to commit suicide for his adherence to Piso's plot against Nero. This sentence is almost certainly not original, but an interpolation, based on Poggio's statement in the *Defense*, §24.

87. Poggio has mixed the dates up: Socrates was tried, condemned, and executed in 399 BCE, four years after the restoration of democracy. Nonetheless, in doing so, he appears to show the antimonarchical tendencies displayed in the *Caesar-Scipio Controversy*. So Canfora suggests that Poggio may have misremembered Sen. *Tranq.* 5.1–3, where the first two sections show Socrates under the tyrants, while the third clearly shows his death under the restored democracy (*De otio* 8.2 does not appear relevant here, as there is no temporal marker at all).

88. Anicius Manilius Severinus Boethius (ca. 480–ca. 524 CE), author of the *Consolation of Philosophy*, appointed consul in 510 by the Ostrogothic king Theoderic. He was implicated in a conspiracy, imprisoned, and executed. Canfora suggests that Poggio may be thinking of Dante's reference to him at *Paradiso* 10.124–29, although, since the reader of that passage needs already to know about Boethius in order to see the reference is to him, it is likelier he recalled this information from an *accessus* to the *Consolation* (see, e.g., Wheeler, *Accessus*, 80–83, §§1–5, where it is said that Theoderic ordered him to be imprisoned at Pavia, but nothing is said about his death).

89. Quintilian (Marcus Fabius Quintilianus), first-century CE author of the *Education of an Orator*, a complete copy of which Poggio had discovered in 1417 (see n. 20). The information comes from Jer. *Chron.* at 88 CE (p. 190 Helm).

90. Lucius Caecilius (or Caelius) Firmianus Lactantius (ca. 240–320 CE), author of *Div. inst.* and *Opif. Dei*—rediscovered by Poggio (see n. 20)—among other works, was a convert to Christianity and a Christian apologist who lived under Diocletian and Constantine I. The information about his teaching post comes from Jer. *Chron.* at 318 CE (p. 230 Helm).

91. Dante Alighieri (1265–1321), born in Avignon of Florentine parents in exile, wrote his *Divine Comedy* in the Tuscan vernacular. In the poem's

three books, the poet is led through Hell and Purgatory by Vergil, and on into Heaven by Beatrice, with whom he was in love. Note the proviso that the poem would be as good as any other *if it had been written in Latin*, which reprises Niccoli's critique of Dante in Leonardo Bruni's *Dialogues to Pier Paolo Vergerio*.

92. Can Grande della Scala (1291–1329), leader of Verona and of the North Italian Ghibellines, and patron of Dante.

93. The anecdote is found in Billanovich, *Petrarca. Rerum memorandarum libri*, 2:83, but in a different form, with Can Grande as the one asking the question to which Dante gives the insulting answer and with a preface suggesting that Dante was a bit too free with his tongue. The fact that Poggio uses the version seen here in his own *Witticisms* 57 tends to suggest he himself had done the adaptation, which in any case is told here with a distinctly antimonarchical twist quite alien to Petrarch.

94. Francesco Petrarca (1304–74), was a vernacular poet (*Canzoniere* and *Trionfi*) and writer of many important prose works in Latin (such as the *Secret*, *On the Solitary Life*, and *On the Remedies for Either Fortune*), as well as the epic *Africa*. He is still widely regarded as the initiator of humanism, because of his abiding interest in Cicero (whose letters to Atticus he rediscovered), Vergil, and Seneca. The information given here (apart from the attack on Robert of Anjou) was widely available, for example in Leonardo Bruni's *Life of Petrarch*.

95. Robert of Anjou (1275–1343) was king of Naples, titular king of Jerusalem, and count of Provence and Forcalquier from 1309 until his death. Petrarch himself has only good things to say about him (Billanovich, *Petrarca. Rerum memorandarum libri* 1:10.1 and 1:37.4–17), suggesting that it is Poggio's antimonarchical stance that has led to his scant support for Petrarch (although his attitude may rather be informed by his concern for his own status — and that of his circle — as harbingers of humanism). See also §41.

96. Giovanni Boccaccio (1313–75), a correspondent and friend of Petrarch, who like him wrote both in prose and in verse, in the vernacular (the *Decameron*, for example) and in Latin (e.g., *On Famous Women* and *Genealogy of the Pagan Gods*).

97. Gian Galeazzo Visconti (1351–1402), the first duke of Milan (1395). It is perhaps surprising to find here an encomium not only of a monarch but of one who had also been a fierce enemy of Florence (his death saw him in the midst of a campaign against that city and Bologna). It is also worth recalling that Florence was again at war with Milan while Poggio wrote these words.

98. Verg. *Aen.* 1.118.

99. For this group of Roman emperors, see above, §15 with n. 46. For Augustus, see §§17, 18, 31, 42, and 45 with notes. For the problems of succession, see *Hist. Aug., Septimius Severus* 21.3–5.

100. *Hist. Aug., Septimius Severus* 20.4–5 (thought in Poggio's time to have been written not by Avidius Cassius but by Aelius Spartianus. See Canfora, "Topica del 'principe,'" 23, on this error of Poggio's).

101. Sen. *Prov.* 1.6.4.

102. Micyllus, a cobbler. The rest of this section translates and paraphrases Lucian, *Gall.* 24–25. This work was fully translated into Latin only much later in the fifteenth century (by Rodolphus Agricola), so Poggio was either working from a Greek text or someone had supplied him with the material. Since this was the period of his life to which we can ascribe the renewal of his Greek studies and the perfection of his knowledge (given that over the next decade he would translate not only shortish works of Lucian—*Juppit. refut.* and the *Asinus*—but also Xen. *Cyr.* and Diod. Sic.), it is clearly the first, as is shown by his use of *Menippus*, another hitherto untranslated Lucianic piece (see §45 with n. 151). We also know that Poggio owned a MS of Lucian, and he tells us in the dedication letter to his *Ass* translation that he was reading through such a codex when he came upon that work. The fact that his knowledge is direct allows us to see his method of approach to the Greek satirist: he paraphrases, skips portions he dislikes, and flattens out the wittiness of Lucian's style. He was, here as elsewhere, interested in the moralistic utility of what he found there and not in Lucian's famous ironical wit. He was also either using a faulty text that did not have the correct character changes marked or reading too quickly, or decided, for the sake of mak-

ing his point without undue explanation of the fantasy inherent in Lucian's scenario, to suppress the fact that it is Micyllus' cockerel who was once a king, not Micyllus himself. It is probably the second, as the whole premise of the dialogue is the paradoxical ability of the cockerel to speak, and this is in any case mentioned by Poggio here, and it would have taken a monumentally corrupt and lacunose text to hide this.

103. Phidias, the fifth-century BCE Athenian sculptor, most famous for his statue of Zeus at Olympia. Myron, the fifth-century BCE sculptor from Eleutherae, whose oeuvre included statues of gods, heroes, athletes, and animals.

104. At this point in Lucian's text, Micyllus asks the cockerel a question about what the disadvantages of ruling actually were, that are figured in the image of the statue, the answer to which is the account that follows. Poggio omits this, as he appears to have decided to simplify the original. Canfora's edition misses the fact that this response closely paraphrases — indeed nearly translates — Gall. 25.

105. These exempla all form part of the Lucian text and were not, as Canfora thought (see his edition), imported from a variety of different sources by Poggio. Nonetheless, Poggio has expanded the original by glossing (e.g., the quotation from Hom. Il. 10.3–4 is not ascribed to him in Lucian, and "the Lydian" appears in Poggio as "Croesus"), which makes it clear that he had thought about the points of reference. But he misremembers the Homeric quotation, confusing Agamemnon's sleeplessness (Il. 10.3–4) with that of Menelaus from just below in the same book (10.25–26). Croesus, sixth-century BCE king of Lydia, whose deaf and dumb son's story is related at Herod. 1.33 and 85. Artaxerxes, king of Persia (405/4–359/8 BCE), was challenged for the throne by Cyrus the Younger, supported by a group of Greek mercenaries that included the Spartan Clearchus. The coup failed when Cyrus was defeated in 401 at the battle of Cunaxa. Dionysius II, tyrant of Syracuse (367–357 BCE), was ousted from power in 357 by Parmenion (ca. 400–330 BCE), a general under the Macedonian kings Philip II and Alexander the Great — here simply referred to as "someone else": there was a tradition that Parme-

nion and Alexander disagreed with one another. Perdiccas (d. 321 BCE), a Macedonian nobleman and commander under Alexander the Great, quarreled with Ptolemy I (367/6–282 BCE), who had taken control of Egypt after Alexander's death, invaded his territory in 421 and was killed. The Ptolemy who quarreled with Seleucus II, king of the Seleucid empire (246–241 BCE), was Ptolemy III Euergetes, king of Egypt (246–221 BCE).

106. Lucian, *Cal.* 10. In contrast with *Gall.* (and *Men.*, for which see §45 with n. 152), *Cal.* had already been translated at least twice before the date of *On the Unhappiness of Leaders* (by Guarino of Verona ca. 1403–8, during his sojourn in Constantinople, and by Lapo da Castiglionchio, il Giovane, before 1438), and its description of Apelles' painting *Calumny* was utilized by Leon Battista Alberti in his *On Painting* (1435). Its popularity was in the first instance due to Manuel Chrysoloras, who used it in his Greek lessons at the Florentine *Studio* (1397–1400), as can be seen from the text, glosses, and scholia written up by one of his pupils in Vat. Urb. gr. 121 (Berti, "Scriba greco-latino" and "Scuola di Manuele Crisolora," with Deligiannis, *Fifteenth-Century Latin Translations*).

107. Cf. Cic. *Div.* 2.28.61, although Cicero actually uses the word *sapientem* (wise man), rather than *bonum* (good man): "For if that which rarely occurs is to be considered a portent, then it is a portent for a wise man to exist. I reckon in fact that a mule has more often given birth than wise men have existed" (*Nam si, quod raro fit, id portentum putandum est, sapientem esse portentum est; saepius enim mulam peperisse arbitror quam sapientem fuisse*). Poggio discovered F = Florentinus Marcianus 257, containing *Div.* among other Ciceronian philosophical works, probably on his trip to the north in 1417; he left it with Niccoli when he went to England, from where it passed to San Marco and had numerous progeny (Rouse, in Reynolds, *Text and Transmission*, 126 and 128).

108. Stoicism was a philosophical movement initiated by Zeno of Citium, after he moved to Athens in 313 BCE, and based in the *Stoa Poikile* (Painted Stoa). Its doctrines concerned logic, physics, and ethics. It is the Stoic position on ethics that is referred to here, in particular, the idea that virtue is sufficient for happiness, nothing but virtue is good and emotions bad, so that the *sapiens*, the Stoic sage, will be bothered by no experience, however awful. See §41 for another reference, again in Nic-

coli's mouth. For the thought in "I regard as good . . . life requires," cf. Cic. *Amic.* 5.19 and 6.21 (and also §41 below).

109. Poggio appears to cite a group of "ancient" tragedies by title, then to allude separately to plays by Greek authors. If so, then five of the titles (*Oedipus, Troas, Thyestes, Medea,* and *Agamemnon*) could refer to Senecan plays (although Cicero's brother Quintus also wrote a play called *Troas*: Cic. *Q. Fr.* 3.5.7—where, however, *Troadam* is deeply problematic. Poggio is evidently simply reproducing the reading he found in a MS). There was an *Atreus* by the early Roman tragedian Accius that Canfora thinks (see his edition) Poggio may have known from Cic. *Off.* 1.28.97, but the title is not given in that passage.

110. For Croesus, see n. 105. The reference here is to the story of his claim to be the happiest of men in a conversation with Solon, contrasted with his ultimate fate—losing his empire to the Persians after his misinterpretation of a Delphic oracle (Herod. 1.29–91). Syphax was chief of a Numidian tribe in North Africa, who revolted from Carthage ca. 214 BCE, but died in prison in Italy after losing a battle to the Romans at the Great Plains. Jugurtha inherited the throne of Numidia after the death of his adopted father Micipsa in 118 BCE. In continual conflict with Rome, he was finally captured and executed after Marius' triumph (104). Perseus, king of Macedon (178–168 BCE), came into conflict with the Romans, lost to them at the battle of Pydna in 168, was later captured, and died in captivity. Mithridates VI Eupator (120–63 BCE), king of Pontus, who fought Rome in three wars, was killed after his son Pharnaces led a revolt against him. Canfora's edition suggests as the main sources for these anecdotes Sen. *Tranq.* 11.12, which mentions together Croesus, Jugurtha, and Mithridates, and Val. Max. 5.1.1b–c, where the fates of Perseus and Syphax are related. See also Just. *Epit.* 1.7.6 and 33.2.5.

111. One might compare Cic. *Off.* 1.4.11 and 1.17.58.

112. Ninus, king of the Assyrians, supposed founder of Nineveh. His wife was Semiramis, but the son who killed her, after she had tried to make him her husband, was called Ninias. Poggio has slightly misremembered Just. *Epit.* 1.2.10.

113. Artaxerxes, king of Persia (see n. 105). The anecdote is recalled from Just. *Epit.* 10.1–2.

114. Alexander and Perdiccas were the brothers of Philip II (382–336 BCE; king of Macedon, father of Alexander the Great), all the sons of Eurydice. The story is derived from Just. *Epit.* 7.4–5.

115. Philip of Macedon (see previous note). The story of Pausanias' assassination of Philip is taken from Just. *Epit.* 9.6.3–8, and that of the involvement of Olympias from 9.7.1–2.

116. Candaules, king of Lydia, conceived a passion for his own wife to such an extent that he felt the need to prove her superiority in beauty to his bodyguard, Gyges. His wife, whom Candaules contrived to show to this bodyguard naked, supposedly without her knowledge, offered Gyges the choice of killing Candaules or being executed for his temerity. He chose to kill Candaules and take over the throne. The story derives from Herod. 1.8–12, but given the early stage of Poggio's Greek studies, it is more likely that, as with many of the anecdotes in this section, he was thinking of Just. *Epit.* 1.7.14–19.

117. Xerxes, king of Persia (see n. 72), was killed by his administrator Artabanus after his return from the unsuccessful Greek campaign in 479 BCE. Artabanus was killed in turn by Xerxes' son, Darius. The anecdote is taken from Just. *Epit.* 3.1.1–2.

118. Dionysius II, tyrant of Syracuse (see n. 105). The anecdote combines material from Just. *Epit.* 21.1.1–3 (accession and killing of his uncles) and 5.8 (teaching boys at Corinth).

119. Ptolemy IV Philopator, ruler of Egypt (221–205 BCE). The anecdote combines material from Just. *Epit.* 29.1.5 (parricide and matricide) and 30.1.2 (fratricide), but Poggio has either misremembered the murder of the sister or has used another source.

120. Nicomedes II Epiphanes, son of Prusias II Cynegus (182–149 BCE), was king of Bithynia (129–ca. 127). The anecdote summarizes Just. *Epit.* 34.4, where the parricide is said to stem from a plot by Prusias to kill Nicomedes. In other accounts, Prusias fled to Nicomedia, where he was stoned to death by the citizens.

121. Ptolemy II Philadelphus (308–246 BCE), king of Egypt (from 282). His sister and wife was not in fact called Cleopatra, but Arsinoe. The error in the name and the coincidence with Just. *Epit.* 38.8.3 and 13 shows that this was Poggio's source.

122. Eucratides I, king of Bactria (ca. 170–145 BCE). The anecdote derives from Just. *Epit.* 41.6.5.

123. Phraates IV (ca. 38–3/2 BCE), king of Parthia. His father's name was Orodes, not Oras (the reading of the MSS). The anecdote is taken from Just. *Epit.* 42.4.16 and 42.5.1–2.

124. Attalus III, last king of Pergamum (138–133 BCE), son of Eumenes II (king of Pergamum, 197–158). Poggio follows, but not in detail, the account at Just. *Epit.* 36.4.1–5.

125. Alexander the Great (see n. 67). His murder of Caranus comes from Just. *Epit.* 11.2.3, and the story that he claimed he was the son of Jupiter from 11.11.7–8. For Alexander's career, Poggio follows the account in Just. *Epit.* Books 11–13.

126. Cf. Sen. *Ira* 3.17.1 for the general thought, although here the reference must also be to contemporary "barbarians," the most obvious of whom for this period would be the Ottoman Turks.

127. The scar image and its language are borrowed from Cic. *Leg. agr.* 3.2.4, one of the eight new speeches of Cicero discovered by Poggio during his time at the Council of Constance (see n. 20).

128. It is difficult to see precisely which incidents Poggio is alluding to here, as the history of the Italian *communi* was bespattered with such familial rivalries. Giovanni Malatesta of Rimini, for example, in 1285 killed his younger brother Paolo and his own wife for committing adultery: although this was not a power struggle, it was a famous case (Dante, *Inferno* Canto 5).

129. The phrase "more than civil conflicts" (*plus quam civilia bella*) is taken from Lucan 1.1.

130. It is not quite clear precisely which conflicts Poggio refers to here. What we now call the "Hundred Years War" was still in progress, and

this had involved internecine conflict in Spain (the so-called "Castilian War" of 1366–69 and the "War of the Two Peters" of 1356–69 in Aragon), while the "Edwardian War" between Edward III of England and Philip VI of France (1337–60) might be considered "internecine" in the sense that it was fought over Edward's claim to Aquitaine, denied by the French crown, as might the "Lancastrian War" of 1415–53, begun by Henry V's invasion of Normandy, although perhaps Poggio is thinking rather of the "War of the Breton Succession," fought between the Counts of Blois and the Montforts of Brittany between 1341 and 1365. Of English Civil Wars, perhaps the "Despenser War" of 1321–22 or the "Peasants' Revolt" of 1381 might have come to his mind, if he was not looking further back to the "Anarchy," the civil war in England between Matilda and Stephen, which lasted from 1135 to 1153. Depending on what Poggio means by "Germany," which was not a state until the nineteenth century, and in this period is used generally for the territory now covered by Belgium and the Netherlands, as well as that across the Rhine, he may perhaps have been recalling the "War of the Vetkopers and Schieringers," which had begun in Frisia in 1350 and would last until 1498, or various conflicts involving the Teutonic Knights (e.g., the "Polish-Lithuanian-Teutonic War" of 1409–11, or the "Polish-Teutonic War" of 1431–35).

131. The phrase "in ruling there is no loyalty" (*Nec fides regni est*) is taken from Cic. *Off.* 1.8.26, where the orator is quoting from an unknown play by Ennius.

132. In fact, it was Cosimo himself, not Carlo, who at §15 gave a list of such good rulers, although his comment did follow on from Carlo's defense of the role of leader as in itself good, based on Cicero's dictum. As Kajanto, "Poggio Bracciolini's *De infelicitate principum*," and Canfora, "Topica del 'principe'" have both remarked, this is probably a sign of overhasty composition (see also n. 13 above and n. 146 below).

133. For King David, see 1 Samuel 17:12–2 Samuel 24, and 1 Kings 1–2. Flavius Arcadius, Eastern Roman emperor (383–408 CE), son of Theodosius. Honorius, younger son of Theodosius, Western Roman emperor (395–423). Theodosius I, Eastern Roman emperor (379–395). Charlemagne (742–815), king of the Franks (from 768) and Lombards (from 774), crowned Holy Roman Emperor in 800.

134. See §32.2 and n. 95.

135. See previous note. Poggio had used Robert as an example of avarice in his earlier dialogue *On Avarice* (1428): Germano, *Poggio Bracciolini. Dialogus contra avaritiam*, 13.3 and 19.10.

136. Verg. *Aen.* 6.129–30.

137. See 2 Samuel 11:2–5, for David's adultery with Bathsheba, wife of Uriah, and 14–20, for his arrangement to try to have Uriah die in battle. *Contra* Canfora in his edition, Poggio would probably not have counted as homicide the killing of Goliath (1 Samuel 17:48–54), as this happened during battle against an aggressor and was not an "arranged killing" of a friend, like Uriah's.

138. For another reference by Niccoli to Stoicism, see §37, and for explanation see n. 108.

139. The quotation, a *bon mot* of Demetrius the Cynic, is slightly truncated from Sen. *Prov.* 1.3.3.

140. A close paraphrase of Sen. *Ad Polyb.* 9.5.

141. Poggio has misremembered the source. He is quoting, obviously from memory, as he misses some phrases, remodels others, and misplaces others (such as the opening words), and not from *Tranq.* but *Ad Polyb.* 6.4–5.

142. Ixion, a legendary king of Thessaly, offended Zeus by attempting to rape his wife, Hera. Zeus substituted a cloud-Hera (and from this union was born Centaurus, eponymous ancestor of the Centaurs). Ixion was punished for eternity by being attached to a fiery wheel (see, e.g., Verg. *Aen.* 6.601).

143. See §17.

144. The anecdote is paraphrased from Val. Max. 4.1 ext. 9; cf. also Cic. *Deiot.* 36.

145. Poggio appears to be referring to the idea that ruling brings unhappiness, although the reason why the former kings of Gaul and Britain were "enabled" to set aside such a burden was that they had been conquered by the Romans.

146. Alcibiades (451/0–404/3 BCE), a prominent and controversial fifth-century Athenian politician and general. Themistocles (ca. 524–459 BCE), Athenian politician and general during the Persian Wars of 480–479, responsible for the naval victory at Salamis. Pericles (ca. 495–429 BCE), most important leader of democratic Athens from the 440s to his death. Aristides (early 5th century BCE), major Athenian politician and general, nicknamed "the Just." Hannibal (247–183 or 182 BCE), Carthaginian general. Camillus (Marcus Furius Camillus), conqueror of Veii while dictator of Rome in 396 BCE. Quintus Metellus: there were a number of individuals named Quintus Caecilius Metellus, one of whom (Q. Caecilius Metellus Macedonicus) is mentioned in the next chapter as a private individual (although in fact he was consul in 143 BCE). But the reference is more probably to Q. Caecilius Metellus Numidicus (cos. 109 BCE), who figures in the exempla-tradition as one who fell from high standing to the misfortune of exile (Val. Max. 3.8.4 and 4.1.13). The Scipios — presumably Publius Cornelius Scipio Africanus (236–183 BCE), victor over Hannibal at the battle of Zama (202), and Publius Cornelius Scipio Aemilianus Africanus (185/4–129 BCE), conqueror of Carthage in 146. Rutilius: probably Publius Rutilius Rufus (b. ca. 160 BCE), consul 105, but prosecuted and condemned for corruption in 92, and exiled (unless Poggio is thinking of a later Rutilius: see below). But given Poggio's strong reliance on Seneca, he is probably thinking of *Prov.* 1.3.7, where this Rutilius is the subject of a contrast in happiness with Sulla (who is brought up here just below), even if this is a contradictory instance. Caesar (C. Julius Caesar; 100–44 BCE), conqueror of Gaul and victor in the Civil War against Pompey, perpetual dictator at the time of his assassination. Pompey (Gnaeus Pompeius Magnus; 106–48 BCE), lost the Civil War to Caesar. Marcus Antonius: see n. 49. Lepidus: see n. 49. The list looks at first sight as though it is not confined to "leaders of the state in their republics." But an argument could be made for a trajectory from democratic Athens via Hannibal's Carthage (which was an oligarchic republic) to republican Rome, stopping short before it reaches the fully constituted empire. This sequence would, however, be disrupted if in fact Rutilius referred to Gaius Rutilius Gallicus, who served as governor of

Lower Germany (ca. 76–79 CE) and proconsul of Asia (soon after 81), who might possibly have been chosen because his career is celebrated in one of Statius' *Silvae* (1.4), which had been rediscovered by Poggio (see n. 20), although this is unlikely for reasons given above (and in *Ep. Fam.* 1.5.1, ll. 163–68 [= Harth 2:186], the consolation letter for Cosimo's exile, it is the republican Rutilius who is given as an example: see Introduction).

147. Lucius Cornelius Sulla Felix (138–78 BCE), dictator at Rome after taking the city by force in 84, a post he retired from in 80. Poggio may depend on a number of sources here: for Sulla's cruelty, on Val. Max. 9.2.1; for his self-asserted happiness and his excesses as dictator, on Sen. *Prov.* 3.7–8, *Ad Marciam* 12.6, *Brev. vit.* 13.6–8, *Ira* 1.20.4. Note the pun on Sulla's cognomen: *felix* means "happy."

148. Gaius Marius (ca. 157–86 BCE), consul seven times (cf. Broughton, *Magistrates*, 2:589) and a highly successful commander against the Teutones, Ambrones, and Cimbri, he was obliged to flee when Sulla (see preceding note) took Rome. He returned and alongside L. Cornelius Cinna recaptured Rome in 87, took up the consulship of 86, but died on January 13. Poggio's main source may have been Cic. *De or.* 3.8, which mentions Marius' exile and the bloody revenge he inflicted upon his return, although many other ancient writers mention his name and crimes (e.g., Sen. *Ben.* 5.16.2).

149. Daughter of Zeus and Themis, goddess of justice, she was the last immortal to abandon the earth (Ov. *Met.* 1.149–50).

150. Poggio's example of Gyges and Aglaus comes from Val. Max. 7.1.2. Poggio paraphrases, in one case (*qui metas agelli sui nunquam cupiditate excesserat*) misinterpreting the text: by adding *cupiditate* he makes it clear that he took *excesserat* to mean "exceed," while Valerius seems only to imply that Aglaus had never left his own property.

151. Val. Max. 7.1.1 mentions Metellus (for whom see n. 146) as a prime example of good fortune. In the following chapter, which Poggio recalls here by mentioning the source for the Gyges story, this is specifically called "happiness" (*felicitas*).

152. Lucian's dialogue has the alternative title *Consultation of the Dead*. Menippus was a third-century BCE Cynic philosophical writer whose persona and, possibly, works Lucian utilized in his own satirical pieces. Teiresias was the famous legendary Theban seer, consulted by Odysseus in Book 11 of Homer's *Odyssey*. The *Menippus* was not translated into Latin until much later (Thomas More's version appeared with the more famous Lucian translations of Erasmus from the press of Josse Bade in Paris, 1506). But Poggio was interested in Lucian, owned a MS of some of his works (Sidwell, "Manoscritti umanistici di Luciano"), and uses other as yet-untranslated works earlier in this dialogue (see nn. 17, 18, 23, 24, 29, 82, 102, 104, 105, 106). His outline covers more or less chapters 3–21 of the work. As Canfora's edition notes, however, Poggio omits the second half of Teiresias' response, which centers not on avoiding positions of power but on scrapping all pretensions to intellectual inquiry— which the next part of Niccoli's discourse goes on to praise. Such eclectic use of Lucian is typical not only of Poggio but of other fifteenth-century writers. The passage about Gyges and Menippus was pillaged wholesale by Aeneas Sylvius Piccolomini in *On the Miseries of Courtiers* (Wolkan, *Briefwechsel*, 454–55). See also nn. 77 and 81, and Introduction.

153. Canfora's edition suggests various ancient sources here (Lucr. 1.54–61; Sen. *QNat.* pref. 7, *De otio* 4.2 and 5.5–8). But although Lucretius was rediscovered by Poggio (n. 20), there is little sign anywhere in the dialogue of any serious impact, and even the mention of Epicurus (§10) seems closer to a passage in Cicero than to Lucretius (n. 27). The Senecan passages listed by Canfora are specifically concerned with scientific inquiry, which is a very small part of the range covered here. Rather than a *mélange* of ancient sources, then, we are dealing here with a statement of the central tenets of fifteenth-century humanism, which have their own contemporary rationale and context, even though driven by the worship of antiquity.

154. Canfora's edition suggests Cic. *Sen.* 71 as a parallel for this image, but the idea of the harbor as a bourne is very common in ancient literature, especially Cicero.

155. For the image of traveling through life, cf. Sall. *Cat.* 2.8.

156. Canfora's edition suggests Lucr. 2.6–16 as a parallel for this passage, but the relationship is, at best, vague.

157. The phrase "content with little" (*parvo contentus*) is quite common. Poggio might have had it in mind from, e.g., Hor. *Sat.* 2.2.110 or Cic. *Att.* 12.19.1.

Bibliography

❧❦❧

EDITIONS AND TRANSLATIONS

Baldassarri, Stefano, ed. *Leonardo Bruni. Dialogi ad Petrum Paulum Histrum.* Florence: Leo S. Olschki, 1994.

——. *Leonardo Bruni. Laudatio Florentine Urbis.* Florence: SISMEL – Edizioni del Galluzzo, 2000.

Berti, Ernesto, ed. *Luciano di Samosata. Caronte; Timone.* Florence: SISMEL – Edizioni del Galluzzo, 2006.

Billanovich, Giuseppe, ed. *Petrarca. Rerum memorandarum libri.* Edizione nazionale delle opere di Francesco Petrarca 14. Florence: G. C. Sansoni, 1945.

Bodnar, Edward, and Charles Mitchell, eds. *Francesco Scalamonti. Vita viri clarissimi et famosissimi Kyriaci Anconitani.* Philadelphia, PA: American Philosophical Society, 1996.

Canfora, Davide, ed. *Poggio Bracciolini. De infelicitate principum.* Edizione Nazionale dei Testi Umanistici 2. Rome: Edizioni di Storia e Letteratura, 1998.

——. *La Controversia di Poggio Bracciolini e Guarino Veronese su Cesare e Scipione.* Florence: Leo S. Olschki, 2001.

Carmody, Francis, ed. *Brunetto Latini. Li Livres dou Tresor.* Geneva: Slatkin Reprints, 1998.

Cortesi, Mariarosa, ed. "La 'Caesarea Laus' di Ciriaco d'Ancona." In *Gli Umanesimi medievali: Atti del II Congresso dell' Internationales Mittellateinerkomitee, Firenze, Certosa del Galluzzo,* edited by Claudio Leonardi, 37–65. Florence: Sismel – Edizioni del Galluzzo, 1998.

Crevatin, Giuliana, ed. "La politica e la retorica. Poggio e la controversia su Cesare e Scipione. Con una nuova edizione della lettera a Scipione Mainenti." In *Poggio Bracciolini, 1380–1459: nel VI centenario della nascita,* edited by Riccardo Fubini, 281–342. Florence: G. C. Sansoni, 1982.

——. *Petrarca. De gestis Cesaris.* Pisa: Scuola normale superiore, 2003.

535

De Keyser, Jeroen, ed., and Scott Blanchard, trans. *Francesco Filelfo. On Exile*. I Tatti Renaissance Library 55. Cambridge, MA: Harvard University Press, 2013.

De Keyser, Jeroen, and Hester Schadee, eds. and trans. *Poggio Bracciolini. Eulogies: Six Laments for Dead Friends*. Ghent: Lysa, 2023.

Di San Luigi, Ildefonso, ed. *Giovanni di Pagolo Morelli. Ricordi*. In *Delizie degli eruditi toscani*, 19:1–164. Florence: Gaetano Cambiagi, 1785.

Fubini, Riccardo, ed. *Poggii Opera omnia*. 4 vols. Turin: Bottega d'Erasmo, 1964–69.

Germano, Giuseppe, ed. and trans. *Poggio Bracciolini. Dialogus contra avaritiam (De avaritia)*. Livorno: Belforte editore libraio, 1994.

Haller, Johannes, ed. *Piero da Monte. Ein Gelehrter und päpstlicher Beamter des 15. Jahrhunderts*. Rome: W. Regenberg, 1941.

Hankins, James, ed. and trans. *Leonardo Bruni. History of the Florentine People*. 3 vols. I Tatti Renaissance Library 3, 16, 27. Cambridge, MA: Harvard University Press, 2001–7.

Harth, Helene, ed. *Poggio Bracciolini. Lettere*. 3 vols. Florence: Olschki, 1984–87.

Kallendorf, Craig, ed. and trans. *Leonardo Bruni. The Study of Literature to Lady Battista Malatesta*. In *Humanist Educational Treatises*, 93–125. I Tatti Renaissance Library 5. Cambridge, MA: Harvard University Press, 2002: .

Laurens, Pierre, ed. and trans. *Pétrarque. L'Afrique*. 2 vols. Paris: Les Belles Lettres, 2006–18.

Macleod, M. D., ed. *Luciani Opera*. 4 vols. Oxford Classical Texts. Oxford: Clarendon Press , 1972–87.

Martellotti, Guido, ed. *Petrarca. De viris illustribus*. 2 vols. Edizione nazionale delle opere di Francesco Petrarca 2. Florence: G. C. Sansoni, 1964.

Mitchell, Charles, Edward Bodnar, and Clive Foss, eds. and trans. *Cyriac of Ancona: Life and Early Travels*. I Tatti Renaissance Library 65. Cambridge, MA: Harvard University Press, 2015.

Moravus, Augustinus, ed. *Antilogion Guarini et Poggii, de praestantia Scipionis Africani, et C. Iulii Caesaris*. Vienna: Hieronymus Vietor and Ioannes Singrenius, 1512.

Mustard, Wilfred P., ed. *Aeneas Sylvius Piccolomini. De curialium miseriis.* Baltimore, MD: Johns Hopkins Press, 1928.

Nederman, Cary, trans. *John of Salisbury. Policraticus.* Cambridge: Cambridge University Press, 1990.

Nisbet, Hugh Barr, trans. *Georg W. F. Hegel. Lectures on the Philosophy of World History.* Cambridge: Cambridge University Press, 1975.

Powell, Jonathan G. F., ed. *Cicero. Cato Maior de Senectute.* Cambridge: Cambridge University Press, 1988.

Rossi, Vittorio, ed. *Petrarca. Le familiari.* Vol. 2, *Libri V–XI.* Edizione nazionale delle opere di Francesco Petrarca XI. Florence: G. C. Sansoni, 1934.

Sabbadini, Remigio, ed. *L'epistolario di Guarino Veronese.* 3 vols. Venice: C. Ferrari, 1915–19. Reprint, Turin: Bottega d'Erasmo, 1967.

Shackleton Bailey, David R., ed. *Anthologia Latina.* Vol. 1.1. Stuttgart: B. G. Teubner, 1982.

Wolkan, Rudolf, ed. *Der Briefwechsel des Eneas Silvius Piccolomini. Fontes Rerum Austriacarum* 61. Vienna: Hölder, 1909.

SECONDARY SOURCES

Baldassarri, Stefano. "Like Fathers Like Sons: Theories on the Origins of the City in Late Medieval Florence." *Modern Language Notes* 124.1 (2009): 23–44.

Baron, Hans. *The Crisis of the Early Italian Renaissance: Civic Humanism and Republican Liberty in an Age of Classicism and Tyranny.* 2nd ed. Princeton, NJ: Princeton University Press, 1966.

Berti, Ernesto. "Uno scriba greco-latino: il Codice Vaticano Urbinate gr. 121 e la prima versione del Caronte di Luciano." *Rivista di filologia e di istruzione classica* 113 (1985): 416–43.

———. "Alla scuola di Manuele Crisolora. Lettura e commento di Luciano." *Rinascimento* s. II, 27 (1987): 3–73.

Broughton, T. R. S. *Magistrates of the Roman Republic.* Vol. 2. New York: American Philological Association, 1952.

Canfora, Davide. "Due fonti di *De curialium miseriis* di Enea Silvio Piccolomini: Bracciolini e Lucrezio." *Archivio Storico Italiano* 64 (1996): 479–94.

——— . "La topica del 'principe' e l'uso umanistico delle fonti in Poggio Bracciolini." *Humanistica Lovaniensia* 45 (1996): 1–92.

Cognasso, Francesco. *Storia di Milano 6.1: Il Ducato Visconteo da Gian Galeazzo a Filippo Maria.* Milan: Fondazione Treccani degli Alfieri, 1955.

Davies, Charles Till. *Dante and the Idea of Rome.* Oxford: Clarendon Press, 1957.

De la Mare, Albinia C. *The Handwriting of Italian Humanists.* Vol. 1. Oxford: Oxford University Press, 1973.

Deligiannis, Ioannis. *Fifteenth-Century Latin Translations of Lucian's Essay on Slander.* Pisa-Rome: Gruppo Editoriale Internazionale, 2006.

Fenzi, Enrico. "Grandi infelici: Alessandro e Cesare." In idem, *Saggi petrarcheschi,* 469–92. Florence: Cadmo, 2003.

Finzi, Claudio. "Cesare e Scipione: due modelli politici a confronto nel Quattrocento italiano." In *La Cultura in Cesare,* edited by Diego Poli, 2:689–706. Rome: Il Calamo, 1993.

Fubini, Riccardo. "Problemi di politica fiorentina all'epoca del Concilio." In *Firenze e il Concilio del 1439,* edited by Paolo Viti, 27–57. Florence: Olschki, 1994.

Gualdo Rosa, Lucia. "Le traduzioni latine dell' *A Nicocle* di Isocrate nel secolo XV." In *Acta Conventus Neo-Latini Lovaniensis,* edited by Josef IJsewijn and Eckhardt Kessler, 275–303. Leuven: Leuven University Press, 1973.

Kajanto, Iiro. "Poggio Bracciolini's *De infelicitate principum* and Its Classical Sources." *Journal of the Classical Tradition* 1.1 (1994): 23–35.

Kent, Dale. *The Rise of the Medici: Faction in Florence, 1426–1434.* Oxford: Oxford University Press, 1978.

——— . *Cosimo de' Medici and the Florentine Renaissance: The Patron's Oeuvre.* New Haven: Yale University Press, 2000.

Kohl, Benjamin. "The Changing Concept of the *studia humanitatis* in the Early Renaissance." *Renaissance Studies* 6 (1992): 185–202.

Marsh, David. *Lucian and the Latins.* Ann Arbor: University of Michigan Press, 1998.

Martellotti, Guido. "Petrarca e Cesare." In idem, *Scritti petrarcheschi,* 77–89. Padua: Antenore, 1983.

Martines, Lauro. *The Social World of the Florentine Humanists, 1390–1460.* Princeton: Princeton University Press, 1963.

Mattioli, Emilio. *Luciano e l'Umanesimo.* Naples: Istituto per gli studi storici, 1980.

McCahill, Elizabeth. "Civility and Secularism in the Ambit of the Papal Court." In *After Civic Humanism: Learning and Politics in Renaissance Italy, 1300–1600,* edited by Nicholas Scott Baker and Brian Maxson, 131–51. Toronto: Centre for Reformation and Renaissance Studies, 2015.

Moreau, Philippe. *Clodiana religio: un procés politique en 61 avant J.C.* Paris: "Les Belles Lettres," 1982.

Morstein-Marx, Robert. *Julius Caesar and the Roman People.* Cambridge: Cambridge University Press, 2021.

Mueller, Giuseppe. *Documenti sulle relazioni delle città toscane nell'oriente cristiano e coi Turchi fino all'anno MDXXXI.* Florence: M. Cellinie, 1879.

Najemy, John. *A History of Florence: 1200–1575.* Oxford: Wiley-Blackwell, 2006.

Oppel, John. "Peace vs. Liberty in the Quattrocento: Poggio, Guarino, and the Scipio-Caesar Controversy." *Journal of Medieval and Renaissance Studies* 4 (1974): 221–65.

Otto, Andreas. *Sprichwörter und sprichwörtliche Redensarten der Römer.* Leipzig: B. G. Teubner, 1890.

Pade, Marianne. "Guarino, His Princely Patron, and Plutarch's *Vita Alexandri ac Caesaris*: an ineditum in *Archivio di S. Pietro H 31.*" *Analecta Romana Instituti Danici* 17–18 (1988–89): 133–49.

———. "Guarino and Caesar at the Court of the Este." In *La corte di Ferrara e il suo mecenatismo 1441–1598,* edited by Marianne Pade, Lene Waage Peterson, and Daniela Quarta, 71–91. Copenhagen: Museum Tusculanums Forlag, and Modena: Edizioni Panini, 1990.

———. *The Reception of Plutarch's Lives in Fifteenth-Century Italy.* 2 vols. Copenhagen: Museum Tusculanum Press, 2007.

Pedullà, Gabriele. "Scipio vs. Caesar: The Poggio-Guarino Debate without Republicanism." In *Republicanism. A Theoretical and Historical Perspective,* edited by Fabrizio Ricciardelli and Marcello Fantoni, 275–305. Rome: Viella, 2020.

Pellizzari, Giovanni. *Variae humanitatis silva. Pagine sparse di storia veneta e filologia quattrocentesca*. Vicenza: Accademia Olimpica, 2009.

Petrucci, Armando, and Emilio Bigi. "Bracciolini, Poggio." In *Dizionario Biografico degli Italiani*, 13:640–46. Rome: Treccani, 1971.

Revest, Clémence. "Poggio's Beginnings at the Papal Curia. The Florentine Brain Drain and the Fashioning of the Humanist Movement." In *Florence in the Early Modern World. New Perspectives*, edited by Brian Maxson and Nicholas Scott Baker, 189–212. London 2019.

Reynolds, Leighton D., ed. *Texts and Transmission: A Survey of the Latin Classics*. Oxford: Clarendon Press, 1983.

Rundle, David. "Carneades' Legacy: The Morality of Eloquence in the Humanist and Papalist Writings of Pietro del Monte." *English Historical Review* 117 (2002): 284–305.

——. "The Scribe Thomas Candour and the Making of Poggio Bracciolini's English Reputation." *English Manuscript Studies 1100–1700* 12 (2005): 1–25.

—— "Beyond the Classroom: International Interest in the *studia humanitatis* in the University Towns of Quattrocento Italy." *Renaissance Studies* 27 (2013): 533–48.

Sabbadini, Remigio. *Le scoperte dei codici latini e greci ne' secoli XIV e XV.* Florence: Sansoni, 1905. Reprint with corrections by Eugenio Garin. Florence: Sansoni, 1967.

Salmi, Mario. "La 'Divi Julii Effigies' del Pisanello." *Commentari* 8 (1957): 91–95.

Saygin, Susanne. *Humphrey, Duke of Gloucester (1390–1447) and the Italian Humanists*. Boston and Leiden: Brill Academic Publishers, 2002.

Schadee, Hester. "*Caesarea Laus*: Ciriaco d'Ancona Praising Caesar in a Letter to Leonardo Bruni." *Renaissance Studies* 22 (2008): 435–49.

——. "The First Vernacular Caesar: Pier Candido Decembrio's Translation for Inigo d'Avalos. With Editions and Translations of Both Prologues." *Viator* 46 (2015): 277–304.

——. "After Caesar: The Man and His Text after Two Millennia." In *The Landmark Caesar*, edited by Kurt Raaflaub, 275–81. Penguin Random House, 2017.

———. "A Tale of Two Languages: Latin, the Vernacular, and Leonardo Bruni's *Civic Humanism.*" *Humanistica Lovaniensia* 57 (2018): 11–46.

———. "'I Don't Know Who You Call Tyrants': Debating Evil Lords in Quattrocento Humanism." In *Evil Lords: Theory and Representations from Antiquity to the Renaissance,* edited by Nikos Panou and Hester Schadee, 172–190. Oxford: Oxford University Press, 2018.

Sidwell, Keith. "Lucian of Samosata in the Italian Quattrocento." PhD diss., University of Cambridge, 1975. Online at: https://www.reposi tory.cam.ac.uk/handle/1810/250690.

———. "Manoscritti umanistici di Luciano, in Italia, nel Quattrocento." *Respublica Litterarum* 9 (1986): 241–53.

———. "Il *De infelicitate principum* di Poggio Bracciolini e il *De curialium miseriis* di Enea Silvio Piccolomini." *Studi Piceni* 14 (1994): 199–206.

———. "Aeneas Silvius Piccolomini's *De curialium miseriis* and Peter of Blois." In *Pius II 'el più expeditivo pontifice': Selected Studies on Aeneas Silvius Piccolomini (1405–1464),* edited by Zweder von Martels and Arjo Vanderjagt, 87–106. Leiden: Brill, 2003.

———. "Editing Neo-Latin Literature." In *A Guide to Neo-Latin Literature,* edited by Victoria Moul, 394–407. Cambridge: Cambridge University Press, 2017.

———. "*Sodalitas* and *inimicitia* in the Lucianism of Poggio Bracciolini." In *Sodalitas: Studies in Memoriam Philip Ford,* edited by Ingrid De Smet and Paul White, 137–61. Geneva: Droz, 2019.

Strasburger, Hermann. *Caesar im Urteil seiner Zeitgenossen.* Darmstadt: Wissenschaftliche Buchgesellschaft, 1968.

Tatum, W. J. *The Patrician Tribune: Publius Clodius Pulcher.* Chapel Hill: University of North Carolina, 1999.

Ullman, Bertold. *The Origin and Development of Humanistic Script.* Rome: Edizioni di storia e letteratura, 1960.

Viti, Paolo. "Leonardo Bruni e il Concilio del 1439." In *Firenze e il Concilio del 1439,* edited by id., 509–75. Florence: Leo S. Olschki, 1994.

Walser, Ernst. *Poggius Florentinus: Leben und Werke.* Leipzig and Berlin: Teubner, 1914.

Weiss, Roberto. *Humanism in England during the Fifteenth Century.* 4th ed. Edited by David Rundle and A. J. Lappin. Oxford: The Society for the Study of Medieval Languages and Literature, 2014 (online) and 2019 (hard-copy).

Wheeler, Stephen M. *Accessus ad Auctores: Medieval Introductions to the Authors (Codex Latinus Monacensis 19475).* Kalamazoo, MI: Medieval Institute Publications, 2015.

Witt, Ronald. *Hercules at the Crossroads: The Life, Works, and Thought of Coluccio Salutati.* Durham, NC: Duke University Press, 1983.

Index

❧❧❧

Publication of this volume has been made possible by

The Myron and Sheila Gilmore Publication Fund at I Tatti
The Robert Lehman Endowment Fund
The Jean-François Malle Scholarly Programs and Publications Fund
The Andrew W. Mellon Scholarly Publications Fund
The Craig and Barbara Smyth Fund
for Scholarly Programs and Publications
The Lila Wallace–Reader's Digest Endowment Fund
The Malcolm Wiener Fund for Scholarly Programs and Publications